D0778938

collector without walls

NORTON SIMON *and* HIS HUNT *for the* BEST

collector

YALE UNIVERSITY PRESS | NEW HAVEN AND LONDON

Bob -

I think you will
encounter many memories
herein - I hope some are
fond ones. As you will
see from your many quotes,
much of this story could
not have been told without
your eloquent contributions.
Many thanks for your
help -

Sara

The Artist's Garden at Vetheuil
Claude-Oscar Monet, French (1840–1926)
Oil on canvas, 1881
The Norton Simon Foundation

© 1992 NSM
125 BN 10
Printed in Hong Kong

Sara Campbell

without walls

Norton Simon and His Hunt for the Best

NORTON SIMON ART FOUNDATION

COLLECTOR WITHOUT WALLS
NORTON SIMON AND HIS HUNT FOR THE BEST

The Norton Simon Art Foundation
in association with
Yale University Press New Haven + London

©2010 Norton Simon Art Foundation

All rights reserved. This book may not be
reproduced, in whole or in part, including
illustrations, in any form (beyond that
copying permitted by Sections 107 and
108 of the U.S. Copyright Law and except
by reviewers for the public press), without
written permission from the publishers.

Printed in China
LCCN 2010926479
ISBN 978-0-9726681-8-7

Note to the Reader

This is a history of the formation and evolution of Norton Simon's art collection.[1] It covers the thirty-five year period from his first purchase at the end of 1954 to his last in 1989. A catalogue of acquisitions follows the narrative. A few dealers and auction houses have operated under different names over time. In the narrative and catalogue I have used the name in effect at the time of the acquisition. Unless otherwise noted, cited material resides in the curatorial archives of the Norton Simon Museum. The citations for references and exhibitions have been abbreviated; full lists of each appear at the end of this book.

In discussing Norton Simon's art collections, I refer to not only his private collection but to several separate entities that bear the Simon name.

THE NORTON SIMON PRIVATE COLLECTION began with the purchase of two paintings in December 1954. A portion of the collection passed to Norton's first wife, Lucille Simon, when they divorced in 1970. Over the years Simon refined the collection with purchases and sales, and, in addition, he donated works to The Norton Simon Foundation and the Norton Simon Art Foundation. His last purchase for the private collection occurred in 1988. Upon his death in 1993, the collection passed to a trust created for the benefit of his wife, the Jennifer Jones Simon Art Trust. The terms of the Trust provided that the objects remaining in the collection upon her death pass to the Norton Simon Art Foundation. Mrs. Simon died in December 2009.

THE NORTON SIMON FOUNDATION was created in February 1952 for educational and charitable purposes. Its first acquisitions were two drawings by Rembrandt van Rijn in January 1964 (cats. 169, 170), followed that April by the acquisition of the remaining inventory of Duveen Brothers. Its last purchase was a painting by Jean-Baptiste Pater in 1985 (cat. 1721).

THE NORTON SIMON ART FOUNDATION was established in 1954 as The Hunt Foods Charitable Foundation. In 1959 The Ohio Match Charitable Foundation and United Can & Glass Company Charitable Foundation merged into The Hunt Foods Charitable Foundation, which then changed the name to the Hunt Foods & Industries Foundation. Reflecting the foundation's interest in purchasing and lending artworks as a "museum without walls," the name was changed in 1966 to the Hunt Foods & Industries Museum of Art. Coinciding with the merger of Hunt Foods with McCall and Canada Dry Corporations to become Norton Simon Inc., in 1968 it became the Norton Simon, Inc. Museum of Art. The name changed twice more. In 1975 it operated as the Norton Simon, Inc. Foundation, and when the corporation was sold in 1983, the name was changed to that by which it is known today, the Norton Simon Art Foundation. The foundation's first two purchases, in July 1965, were two large bronze figures by Alberto Giacometti (cats. 289, 290). Its last during Mr. Simon's lifetime was a painting by Gustave Courbet in 1989 (cat. 1732).

A fourth entity, the NORTON SIMON MUSEUM OF ART AT PASADENA, was established in 1924 as the Pasadena Art Institute. In 1954 its name was changed to the Pasadena Art Museum. Reflecting its emphasis on modern art, the museum changed its name in 1973 to the Pasadena Museum of Modern Art. In 1974 the name reverted to the Pasadena Art Museum, and the following year, 1975, it became the Norton Simon Museum of Art at Pasadena. Only works purchased by the museum between 1974 and Mr. Simon's death in 1993 are listed in the accompanying catalogue.

Throughout this narrative the reader will find repeated references to profits. Norton Simon was extraordinarily conscious of the value of the objects he was buying and later selling. When he made sales, he was absolutely mindful of the profit he was making, and he used these profits to enhance the collection. In that regard, it is faithful to his way of thinking to reference these profits as they occurred.

1. For an account of Simon's life and his influence on business, higher education, and culture, see Muchnic, 1998

Contents

Preface

NORTON SIMON DIED OF PNEUMONIA in his sleep on 2 June 1993. His passing was widely reported in the national press, and his many extraordinary accomplishments in business and art were lauded. The *New York Times* described him as "a Renaissance man among the self-made business titans of his generation."[1] The director of the Metropolitan Museum of Art, Philippe de Montebello, called the Norton Simon Museum "one of the great collections of our age."[2]

As the understanding of Simon's importance in the pantheon of art collectors emerged, it became obvious that the story of his influence on the cultural history of Southern California needed to be told. A few months after his death, *Los Angeles Times* writer Suzanne Muchnic discussed with me the possibility of writing Simon's biography. With the permission of his widow, Jennifer Jones Simon, Muchnic spent several years researching and writing *Odd Man In: Norton Simon and the Pursuit of Culture* (1998), during which time she had open access to the archives of the Norton Simon Museum, along with other sources, and interviewed dozens of dealers, business associates, and cultural leaders.

At about the same time, the Norton Simon Art Foundation hired documentary filmmakers Charles and Davis Guggenheim to create a film about Simon. An award-winning documentary, *The Art of Norton Simon* is shown daily at the museum.[3] As part of their research, the Guggenheims interviewed several dozen of Simon's friends and colleagues, as well as art dealers, conservators, museum professionals, and former staff. These people shared anecdotes and opinions about the man and discussed his impact on business, art, education, and cultural life in California and the United States. Full transcriptions of these interviews are in the Norton Simon Museum curatorial archives.

In 2007 the Norton Simon Museum hosted a symposium celebrating the centennial of Simon's birth. Called "Collector without Walls: A Symposium on Norton Simon," the conference was held on 27 October 2007. Museum curators, art conservators, business associates, dealers, and former staff members gathered for a day to remember Simon. Along with the Guggenheim interviews, the transcriptions of the symposium have provided a colorful palette from which to paint a portrait of Norton Simon.

OPPOSITE
Norton Simon, 1970, in front of Aristide Maillol, *Standing Bather with Raised Arms.* CAT 410

This book chronicles Norton Simon's extraordinary role as a collector from his first purchase of two paintings in late 1954 until his last two acquisitions in 1989. It is based on my forty-year association with Mr. Simon and the Norton Simon Museum and foundations. From 1969 until his death in 1993, I witnessed his negotiations over artworks—from their acquisition to their care and loan, and occasionally their sale, and I was involved in countless conversations with him over the years. I started to work for Norton Simon in late 1969, when his art team consisted of a few staff members working out of his offices at Hunt Foods Inc. in Fullerton, California. I initially provided curatorial research and clerical support, and soon helped to implement Simon's "museum without walls" exhibition program of lending his foundations' collections to museums and university art galleries throughout the United States. When Mr. Simon assumed responsibility for the Pasadena Art Museum in 1974, he invited me to oversee the care and exhibition of the collection, initially as the curator and then as Chief Curator. From 1993 until 2002 I was the Norton Simon Museum's Director of Art. I have served as Senior Curator since 2002, consulting on the museum's exhibition and publication programs, serving as general editor and writer for three of its comprehensive collections catalogues, and cataloguing Norton Simon's archives. A great deal of this book is based on my personal recollection, but for earlier transactions occurring before the beginning of my tenure in 1969, my primary sources have been the Norton Simon Museum archives, foundation documents, and myriad conversations with Simon's colleagues and dealers and art historians who also were directly involved with him.

THIS ACCOUNT WOULD NOT HAVE BEEN POSSIBLE without the influence and assistance of many people, and I am very pleased to have this opportunity to recognize them. First, I want to thank my husband, George Abdo, for his friendship, encouragement, and counsel, and for listening to my stories for thirty-seven years. I am indebted to my friend and college classmate Darryl Isley for introducing me to the Simon collection and recommending me for a job with Norton forty-one years ago. The grace and talent of three women—Angelina Boaz, Julia R. Mayer, and Barbara Roberts—remain an inspiration, and I am deeply appreciative for the opportunity of working with them. Lucille Ellis Simon graciously welcomed me into the Simon family and organization. Marion Blackburn and Chris Klein provided advice, friendship, and good humor.

Jennifer Jones Simon chaired the museum's board of trustees during my term as Director of Art, and I am grateful for her support in seeing Norton Simon's life and collection recorded and honored. My gratitude goes to Walter Timoshuk and the board of the Norton Simon Art Foundation for suggesting this project and for their guidance. The following people provided valuable assistance: Julian Agnew, Amy Albright, Giselle Arteaga-Johnson, Richard R. Brettell, David Bull, Cindy Burke, Jacquie Cartwright, Barnaby Conrad, Desmond Corcoran, Ronald Dykhuizen, Milton Esterow, Michael Findlay, Bud Glickman, Tessa Helfet, Ben Heller, Perry Hurt, Christine Knoke, Robert Macfarlane, Susan Mason, Simon Matthews, Achim Moeller, Thomas Norris, Evelyn Prell, Clare Preston, Dorothy Rabin, Michelle Rabin, Javier Ramirez, Elaine Rosenberg, Eliot Rowlands, Caroline Sam, Gloria Williams Sander, Judith Sobol, David Steadman, Sally Swaney, Donna C. Swartz, and Lillian Weiner. The catalogue portion of this book benefited enormously from the kindness of many art specialists, dealers, and collectors, and I would especially like to thank Guy Bennett, Robert Light, David Nash, and Eugene V. Thaw. Lilli Colton provided valuable understanding about the subject as well as her considerable design talent. David Abdo patiently guided me through countless technical issues. As always, Frances Bowles and Fronia W. Simpson are a pleasure to work with. My thanks, finally, go to Maryanna Abdo, Leah Lehmbeck, Suzanne Muchnic, Thomas Pfister, and Carol Togneri for their encouragement and suggestions.

While a history of Norton Simon's collecting, organized largely on chronological lines, this book is also intended as a window on his extraordinary, powerful personality, his remarkable emergence as a great and knowledgeable connoisseur, and his belief in the capacity of art to humanize and educate. It was an exasperating, demanding, and utterly magnificent experience to work for him and to watch the collection change and grow. Discussing the collection, planning the exhibitions, and trying to keep up with such an intense questioner constituted an unparalleled experience for which I am unreservedly grateful. ✶

SARA CAMPBELL
SPRING 2010

1. Pace, 1993, p. 1.

2. Muchnic, 1993, p. 1.

3. *The Art of Norton Simon*, 1999, Davis Guggenheim, director, Charles Guggenheim, producer. The film won the Chris Award at the 48th Annual Columbus International Film & Video Festival and the Gold Award for Arts/Culture at the Worldfest-Houston Festival.

CHAPTER ONE

From Portland to Pasadena

An essential port of call for scholars.—CONNOISSEUR[1]

AT NOON ON SATURDAY, 1 MARCH 1975, Norton Simon officially reopened the art museum in Pasadena, California, that had been reorganized under his leadership. At his insistence, the day was understated: no press previews, no glittering crowds, no opening parties, no refreshments. He wanted merely to open the doors and admit the waiting public.[2] Accompanied by a few members of the museum's board of trustees, friends, and staff, he walked the galleries and observed visitors as they reacted to the artworks on display (fig. 1).

The building had been home to the financially troubled Pasadena Museum of Modern Art, for which the two Simon-led foundations had assumed fiscal responsibility the previous April. For most of the ensuing year, it was closed while he directed remodeling efforts and determined every aspect of how the institution should be run. As with the many companies he led, Simon concerned himself with every detail of the museum's functions. Months of meetings were spent determining the hours of operation; the inventory and staffing of the bookshop; the colors for each gallery; detailed floor plans and installation design; and, of course, the arrangement of the artworks. The renewed museum represented the culmination of Simon's dream, a chance finally to *do it right*, correcting the mistakes he had criticized in so many other museums. After sharing his art with museums for twenty years and serving on the board of the Los Angeles County Museum of Art for fourteen, Simon was determined that this museum would be run the correct way—and to him that meant his way. To the dismay of many, he eliminated children's art workshops, dance classes, music programs, the café, and docents. He dismantled volunteer support and fund-raising groups. He wanted to focus completely and exclusively on the art and do away with anything he regarded as not essential to the core mission of a museum: allowing the individual visitor to encounter the artworks. The art collection alone would be the heart of the museum. Less than two years later, the art journal *Connoisseur* provided validation that he had achieved his goal. Devoting an entire issue to the collection, *Connoisseur* acclaimed Simon's collection as "one of the most remarkable in the world" and "an essential port of call for scholars."[3]

OPPOSITE
Norton Simon Museum entrance

ABOVE LEFT
Norton Simon

ABOVE
FIG. 1. Norton Simon (center) and friends at the reopening of the Pasadena Museum, 1 March 1975

FIG. 2, FROM LEFT. Evelyn, Marcia, and Norton Simon, c. 1920

THIS IS A STORY ABOUT Norton Simon the collector, but that phase of his life is utterly dependent on his business success and the wealth that he accumulated. The lessons he learned in business were brought to bear in collecting. His business career, before he began his fervent collecting of art, demonstrates that he had long established the modus operandi that would serve him well for all of his acquisitions—both artistic and corporate.

Norton Simon grew up in Portland, Oregon, born the eldest child and only son of Myer and Lillian Simon on 5 February 1907.[4] Norton was followed by two younger sisters, Evelyn in 1913, and Marcia in 1918 (fig. 2). Norton's earliest lessons in commerce came from observing his father's entrepreneurial practices, such as buying the stock of bankrupt businesses—predominantly groceries and consumer goods—which he sold at his small department store, Simon Sells for Less.

Lillian died in 1921, when Norton was fourteen. A year later, Myer moved the family to San Francisco, where Norton enrolled at Lowell High School and where he met his classmate and lifelong friend Edmund G. "Pat" Brown, later attorney general and governor of California. Remembering their friendship and their time playing cards and shooting craps, Brown recalled Simon's talent with numbers at this early age: "It was amazing how Norton could always figure out the odds. He might be playing against half a dozen others, but somehow he kept all the odds in his head."[5]

Simon's precocious aptitude for numbers was put to use after school hours when he began his business career selling paper bags and other paper products to grocery stores.[6] When he graduated from Lowell in 1923 at the age of sixteen, his father hoped he would continue his education and study law. At Myer's insistence, Norton enrolled at the University of California, Berkeley. He lasted less than a month before dropping out.[7] For the next two years Norton worked with his father as an importer and exporter of surplus goods and began his own independent business ventures, which included a San Francisco theater. In 1925, at eighteen, he moved to Southern California, where his intelligence and energy led to his managing

Simon was not a man who had grown up around fine art, nor had he come from a family of collectors. On the contrary, he purchased his first important painting just twenty years before this opening day, at age forty-eight, and he had been collecting with the aim of developing a public collection for only a decade. Nevertheless, by this day in March 1975, Norton Simon was widely acknowledged as one of the most important art collectors in the world. No one questioned his ability to run a major museum or to populate it with suitable artworks. He came to Pasadena with more than four thousand works of art and a passionate drive to make the new museum as great as those he regarded as models of excellence, such as the Kimbell Art Museum in Fort Worth, the Kröller-Müller Museum in Otterlo, the Netherlands, and especially the Frick Collection in New York.

an exporting business and several other enterprises. In 1927 he bought his first company, Los Angeles Steel Products, a sheet metal distributor. Within two years, he convinced his father and new stepmother to resettle the family in Los Angeles.[8]

Norton's financial success through the Great Depression is well documented.[9] His three-thousand-dollar investment in the steel company in the late 1920s increased more than tenfold by the end of the depression. By 1931 the company yielded enough profit for Norton, then just twenty-four, to invest in a bankrupt Fullerton, California,[10] bottling plant that over the next two decades became Hunt Foods, Inc. With Myer's expertise as general manager, they turned the business into a successful food-processing plant that canned fruits and vegetables under the name Val Vita Food Products Company (fig. 3). Over the next ten years the annual sales increased from $43,000 to nearly $9 million.[11]

At a Thanksgiving party in 1932, Norton met Lucille Ellis, a graduate of Wellesley College, who was studying social work at the University of Southern California. They married just three months later, in February 1933. Their first home was in Fullerton, where sons Donald and Robert were born, but by 1941 they had moved the family back to Los Angeles.

In November 1941, through Val Vita Food Products, Simon acquired nearly 10 percent voting control of the Hunt Bros. Packing Company of Hayward, California.[12] In February 1943—at thirty-six—Simon became the largest stockholder, president, and active manager of Hunt Bros. In 1945 Hunt made its fourth and biggest purchase in three years when it used $3 million of its own stock to buy the Hayward, California, food-packing enterprise California Conserving Co., Inc. This made Hunt the largest food-processing company on the West Coast with sixteen canning plants that produced seventy products. According to *Time*, "Norton Simon climbed to his tin-can throne by a simple formula: don't start a business yourself; buy up those already started and run them better."[13] The business journal *Sales Management* in 1948 described him as "aggressive, but not slapdash.... He makes quick decisions, but they are based on keen analysis of conditions. He is a brilliant statistician, using figures creatively."[14]

FIG. 3. Val Vita packing plant, Fullerton, Calif., c. 1935

In 1946 Simon changed the name Hunt Bros. to Hunt Foods, Inc. and adopted a new sales and advertising slogan, "Hunt for the Best," and in the next two years spent more than $3.2 million on national advertising.[15] He proved to be a marketing innovator. When he purchased full-page, four-color advertisements in *Life* magazine that appeared every week of the year, it was the first time an advertiser had bought fifty-two consecutive advertisements in a national weekly.[16] In a particularly bold move, Hunt placed ads in such upscale magazines as *Vogue* and *Harper's Bazaar*, advancing the concept that a product as commonplace as tomato catsup was in fact chic (figs. 4, 5). Harold Williams, former Hunt Foods executive and later president of the J. Paul Getty Trust, saw Simon's use of such advertising as a sign of his enormous creativity:

> Norton's Hunt's Catsup ads in the 1950s were incredible works of art. The idea that Vogue Magazine [used] an entire page showing a white table setting, all white, and the red bottle of Hunt's Catsup in the middle. No words. They were incredible ads. It takes a creative person with aesthetic sense to appreciate something like this—to be willing to invest an advertising budget in something that's as unconventional as those ads were. They were enormously powerful.[17]

FIG. 4. Advertisement for
Hunt's Tomato Catsup,
Vogue, 1 April 1956

FIG. 5. Advertisement for
Hunt's Tomato Catsup,
Vogue, 1 May 1956, and
Harper's Bazaar, June 1956

In 1950 Simon added television to his advertising campaign, and Hunt became the first company to advertise a single label on a coast-to-coast television network five days a week.[18] By then Hunt Foods, Inc. was a national food-processing giant. Simon was equally aggressive in his pursuit of other companies, including Ohio Match Company. He used profits from Ohio Match to buy into the Wesson Oil and Snowdrift Company, and the Northern Pacific Railway Company. Simon was often called a corporate raider, a description he resented.[19] Former Norton Simon Inc. president David Mahoney agreed that the term was unwarranted and believed that Simon improved the companies he took over: "Norton never raided anything. I think he was difficult to managers who were not doing a good job. He went out and tried to recruit the best management that he could. I don't know of any company that Norton ever controlled that didn't come out better in the long run."[20]

In December 1953 Norton Simon was featured in a *Fortune* magazine article entitled "Norton Simon—Like Him or Not." As the title suggests, the author wrote about Simon's unpopularity as well as his success. The article pointed out that Simon felt an obligation to improve any company he invested in and described what he called his "ownership complex":

> There's someone like him in every industry—
> the man voted least popular but most likely to
> succeed. He operates on the theory that success
> depends…on sweeping obsolete or inefficient
> structures out of the way and building new.
> His theory has worked to bring Simon hand-
> some returns, for although he is only forty-six,
> he has already accumulated for himself and his
> immediate family a stake of some $35 million.
> Presumably he still has a long way to go.[21]

In 1954 the Simons sold their first home and moved into a comfortable ranch-style house they built on North Hudson Avenue in the Hancock Park area of Los Angeles. Unhappy with the artworks chosen by their decorator, Norton began searching for art to fill the walls. The Simon family and many friends credit Lucille with initiating Norton's interest in art, and in later years she complained that he had "never acknowledged my help in getting him started."[22] All the same, even Lucille was surprised by the intensity he brought to collecting. Longtime Simon assistant Angelina Boaz recalled, "She [Lucille] decided she would buy paintings, and she wanted to get him interested, but she said, 'Little did I know, this was the first olive out of the bottle.' When he got interested it was like an explosion."[23] ❧

1. *Connoisseur*, 1976, p. 161. The November 1976 issue was entirely devoted to the Norton Simon Museum of Art.

2. For Simon's explanation for the low-key opening, see p. 167.

3. *Connoisseur*, 1976, p. 161.

4. Myer Simon (1885–1953) was born in San Francisco, the son of a scrap-metal dealer, and Lillian Glickman (1884–1921) was born in Chicago and raised in Sacramento.

5. Berges, 1965, p. 75.

6. Conrad, 1968.

7. Norton Simon was enrolled from 21 August until 17 September 1923. Office of the Registrar, University of California, Berkeley, 26 August 1997.

8. In 1923 Myer married Lucille Michaels, a woman Norton deeply admired, who lived until 1969.

9. *Time*, 1945; Lincoln, 1953; *Time*, 1955; Berges, 1965; Roberts, 1970; Muchnic, 1998

10. Fullerton is about twenty-five miles southeast of Los Angeles.

11. Hunt Foods executive vice president (and later president of the J. Paul Getty Trust) Harold Williams remembered, "Within the company Myer was kind of a legend when I joined. He was referred to often and Norton talked about him a lot. Apparently there was quite a close relationship between father and son." Williams, interview by Davis Guggenheim, 18 July 1996.

12. *San Francisco Examiner*, 1941; and Collins, 1948. The more than 22,000 shares of common stock and 5,757 shares of preferred stock came from the estate of G. H. Brandt, former president of Hunt.

13. *Time*, 1945, p. 87.

14. Collins, 1948, p. 57.

15. This represented about 7 percent of sales at a time when the rest of the industry was spending about 2–2 ½ percent.

16. Collins, 1948, p. 57.

17. Williams, interview by Davis Guggenheim, 18 July 1996.

18. By 1951 Hunt's tomato sauce was the number-one seller in the nation; Hunt's peaches were now ranked second among all brands; Hunt's catsup was the number-three brand; and Hunt Foods had become the nation's fourth largest company in its field.

19. Williams, interview by Davis Guggenheim, 18 July 1996.

20. David Mahoney, interview by Charles Guggenheim, 29 October 1996.

21. Lincoln, 1953, p. 142.

22. Whitman, 1979, p. SC-32.

23. Angelina Boaz, interview by Davis Guggenheim, 24 July 1996.

CHAPTER TWO

Learning to Collect
1954–1959

Nobody believes me, but the fact is that I never have a fixed idea about where I am going. I follow the road with the unknown end. I go where the going looks best.—NORTON SIMON[1]

SEARCHING FOR ART FOR HIS NEW Hancock Park home, Norton Simon found his first paintings, not in New York or London, but at a Los Angeles art gallery within walking distance of his office. The historic Ambassador Hotel, site of the celebrated Coconut Grove lounge and early Academy Award ceremonies, was located near Simon's house and one block from his Wilshire Boulevard headquarters.[2] In addition to ballrooms, restaurants, and shops, in the 1950s the hotel housed both the barbershop where Simon had his hair trimmed and the Dalzell Hatfield Gallery. When he walked to and from the barbershop, he passed the gallery's display windows,[3] and it was at Dalzell Hatfield on 22 December 1954 that he bought two paintings, beginning a lifetime of collecting.

For just $300 Simon purchased an oil painting by the American Dan Lutz entitled *Bass Section* (cat. 1). A small and colorful but otherwise unremarkable canvas, it depicts the bass fiddle players in a jazz ensemble. Though Simon's sister Evelyn owned a painting by Dan Lutz, and he often saw it in her home,[4] his interest in this modest picture is puzzling in light of the astounding quality of the art collection he later assembled. However, there may be no greater testimony to the enormous leap he made in an incredibly brief period of time. He spent considerably more money on the second painting bought that day. For $16,000 he bought a late portrait by the French Impressionist Pierre-Auguste Renoir entitled *Andrée in Blue*, depicting the artist's model and future daughter-in-law Andrée Heuchling seated and wearing a blue hat and blouse (fig. 1).[5] As a complete novice, Simon would have been especially pleased to own a painting by such a well-known artist, and certainly a portrait by the Impressionist master points to the direction that Simon presently took in building his collection. Nevertheless, the subsequent development of Simon's discriminating eye ensured that he would lose interest in both of these pictures, and ultimately he kept neither in his personal collection. He never hung the Lutz at home but kept it in the corporate offices, and in 1966 he donated it to the Norton Simon Art Foundation. The Renoir left his collection more rapidly, when he gave it anonymously to Pomona College in December 1956.

OPPOSITE
Edgar Degas, *Women Ironing*, begun
c. 1875–1876; reworked c. 1882–1886 (detail),
Norton Simon Art Foundation. CAT. 78

ABOVE LEFT
Norton Simon

ABOVE
FIG 1. Pierre-Auguste Renoir, *Andrée in Blue*, 1916–1918,
private collection, U.S.A. CAT. 2

FIG 2. E. J. Rousuck of Wildenstein & Co.

When compared with the Renoirs Simon later acquired, it is understandable that a late portrait might lose its staying power.[6] This may have happened in the summer of 1955 when the Simons lent the painting to the Los Angeles County Museum for a major exhibition of Renoir's works.[7] The dealer Hatfield played a role in the show's organization and lent five objects.[8] Considering the brief time between the purchase of *Andrée in Blue* and the exhibition, it is likely that Hatfield had tentatively agreed to lend the picture and may even have used the request by the exhibition organizers as a selling point. In any event, Hatfield pushed for its loan by advising Simon, "I would encourage you to lend it because to be shown in such important exhibitions adds luster to the record of the picture."[9]

The exhibition offered the fledgling collectors an essential introduction to the rarefied world of art museums and donors. The other lenders were eminent American and Canadian museums, including the Art Institute of Chicago, the Museum of Fine Arts, Boston, the Metropolitan Museum of Art, and the Philadelphia Museum of Art. The private collectors were equally distinguished: Edward G. Robinson, Sidney and Frances Brody, Anna Warren Ingersoll, Robert Lehman, J. K. Thannhauser, Jean Renoir, and Grover Magnin. These were names Simon later referred to when discussing great American collectors, and this exhibition was, in a way, his coming out as a collector. In the seven months between buying the Renoir and the opening of the exhibition, he had been to New York, met several important dealers, and seen the superb quality of artworks that were available. Taking into account Norton Simon's competitive nature, he surely compared *Andrée in Blue* with the other Renoirs in the exhibition, and he knew he could do better.[10]

The two paintings purchased in December were followed the next month by a few inconsequential acquisitions from Los Angeles dealers. In a 1972 interview, Simon justified his early—and what would later seem almost casual—purchases: "At the time looking around for art was not a terribly serious endeavor for me, as it became later. In those days I bought anything that had a personal aesthetic appeal to me."[11] It was a modest beginning, but by the end of the decade, Simon's collecting had become an obsession.

In early March 1955, while in New York on business, Simon met the artist Helen Frankenthaler, who was instrumental in introducing him to New York art galleries and dealers.[12] The twenty-seven-year-old Frankenthaler had just returned from seeing an exhibition of works by Hans Hofmann at the Samuel M. Kootz Gallery.[13] Simon was so taken with her enthusiastic response to the exhibition and their animated discussion about art that he asked her to accompany him to the gallery, where he bought Hofmann's 1954 *Floral Composition* (cat. 6) for $1,200. On this visit to New York, he also met E. J. "Mannie" Rousuck (fig. 2), vice president of the esteemed art gallery Wildenstein & Co., beginning a mutually advantageous three-decade relationship between collector and dealer. Immediately recognizing Simon's potential importance, Rousuck showed him major nineteenth-century paintings—landscapes by Camille Corot, Paul Gauguin, and Camille Pissarro. The early Rousuck letters to Simon reveal that the dealer tried subtly to educate the collector while promoting his stock. These letters read like museum wall labels: "Pissarro has been called the purest of the great Impressionist painters, and his particular greatness is coming to be increasingly recognized as the time passes. If Monet was the leader of the Impressionist movement, Pissarro was its prophet."[14] Further, Rousuck assures Simon he is getting the very best: "It was at Pont-Aven that, in the opinion of many, [Gauguin] painted most of his *greatest pictures*. This Gauguin is the greatest example of the Pont-Aven period. It is world-famous."[15] Simon agreed, and his first important art acquisitions took place on 22 March 1955—Paul Gauguin's 1888 *Brittany Landscape with Swineherd* for $60,000 (fig. 3) and Camille Pissarro's 1872 *Banks of the River at Pontoise* for $28,000 (fig. 4). Simon was uncomfortable with his relative inexperience and lack of expertise, and since the purchase prices were a great deal larger than anything he had previously paid, he negotiated an agreement with Wildenstein that the dealer would exchange the works at any time or repurchase them at full price up to one year from the sale date.[16] He later explained his strategy:

> The first pictures I bought from Wildenstein, knowing that I didn't know too much about them, I said, "I want to know how much I can sell them back to you for cash in one year if I don't like them, or two years." They said, "Well you can trade them in for full value, you can do that any time." I said I didn't talk about trading them, I understand trading. I want to know what I can get for cash and take my loss and run. So the first half a dozen pictures I bought with a guarantee. I turned none back, but I think also that they probably were more cautious in what they might have sold me than if I didn't do that.[17]

These early acquisitions from Wildenstein represented a giant leap for the new collector and brought Simon into the orbit of the most important dealers, helping to establish his reputation as a serious buyer.

A month later, the art historian John Rewald wrote to Simon asking for permission to include a reproduction of the Gauguin in his seminal study *Post Impressionism: From Van Gogh to Gauguin*.[18] Rewald had intended to illustrate the

FIG 3. Paul Gauguin, *Brittany Landscape with Swineherd*, 1888, Los Angeles County Museum of Art. CAT 7

FIG 4. Camille Pissarro, *Banks of the River at Pontoise*, 1872, private collection, Chicago. CAT 8

work in black and white, but Simon, drawing on his experience with corporate advertising campaigns and understanding the importance of appearance in promoting a product, decided to pay $500 to have the work reproduced in color.[19]

The paintings by Gauguin and Pissarro were profoundly significant in the formation of the Simon collection and indicative of its future greatness. Early and noteworthy acquisitions, they stayed with the collector longer than any other pictures, which gave them added sentimental value. The Pissarro also represented the beginning of a long professional and personal relationship with the art historian and Pissarro expert Richard F. "Ric" Brown (fig. 5), the newly appointed chief curator—and later director—of the Los Angeles County Museum. Formerly with the Frick Collection in New York, the charismatic Brown was enormously enthusiastic about his new position and very popular with museum supporters. As *Life* magazine noted, "In addition to running an art museum…he assumed with rare relish and skill a triple role as politician, evangelist, man-about-town. His boyish face, his eloquent tongue, his zeal for the beautiful swept over the city like a great wind."[20] When Brown walked into Simon's living room for the first time and saw the Pissarro, he fell to his knees as if before an altar—an endearing gesture that greatly amused the collector. As Simon family friend Lillian Weiner remembered, "Ric got down on his knees and paid homage to the fact that here was the Pissarro, here in Los Angeles, and Ric had done his thesis at the Fogg on Pissarro. And lo and behold, here it was greeting him in Los Angeles, where he would never ever have expected it."[21]

FIG. 5. Richard F. Brown

Except for the few times they were lent to exhibitions, the Pissarro and Gauguin always hung in the living room of the Simons' home on North Hudson Avenue. When Norton and Lucille divorced in 1970, both paintings passed to Lucille as part of the property settlement. Norton moved to a Beverly Hills Hotel bungalow after the divorce, where a framed color reproduction of the Gauguin landscape by pure chance decorated the sitting room.[22] He found this striking coincidence very amusing and pointed it out to friends and staff, joking that he still had his Gauguin.[23]

Visits to art galleries naturally became part of the travel itinerary for the new collectors, and the Simons returned from a holiday in Paris in July 1955 with several objects, including his second Renoir, a small oil painting of a woman (cat. 10). A trip to New York that same month yielded his first purchase from the New York dealer M. Knoedler & Co., a small bronze sculpture by Henri Matisse (cat. 11). Knoedler sold him a second bronze sculpture in September—the first work by Edgar Degas to enter the collection—*Dancer in the Role of Harlequin* (cat. 15). At this time the Knoedler gallery was deeply involved in Degas's sculpture. Since 1918, the artist's wax and plastiline originals had remained at Hébrard's, the Paris bronze foundry, where they were used as the matrices to cast bronze versions of Degas's sculpture. Because it was thought the waxes had been destroyed as part of the lost wax process of bronze casting, their survival was a surprise to art historians. In 1955 Hébrard's heir, Nelly Hébrard, consigned the waxes to Knoedler, and the dealer organized a major exhibition and catalogue to publicize their "rediscovery."[24] As a result, this period saw Knoedler promote and sell many dozens of Degas bronzes, more than any other dealer over the next decade.[25] In any event, *Dancer in the Role of Harlequin* was the beginning of Simon's abiding appreciation of the artist; its purchase led to three decades of collecting more than 130 paintings, drawings, and sculptures by Degas.

Through the remainder of 1955, Simon's collecting focused on the works of nineteenth- and twentieth-century artists. In October, he purchased two paintings, a Cubist still life by Georges Braque and his first pastel by Degas (cats. 17, 18).[26]

Also in October, Wildenstein sent on approval *The Studio* by Honoré Daumier (fig. 6), which Simon kept for eight months before committing to buy. Ric Brown, who had by now become one of several unofficial advisors, often discussed potential purchases with Simon and weighed in on the Daumier. After an October dinner party at the Simons', Brown wrote in his thank-you note:

> The more I think about the Daumier, the more I realize that such quality pictures by this particular master are definitely going to be harder to come by in the near future. In addition to this, it helps to round out your collection, and complements perfectly the other things which you have. And it is most amenable for a private home. If there is any way in which I can be of help to you as far as research or in checking up on things in which you may be interested, please feel free to call upon me and the resources of this museum.[27]

Before making up his mind on *The Studio*, Simon bought from Wildenstein in December another painting by Daumier, this one of circus performers entitled *Saltimbanques Resting* (cat. 19). As he began to spend larger amounts on pictures, Simon arranged with Wildenstein to guarantee to repurchase the painting for $75,000 within one year, or to exchange it for the full price of $85,000 at any time that Simon wished.[28] In his first full year of collecting, Simon spent more than $230,000 on seventeen artworks.

INCLINED AT THAT TIME TO Impressionist and modern objects, Simon bought six more examples in the first half of 1956, including a ceramic vase painted by Georges Rouault, another still life by Braque, a drawing and a painting by Henri Matisse, and his third and fourth works by Degas (cats. 21–25, 27). It was not until the end of May 1956 that Norton Simon decided to consider older art, and he started with an artist he must have regarded as the definitive old master—Rembrandt van Rijn.

FIG 6. Honoré Daumier, *The Studio*, 1870, The J. Paul Getty Museum, Los Angeles. CAT. 29

FIG. 7. Formerly attributed to Rembrandt van Rijn, *A Jewish Philosopher*, c. 1656, location unknown. CAT. 28

FIG. 8. Formerly attributed to Rembrandt van Rijn, *Portrait of a Lady, Traditionally Said to Be Hendrickje Stoeffels*, Alfred and Isabel Bader, Milwaukee. CAT. 26

As early as 1955, on one of his initial visits to New York galleries, Simon visited Duveen Brothers, one of the preeminent dealers in old masters.[29] By May 1956 he was looking at two paintings at Duveen then attributed to Rembrandt: a head of a man called *A Jewish Philosopher* (fig. 7), for $100,000, and *Portrait of a Lady, Traditionally Said to Be Hendrickje Stoeffels* (fig. 8), for $200,000.[30] While he was considering the works, Simon was trying to learn everything he could about the Duveen business—its reputation, its financial stability, and its reliability. He went so far as to investigate the dealer through the credit information provider Dun and Bradstreet,[31] as well as through contacts inside Duveen's bank. The bank's response, "They sell [to] a wealthy clientele and we feel your customer may deal in complete confidence as [the] company is reputable and reliable," was followed by a letter that described Duveen's business in detail.[32]

Although Simon was doing his homework, he was up against formidable, and not necessarily forthcoming, negotiators. Indeed, Duveen withheld the suggestion of doubtful authorship about both pictures. Three years earlier the gallery's owner, Edward Fowles, had offered *Hendrickje* to the Rijksmuseum in Amsterdam for far less money, $105,000. Despite the lower price, the work was turned down by the Dutch museum's director general David Roell, who wrote of the picture:

> It is very unfortunate that, though we greatly admire this painting, neither Dr. van Schendel [director of the Department of Paintings] nor I do feel the inner conviction that it is entirely by the hand of Rembrandt. Under these conditions you will no doubt understand that we could not consider paying a Rembrandt price for it.[33]

Additionally, the art historian Abraham Bredius had published doubts about *A Jewish Philosopher* in his 1936 catalogue of Rembrandt's works.[34] Duveen obviously knew about Bredius's twenty-year-old opinion but shared neither it nor the failed Rijksmuseum transaction with Simon.

By May 1956 *Hendrickje* was in Los Angeles, hanging in the Simons' home. The initial agreement written by Duveen vice president Bertram S. Boggis in May 1956 dealt only with this work, and it stipulated that Simon would purchase the portrait for $200,000. He was to pay a deposit of $50,000 to be held by Duveen for a year, at which time he would either pay the remaining $150,000 or return the painting and receive a refund of his deposit.[35] By coincidence, Ric Brown was traveling in New York at the time. Simon asked him to visit Duveen, examine the *Philosopher*, and give him his opinion by comparing it with *Hendrickje*, which Brown had already seen at the Simons'. Brown (a nineteenth-century scholar) was evidently reluctant to pass judgment on the paintings' authenticity. He wrote to Simon that while he was impressed with the passion reflected in the man's face, he ultimately felt more drawn to the subtlety evident in the woman's portrait, noting:

> There is more of that old Rembrandt "magic," in seemingly having "breathed" the paint on, in the portrait you have out there now. Nothing in the *Philosopher* quite reaches the tantalizing level to be found in the girl's eyes. I have been doing some "informal" research on Rembrandt prices and have decided that Duveen's should come down quite a bit.[36]

In fact, Duveen did lower the price by $60,000 to $240,000 for the two, subject to Simon's right to return one of the pictures at the end of June 1958 for a credit of either $140,000 for *Hendrickje* or $100,000 for the *Philosopher*. In the jockeying for advantage, Simon arranged an agreement whereby he kept both paintings for his $50,000 deposit, instead of just the woman's portrait. *Hendrickje* was the most expensive artwork Simon had ever considered, and he took as long as possible to conclude the arrangements. The negotiations continued for several months, and in November 1956 Simon and Duveen exchanged letters of understanding. Duveen suggested that the New York conservator William Suhr clean the portrait of Hendrickje at the dealer's expense, and Simon avoided paying for the insurance by having Duveen cover it until the cleaning was accomplished. Simon wrote to Duveen:

Until the matter of the cleaning is finally resolved you will carry insurance coverage for both paintings. It shall be my responsibility to carry the insurance coverage for both paintings when this agreement takes effect, that is, when I have accepted the portrait of Hendrickje Stoeffels after it has been cleaned and restored, or after I have waived such work.[37]

Simon was vague about whether the treatment should occur at all, saying, "I may or may not request this, depending upon the length of time it will take, and other factors,"[38] although Suhr eventually worked on the picture. Eleven months later, in October 1957, Simon confirmed that the payment due that month would be postponed, "until such time as I have had several days in which to inspect the [restored] painting."[39] Simon wrote in December that he had examined the results of the cleaning and would send money to be applied to the purchase price plus interest.[40] He also agreed that the purchase price for *Hendrickje* was now $133,500. He spent the next eighteen months thinking about the pictures and asking for the opinions of Jakob Rosenberg and Seymour Slive, scholars of seventeenth-century Dutch art.[41] The *Philosopher* was particularly troubling, because there was another, almost identical painting of the same sitter in the National Gallery of Art, Washington, D.C., which most scholars believed to be the original.[42] Concerned about the continuing questions over the two versions, and wanting an example with impeccable credentials, Simon let other dealers know that he was in the market for a "fine late Rembrandt."[43] After talking to experts and looking at other works by Rembrandt, by May 1959 Simon had enough doubts about the *Philosopher* that he notified Duveen that he was exercising his option to require the firm to repurchase the painting.[44] He decided to keep *Hendrickje* and made his final payment on it in June 1960, four years after he had first discussed the picture with Duveen. The painting hung in his living room for the next decade, until it went to Lucille at the time of their divorce. Present scholarship attributes neither work to the Dutch artist.[45]

FIG. 9. Édouard Manet, *Madame Manet*, 1874–1876,
Norton Simon Art Foundation. CAT. 30

In the summer of 1956, as Norton Simon was beginning his negotiations with Duveen, he was also looking at other major paintings, including from Wildenstein his first Édouard Manet, a portrait of the artist's wife. Also from Wildenstein he finally committed to buy Daumier's *The Studio*. The dealer first sent information on Manet's portrait *Madame Manet* (fig. 9) in April 1956. As he had done with *The Studio*, Simon bargained to keep *Madame Manet* hanging in his home at no cost other than interest for as long as he could—in this instance eighteen months—before he finally paid for it in October 1957.

The other significant artworks already in his home by this time were the Gauguin and Pissarro landscapes and the two Daumiers. Undoubtedly Simon was learning from these pictures, as well as the two dozen or so other paintings, drawings, and sculptures he had collected to this point. Both *Madame Manet* and *Hendrickje Stoeffels* were in his living room in May 1956, as he considered their acquisition. In spite of their being painted more than two hundred years apart, their remarkable similarity clearly fascinated Simon. Each painting depicts the artist's mistress or wife. Each subject faces the viewer with the same pose and the same placid expression. Even the tonalities and sizes are comparable. He eventually committed to buy the paintings within weeks of each other.[46]

Simon relished making comparisons and asking for opinions, and he would spend as much time as possible before reaching a decision. It was not uncommon for him to compare an old master with a modern work, or a still life with a portrait. *Madame Manet* and *Hendrickje Stoeffels* made an especially compelling combination, and Simon used their pairing to invite comments from every guest. Duveen director Edward Fowles, for example, wrote to Simon after a visit, "I had an interesting journey to the airport with your son, a… keen, intelligent, inquiring mind, quite anxious to learn. He asked me many apparently simple questions…for example the comparison between a portrait by Rembrandt and a portrait by Manet."[47] The son was probably nineteen-year-old Robert, coached by his father to ask seemingly casual questions, both to teach him about art and to help Simon learn Fowles's opinion.

A sublime study that recalls the eighteenth-century delicacy of Honoré Fragonard, Daumier's *The Studio* (fig. 6) was on approval in Simon's home for eight months. The $50,000 purchase price was reduced by $14,400, in trade for the Renoir painting that Simon bought in Paris the previous July for $13,000 (cat. 10). Keeping his options open and continuing, in a sense, an "approval period," Simon wrote in May 1956 to Rousuck at Wildenstein:

> Now in regard to the sale of the little Renoir—you know I did want $20,000; however, I am satisfied with getting the $14,400 as long as we have the understanding we have—that is, the balance of $35,600 on the little Daumier is not to be paid for a year from this date, and that if for any reason I don't want to pay the balance of $35,600 I will just forfeit the $14,400 credit from the Renoir. Now certainly you know the likelihood of my doing anything like that is remote, for we both enjoy the picture immensely; however you never know what may happen.[48]

In the fall of 1956 Simon arranged with his broker, Gustave Levy of Goldman Sachs, Inc., to meet the great collector Arthur Sachs, who had placed the Daumier *Studio* on consignment with Wildenstein. Sachs replied to Levy's letter that he would be happy to meet Simon, who still had not paid for the painting. Based on a December 1956 letter from Daniel Wildenstein, it is possible that Simon tried to negotiate separately with Sachs, to the exclusion of Wildenstein, and may have mentioned a possible trade for a "Rembrandt."[49] A peeved Daniel Wildenstein wrote:

> I just received a letter from Mr. Arthur Sachs who was very astonished by your telephone call. He seems to have been amazed that you want to exchange the Daumier against a Rembrandt. I would like to point out that I don't know to which Rembrandt you refer, but that if it is

as important a work of that master as your Daumier is in the work of Daumier, it must be *The Night Watch*.[50]

Wildenstein not so subtly staked his claim on Sachs by notifying Simon that the collector had consigned his pictures to Wildenstein. He followed up with two paragraphs describing other works Sachs had placed with the dealer and offered to send photographs if Simon was interested. Simon responded in kind, by first declaring his right to contact Sachs on his own: "I know Mr. Walter and Mr. Howard Sachs quite well, and the Goldman Sachs Company also. Through them I contacted Mr. Arthur Sachs…for I too recognize his very eminent position in the art world." Letting Wildenstein know he could very well find good pictures without going through the dealer, Simon arrogantly added, "You probably will be interested in knowing that we have had the good fortune to purchase a superb late Rembrandt [*Hendrickje Stoeffels*]. We are now enjoying it as we are enjoying the Daumier."[51] There is no evidence in the archives of any further communication between Simon and Arthur Sachs. It is possible that Sachs took Simon's overture as much amiss as Wildenstein did. In any event, in spite of this testy exchange, Simon continued to buy artworks from Wildenstein. But he was meeting and buying from other dealers as well.

Through Frankenthaler, Simon met Ben Heller, a dealer in contemporary art who also later sold Simon examples of Asian sculpture when he began collecting such work in the 1970s. Heller recalled their introduction:

> Helen Frankenthaler called me up. She was having a visit from a gentleman by the name of Norton Simon, and she thought that we each might benefit from knowing one another, because she knew that I had interests beyond just the contemporary world and had all kinds of contacts and had an eye, and so we met at Helen's apartment. Norton was just very early in the game. We met there and then we began to see each other and go around to galleries together.[52]

In August 1956 Simon added his first work by Paul Cézanne, which was also his first purchase from the New York dealers Rosenberg & Stiebel, the seated man called *Portrait of a Peasant* (fig. 10). In the same interview, Heller described escorting Simon to dealers in these early days and finding this painting:

> The Cézanne was the biggest thrill for me. This was at Rosenberg and Stiebel. I had never gone in there on my own. I had never thought of buying a Cézanne on my own. This was not only a Cézanne and a late Cézanne but a gorgeous painting of his gardener, and it was $70,000. It was so far out of my dollar league that the only way I could think about it was poker chips and just the purity of whether the painting was good. And it was gorgeous and he [Simon] walked a little bit by it the first time and I asked him to go back and look at it because I thought it was so ravishing, which he did, and he bought it.

Heller was greatly disappointed when Simon sold the Cézanne in 1973 to the New York dealer Eugene V. Thaw for $1,000,000, recalling, "It broke my heart, he subsequently traded it in to buy an old master work and I never would have let go of that thing, no matter what. It was like a building block in the collection."[53] The painting is now in the Thyssen-Bornemisza Collection, Madrid.

In 1956 Simon bought twenty-three artworks, spending more than $505,000. By the end of the year, after buying art for just over two years, he had purchased forty-two objects. Four had already been donated or traded for other works.[54] Also on display in his home were other works being considered for purchase that he did not yet own.

He had spent about $753,000 on his entire art collection. That December he asked Wildenstein's Rousuck to give him new insurance values for the twelve most expensive paintings.[55] Since five of these had been sold to the collector by Wildenstein, the numbers understandably reflected the dealer's efforts to assure Simon that he had invested wisely: the total appraised value was $1,091,000.[56]

Although he was still relatively new to the art world and had yet to make his first purchase at auction, Simon already commanded the attention of the London auction houses and their managers. In November 1956 Peter Wilson, a director of Sotheby & Co. in London, sent him the catalogue of an upcoming sale, asking that Simon introduce him to the actor and collector Edward G. Robinson in the hopes of convincing Robinson to sell his collection through Sotheby's.[57] It is not known if Simon made the introduction, but over the years he and Wilson established a very profitable relationship, almost to the exclusion of Sotheby's rival, Christie's.

Simon bought his first Cézanne watercolor, *Mont Sainte Victoire* (cat. 43), from Dalzell Hatfield, his first dealer back in Los Angeles, shortly after the New Year 1957. Later in January he began a friendship and enduring business relationship with another New York dealer, Alexandre Rosenberg, of Paul Rosenberg & Co.[58] From him, Simon purchased his second Cézanne watercolor, recto/verso depictions of a wooded road and Mont Sainte Victoire (cat. 44), and Degas's pastel study for the more finished portrait at the Art Institute of Chicago, *Madame Dietz-Monnin* (cat. 45).

With his father's advice, nineteen-year-old Robert Simon acquired from Rosenberg Henri de Toulouse-Lautrec's haunting portrait of a prostitute, *The Streetwalker* (cat. 46). Robert and his father agreed that Simon would pay the insurance, framing, conservation, and other expenses related to the care of the art, as well as make decisions about loans and deaccessions. Norton encouraged both of his sons to learn about and collect art, and to relish it with the same passion he and Lucille did. He gave them gifts of artworks and had a strong hand in directing their own purchases. As is the case with many wealthy families, trust accounts had been established for the children when they were infants. Simon had also created a family foundation—The Norton Simon Foundation.[59] In 1964 the family members entered into an agreement pledging to support the foundation by donating to it shares of stock and artworks over the course of ten years.[60] Simon believed that this arrangement made it possible for him to teach his children

about philanthropy and at the same time build the foundation's art collection.

Simon added his second Pissarro landscape in March, *Boulevard des Fossés, Pontoise* (fig. 11), from the renowned Jakob Goldschmidt collection. Simon had known about this painting for some time, since Knoedler had offered it to him nearly two years earlier. As Ric Brown informed the Simons at that time, "In my wanderings I had another good look at Jakob Goldschmidt's early Pissarro. Knoedler's is asking too much for it, of course [$38,000], but it is *absolutely* one of the best in existence!!!"[61] Unsold by Knoedler, it appeared in a sale featuring some of Goldschmidt's collection at Sotheby's in November 1956, selling for $23,800 jointly to the London dealers Thomas Agnew and Arthur Tooth.[62] They immediately consigned it back to Knoedler, from whom Simon acquired it the following March for $34,000.

ABOVE LEFT
FIG. 10. Paul Cézanne, *Portrait of a Peasant*, c. 1900–1906, Thyssen-Bornemisza Collection, Madrid. CAT. 31

ABOVE RIGHT
FIG. 11. Camille Pissarro, *Boulevard des Fossés, Pontoise*, 1872, Norton Simon Art Foundation. CAT. 47

Simon was paying more attention to the art market in early 1957. He started subscribing to Sotheby's sales, noting prices in the catalogues, which he often sent to Brown for comment. He quickly compared prices and quality, and sharpened his eye. Although he did not buy any old master paintings in 1957, he was considering three, which had been at his home on approval from Wildenstein since the previous June; he paid the dealer close to $2,000 in interest to do so. The paintings were a lively oil sketch then attributed to Jean-Honoré Fragonard entitled *Portrait of the Artist's Cook* (cat. 60) and a pair of still lifes by Jean-Siméon Chardin, *Still Life with Cooking Utensils* and *Still Life with Fowl* (cat. 61A–B). In December 1957 Frederick Wight of the University of California, Los Angeles asked Simon to lend the two Chardins to an exhibition at UCLA and the California Palace of the Legion of Honor in San Francisco. Simon agreed, and he paid Wildenstein for them on 14 January, the day after they were lent to UCLA. Ever in the market for the best deal on the best pictures, Simon had a similar pair from Knoedler also hanging in his house on approval at the time the Wildenstein pair was under consideration. A file memorandum notes:

> All four were accepted as autograph works. Edward G. Robinson was considering the Wildenstein pair before the Simons became involved and was able to negotiate the price to $24,000. Wildenstein was asking the Simons $35–40,000, whereas Knoedler wanted $80,000 for their pair. The Simons were finally able to settle at $23,500 for the Wildenstein pair. Valentiner[63] and Ric Brown both saw both pairs and concluded that the Wildenstein pictures were better.[64]

In early March 1958 the Los Angeles County Museum opened an important exhibition devoted to the works of Edgar Degas.[65] Organized with the curatorial assistance of the Degas scholar Jean Sutherland Boggs, then a professor at the University of California, Riverside, the exhibition displayed 113 paintings, drawings, prints, and sculptures from American public and private collections. Norton and Lucille owned seven works by Degas, and all were lent to the exhibition.[66] Two of their most recent acquisitions were featured prominently in the catalogue. *Madame Dietz-Monnin* (cat. 45) served as the cover illustration in color, and *Young Girls beside the Sea* (cat. 56) was illustrated in color as the introduction to Boggs's essay. As with Rewald's history of Post-Impressionism, Simon paid for the color reproductions and was thanked by Ric Brown in the catalogue's foreword for having "provided considerable financial assistance for making additional color illustrations."[67] In addition to the exposure Simon's collection received, the exhibit allowed him to shape his understanding of Degas. He was able to examine firsthand a wealth of objects by the artist and meet a number of important Degas scholars. Indeed, he maintained a long acquaintance with Boggs and often turned to her for advice regarding Degas connoisseurship.

In September 1958 Simon discussed with Geoffrey Agnew of the London firm Thomas Agnew & Sons another group of paintings from the Jakob Goldschmidt estate to be sold on 15 October at Sotheby's. Simon admitted that he was put off by the presale interest and potentially high prices: "From what I hear, the general indication is such that I question whether I will be bidding at all. It seems as though everyone has pretty high ideas on prices."[68] Agnew tried his best to persuade Simon of the extraordinary quality of the objects. Among the best from Goldschmidt's collection, the group included three superb Manets, two Cézannes, a Vincent van Gogh, and a Renoir. Of Manet's *Rue Moisnier with Flags*, Agnew said, "This is a perfect Impressionist picture, in that it is really a picture of light and its effects.... I know of few Impressionist pictures which are as beautiful."[69] Agnew described Cézanne's *Boy in a Red Waistcoat* as "A superb picture, one of Cézanne's finest, which could hang with the greatest pictures of any period or school. Certainly the most valuable picture in the collection."⁷⁰ Unfortunately for the present collection, Simon chose not to bid on any of the pictures, although he did follow the sale closely. It is unlikely that at this early date he would have felt comfortable quickly making the decisions necessary to purchase an expensive work at auction. He had only recently made his first auction purchase when in July he arranged for Agnew to bid on a Jean-François Millet pastel. More to the point, the seven paintings in Sotheby's sale each went for more than he had spent on any single artwork; the sale's proceeds were £781,000 (about $2.2 million). Simon was not yet willing to spend that much. After the October Goldschmidt sale he went through a similar exercise with Wildenstein when he asked Rousuck to evaluate the lots in the 19 November Parke-Bernet sale of the Arnold Kirkeby collection. Simon again refrained from buying anything. Then, at the end of the year, he directed Agnew to buy a few objects for him at Sotheby's 3 December sale of Impressionist and modern works. While the works in the sale were certainly not of the Goldschmidt caliber, Simon dipped his toe in the water and obtained a few good pictures at modest prices. With Agnew's advice, he purchased for Robert Simon seven paintings and drawings, including landscapes by Louis-Eugène Boudin, Henri-Joseph Harpignies, and Paul Signac (cats. 67–73). Simon was especially delighted with the Boudin and the Signac but equivocal about the Harpignies (cat. 71), noting, "At this point the only question in our minds is whether or not we like these darker paintings for our home. Our experience has been that particularly on the dark things one has to live with them for a while to thoroughly appreciate them."⁷¹ Evidently living with the "dark things" proved informative. He eventually sold all but the Harpignies.⁷²

Through his association with Ric Brown during this early period in his collecting, Simon became involved with the activities of the Los Angeles County Museum, and in 1957 he was invited to join its board of governors. The museum was at that time a multi-interest county facility in Exposition Park that housed science and history collections along with artworks. Brown and Simon were soon working on a plan to separate the art collection in what was the genesis of the present Los Angeles County Museum of Art. They approached board member Edward W. Carter, president of the Broadway-Hale department store chain, asking him to lead the necessary fund-raising. Carter agreed, contingent on the cooperation of the County Board of Supervisors and the availability of a county-owned site. They agreed that the operating expenses should be underwritten by the county, while management of the museum would be vested in a self-perpetuating board of trustees independent of public agencies.⁷³

Shortly after the opening of the Degas exhibition in March 1958, the museum's board of governors met to discuss the construction of a new art museum in the Hancock Park district of Los Angeles, a short distance west of the Simons' home. A few days later Simon underscored to the board president his commitment to the project, writing:

> This will confirm my conversation with you and Mr. Edward Carter, which developed in connection with the resolution of the Board of Governors of the Los Angeles County Museum of March 15, 1958. I am happy to be able to advise you that various trusts, foundations, and members of my immediate family have authorized me to advise the Board of Governors that we are willing to contribute a total of $1,000,000 towards the cost of erecting a separate building designed exclusively as a museum for art, to be located on the Hancock Park site. In preparation for such a contribution, my associates and I have made a contribution of $26,500 in December 1957, which will apply against the total of $1,000,000.⁷⁴

ABOVE
FIG. 12. Frans Hals, *Portrait of a Young Man*, 1650–1655, Norton Simon Art Foundation. CAT. 93

OPPOSITE ABOVE
FIG. 13. Edgar Degas, *Women Ironing*, begun c. 1875–1876; reworked c. 1882–1886, Norton Simon Art Foundation. CAT 78

OPPOSITE BELOW
FIG. 14. Edgar Degas, *Women Ironing*, c. 1884–1886, oil on canvas, 30 x 31 ⅞ in. (76 x 81 cm), Musée d'Orsay, Paris

Notwithstanding the generous tone of the letter, Simon made the gift conditional: "My associates have asked that the gifts be subject to the condition that the architect for the proposed museum will be one of my choice and that the plans for the project will be subject to my approval."[75]

In spite of some progress on the County Museum's capital campaign, by the end of 1958 dissension broke out within the board of governors centering on Simon's competition with board member Howard Ahmanson, chairman of Home Savings and Loan Association. The board at its December meeting agreed to Ahmanson's proposal that he give $2,000,000 toward the building contingent on his choosing the architect for the building, which was to be named the Ahmanson Gallery of Fine Arts.[76] It is likely that the museum board never formally agreed to Simon's gift condition of architect approval, since it was not the basis of his objection to the Ahmanson provision. Instead, Simon strongly objected to anyone's name appearing on what would be a museum funded by many of the citizens of Los Angeles County, and he subsequently lowered his own $1-million pledge to $100,000.[77]

Seen in its entirety, 1958 was not a noteworthy year for Simon's collecting, either in terms of artistic quality or value of works purchased. His entire expenditure was a little less than $100,000 for seventeen objects. But if it had not been a big year in terms of dollars spent, he had learned a great deal about many different aspects of the market, including scholarship, museums, auction houses, and dealers. Simon had honed his skills in working with art dealers and developed a reputation to the point that the young dealer Ben Heller went to him for advice on handling price discussions, asking, "Are [prices] firm? Do they drop a normal 10 percent? Or is it only catch as catch can on each particular painting? Perhaps you could give me your advice and counsel in this matter."[78] Simon offered to meet with him on his next trip to New York and help him with his negotiating skills, writing, "As far as Wildenstein is concerned, they drop 10 percent, and then are subject to a little trading. Regarding Rosenberg, they are not that specific in their dropping. They drop and are subject to trading."[79]

SIMON BOUGHT ONLY FIVE ARTWORKS in 1959, all within the first six months, yet his interest in collecting was still keen. He attended the modern paintings sale at Parke-Bernet on 14 January, diligently noting the knockdown prices of all ninety-eight objects in his catalogue, but nothing intrigued him enough to place a bid. In March Alexandre Rosenberg notified him that he was sending four paintings on approval. Rosenberg also responded pointedly to Simon's practice of asking one dealer about another's stock, writing, "Let me say that I appreciate and follow with interest your efforts to assemble a great collection from any source, and that I shall always be glad to help whenever it does not conflict with the propriety and obligations imposed on us by our professional responsibility."[80]

The slowdown in acquisitions in 1958 and 1959 can be attributed in part to the fact that Simon was considering at least seven paintings that were already hanging in his home on approval. The two most important were Frans Hals's *Portrait of a Young Man* (fig. 12) from Wildenstein that he had been living with for two years, since January 1957, and Manet's *Still Life with Fish and Shrimp* (cat. 82) that arrived from Rosenberg in March 1959. There were five other works from Rosenberg and Wildenstein with a value of almost half a million dollars. Simon bought none of the seven in 1959 but did eventually acquire four of them.[81]

Additionally, Simon had decided by the last year of the decade to acquire his first major painting by Degas. The dynamic and masterful *Women Ironing* (fig. 13) was the most expensive work of art he had ever considered.[82] The lavishly painted composition features two women in a laundry; one arches her back as she leans on her iron while the other stretches her arms and yawns. At $260,000, it was almost twice as costly as his next most expensive painting, Rembrandt's *Hendrickje*. Aside from its beauty and iconic subject matter, Simon appreciated the painting's provenance. The picture previously resided in two distinguished collections, first with the famed Dresden and later Swiss collection of Oscar Schmitz, and then with the renowned Edith Dunn Beatty in London. It passed by inheritance to Edith's husband, Sir Alfred Chester Beatty,

who consigned the painting in December 1958 to the esteemed London firm of Arthur Tooth & Sons. According to an article in the London *Daily Telegraph*, Dudley Tooth took the painting to Los Angeles in February 1959 and displayed it in Ric Brown's office at the Los Angeles County Museum. Brown was hopeful that one of the museum's patrons would buy the painting and invited most of the prominent art collectors in the area to see it. Brown commented, "I concentrated on trying to get one of the members of our board to buy it. Mr. Simon is on the museum board and one of our most generous supporters. The museum could not afford it, but at least the painting has stayed in Los Angeles. And it's a humdinger, to say the least."[83]

By this time Simon owned seven works by Degas in various media, but this large oil on canvas would be by far the most important. Called "one of the icons of late-nineteenth-century Realism,"[84] the painting is one of a series depicting Parisian laundresses at work. Women ironing is a subject the artist explored many times, and that gave Simon the occasion to engage in one of his favorite amusements, that of comparing works of art. Brown was certainly aware of this penchant. A year later, for instance, he wrote to Simon from Paris saying he had just seen the Louvre's version (fig. 14, now in the Musée d'Orsay). Complimenting Simon's choice, he noted, "This is a very great picture, which I have just been studying carefully—but I know of another one by the same guy of the same subject, that is in Los Angeles, and that one is even better!!!"[85] *Women Ironing* is one of the great works that Norton Simon enjoyed living with—and enjoyed discussing. The television newsman Tom Brokaw, Simon's friend and Norton Simon Museum trustee, said of the painting:

I love it in part because Norton took me into that picture. He talked about the strength of those women, and the lines, and their vitality. He would always look at Impressionist art and he would talk about how contemporary it was. And he was pretty dismissive of abstract stuff because he said we don't know the test. He said, "In this picture you know the test of time. Look at those human forms and how they were captured by Degas and you see the lines and how graceful they are." And it began to take on different lines for me as I looked at it. He took me inside the painting.[86]

The last work bought in 1959 was purchased in June. Brown had written to Simon a year earlier to inform him that Peter Paul Rubens's *Isabella Clara Eugenia, Governor of the Spanish Netherlands, as a Poor Clare* (cat. 80) was being offered by Rosenberg & Stiebel for $45,000. Brown evidently tried to get another Los Angeles collector to buy it, but, according to Brown, the deal fell through because "she is not 'pretty' enough!!!!"[87] Simon arranged for the painting to be shipped on approval in November, and he kept it for seven months before finally buying it. Although only five objects were purchased in 1959, the total expenditure on art that year was an impressive $359,500, monetarily his second most active collecting year.

By mid-1959 Norton Simon was well on his way to forming an art collection internationally known for its excellence. In the front-page *Daily Telegraph* article announcing the sale of *Women Ironing*, for instance, the collection was described as "not just the best in California but probably the finest west of the Hudson River in New York."[88] Less than five years after his first modest purchase of paintings to decorate his house, he had compiled a collection recognized even in London for its quality, and with *Women Ironing*, he had made one of the major art acquisitions of 1959. He had completed eighty acquisitions for a little more than $1.5 million. Presaging the brilliance of his activities to follow, Simon's actions infiltrated all aspects of the art market, which would serve him extraordinarily well over the next two decades as he continued to shape his collection. ❧

1. Norton Simon, in Lincoln, 1953, p. 144.

2. The Ambassador was located at 3400 Wilshire Boulevard; Simon's office was at 3440. The hotel closed in 1989; the property has been owned by the Los Angeles Unified School District since 2001. The Myron Hunt-designed building was demolished in February 2006 to make way for an elementary school and a high school.

3. Lillian Weiner, interview by Davis Guggenheim, July 1996.

4. Evelyn Prell, interview by Davis Guggenheim, 23 October 1996.

5. Andrée Heuchling (also spelled Hessling), known as Dédée, married Renoir's son Jean in 1920.

6. See, for example, *Young Woman in Black* (cat. 142), *Couple Reading* (cat. 414), *The Pont des Arts, Paris* (cat. 531), and *At Renoir's Home, rue St.-Georges* (cat. 1522).

7. Los Angeles, County Museum, *Pierre Auguste Renoir, 1841–1919: Paintings, Drawings, Prints and Sculpture*, 14 July–21 August 1955 (traveled to San Francisco Museum of Art, 1 September–2 October 1955).

8. In the exhibition catalogue's foreword and acknowledgments, the assistant chief curator of art, Richard F. Brown, thanked "Mr. and Mrs. Dalzell Hatfield for indispensable help in assembling the exhibition and catalogue."

9. Dalzell Hatfield to Norton Simon, 6 May 1955.

10. At this exhibition, for instance, Simon first saw Renoir's *Pont des Arts* (cat. 531), which The Norton Simon Foundation purchased at auction in 1968.

11. Seldis, 1972b, p. 27.

12. Helen Frankenthaler, conversation with Sara Campbell, 20 March 1996.

13. Samuel Kootz, interview by Dorothy Seckler of the Archives of American Art, 13 April 1964. The exhibition, on view for about two weeks, was organized by Clement Greenberg.

14. E. J. Rousuck to Norton Simon, 8 March 1955.

15. Ibid.

16. Wildenstein & Co. to Norton Simon, 22 March 1955.

17. Berges, 1975.

18. Rewald to Simon, 19 April 1955.

19. Simon to Rewald, 29 April 1955.

20. Wernick, 1966, p. 103.

21. Lillian Weiner, interview by Davis Guggenheim, July 1996.

22. A life-size reproduction of the painting was published by Harry N. Abrams in 1958.

23. Norton Simon, conversation with Sara Campbell, July 1970. The Gauguin never lost its appeal for Simon, and in 1975 he bought a Brittany landscape by Émile Bernard (cat. 1124) principally because it reminded him of the other painting.

24. New York, M. Knoedler and Co., *Edgar Degas: Original Wax Sculptures*, 9 November–3 December 1955. See pp. 180–181 for a discussion of Simon's acquisition of the Degas modèle bronzes.

25. Campbell, 1995.

26. The pastel, *Dancer in Green* (cat. 18), is now thought to have as its foundation an original charcoal drawing by Degas that was worked over in pastel by a later hand. See Campbell et al., 2009, cat. 29.

27. Richard Brown to Lucille and Norton Simon, 21 October 1955. The Simons expressed their appreciation for Brown by making a $500 gift to the museum in his honor. Museum Membership Secretary Signa Broline to Mr. and Mrs. Simon, 2 March 1956, thanks them for the gift given "because of your esteem for our Chief Art Curator, Dr. Richard F. Brown."

28. Rousuck to Simon, 20 December 1955.

29. Muchnic, 1998, pp. 71–72. According to Muchnic, Simon was interested in many objects in the Duveen inventory and dropped by the gallery several times each year.

30. Hugh Satterlee (attorney for Duveen Brothers) to Duveen vice president Bertram Boggis, 7 May 1956. The two paintings are cited in Bredius, 1936 as nos. 112 and 260.

31. Dun and Bradstreet reports, 18 October 1955 and 6 June 1956.

32. Memorandum from George P. Rea to Norton Simon, 12 June 1956, quoting a source at Bankers Trust Company.

33. David Roell to Edward Fowles, 20 April 1953, Duveen Brothers records, Getty Research Institute, Los Angeles.

34. Bredius, 1936, no. 260. Bredius wrote about *A Jewish Philosopher*, "Signed: Rembrandt f.1656. I am not convinced either by the authenticity of the signature, or by the attribution."

35. Boggis to Simon, 28 May 1956.

36. Brown to Simon, 2 June 1956.

37. Simon to Boggis, 24 November 1956; agreed to by Edward Fowles, 15 January 1957.

38. Simon to Boggis, 24 November 1956.

39. Simon to Boggis, 14 October 1957.

40. Simon to Boggis, 31 December 1957.

41. On 4 April 1958 Ric Brown wrote to Simon that he had talked with Rosenberg and Slive: "now we have *both* of them trying to get the full dope."

42. *The Philosopher*, c. 1653, now thought to be Rembrandt Workshop (possibly Willem Drost), 1942.9.66. See, for instance, Valentiner, 1931, no. 108; Rosenberg, 1948, vol. 1, p. 59.

43. Geoffrey Agnew to Simon, 1 September 1958.

44. Simon to Edward Fowles, 19 May 1959.

45. J. Bruyn (of the Rembrandt Research Project) to Norton Simon, 9 November 1976: "Portrait of Hendrickje (?): The in parts unconvincing brushwork and, particularly, the most unusual colour scheme…make an attribution to Rembrandt or his circle unlikely." Regarding the *Philosopher*, see Bredius and Gerson, 1969, no. 260A. Gerson wrote that Bredius had been unwilling to attribute the painting to Rembrandt and added, "So am I."

46. In January 1957 Simon added Frans Hals's *Portrait of a Young Man* (fig. 12) to the growing collection of bust portraits in his living room. On approval from Wildenstein, Simon kept the work for 4 ½ years before finally buying it in August 1961.

47. Fowles to Simon, 11 December 1956.

48. Simon to Rousuck, 31 May 1956. Simon did not finally pay for the Daumier until July 1957, at which time he paid the $35,600 principal plus $6,888.90, which represented 8 percent interest on the full $50,000 for the twenty-one months he had kept the painting (October 1955–June 1957).

49. The Rembrandt in question may have been the *Philosopher*, although Simon was possibly just making conversation with Sachs.

50. Daniel Wildenstein to Simon, 15 December 1956.

51. Simon to Wildenstein, 21 December 1956. Lucille Simon received the Daumier in 1970 and sold it in 1985 to the J. Paul Getty Museum, Los Angeles.

52. Ben Heller, interview by Davis Guggenheim, 31 October 1996.

53. Ibid.

54. Cats. 2, 5, 10, 12.

55. They were works by Gauguin, Daumier, Pissarro, Rembrandt, Degas, Cézanne, Matisse, Manet, and Braque.

56. Rousuck to Simon, 12 January 1957.

57. Wilson to Simon, 5 November 1956.

58. Alexandre Rosenberg (1921–1987) was the founding president of the Art Dealers Association of America.

59. See Note to the Reader for a discussion of the foundations and their history.

60. Charitable Subscription Agreement, 7 March 1964. Each Simon family member pledged to support The Norton Simon Foundation because of "a keen interest in philanthropic work" and a mutual desire to "promote the programs of The Norton Simon Foundation." The agreement went on to say that each member planned to support the charitable work of the foundation and its proposed program to acquire a substantial collection of works of art for loan to museums and universities for exhibition to the general public. From 1957 to 1963 Donald purchased four objects (cats. 53, 82, 143, 150) that he donated to the foundation in 1971. Robert purchased eighteen artworks from 1957 to 1967 that passed to the foundation after his death in October 1969 (cats. 46, 49, 55, 56, 61a–b, 67–73, 84–86, 90, 363, 372).

61. Brown to the Simons, 2 June 1956.

62. Simon had been following the picture and had noted the price in his copy of the sale catalogue.

63. William R. Valentiner, head of the art division of the Los Angeles County Museum, 1946–1954.

64. Memorandum from Darryl Isley, 11 October 1973. Chardin painted several versions of this subject with similar dimensions. The two in the Norton Simon Foundation collection are Wildenstein, 1933, nos. 913 and 943.

65. Los Angeles, County Museum, *Edgar Hilaire Germain Degas*, 3 March–6 April 1958.

66. Cats. 15, 18, 24, 25, 35, 45, and 56.

67. Richard F. Brown, foreword, in Boggs et al., 1958, p. 8.

68. Simon to Agnew, 29 September 1958.

69. Agnew to Simon, 3 October 1958. The Manet (Rouart and Wildenstein, 1975, no. 270) is now in the J. Paul Getty Museum, Los Angeles.

70. Agnew to Simon, 3 October 1958. The Cézanne (Rewald, 1996, no. 659) was bought by Paul Mellon for £220,000 and is now in the National Gallery of Art, Washington, D.C.

71. Simon to Agnew, 9 January 1959.

72. Simon sold the six pictures for $117,550, a profit of almost $92,000.

73. Seidenbaum, 1965, p. 29. It was eight more years before the new museum was completed.

74. Simon to William T. Sesnon Jr., 27 March 1958.

75. Ibid.

76. The minutes of the 16 December 1958 meeting of the Museum Associates stated, "Such name shall be the sole name, title, or designation of said Art Gallery ever to be used to identify it, and such name, title or designation shall be used not only on the original structure comprising the Art Gallery but any additions thereto."

77. Simon to Sesnon, 15 May 1959.

78. Heller to Simon, 8 October 1958.

79. Simon to Heller, 14 October 1958.

80. Rosenberg to Simon, 12 March 1959.

81. Manet, *Still Life with Fish and Shrimp* (cat. 82); Daumier, *The Reader* (cat. 92); Hals, *Portrait of a Young Man* (cat. 93); Renoir, *Seated Nude* (cat. 106).

82. Funding may have proved difficult, as the painting was paid for, and owned jointly by, Norton Simon (one-quarter interest), Lucille Simon (one-quarter interest), and their son Robert Simon (one-half interest). The picture has an incredible history of ownership within the Norton Simon entities: Robert's one-half interest passed to The Norton Simon Foundation in 1969, and Lucille's quarter went to Norton in 1970 as part of their divorce settlement. Norton gave his half-interest to the Norton Simon Art Foundation in 1971, and The Norton Simon Foundation sold its half-interest to the Norton Simon Art Foundation in 1979.

83. *Daily Telegraph*, 1959, p. 1.

84. Richard Kendall, in Campbell et al., 2009, cat. 7.

85. Picture postcard, Brown to Simon, 25 May 1960.

86. Tom Brokaw, interview by Charles Guggenheim, 29 October 1996.

87. Brown to Simon, 4 April 1958.

88. *Daily Telegraph*, 1959, p. 1.

CHAPTER THREE

Greater Depth, Greater Quality
1960–1963

The more pictures I see, the more selective I want to be.
—NORTON SIMON[1]

IN FOUR YEARS NORTON SIMON had created the esteemed collection lauded in the London *Daily Telegraph* as the finest west of the Hudson River, and over the next four years it expanded significantly in both depth and quality. During this period he bought his first paintings by Pablo Picasso and Vincent van Gogh, as well as works by Frans Hals, Peter Paul Rubens, Francisco de Goya, and Lorenzo Monaco. At the same time, he evolved from the hesitant, somewhat deferential buyer to an intelligent, shrewd, and sometimes difficult negotiator. He displayed these traits as early as January 1960, for instance, when for $110,000 he acquired Édouard Manet's *Still Life with Fish and Shrimp* (p. 188) from Alexandre Rosenberg. Simon kept the painting on approval for almost a year and engaged in negotiations that sorely tried Rosenberg's patience.[2] The usually unflappable dealer (fig. 1) ended his January 1960 letter, in which he discussed several billing variations, by asking, "May I say again that I would be much happier if you could make it a straight deal?"[3]

Although Simon bought other objects after the Manet in January, including sculptures by Daumier and Matisse and Greek and Egyptian figures, it was not until December 1960 that he made another significant acquisition, and again it came from Rosenberg. In October the dealer offered him a 1932 oil painting by Pablo Picasso, *Woman with a Book* (fig. 2). Inspired by Jean-Auguste-Dominique Ingres's magnificent portrait *Madame Moitessier* in London's National Gallery (fig. 3), Picasso created a portrait of his mistress at the time, Marie-Thérèse Walter. In both paintings the sitters face the viewer, resting their right arms on upholstered chairs, and pensively touch their right cheeks. Behind them, mirrors reflect their profiles. But where Madame Moitessier holds a closed fan in her left hand, Marie-Thérèse holds a book, her splayed fingers and the pages mimicking an open fan. The portrait's vibrant colors and sensuous lines are characteristic of Picasso's

ABOVE LEFT
Norton Simon

ABOVE
FIG. 1. Alexandre Rosenberg

OPPOSITE
FIG. 2. Pablo Picasso, *Woman with a Book*, 1932 (detail), The Norton Simon Foundation. CAT. 90

LEFT
FIG. 3. Jean-Auguste-Dominique Ingres, *Madame Moitessier*, 1856, oil on canvas, 47 ¼ x 36 ¼ IN. (120 x 92.1 CM), The National Gallery, London

other 1932 depictions of Marie-Thérèse. Simon asked Rosenberg to send the painting to California on approval and bought it in December for $115,000. For many years it hung in the Simon dining room, later joined by other paintings by Picasso (fig. 4). It is now the highlight of the Norton Simon Museum's twentieth-century galleries.

In late January 1961 Dudley Tooth, of London's Arthur Tooth & Sons, visited Simon, who told the dealer he and Lucille were looking for a "major purchase" for 1961:

> We are convinced that we want a real masterpiece of the "Ironers" [Degas's *Women Ironing*] or the Rembrandt caliber for our next purchase. Over a period of years, even though infrequently, we know that many of these major pieces come up and this is the direction of our thoughts now.[4]

Tooth took their desire to heart and over the next few months offered them important artworks, such as a van Gogh from the prominent Chester Beatty collection, a drawing by the fifteenth-century Netherlandish master Hugo van der Goes, and a painting by Claude Monet of Argenteuil. Unfortunately,

FIG. 4. Dining room in the Simon house, Los Angeles, 1967, with artworks by Pablo Picasso

the Simons' imagination was not captured by any of these, and Tooth did not provide the Simons with their "real masterpiece" for 1961.

Simon found an extremely likely candidate for his major purchase in Rembrandt's *Aristotle with a Bust of Homer* (fig. 5) from the estate of Anna E. Erickson.[5] When he learned that the collection would be placed on the market, he wrote to the executor of the estate about the Rembrandt, "I want to express my interest to you in purchasing this painting and the hope that you will inform me when this picture will be available for sale, as I would like to make a definite bid on it."[6] He also indicated that he would like to find out about other artworks in the collection, "and whether there is any probability that they will be for sale at this time or at some future date."[7]

A few weeks later Simon learned that Parke-Bernet would sell the entire Erickson collection, when Parke-Bernet president Leslie A. Hyam confirmed that the sale would take place on 15 November 1961.[8] Simon responded that he was considering several of the items, but especially the Rembrandt:

> I am interested in a number of these pictures—particularly the three Rembrandts, the Hals, the Crivelli, the Fragonard, and the Nattier. If there would be any chance of your obtaining a transparency of the major Rembrandt of Homer and Aristotle, I would be happy to stand a portion of the cost. If you think this would be possible, I would like to have it at your earliest convenience in order to contemplate it as a prospective bidder. In the past, it has helped me immeasurably in bidding to study photos, or in the case of important works, a transparency, for some months prior to the sale. Also, it would be my guess, based on the favorable reputations of these pictures, that a greater familiarity would be more apt to help bidding than hurt it. I would also appreciate being advised as to when the paintings may be inspected.[9]

FIG. 5. Rembrandt van Rijn, *Aristotle with a Bust of Homer*, 1653, oil on canvas, 56 ½ x 53 ¾ IN. (143.5 x 136.5 cm), The Metropolitan Museum of Art, New York

Hyam replied that he would send photographs of the seven paintings that Simon mentioned, and, he added archly, "I should warn you, however, that there are so many people interested in this picture that it is probably going to be little use bidding for it under seven figures."[10] Hyam seems not to have understood that Simon was a serious collector, something Parke-Bernet would later come to realize. In 1961 Parke-Bernet in New York and Sotheby's in London were separate businesses; the firms did not merge until 1972. Clearly, Parke-Bernet's research about Simon and his collection was not on a par with its London competitors: Sotheby's had been courting Simon since 1956, and Christie's since at least 1960.[11]

After waiting a month to receive the photographs, Simon again wrote to Hyam and pointed out his ability to afford expensive paintings, "I am extremely anxious to receive [the Rembrandt transparency] particularly since you mention that it will probably be bid up to seven figures." Simon added for good measure, "For your information, I am on the Board of the Los Angeles County Museum and have a definite interest in these paintings not only for my own collection, but also as a possibility for loan or gift to the museum."[12]

Simon arranged to see the picture in New York in September and requested two tickets to the sale (Hunt Foods executive vice president Harold Williams was to accompany him). The tickets he received were not in the reserved section. Although Parke-Bernet later resolved the problem, in a reaction that seems steeped in insecurity, Simon felt the need to validate himself:

> I can readily appreciate the many problems which you are encountering in the seating arrangement for this sale and you have my sympathy. However, inasmuch as I made inquiry to the attorney handling the Erickson estate regarding the collection prior to the time that it was awarded to Parke-Bernet for auction and since you have known of my deep interest, having been a consistent buyer of important pictures in this country for many years, I feel I have the right to make this request and I am pleased that you recognize this right.[13]

In spite of his interest in the painting and his determined advance planning, the sale itself was not only an education for Simon; it was a rude awakening. The bidding rapidly passed him by, and, ironically, Simon proved himself the novice Hyam seemed to think. Williams later recalled their hours of preparation, as well as their rapidly foiled plans:

> The Erickson Collection was coming to auction, and that was a collection that included among other things the *Aristotle with a Bust of Homer* by Rembrandt. Norton decided that this was something we ought to have, so the night before the auction, Ric [Brown] and Norton and I were in a hotel room, working out our strategy. After hours of debating all kinds of strategy we decided that I was to start the bidding at $800,000, and then when it got to some number Norton would pick up the bidding from there and use his judgment because it was his money. So here we are seated in the auction house, the Rembrandt comes up and the first bid's $1.2 million. We were out of the market before we even got started—didn't even make a bid.[14]

Simon's earlier posturing aside, on this occasion he was clearly out of his depth. Perhaps realizing his naïveté, five days after the Erickson sale, he wrote to Sotheby's director Peter Wilson regarding an upcoming sale in London on 6 December. "I will probably bid through a dealer as I usually do; however it may be possible for me to bid directly to you."[15] Although he bought a few minor works at Parke-Bernet in late 1964, six years passed before he made his first significant purchase at the New York auction house. In October 1967 he paid $310,000 for Jean-Baptiste Camille Corot's *The Cicada* (cat. 390), at the time a world auction record for the artist.

Simon's loss of the *Aristotle* meant that he was still looking for his major purchase of 1961, and a month after the auction he bought two paintings by Vincent van Gogh: *St. Paul's Hospital at St. Rémy* (fig. 6) from Paul Rosenberg & Co. and *The Mulberry Tree* (fig. 7) from Marlborough Fine Art Ltd.

The Mulberry Tree cost $300,000, and the price for *St. Paul's Hospital* was almost $400,000.[16]

IN 1962 SIMON ADDED twenty-three more artworks to his ever increasing collection. Only two purchases were old masters, as he continued to place overwhelming emphasis on nineteenth- and twentieth-century objects. In January, he bought Paul Cézanne's sublime *Tulips in a Vase* (fig. 8). A simple arrangement of flowers sits in a green-glazed Provençal olive jar on a table with a few apples and oranges. In this solid, perfectly constructed composition, the negative spaces carry as much weight as the objects. The tall, narrow proportions, unlike the standard-size stretched canvases Cézanne typically used, are explained by the fact that it was painted on paper rather than canvas. The Cézanne came from the collection of Chester Beatty and was a picture Simon knew about and pursued for more than a year.[17] Dudley Tooth had cabled him the previous fall that Beatty already had another deal pending, but that "if deal falls through he promises us cast-iron option but thinks picture sold. Many regrets."[18] Simon responded to Tooth:

> I am certainly sorry that we missed the opportunity of buying this picture and feel very badly that I did not get in touch with you a week or 10 days sooner. Let's be hopeful that you will still hear from Beatty or that another opportunity will occur in the not too distant future. Certainly we are due to "click" on something soon.[19]

Fortunately for Simon, the other deal fell through, and five weeks later Tooth relayed their advantageous position but spoke of the need to be aggressive because of interest expressed by other parties:

> Thanks to Sir Chester Beatty who insisted that we should have the option on the Cézanne if the original deal was not completed, we now seem to have a clear course. Beatty has obtained an option in writing in our favour until noon on *28th February*. Other people have tried to get between him and the picture on behalf of

OPPOSITE, ABOVE
FIG. 6. Vincent van Gogh, *St. Paul's Hospital at St. Rémy*, 1889, Armand Hammer Museum of Art and Culture Center, Los Angeles. CAT. 99

OPPOSITE, BELOW
FIG. 7. Vincent van Gogh, *The Mulberry Tree*, 1889, Norton Simon Art Foundation. CAT. 101

ABOVE
FIG 8. Paul Cézanne, *Tulips in a Vase*, 1888–1890, Norton Simon Art Foundation. CAT. 103

Mellon but he has successfully averted this. I expect that any offer below the stated 2 million new francs would destroy our option.[20]

Tooth, as mentioned above, was aware that other dealers were interested in the picture. Simon himself had discussed the painting with others, including the Beverly Hills dealer Frank Perls. Presumably unaware of Simon's involvement with Tooth, Perls wrote to him in January:

> The man who has an option on the picture is trying to chisel with the owners, and therefore my man is sure that we will get the picture in the very first days of February. He has assured me that I should not worry, that we will get the picture. As I told you on the phone, it would be to your benefit if you kept quiet and uninterested about the picture, as in any case, I will be able to get it for you for *less money* under the arrangements which I have made with my man in Paris.[21]

Simon wrote two drafts of a response to Perls (in one saying, "I cannot believe that he [Tooth] would, as you say, 'chisel' the owner, as he is a very responsible person in whom I have a great deal of confidence")[22] and finally settled on a brief confirmation of his respect for Tooth and the London dealer's earlier claim to the sale:

> The dealer who has the option on the Cézanne still life of tulips is Dudley Tooth. Dudley is the man I have been working with on the picture and, of course, is very reliable. Dudley had promised me first refusal on the picture and I feel fortunate. I am sending you this letter as I want you to know the facts.[23]

Notwithstanding Tooth's caution that an offer of less than two million francs would destroy their option, Simon succeeded in buying the painting for 1,900,000 francs (slightly more than $400,000). When confirming the transaction, Tooth reminded Simon of how long they worked to acquire the picture: "it must be well over a year ago that you first brought up the question of this Cézanne…. I am convinced that this is one picture in a million and congratulate you on your courage and patience in getting it."[24] In his note to Tooth enclosing a $14,000 commission, Simon said, "I want to tell you again how much Mrs. Simon and I appreciate the painting and your efforts in our behalf in the acquisition of it. It is really beautiful!"[25] While Simon was famous for urging staff, friends, and others to compare artworks and give opinions, he did not readily share his own thoughts about his art. Yet in one candid moment years later, he confessed that *Tulips in a Vase* was his favorite.[26]

At the end of January 1962 Simon purchased Degas's *After the Bath, Woman Drying Herself* (fig. 9). He had studied Degas's bathers for so many months that he was able to cite them by their numbers in the Degas catalogue raisonné by Paul Lemoisne. The previous December, for instance, in a typically convoluted paragraph, he had asked Tooth to comment on several bathers then on the market:

> I understand there are three Degas which are now for sale or have been for sale recently. They are Lemoisne nos. 958, 1341, and 749. Apparently [according to Lemoisne] no. 749 was owned by you at one time. This picture looks quite beautiful to us; however the price is very high, in fact over 50% more than no. 958. Friends of ours have been giving some consideration to 749 and 958 and we have been considering no. 749 ourselves. I thought perhaps, since you are one of the historic owners, you might be able to enlighten me a little; I would be particularly interested in a comparison of the two pictures, as well as a today's market appraisal on no. 749.[27]

Simon was not being completely forthcoming with Tooth. At that time he was in fact considering the purchase of all three bathers he mentioned in the letter: Lemoisne 958 (fig. 9), which he bought from Knoedler one month after this letter, and the other two from Alexandre Rosenberg, which he did not buy. In any event, Tooth seems not to have risen to the bait by commenting on works being offered by other dealers. Simon had had one of them (no. 749, *La Toilette*) on approval from Rosenberg since the previous October and kept it until mid-April, when the exasperated dealer wrote:

> As you know, every business has its exigencies and limitations. Despite my desire, often proven, to oblige you in a genuinely friendly manner, it becomes necessary for me to know the disposition of our Degas.... I am sure you realize that it is an important picture which has been out of our hands since October 31st, 1961. Although I always have a particular satisfaction when this firm contributes a painting to your collection, I cannot help remaining mindful of the rest of the market.[28]

Simon returned it immediately. Rosenberg's frustrated request may be attributable to his having other works from his inventory with Simon not only for months but for years. An 1872 *Seated Nude* by Renoir originally came to California in March 1959; another watercolor of Mont Sainte Victoire by Cézanne and a bronze horse by Degas arrived in July that same year. After keeping them for three years, Simon finally bought them in 1962 (cats. 106, 110, 111).[29]

When Simon first began to buy artworks at auction, he relied on the London dealers Geoffrey Agnew (fig. 10) and Dudley Tooth (fig. 11) not only to advise him of the availability

FAR LEFT
FIG. 9. Edgar Degas, *After the Bath, Woman Drying Herself*, 1888–1892, Harmon Fine Arts/Leonard Stern, New York. CAT. 104

LEFT
FIG. 10. Sir Geoffrey Agnew

ABOVE
FIG. 11. Dudley Tooth

and value of objects coming up for sale but to bid on his behalf. However, as he gained experience, he began to establish his own relationships with the auction houses. Simultaneously, with his growing reputation as an important buyer, they pursued him. The previous December (1961) Sotheby's director Peter Wilson visited Simon, promising to inform him when anything of importance came up, yet indicating that he did not "in any way want to interfere with your relationship with Dudley Tooth, through whom no doubt you would bid were you by any chance interested."[30] Simon responded that he would continue to work through Tooth, who had become his primary art advisor in London.[31] Yet when Wilson asked in July 1962 whether "In future if there is anything very fine coming up here which I think you should consider buying, would you like me to get in touch with Dudley Tooth or write to you direct?"[32]

ABOVE

FIG. 12. Peter Paul Rubens, *Meleager and Atalanta and the Hunt of the Calydonian Boar*, c. 1618–1619, Norton Simon Art Foundation. CAT. 112

OPPOSITE ABOVE

FIG. 13. Lorenzo Monaco (Piero di Giovanni), *Virgin Annunciate*, c. 1410–1415, Norton Simon Art Foundation. CAT. 124

OPPOSITE BELOW

FIG. 14. Edgar Degas, *Dancer Bowing (Green Dancer)*, c. 1879, pastel, Thyssen-Bornemisza Collection, Madrid. CAT. 140

Simon answered, "I would very much appreciate your letting me know directly of anything you may have coming up which you feel is of exceptional importance, rarity or beauty in any classification."[33] Yet there was no apparent disagreement with Tooth, who in early 1962 sold Simon (in addition to *Tulips in a Vase*) his first work by Monet, *Sailboat at Argenteuil*, and interior scenes by Pierre Bonnard and Édouard Vuillard (cats. 105, 108, 109).

While Simon's chief collecting interest was clearly nineteenth-century French paintings, he was considering old masters as well, and for about six months he had on approval Peter Paul Rubens's *Meleager and Atalanta and the Hunt of the Calydonian Boar* (fig. 12). It went to the Los Angeles County Museum for technical examination while Simon solicited opinions from Rubens experts, in particular Michael Jaffé and Julius Held, both of whom enthusiastically recommended the painting.[34] Simon finally bought it from Rosenberg & Stiebel in June 1962 for $118,750. Drawn from Ovid's narrative in *The Metamorphoses*, the Rubens is an oil study for a much larger painting in Vienna. Simon never tired of comparing Rubens's briskly painted studies with their larger counterparts, rightly believing that the oil sketches imparted a sense of immediacy through rapid and spontaneous brushstrokes that was sometimes lacking in the finished composition.

After the Rubens, Simon bought only one other old master painting in 1962 and his second painting from London's Thomas Agnew & Sons: Lorenzo Monaco's *Virgin Annunciate* (fig. 13). At this time earlier European paintings were rare in Simon's collection, but he did own works by Thomas Gainsborough, Jean-Siméon Chardin, Jean-Honoré Fragonard, Rubens, and Rembrandt, as well as Jacob van Ruisdael and Frans Hals. As a fifteenth-century painting, however, the Lorenzo Monaco was indeed the earliest example, and when Agnew first brought it to his attention to June 1960, Simon responded, "Although we agree with you that this is an amazing picture, it is not the type we normally are interested in purchasing. If we were to see the picture, we probably would fall in love with it too."[35] While he could have been talking about its age, Simon almost certainly meant that the religious subject matter would look out of place in his home. His other old master pictures were secular portraits or mythological scenes. In the intervening two and one half years, however, the Simons changed their minds about this elegant representation of the Virgin Mary hearing of her Immaculate Conception. In October 1962 Geoffrey Agnew wrote that he understood that Simon was prepared to buy the Monaco, "once Ric Brown has satisfied you as to the condition."[36] Still somewhat insecure about his standing as an independent connoisseur, Simon bristled a little at this comment. He replied:

> You stated in your letter that Ric Brown has to satisfy me as to the condition of the Monaco. I would like to clarify this. I wouldn't want to put the responsibility on Ric Brown to satisfy me as to the condition and authenticity of the painting. I must satisfy myself. Although there are several people here in Los Angeles with whom I consult, fundamentally, I find I must use my own judgment.[37]

Agnew answered, "of course you must satisfy yourself about the condition. Of the authenticity there is of course no question. The price, as you know, is $130,000."[38]

The following account demonstrates Simon's penchant for prolonging negotiations and wearing down his opponents. The longer he had an artwork in his possession without paying for it, the longer his money was earning interest. Further, in an effort to bring down the price, he used a strategy he would perfect in years to come. He knew that dealers enjoyed the prestige of placing works of art in a museum collection and might lower their prices if that was an object's destination. Rather than admitting that he was buying the painting for his private collection, he hinted to Agnew that the picture could be a gift to the Los Angeles County Museum. The dealer then immediately dropped the price to $125,000. As a further bargaining maneuver Simon wrote that he talked with a tax appraiser in New York, who suggested a lesser amount:

> There is no budging him in his opinion. Although the painting was priced at $100,000 three years ago, his feeling is that the market

is now down enough that he feels he could not change his appraisal. I have thought the matter over, and under the circumstances, I am not willing to pay the $125,000 price that you mentioned over the telephone. The most I personally would pay is $115,000 and I could mail you a check immediately if this figure is acceptable. If I purchase the picture it will probably end up in the museum here in Los Angeles.[39]

The archives do not disclose any correspondence with a tax appraiser, and most likely Simon fabricated an expert to judge the value of a potential donation to convince Agnew the price was too high. Simon went on to say that if that was not acceptable, he would try to arrange for the Los Angeles County Museum to buy the painting, but it would be with "fairly lengthy deferred terms." Agnew accepted Simon's offer of $115,000. The painting went, of course, to the Simons' personal collection, and not to the County Museum.

IN 1962 NORTON SIMON spent more than $1.3 million on twenty-three artworks. In 1963 he picked up the acquisition pace with forty-four purchases—almost double the number of any previous year—and spent almost $2 million. The objects ran the art historical gamut from Albrecht Dürer to Edvard Munch (cats. 154, 139). Works on paper accounted for more than half the total acquisitions, and he purchased prints and drawings by Lucas Cranach the Elder, Rembrandt, and Ingres, among others. He also increased his purchases at auction,

OPPOSITE ABOVE
FIG. 15. Bedroom in the Simon house, 1964

OPPOSITE BELOW
FIG. 16. Attributed to Giorgione, *Bust Portrait of a Courtesan*, The Norton Simon Foundation. CAT. 152

buying nine. He again called on the advice and assistance of Dudley Tooth, and that spring the two focused on one offering in particular, the estate sale on 11 June of the Scottish collector William Cargill. The auction consisted of forty-nine Impressionist paintings and sculptures, including works by Degas, Monet, Gauguin, and Renoir. Tooth bought three for Simon: Degas's pastel *Dancer Bowing (Green Dancer)* (fig. 14), his oil *Portrait of a Polytechnician*, and Renoir's *Young Woman in Black* (cats. 140–142), spending more than $460,000. After the sale, Tooth wrote, "I am extremely glad that I got you the three pictures you most wanted. The Degas pastel was of course a very high price but you will never get a chance at such a beautiful pastel again."[40] Simon responded,

You are certainly correct! We are delighted with the purchases, particularly the pastel. The more pictures I see, the more selective I want to be. The Degas pastel, as well as the Renoir, give us the same types of reactions as the Cézanne *Tulips* and the van Gogh *Mulberry Tree*. Please continue to keep your eyes open for these types of things and be as selective as possible.[41]

A 1964 photograph (fig. 15) shows two of the three paintings (Degas's *Dancer Bowing* and the Renoir) in a bedroom of the Simons' home. The Renoir portrait, the Cézanne *Tulips*, and the van Gogh *Mulberry Tree* hang in the Norton Simon Museum. Unfortunately, in spite of Simon's good opinion, neither Degas is still in the collection, since both were sold in 1971.

Norton Simon made his third purchase from Duveen Brothers in September 1963, when he finally bought Giorgione's *Bust Portrait of a Courtesan* (fig. 16), a painting he first considered six years earlier when he discussed it with Duveen vice president Bertram Boggis. But Simon was concerned about its authorship, after learning that the painting was published with attributions to various Venetian artists, including Giovanni Cariani[42] and the young Titian,[43] as well as Giorgione.[44] Even Duveen Brothers, now selling the portrait as by Giorgione, listed the picture in its stock books in the 1930s as by Titian.[45] Duveen quoted a price of $190,000, and Simon offered $125,000. Boggis answered:

There is no question regarding the attribution. Modern opinion is for Giorgione and we sell it only as a Giorgione. When you talked about $125,000 as a basis, I had the impression that you had a scheme to combine the three paintings [along with Rembrandt's *Philosopher* and *Hendrickje Stoeffels*] and in some way compensate us for the difference between 125 and 190. I could not see how it could be done, but I was willing to listen, as in your own words, it had to be a mutually satisfying arrangement.[46]

Simon, who had clearly done his homework, replied:

As you know, there are only about a half dozen Giorgiones that are not controversial as to their attribution. Obviously, you cannot sell this unqualifiedly as a Giorgione, nor can anyone buy it on that basis. I would like to live with the painting for some time, and I would also like to have Dr. Brown help me on the degree of assurance we can feel about its attribution. I thought it was quite clear that the basis we talked about is definitely $125,000 over a three-year term; the only question was the exact terms and arrangements.[47]

Simon kept the painting for four additional months but decided to send it back at the end of October 1957. In reporting its safe return, Boggis reiterated Duveen Brothers' belief in the picture, "We are very happy to know that you enjoyed her stay with you, but the fact that the question of attribution gave you considerable concern is very perturbing to us."[48] More than four years later, Simon renewed his interest in the picture and discussed it with Duveen's Edward Fowles, who wrote, "As promised on the telephone, I agree to hold the picture for you …for a period of ten days from this date."[49] Simon responded that he could not consider it, as "I have just purchased two major works and cannot see my way clear to purchase the Giorgione until I have given it further consideration." Saying he would be in New York soon, Simon continued, "If you still have the picture available at that time, maybe I will have 'recovered' from my

other purchases by then and we can talk again."[50] He had in fact recently purchased three "major works," not two: van Gogh's *Mulberry Tree* and *St. Paul's Hospital* and Cézanne's *Tulips in a Vase*. Simon's cost for the three bought in December 1961 and January 1962 was almost $1.1 million.

While his outlay for the "major works" might have caused Simon to wait a bit for a recovery, it is more likely he was trying to gauge Fowles's eagerness to sell the painting by dropping the price. Instead, in the intervening years Fowles had raised the amount another $2,500, and when the Giorgione was finally shipped back to California in late August 1963, the purchase price was $192,500. To make up for the fact that he could not get the price dropped to $125,000, Simon set out terms stating that the balance together with interest would be paid in two years, "unless for any reason I should desire to extend the payment period for an additional two years."[51] Fowles responded with some concern, "Perhaps I should remind you that I shall soon complete my 79th year, and I feel that the terms set forth in your letter, inasmuch as there would be no further payment for a period of two years, with the possibility of this period of time being extended for a further two years, is not to be commended."[52] However, after Simon further explained the numbers to Fowles and encouraged him about the state of his health, Fowles answered that the terms were "entirely acceptable."[53] Simon's apprehension about the painting's attribution to Giorgione continued for many years. After it was installed in his museum in Pasadena, he often asked his curators to rewrite the exhibition label to reflect alternative opinions, shifting back and forth between "Giorgione," "Early Titian," and "attributed to" one or the other. At one point, in March 1984, he asked that the label list the names of all the scholars in favor of Giorgione and those experts who believed it was by Titian. Present scholarship has leaned toward the latter.[54]

In spite of Simon's years of consideration and negotiation, and its eventual purchase in September 1963, the painting went back to New York one more time a year later. In September 1964 Fowles returned the initial deposit of $20,000, and Simon returned the painting. The previous April, The Norton Simon Foundation had agreed to the purchase of Duveen's entire inventory, along with *Bust Portrait of a Courtesan*, for $4,000,000. In 2009 the *Courtesan* alone would be worth five times that amount. ❧

1. Norton Simon, in *Time*, 1963, p. 64.

2. The Manet was purchased with funds from Donald Simon, who gave it to The Norton Simon Foundation in 1971 (see chap. 2, n. 60).

3. Alexandre Rosenberg to Simon, 20 January 1960. Simon's later transactions concerning this painting continued to veer far from a "straight deal" (see pp. 147, 188).

4. Simon to Dudley Tooth, 30 January 1961.

5. Erickson was the widow of Alfred W. Erickson, cofounder of the advertising firm McCann-Erickson, Inc.

6. Simon to Earl A. Darr, 28 April 1961.

7. Ibid.

8. Leslie A. Hyam to Simon, 15 June 1961.

9. Simon to Hyam, 26 June 1961.

10. Hyam to Simon, 30 June 1961.

11. Simon first bought at Sotheby's in 1958 but not at Parke-Bernet until 1964. Simon's first purchases at Christie's were not until 1964, but Christie's U.S. representative and general manager Robert M. Leylan visited the Simons' home in 1960 and again in 1962.

12. Simon to Hyam, 31 July 1961.

13. Simon to Hyam, 8 November 1961.

14. Harold Williams (former president of the J. Paul Getty Trust), interview by Davis Guggenheim, 18 July 1996. The Rembrandt was bought by the Metropolitan Museum of Art.

15. Simon to Wilson, 20 November 1961.

16. *St. Paul's Hospital* was on approval since May 1961, and in December Simon paid half the purchase price plus interest; he paid the second half along with interest the following May. He sold *St. Paul's Hospital* for $1,200,000 at the 5 May 1971 auction of works from his personal collection. Although his reasons for selling the painting are not fully understood, in part he objected to the upper portion of the composition, which he worried

was unresolved. The criticism heaped on him for allowing an important van Gogh to leave Los Angeles was quelled when the buyer turned out to be another prominent local collector, Armand Hammer. In a meeting in Simon's office after the sale, he celebrated its success with his staff. He quipped that the city would keep its van Gogh, but that Hammer would have to pay for it (Simon, conversation with Sara Campbell, 6 May 1971).

17. As recounted in Tooth to Simon, 15 January 1962.

18. Tooth to Simon, 14 November 1961.

19. Simon to Tooth, 20 November 1961.

20. Tooth to Simon, 30 December 1961.

21. Perls to Simon, 10 January 1962.

22. Undated draft, Simon to Perls, c. 12 January 1962.

23. Simon to Perls, 12 January 1962

24. Tooth to Simon, 15 January 1962.

25. Simon to Tooth, 30 January 1962.

26. Norton Simon, conversation with Sara Campbell, July 1990. In spite of his affection for the painting, Simon arranged to sell *Tulips in a Vase* at auction in 1973, only to have second thoughts and buy it back (see p. 147).

27. Simon to Tooth, 11 December 1961, citing Lemoisne, 1946–1949.

28. Rosenberg to Simon, 14 April 1962.

29. The Renoir was finally purchased in March and the Cézanne and Degas in May. The final invoices included 8 percent interest.

30. Wilson to Simon, 8 February 1962.

31. Martin Summers, of Lefevre Gallery, who worked for Tooth in the early 1960s, has called Dudley Tooth Simon's "eyes and ears" in London (Martin Summers, interview by Davis Guggenheim, 6 June 1996).

32. Wilson to Simon, 16 July 1962.

33. Simon to Wilson, 29 July 1962.

34. Julius Held to Norton Simon, 26 January 1962; Michael Jaffé to Richard Brown, 16 February 1962.

35. Simon to Geoffrey Agnew, 10 June 1960.

36. Agnew to Simon, 10 October 1962.

37. Simon to Agnew, 26 October 1962.

38. Agnew to Simon, 29 October 1962.

39. Simon to Agnew, 27 November 1962.

40. Tooth to Simon, 12 June 1963. In addition to the Renoir and two Degas works, two other paintings from the Cargill sale eventually entered the Simon collections: Pierre Bonnard, *Madame Lucienne Dupuy de Frenelle* (cat. 276) and Henri Fantin-Latour, *White and Pink Mallows in a Vase* (cat. 398).

41. Simon to Tooth, 1 July 1963.

42. Baldass, 1929, and Troche, 1932, attribute the painting to Cariani.

43. Scholars attributing the picture to Titian included Suida, 1933; Morassi, 1942; and Valcanover, 1960.

44. See, for instance, Richter, 1937; Pignatti, 1955; and Berenson, 1957.

45. Duveen records, Getty Research Institute, Box 185, General Stock books New York, Paris, and London, 1935–1937.

46. Boggis to Simon, 17 June 1957.

47. Simon to Boggis, 3 July 1957.

48. Boggis to Simon, 31 October 1957.

49. Fowles to Simon, 7 February 1962.

50. Simon to Fowles, 21 February 1962.

51. Simon to Fowles, 10 September 1963.

52. Fowles to Simon, 30 September 1963.

53. Fowles to Simon, 3 December 1963.

54. The following writers attribute the painting to Titian: Lucco, 1995; Anderson, 1996; and Joannides, 2001.

Turning Point
1964

I know of no successful art dealer who isn't a really solid businessman.—NORTON SIMON[1]

NORTON SIMON'S TENTH YEAR as an art collector, 1964, marked a profound turning point in his level of activity and dedication. It was unquestionably the most important year to date in the development of his collection (see Appendix). If nothing else, he bought the monumental Duveen inventory. In addition, he made ninety other acquisitions in 1964, more than twice the number of works he bought in 1963 and five times that of any other year. While the numbers are impressive, the sum paid was even more so, with more spent on art in 1964 than in the ten previous years combined. From 1954 through 1963, Simon made 168 acquisitions and spent about $6 million. In 1964 alone he spent almost $7 million.[2]

Although at this point about 75 percent of Simon's collection dated to the nineteenth and twentieth centuries, he was intrigued by a varied assortment of objects. In 1964 he bought everything from a riveting fifteenth-century depiction of Christ by Hans Memling to a twentieth-century still life by Georges Braque. Dealers who specialized in later material, such as Alexandre Rosenberg and Dudley Tooth, sold him Impressionist and modern art, but he dealt as well with firms whose offerings spanned many centuries, such as Wildenstein, Thomas Agnew, and M. Knoedler & Co. From these latter dealers he acquired most of his old masters. He also purchased three paintings from the firm of Duveen Brothers.

Duveen specialized in works from the eighteenth century and earlier. Established in 1879 in England and eventually made eminent by Lord Joseph Duveen, the firm was responsible for placing major works of art with the greatest early-twentieth-century American collectors, such as Henry Clay Frick, Andrew Mellon, and Henry Edwards Huntington. Duveen Brothers was one of the first dealers Norton Simon visited, probably in early 1955. From them in 1956 he acquired two paintings attributed to Rembrandt, *A Jewish Philosopher* and *Portrait of a Lady, Traditionally Said to Be Hendrickje Stoeffels* (p. 22). As noted in chapter 3, Simon also acquired from Duveen in September 1963 *Bust Portrait of a Courtesan* attributed to Giorgione (p. 47). With the exception of these three paintings, Simon had displayed little interest in this venerable if somewhat antiquated institution.

OPPOSITE
Claude Michel, called Clodion, *Bacchante Supported by Bacchus and a Faun*, 1795 (detail), The Norton Simon Foundation. CAT. D68.

ABOVE LEFT
Norton Simon

FIG. 1. Mr. and Mrs. Edward Fowles in a showroom at Duveen Brothers, c. 1964

All of this changed with surprising speed in late 1963. Shortly after Simon finalized the Giorgione transaction, he began investigating other objects at Duveen. By November 1963 he had reserved seven artworks.[3] In January 1964 he requested that five additional paintings be sent to the Los Angeles County Museum, with all transportation and insurance costs borne by Duveen.[4] The next month, seven paintings and two sculptures were shipped.[5] An undated draft in early February outlines a purchase agreement for fourteen objects, some already in California. Simon's handwritten notes on the draft advise that the remaining items be "shipped to LA museum promptly for purpose of [The Norton Simon Foundation] getting possession." The draft further stated that the foundation agreed that all pictures would be offered for loan to the Los Angeles County Museum of Art (then under construction) for a minimum of three years, in an effort to be "helpful in the development of the new museum in Los Angeles."

In the meantime, there was a flurry of activity by Simon and his staff, as he weighed the advantages of buying parts of the firm's inventory or buying the company outright. Duveen's owner, Edward Fowles, then seventy-nine years old, was interested in dissolving the business while providing for himself and his employees, most also past retirement age. The job of smoothing the way with Fowles and his wife Jean (fig. 1), fell to Simon's assistant Barbara Roberts.

For the first decade of his collecting life, Simon worked without a curator to help him with his acquisitions and research. He communicated directly with dealers and scholars, occasionally relying on the corporation's clerical staff to deliver messages. It was not until 1964 that he secured an assistant whose sole purpose was to help him with art acquisitions. Roberts had a journalism background and was a former copywriter at McCall Corporation (a Norton Simon company), but she had no art experience. In 1963 she initially worked as an executive assistant reading and distilling the many reports Simon needed to digest before attending meetings of the several boards on which he served, especially those of the Regents of the University of California. By early 1964 she was interacting full-time with art dealers. With the acquisition of Duveen Brothers, Roberts not only became Simon's liaison with Edward and Jean Fowles, but she also supervised the company's dismantling and the distribution of loans from its inventory to museums around the country.

The prospect of acquiring an entire business operation was certainly not new to Simon, who had taken control of such disparate companies as McCall Corporation, Ohio Match Company, and Wheeling Steel. Now, with Duveen, he moved at an incredible pace: in less than three months, he went from discussing a minor transaction for a few pictures to negotiations to take over the whole company. On 19 February Fowles and Simon signed two separate agreements. In the first, both parties agreed to a ninety-day option on Duveen's outstanding inventory for $4 million, at $400,000 per year.[6]

In the second contract, the foundation agreed to buy eighteen artworks, divided into groups, acquiring one group a year over nine years at a total price of $1,525,750. The foundation was granted an option to purchase three additional paintings at a total price of $835,000.[7] Simon and Los Angeles County Museum director Ric Brown had picked the twenty-one paintings and sculptures they considered the best of the dealer's holdings, among them works by Claude Michel (called Clodion, fig. 2), Nicolas Largillière, Desiderio da Settignano, Francesco di Giorgio, Bernardino Luini, Anthony van Dyck, Peter Paul Rubens, Jean-Honoré Fragonard, and Sandro Botticelli (fig. 3). The two agreements were complementary and effectively gave the foundation the opportunity to investigate Duveen's inventory and accounts. If, for any reason, Simon did not like what was discovered during the examination, he could relinquish the ninety-day option on the entire inventory and still have an option to buy what he considered the cream of the stock.

Before the end of the option period, The Norton Simon Foundation decided to buy it all—art inventory, library, and building.[8] The foundation and Fowles signed a purchase agreement on 18 April 1964, which for $200,000 gave the foundation the option to purchase the entire outstanding inventory of Duveen Brothers, for a total price of $4 million payable in ten equal annual installments. Within days, the sale was reported in the newspapers. The $4-million price was not disclosed, but the collection was purportedly valued at $15 million, which became the amount eventually mentioned in every news report.[9]

The entire Duveen inventory numbered about 780 objects: 21 drawings, 164 paintings, and 61 sculptures by Italian, French, and British artists. There were more than 100 pieces of furniture, consisting of French and Italian tables, chairs, desks, and assorted odds and ends. The approximately 400 remaining objects ranged from Flemish and French tapestries (fig. 4) to paneled rooms, mantelpieces, chandeliers, and Chinese porcelain. Finally, there were some copies, second-rate pieces, and outright fakes.

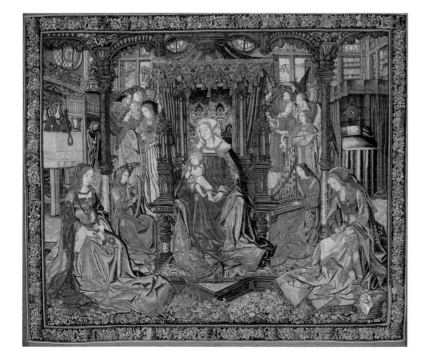

TOP

FIG. 2. Claude Michel, called Clodion, *Bacchante Supported by Bacchus and a Faun*, 1795, The Norton Simon Foundation. CAT. D68

ABOVE

FIG. 3. Sandro Botticelli, *Madonna and Child with Adoring Angel*, c. 1468, Norton Simon Art Foundation. CAT. D8

LEFT

FIG. 4. Flanders, Brussels, *Holy Family with Music-Making Angels*, c. 1520, The Norton Simon Foundation. CAT. D90

To learn more about the paintings, Roberts invited noted art historians to the New York gallery. The specialists included the Renaissance scholars Everett Fahy and Creighton Gilbert, the art critic Clement Greenberg, the director of the Worcester Museum of Art, Daniel Catton Rich, the chief curator of the Metropolitan Museum of Art, Theodore Rousseau, and the paintings conservator William Suhr. Roberts created spreadsheets with each expert's remarks arranged in columns next to the painting in question, so that Simon could take in all at once the usually consistent but occasionally conflicting opinions (see spreadsheet in Notes section). The experience of poring over the comments was enlightening, but it also honed Simon's ability to judge the quality of his holdings and possible acquisitions. Over the next few years, Simon weighed these responses when considering paintings to deaccession. Among those he sold in the late 1960s was a portrait of a man attributed to Botticelli (D110) that engendered these negative comments: "Ugh, awful," "Oh, no," and "Good God." Yet Simon did not always completely rely on the remarks. He kept some paintings in spite of negative opinions, perhaps because he saw something promising. He retained until 1980 a *Virgin and Child with Saint John* by Biagio d'Antonio (D106) that the specialists found "pedestrian" and "so-so." He also later sold a few that the specialists liked very much, notably a selection of fine portraits by British painters. When Simon sold these works by Thomas Gainsborough, George Romney (fig. 5), and others in the May 1971 sales, he said it was because he did not wish to collect and compete in an area in which the Huntington Library in neighboring San Marino already had spectacular holdings.

As in the past, Simon also relied on Ric Brown. Brown, in fact, had originally advised against the Duveen purchase, believing that there were too many questionable attributions in the group. He was often incautious in sharing his thoughts, which resulted in a strained relationship with Edward and Jean Fowles. In a memorandum to Simon, Roberts reported:

> The Fowles's bitterness toward Ric has deepened to overt hatred. They not only did not get over their anger toward him during their two-week stay in Rome but gained added fuel. They saw Dr. Faldi, Director of the Doria Pamphili Gallery [who] told them, "Dr. Brown has almost convinced me that your *Salome* is a sixteenth-century copy of ours." This comment, added to Luisa's[10] story of Ric's attitude toward the Duveen collection makes them certain that Ric is doing his best to negate their pictures.[11]

According to Roberts, Jean Fowles tried to undermine Brown's comments by saying that the museum director was "becoming obsessed with his own importance":

> He receives red carpet treatment in Europe but he doesn't realize this is afforded him not personally but because he represents a number of important collectors. Edward suggests that what Ric really desires is to have the money represented by the Duveen sale to use in European buying trips. Thus, he could play a more meaningful role in building [LACMA's] collection, and build his own reputation and status at the same time.[12]

Roberts went on to relay to Simon the Fowleses' overt flattery:

> Jean said you must always remember that it is rarely the director who makes a museum great; it is done by one or more collectors of courage and conviction, i.e., Altman, Bache, Morgan, and Rockefeller for the Metropolitan, Mellon, Kress, and Widener at the National Gallery, Frick for his own museum, etc.[13]

It was understood that Fowles would continue to sell some of the inventory. The foundation did not intend to keep everything, and from 1964 until 1969 sold about 125 objects, including carpets, chairs, decorative objects, porcelain, and a handful of paintings.[14] The foundation placed Duveen artworks on loan at several museums, including the Metropolitan Museum of Art, the Museum of Fine Arts, Boston, the Wadsworth Atheneum, the Worcester Art Museum, and the M. H. de Young Memorial Museum in San Francisco.

In Los Angeles, Simon donated a few pieces of Italian furniture to the Elmer Belt Library of Vinciana at the University of California, Los Angeles (UCLA), and at the request of Simon's friend and fellow University of California regent, Dorothy B. Chandler, the foundation lent nine paintings to the Founders' Room in the concert hall named after her at the newly completed Los Angeles Music Center. The vast majority of the objects, however, Simon had shipped to the Los Angeles County Museum of Art (LACMA) just in time for its public opening in March 1965. More than 200 paintings, drawings, tapestries, decorative art objects, and pieces of furniture substantially supplemented LACMA's permanent collection and, it was hoped, would serve as a catalyst for gifts or other loans. At the time of the opening, the *Los Angeles Times* optimistically reported:

> The cream of the famous Duveen Collection, acquired by Los Angeles industrialist Norton Simon some months ago, constitutes the most important long-term loan of great art on view in the new museum. The history of America's greatest museums in New York, Boston, Philadelphia and Chicago proves that their world-famous collections had their start in similar loans which were eventually converted into gifts by this country's great art patrons.[15]

The Duveen artworks continued to be on exhibit at LACMA until early 1971, when Simon decided to sell a major portion of his personal collection and works from the foundation at auction at Parke-Bernet in New York. At the two-day sale on 7–8 May 1971, more than 300 objects from the collection were sold, bringing in about $860,000. Other sales followed in 1973 and 1974. Today the Norton Simon collections retain only about 130 artworks from the 1964 Duveen inventory.

FIG. 5. George Romney, *Miss Kitty Calcraft*, c. 1787, Brigham Young University Museum of Art, Provo, Utah. CAT. D156

Wildenstein had offered it to Simon in 1963, and they agreed that he would keep the pastel for one year at the asking price of $210,000 plus 8 percent interest, with principal and interest due in January 1964. The work appealed to Simon on several levels: the brilliant application of pastel, the subject of a nude bather, and, especially, its provenance—it was at one time in the collection of Claude Monet. To distinguish the pastel from his other works by Degas, and because of the woman's distinctive slippers, Simon gave it the nickname "Red Shoes." He already owned another Degas pastel of a woman drying herself, the seated bather from Knoedler (p. 43). Of almost identical size, the works were superficially similar, but the compositions and medium are quite different. These circumstances again offered Simon the opportunity to compare artworks, and the $16,800 interest was a relatively small price to pay to live with the bather for a year before reaching a decision. Just as he had relished comparing the portraits of Suzanne Manet and Hendrickje Stoeffels, he was fascinated by juxtaposing disparate works. Simon displayed the Degas bather, for instance, alongside paintings by Hans Memling, Honoré Daumier, and Giorgione in his study (fig. 7). Ten years later he sold the Degas back to Wildenstein for $700,000. In spite of his affection for the pastel, the $490,000 profit was no doubt irresistible. He never lost interest in the work, however, and in 1978 again bought it from the dealer, this time for $40,000 less than he sold it for.[16]

WHILE NORTON SIMON WAS NEGOTIATING with Duveen in early 1964, he continued to buy other works of art at an astonishing rate. He bought thirty-nine artworks from other dealers before the Duveen agreement in April, and by the end of the year the total numbered ninety. In January alone he spent almost $450,000 on two drawings by Rembrandt, a suite of one hundred linocuts by Pablo Picasso, a cityscape by Jan van der Heyden, and a pastel by Degas (cats. 169–173). The Degas, *Woman Drying Herself after the Bath* (fig. 6), is a monotype reworked in pastel depicting a nude woman standing in front of a mirror drying her back. A monotype is a print created by applying ink directly to a metal plate and transferring the illustration to paper. Generally only one image is printed, although Degas would on occasion print two, the second fainter than the first. He would set aside the first image and rework the second with pastel, as he did with *Woman Drying Herself after the Bath*. The artist has placed the bather in shadow and skillfully highlighted just the edges of her right side, bed, and petticoats. He further enlivened the whole by dressing his model in a pair of bright red slippers.

FIG. 6. Edgar Degas, *Woman Drying Herself after the Bath*, 1876–1877, The Norton Simon Foundation. CAT. 172

FIG. 7. Study in the Simon house, 1964

In February 1964 Simon bought his first sculpture by Aristide Maillol, *Young Girl with Arm over Her Eyes* (cat. 176). Maillol became a favored artist, and Simon eventually owned over fifty works by the French sculptor. On more than one occasion, he bought the same likeness, as he did in June 1964 when he purchased a second cast of *Young Girl with Arm over Her Eyes* from Alexandre Rosenberg (cat. 224). Since this was only Simon's fifth Maillol, it is hard to imagine he was having trouble telling them apart. On the other hand, at this time he was grappling most intensely with the Duveen purchase, and it is possible that with the relatively low price of $6,500, he may not have been paying much attention. He kept both bronzes for six years, allocating one to his home and the other to his office in Fullerton. In 1970 he sold one at auction, and the other went to Lucille Simon.

Although Simon owned a selection of drawings by nineteenth- and twentieth-century artists, before 1964 he had acquired only two drawings by old masters, one by Jean-Antoine Watteau (cat. 97) and one attributed to Peter Paul Rubens (cat. 162). In this year, however, he bought twenty-three Dutch, French, and Italian drawings by artists from the sixteenth to eighteenth centuries. His focus on the old masters is attributable in part to his concentrated interest in the Duveen stock, which also contained twenty-one drawings. But these particular purchases might also have been inspired by a Smithsonian Institution exhibition of eighteenth-century Venetian drawings that was shown at the Los Angeles County Museum of Art in early 1964.[17] The exhibition included works by Francesco Guardi, Pietro Longhi, Bernardo Bellotto, and Giovanni Battista Tiepolo, among others. Simon had many Italian drawings on approval that spring, stacked on the sofa and floor of his study (fig. 7), and bought nine within three months of the exhibition.[18] He was also discussing the market and upcoming sales with Peter Wilson at Sotheby's and asked Wilson to keep him informed of good old master paintings and drawings.[19]

In April, the same month as the Duveen purchase, Simon bought twenty-one other objects, fifteen of which were old master drawings, as well as paintings by Anthony van Dyck (cat. 211), Claude Monet (cat. 213), and Hans Memling. *Christ Giving His Blessing* by Memling (fig. 8) is a compelling depiction of Jesus gazing directly and benevolently at the viewer. Simon first discussed the painting with M. Knoedler & Co. in 1962, reserved it in late 1963 pending Ric Brown's review, and arranged for its shipment in February 1964, along with the van Dyck portrait, *Marchesa Lomellini Durazzo* (cat. 211; see fig. 15). Knoedler wanted $455,000 for the two paintings. Ever the negotiator, Simon proposed to pay $400,000 in the form of a three-year promissory note.[20] Later, in March 1967, Simon became aware of another Memling of the same subject in the William A. Coolidge collection (fig. 9).[21] He learned that Knoedler sold it to Coolidge in 1955, and that Coolidge had known about a second version at the time. Angered by the fact that another collector was better informed than he, Simon spent a few weeks studying the differences between the two works. He postponed the final payment almost a month, and then wrote indignantly to the dealer to state his reason for the delay:

> I have always considered Knoedler among the dealers from whom I would prefer to buy my paintings—because of faith in Knoedler's

ABOVE
FIG. 8. Hans Memling, *Christ Giving His Blessing*, 1478, Norton Simon Art Foundation. cat. 210

RIGHT
FIG. 9. Hans Memling, *Christ Blessing*, 1481, oil on panel, 13 13/16 x 9 7/8 in. (35.1 x 25.1 cm), Museum of Fine Arts, Boston

integrity of communication concerning all important matters on paintings. In the case of the Memling I was quite disturbed when I found that in 1955 Knoedler had sold a Memling which was representationally quite similar to the Memling which was sold to me. In selling that Memling Knoedler used good care to inform the purchaser of the existence of the Memling I ultimately purchased. However, in my case, although you had sold the similar Memling only seven or eight years before, you failed to call this to my attention. Respecting your integrity, I do not feel it appropriate to hold up payment any longer or ask you for adjudication of some kind in regard to the picture. Obviously I like the picture and would like to keep it, but if it becomes apparent to me that lack of the information which was at your disposal did not give me the opportunity to check as thoroughly as I would have before making such a purchase, I may feel otherwise. I hope that the occasion does not present itself, but I do know that you should appreciate my position.[22]

Knoedler responded that Coolidge already knew of the other version and that they thought he wished to remain anonymous, noting at any rate that both paintings were published as genuine Memlings.[23] Knoedler continued assuringly, "There has never come to our attention any opinion reflecting adversely upon the genuineness, authenticity, or artistic quality of the painting."[24] Art historians continued to assure Simon about his painting, yet the fact that there were two similar Memlings haunted him for many years, and he asked for a comparison of the two versions almost every time he discussed his picture.

Shortly after buying the Memling, Simon added several important Impressionist paintings, including works by Cézanne, Monet, and Degas. The Cézanne, *Still Life with Pears and Apples, Covered Blue Jar, and a Bottle of Wine* (cat. 225), is a glorious and spare watercolor bought for $90,000. Concerned about continuously displaying works on paper, and tempted by the handsome profit he would reap, Simon sold it in 1981 to the art dealer Eugene Thaw for $500,000. (Thaw later gave it to the Morgan Library in New York.) Simon purchased Monet's *Water Lilies, Giverny* (fig. 10) from Sam Salz in New York for $240,000. The painting was displayed in his home until his divorce in 1970, when it was allotted to him as part of the settlement. Simon decided to place it in the Parke-Bernet sale of his

FIG. 10. Claude Monet, *Water Lilies, Giverny*, 1919, private collection. cat. 222

collection in May 1971, where it brought $320,000. This small profit was utterly dwarfed when it was resold at auction in June 2008, this time bringing $80 million.[25]

Degas's *Actress in Her Dressing Room* (fig. 11) also left the collection, but later returned for good. Dudley Tooth approached Simon about two pictures in April 1964. The first was a Johannes Vermeer from the collection of Sir Alfred Beit;[26] the second was the Degas. Tooth rightly gauged his client's penchant for nineteenth-century objects and especially for Degas. More than one-half the collection dated from the nineteenth century, including seventeen works by Degas. Therefore, although Tooth mentioned the Vermeer in every letter, he was more aggressive with the Degas, tempting Simon with flattery and negotiation strategy: "The owner is a lady who gave it to me for sale on condition I only showed it to serious collectors. She would want quick cash if she accepted an offer but I know this will not worry you."[27] Simon asked for the Degas to be shipped to him on approval. Once he had it in hand, and knowing he put both the dealer and the owner at a disadvantage, Simon pushed back, offering less than the asking price of £50,000. Tooth cabled, "After very tough fight with owner have bought Degas for £44,000 [about $123,000]. Feel certain would have fetched more at Sotheby's."[28]

After installing *Actress in Her Dressing Room* in his home and living with it for a few years, Simon developed something of a love/hate relationship with the picture. While he was drawn to the intense coloring, bold brushwork, and mysterious aspect of the figure seen from the back, he struggled with what he perceived to be her ugly reflection in the mirror. This ambivalence led first to his selling the painting at auction in May 1971 for $100,000, but then repurchasing it nine months later for $135,000.

In June, in an article entitled "The Abstract Businessman," *Time* magazine described Simon as the most discriminating art collector on the West Coast. The article quoted a museum curator as saying, "in the same way he picks up a company that could be doing better, Simon makes a good painting more important by adding it to his collection." Ric Brown added, "Simon's primary consideration is esthetic quality without regard for periods, and he lives with it just that way, hanging a Van Dyck alongside a Gorky in his office, a Memling alongside a Degas at home. This takes courage and taste."[29]

The remainder of the year saw no letup in Simon's acquisitions, for either his personal collection or the foundation's. Most significant for the foundation's present collection were his acquisitions of Canaletto's *The Piazzetta, Venice, Looking North* (cat. 229) and Georges Braque's *Still Life with Musical Instruments* (cat. 232). Of less importance were works such as a beach scene by Maurice Prendergast (cat. 236) bought at auction for $21,000. Simon sold it a little over a year later to the Los Angeles collector Justin Dart for $25,000 through the dealer Paul Kantor. Even at these small dollar amounts, however, Simon was meticulous in noting profits and losses. His notation on Kantor's bill for a $3,500 commission states, "Please pay and reduce from selling price. Picture also cost I think $250 to clean and about $80 freight which means I came out with a *little* profit."[30] The profit was $170.

During the last two months of 1964 Simon continued to add artworks from a range of periods. From Christie's he acquired the oil sketch *Study for "Leda and the Swan"* by the English painter William Etty (fig. 12). It was one of his favorite pictures, no doubt owing to the appealing nude, yet he never owned another work by Etty. His last purchase of the year, from Rosenberg, was Paul Gauguin's colorful and riveting *Self-Portrait with Palette* (fig. 13). Painted in France after Gauguin's first trip to Tahiti, the picture shows the artist against a red background prominently holding his brush and palette. Simon had known about the painting for at least eighteen months, when it was first offered by Dudley Tooth, who wrote:

ABOVE LEFT
FIG. 11. Edgar Degas, *Actress in Her Dressing Room*, c. 1875–1880 and c. 1895–1905, The Norton Simon Foundation. CAT. 221

LEFT
FIG. 12. William Etty, *Study for "Leda and the Swan,"* c. 1840, Jennifer Jones Simon Art Trust, Los Angeles. CAT. 248

ABOVE
FIG. 13. Paul Gauguin, *Self Portrait with Palette*, 1893–1894, private collection, New York. CAT. 258

The Gauguin *Self-Portrait* is physically in front of me now. As I told you, the starting price is $300,000, without our commission. I have an English client negotiating for it and when I find out what is the really lowest price, and if my client eventually gives up, I will let you know. It is a tremendously impressive picture and belongs to Arthur Sachs in Paris.[31]

Tooth wrote again a few weeks later, "My London client's offer of £80,000 [about $223,000] for the Gauguin *Self-Portrait* has been turned down. I know you find fault with the tonality of the hand [which] Gauguin has purposely understated."[32] In March 1964 the painting went to Alexandre Rosenberg, who sold it to Simon in December for $275,000. Simon kept the *Self-Portrait* for six and a half years, finally selling it in 1971. It is not known either why he was unhappy with the painting or why he sold it. Perhaps the understated hand mentioned by Tooth continued to bother him, but it is more likely that—as with most of his other deaccessions—he wanted to capitalize on its increased value. When he sold it at Parke-Bernet in 1971, the $420,000 sale price was a world auction record for the artist.

As their personal collection grew, the Simons had increasing difficulty finding places to display it.[33] They were able to buy the house next door in early 1963 and by that October hired architects.[34] The house was demolished, and construction on an addition to their existing home began in July 1964. In describing the remodeled house, the writer Barnaby Conrad noted its unpretentiousness, declaring that with no grand driveway or high walls, "it might be the house of a successful contractor or orthodontist." Conrad was especially struck by its unassuming design compared with the magnificent art collection within: "If the house is undistinguished on the outside it is undistinguished in the same way the Prado in Madrid is undistinguished; inside is a priceless trove."[35] A winding hallway gallery connecting the house and the addition (fig. 14) was lined on one side with paintings and low bookshelves and on the other with a two-sided floor-to-ceiling glass exhibition case for sculpture that afforded a view of the interior garden. The highlight of the new addition, however, was a large and comfortable sitting room flanked on one side by Norton's office and on the opposite wall by an alcove holding a set of sliding panels on which were mounted an assortment of paintings. The panels could slide into and out of view, depending on what works the Simons or their visitors wanted to see (figs. 15, 16).

The Simons stored most of their private art collection at the Los Angeles County Museum while construction continued through late 1964 and early 1965. Before returning home, however, the collection had the distinction of being the first exhibition at the newly built Los Angeles County Museum of Art on Wilshire Boulevard. ❧

OPPOSITE LEFT
FIG. 14. Norton Simon in the gallery hallway of his house, 1970

OPPOSITE RIGHT
FIG. 15. Sitting room in Simon house, 1967

ABOVE
FIG. 16. Norton and Lucille Simon in their sitting room with moveable exhibition walls in the background, 1967

1. Norton Simon, in *Newsweek*, 1964, p. 61.

2. The ninety acquisitions, excluding the $4,000,000 Duveen purchase, cost $2,979,949.

3. Fowles to Simon, 22 November 1963. The reserved artworks were by (or attributed to) Fra Angelico (D1), Francesco di Giorgio Martini (D19), Sebastiano Mainardi (D35), Donatello (D71), and Botticelli (D110). Two frescoes of angels attributed to Giotto were also mentioned, but do not appear with that name on the Duveen stock list. The "D" numbers herein refer to the Duveen inventory list, which begins on p. 441.

4. Triumph Insurance Agency to Duveen Brothers, 10 January 1964. The paintings, chosen with the aid of Los Angeles County Museum director Ric Brown were *Rest on the Flight into Egypt* now attributed to Vincenzo Catena (D12); Bernardino Luini, *The Toriani Altarpiece* (D33a–e); and Peter Paul Rubens, *King Louis XIII* and *Anne of Austria* (D50a–b). A *Madonna and Child* attributed to Paolo Veneziano is also listed but does not appear with that name in the Duveen stock list.

5. Duveen Brothers to Frenkel & Co., Inc., 6 February 1964. In addition to the Fra Angelico, *Virgin and Child* (D1) and Francesco di Giorgio, *Fidelity* (D19), both reserved in November, the artworks were Francesco d'Antonio, *Virgin* and *The Archangel Gabriel* (D18a–b); Desiderio da Settignano, *Madonna and Child* (D69); Giambologna, *Rape of Proserpina* (D74); Sandro Botticelli, *Virgin and Child with Saint John* (D112); Bernardo Daddi, *Virgin and Child* (D120); and Anthony van Dyck, *The Princess of Orange* (D125).

6. Two-page Purchase Agreement, 19 February 1964, between Duveen Brothers, Inc. and The Norton Simon Foundation.

7. Purchase Agreement, 19 February 1964, between Duveen Brothers, Inc. and The Norton Simon Foundation. The eighteen were the artworks mentioned in notes 4 and 5 above, by Francesco d'Antonio (D18a–b); Francesco di Giorgio Martini (D19); Luini (D33a–e); Rubens (D50a–b); Desiderio da Settignano (D69); Giambologna (D74); Daddi (D120), and van Dyck (D125); as well as Nicolas de Largillière, *The Marquis d'Havrincourt* (D30) and *The Sculptor Pierre Lepautre* (D31); Claude Michel, called Clodion, *Bacchante Supported by Bacchus and a Faun* (D68); and Carlo Crivelli, *Madonna and Child* (D119).

8. The library was sold to the Sterling and Francine Clark Art Institute in 1965. The building was sold to the dealer William Acquavella in 1967 (see p. 87).

9. See, for instance, Esterow, 1964; *Newsweek*, 1964; Seldis, 1972b, p. 27.

10. Luisa Vertova-Nicolson was a notable art historian and close colleague

	Clem Greenberg	Willy Suhr	Dan Rich	Ted Rousseau	Creighton Gilbert
Red Curtain Bellini	"Lovely" Was one of his two favorite pictures on first floor.	Only Bellini he liked, and he wasn't too sure of that. Never maintained it was a Bellini.	Liked a great deal and would hang with Bellini attribution.	"Lovely, but some of the restoration not advantageous."	This one really puzzled him and he was unwilling to take a definite stand. Cited certain technical and artistic contradictions.
Loeser Bellini	Didn't care for	"No"	"Definitely not right."	"Bad."	Liked Loeser least of all.
Luini's	Thought both were great.	"Nice, and you don't have any trouble deciding between them."	"Excellent, perfect. Condition is fine too."	"Very good. You'll take both, won't you?"	"Excellent; no problem either as to artistic merit, condition or attribution."
Francia's	Preferred one of St. Catherine	Liked both and suggested taking both.	"I would only select one." Preferred one with 2 saints.	Preferred one with 2 saints.	Definitely and positively preferred one with St. Catherine (which Ric has always favored). No attribution problem.
Bassano	"It's a real Venetian picture but rather dull."	Liked it. Said it was better than Giorgione Man. No comment.	"Dull and uninteresting"	"Good, and probably by Bassano"	Liked academically, although he felt picture rather dull. Attribution should be Venetian, 15th C. Costume will pin down date.
Nuzi		No comment	"Very mediocre. It's out."		"Nothing really"
Grasset Botticelli	"Beautiful"- his other favorite.	"Lovely, but I wouldn't risk calling it Botticelli. Should read Bot. - attrib. to."	"Very interesting. I'd take it and call it Botticelli-?."	"Very pretty. Would call it Bot. and assts. It's far better to under-attribute."	"Good pricture. It's School of Bot. but late school by artist who had talent. Superior to other School pictures."
Dossi	"Terrible"	Was very enthusiastic about it.	Didn't like it at all.	He and Liz Gardner both liked. They felt it was by Dossi too.	"Definitely possible that it's a Dossi. Check further and restore."

Spreadsheet with comments about artworks in the
Duveen collection, 1964

of the major Italian scholar Bernard Berenson, who provided Joseph Duveen with favorable attributions for many paintings.

11. Barbara Roberts to Simon, 23 November 1964. The "Salome" (D55) is a painting formerly attributed to Titian.

12. Ibid.

13. Ibid.

14. Several of these had been roundly panned by the specialists Roberts interviewed.

15. Seldis, 1965a, pp. 25, 38.

16. In December 1978 the Norton Simon Foundation repurchased the pastel for $310,000 plus the trade of *Water Lilies* by Monet (cat. 1332) valued at $350,000, for a total of $660,000 (see p. 182).

17. Los Angeles County Museum of Art, *Eighteenth-Century Venetian Drawings from the Correr Museum*, 16 January–18 February 1964 (traveled to the National Gallery of Art, Washington, The Museum of Fine Arts, Houston, and the California Palace of the Legion of Honor, San Francisco).

18. Cats. 180, 193, 196, 200, 202–204, 206, 207.

19. Wilson to Simon, 2, 5, 6 March 1964; Simon to Wilson, 3 March 1964. Additionally, Simon informed Wilson of the impending deal with Duveen Brothers (Simon to Wilson, 16 April 1964).

20. The note, dated 1 April 1964, promised to pay Knoedler $290,000 payable as follows: $90,000 on 1 April 1965, with interest on $290,000 at 8 percent per annum; $95,000 on 1 April 1966, with interest on $200,000 at 8 percent per annum; and $105,000 on 1 April 1967, with interest on the sum of $105,000 at 8 percent per annum.

21. The art collector William Coolidge was a trustee of the Museum of Fine Arts, Boston. His bequest to the museum includes his version of Memling's *Christ Giving His Blessing*, as well as other works by old masters and the Impressionists.

22. Simon to Roland Balay, 28 April 1967.

23. Friedländer, 1967–1976, vol. 6, p. 124.

24. Balay to Simon, 8 May 1967.

25. London, Christie's, 24 June 2008, lot 16.

26. Probably *A Young Woman Seated at the Virginal*, attributed to Vermeer, c. 1670, purchased by Steve Wynn, Las Vegas at London, Sotheby's, 7 July 2004, lot 8.

27. Tooth to Simon, 1 May 1964.

28 .Tooth to Simon, 8 June 1964.

29. *Time*, 1964.

30. Invoice from Paul Kantor Gallery to Simon, 11 January 1966.

31. Tooth to Simon, 20 June 1963.

32. Tooth to Simon, 1 July 1963.

33. By the end of 1963 they had more than 180 objects in their personal collection.

34. The lot, which sold for about $250,000, was at 110 North Hudson Avenue. The Simons hired the architects Henry Lawrence Eggers and Walter William Wilkman, designers of the graduate residence houses at the California Institute of Technology and the classrooms and library at Westridge School, Pasadena. In 2005 the Simon house and addition were razed and a new mansion was constructed on the site.

35. Conrad, 1968.

CHAPTER FIVE

Collector and Patron
1965

Simon in recent years has leaped from catsup to culture by assembling a $45 million assortment of art that ranks as one of the U.S.'s most impressive private collections.—TIME, 1965[1]

IN JANUARY 1965 LACMA's Ric Brown was not just overseeing the final phase of construction for the new museum, which was scheduled to open at the end of March. He was also serving his second year as president of the College Art Association, a national professional organization devoted to the visual arts. The association's annual conference brings together scholars, curators, critics, and artists to float new ideas, in a host city that readies all of its best art for the influx. The 1965 annual meeting was to be held in Los Angeles, giving Brown the opportunity to showcase the new museum for his colleagues. Norton Simon understood that among the delegates were the foremost scholars in the field of art history, and from his point of view their assessment of his collection was just as important as their preview of LACMA. Moreover, since his home was undergoing renovation, he was already storing his artworks at the museum. In a move that only Simon could orchestrate, he arranged for the best of his collection to be displayed in the galleries, well before the museum officially opened its doors to the public.

The exhibition, which opened 18 January 1965, ten weeks before the museum's official opening, featured more than 120 of Simon's paintings, drawings, prints, and sculptures (fig. 1).[2] It was on view for almost two months and taken down on 7 March, just three weeks before the museum was officially to open.[3] The LACMA curatorial staff was already upset with the administration's decision to move to the new building before construction was completed.[4] They surely suffered even more inconvenience by the additional responsibility of mounting and dismantling Simon's temporary exhibit as they rushed to complete the installation of the permanent collection. But aside from Simon's position as a board member, Brown and the board counted him as a formidable patron, since he was a generous lender to the museum in its former location as well as the new one.

The exhibition stressed the difference between The Norton Simon Foundation collection and the Simons' personal collection. The title, *A Selection from the Mr. and Mrs. Norton Simon Collection Honoring the College Art Association*, highlighted the private nature of the assemblage, as well as the fact that the works on display did not

OPPOSITE
Rembrandt van Rijn, *Portrait of a Boy in Fancy Costume*, c. 1655–1660 (detail), The Norton Simon Foundation. CAT. 266

ABOVE LEFT
Norton Simon

ABOVE
FIG. 1. Installation photograph: *A Selection from the Mr. and Mrs. Norton Simon Collection Honoring the College Art Association*, Los Angeles County Museum of Art, 18 January–7 March 1965

represent everything he owned. The *Los Angeles Times* likened Simon to the country's great art patrons:

> In less than 10 years' time Simon has become such a patron as this, and the owner of one of the top private collections anywhere. His benefactions to the County Art Museum have been great. Recently, when more than 1,000 members of the College Art Association met in Los Angeles and previewed our new museum, the Simons emptied their own home in order to put on display for the first time their private collection. Its scope dazzled these professional visitors.[5]

The national media also took note, calling the Simons' private collection "the finest single group of art works on the West Coast and for that matter one of the finest in the entire country. Here is a collection with strong personal identity and uncompromising standards. No showy, obvious, or routine work is included. Restraint and quality are the key words."[6] Among the works in the exhibition were his two earliest important acquisitions, Paul Gauguin's *Brittany Landscape with Swineherd* and Camille Pissarro's *Banks of the River at Pontoise* (p. 19.)[7] Yet it also included objects he was buying right up to the last minute before the exhibition opened, such as Gauguin's *Self-Portrait with Palette* (p. 61) and *Tahitian Woman and Boy* (fig. 2).

Simon first heard about the Tahitian Gauguin when Sotheby's notified him that it would appear in a November 1964 sale in London.[8] Simon decided not to bid, however, and the picture was bought by Hammer Galleries (which was co-owned by the Los Angeles collector Armand Hammer) for $252,000. Simon bought it for considerably more when he paid Hammer $365,000 six weeks later. Uncharacteristically, he did not balk at the tremendous markup. In fact, he boasted about the deal to friends and members of the trade, as the dealer David Nash later remembered:

> Norton had a story about the acquisition of every single picture, and he loved the story of the Gauguin. At that time, there was really only one other person in the Los Angeles community who was an active buyer and that was Armand Hammer. [The painting] was filthy dirty, having been untouched for many, many years, and Norton didn't want to be the person to buy it and have it cleaned and then discover that it was not in such good condition. So according to him, he allowed Armand Hammer to buy and then Hammer had the painting cleaned, and then Norton looked at it again and discovered how beautiful it was underneath and offered Hammer a fairly big profit. And Norton felt this had been a very clever move because if he competed against Hammer, he might have driven up the price much higher. This way, he allowed Hammer to take the risk and gave him a profit.[9]

During the early months of 1965, Simon was engaged in the activities surrounding LACMA's College Art Association exhibition as well as preparations for the museum's official opening at the end of March (fig. 3). He was also overseeing his corporate foundation's acquisition of land for a proposed art museum in the city of Fullerton, a move that somewhat belied his commitment to lend artworks and support to the County Museum.[10] Further, in addition to the purchase of the Gauguin, that January he learned about a painting coming up at auction that over the next few months became his sole preoccupation.[11] Against the backdrop of buildings and exhibitions, Simon concentrated his attention and energy on what would become possibly the most important acquisition of his life: Rembrandt's *Portrait of a Boy in Fancy Costume* (previously presumed to be the artist's son, Titus, fig. 4).[12]

Simon had known about the painting since at least 1957, when Claude Partridge of Frank Partridge & Sons in London wrote to him, "You mentioned you would like a late Rembrandt. There are now very, very few of these left in private

OPPOSITE

FIG. 2. Paul Gauguin, *Tahitian Woman and Boy*, 1899, Norton Simon Art Foundation. CAT. 262

RIGHT

FIG. 3. Lucille Simon, Mr. and Mrs. Edward Carter, Richard F. Brown, and Norton Simon at the opening of the Los Angeles County Museum of Art, March 1965

ABOVE

FIG. 4. Rembrandt van Rijn, *Portrait of a Boy in Fancy Costume*, c. 1655–1660, The Norton Simon Foundation. CAT. 266

hands. The Cook picture of his son Titus does not seem to be for sale: I know for a fact he was offered £120,000 [about $335,000] for it."[13] Simon responded, "In regard to the Rembrandts, the prices seem quite high. Of course, one never knows until one sees the actual paintings, but based upon the picture I have seen, the most outstanding is the Cook picture and the price is rather high for this relatively small picture."[14] Almost six years later in 1963, the price of the painting had risen considerably: Thomas Agnew & Sons offered it for £550,000 ($1,540,000). Geoffrey Agnew sent Simon several pages of the history of the painting, saying,

> There is no doubt that this is one of the most desirable and beautiful Rembrandts in the world. May I emphasize how important it is that no word should get out about the negotiations? I will look forward to hearing from you when you have consulted Ric Brown.[15]

As usual, Simon could not refrain from letting the word out and immediately talked with Edward Fowles of Duveen Brothers, who sent him a history of his own interest in the painting. Fowles wrote that it was probably worth "over half a million dollars" and advised him to buy it if possible.[16] After discussing the painting with Brown, Simon wrote back to Agnew:

> On thinking it over, the price seems quite high. I do not believe I would want Ric to go over there unless we could settle on a definite price with the owners that would be somewhat below the price you indicated. Furthermore, I feel that they should agree to give us a firm option for perhaps two or three days, which would be enough time for Ric to fly to London (and I might also accompany him) and also give him an opportunity to come to some definite judgments as to the condition of the picture. I don't believe these conditions are unreasonable, but I would like to have your views on them.[17]

Agnew responded by return mail, telling Simon that the painting was not in London but on the Isle of Jersey off the coast of Normandy, adding,

> In my opinion, which is, I think, universally shared among connoisseurs and experts, there is no problem about this picture as to its authenticity, condition, aesthetic quality, attractiveness, desirability and importance. The only problem is one of price. That can only be resolved by negotiation. As I have told you, I believe a fair price for the picture would be £550,000, but there is no possibility of getting the owner to agree to lowering his price unless one makes a firm offer. We have tried several methods of approach and our experience of dealing with this family extending over the last twenty-five years teaches us that a direct offer is the only way to achieve success.[18]

Simon wanted to examine the painting in a more convenient, neutral setting rather than in the home of the owner on the Isle of Jersey. Furthermore, he was not prepared to make a firm offer that was $1.1 million more than he had ever paid for a single work of art.[19] He answered Agnew two weeks later that he could not make the trip until at least April and that at any rate it was inconvenient for him and Brown to go to Jersey.[20] He told Agnew not to feel obligated to hold the painting for him, and it was another year—early 1964, around the time of the Duveen negotiations—before Agnew wrote again, mentioning that the owners were prepared to take the slightly lower price of £500,000 [$1,400,000], adding, "They do not wish to bring it to England for fear of complication about an export license, which they feel would not arise if the picture remained in Jersey."[21]

Simon responded on 18 March, "Surely I am still interested in the Cook Rembrandt, but it is so inconvenient to go over to Jersey—I'm also concerned that lighting conditions would not be of the best, and feel the chances of seeing it under the most favorable circumstances are remote." Agnew answered on 22 April that of course the light would be good in Jersey and that the painting could be seen in favorable circumstances ("The more I think of it, the more I feel it would be a wonderful addition to your collection"). He asked Simon to let him know the next time he planned to be in London so they could arrange a trip to see it. Since at the time Simon's mind, as well as his financial resources, was occupied with the acquisition of Duveen Brothers, he replied, "At this time, I am not too interested in pursuing the Cook Rembrandt."[22]

Over the next eight months, the owner decided to abandon the idea of selling the painting privately. To avoid an impending capital gains tax law in Great Britain that would take effect on 1 April 1965, the owner placed the picture with Christie's. On 18 January 1965, the day Simon's private exhibition opened at LACMA, Agnew again brought up the Rembrandt portrait. He informed him, "Now some important news. The Cook Rembrandt is coming up at Christie's. If possible, you should come and see it and, once again, I recommend it with all my heart and all my head." On 20 January Robert M. Leylan, Christie's U.S. representative and general manager, also wrote to advise Simon that the sale would take place in London in just two months, on 19 March, and that the presale estimate was about $1,500,000.[23] Remembering his unpleasant initiation in public auctions at the 1961 sale of *Aristotle with a Bust of Homer*,[24] Simon prepared himself for all eventualities, including making inquiries about the procedure for obtaining an export permit and alternative forms of financing.

On 15 March Leylan confirmed that Simon would arrive in London late in the evening of the 18th. At the airport he would be met by Christie's director John Herbert, who would take him to the headquarters of the two-hundred-year-old auction house on King Street. There he would meet chairman of the board I. O. "Peter" Chance, who would conduct the sale and give Simon the opportunity to examine the painting with an ultraviolet light. Because Simon was determined to remain anonymous, Leylan also verified that Christie's had reserved a suite under an assumed name at Claridge's: "Please be assured that I and all concerned at Christie's in London have done and will do everything possible to ensure anonymity on your behalf." To further cloak his identity, Simon arranged what he conceived to be an inscrutable mode of bidding. It was so complicated, however, that Christie's director Patrick Lindsay was obliged to make notes of Simon's instructions (fig. 5):

> Friday March 19th. Rembrandt. Lot 105. Portrait of Titus. When Mr. Simon is sitting down he is bidding. If he bids openly when sitting down he is also bidding. When he stands up he has stopped bidding. If he then sits down again he is not bidding until he raises his finger. Having raised his finger he is continuing to bid until he stands up again. P. Lindsay.[25]

FIG. 5. Notes by Christie's Patrick Lindsay regarding Norton Simon's bidding strategy

FIG. 6. Norton Simon protesting the winning bid at Christie's, 19 March 1965

During the bidding process, Simon confused Chance by bidding aloud, then remaining silent. Chance became convinced that although Simon was seated, he had stopped bidding. When the bid rose to $2.1 million, Simon stayed seated and silent despite Chance's entreaties for another bid. When Chance knocked down the painting to Marlborough Fine Art (on behalf of Stavros Niarchos),[26] Simon rose to his feet in protest (fig. 6). Eventually, in full view of the press, and in spite of objections from Marlborough, an embarrassed and shaken Chance put the painting back on the block and reopened the bidding. Marlborough did not bid again, and Simon bought the Rembrandt with the next bid of $2.2 million. Although Christie's conditions of sale regarding disputed bids require the auctioneer to reopen the bidding, it was utterly unheard of at a sale of this magnitude. The brouhaha, coupled with the extraordinary price, made headlines in papers around the world. Dudley Tooth, who had been sitting with Simon at the sale, dashed off a note to Simon that same afternoon, "You are flying to New York while I am writing this. What a party! I shall never forget it."[27]

Members of Simon's staff in Fullerton had worked for weeks to keep his interest in the picture—as well as his identity—a secret. At one point they discussed issuing clandestine code words to talk about the details of the sale. As a result, and along with everyone else, they were extremely surprised and amused by the ensuing publicity. His assistant Angelina Boaz confirmed his determination to remain anonymous as well as the extraordinary public end to the secrecy:

> Before he left [for London] he really wanted that painting. He said to me, "I'm going to the auction, but nobody will know I'm bidding. When I call you, I'll just say, 'Have so and so wire so much money.' I'll give you a password, and then you just go ahead, and have that money wired. But I won't say why. I don't want anybody to know that I've got the painting." On the way home from work the night of the auction, I heard on the radio, "Norton Simon just spent $2.2 million to buy a Rembrandt painting." When he next phoned, I said, "Oh that was a big secret!"[28]

Although Simon went through these complex, almost legendary lengths to keep his identity hidden, there was some speculation in advance that he would be the bidder, as David Nash later recounted:

> When Titus appeared on the market, I think it was at a time when everybody expected that the logical buyer was going to be Norton Simon. One has to remember that in those years, the art market was much, much smaller than it is now. Most of the people in it knew each other. It wasn't the huge international industry that it is today. And I know that everybody was expecting Norton to buy it, which is why he went, I think, through this elaborate plan to conceal the fact that he was going to bid for it.[29]

While stories of what transpired in the salesroom were widely circulated in newspapers and books,[30] Simon's own explanation has never been published. In 1975, in an interview in preparation for a possible biography with *Time* magazine Los Angeles bureau chief Marshall Berges, Simon related his version of the proceedings:

> What was the most colorful thing about the Titus? It was the way I really bid and the battle because of it. The truth of the matter is when I look back the only thing I can say is, I was worried and I was upset and it said right in the catalogue that if there is an argument, the auctioneer puts it up to bid again. It's just as clean cut as that. But everybody was emotionally involved. I was emotionally upset, so it stirred up something. When I was sitting down, as long as I was sitting down I was bidding. And what happened was, when I got up to a certain price, I'm sitting down and [Peter Chance] turns and looks at me—I told him I didn't want to be disclosed—and says, "I have a bid of so much over here, do I get any more?" He didn't point his finger at me, but did everything else but. "I'm going to knock it down. Once, twice, do I hear any more?" and he looks right at me. And I look at him with daggers in my eyes, but I wouldn't open my mouth, and he knocked it down to the other guy. I stood up and hollered and I was so goddamned emotional, I gave [the bidding instructions] to a dealer sitting next to me, who knew nothing about it, and I said, "Dudley [Tooth], they're screwing me, read this letter." He said "Norton, you didn't bid." I said, "Read the letter." And he reads the letter out loud. So that became the important event—not the price I paid for the picture or how good the picture was. And my God he gave me all kinds of time by saying, "Do I hear any more?" As far as I was concerned as long as I was sitting down, he was hearing more. He knew the reason I did that was that I didn't want anyone else to know that I was bidding. Finally they had a consultation up there on that platform and decided to throw it open to bidding again and the other bidder was so goddamned mad because it was already knocked down to him, that I made one more bid and he wouldn't bid again.

In the intervening years, Simon thought a good deal about Chance's behavior, and during the interview he offered an interpretation that was less about confusing instructions and more about strategy:

> Some way or another that auctioneer knew that was the last bid he was going to get out of the other fellow, and therefore he wanted to be damned sure I was bidding. Some way or another he got a signal, "This is it and I'm through." So now he figures, "I've got two and a quarter million at stake and nobody sees this man Simon bidding. Supposing he walks out on it, all I've got is a copy of a letter." Well that really should be enough. There's no excuse, except for the fact that nobody would know that I was bidding and therefore, he'd have to knock it down to me. He must have gotten nervous because it brought a lot more money than they expected. Really, the picture was great, everybody knew about the picture and they were all excited, but the thing that really caused the drama was something completely different.[31]

For the next two months Christie's engaged in negotiations both with the British Board of Trade over the granting of an export permit and with lawyers for Niarchos, who contended that Marlborough's bid was binding. The Reviewing Committee on the Export of Works of Art for Britain's Department of Education and Science met to review the petition for an export permit. The National Gallery opposed the export, citing the painting's national importance, its long history in an English collection, its outstanding aesthetic significance, and its rarity and charm.[32] Christie's countered that Rembrandt was well represented in Britain, and that the National Gallery in particular already possessed more Rembrandts than any other museum in Europe, including types exemplified by *Titus*. They believed that "The need to retain the Cook portrait for England seems to us to be unarguable on grounds either of artistic importance or of rarity."[33] Nevertheless, the Reviewing Committee recommended that the export license be withheld for one month to allow for a £798,000 (approximately $2.2 million) public subscription in England. In the absence of such an offer by 10 May 1965, the export license would be granted. In a gesture that could be seen as exceedingly generous, but more likely was a bid for favorable publicity and a way to force the National Gallery's hand, Simon offered to open a public subscription to keep the picture in London by lending it to the National Gallery for sixty days, and he promised to contribute between £50,000 and £100,000 to the subscription. Only three years earlier the National Gallery had pushed through a successful public appeal for Leonardo da Vinci's *Virgin and Child with Saint Anne and John the Baptist*. The museum decided it was too soon for another appeal and did not pursue *Titus*.[34] The export license was granted on 12 May.

Niarchos, in the meantime, continued to threaten Christie's with a lawsuit, clouding the issue of export and demanding assurances from the auction house that it would not release the painting to Simon without notice. A month after the sale, Niarchos withdrew his claim,[35] but days later his representative tendered an offer to Simon directly, writing, "I think Mr. Niarchos would still be interested to acquire the Rembrandt and, I have a feeling he would be prepared to pay you a profit of £100,000 ($280,000) if you were interested in disposing of it."[36]

Simon had no intention of selling, but there was still the question of payment to Christie's. Despite the delays in the export license, Christie's was obligated to pay the seller seven days after the sale. Because they had to borrow the money, Christie's asked Simon to reimburse some of the expenses.[37] Simon consulted with an attorney for the Norton Simon Foundation on this issue and delayed in taking a position on Christie's request for payment of interest. Although Christie's asked for interest on a thirty-day period, which amounted to £5,247, the foundation agreed to nine days, or £1,574. This continued to be a sore spot, and a rankled Peter Chance wrote that because he had agreed that Simon needed to pay for the picture only when it was delivered in New York, he had been advised he had no grounds to make a claim. He added, "While I have no alternative but to accept this legal interpretation, I feel that it works so inequitably that I am driven to write to you personally."[38] In a letter to Chance, the attorney for The Norton Simon Foundation, Milton Ray, responded that he could not permit the foundation's trustees to abrogate its legal rights. Ray concluded, "The only balm which we can hold out is the hope that you will more than recoup your loss in the course of future dealings."[39]

When *Titus* arrived in the United States accompanied by considerable fanfare, its first public exhibition was at the National Gallery of Art in Washington, displayed in a room by itself (fig. 7). In December, it moved to the Los Angeles County Museum of Art, where it was again given a special gallery. It remains one of Simon's most costly—and popular—acquisitions, and certainly the one for which he is best known. At the time of its acquisition, it was the second-most expensive painting to be sold at auction after Rembrandt's *Aristotle with a Bust of Homer*.[40] His longtime friend and colleague (and future president of the J. Paul Getty Trust) Harold Williams recalled, "I remember how proud Norton was. He was so excited. Probably the most excited I've ever seen Norton about an acquisition was Rembrandt's *Titus*."[41]

In the eleven months between the acquisitions of Duveen and *Titus*, Simon made almost sixty other purchases, and only nine were by old masters. After *Titus*, the shift to more modern artworks became even more dramatic, and over the next few years Simon bought objects that were almost exclusively from later periods. In part, he may have been making a conscious effort to balance the Duveen collections with Impressionist and modern art. On the other hand, his heart still remained in the later centuries.

FIG. 7. Norton and Lucille Simon with National Gallery of Art director John Walker at the exhibition for Rembrandt's *Portrait of a Boy in Fancy Costume*

IN SPITE OF THE TIME, MONEY, and energy that went into the *Titus* purchase, it was not Simon's only acquisition the spring and summer of 1965. In April, for instance, he acquired eight artworks, including two more by Degas. Simon had long been in the market for a cast of Degas's *Little Dancer, Aged Fourteen* (fig. 8) when Frank Lloyd of Marlborough Gallery notified him in February 1965 that he had secured a cast. It arrived in Los Angeles in mid-March. Indicative of Simon's inquisitiveness and burgeoning knowledge about bronze casting are the complaints he wrote on Marlborough's invoice (fig. 9). He criticized the insufficient information provided regarding the bronze's provenance and his inability to find an inscription on the cast, and he questioned whether the bow and skirt were original. He knew about the foundry marks and tried to find the inscription, which in fact was hiding on the dancer's thigh under the skirt. Simon did buy it, however, and displayed it in his home for six years before selling it in his large May 1971 auction sales. His curatorial staff suspected that he regretted selling the bronze. He certainly never lost his appreciation for Degas's sculptural works, and he acquired another cast of the *Little Dancer* in 1977, when he bought the entire set of Degas foundry models. When he sold this first example at Parke-Bernet in 1971, the bronze brought $380,000, which was a world auction record for both modern sculpture and the artist. When this same cast sold again in 1988, the price was $10,000,000.[42]

OPPOSITE

FIG. 8. Edgar Degas, *Little Dancer, Aged Fourteen*, private collection, Brunei. CAT. 269

ABOVE

FIG. 9. Marlborough-Gerson Gallery, New York, invoice for Edgar Degas's *Little Dancer, Aged Fourteen*, 12 March 1965, with Norton Simon's notes

TOP

FIG. 10. Edgar Degas, *Rehearsal of the Ballet*, c. 1876, The Nelson-Atkins Museum of Art, Kansas City, Mo. CAT. 271

Simon's second Degas acquisition that April, and another example of a great Degas no longer in the collection, is the beautiful *Rehearsal of the Ballet* (fig. 10). The dealer Stephen Hahn brought the work to Simon's attention and bought it for him at the 14 April Parke-Bernet auction. The pastel depicts the Paris ballet master Jules Perrot directing dancers on the stage, and it is thought to be one of the first—if not the first—Degas pastels in America, originally purchased from the artist by the American collector Louisine Havemeyer. It remained with her descendants until the sale, when the $410,000 price Simon paid set a world record for the artist. Unfortunately, Simon soon became concerned about its condition. His apprehension began shortly after its purchase, when it was lent to the Museum of Fine Arts, Boston. The museum's conservator, noting that there were several areas of flaking pigment and an acidic secondary mount, suggested securing the flaking and remounting the primary support, work that was accomplished before the pastel was sent to California. Simon continued to fear possible problems with its condition and potential losses. He again consulted experts, who assured him the pastel was stable. In spite of its beauty and historical significance, as well as reassurances from conservators, Simon's anxiety finally caused him to place it in Parke-Bernet's 1973 sale of objects from his personal collection. The picture was so noteworthy that its sale price of $780,000 set its second world record. It is now in the Nelson-Atkins Museum of Art in Kansas City.

FIG. 11. Leonardo da Vinci, *Ginevra de' Benci*, c. 1474/1478, oil on panel, 16 13/16 x 14 9/16 in. (42.7 x 37 cm), National Gallery of Art, Washington, D.C.

Because of the notoriety garnered from the Rembrandt sale, Simon was almost overnight transformed into the definitive A-list collector. He received dozens of offers of art from dealers and collectors, business propositions from would-be millionaires, and even fan letters addressed to *Titus* himself. As one of the world's most likely prospective buyers, Simon no longer paid interest on objects he kept at his home on approval. Dealers were willing to send him works to consider just for the opportunity to be associated with his collection, and he took full advantage.

Yet there was one opportunity that Simon considered— and finally declined—in which the owner would not allow the work to go to California under any circumstances before its sale. Arguably even more important than a Rembrandt painting, this was a portrait by Leonardo da Vinci. Sotheby's Peter Wilson telephoned Simon in May 1965 about Leonardo's *Ginevra de' Benci* (fig. 11), owned by Prince Franz Josef of Liechtenstein, at an asking price of $7 million.[43] He was assured that the owner was not showing the picture to anyone else, although Simon heard later from "museum friends" that the picture was being offered to others at $6 million.[44] Simon talked about the possibility of "good faith money" and removing the painting from Liechtenstein for examination before determining a value. This was unacceptable to the prince, whose terms were as steep as the price. He arranged through his agent that Parke-Bernet propose to Simon that he had ten days to pay $500,000 for a six-month option to buy the painting for $6 million. Although the option money was included in the price, if Simon decided

not to buy, he would forfeit the half million. Further, Simon was not allowed to have possession of the painting during the six months. The prince would keep it under seal and surveillance "in a strong room in the Prince's castle at Vaduz and shall not during the option period show it to or allow it to be inspected by any person other than you or your representatives."[45] Simon certainly intended to discuss the painting with others, and the offer stipulated that he would be able to discuss it with museum directors, collectors, and museum trustees, "subject to their understanding its confidential nature and on the footing that no further disclosure may be made by them."[46] Wilson arranged for Simon and Ric Brown to meet the prince in Liechtenstein in late June to examine the painting.[47] Simon persisted in wanting to borrow the Leonardo for a thorough pre-purchase examination, a move still unacceptable to the prince. Under the circumstances, Simon neither agreed to a deposit nor made an offer. Before the end of the year, however, newspapers announced that Simon had offered $6 million and reported that the prince had turned it down.[48] Simon responded in the *New York Times*, "I couldn't possibly acquire pictures if I talked about what I'm going to buy or not buy. I've seen the picture and it's very beautiful. But I've seen lots of other beautiful pictures. You don't buy them all."[49] Simon made no further overtures to buy the portrait. A little more than a year later, in February 1967, the National Gallery of Art in Washington, which already owned several works from the Liechtenstein collections, bought the painting for a reported $5.8 million.

Norton Simon and the Los Angeles County Museum of Art started the year 1965 with optimism and cooperation. After Simon's private exhibition for the College Art Association, the museum moved to ready the facility for its 31 March public opening (fig. 3). During the buildup, there was a good deal of positive publicity. *Time*, for instance, reported that the new museum made Los Angeles "the artistic capital of the U.S. west."[50] The *Los Angeles Times* published a special supplement devoted to the museum and declared the opening "a milestone in the cultural history of Southern California."[51] Simon's pivotal role in the museum's success was manifest: "Other names may have been on the museum buildings, but it was Norton Simon's collection, on loan only, that was the centerpiece."[52] Without Simon's paintings, the museum collection was, in the words of the art critic Alfred Frankfurter, "little more than non-vintage wine in shiny modern bottles."[53]

Favorable publicity and strong public interest in the new museum brought a new set of problems. At LACMA's April board of trustees meeting, Simon expressed concern over both the excessive crowds (47,000 on the first weekend) and the ineffectiveness of museum security.[54] He was upset about other issues beyond security, particularly the fact that the board itself still governed the Natural History Museum as well as the art museum, and he was especially critical of the board's failure to establish an art acquisitions policy. In delaying his agreement to a proposed two-year loan commitment, he complained about the board's failure to adopt a policy governing the museum's operation, laying most of the blame at the feet of the board chair, Edward Carter:

> I have come to the inescapable conclusion that you, as Chairman, are primarily responsible for the acts and omissions which pushed us to this decision. Although you undertook to separate the art museum and its Board from the museum of history and science, this has not been done. I appreciate that there are many important elements in building a social and cultural institution, but there comes a time when its main and ultimate purposes—public exposure to art—must be brought sharply back into focus. I feel that these matters, which have been discussed behind the scenes by many, should be brought out into the open and faced forthrightly at the next Board meeting.[55]

Questioning Simon's own commitment to the institution, Carter replied, calling Simon's allegations gross distortions:

> To date your own contributions of service, money or art to the County Museum have really been relatively modest. Despite this and because you have stated your intention to do

substantially more in the future, I have endeavored to accommodate your wishes regarding the museum to the extent that they squared with good practice and the maintenance of reasonable harmony. You should, however, be aware that along with other board members, I am becoming increasingly impatient with your unwarranted personal attacks and the recurring threats to remove your pictures.[56]

Simon answered in kind:

> Your letter shows clearly that you do not understand my intentions to assist the museum and that you do not appreciate the assistance I have rendered to date. Let me make my position clear—I want to help make the Los Angeles County Museum become one of the great museums of this country. You and I appear to be in fundamental disagreement as to how this is to be accomplished.[57]

Simon no doubt relayed his displeasure to the *Los Angeles Times* art writer, since it can hardly be a coincidence that only a few days later Henry Seldis wrote:

> It is no mere speculation to report that Simon's decision to bring the famous canvas [Rembrandt's *Titus*] to Washington first has to do with his growing dissatisfaction with developments within our new museum. "My hope still lies here," Simon told me after his decision regarding *Titus*. "I would like to see the majority of my current loans stay in the County Museum of Art for good. Without question the civic and social parts of a museum are important but its main purpose is and must be art." Simon seems to be unhappy with the lack of developing an overall acquisitions policy, with the relatively small number of art-minded members on the museum board and with incomplete separation of the County Museum of Art from other county museum branches.[58]

The difficulties at LACMA extended to the director's office, and Simon's longtime ally Ric Brown soon lost the support of the board, which urged his resignation. By year's end he left to direct the Kimbell Art Foundation in Fort Worth. The deputy director, Kenneth Donahue, from the Ringling Museum in Sarasota, Florida, was eventually named director. While Simon joined the other members of the LACMA board in unanimously accepting Brown's resignation, he remained his friend and admirer. In later years he pronounced LACMA a museum with too many bosses who failed to give Brown enough authority to do a good job.[59]

Although Norton Simon continued to be displeased with the leadership of the County Museum, he gave it considerable support through substantial loans of his artworks. At the same time, he was using the institution as a massive storage and exhibition facility. Exposure for his collection garnered Simon numerous accolades. However, he soon began to make it available to a wider audience beyond Los Angeles County. ❧

1. Berges, 1965.

2. The exact number in the exhibition is unknown. There was no catalogue and the only official museum record is an 8 January 1965 receipt for delivery of seventy-two artworks. The identity of other objects on view has been pieced together from installation photographs in the Norton Simon Museum curatorial archives.

3. Barbara Roberts to Theodore Rousseau, 17 March 1965. Roberts informed the Metropolitan Museum's chief curator Rousseau that Simon's collection was taken down on 7 March and placed in storage at the museum, adding, "Mr. Simon regrets that the conditions are so far from ideal, but since the remodeling of his home is not yet completed, he has no other alternative."

4. Barbara Roberts to Norton Simon, 9 February 1965. Roberts told Simon of staff concerns, in particular, the issue of artworks becoming soiled as a result of sandblasting.

5. Seldis, 1965a, pp. 25, 38.

6. Kuh, 1965, 35.

7. The Gauguin *Brittany Landscape* eventually became part of LACMA's collection, a gift from Lucille Simon in 1991.

8. Peter Wilson to Simon, 30 October 1964.

9. David Nash, interview by Davis Guggenheim, 14 July 1996. Before becoming a private dealer, Nash was a specialist in the Impressionist and Modern Department at Sotheby, Parke-Bernet in New York.

10. *Los Angeles Times*, 1965. See also chap. 6.

11. Geoffrey Agnew to Simon, 18 January 1965.

12. It is now generally agreed that the painting is not a portrait of the artist's son, and the work is simply titled *Portrait of a Boy in Fancy Costume*.

13. Partridge to Simon, 1 April 1957.

14. Simon to Partridge, 9 April 1957.

15. Agnew to Simon, 8 January 1963.

16. Fowles to Simon, 21 January 1963.

17. Simon to Agnew, 8 February 1963.

18. Agnew to Simon, 12 February 1963.

19. Simon's most costly artwork until this time was Cézanne's *Tulips in a Vase* (cat. 103), bought in 1962 for $404,472.

20. Simon to Agnew, 26 February 1963.

21. Agnew to Simon, 17 February 1964.

22. Simon to Agnew, 4 May 1964. Considering his later interest in the Rembrandt, and the notoriety surrounding its acquisition as well as its higher price, it is unfortunate that he did not buy it then. On the other hand, the circumstances of the auction sale and the publicity made Norton Simon famous.

23. Leylan also called Simon's attention to another Cook picture, Diego Velázquez's full-length portrait *The Jester Calabazas* and its presale estimate of $5–700,000. Simon wrote back on 1 February asking for more information about the Velázquez. Leylan wrote again on 22 February to say that he would be in Los Angeles in late March. Simon instructed his secretary Angelina Boaz to respond, and her dictation notes are on Leylan's letter: "Do you have estimate on Cook Rembrandt? What will it bring?" He also asked again for an estimate on the Velázquez but did not bid on it at the sale.

24. See chap. 3, pp. 38–40,

25. Patrick Lindsay, memorandum, 19 March 1965.

26. Principally a collector of Impressionist art, in 1957 the Greek shipping mogul Niarchos acquired most of the collection of the actor Edward G. Robinson for $3 million.

27. Tooth to Simon, 19 March 1965.

28. Angelina Boaz, interview by Davis Guggenheim, 24 July 1996.

29. David Nash, interview by Davis Guggenheim, 14 July 1996.

30. For a concise description, see Muchnic, 1998, pp. 1–5.

31. Berges, 1975.

32. Sir Philip Hendy, director of the National Gallery, in a written statement prepared for the Department of Education and Science Reviewing Committee, 9 April 1965.

33. Christie, Manson & Woods Ltd., in a written statement prepared for the Department of Education and Science Reviewing Committee, 9 April 1965.

34. Lord Robbins, chairman of the National Gallery, to Simon, 15 April 1965; National Gallery Press Release, 21 April 1965; *New York Times*, 1965.

35. Anthony Lousada to Milton Ray, 20 April 1965.

36. Francis K. Lloyd to Simon, 29 April 1965.

37. I. O. Chance to Simon, 26 March 1965.

38. Chance to Simon, 10 August 1965.

39. Ray to Chance, 23 August 1965.

40. In 1961 the Metropolitan Museum of Art paid a record $2.3 million for the Rembrandt, a painting Simon had hoped to buy (see pp. 38–40). J. Carter Brown, former director of the National Gallery of Art, Washington, suggested: "I think he was hoping it would go for more money rather than less. If you're going to pay $2.2 million, why not pay $2.3 and one half, and then have the most expensive picture in the world? I think that probably the figure for which *Aristotle* had sold was burned into his head and became a kind of benchmark for his own thinking. We were quite interested in it ourselves, the National Gallery, but deferred to another branch of the Mellon family who were fully prepared to pay whatever it cost." J. Carter Brown, interview by Charles Guggenheim, 4 October 1996.

41. Harold Williams, interview by Davis Guggenheim, 18 July 1996.

42. Another cast of *Little Dancer, Aged Fourteen* sold at Sotheby's, London, 3 February 2009, for more than £13 million ($19 million).

43. Simon to Norman Cousins, 17 December 1965.

44. Simon to Cousins, 17 December 1965: "I wasn't interested in talking if they were shopping the picture around."

45. Peter Wilson to Simon, 1 June 1965.

46. Ibid.

47. Esterow, 1965, quotes Brown as having been permitted to take the painting from the wall to examine it with a magnifying glass, and Simon is quoted as having seen it as well, but it is unclear when it was seen or whether they viewed it together; Brown was interviewed after his resignation from LACMA and did not say whether he went to Liechtenstein on behalf of Simon.

48. Esterow, 1965; Kamm, 1965; Seldis, 1965c.

49. Esterow, 1965. Esterow also quoted one unnamed dealer, who was "unimpressed with all the wheeling and dealing. 'Norton Simon thinks he can buy anything. One of these days he is going to sit down with de Gaulle and offer to buy the Louvre.'"

50. Berges, 1965.

51. *Los Angeles Times*, 28 March 1965, magazine supplement. In the same issue celebrating the museum opening, Simon placed a full-page ad, illustrating a stone head from the Duveen collection, and with a sly dig at donors whose names were attached to various museum buildings: "This Gothic masterpiece is a monument to an unknown sculptor. The new County Museum of Art is a monument to thousands of people, many of them anonymous, whose generosity has helped create this museum for Los Angeles and for America." The sentiment was disingenuous, considering the attention he received surrounding the College Art Association exhibition.

52. Davis, 2007, p. 79.

53. *Newsweek*, 1965, p. 86.

54. Minutes, Board of Trustees Meeting, Los Angeles County Museum of Art, 6 April 1965.

55. Simon to Edward Carter, 20 April 1965. Simon and Carter also frequently sparred at meetings of the University of California Board of Regents (Muchnic, 1998, pp. 139–140, 146).

56. Carter to Simon, 10 May 1965.

57. Simon to Carter, 2 June 1965.

58. Seldis, 1965b.

59. Muchnic, 1990, p. 93.

CHAPTER SIX

Museum without Walls I
1966–1969

A little more than ten years after launching seriously into art collecting, the works held by him privately or through his foundations constitute this country's foremost museum without walls.—LOS ANGELES TIMES[1]

FROM THE TIME NORTON SIMON first took on the enormous holdings of the Duveen collection, he lent portions to venues outside Los Angeles, including the Metropolitan Museum of Art, the Worcester Art Museum, the Wadsworth Atheneum, and others. He had also been considering forming his own museum for some time, at least a year before LACMA opened its new facility in 1965. In March 1964, while he was negotiating the Duveen Brothers sale, Simon's corporate Hunt Foods & Industries Foundation announced a $500,000 gift to the city of Fullerton, California, to construct an art museum, provided there was city participation in the project. The Hunt Foods & Industries Foundation and The Norton Simon Foundation, along with Simon and his family, would "loan works of art to the museum, and, from time to time, donate art objects to the museum."[2] Hunt Foods & Industries had built its new corporate headquarters in Fullerton in 1962 (fig. 1). Designed by the architect William Pereira, who was later to design LACMA, the plan included a twelve-thousand-square-foot library situated on the company grounds, which the Hunt Foods & Industries Foundation donated to the city (fig. 2). Donating art books and lending artworks to the library, Simon envisioned the facility as the "first step in the development of an important cultural center and landscaped park area in Fullerton."[3]

After the March 1964 offer, negotiations with the city of Fullerton about the prospective art museum dragged on for more than two years amid political wrangling regarding land use. Unconvinced that the project would move forward, Simon directed Barbara Roberts to investigate other sites. In May 1966 she reported on the Beverly Hills estate Greystone Mansion, saying, "it would make an absolutely magnificent museum," but cautioned that parking would be a problem.[4] In addition to investigating existing sites and potential architects for a new building, Roberts was scouting prospects to serve as the foundation's first director and interviewed a number of Southern California art historians, including Thomas Leavitt, James Demetrion, John Coplans, and Robert Wark.[5] Finally frustrated by Fullerton's

OPPOSITE
Pierre-Auguste Renoir, *The Pont des Arts, Paris*, 1867–1868 (detail), The Norton Simon Foundation. CAT. 531

ABOVE LEFT
Norton Simon

TOP
FIG. 1. Hunt Foods & Industries headquarters, Fullerton, Calif., 1968, with sculpture by Henry Moore (CAT. 283) in the foreground

ABOVE
FIG. 2. Hunt Branch Library, Fullerton, Calif., 1968

FIG. 3. Entrance and reflecting pool, Hunt Foods & Industries headquarters, Fullerton, Calif., 1968, with sculpture by Aristide Maillol (CAT. 325)

inaction, the foundation withdrew its pledge to the city in October 1966 and announced that it would instead use the funds to buy art. One can only speculate on the magnitude of this loss to the Fullerton community and Orange County.

At the end of November 1966, the Hunt Foods & Industries Foundation changed its name to the Hunt Foods & Industries Museum of Art.[6] Borrowing from André Malraux's concept of *le musée imaginaire*, Simon explained the significance of the change by declaring that rather than existing as an edifice, it would be a "museum without walls," whose mission was to buy artworks and lend them to museums and university art galleries.[7] The first such presentation was an exhibition of thirty-one nineteenth- and twentieth-century paintings and sculptures held at the University of California, Irvine.[8] The exhibition included paintings by Willem de Kooning, Henri Matisse, Piet Mondrian, and Pablo Picasso, and sculptures by Aristide Maillol and Jacques Lipchitz.[9]

Simon was interested in enhancing the corporation's image through the display of art, and he used the corporate headquarters to showcase artworks for the benefit of both visitors and company employees. The long entry walk flanked a reflecting pool, and during the course of 1966 Simon bought several nineteenth- and twentieth-century sculptures to populate the pool and nearby gardens. The sculptures included Henry Moore's *Standing Figure: Knife Edge* (cat. 297), Jacques Lipchitz's *Bather* (cat. 300), and Auguste Rodin's *Monument to*

FIG. 4. Norton Simon and Angelina Boaz, 1965

Balzac (cat. 321) and *Walking Man* (cat. 323).[10] He acquired his first monumental lead figure by Aristide Maillol, entitled *Air* (cat. 325), placing it first near the Hunt Branch Library and later in the reflecting pool (fig. 3). Hunt advertising executive Robert Glickman recalled the creation of the sculpture garden:

> When we built that beautiful building Norton created a park with sculpture in it, and there were Giacomettis and Henry Moores and Rodin sculptures and it was just incredible. We used to spend more money on the gardeners than we spent on lots of other things for that company. But it was a beautiful place to come to work.[11]

Simon's assistant Angelina Boaz remembered the reaction of the Hunt employees unused to seeing modern sculptures:

> You can't imagine the controversy to start with, but it was a real learning experience for people who worked there. They appreciated the fact that here were these treasures just on the lawn that they could see. So he did offer and expand the knowledge of people who worked for him, and they began to see things, and try to learn a little about it, because they saw it every day.[12]

The corporation enhanced its image as a culturally minded organization by exhibiting artworks not only in the garden but also in its offices. Smaller sculptures, prints, and paintings were displayed throughout the reception areas, hallways, and executive office suites. Boaz described the executive floor and Simon's office (fig. 4):

> The fourth floor was very special. Rouault and Daumier lithographs lined the corridors. There were large paintings in some areas. He made sure that almost every office had some sort of original art in it. Joining [his office] was a living room with art on the walls. You were surrounded with these wonderful things. He would ask almost everyone who walked into his office, "How do you feel about that one? How do you feel about that one?"[13]

That summer of 1966 the Hunt Foods & Industries Museum of Art bought important twentieth-century paintings, including works by Piet Mondrian and Henri Matisse (cats. 320, 326) and Picasso's *Open Window in Paris* (fig. 5). Bought from the New York dealer Alexandre Rosenberg for $225,000, the Picasso was exhibited first at the Hunt Branch Library, then at the Los Angeles County Museum of Art as part of its regular exhibition program, and later in *The Cubist Epoch* exhibition at both LACMA and the Metropolitan Museum of Art.[14] It then traveled with other works from the Simon collections to the Princeton University Art Museum. While the painting was at Princeton, Simon learned of its remarkable journey during World War II. The Princeton registrar informed him that there were severe cracks and losses along all four edges.[15] Alexandre Rosenberg responded to Simon's inquiries concerning previous conservation by saying that the condition of the painting was due to its dramatic past:

> The picture was stolen, along with many others, from the premises of my father's gallery in Paris shortly after the occupation of the city by the invading Germans, in 1940. It was recovered in 1946 among a bundle of about a dozen paintings, loosely and rather carelessly rolled up, one inside the next. The "Open Window," being the tallest, was located on the outside of the package, and its edges were slightly frayed. This roll of canvases had been kept in hiding by a French dealer who had obtained it from the Germans. He had been arrested on suspicion, and he won his release by turning over his loot to my father, in a deal worked out by the police.[16]

Although Rosenberg had relined the painting, Simon worried that it needed further treatment. He scribbled notes on Rosenberg's letter, "What are we doing about this? Get estimate for sale purposes; also I would like to consider selling privately." He either was not that fond of the painting or, at best, was not

FIG. 5. Pablo Picasso, *Open Window in Paris*, 1920, Museum of Modern Art, Tehran. CAT. 327

fond enough of it to ignore the conservation needs. It stayed on loan at Princeton while he negotiated its sale through Eugene Thaw. Simon's curator Darryl Isley reported on an October 1973 conversation with Thaw:

> The man who was interested earlier has come back a couple of times to see if it is available. I told him [Thaw] I would hate to see it go since our Picasso collection is so good. Thaw said he thought *Open Window* is an impressive big bore. If the money could be spent somewhere better, say another Renaissance masterpiece, it would be advisable to sell the Picasso.[17]

In spite of Thaw's opinion, however, he bought it in 1974 for $1,000,000. Its extraordinary history continued. Thaw sold it to Iran's Empress Farah Pahlavi. It remained in Tehran when she and the shah left the country, and after the 1979 Iranian revolution, the painting went to the Museum of Modern Art in Tehran.

Simon and the Pierre Matisse Gallery began discussing Henry Matisse's famous *Back, I–IV* series (fig. 6) in May 1966, and the four were sent on approval in September. The four large bronzes depict a female form in relief, seen from the rear. The backs become progressively more abstract from the first panel to the last. Although the four reliefs are among Matisse's most important sculptures, a discrepancy over the inscriptions made Simon doubt their quality. The bronzes are inscribed "0/10," and the dealer Pierre Matisse, the artist's son, represented them as cast number zero of ten, from the collection of his mother.[18] However, after their arrival in California, the dealer wrote that he was in error; the Hirshhorn Museum already owned *Backs* numbered "0/10" from his mother's collection, and the erroneously numbered bronzes now with Simon were in fact "10/10" (set ten of ten).[19] Simon bought the four bronzes in January 1967 for $190,000. The confusion over the inscription and bronze numbering persisted until 1975, when, after consultation with the foundry, Pierre Matisse concluded that the foundry simply forgot to add the number "1" before the "0." He recommended Simon add a "1" in front of the "0" on each bronze and suggested that "a sculpture student from UCLA chisel the number on."[20]

Needless to say, Simon did not follow this unethical recommendation. He remained troubled by the unorthodox numbering and began investigating selling the group in 1976. Unconcerned about the numbering, the dealer Ernst Beyeler bought the set in 1982 for $1,750,000. As with other important works Simon deaccessioned, such as Degas's *Rehearsal of the Ballet* (p. 77) or Picasso's *Open Window in Paris* (fig. 5), it is difficult to ascertain whether the sale was prompted by the tremendous profit he would realize or a true concern over a work's quality and condition. While their fame and marketability may have played some part in Simon's decision to sell the Matisse suite, ultimately the question of duplicate cast numbering arose as a major factor.[21]

IN 1966 SIMON MADE THIRTY-FOUR acquisitions and spent almost $1.5 million. The following year, 1967, he spent more than twice that amount, $3,185,000, more than doubling the number of acquisitions (see Appendix). Fully half of the objects were nineteenth- and twentieth-century sculptures. Aside from the Matisse *Backs*, mentioned above, there were bronzes by Jacques Lipchitz, Pablo Picasso, and Barbara Hepworth, as well

FIG. 6. Henri Matisse, *The Back, I–IV*, c.1904–1929, The Burnett Foundation, Fort Worth. CAT. 328 A–D

as his second Maillol lead figure, *The River* (cat. 339), which was put on display in the corporate gardens reflecting pool. In addition to Maillol's two monumental lead sculptures now on the office grounds, Simon bought for his private collection another entitled *The Three Nymphs* (cat. 376), which he put in his garden at home. Smaller, life-size Maillols were exhibited in the Hunt Branch Library, and tiny maquette-size bronzes decorated both the offices and his home. Most of Simon's Maillol acquisitions came from the Paris dealer Dina Vierny, Maillol's former model with whom Simon formed a friendship in spite of the misunderstandings that often accompanied their transactions. Vierny preferred to write her letters and invoices in French, a language Simon knew only slightly. Vierny would send long lists of small bronzes that were available, and the titles (in French) did not always correspond to the pieces that were ultimately shipped. The large number of bronzes criss-crossing between Paris and Fullerton added to the confusion and on more than one occasion led to the purchase of dupli-cate bronzes. Simon bought twenty-five Maillols in 1967 alone and eventually held the largest collection of this artist's works outside France. Today, twenty-three remain in the collections in Pasadena.

In addition to the sculptures, Simon added several important paintings and watercolors during 1967. He bought two Picassos from Alexandre Rosenberg—for his private collec-tion for $215,000 he acquired *Woman in an Armchair* (cat. 347) and for $175,000, the artist's striking, monumental study in black and gray, *Bust of a Woman* (cat. 377), which hung in the entrance lobby of the Hunt Foods headquarters. Simon's most expensive purchase of the year was Paul Cézanne's *Still Life with Kettle, Milk Pitcher, Sugar Bowl, and Seven Apples* (fig. 7), a delicately rendered, colorful watercolor bought at Sotheby's in London for the auction record price for the artist of more than $400,000. He sold the still life at auction in 1973 for $620,000, and it is now in the J. Paul Getty Museum. Another auction purchase—and also a world auction record for the artist—was Jean-Baptiste Camille Corot's *The Cicada* (cat. 390), bought at Parke-Bernet in New York for $310,000.

ABOVE
FIG. 7. Paul Cézanne, *Still Life with Kettle, Milk Pitcher, Sugar Bowl and Seven Apples*, c. 1895–1900, The J. Paul Getty Museum, Los Angeles. CAT. 348

LEFT
FIG. 8. Henri Fantin-Latour, *White and Pink Mallows in a Vase*, 1895, Norton Simon Art Foundation. CAT. 398

When Simon acquired Duveen Brothers, the sale included not just the inventory, the library, and archives but also the building itself, at 18 East Seventy-ninth Street in New York. In November 1967 he sold the building to Acquavella Galleries for $425,000. William Acquavella used two paintings as partial payment, Henri Fantin-Latour's *White and Pink Mallows in a Vase* (fig. 8) at a value of $75,000 and Pierre-Auguste Renoir's *Woman with a Rose* (cat. 399) at a value of $175,000. Simon sold the Renoir to the New York dealer William Beadleston in 1981 for $526,750. The files do not reflect his reasons for deac-cessioning the painting. Certainly he liked the artist, since he bought twenty-two paintings, drawings, and sculptures by Renoir over the course of his collecting. Moreover, in the two and one half years between the November 1967 trade and his first investigations into selling *Woman with a Rose* in April 1970, he bought ten additional Renoirs, spending almost $3 million. The number of Renoirs he bought might be assumed to reflect his admiration for the artist, yet he ultimately kept only seven of the twenty-two. To some extent, it is futile to analyze Norton Simon's reasons for selling particular works: in the end, it probably had to do with profitability. Simon realized a $2,033,290 profit on the fifteen Renoirs he sold.

At the time he was negotiating with Acquavella to sell the Duveen building, Simon was also concluding arrangements to hire a trained art historian to oversee the art collections. In November 1967 he appointed the Oakland (California) Museum director James M. Brown as the first director of the Hunt Foods & Industries Museum of Art. Since Brown successfully shepherded construction of the Oakland Museum, the *Los Angeles Times* speculated that he was hired to oversee construction of a Simon museum. The idea of a Hunt Foods museum building had been tabled in late 1966, when Simon announced his "museum without walls" exhibition program, and Brown downplayed to the press the idea of a new building by saying, "It is certainly Mr. Simon's intent to supplement rather than to compete with existing cultural facilities."[22] In spite of his message to the press, however, Brown's directive was to develop plans for the best possible use of the collections and then to recommend a site and architect.[23] In the meantime, he managed the foundations' art collections, arranged loan exhibitions throughout the United States, and acted as liaison with the Los Angeles County Museum of Art.[24]

While Simon was building the collections for his two foundations and directing their growing loan programs, he was also attending to his personal collection and its display, welcoming visits from dealers and scholars to his remodeled home. In early 1968, for instance, the art historian John Rewald wrote to thank Simon for his hospitality during a recent visit:

> Alice and I were impressed not only with your new acquisitions, but also with the installation through which your collection remains part of your daily life and does not become a "gallery of masterpieces." We thought that the glass case with shelves for sculpture, set against the natural light, was possibly the most felicitous solution we have ever seen.[25]

Christie's U.S. representative was even more effusive, telling Simon his collection was "far and away the finest and most serious collection being formed today."[26]

In February 1968 Simon acquired his sixteenth sculpture by Auguste Rodin, cast number 10 of the monumental *Burghers of Calais* (cat. 413). This was the sixth Rodin purchased directly from the Musée Rodin in Paris, an arrangement Simon initiated in 1966 with the acquisition of the artist's *Monument to Balzac* (cat. 321) and which continued until 1984, near the end of his active collecting, when he bought three large individual studies for the *Burghers* (cats. 1709–1711).[27]

Acquisitions of nineteenth- and twentieth-century works prevailed throughout the spring and summer of 1968 with paintings by Pierre-Auguste Renoir, Chaim Soutine, Jackson Pollock, and Juan Gris. Simon's most important purchase, however, was Édouard Manet's *The Ragpicker* (fig. 9) from Wildenstein. After Rembrandt's *Titus*, Simon's next most costly painting had been Degas's *Rehearsal for the Ballet*, purchased in 1965 for $410,000. The Manet at $850,000 was twice as expensive. The over-life-size depiction of a Parisian beggar is part of a series of "four philosophers," single rumpled male subjects standing against dark backgrounds.[28] Inspired by the Spanish artist Diego Velázquez's large canvases in the Museo del Prado, especially his *Moenippus* and *Aesop*, Manet began painting *The Ragpicker* shortly after his trip to Spain in 1865. Simon first considered the work in 1967, finally agreed to a thirty-day option in February 1968, and bought it in March. He managed to keep a good part of his money over the next year, however, by extending the payment schedule and paying one-third down, one-third at the end of 1968, and one-third at the end of 1969. It was not a question of whether or not he could afford it, but how he could better invest the money over twenty-one months.

By this point in 1968 Simon was a very good client of Sotheby's and its New York affiliate Parke-Bernet. Indeed, his reputation as a serious buyer was vastly greater than when he was forced to justify his status at the Erickson sale in 1961.[29] He had purchased dozens of artworks at each auction house, and the previous October he had paid the record price for Corot's *Cicada* at Parke-Bernet. In an incredible about-face of Simon's treatment by the firm seven years earlier, Parke-Bernet's president, Peregrine Pollen, offered him the extraordinary opportunity to preview privately any works in which he was interested:

> I so much enjoyed seeing you and having the opportunity again to look at the finest collection in any private house in America. You told me that on some occasions it is not possible for you personally to come to London or New York to satisfy yourself about the condition of important paintings which interest you; and that as a result you have been obliged to buy these paintings privately at prices vastly in excess of the prices realized at the sales. I do feel that this could be avoided. If, in future, there are important paintings in any of our sales which interest you, I am certain that it could be arranged in many instances for the paintings themselves to be sent to you before the sale so that you could satisfy yourself about their condition and color.[30]

There is no evidence that Simon accepted Pollen's offer. In any event, he remained a good customer, and, when he sold objects, he most often used Sotheby's and Parke-Bernet.

In May 1968 James Brown organized an exhibition of sculptures from the Hunt Foods & Industries Museum of Art at the Los Angeles County Museum of Art to open in August.[31] The objects were to be placed at the entrance plaza at LACMA (at that time called the Mr. and Mrs. Norton Simon Sculpture Plaza).[32] Most of the pieces were then on display at the Hunt Foods corporate headquarters garden in Fullerton, and two, Maillol's *Mountain* (cat. 495) and Marino Marini's *Miracolo* (cat. 505), acquired just that summer, were sent directly to LACMA. Citing the previous loans from the Simon collections that "have provided County citizens and visitors with a rich variety of works from all periods in art history, and have greatly augmented the museum's growing permanent collection," the LACMA press release emphasized that the exhibition

FIG. 9. Édouard Manet, *The Ragpicker*, c. 1865–1870, The Norton Simon Foundation. CAT. 433

"represents a major step in a continuing program of cooperation in the public interest."[33] Lauding the display for its "outstanding landmarks in the development of sculpture," the *Los Angeles Times* art critic Henry Seldis inferred that this cooperation might lead to even better things for the museum:

> The museum trustees' renewed wooing of [Simon] seems to make it probable that his major loan of outdoor sculptures will soon be followed by a substantial program of loans from the great resources of paintings controlled by him. In the past ten years Simon has become not only the most important but the most dedicated and personally involved collector in the country.[34]

ABOVE
FIG. 10. David Smith, *Cubi XXVIII*, 1965, The Broad Art Foundation, Los Angeles, © Estate of David Smith/ Licensed by VAGA, New York, NY. CAT. 515

OPPOSITE LEFT
FIG. 11. Pierre-Auguste Renoir, *The Pont des Arts, Paris*, 1867–1868, The Norton Simon Foundation. CAT. 531

OPPOSITE RIGHT
FIG. 12. Claude Monet, *Garden at Sainte-Adresse*, 1867, oil on canvas, 38 5/8 x 51 1/8 in. (98.1 x 129.9 cm), The Metropolitan Museum of Art, New York

Simon's interest in modern sculpture was not confined to the figurative works of Maillol and Rodin. In July 1968 he bought from Marlborough-Gerson Gallery David Smith's *Cubi XXVIII* for $65,000 (fig. 10). This completely abstract sculpture was an aesthetic leap. Simon knew the artist's work and certainly trusted the dealer, having previously bought dozens of objects from Marlborough. Simon was moving toward abstract sculpture with the works of Henry Moore, and even more so with those of Barbara Hepworth, whose simplified organic forms seemed to lead Simon to Smith. However, he considered selling *Cubi XXVIII* several times between 1976 and 1980.[35] His interest in deaccessioning probably had more to do with the potential profit on his $65,000 investment than it did with his opinion of the sculpture, and in 1982 he sold *Cubi XXVIII* back to Marlborough for a phenomenal $1,100,000.[36] Its value continued to escalate, and when the sculpture sold at Sotheby's in November 2005, the Los Angeles collector Eli Broad paid $23.8 million.

As Simon continued to add artworks to the rapidly expanding collections, the need for researching and cataloguing became paramount, and in the summer of 1968 James Brown hired Darryl Isley, a recent art history graduate. A Fullerton resident who as a student worked summers in the Hunt Foods cannery, Isley was Simon's first employee (after Brown) with an art history background. He worked first as a research curator cataloguing the collections, and, after Barbara Roberts's departure in 1971, became Simon's chief art aide and negotiator.[37]

Simon stepped back into the old master market in June 1968 with the purchase of sixteen paintings at Sotheby's from the Chicago collection of Morris L. Kaplan (cats. 470–485).[38] Accustomed to spending six figures on Impressionist and modern paintings, Simon felt that the works in the sale, although of mixed quality, offered a chance to acquire a few paintings at extremely modest prices. He spent about $97,500 for the group, which included paintings by Thomas de Keyser and Peter Paul Rubens, but also some by lesser-known sixteenth- to eighteenth-century artists. Simon believed that he had made a good investment, since he later sold six of them for about $67,000. A few years later he asked Isley for a list of the pictures that had been in the Kaplan sale, along with the prices. Simon wrote next to eight of the works "good," "excellent," or "bargain and good," and at the bottom of the page penned, "Glad to know we have some reasonably priced pictures."[39] Yet he understood that bulk buying did not always work and later confessed to an interviewer, "A certain amount of very significant things are important within a collection. Oftentimes when you buy the lesser ones you rationalize and you wind up with a lot of junk."[40]

At Parke-Bernet in October 1968 Simon added to his collection its earliest, largest, and most important Renoir, *The Pont des Arts, Paris* (fig. 11). Renoir worked on a series of views of Paris in the summer of 1867, and this cityscape was probably begun at that time. Looking east, up the Seine, one sees the cast-iron Pont des Arts and the dome of the Institut de France. Afternoon sun bathes the people strolling on the riverside quai. It has been called one of the "most important urban view paintings of the Second Empire,"[41] capturing not only a sunny Parisian afternoon by the Seine but buildings, bridges, and urban commerce. After *Titus*, its $1,550,000 price was the highest Simon had paid for a single work of art, and it set the world auction record for an Impressionist painting. David Nash, for many years a specialist in the Impressionist and

Modern Department, and later vice president at Parke-Bernet, recalled that Simon was especially keen to have *The Pont des Arts* because he had missed buying another early Impressionist landscape, Monet's *Garden at Sainte-Adresse* (fig. 12), which had been bought by the Metropolitan Museum of Art at auction the previous year in London for $1.4 million:[42]

> Although he greatly admired [the Monet], he never quite got up the courage to go all the way for that picture. And he regretted it forever after. And later this Renoir came up for sale in New York. Like the Monet, it was an early masterpiece by the artist and Norton was, I think, determined not to repeat the mistake that he'd made in being outbid for the Monet. So he really went for this picture and brought it up over a million dollars, which was the first time that any [Impressionist] picture in the United States sold for that price. I'm not sure if it wasn't a purchase on the rebound, as it were. He was forever afterwards justifying that he bought the right one, that it was a better purchase to buy the *Pont des Arts* than it was to buy the Monet.[43]

FIG. 13. Henri-Horace Roland de la Porte, *Still Life*, c. 1765, Norton Simon Art Foundation. CAT. 561.

Simon's biographer Suzanne Muchnic writes that he was so interested in Monet's *Garden at Sainte-Adresse* that he tried to persuade Christie's in London to withdraw the painting from the auction and sell it to him privately.[44] When *The Pont des Arts* was on the block, he arranged for the dealer Stephen Hahn to bid for him up to $1 million. At that point, Simon took over the bidding by telephone to Sotheby's chairman Peter Wilson, who was behind a screen on the salesroom stage. Wilson then relayed Simon's bids to the podium.[45]

Simon bought his fourth most expensive picture in November, when he acquired a major 1906 Picasso, *Nude Combing Her Hair*, for $680,000 (p. 199).[46] Alexandre Rosenberg made the "maximum possible allowance on price" because of the understanding that the amount would be payable on demand.[47] The painting was in Los Angeles on approval for a few months before the purchase, and Simon planned to buy it for his personal collection.[48] Rosenberg intended to wait until after the first of the year to send the bill, but on 18 November he wrote that he contemplated making several purchases on a trip abroad and needed the money right away. Either Simon lacked readily available personal funds or he had a change of heart about hanging the painting in his home, because he directed the Art Foundation, rather than his personal account, to pay for it. The picture was exhibited in Philadelphia, LACMA, the University of California, Berkeley, and the Princeton University Art Museum before coming to Pasadena. Unfortunately for the collection, Simon sold the painting to the Kimbell Art Foundation in Fort Worth in 1982.[49]

In 1968 Simon more than doubled the previous year's purchases. He made 164 acquisitions and spent a phenomenal $11 million (about $68.5 million in 2010 dollars). Expensive works such as the David Smith sculpture and the Renoir and Picasso paintings point to his overwhelming attention to the nineteenth and twentieth centuries, and in fact more than 83 percent of the objects purchased during the year were made after 1800. In spite of what is revealed in the numbers, he continued to investigate pictures from earlier periods, writing for example to the London dealer Geoffrey Agnew in December 1968, "I have turned to the field of old masters with considerably increased interest and I would appreciate any outstanding examples you might bring to my attention."[50] His last purchase in 1968 was an old master that he bought the same day he wrote to Agnew, the exquisite *Still Life* by Henri-Horace Roland de la Porte (fig. 13). Bought from the London dealers Herner & Wengraf for $14,000, the glowing, meticulously executed arrangement of fruit and tableware by the rival of Jean-Siméon Chardin was clearly a bargain, and Simon no doubt was looking for other hidden treasures. He continued to pursue and acquire old master artworks in 1969 with renewed emphasis.

SIMON MAINTAINED HIS EXCEEDINGLY active buying pace in 1969, with 150 acquisitions at a cost of more than $10.6 million (see Appendix). The nineteenth- and twentieth-century objects still outnumbered older works, this year by two to one, but 1969 proved a turning point for Simon's interest in old master works. With the exception of the 1964 Duveen inventory acquisition, he bought as many old master paintings in 1969 alone—thirty-eight—as in the previous fifteen years combined. He began the year with two distinctive and notably different paintings. Aristocratic society in the eighteenth century is represented by Élisabeth Vigée-Lebrun's 1793 portrait *Theresa, Countess Kinsky* (cat. 567). A friend of Queen Marie-Antoinette, Vigée-Lebrun painted the luminous portrait while she was in exile during the French Revolution. The lives of commoners are seen in Jan Steen's 1663–1664 *Wine Is a Mocker* (cat. 569), a bawdy yet moralizing depiction of an inebriated woman by the master of Dutch genre painting.

A few weeks later, in March 1969, Simon acquired one of the earliest paintings to enter the collection, Giovanni Bellini's 1474 portrait of Joerg Fugger (fig. 14). Thought to be Bellini's first known portrait, it depicts a young member of the great Augsburg banking family and is one of the first examples by an Italian artist in oil instead of tempera. Simon bought the painting for $220,000 from Lorenzo and Donatella Papi, the heirs to the Florentine collector-dealer Alessandro Contini-Bonacossi.[51] Simon first became acquainted with the Papi family in October 1968. He instructed Barbara Roberts to meet them in Florence in early March to see the collection, and Simon did the same shortly thereafter. He hoped that by establishing a good relationship with the Papis, he would secure access to the best of their collection's works. Although the relationship was cordial, Simon acquired only one other painting directly through the Papis, a portrait by Giovanni Battista Moroni (cat. 671). The other works Simon bought from the Contini-Bonacossi collection, paintings by El Greco, Giovanni Battista Tiepolo, and Francisco de Zurbarán, were acquired through the dealer Eugene Thaw (cats. 643, 738, 769, 829).

The astonishing number of objects Simon was buying placed an extraordinary burden on the Los Angeles County Museum of Art, which received the bulk of his loans. However, he also lent to other institutions across the country, such as the Phoenix Art Museum, the Cleveland Museum of Art, and the Museum of Fine Arts, Boston. Other venues included museums in Brooklyn; Chicago; Cambridge, Massachusetts; Kansas City; New York; Minneapolis; Washington, D.C.; Philadelphia; Portland, Oregon; Richmond, Virginia; and Worcester, Massachusetts. Aside from publicizing the art collection and benefiting borrowing institutions, loans to out-of-state museums provided another advantage. California collectors could qualify for an exemption from the state use tax on artworks purchased outside California by making them available for public display outside the state during the first three months of ownership. Many works were exhibited for three months and then moved to LACMA for display; others stayed away for longer periods. Most often the object was incorporated into an exhibition of the borrowing museum's permanent collection, but occasionally museums organized special displays of the Simon collections. Portland and Philadelphia, for instance, held exhibitions in 1968–1969, each named *Recent Acquisitions by the Norton Simon, Inc. Museum of Art.*

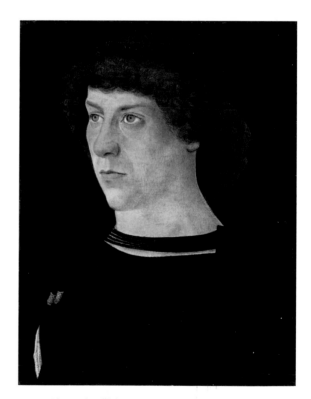

FIG. 14. Giovanni Bellini, *Joerg Fugger*, 1474, Norton Simon Art Foundation. CAT. 584

In March 1969 the *Los Angeles Times* writer Henry Seldis addressed rumors of trouble at the Los Angeles County Museum of Art. In an article titled "After Four Years, Goals Undefined," he wrote, "less than four years after its opening the County Museum of Art has become the source of running controversies." Citing the museum's shortage of top artworks, Seldis praised Simon's "museum without walls" loan program and once again fanned the flames of hope that he would single-handedly come to the museum's rescue:

> A little more than ten years after launching seriously into art collecting, the works now held by him privately or through his foundations constitute this country's foremost museum without walls. There is evidence that plans for building a separate facility for the Norton Simon Inc. Museum have been suspended while Simon considers his possible future commitments. At the moment he seems closer to the museum than ever, having lent his major works of sculpture to be displayed for a year on the museum's Norton Simon Plaza. In all likelihood an entire floor of the museum's Ahmanson Gallery will soon be filled with Simon loans, giving the weak permanent collection, already strengthened in many key areas by Simon-owned paintings, an immeasurable boost.[52]

Simon did continue to lend artworks, including six large tapestry cartoons by Giovanni Francesco Romanelli, bought in March at Sotheby's in London. The six massive, full-scale cartoons tell the story of the love affair between Dido and Aeneas (cats. 591–593, 657, 682, 683).[53] This was a curious acquisition, since Simon had no permanent building in which to house his collection, and the paintings' enormous size (nine feet high and twelve to twenty feet wide) make them especially difficult to move and lend. While the purchase was unusual in this way, it was nevertheless not surprising, considering the splendid quality of the paintings. An object's potential popularity with visitors was quite often a factor in Simon's ultimate decision to buy, and in this case he rightly assumed that the skilled, painterly rendering of the figures and the sweeping Baroque theatricality would be greatly admired by visitors. Because of the size of the paintings, they presented challenges with display, and while on loan to the Los Angeles County Museum of Art they hung in the atrium of the Ahmanson Building, overlooking the central court three floors below.

The museum without walls loan program had proved successful, as evidenced by the number of museums that were borrowing Simon works and the exposure the collection received. As the program expanded, Brown's mandate to find the best possible use for the collections seemed to focus more on loans and less on a new building. In June 1969, after just eighteen months on the job, he accepted the position of director at the Virginia Museum of Fine Arts. The press speculated that he left because the building project in Fullerton had been shelved and Simon was lending more to LACMA and elsewhere.[54] While the Simon archives do not reveal any disagreement between Simon and Brown, it is easy to construe that Brown had become frustrated in the role of loan broker, but he emphasized that his departure was amicable, and that the Virginia offer was just too good to pass up.[55]

By mid-1969 Simon had purchased three paintings, four drawings, and eighty-five prints by Rembrandt van Rijn, with *Titus* still the most celebrated example.[56] A fourth painting was acquired in 1969, a self-portrait (cat. 654), painted in the late 1630s. Rembrandt portrayed himself wearing an elegant velvet beret and gold chain around his neck. The chain was a symbol of prestige often awarded to artists. Simon had first learned of the painting's availability from the dealer Stephen Hahn in December 1968.[57] Christie's informed Simon a few months later that it would appear in the 27 June 1969 sale, describing it as "a remarkably handsome and well preserved work."[58] Determined to keep a lower profile at this Christie's auction than at the *Titus* sale in 1965, Simon commissioned the Boston dealer Robert Light to bid, buying the picture for $1,150,000.[59] Light, remembering Simon's unsuccessful effort to remain anonymous at the *Titus* sale, asked if he wanted anonymity this time:

> I remember saying to him by phone just before the sale, "Now let's assume for the moment that I'm successful and I buy this picture. There will be a certain amount of publicity about this, now do you want me to reveal your name as the buyer?" And he—I remember being rather surprised—he said, "Oh absolutely."[60]

Continuing his acquisitions of old master pictures, Simon bought several Dutch paintings, including his third Jan Steen (cat. 660), two works by Jean-Honoré Fragonard (cats. 669, 670), a portrait by Giovanni Battista Moroni (cat. 671, his third painting from the Contini-Bonacossi collection), and a landscape by Jacob van Ruisdael (cat. 680), bought in September from Colnaghi. Simon had been seeking a painting by Ruisdael for some time, going so far as to place an advertisement in *Apollo* magazine that read, "We are interested in acquiring a fine Jacob van Ruisdael painting. Please send good photograph and/or transparency along with provenance, documentation and price."[61]

Still in the old master market, Simon again turned his sights toward Christie's when he decided to contend for the grand yet sublime *Flight into Egypt* by the Venetian painter Jacopo Bassano (fig. 15).[62] A friezelike group of figures is led by an angel who gestures toward an unseen refuge. The angel's massive, rainbow-colored wings and swirling garments capture

FIG. 15. Jacopo da Ponte, called Jacopo Bassano, *The Flight into Egypt*, c. 1544–1545, Norton Simon Art Foundation. CAT. 702

the urgency of their flight. Saint Joseph follows directly behind the angel, his legs and trailing robes mirroring those of the angel. At the center of the composition the Virgin Mary sits serenely on a donkey holding the Christ Child. The two regard each other lovingly and tenderly, oblivious of the turmoil around them. The realistic, expressive, colorful rendering of people, animals, and landscape epitomizes the best of Venetian painting.

In a British private collection since the eighteenth century, the Bassano was given in the 1950s to Prinknash Abbey in Gloucester, where it hung in the refectory. To generate cash for a building program, the abbey placed the painting in the Christie's 5 December sale, expecting it to fetch about £20,000–30,000. The painting drew a good deal of attention at the auction, and the bids escalated to almost ten times that amount, with the final price at £273,000 ($655,000). The London dealer Edward Speelman was one of the underbidders, and in a congratulatory letter to Simon he wrote, "This is really a great masterpiece. I bid up to 200,000 guineas, and before the sale was rather confident that I might get it!"[63] Simon's successful bid was enough to complete the abbey's entire construction project. The grateful Benedictine monks wrote thank-you letters to Simon, and he sent a representative to the ceremonies dedicating the new building.[64]

Even as Simon aggressively sought out old masters throughout 1969, he was just as actively accumulating Impressionist and modern works. He bought examples by nineteenth-century artists he had not previously acquired, such as Jean-Frédéric Bazille's *Woman in a Moorish Costume* (cat. 709), and fine examples by artists with whom he was more familiar, such as Gustave Courbet, Claude Monet, Vincent van Gogh, and Edgar Degas. Two of those by Degas, ballet paintings bought in October on consecutive days, reflect the extremes of Simon's collecting style. The first was a picture he never learned to love. The second he had known about for years, and it remains one of the highlights of the collection.

He first bought *Three Dancers* (fig. 16) on 14 October from Alexandre Rosenberg. Although the sales transaction for this work was ordinary, Simon's opinion and treatment of the artwork were anything but. He initially bought the painting because he was drawn to the seated figure on the right, but he disliked the two on the left, which he perceived as sketchy and awkward. He discussed with Ben Johnson, conservator at LACMA, the extraordinary idea of actually cutting the picture in half so that he would not have to look at the two standing dancers. A distressed Johnson offered instead a system to hide the left-hand side that he hoped would protect the picture and at the same time satisfy the collector. Johnson made a stretcher with a rounded left edge so that the support (paper mounted on silk) would bend around it without being sharply creased. The conservator very much opposed the procedure, pointing out that the condition would be affected and, appealing to Simon's monetary interests, warned that the painting's value would consequently be diminished.[65] Nevertheless, in early 1973 Simon ordered the work to be done, and Johnson reluctantly agreed, only because he was afraid that if he refused, Simon would hire someone else who might do it poorly.[66] It remained in this condition, framed showing only the right-hand side, for ten years and even appeared in an exhibition and catalogue in this truncated form.[67] At the urging of other conservators and his curators, Simon finally reversed his decision in 1983 and agreed to have the work removed from the curved stretcher, unbent, flattened, and reframed. Conservator Bernard Rabin (p. 239) later recalled walking through the museum with Simon and stopping in front of the *Three Dancers*. I was often asked to accompany them and take notes of Rabin's comments. Rabin described his exchange with Simon: "I said to him, 'This looks to me as if it were folded.' He said, 'Yes, it was folded.' I said, 'What damn fool would fold a thing like that?' He said, 'Me,' and turned around and said to Sara, 'Don't put that down.'"[68] Simon's proprietary disregard of the artist's intent was unusual for him. Customarily, he would sell a work he found unsatisfactory. It is likely that in this instance he kept the picture because of his attraction to the seated dancer.

Simon found the second Degas ballet scene far more appealing, and the composition remained a favorite. The day after he purchased *Three Dancers*, he bought *The Star: Dancer on Pointe* (fig. 17) at auction at Parke-Bernet. This lush pastel depicts a lone ballerina moving across the stage. Degas has caught the fleeting moment in which she is adroitly balanced on one leg. Simon first encountered *The Star* at the 1958 Los Angeles County Museum Degas exhibition, which introduced him to the world of Degas. He always referred to the picture as the "Magnin Degas," since it came from the estate of Grover A. Magnin, a prominent San Francisco retailer. It was also once in the collection of the Earl of Avon, Sir William Eden (Prime Minister Anthony Eden's father), and, aside from the object's obvious beauty, the two prestigious names in the provenance appealed to him. This pastel was Simon's thirty-eighth work by Degas.[69]

Simon now owned an impressive number of works by Degas and other Impressionist artists. He continued to expand his twentieth-century sculpture collection, buying eight works by Henry Moore in 1969, spending almost $250,000. Early in the year he bought *Upright Motive No. 8* (cat. 562). Moore had given to his wife and daughter the rights to this sculpture as well as to the similar *Upright Motive No. 5* (cat. 666). Simon successfully enlisted the help of *Los Angeles Times* writer Henry Seldis, a friend of Moore's and curator of the 1973 exhibition *Henry Moore in America*, to convince the sculptor to let his daughter sell one or both *Uprights* directly to Simon rather than through a dealer. In addition to works by Moore, in 1969 Simon acquired two sculptures each by Picasso and Wilhelm Lehmbruck and three by Constantin Brancusi. His most striking sculpture acquisition of 1969, however, was another monumental abstract bronze, entitled *Four Square: Walk Through*, by the English sculptor Barbara Hepworth. Simon bought the work from Marlborough for $45,000 and arranged to have it shipped to the Yale University Art Gallery for exhibition. It traveled to two other universities—the University of California, Los Angeles in 1972 and Stanford University in 1975—before coming to the Norton Simon Museum in Pasadena, where it has enjoyed pride of place outside the entrance to the museum since 1978 (fig. 18).

FIG. 16. Edgar Degas, *Three Dancers*, c. 1872–1874, The Norton Simon Foundation. CAT. 686

FIG. 17. Edgar Degas, *The Star: Dancer on Pointe*, c. 1878–1880, The Norton Simon Foundation. CAT. 687

FIG. 18. Barbara Hepworth, *Four Square: Walk Through*,
1966, Norton Simon Art Foundation. CAT. 586

The end of October 1969 was marked by profound tragedy for the Simon family, when Norton's younger son, Robert, committed suicide. This calamity was a contributing factor in his divorce from Lucille the following July and no doubt prompted his finally removing himself from the day-to-day operations of Norton Simon Inc. He had been gradually disengaging himself from the business for some time and in December resigned as director and finance committee member. The overwhelming misfortune that befell his family surely accelerated his move away from business, although he publicly gave another reason. His decision was based, he said, "on my great satisfaction with the company's performance and outlook and on my own desire to concentrate more fully on my educational and cultural interests."[70]

Simon also stepped back from art purchases, but the momentum of his former frenetic buying pace meant that multiple transactions were in various states of completion and still needed attention. Illustrative of this situation is a memorandum from Barbara Roberts dated 10 November 1969, listing forty-nine paintings under consideration from about a dozen dealers. Roberts arranged the list according to ratings assigned by LACMA's director Kenneth Donahue and conservator Ben Johnson. Simon put his own notations next to twenty-five, commenting on the prices and assigning his own grades (fig. 19). From this group, he bought eleven paintings, five before the end of the year and six spread out over most of 1970. Simon's notations reveal not only the extent of his direct involvement with acquisitions but also his opinions about quality and prices.

I joined the Norton Simon Inc. Museum of Art in Fullerton in November 1969, the same day as Roberts's memorandum cited above. Simon no longer had a day-to-day role in the management of Norton Simon Inc., and his staff of seven handled his foundation and personal business, including the oversight and administration of his art collection.[71] In addition to assisting Roberts, I kept records of Simon's acquisitions and researched potential purchases. With Simon's retirement from the company, Norton Simon Inc. president David Mahoney transferred its headquarters to New York City. With no reason to stay in Fullerton, Simon moved to his Los Angeles office on Wilshire Boulevard, closer to his home. Four of us followed him to Los Angeles.[72] Although 1970 saw a slowdown in art purchases, the year itself—especially the first six months—was a tumultuous and challenging period, since, in addition to the changes in his personal life, Simon struggled with the administrative staff of the Los Angeles County Museum of Art, began to deaccession portions of his art collection, set in motion a project to catalogue the art collections, and—most surprising to his staff—turned entirely away from art and entered politics. ❦

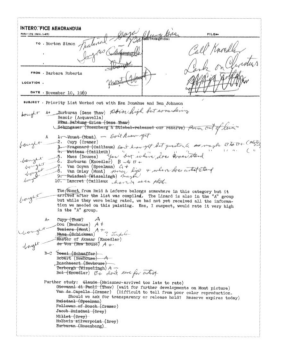

FIG. 19. Page one of memorandum, 10 November 1969, regarding artworks under consideration, with Norton Simon's notes

1. Seldis, 1969.

2. Hunt Foods & Industries Foundation, press release, 10 March 1964.

3. Hunt Foods President Carl Kalbfleisch to Fullerton City Administrator Herman Hiltscher, 10 March 1964.

4. Barbara Roberts to Norton Simon, 27 May 1966. Greystone became a public park in 1971.

5. In February 1966 Roberts interviewed Thomas Leavitt, director of the Santa Barbara Museum of Art (Roberts to Simon, 1 March 1966). In July she interviewed James Demetrion, assistant director of the Pasadena Art Museum (Roberts to Julia Mayer, 7 July 1966), and John Coplans, director of the art gallery at the University of California, Irvine (Roberts to Simon, 7 July 1966). In August she met with Robert Wark, director of the Huntington Art Gallery (Roberts to Simon, 15 August 1966). Also in August she interviewed the architect Quincy Jones about the possibility of designing the museum (Roberts to Mayer, 17 August 1966).

6. Minutes of Special Meeting of the Trustees of Hunt Foods & Industries Foundation, 30 November 1966.

7. Hunt Foods & Industries Foundation, press release, 26 October 1966, p. 1. The notion was famously espoused by novelist and art historian André Malraux (1901–1976) who proposed that art books and the reproduction of artworks served as a "museum without walls" (Malraux, 1967).

8. Irvine, 1967.

9. Although the Hunt Foods & Industries Museum of Art acquired art from all cultures, its collection was usually identified with Impressionist and modern paintings and monumental twentieth-century sculpture. The Hunt Foods & Industries Museum of Art eventually was renamed the Norton Simon, Inc. Museum of Art, as Simon aggregated his companies into a consumer conglomerate bearing his name. Now severed from its corporate history, it is known as the Norton Simon Art Foundation, which, along with The Norton Simon Foundation, holds the Simon collections. Today the character of the artworks of the two foundations is indistinguishable. For a description and history of the foundations, see Note to the Reader.

10. At the time Simon commissioned the *Monument to Balzac*, he bought another cast of *Walking Man*, which he gave to the University of California, Los Angeles in honor of university chancellor Franklin D. Murphy. He had arranged the anonymous gift through H. R. Haldeman, at that time the chairman of the board of trustees of the UCLA Foundation (H. R. Haldeman to Norton Simon, 21 March and 18 April 1967). The bronze, cast no. 11 from an edition of 12, was bought on 16 June 1966 for $32,470 and given to UCLA on 31 March 1967. Simon bought a third *Walking Man* (edition of 12, cast no. 12) from the Musée Rodin on 10 September 1969 for $30,680, which he donated to Wellesley College.

11. Robert Glickman, interview by Davis Guggenheim, 23 October 1996.

12. Angelina Boaz, interview by Davis Guggenheim, 24 July 1996.

13. Ibid.

14. Los Angeles County Museum of Art, *The Cubist Epoch*, 15 December–21 February 1971; New York, The Metropolitan Museum of Art, 7 April–7 June 1971.

15. Robert Lafond to Darryl Isley, 29 February 1972.

16. Alexandre Rosenberg to Isley, 25 May 1972.

17. Isley to Simon, 5 October 1973.

18. Pierre Matisse to Simon, 13 June 1966.

19. Matisse to Simon, 10 November 1966.

20. Matisse to Isley, 5 May 1975.

21. Simon curator Tessa Helfet, memorandum to file, 30 March 1982.

22. Seldis, 1967b.

23. James Brown to Cleveland Museum of Art director Sherman E. Lee, 23 April 1968.

24. Brown to Simon, 8 August 1968.

25. John Rewald to Simon, 6 January 1968.

26. John Richardson to Simon, 23 May 1969.

27. In all Simon acquired twenty-six works by Rodin, fourteen from the Musée Rodin.

28. Moreau-Nélaton, 1926, vol. 1, p. 130. The other three are *Beggar with a Duffle Coat (Philosopher)* and *Beggar with Oysters (Philosopher)*, The Art Institute of Chicago, and *The Absinthe Drinker*, Ny Carlsberg Glyptotek, Copenhagen.

29. See pp. 38–40 for a description of the Erickson sale of *Aristotle Contemplating the Bust of Homer*.

30. Peregrine Pollen to Simon, 22 March 1968.

31. Brown to Kenneth Donahue, 15 May 1968.

32. Los Angeles, 1968. In spite of Simon's stated opposition to naming county buildings for donors, he did not object to his name on the sculpture plaza.

33. Press release, Los Angeles County Museum of Art, 15 August 1968.

34. Seldis, 1968, p. 46.

35. In 1976 he arranged with David Nash of Sotheby Parke Bernet to try a private sale at $450,000 less 10 percent commission. In 1979 there were brief discussions with the Los Angeles dealer James Corcoran, who said that if it were for sale at $800,000, he had an interested client. Also in 1979 and then in 1980 Martha Baer at Christie's asked to put it in a fall sale with a reserve of $750,000 with no commission except for 1 percent if it went over $850,000.

36. Marlborough bought it for the Sid W. Richardson Foundation, Fort Worth.

37. From 1975 until 1977 Isley was director of the Norton Simon Museum at Pasadena. After leaving Simon, he worked for Wildenstein Gallery and later as a private dealer. He died in 1990 in London.

38. Morris L. Kaplan sale, London, Sotheby & Co., 12 June 1968.

39. Simon, on a memorandum from Isley to Simon, 19 July 1974.

40. Berges, 1975.

41. Brettell and Eisenman, 2006, p. 336.

42. London, Christie's, 1 December 1967, lot 26.

43. David Nash, interview by Davis Guggenheim, 14 July 1996.

44. Muchnic, 1998, p. 63.

45. Glueck, 1968.

46. Rembrandt's *Titus* cost $2,245,453; Renoir's *The Pont des Arts*, $1,550,000; Manet's *The Ragpicker*, $850,000.

47. Rosenberg to Simon, 18 November 1968.

48. File memorandum from Angelina Boaz dated 16 August 1968.

49. For a discussion of the Picasso sale, see pp. 198–199.

50. Simon to Agnew, 17 December 1968.

51. In 1998 the collection of Alessandro Contini-Bonacossi, which included works by Duccio, Paolo Veneziano, Sassetta, Paolo Veronese, Jacopo Tintoretto, and many others, was bequeathed to the Uffizi Gallery in Florence.

52. Seldis, 1969.

53. A set of tapestries made from Romanelli's cartoons is in the Cleveland Museum of Art.

54. McGuinness, 1969.

55. Ibid.

56. In 1969 the Simon collections still owned two Rembrandt paintings, the portrait presumed to be Hendrickje Stoeffels and *Titus*. He had returned *A Jewish Philosopher* to Duveen in 1959.

57. Stephen Hahn to Simon, 13 December 1968.

58. Patrick Lindsay to Simon, 7 May 1969.

59. *Self-Portrait* was initially rejected by the Rembrandt Research Project (Bruyn et al., 1989, no. C97). Ernst van de Wetering, a member of the original group who currently directs the project, will include the Norton Simon painting as an autograph Rembrandt in a forthcoming volume dedicated to Rembrandt's self-portraits. In 2001 and 2003 van de Wetering was able to perform a detailed technical examination of the work, a procedure not available to the original RRP team and concluded the work is an autograph Rembrandt.

60. Robert Light, interview by Davis Guggenheim, 20 June 1996.

61. Isley to Apollo advertising department, 3 July 1969. The notice, which appeared in the September 1969 issue, was an anonymous listing, with responses to go to a box number. The museum archives do not record any responses to the advertisement. Cat. 680, the landscape bought from Colnaghi in September, is now attributed to Jacob van Ruisdael and Nicolaes Berchem (Walsh, forthcoming).

62. Simon arranged for Robert Light to bid on his behalf at Christie's.

63. Edward Speelman to Simon, 8 December 1969.

64. Since the painting was purchased by the corporate foundation (the Norton Simon, Inc. Museum of Art), Simon requested that a representative of Norton Simon Inc. (Herbert Mayes) attend the opening.

65. Sara Campbell to Simon, memorandum, 31 January 1973.

66. Isley to Simon, memorandum, 9 March 1973.

67. San Francisco, 1973, no. 30.

68. Bernard Rabin, undated [1996] interview with Davis Guggenheim.

69. Since 1955 he had bought thirteen bronzes, eight oil paintings, eleven pastels, two drawings, and three monotypes.

70. *Wall Street Journal*, 1969.

71. At that time the art department consisted of Barbara Roberts, who handled negotiations for acquisitions; her assistant Marion Blackburn; the registrar Chris Klein; and research curator Darryl Isley. Because much of Simon's dealings by late 1969 involved art rather than business transactions, his executive assistant Angelina Boaz frequently interacted with the art staff, as did The Norton Simon Foundation's vice president, Julia R. Mayer, and accountant, Virginia O'Hern.

72. Barbara Roberts, Darryl Isley, Julia Mayer, and I moved to the Wilshire Boulevard office.

CHAPTER SEVEN

Transformations
1970–1971

Working with Norton was mostly creative chaos.
—ROBERT MACFARLANE[1]

THE EARLY 1970S SAW EXTREME CHANGES in almost every aspect of Norton Simon's life: his personal relationships; his business interests; his affiliation with the Los Angeles County Museum of Art as trustee and lender, and—for the purposes of this narrative—a profound transformation in the scope, size, and character of his art collection. Up to now, this account of Simon's collecting has largely followed a chronological sequence. But because of the extraordinary complexity of Simon's activity in 1970 and 1971, the narrative necessarily moves to parallel but intertwined tracks to cover these years. The first track is the shift in Simon's public and private life, which to a great extent affects what followed. Next is Simon's tumultuous relationship with LACMA and his eventual break with the institution. Closely linked to these events are a series of massive deaccessions from his art collection that occurred from 1970 to 1974 and a major cataloguing project by some of the world's most distinguished art historians. Finally, renewed acquisition zeal in 1972 resulted in an incredible realignment of the Simon collections.

During the spring of 1970 Simon's attention briefly turned from art to politics, when on 20 March he announced his candidacy in the California Republican primary election (fig. 1) to be held in June for the U.S. Senate seat held by George Murphy.[2] Although he called himself a Republican, Simon was a maverick who supported issues without regard to party lines. A longtime friend and supporter of former Democratic California governor Edmund G. "Pat" Brown, he had contributed to the Senate campaign of John Tunney, who would oppose Murphy in the general election. Concerned that Murphy was running unopposed in the primary, which would increase his strength in November, Simon took the advice of friends and challenged him by filing a Declaration of Candidacy. He did so on the last possible day to file.[3] To critics who said he had no political experience, he responded, "Of course I'm brand new to politics. But I was brand new to magazine publishing and soft drink bottling and art collecting, for that matter when I first started. I will find my way."[4] Overnight, his Wilshire Boulevard office was turned into a campaign headquarters. Barbara Roberts was enlisted to solicit campaign contributions from art dealers,

Can Norton Simon A Businessman Be Elected to the United States Senate?

OPPOSITE
Vasily Kandinsky, *Open Green*, 1923 (detail), The Norton Simon Foundation. CAT. 747

ABOVE LEFT
Norton Simon

ABOVE
FIG. 1. Norton Simon senatorial campaign poster, 1970

while Darryl Isley and I were left to manage the art department. Simon hired a professional campaign staff but relied on his friend and fellow University of California regent Frederick Dutton to advise the campaign. A prominent Democrat, Dutton was uneasy in the role of advisor to a Republican, but nonetheless agreed to assist him.[5] According to Dutton, Simon viewed his entry into politics as an opportunity to annoy the Republican Party rather than a bid to win an election. In a 1996 interview, he labeled Simon's decision to run as characteristically impulsive:

> It was not untypical of how he often jumped off the cliff. Norton thought he was bringing some fresh air into his party, rather than that he really had a serious chance of winning. I don't think he wanted to win. What would Norton Simon have done in the U.S. Senate? That's an old boys' club. No, no, I don't think so.[6]

Simon was uncomfortable in the role of campaigner and gave few press conferences. "I realized that Norton was not a back slapper or articulate," Dutton recalled. "He was one of the most inarticulate men I ever saw. But he was also one of the brightest."[7] Simon lost the primary race to Murphy but in doing so damaged Murphy's standing, enabling an ultimate Tunney victory. Dutton rightly believed Simon was unfazed by the loss, and that whether it was business, art, or politics, it was the process, not the winning, that was important. Simon agreed that in spite of losing, it was a heartening experience. Speaking in his very characteristic prose, he said:

> I felt that in my Senate race, having 32 or 33 percent of the people who were for me, not having been in politics and not being my life's work, but just being an experience, was a very positive, encouraging thing because I wasn't a politician—I was running against an incumbent, was running against the basic party principles that were far to the right of me and still to get that much of the vote, I felt, well gee, that's pretty good. I've got to expect that it's normal and natural not to be loved by everyone, even though I, like a lot of other people, would like to be.[8]

The Senate campaign offered Simon a heady diversion from business and art, but it did nothing to prevent the collapse of his thirty-seven-year marriage to Lucille. The difficulties that had been building for years were exacerbated by the suicide of their son Robert the previous October, and after the June election, Norton and Lucille agreed to divorce. When Simon moved out of his house, he rented a bungalow at the Beverly Hills Hotel. Almost overnight he stepped away from art acquisitions and the day-to-day management of his collection and arranged for his curatorial staff—Barbara Roberts, Darryl Isley, and me—to move from the foundation offices to LACMA, where we were to aid the museum in the administration of the Simon loans. Roberts, sensing the downturn in Simon's attention to his collection, and not interested in the proposed position as assistant to Director Donahue, left to become the first West Coast representative of Christie's. The museum, still hopeful that Simon's collections would eventually come to LACMA and striving to curry his favor, agreed to add us to its payroll. As Simon's biographer Suzanne Muchnic described it, "When Simon talked, people at the museum listened."[9]

LACMA was indeed listening, and in September 1970 Kenneth Donahue proposed creating a Norton Simon Collections Committee with Simon as chair. The committee would establish policy for all matters relating to the Simon collection, and LACMA would appoint a curator, conservator, registrar, and two preparators responsible solely for the collection and answering to the committee. In addition, Donahue created a list that he called "Mr. Simon's suggestions for improving the museum." First on the list was the removal from the museum's entrance of a large sculpture by Norbert Kricke that Simon thought inferior. Other items included such concerns as relandscaping, rearranging gallery spaces, moving the conservation center, ridding the galleries of all "questionable material and objects of quality not deserving to be shown in a major museum," and—for reasons that are not clear—removing the museum's architect, William Pereira, from any role.[10] Many of Simon's suggestions were sound. He had, for instance, urged that the reflecting pools surrounding the museum be replaced with lawns, since the pools were leaking water into the building's foundations.

The following month Donahue, LACMA board president Franklin Murphy,[11] board members Sidney Brody, Kathryn Gates, and John Walker (former director of the National Gallery of Art, Washington)[12] met with Simon and his staff to iron out questions ranging from insurance and exhibition costs to ongoing perceptions by LACMA curators that all of the museum's priorities were directed toward Norton Simon.[13] Murphy acknowledged that he accepted the board presidency only to facilitate obtaining Simon's collections, thereby garnering for the museum national recognition. Administrative and board restructuring, he argued, was taking place as evidence of goodwill.[14] Simon countered that he wanted to eliminate the negative perception of changes made "just for Norton Simon" and stressed the importance of conveying that they were being made "strictly because it is the only way the museum can survive."[15] Yet, in spite of the anxiety over pleasing Simon, by the end of the year, the museum had implemented none of his suggestions. Simon was so frustrated by what he saw as the museum's inefficiency that at one point he considered removing all of his artworks and sending them to other museums.[16]

During this period, Donahue was trying to secure a long-term loan of the Simon collections, which would include an exhibition catalogue edited by Walker. Because Walker was so deeply involved in the pending project, Simon enlisted his aid in moving matters along. Walker wrote to Donahue outlining all of Simon's complaints. Besides those mentioned above, they included fairly benign suggestions such as softening the appearance of the sculpture plaza with plants, performing needed conservation on artworks, and cleaning up basement corridors. There were, however, also more astonishing proposals, such as giving the textile department to another museum.[17] Walker met with members of the museum staff to push for the changes. He discussed his report with the board's Operating Committee, which decided that, before any action was taken, a budget needed to be created.[18] In March 1971 the board's Executive Committee suggested that in light of the "tight budget situation," additional money might have to be raised to pay for the changes Simon wanted.[19] Yet no money was forthcoming.

Despite these distractions, his personal life took precedence. Invited to a party given for *Newsweek* editor in chief Osborn Elliott at Chasen's restaurant in Los Angeles, Simon was asked to escort the actress Jennifer Jones Selznick, widow of film producer David O. Selznick. At first Simon was reluctant to accept, since the event was to occur on 5 May—the same night as the sale of works from his private collection. Further, he confessed to his secretary Beverly Perkins, since he did not often go to the movies, he was not sure who Mrs. Selznick was. Perkins enthusiastically urged Simon to attend and assured him that Mrs. Selznick was both charming and beautiful.[20] Simon agreed to be her escort and found her not only lovely but also interested in many of the same social causes that he was concerned with, such as mental health and drug abuse. After the Chasen's party, they began a whirlwind courtship that led to a trip to Europe. While in London before flying home, they decided to marry. It was a holiday weekend and they were unable to secure a marriage license. In a characteristically unorthodox Simon move, Sotheby's chief Peter Wilson obtained a yacht for the couple, and they were married five miles off the coast of England on 30 May 1971, less than four weeks after they met. Recounting the ceremony to the *Los Angeles Times*, Simon said, "It was great fun. We were bobbing around in the sea, and in the early morning light, I could just make out the white cliffs of Dover." He added, "To say that we are tremendously happy would be the understatement of 1971" (fig. 2).[21]

ABOVE AND BELOW RIGHT
FIG. 2. Jennifer and Norton Simon, May 1971

Notwithstanding Simon's newfound domestic happiness, he continued to be frustrated with LACMA and finally resigned from the museum board in late August 1971, after fourteen years of service. However, he continued to meet with board members and museum administrators about his loans. He complained about the treatment of his artworks, citing Rodin's *Monument to Balzac*, whose patina was being compromised by chemicals in the water of a nearby fountain. He criticized Donahue's ability to manage as well as his handling of the proposed exhibition catalogue and its writers. He declared he would not make a commitment for an exhibition at LACMA "because of the mess it is in." Board member Gates agreed with him, saying, "Norton is right. We have been pointing to these things for years."[22] In the summer of 1971 he removed Isley and me from LACMA, returning us to his office on Wilshire Boulevard.

As his dissatisfaction grew, Simon looked for other venues for the collection. Although at the time he had decided against building his own museum, he began to look at the possibility of remodeling existing structures to suit his needs. Returning to an idea he considered five years earlier, he suggested that a grand private home might offer enough room to display the collection in elegant surroundings.[23] In late 1971 Isley, Perkins, and I visited several estates in the Holmby Hills, Beverly Hills, and Bel Air areas of Los Angeles. They included the 27,000-square-foot Leigh Battson estate known as The Knoll, as well as the 23,000-square-foot Casa Encantada, home of hotelier Conrad Hilton, who personally escorted us through the mansion.[24] We reported back to Simon about the estates' suitability, but he soon dropped the idea, since he became more interested in his collection appearing at other venues around the country rather than in committing to his own museum.

In March 1972 Simon met with LACMA trustee Gates to discuss the County Museum's handling of his artworks. He proposed changing his arrangement to a contractual one similar to what he was considering at other museums[25] and suggested it was no longer the case that "a privilege [i.e., LACMA's possession and use of Simon's loans] long extended becomes a right." He and his staff would create a list from which the museum could select works for loan, and everything else would be removed from the premises.

Even as Simon was dealing with great changes in his personal life and recasting his relationship with LACMA, he began to sell large portions of his collections. Up until 1970, in fifteen years of collecting (1954–1969), Simon had made 711 acquisitions.[26] With the exception of sales from the Duveen inventory,[27] there were only forty-three deaccessions during the entire fifteen years, and these most often took the form of gifts and donations, or returns and trades, rather than sales.[28] Simon sold outright only four objects from 1954 to 1969. Three were private sales to friends or relatives, and one was to a dealer. However, in the next five years he completely altered this practice and thoroughly revised the composition of his collection by selling, trading, and replacing almost half of what he owned.

With only one exception, nothing was sold at auction until 1970.[29] Simon was certainly no stranger to the auction salesrooms, since about a sixth of his art up to this time had been bought at auction, but before 1970 he had virtually no experience with selling in this manner. Then, in early March, Peregrine Pollen, president of Parke-Bernet Galleries, and Peter Wilson of Sotheby's (Parke-Bernet's parent company in London) met with Simon to discuss the possibility of a sale. In an effort to woo the collector, Wilson drafted a glowing preface to the proposed catalogue, which said in part, "The Norton Simon collection includes perhaps fifty works which would grace the National Gallery of Art, the Jeu de Paume, the Cabinet des Dessins of the Louvre or the Metropolitan Museum, and moreover rank as stars in such illustrious company."[30] Wilson then offered Simon a way to justify deaccessioning:

> A collector cannot control or even anticipate the order in which the precious objects he covets become available. Thus it is natural that in a collection which has been continuously growing over the last fifteen years, examples of some of the artists represented should be eclipsed by later purchases.

He ended with another encomium to the collection and the collector:

> As will be seen by glancing through the following pages, this group of paintings and drawings ranks in importance with any auction held by Parke-Bernet over the last years. That this should be the case is a measure of the stature of Mr. Simon in a field which he has made his own.[31]

While Wilson and Pollen pushed for a large and heavily marketed sale devoted exclusively to his collection, Simon decided to test the waters first with a smaller selection sold anonymously. The initial auction sale of objects from the Simon collections took place in May 1970, when he agreed to sell thirty-nine paintings, drawings, and sculptures at Parke-Bernet in New York.[32] Simon selected a group of works by nineteenth- and twentieth-century artists, including watercolors and drawings by Jules Pascin and Marcel Gromaire, paintings by Jean Metzinger and Henri Fantin-Latour, and small sculptures by Aristide Maillol and François Pompon. To enhance the sale, the auction house wanted to see more important objects included and encouraged him to upgrade the grouping. Simon added a few better-known examples—paintings such as Amedeo Modigliani's *A Young Italian Girl* (fig. 3) and Pierre-Auguste Renoir's *Young Woman (Gabrielle)* (cat. 350). Parke-Bernet agreed to charge no commission on any item that did not reach the low estimate, and in a sale that grossed more than $800,000, its commission was about $11,000. Simon netted $210,000 over his original purchase prices, with almost half the profits coming from one work: Alberto Giacometti's *Standing Woman I* (fig. 4, right). Purchased for $32,000 five years previously, it sold for $130,000. When the same cast sold in 2000, it brought $14.2 million.[33]

Why did he sell a group of objects at this time, after years of escalating acquisitions and virtually no sales? It was not to replenish capital expended in recent purchases, since the amount from the sale was insignificant—in 1968 and 1969 alone he bought more than three hundred objects for $21.8 million. However, it did not escape his notice that auctions offered an anonymous and painless way to divest the collection of works that were no longer of interest or that held the opportunity for profit.

Five months after the May 1970 sale, Isley again discussed the art market with Pollen. It began as a conversation about bought-in lots, with Pollen advising against "putting the things up for auction again so soon," saying that "the next opportunity for a good sale will be the spring."[34] Pollen suggested that he and Wilson talk to Simon about future sales, and they soon drafted consignment and sales agreements for both his private collection and art belonging to The Norton Simon Foundation (primarily objects from the Duveen Brothers inventory). The first sale, "Highly Important 19th and 20th Century Paintings, Drawings, & Sculpture from the Private Collection of Norton Simon," took place on the evening of 5 May 1971.

The sale presented a stellar group of seventy-four nineteenth- and twentieth-century drawings, paintings, and sculptures. At least two lots brought record auction prices, Degas's *Little Dancer, Aged Fourteen* (p. 76) and Paul Gauguin's *Self-Portrait with Palette* (p. 61). No fewer than fourteen artworks went to museum collections in the United States and abroad. Degas's *At the Stock Exchange* (fig. 5) is now in the Metropolitan Museum of Art, while his *Dancer Bowing (Green Dancer)* (p. 45) is in the Thyssen-Bornemisza Collection, Madrid. Four paintings bought by the collector Armand Hammer are now in Los Angeles at the Armand Hammer Museum of Art, including Camille Pissarro's *Boulevard Montmartre, Mardi-Gras* (fig. 6) and Vincent van Gogh's *St. Paul's Hospital at St. Rémy* (p. 40, fig. 6).[35] Artworks that originally cost Simon about $3.5 million sold for more than $6.2 million; only four went unsold.

ABOVE
FIG. 6. Camille Pissarro, *Boulevard Montmartre, Mardi-Gras*, 1897, Armand Hammer Museum of Art and Culture Center, Los Angeles, cat. 421

ABOVE RIGHT
FIG. 3. Amedeo Modigliani, *A Young Italian Girl*, 1918, location unknown. CAT. 114

RIGHT
FIG. 4. Alberto Giacometti, *Standing Woman I*, 1960, location unknown. CAT. 289, *right*

FAR RIGHT
FIG. 5. Edgar Degas, *At the Stock Exchange*, 1878–1879, The Metropolitan Museum of Art, New York. CAT. 123

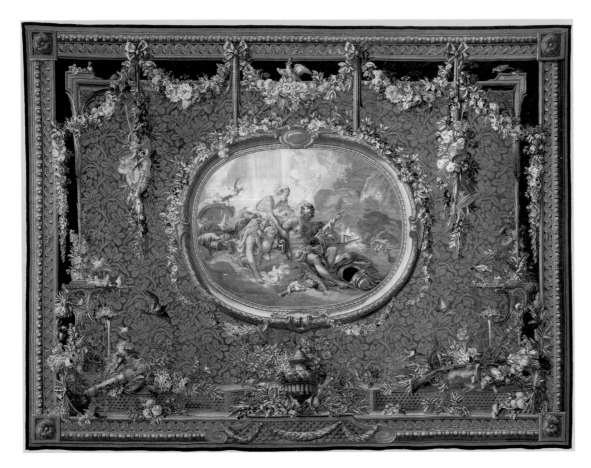

LEFT

FIG. 7. France, Gobelins, after cartoon by François Boucher, *Venus at the Forge of Vulcan*, The J. Paul Getty Museum, Los Angeles. CAT. D216

BELOW LEFT

FIG. 8. Claude Monet, *The Wooden Bridge at Argenteuil*, 1872, Fondation Rau, Zurich. CAT. 213

BELOW

FIG. 9. Pierre-Auguste Renoir, *Young Woman in Black*, C. 1875–1877, Jennifer Jones Simon Art Trust, Los Angeles. CAT. 142

A further massive two-day sale occurred on 7 and 8 May, with more than three hundred objects from The Norton Simon Foundation Duveen inventory. Among the twenty-two French and Flemish tapestries that were sold is the fine set of Gobelins after designs by François Boucher, bought by the J. Paul Getty Museum for $190,000 (fig. 7).[36] The Getty Museum also bought a large walnut cabinet (cat. D227) for the very low price of $1,700. The chest was thought to be an eighteenth-century copy of a sixteenth-century Burgundian cabinet, and that the date "1580" painted on one panel was counterfeit. The Getty's subsequent research has determined that the cabinet is indeed original late Renaissance furniture, and that the 1580 date is genuine.[37] Simon added to the 7–8 May sale sixteen old master drawings and two paintings from his private collection, including a portrait then attributed to Fragonard (cat. 60), now in the collection of the Frick Art Museum in Pittsburgh. The two-day sale brought about $860,000 for the foundation, and $120,000 for Simon's eighteen works.

In the world of auction houses, Sotheby's prime competitor was Christie's, which had recently hired Simon's former curator Barbara Roberts as its U.S. West Coast representative. Roberts spent the first few months after the May 1971 Parke-Bernet sales striving to bring some of Simon's business to her new employer.[38] Christie's proposed selling about a dozen paintings from his private collection, and he eventually consigned three to its 30 November 1971 sale: Edgar Degas's *Portrait of a Polytechnician* (cat. 141, now in the Murauchi Art Museum, Tokyo), Claude Monet's *Wooden Bridge at Argenteuil* (fig. 8), and Pierre-Auguste Renoir's *Young Woman in Black* (fig. 9). Fortunately, the Renoir did not sell and is still in the collection.

Although his profit on the sale of the Degas and the Monet was more than $300,000, for many years Simon did not consign to Christie's anything else of importance. This did not go unnoticed by the auction house. At one point, for instance, Isley asked J. A. Floyd of Christie's to send objects to California before Simon paid for them. Floyd consented, but warned that Simon should not assume this would happen as a matter of course. Isley reported to Simon, "I told him we do not have

this trouble with Sotheby's. He said if Christie's got the kind of merchandise Sotheby's got from us, he might be more favorable. All he gets are the leftovers."[39]

In spite of the monetary success of the sales for Simon and the need to refine the collection, the 1970–1971 sales caused considerable consternation at the Los Angeles County Museum of Art, where the loss of the artworks was keenly felt.[40] This was particularly true as it affected the planned catalogue project, guided by John Walker, who had served with Simon on the museum's board. Simon lent Rembrandt's *Titus* to the National Gallery of Art when Walker was director there (p. 75), and their cordial relationship continued after Walker's retirement in 1969. That fall the two met to discuss Simon's "museum without walls" loan program and a possible traveling exhibition to Europe, Canada, and several museums in the United States. They agreed that a definitive catalogue would accompany the exhibition and that it would be prepared by distinguished experts in those fields represented in the Simon collections. The catalogue would be distributed to Norton Simon Inc. stockholders and sold at the host museums. Walker would be responsible for recruiting and supervising the scholars, as well as serve as the consulting curator for the exhibitions. In clarifying his role, Walker wrote, "You spoke of my 'Masterminding' the operation. If I cannot significantly assist your project, then our arrangements will come to an end. But whatever happens I am sure our friendship will continue."[41]

Simon responded shortly afterward, "I am convinced that we need your organized mind and expertise, and your spirit of enthusiasm in the project we are about to undertake."[42] When Walker received a list of the objects, he was amazed at the extent of the collections, declaring, "I believe there are close to a thousand items if one includes prints and drawings."[43] He was only slightly exaggerating, since Simon's holdings at that time numbered more than seven hundred items, and the Duveen paintings and sculptures added at least two hundred more. Walker suggested four different catalogue options, ranging from an elaborate four-volume catalogue raisonné to a simple checklist and picture book, promising the project could be accomplished in two years.[44]

Drawing on his experience, superlative contacts among art historians, and the lure of Simon's collection, Walker recruited a group of the most eminent scholars perhaps ever assembled for one publication. Sir John Pope-Hennessy,[45] director of the Victoria and Albert Museum, would catalogue the Italian paintings and sculpture. Wolfgang Stechow,[46] professor emeritus at Oberlin College, would write about the Dutch paintings, while the Flemish works fell to Michael Jaffé,[47] head of the University of Cambridge Department of Art History. Ellis Waterhouse,[48] director of the Yale Center for British Art, agreed to write about the eighteenth-century British paintings, and Francis Watson,[49] director of the Wallace Collection, would take on the French eighteenth-century works. Diego Angulo Íñiguez,[50] director of the Diego Velázquez Institute in Madrid, would write about Spanish paintings, while Hans Naef would catalogue the drawings by Jean-Auguste-Dominique Ingres.[51] The nineteenth and twentieth centuries were allocated to George Heard Hamilton,[52] director of the Sterling and Francine Clark Art Institute in Williamstown, Massachusetts, who would catalogue the sculpture, while John Russell[53] and John Rewald[54] would write about the paintings.

The projected catalogue was to consist of four volumes. The first would contain about two hundred entries on the most important paintings. The second and third volumes would be devoted to sculptures and drawings, respectively, while the fourth would comprise less important paintings, along with any new acquisitions. The first volume would also serve as the catalogue for an exhibition at the Los Angeles County Museum of Art that would take place in early 1972. The scholars would be paid a fee per entry, with provisions for travel, research assistance, and typing services. The County Museum agreed in July 1970 to assume responsibility for printing costs, but the foundation would reimburse the museum for the writers' expenses.[55] In November, it was decided to reduce the size of the catalogue to two volumes.[56]

With a large Simon exhibition in the offing, Walker assembled the writers to produce the catalogue. As the scholars arrived in Los Angeles during late 1970 and early 1971, Isley and I escorted them through the collections, and we recorded their opinions not only about the art of their own areas but about everything else they looked at as well. Every writer rated each artwork in one of three categories—A was reserved for objects of the highest caliber that would automatically go into the catalogue; the B group consisted of items that were not as important but should stay in the collection and possibly find a place in the catalogue; and the C category contained artworks that the scholars deemed unworthy of the collection. We noted every comment and compiled lists of each relevant group for Simon's review. He often solicited opinions about his artworks, but owing to the eminence of the scholars, and the number of objects they examined, these sessions were by far the most intense and thorough. When compiling lists of objects for possible inclusion in the May 1971 auctions, Simon relied heavily on these judgments.

The auction sales angered many of the catalogue writers, who believed that their opinions aided, not the County Museum, but a private collector. They knew in advance that their reactions would help to refine the catalogue by weeding out questionable works,[57] but the enormous scope of the sales went far beyond their understanding of how their connoisseurship was to be used. Furthermore, they had already completed catalogue entries for many of the works that were sold. Simon refused Walker's suggestion to scuttle the project, and, in an effort to placate the writers, Walker proposed a letter to each and sent Simon a draft. The copy (with Simon's strikethroughs) reads:

> [Norton] still intends to go ahead with the catalogue. There is less urgency, however, about the delivery of the text. The Norton Simon Foundation will continue to buy, more probably in the field of old masters. His own enthusiasm for collecting, he emphasized, ~~has in no way diminished~~ [here, Simon substituted "is still very dynamic"]. This is simply an interim communication, which I felt had to be sent at once ~~following a long period of uncertainty on my part and I am sure puzzlement on yours~~. [Simon adds: "Mr. Simon assures me he had good reason for all the things sold in the recent sale."][58]

The Simon archives contain no copies of the final letter, and it is possible that Walker never sent it. In any event, the scholars remained confused about their role. Russell, for instance, asked Isley to confirm whether the catalogue was moving forward, "but I admit to having both lost interest and belief in the whole venture."[59]

As the summer of 1971 wore on, Isley and Walker tried to keep the catalogue and a possible exhibition at LACMA on track, but Simon's dissatisfaction with the County Museum and his own undermining of the project through his sales made it increasingly unlikely that either project would be realized. Board president Murphy and Walker met with Simon in October, and it was decided that the catalogue should continue. However, Simon would not commit to an exhibition at LACMA. Furthermore, he stressed that he intended to sell more artworks.[60] Walker sent letters to the writers, allaying their concerns about the sales by informing them of recent important acquisitions of works by Henri Rousseau, Jacob van Ruisdael, Henry Moore, and Vasily Kandinsky, adding optimistically, "Thus, as you see, the collections are being brought into better balance. In any event, you will not be quoted in connection with any sale."[61]

Walker had spent months trying to placate the scholars and keep the project moving forward and felt that Simon had undercut his efforts at every turn. In early 1972 he reminded Simon, "I have been doing my utmost to keep together the team of scholars I assembled for your catalogue…this is the most distinguished group of experts who have ever worked together cataloguing a collection."[62] He summarized the thoughts of his team, which varied from that of Rewald, who was angry not to have been told of the sales in advance, to Waterhouse, who offered to advise Simon on future sales. Russell and Pope-Hennessy were resentful and wanted assurances that no additional objects would be sold, the position that Walker himself took. Several authors—Jaffé, Stechow, Angulo Íñiguez, and Hamilton—were willing to continue.

Furious that Walker had not more strongly defended his position with the writers, and determined to manage his collection as he wished, Simon composed several drafts of a response, including one that stated, "I want it clear from here on out that I have no intention to go along with any commitments about selling. I presume your allegiances are such that you will not be able to edit any catalogue for me anyway. I am sorry the whole experience has created such a fiasco."[63] In the end, Simon decided not to answer Walker himself and instead directed foundation vice president Julia Mayer to write in early February 1972 that he was distressed and would talk to Walker when he, Simon, returned from a trip.[64] A miffed Walker replied, "It occurs to me that in the years we have known each other I have had very few letters directly from you. It would be heartening to receive one."[65] In Simon's March 1972 meeting with LACMA trustee Gates he discussed the moribund catalogue. He told her he wanted ownership of all of the finished material "for a catalogue for an unspecified date in the future" but wished to terminate Walker.[66] Later in the month, Walker wrote to LACMA director Donahue, "Norton has been in the end too cavalier in his treatment of me to make me want to continue as editor of his catalogue…It has been an unhappy experience, and one I endured only because I thought I could be of use to the Los Angeles County Museum. Otherwise I would have withdrawn a year ago."[67]

In the spring of 1972, in spite of the turmoil caused by the art sales, the failed catalogue, and Simon's continued displeasure, Donahue and the LACMA staff were still preparing for an exhibition of the Simon collection to open in June. Much to Donahue's disappointment and embarrassment, he learned that Simon was negotiating for a large exhibition of artworks from the corporate foundation collection, the Norton Simon, Inc. Museum of Art, to open in December 1972 at the Princeton University Art Museum. Donahue soldiered on and by the end of March 1972 was able to reach an agreement for an exhibition to begin no later than the first of June. Simon finally wrote personally to Walker on 31 March telling him of the appointment of Robert Macfarlane as president of The Norton Simon Foundation.[68] Macfarlane would handle its affairs, including "getting our relationship with LACMA on a more constructive basis." He informed Walker that there would not be a catalogue "as originally conceived," but that Macfarlane would work directly with each of the scholars to resolve any questions, and finally that "Franklin [Murphy] concurs that we should accede to your past request that you be relieved of the burden of editorship." He ended on a conciliatory note:

> You must know that we are all saddened by the difficulties which have arisen in relation to both an exhibition as well as a catalog. I know that your patience and persistence with the project were related not only to your interest in the Los Angeles County Museum of Art but also to our long-standing and warm relationship, and I am therefore most grateful. I hope that in the days and years ahead it may further be enlarged and enriched.[69]

A mollified Walker responded, saying that he "greatly appreciated the last paragraph of your letter," and that "I understand your reasons for giving up the catalogue . . . and am only sorry that this decision was not made a year ago as I suggested."[70] The scholars sent their notes and completed entries to Isley, and these art historically vital documents reside in the Norton Simon Museum curatorial files. The catalogue was never published.

IN LIGHT OF THE SALES IN THE EARLY 1970S, it seemed that the Simon collection was headed toward extinction. During a ten-month period in late 1970 and early 1971, when Isley and I were administering the collection from LACMA and watching it systematically depart to New York and the auction block, we wondered if Simon would eventually sell the entire collection. He had radically slowed his incredible 1968–1969 buying rate (see Appendix). Although in the midst of the Senate campaign and negotiations for the May sale, he still found time to buy twenty-three artworks—fourteen in January alone—a major downturn occurred after his divorce, when he added only six objects from July through December. Total acquisitions for the year fell to 30 from the previous year's 152. Our fears were only temporary, however, since he soon picked up his pace to earlier levels after his remarriage the next May.[71]

Simon acquired several important old master paintings in 1970, including two by Francisco de Zurbarán, *Fray Diego Deza* (cat. 720) and *The Birth of the Virgin* (cat. 738), as well as Lucas Cranach the Elder's *Adam* and *Eve* (cats. 742, 734). He also made three significant purchases of works on paper. The first was a collection of 139 drawings purchased in January from the Los Angeles bookseller Jacob Zeitlin. The chalk drawings by Jean-Honoré Fragonard were copies after the old masters made while traveling in Italy as a student (fig. 10). Fragonard's exquisite copies of paintings by Tintoretto, Titian, Veronese, Tiepolo, and many others reveal both the works to which he was attracted as well as his own style and sensibilities. The same day in January 1970 Simon bought Rembrandt's *Christ with the Sick around Him, Receiving the Children* (cat. 713). The artist combined several stories from the Gospel of Matthew into one image, as Christ is seen debating with scholars, healing the sick, and calling the children around him. The beautiful etching, with its masterful use of light and dark, is also called *The Hundred Guilder Print*, referring to the fact that Rembrandt was able to charge the handsome sum of one hundred guilders, significantly more than his usual fee. Simon's interest in works on paper continued when at the end of the year he bought from Wildenstein an album of sixty drawings by the great seventeenth-century landscape artist Claude Lorrain (fig. 11). The

TOP
FIG. 10. Jean-Honoré Fragonard, *Madonna and Child with Saints Jerome and Mary Magdalene, after Correggio*, 1760–1761, The Norton Simon Foundation. CAT. 716
ABOVE
FIG. 11. Claude Gellée, called Claude Lorrain, *Hilly Countryside*, c. 1640, Norton Simon Art Foundation. CAT. 740

drawings represent the full range of Claude's skills in chalk, charcoal, and pen and ink and include studio compositions of historical and biblical subjects as well as classical landscapes. In June 1969 Simon agreed to buy them for $1,000,000, payable in four equal six-month installments with the first payment due at the end of the year.[72] He later arranged with the dealer to forgo installments and instead to accept one lump-sum payment at the end of 1970. For the next eighteen months Simon directed conservation treatment, the separation and removal of the drawings from their binding, as well as their framing (fig. 12), and began arrangements for their loan and the publication of an exhibition catalogue. Between 1970 and 1975 the drawings were exhibited at eleven museums and university art galleries.[73] However, to Simon's way of thinking, they garnered little public interest in spite of their scholarly significance. Over the years, he asked specialists and dealers, as usual, to estimate the drawings' values, and in 1980 he determined to sell all but seven, a number that he deemed sufficient for exhibition.[74] The fifty-three drawings were sold to the dealers Thomas Agnew & Sons, Eugene Thaw, and David Carritt for $4,420,000. Thaw later said of the sale, "not one of the best deals I ever made. I thought it was going to be terrific, and got off with a bang when I sold three drawings to the Frick right away. Then everything dried up—too many Claudes on the market at once."[75]

Simon bought nothing during the first six months of 1971.[76] Any attention he would previously have devoted to his collection was directed instead to the May sales and to his courtship and marriage to Jennifer Jones Selznick. Still, he was sensitive to the message his sales were sending dealers, and when the Zurich dealer Peter Nathan wrote that he would be in New York for Simon's sales and in Los Angeles afterward, Simon asked Isley to respond, "Don't let my personal sale of pictures mislead him. I'm still buying for Foundation and am very interested in the Ruisdael."[77] The Jacob van Ruisdael in question was *Three Great Trees in a Mountainous Landscape with a River* (cat. 743), which Simon bought from Nathan that July.

In October Simon took his new wife to New York, and together they went to two auctions at Parke-Bernet on consecutive evenings. At the 20 October sale, Simon was the successful buyer of his first Vasily Kandinsky, *Open Green* (cat. 747), for $155,000.[78] At the 21 October sale the next day, for five times the cost of the Kandinsky, he bought Henri Rousseau's *Exotic Landscape* (fig. 13) for $775,000, his first and only purchase of a work by the enigmatic French artist. He added just ten acquisitions in 1971, spending about $1.9 million.

As Simon accelerated the pace of his acquisitions during the next year and over the next decade, he continued to alter the appearance of his pre-1970 collection by additional extensive deaccessions and simultaneous new acquisitions. In his first fifteen years of collecting, Simon made more than 750 acquisitions. Fewer than 250 of these remain in the collections. Today there are only nineteen artworks that date from his first five years. Further, after 1971 the essential character of the collection was utterly transformed as Norton Simon plunged into collecting in an entirely new, non-European area, the sculpture of South and Southeast Asia. ❧

FIG. 12. Norton Simon studying Claude Lorrain drawings at his home, Los Angeles, May 1970

FIG. 13. Henri Rousseau, *Exotic Landscape*, 1910, The Norton Simon Foundation, CAT. 748

1. Robert Macfarlane, speaking at "Collector without Walls: A Symposium on Norton Simon," 27 October 2007.

2. For a thorough discussion of Simon's Senate campaign, see Muchnic, 1998, chap. 17, pp. 149–158.

3. In a meeting of the Board of Regents of the University of California while aides completed the filing paperwork, Simon had to borrow money to pay the filing fee from his fellow regents.

4. Harvey, 1970, p. 36.

5. Frederick Dutton (1923–2005) served in Governor Brown's administration and was Assistant Secretary of State under John F. Kennedy. Hoping for a degree of anonymity, Dutton insisted on a code name. He and Simon decided on "Percy Pinkerton."

6. Dutton, interview by Charles Guggenheim, 2 October 1996.

7. Ibid.

8. Berges, 1975.

9. Muchnic, 1998, pp. 115–116.

10. Kenneth Donahue, memorandum, 11 September 1970. This is especially curious since Simon used Pereira's firm to design the Hunt corporate office complex and the Hunt Branch Library. There is nothing in the archives to indicate that he was disappointed with the results.

11. Former chancellor of the University of California, Los Angeles, Murphy was chairman of the board and chief executive officer of the Times Mirror Company from 1968 to 1981. He also served as a trustee of the Norton Simon Inc. Museum of Art (now the Norton Simon Art Foundation) from 1968 to 1971.

12. John Walker (1906–1995) was director of the National Gallery of Art from 1956 to 1969.

13. Notes from a meeting of the Operating Committee, Los Angeles County Museum of Art, 10 October 1970.

14. Ibid.

15. Ibid.

16. Office memorandum, 27 January 1971.

17. Walker to Donahue, 25 November 1970.

18. Minutes of the Los Angeles County Museum of Art Operating Committee, 1 February 1971.

19. Minutes of the Los Angeles County Museum of Art Executive Committee, 2 March 1971.

20. Beverly Perkins, conversations with the author, April–May 1971; Perkins to Simon, memorandum, 23 April 1971: "She looked lovely on the Academy Awards show and you might have a good time."

21. *Los Angeles Times*, 1971, p. 1.

22. Julia R. Mayer, memorandum concerning a meeting on 25 October 1971 with Norton Simon, Kathryn Gates, Henry Dreyfus, Franklin Murphy, and John Walker.

23. In May 1966 Simon directed Barbara Roberts to investigate large homes as potential museum sites (see p. 83).

24. Isley to Simon, 5 November 1971.

25. This was a reference (without mentioning the venue) to an exhibition he was planning at the Princeton University Art Museum the following December.

26. The number of artworks differs from the number of acquisitions, since one purchase might be a pair of paintings, or a portfolio of 100 prints. The Duveen acquisition alone numbered 779. Simon's 710 other acquisitions represented more than 2,400 individual examples. The total number of artworks (including Duveen) acquired by 31 December 1969 was more than 3,000.

27. At the time of the Duveen purchase it was understood that the foundation would work with Duveen Brothers to sell many of the items. In addition to 11 Duveen objects donated to the University of California, Los Angeles, 86 were sold during the first two years; by the end of 1969 Simon had sold 100 more.

28. A few artworks had been intended as donations at the time of their purchase, such as works by Rodin (see chap. 6 n. 10). In addition, he gave a cast of Aristide Maillol's *Sorrow*, bought from Dina Vierny in 1968, to the University of California, Berkeley. Other artworks were given to friends and relatives over the years, and some pieces had been traded to dealers.

29. The only artwork Simon sold at auction before 1970 was a Gainsborough School portrait (D133) from the Duveen collection. At the time of the Duveen acquisition the work was owned by Duveen in partnership with a private collector, who agreed that the foundation could sell the painting at public auction. Although Simon had deaccessioned close to one hundred Duveen artworks by the end of 1969, the vast majority—about eighty— was traded or returned to dealers, or were gifts. He had sold only nineteen objects outright, and all but the one mentioned above were private sales to dealers.

30. Peter Wilson, "Draft Preface to Catalogue of Seventy-nine Paintings and Drawings from the Norton Simon Collection," undated handwritten draft.

31. Ibid.

32. Agreement dated 15 April 1970. Thirty-six European objects were consigned to the 13 May sale (eight were bought in); three American paintings were sold on 14 and 21 May. A few of the works came from his personal collection; the remainder from his two foundations; none of the owners was identified in the catalogues.

33. New York, Christie's, 8 November 2000, lot 63.

34. Isley to Simon, memorandum, 20 October 1970.

35. Other paintings in the Hammer Museum are cat. 63, Jean-Francois Millet's *Peasants Resting* and cat. 212, Jean-Baptiste Camille Corot's *Study of Medieval Ruins*. Hammer also bought Pierre Bonnard's *Nude Against the Light* (cat. 444), which was given to the Hammer Museum and returned to The Armand Hammer Foundation in 2007. Other museums that benefited from the 5 May 1971 sale are the National Gallery of Art, Washington (cat. 137, Georges-Pierre Seurat's *The Model*); Museum of Fine Arts, Houston (cat. 81, Odilon Redon's *Trees*); North Carolina Museum of Art, Raleigh (cat. 108, Pierre Bonnard's *The Lessons* and cat. 282, Auguste Rodin's *The Kiss*); Flint, Michigan, Institute of Arts (cat. 109, Édouard Vuillard's *Woman Lighting a Stove*); Fitzwilliam Museum, Cambridge (cat. 536, Walter Sickert's *Mornington Crescent Nude*); Pola Museum of Art, Hakone, Japan (cat. 144, Monet's *Argenteuil*).

36. Another tapestry (cat. D217, *The Annunciation*), was acquired by the Metropolitan Museum of Art.

37. J. Paul Getty Museum, 71.DA.89. Interestingly, Mr. Getty had expressed interest in the cabinet in 1968 (J. Paul Getty to Duveen's Edward Fowles, 31 January 1968). Fowles informed Getty that The Norton Simon Foundation had lent it to the Metropolitan Museum of Art.

38. Isley to Simon, memorandum, 14 June 1971; Barbara Roberts to Simon, 1 July 1971. Christie's international sales took place in London; it did not open its New York saleroom until May 1977.

39. Isley to Simon, 18 June 1974.

40. Curators who had freely given advice to Simon for years, hoping that he would continue to lend the collection and eventually donate it to the museum, were upset to the point that they were no longer interested in advising him (as reported in Isley to Simon, 13 January 1972).

41. Walker to Simon, 8 December 1969.

42. Simon to Walker, 17 December 1969.

43. Walker to Simon, 7 January 1970.

44. Walker to Simon, 6 February 1970.

45. Sir John Pope-Hennessy (1913–1994) was the director of the Victoria and Albert Museum (1967–1973) and the British Museum (1974–1976). He then became the consulting chairman of the Department of European Painting at the Metropolitan Museum of Art (1977–1986).

46. Wolfgang Stechow (1896–1974) was Kress Professor in Residence at the National Gallery of Art and an advisory curator at the Cleveland Museum of Art. Stechow's best-known work is *Dutch Landscape Painting of the Seventeenth Century* (1966).

47. Michael Jaffé (1923–1997) was the director of the Fitzwilliam Museum in Cambridge from 1973 to 1990. He is the author of books on Anthony van Dyck, Jacob Jordaens, and Peter Paul Rubens, among others.

48. Sir Ellis Waterhouse (1905–1985) was Barber Professor of Fine Art at Birmingham (England) University and the director of the Barber Institute from 1952 to 1970. He is the author of many books on Italian and British painting. His *Painting in Britain, 1530–1790* was the first volume in the Pelican History of Art series.

49. Sir Francis Watson (1907–1992) wrote monographs on Giovanni Battista Tiepolo, Canaletto, and Jean-Honoré Fragonard, and the five-volume series on the Wrightsman Collection in the Metropolitan Museum of Art (1966–1973).

50. Diego Angulo Íñiguez (1901–1986) is the author of the three-volume *Murillo: Su vida, su arte, su obra* (1981).

51. Hans Naef (b. 1920) has written extensively about Ingres, including the drawing entries in *Portraits by Ingres: Image of an Epoch* [Exh. cat. The Metropolitan Museum of Art, New York.] New York, 1999.

52. George Heard Hamilton (1910–2004) was the director of the Sterling and Francine Clark Art Institute from 1966 to 1977. He is the author of *Manet and His Critics* (1954) and, for the Pelican History of Art series, *The Art and Architecture of Russia* (1975) and *Painting and Sculpture in Europe, 1880–1940* (1967).

53. John Russell (1919–2008) was art critic for the *New York Times* from 1974 to 1990. He is the author of *Max Ernst: Life and Work* (1967), *Francis Bacon* (1971), *The World of Matisse: 1869–1954* (1972), and *Matisse: Father and Son* (1999).

54. In addition to writing the first catalogue of the sculpture of Edgar Degas (1944), John Rewald (1912–1994) was the author of many books on Paul Cézanne and Paul Gauguin, *The History of Impressionism* (1946), and *Post-Impressionism: From van Gogh to Gauguin* (1956).

55. Donahue to Walker, 29 July 1970.

56. Walker to Simon, 12 November 1970.

57. Barbara Roberts's letter to John Walker, 23 June 1970, for instance, reminded him that the writers knew that questions of quality, attribution, and condition "will assist in the determination of what is to be included not only in the first volumes but what will remain in the collection as well."

58. Walker to Simon, 28 May 1971.

59. Russell to Isley, 17 June 1971.

60. Foundation vice president Julia R. Mayer, memorandum concerning a meeting on 25 October 1971 with Simon, Kathryn Gates, Henry Dreyfus, Franklin Murphy, and John Walker.

61. Walker to the catalogue scholars, 19 November 1971.

62. Walker to Simon, 21 January 1972.

63. Simon draft of unsent letter to Walker, 1 February 1972.

64. Mayer to Walker, 2 February 1972.

65. Walker to Simon, 3 February 1972.

66. Mayer, office memorandum, 9 March 1972.

67. Walker to Donahue, 20 March 1972.

68. Macfarlane, a Presbyterian minister, was an old friend of the Simon family. Macfarlane's father was a longtime business associate of Simon's.

69. Simon to Walker, 31 March 1972.

70. Walker to Simon, 19 April 1972.

71. Norton and Lucille's divorce proceedings began 24 July 1970; the divorce was final on 29 January 1971.

72. Wildenstein's president Louis Goldenberg to Simon, 5 June 1969.

73. San Francisco, 1970.

74. Julia R. Mayer, memorandum, 5 September 1980, regarding a report to the Norton Simon Art Foundation Executive Committee, 4 August 1980.

75. Eugene Thaw, conversation with Sara Campbell, January 1991.

76 He paid for Lucas Cranach's *Adam* in January 1971 but had committed to buy it in May 1970 at the time he purchased *Eve*.

77. Notes on letter from Peter Nathan to Simon, 31 March 1971.

78. Simon spent a good deal of time in late 1971 comparing available Kandinsky paintings, and in December he bought another, *On the Theme of the Last Judgment* (cat. 750), from the dealer Leonard Hutton.

CHAPTER EIGHT

New Loves 1972–1973

Norton Simon was the single biggest bull that ever appeared in the Indian china shop.—PRATAPADITYA PAL[1]

Norton Simon's interest in collecting was rejuvenated after his 1971 marriage to Jennifer Jones, and he gave most of his time to a newfound field: the art of India, the Himalayas, and Southeast Asia. During the next two years he bought 138 examples, spending more than $6.6 million. He was hardly neglecting the rest of his collection, since in the same two-year period he made 123 purchases of Western art for almost $20.5 million. All the while, he was overseeing the loan of hundreds of his artworks to museums and university galleries throughout the country. On any given day or in any one hour, he might be occupied in one or the other of these pursuits. To better elucidate the story of each, I have separated his Asian and European acquisitions and the loan program into three chapters, each treating the two-year period 1972–1973. This first chapter on the period discusses Simon's acquisitions of South and Southeast Asian art.

The early 1970s, however, were not the first time Simon had considered South Asian art. A precursor of what was to follow, Simon's first recorded interest came in early 1967, when he asked Sotheby's about a bronze figure of the goddess Parvati from the South Indian Chola period that had sold in its Indian sculpture auction in February.[2] Peter Wilson answered Simon's inquiry about whether the work was still available by telling him that it had sold for £6,000 ($16,800) to a private collector who wished to remain anonymous. Seeking to discourage Simon from further inquiry, Wilson added, "It would really be hopeless to approach him about it as I am sure he would not wish to part with it."[3] Based on Simon's notations on the cover of the Sotheby's catalogue, at least three Chola bronzes had caught his eye, presaging his later fascination with similar works from South India.[4] The inquiry was evidently no more than a passing interest, and he gave the field no further attention for four years. In the course of the following four, however, Simon became one of the world's foremost collectors of South and Southeast Asian art. In a remarkably short period, he came to dominate the market, and his very presence in the arena raised prices.

Simon's captivation with South Asian art blossomed almost overnight, following one of the slowest years since he had started collecting. After his July 1970

OPPOSITE
India, Tamil Nadu, LEFT: *Parvati*; RIGHT: *Shiva the Bull-Rider*, c. 1000 (detail), The Norton Simon Foundation. CATS. 756, 824

ABOVE LEFT
Norton Simon

FIG. 1. India, Delhi Region, *Chess Set and Board*, c. 1850, The Norton Simon Foundation. CAT. 745

Simon moved quickly and assuredly into the area of South Asian art collecting. This new direction, coupled with the deaccessions of the preceding two years, entirely changed the character and scope of his collection. Upon his return from India he immediately asked Pal to compile a list of the best dealers in the field. On the list was Doris Wiener in New York, who in December sold Simon his first important work from South Asia, *A Dejected Heroine(?)* (fig. 2), an eleventh-century sandstone female figure from Madhya Pradesh. An exquisitely carved architectural detail originally part of a temple wall, the elegant and sensuous lady appears to be sculpted completely in the round. Her torso twists around toward the viewer, while her hips and legs turn away. The elaborate, beautiful carving and dramatic perspective camouflage her impossibly contorted shape as she caresses a strand of her hair.

divorce, he bought only six artworks during the rest of the year and just thirteen in all of the next (see Appendix).[5] Before October 1971 he had never owned a work of art from India, the Himalayas, or Southeast Asia, but a fall 1971 trip to India with his new wife led him in a wholly new direction, and he began acquiring Asian art with a speed and intensity that shocked his staff and delighted dealers.[6] While in New Delhi, Simon telephoned Darryl Isley to inquire about cultural sights and museums he should see. Isley put him in touch with Pratapaditya Pal, the senior curator of Indian and Southeast Asian Art at LACMA.[7] Aside from a trip to the Taj Mahal, Pal suggested he visit the National Museum, which became Simon's introduction to Indian sculptural masterpieces. While in New Delhi, Simon naturally visited art dealers, securing at one his first piece of Indian art, an ivory chess set from the Delhi region, from about 1850 (fig. 1). The thirty-two pieces rest on a black-and-white board inlaid with ivory.[8] The pawns on the two warring sides are represented by foot soldiers carrying spears, and the king, his minister, and his generals ride exquisitely carved elephants and camels. Simon justified the acquisition because he was a chess player, but despite his affection for the set, he dismissed it as merely a pleasant souvenir. In fact, the set is considered to be of fine quality, very well preserved, with an elegant board,[9] and worth considerably more than the $3,000 purchase price. He was not so lucky with the second piece bought at the same time, an ivory *Shiva and Parvati* (cat. 746), which proved to be a twentieth-century tourist trade object and was later sold.

FIG. 2. India, Madhya Pradesh, *A Dejected Heroine(?)*, 11th century, The Norton Simon Foundation. CAT. 751

Wiener went on to sell Simon some of his finest pieces of Asian art, recalling, "For me it was fascinating.... He started at square one. He wanted to know about Hinduism as compared to Buddhism, for example, and he wanted to know everything right away."[10] In January 1972 three more artworks from Wiener followed *A Dejected Heroine(?)*. The first was a bronze Gupta period *Buddha Shakyamuni*, about 550 (fig. 3), bought for The Norton Simon Foundation for the then impressive price of $300,000. Its fine state of preservation may be the result of its having been transported to Tibet as a sacred relic. Portrayed in the classic frontal pose with his right hand lifted in the gesture of reassurance, the figure is seen in the role of the historic Buddha. The beautiful bronze with its silvery patina is of the understated Gupta style of northeastern India, and the body is seen through a layer of diaphanous fabric. Simon enjoyed comparing this first bronze with very similar representations of the Buddha in both the John D. Rockefeller III collection and the Cleveland Museum of Art.

Simon bought two additional sculptures from Wiener in January 1972 for his private collection—an early-twelfth-century Orissan *Celestial Musician* (cat. 755) and a Chola bronze *Parvati* (fig. 4). The *Parvati* was Simon's first work from the Chola period. Chola bronzes were created in what is now the south Indian state of Tamil Nadu, between about 900 and 1300. He went on to acquire five examples of this Hindu goddess and dozens of other Chola bronzes, but this one remained perhaps his favorite. Shiva's wife and daughter of the Mountain King Parvata, this slightly stocky Parvati wears an intricately patterned garment on her lower body while her voluptuous torso is revealed. Bedecked in an elaborate necklace and bracelets, she would have held a lotus in her right hand, and her left hand hangs gracefully at her side.

FIG. 3. India, Bihar, Gupta Period, *Buddha Shakyamuni*, c. 550, The Norton Simon Foundation. CAT. 754

FIG. 4. India, Tamil Nadu, *Parvati*, c. 1000, The Norton Simon Foundation. CAT. 756

In a 1996 interview, Pal discussed Simon's attraction to Chola bronzes and his understanding of their artistic brilliance: "He had an instinctive passionate liking for Chola bronzes, which is why he built the greatest Chola bronze collection outside of India. They are technically and aesthetically among the finest cast bronzes; each is a unique cast. They are very simple and elegant bronzes and I think that's what appealed to him."[11] Pal attributed Simon's interest to the fact that they were usually sculpted in the round and could be viewed from all sides, comparing them to classical Greek sculptures that were familiar to the Western eye. As a matter of fact, Simon wrote about this very relationship in an unpublished 1974 essay:

> A trip to India a few years ago opened my eyes to Eastern art, especially sculpture. I marveled at the connections between some of the ancient Greek sculpture and the [Indian] sculptures. One of the main appeals of that art form is the sense of sculpture in the round; there is homage and reverence for the human body to an intense degree. While there are interesting factors in the mythology and iconographical concepts, I found my main interest in the devotion to the aesthetics of the human body. The fact that the sculptors were able to produce such joy in single bronze castings and in single stone carvings is a marvel.[12]

As Simon accumulated sculptures from South Asia, he compared their value with one another as well as with otherwise unrelated objects. When he studied similar works, he grew to understand their relative value. In addition, by evaluating somewhat unfamiliar Asian artworks against European examples that he knew intimately, he honed his knowledge and perfected his eye in both areas. In January 1972 he drew me into one such reflection, comparing the *Parvati* from Wiener and Degas's *Little Dancer, Aged Fourteen* (fig. 5). The *Parvati* was in his home on approval, and he asked me which bronze I would rather own. The *Dancer* was no longer present for a physical comparison, since he had sold it in May 1971.

Knowing his affection for Degas, I inferred from his question that he regretted selling the *Dancer*, even though its sale price at $380,000 (a record for a Degas sculpture) was almost four times the $100,000 Wiener was asking for the *Parvati*. I hedged by commenting on the difficulty of evaluating apples and oranges, but Simon argued that it was absolutely fair to make a comparison between an eleventh-century Indian sculpture and one from nineteenth-century France. He reasoned that both were bronze female figures of approximately the same height. *Little Dancer, Aged Fourteen* was Degas's pivotal sculpture, yet to Simon's way of thinking, the Chola bronze was far superior in terms of craftsmanship, uniqueness, and beauty, and it was a bargain at the price.[13] The dealer Ben Heller recalled Simon's penchant for comparing dissimilar artworks:

> He loved to compare not apples to apples. He liked apples to oranges better, but I guess he liked apples to pineapples far better. And we spent one night discussing whether he should buy an exquisite tiny Watteau or a marvelous, early Chola, South Indian bronze. That was really apples to pineapples. With Norton, it wasn't sufficient to just make a decision. You had to know all the reasons why.[14]

A restless and inquiring intellect, Simon approached his new interest with curiosity and excitement, not least because the prices for high-quality works in this field were far lower than for the Western artworks he was considering and buying. As with the Western art market, he wanted to see as much as he could as quickly as he could, knowing that he learned best when he could examine, compare, and live with objects. It was a challenge for all of us—Isley and me as well as Norton Simon—to look at a completely non-Western iconography and vast pantheon of saints and gods that were almost altogether new. The learning curve was steep. With the aid of newly acquired books and frequent, lengthy discussions with Asian art curators and dealers, we eventually learned to distinguish Buddhist saints from Hindu gods, western India from southern, and work from Nepal or Tibet from that of Cambodia or Thailand.

Part of the education came from seeing multiple examples of the same subject in the same style, as with another *Parvati* (cat. 778) purchased from Doris Wiener in May, and a third acquired from Ben Heller in July (cat. 822). All three are from South India and very closely dated, but they are very individual representations with distinct and illuminating differences. Stylistically, the first Wiener *Parvati* greatly resembled a Shiva on offer from Spink & Son in London (fig. 6), and it was determined that the two had been sculpted by the same Chola artist and meant to be a pair. Shiva's characteristic relaxed stance and bent left arm reveal that he has assumed the pose known as Shiva the Bull Rider. Shiva and Parvati in this instance would have been accompanied by Shiva's companion, the bull Nandi, or Vrisha, on whose head the god would have been leaning.

In addition to the Doris Wiener Gallery, Pal recommended several other prominent dealers, including Spink & Son in London and William H. Wolff, Ben Heller, and J. J. Klejman in New York. Simon first met Klejman in 1966 while briefly considering a large Greek bronze Dionysus.[15] By late 1971 Klejman wanted to retire from business and divest himself of his inventory, while Simon was interested in forming a collection. Pal and Simon compiled lists from Klejman's stock in early 1972 and arranged for several dozen pieces to be sent to California. The artworks were not only Indian, Tibetan, and Nepalese but also African, Egyptian, and Byzantine. These

seventy works of art were divided into several groups, which Simon committed to buy at different times over the next two years. These fine bronzes and stones from India, Cambodia, and Thailand constitute the backbone of Simon's South Asian collection. Also included were his first Himalayan bronzes, one of the most outstanding being the elegant ninth-century Kashmiri *Bodhisattva Manjusri* (fig. 7). A bodhisattva is a Buddhist enlightened being who forgoes paradise to help others, and Manjusri is the bodhisattva of wisdom. The six-armed figure stands on a lotus base, accompanied by his peacock companion. He displays various characteristic attributes, holding the lotus in his front left hand, while with his front right hand he displays the gesture of charity. Manjusri wears an elaborate tiara and numerous bracelets, necklaces, and garlands, emphasizing his princely, nondivine status.

OPPOSITE
FIG. 5. Edgar Degas, *Little Dancer, Aged Fourteen*, private collection, Brunei. CAT. 269

ABOVE LEFT
FIG. 6. India, Tamil Nadu, *Shiva the Bull-Rider*, c. 1000, The Norton Simon Foundation. CAT. 824

ABOVE RIGHT
FIG. 7. India, Kashmir, *Bodhisattva Manjusri*, 9th century, The Norton Simon Foundation. CAT. 763

FIG. 8. India, Uttar Pradesh, *Celestial Dancer*, 11th century, Jennifer Jones Simon Art Trust, Los Angeles. CAT. 772

William Wolff, another New York dealer recommended by Pal, sold Simon ten sculptures in April and May 1972. The first three went to Simon's private collection, including one of his favorite stones, the fine *Celestial Dancer* (fig. 8). The elaborately carved maiden twists and turns her body as her jewelry and scarves swirl around her. Simon kept the sandstone dancer mounted on the wall above his fireplace. Although he was generous about lending other works from his personal holdings to the Norton Simon Museum, the maiden never left his home until after his death.

Wolff sold Simon what was then the earliest Indian artwork in the collection, a sandstone railing pillar from the Buddhist site at Bharhut (fig. 9). The pillar is decorated with figures arranged in two registers that symbolize fertility and prosperity. The upper register depicts a female nature goddess known as a *yakshi*, who clutches the branch of a mango tree, causing it to bear fruit, and points to the loving couple in the lower register.

RIGHT
FIG. 9. Madhya Pradesh, Bharhut, *Railing Pillar: Goddess and an Amorous Couple*, c. 100 B.C., The Norton Simon Foundation. CAT. 781

ABOVE RIGHT
FIG. 10. Ben Heller

One of the largest sculptures from Wolff was the first massive stone figure to enter the collection, *Krishna Fluting in Brindavan* from the southern Indian state of Karnataka (cat. 780). Simon had neither equipment nor staff to set up and display large pieces, a fact that did not deter him from acquiring many others even larger than the five-foot *Krishna*. With the influx of crate after crate of artworks arriving on approval, Isley and I searched for a suitable site to receive, unpack, and store the objects. Their size made it all but impossible to unpack crates in Simon's suite of offices on Wilshire Boulevard, so we rented space in a moving company warehouse nearby. When sculptures were too large to lift, we would leave them in the crates in the warehouse, lids removed, and then invite Simon to examine them a few at a time.

A number of these large crates came from Ben Heller (fig. 10). Simon and Heller first met in the mid-1950s, when they were brought together by the artist Helen Frankenthaler, who had escorted Simon around New York, introducing him to art dealers.[16] Simon asked Heller to send him a list of his best Asian objects. "It was so nice to speak with you once again yesterday," Heller wrote, "and to hear how happy you are and to find that you, too, have fallen under the spell of India. It is a subject I could go on about for hours."[17] The dealer was admittedly excited not only about the art itself but also about Simon's mushrooming interest. He later recalled the buzz surrounding Simon's entry in the Asian art market, as well as his own strategy for dealing with him:

> The art world has its own telegraph system of who the big buyers are. It learns very quickly who buys how. So that the buyer who wants to bargain, comes up against a seller who already knows he's going to bargain. So, when I negotiated with Norton about a group of Asian objects, knowing what Norton was, I carefully held back the two most significant works for the second half of the purchase, figuring that would give me a greater advantage. Everybody else, knowing he was coming, prepared for him.[18]

FIG. 11. India, Uttar Pradesh, Mathura, *Serpent Deity*, 100–150, The Norton Simon Foundation. CAT. 821

By August 1972 Simon had purchased six artworks from Heller for $740,000, two from Southeast Asia and four from India, including three more South Indian bronzes from the Chola period, *Parvati*, *Shiva with Uma and Skanda*, and *Ganesha* (cats. 822, 823, 830). The largest sculpture purchased from Heller was the immense second-century *Serpent Deity* (fig. 11) that Simon bought for $75,000. Even missing his body below the knees, the deity is still a commanding presence at over six feet high, with an impressive canopy of seven cobras that shelters his head. Carved from the pink sandstone of north-central India's Mathura region, the work is one of the earliest in the collection.

The more Simon became involved with Indian art, the more he learned about the conservation issues associated with old bronzes. Yet until June 1972 he had no reason to regard their condition as anything but theoretical. After their marriage, Norton and Jennifer leased a beach-front house in Malibu. Throughout his years of collecting, it had been Simon's practice to have artworks on approval sent to his house so that he could live with them before deciding to purchase. As a result, he had several dozen small to medium-size Asian stones and bronzes at home during a long and particularly rainy weekend in early June. After a few days, the extra humidity, coupled with the salt air, caused several of the ancient bronzes to blossom with bronze disease, a form of corrosion fed by excess humidity and manifested by powdery, bright greenish spots. *Shiva the Bull-Rider* (fig. 6), the large Chola dynasty bronze then on approval from Spink & Son, was particularly vulnerable, turning almost completely green overnight. A distraught Simon immediately sent all of the pieces to the LACMA conservation laboratory, where conservator Ben Johnson assessed the damage, separated the bronzes that needed treatment, and returned the rest to Simon with instructions on environmental protection.[19]

Once the damaged works were in a secure environment, Simon asked Wiener to recommend a restorer with expertise in ancient bronzes. She suggested the London firm of Anna Plowden and Peter Smith, and within a few weeks the two flew to Los Angeles to assess the collection. Plowden was especially interested in *Shiva*'s condition. Mate to *Parvati* (fig. 4) that Simon had bought from Wiener in January 1972, *Shiva* was made in the same workshop, worshiped in the same temple, and buried in the same soil. After their excavation, *Parvati* was sold to Wiener and *Shiva* to Spink & Son. Before the bronzes were sent to Simon, Plowden had cleaned and was to treat both for bronze disease. However, Spink's Isadore Kahane had directed that *Shiva* be cleaned and shipped to Simon as soon as possible,[20] leaving Plowden only enough time to carry out a surface cleaning. With less pressure from Wiener, Plowden had time to perform an additional, experimental vacuum treatment that infused the Wiener bronze with a chemical solution. In a nearly miraculous set of circumstances, the pair of bronzes, reunited with Simon, was subjected to the same adverse Malibu conditions. Proving beyond any doubt the benefit of the vacuum treatment, *Parvati* showed virtually no signs of bronze disease while *Shiva* was covered in bright green powder. Plowden took *Shiva* back to London and successfully treated it with the same vacuum chemical process.[21]

Simon immediately hit it off with Plowden and Smith (fig. 12), appreciating their no-nonsense attitude, their prodigious expertise in the field of Asian art, and their good spirits. He contracted with the team to examine and repair his entire Asian sculpture collection, and to design and build mounts and bases for the works. They told him that they already knew

FIG. 12. Peter Smith and Anna Plowden, 1972

many of the pieces in his collection because they had treated them for the source who owned them before they were bought by dealers who later sold them to Simon. They identified this source as the Narang brothers' London dealership, Oriental Antiquities. Simon immediately comprehended that he could buy directly from the Narangs, thereby saving the ensuing markup that occurred when he purchased objects from intermediary dealers.

At Simon's request, Isley investigated the Narangs and found that they had branches in London, Delhi, and Bombay (now Mumbai). Simon wrote on one memo, "Remind me on Europe trip to see these people."[22] In September 1972 I accompanied Mr. and Mrs. Simon to London, where, joined by Plowden and Smith, we visited the Narangs. Plowden and Smith had alerted them to Simon's capabilities as a collector, and the eager dealers spread out dozens of stones and bronzes for viewing in their gallery and later at their apartment, on chairs, sofas, coffee tables, and the floor. Simon loved the experience. He was intrigued by their unorthodox presentation and most attracted to the idea of a better deal. He particularly liked Manu Narang, a handsome and mysterious character (reputed also to have been a Bollywood star), and he took pleasure in the banter and dealing at which they were both adept. Plowden and Smith also enjoyed visiting dealers with Simon, observing and admiring his bargaining tactics. After the visits they would return to Simon's hotel room to review photographs and discuss the objects they had seen. Peter Smith recalled:

He had the most amazing, fantastic memory. He would find a few objects and ask, "How much is this?" That's £100,000. "How much is this?" That one was £200,000, and another one was £10,000. He said, "If we put these three things together, what deal will you give me?" And so the dealer quickly throws out some figure with rather a large discount because it's three things, and then Simon would pick another three or four pieces and do the same thing, "What could we do with this little group over here?" And he might make up three or four groups, and ask, "Now if we put group one and two together, what can we do? Now if we put the whole lot together?" And of course the dealer's absolutely sweating and quoting figures without really working out exactly where he is. And when we went back to the hotel he could remember every single price that had been quoted on every single piece and he said, "Well that one on its own was £100,000 but when it was with those three it came down to £80,000. Then when we put these two groups together it must have come down to about sixty, so let's offer him fifty."[23]

At the Narang apartment Simon compiled a list of about thirty bronzes to be sent to Los Angeles on approval. There were additionally eight stones that were to be sent to Peter Smith's workshop in London to be examined. Simon eventually bought fifteen of the sculptures he encountered on his first visit to the Narangs.

In September 1972 Simon purchased from Spink & Son a monumental ninth-century Thai *Buddha Shakyamuni*. Spink's Isidore Kahane originally offered a large bust consisting of the head, shoulders, and upper arms but also sent a snapshot of the bust lying next to two huge, indistinct stone fragments. Perhaps not interested in extra shipping charges, Kahane dismissed the remnants as unimportant and incomplete. When questioned, he said it was up to the buyer to decide whether or not to reassemble it, and stressed that

the bust alone was quite lovely. Simon wanted the extra stones crated and sent to him anyway. On seeing the pieces, he immediately recognized that they should be reassembled. Once Peter Smith reattached the sections, the Buddha was restored to a majestic eighty-eight-inch height (fig. 13). Carved during the Mon-Dvaravati period, 800–899, the work may be the largest of its type outside Thailand and originally stood more than nine feet high. The Buddha's massive body is revealed through a sheer robe that is merely suggested, much like that of the small sixth-century bronze *Buddha Shakyamuni* from Wiener (fig. 3). His gaze is benevolent and reassuring. The hollow in his forehead was probably inlaid with a now missing gemstone and represents the Buddha's *urna*, or auspicious whorl of hair. The sculpture now occupies a place of honor in the center of the Norton Simon Museum's entrance hall.

Considerably smaller than the Thai Buddha, but no less impressive, is the Kashmiri *Buddha and Adorants on the Cosmic Mountain*, purchased from Wiener in November for $225,000 (fig. 14). The Buddha sits in meditation on a pillow inlaid with silver and copper. He rests atop a rocky mountain separated into three dominions. Saints flank the Buddha and occupy the celestial level, while in the middle human worshipers kneel in adoration. Animals dwell at the base of the mountain. The halo that once would have formed an arch behind the Buddha is now missing, but the grand and sumptuous appearance of this altarpiece is not diminished by the halo's absence.

ABOVE
FIG. 13. Thailand, Si Thep, Mon-Dvaravati Period, *Buddha Shakyamuni*, 9th century, The Norton Simon Foundation. CAT. 851

RIGHT
FIG. 14. India, Kashmir, *Buddha and Adorants on the Cosmic Mountain*, c. 700, The Norton Simon Foundation. CAT. 884

RIGHT

FIG. 15. Thailand, Si Thep, Mon-Dvaravati Period, *Bust of a Hindu Deity*, 7th century, before restoration, The Norton Simon Foundation. CAT. 899

FAR RIGHT

FIG. 16. India, Tamil Nadu, Shivapuram, *Shiva as King of Dance*, c. 950, location unknown. CAT. 896

Simon bought five sculptures from Ben Heller in December 1972 (cats. 895–899), including a magnificent Thai bust of a Hindu deity for $175,000 (fig. 15).[24] The god's handsome face is framed by a large halo into which are carved locks of hair. He wears a decorated miter and oversize earrings, which in the past caused him to be identified with the god Surya. Even though the bust was missing its right shoulder and part of the left, the exceptional stone was described by the scholar (and Cleveland Museum of Art director) Sherman Lee as "surely one of the most individual and beautiful remains from early Southeast Asia."[25]

One of Heller's five sculptures consumed a great deal of Simon's time and energy over the next four years. This was a Chola dynasty *Nataraja*, also called *Shiva as King of Dance* (fig. 16).[26] Shiva is depicted in his role of the Hindu god of destruction. His cosmic dance symbolizes the cycle of creation, preservation, and destruction. Surrounded by a circle of fire, the deity rests his bent right leg on a dwarf that came to represent ignorance and raises his left in a graceful arc. Strands of his hair, intertwined with flowers and serpents, fan out on either side of his head. His two upper hands suggest the opposing concepts of creation and destruction. In one hand he holds the drum with which he beats out the creation of the universe, in the other the flame that will destroy it. He reassures the faithful with his lower right hand and with his left gestures toward his uplifted left leg, signifying liberation. Forty-three inches in height, the figure is one of the largest Chola depictions of this subject in bronze.

Simon had known about the bronze since November 1971, when Heller first described it and emphasized its greatness, writing, "I believe it fair to say that mine might well be the most important of Hindu icons."[27] In the 1950s the *Nataraja* was taken from the temple at Shivapuram in South India, and it was published in 1965 as residing in the well-known Bombay private collection of Boman Behram.[28] Behram sold the bronze in 1969, and it was transported from India to New York in April 1969 by Manu Narang,[29] who within a few weeks sold it to Heller. Simon was interested when Heller first offered it to him in 1971 but was concerned about its provenance, removal from the temple, and possible unlawful entry into the United States. He asked for opinions and advice from scholars, curators, and dealers as he weighed the consequences of its purchase. In June 1972 Heller granted him a six-month option to buy the bronze, and Simon used the time to research its history. After assuring himself that it had entered the country legally and that Heller had clear title, he agreed in December 1972 to buy it for $900,000.[30] The *Nataraja* traveled to the Metropolitan Museum of Art, where an exhibition of Simon's Asian collection was scheduled to open in late 1973. In mid-February 1973 it was shipped to Anna Plowden in London for cleaning. Because of its quality and the high price, the bronze was well known among Asian art dealers and curators, and it was only a matter of time until its purchase was in the news. Simon received a great deal of negative publicity in May, when the *New York Times* reported that he had paid $1 million for a sculpture that "Indian Government officials say was stolen from a South Indian temple and smuggled out of India."[31] The writer had asked for a quote from Simon, who impulsively and unfortunately responded, "Hell, yes, it was smuggled. I spent between $15 and $16 million over the last two years on Asian art and most of it was smuggled. I don't know whether it was stolen."[32] He exaggerated the amount he had spent, as it was only about one-third that sum. While he had intended to convey his concern about India's lax exporting laws, the article and his quotes proved very embarrassing. The following day the *Los Angeles Times* carried Simon's denial and clarification. Trying to draw a distinction between a smuggled object (that is, removed from a country without export documents) and one that had been stolen from a temple, Simon pointed out that the Indian government had known for many years that the bronze was owned by a private Indian citizen, but that no one was interested in its return until it sold for such a high price. He believed there was no question that he bought the bronze from its rightful owner and that he had clear title. He went on to say that if the United States signed the United Nations treaty that stipulated countries such as India would be responsible for barring exportation of smuggled art, and if countries of entry were accountable for their importations, he might consider giving the bronze to an Indian museum. "But," he declared, "I will never do so while unfounded claims are being made that I bought a work whose title is clouded."[33]

The controversy lay moderately dormant for over a year. When it resurfaced, it had major consequences for a planned loan of Simon's Asian collection to the Metropolitan Museum of Art, discussed further in chapter ten. Then in late 1974, the government of India filed a $1.5-million lawsuit against Simon for the return of the statue. The lawsuit and its settlement are described in chapter eleven.

By the end of 1972, just a little more than a year after he bought the chess set in New Delhi, Simon had amassed 101 pieces of Indian, Himalayan, and Southeast Asian sculpture, having paid more than $5.6 million, making him an extremely serious contender in the South Asian art market. Pratapaditya Pal remembered that every conversation with Simon involved a discussion about the state of the market, without his realizing

that he was the most important factor in that market, saying that Simon "took the market to a new plateau, there's no question."[34] Indeed, Isley reported to Simon a discussion with Parke-Bernet's David Nash, saying, "Strict orders were given for Parke-Bernet to upgrade its Indian art department because you are now involved in this area."[35]

In January 1973 Simon continued his remarkable pace in acquiring Asian art, and on 5 January alone he bought twenty more examples—eighteen Indian and Himalayan pieces from Klejman and two Cambodian works from Wiener. One from Wiener was the massive Angkor period *Vishnu* (fig. 17), a life-size sculpture made of highly polished sandstone. In his remaining hands, Vishnu carries two of his attributes. In his upper left hand is the conch shell, the fierce sound of which warded off enemies. In Vishnu's lower right is an orb representing the earth and underlining his role as protector of the universe. The second Cambodian stone from Wiener was headless, one of two large torsos Isley noted on his first trip to

FIG. 17. Cambodia, Angkor Period, *Vishnu*, c. 950, Norton Simon Art Foundation. CAT. 904

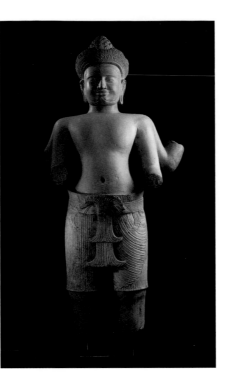

FIG. 18. Cambodia, Angkor Period, *Shiva*, c. 925, Norton Simon Art Foundation. CATS. 779, 903

Simon also bought from Wiener in January 1973 a group of Nepalese paintings that formed a Ragamala album (cat. 924), consisting of thirty-six depictions of ragas, or musical modes. In the ragamala tradition, each musical mode has characteristic personifications. The word *ragamala* in fact translates as a garland of musical modes. The paintings combine the arts of music, poetry, and painting. The musical mode would inspire the poet to create a short poem that appeared at the top of each page, which in turn inspired the artist to paint the picture (fig. 19).

In February 1973 Simon bought from Wiener his second *Nataraja* (cat. 925) for $260,000, affording him the opportunity to compare his two dancing Shivas. The Wiener bronze had no legal entanglements. Smaller than the Shivapuram *Nataraja*, the gracefully balanced deity was made about fifty years later than the Heller bronze. In December Simon purchased his third example (cat. 999), this one with an incomplete circle of flames. This bronze was first offered by a Swiss dealer for $115,000 and was in Los Angeles on approval for one week in May 1972. However, its lack of a complete halo troubled Simon, and he returned it. When it appeared in a December 1973 auction at Christie's, however, he reconsidered. Isley instructed Christie's that Simon would bid up to £55,000 against a dealer and £45,000 against anyone else.[37] In spite of the figure's condition problems, the purchase price of £47,250 ($105,672) was an auction record for an Indian bronze and about twice the previous record.

Wiener's gallery the previous year. In the meantime, in May 1972 Simon had purchased from William Wolff an Angkor period head of Shiva (cat. 779). When Wiener learned Simon owned the head, she suggested to Isley that one of her two torsos might possibly fit with the head, and in September 1972 it was sent to her gallery for study. One of the torsos (cat. 903) matched, and the head and torso were conserved and joined to become one large figure (fig. 18).[36] The Simons were surrounded by so many new pieces of Asian sculpture that they had trouble identifying which was which, especially when many had the same characteristics. It was difficult to distinguish, for instance, the two Angkor stones from Wiener, so for convenience they assigned nicknames to their favorite pieces. The *Vishnu* was irreverently dubbed "Charlie," and the somewhat similar *Shiva* became "Charlie Jr."

Simon spent a little more than $1 million on Asian art in 1973—a great deal less than the $5.5 million in 1972. On the other hand, he still managed to acquire forty artworks, and after just over two years he had accumulated almost two hundred Indian, Himalayan, and Southeast Asian paintings and sculptures. Even though he would add hundreds more in the future, the collection was already so impressive that it was scheduled to be the subject of a major loan exhibition at the Metropolitan Museum of Art. Ultimately canceled amid great controversy over the Shivapuram *Nataraja*, the exhibition was to be part of an extraordinary series of Simon loans scheduled throughout the United States during this period, discussed more fully in chapter ten. ✸

FIG. 19. Nepal, Bhaktapur(?), *Ragamala Album: Kochakari Ragini*, c. 1625, Norton Simon Art Foundation. CAT. 924

1. Pratapaditya Pal, interview by Davis Guggenheim, 20 June 1996.

2. London, Sotheby's, 27 February 1967, lot 131. The 26 5/8-inch bronze figure was described as South Indian, eleventh century.

3. Peter Wilson to Norton Simon, 3 April 1967.

4. In addition to the *Parvati*, Simon noted lot 122, *Figure of a Hero*, now in the Ashmolean Museum, Oxford, and lot 129, *Chandesvara*, location unknown. Three others in the sale he did not note but coincidentally later came into the Simon collections: lot 117, *Shiva and Parvati Embracing* (cat. 818), lot 118, *Shiva with Uma and Skanda* (cat. 1253), and lot 139, *Shiva as the Supreme Teacher* (cat. 817).

5. Simon spent $2.3 million on art in the second half of 1970 and $1.8 million in all of 1971.

6. Because of Jennifer Simon's interest in Indian philosophy and religion, she is credited with first suggesting India as a destination, and with encouraging Simon's interest in Asian art. According to an office memorandum outlining Norton Simon's 1970–1975 travel schedule, between 21 September and 9 October 1971 the Simons visited Japan, Hong Kong, Thailand, India, and Greece.

7. In the 1990s and 2000s Pratapaditya Pal was a research fellow at the Norton Simon Museum and wrote the three definitive collections catalogues for the Simon Asian collection (Pal, 2003a; Pal, 2003b; Pal, 2004).

8. The hinged board is designed also to serve as a case to contain the chess pieces.

9. Pal, 2003a, p. 210.

10. Muchnic, 1998, p. 169.

11. Pal, interview by Davis Guggenheim, 20 June 1996.

12. Simon, 1974, p. 4.

13. Conversation with the author, January 1972. See also Campbell, 1996, pp. 30–31.

14. Ben Heller, interview by Davis Guggenheim, 31 October 1996.

15. Simon to J. J. Klejman, 17 March 1966.

16. Heller dealt in Western art as well as Asian, and in 1973 he sold the American artist Jackson Pollock's large *Blue Poles: Number 11, 1952* to the National Gallery of Australia.

17. Heller to Simon, 12 November 1971.

18. Heller, interview by Davis Guggenheim, 31 October 1996.

19. Johnson was amused that Simon was so panicked by the emerging "epidemic" that he sent all of the stones as well as the bronzes.

20. Isidore Kahane to Simon, 10 February 1972.

21. The dealer Eugene Thaw, and not Spink & Son, eventually sold *Shiva the Bull Rider* to Simon.

22. Memorandum from Isley to Simon, 7 August 1972.

23. Anna Plowden and Peter Smith, interview by Davis Guggenheim, 6 June 1996.

24. In 1974 the bust was reunited with its torso, which Simon acquired from Spink & Son (see p. 170).

25. Lee, 1969, p. 101, no. 1.

26. For a detailed account of the acquisition and controversy surrounding the Shivapuram *Nataraja*, see Muchnic, 1998, pp. 171–177, 223–231.

27. Heller to Simon, 12 November 1971.

28. Barrett, 1965, p. 32.

29. Consumption Entry, Bureau of Customs, 2 May 1969, states it arrived at the port of New York on 24 April 1969.

30. Norton Simon, file memorandum, 9 June 1973.

31. Shirey, 1973, p. 1.

32. Ibid.

33. Seldis, 1973.

34. Pal, interview by Davis Guggenheim, 20 June 1996.

35. Isley to Norton Simon, 2 August 1972.

36. The work was performed by Joseph Ternbach in January 1973. The piece was further restored by Plowden and Smith in 1979. Pal purchased Wiener's second torso for LACMA and had it joined to a head of Vishnu already in the collection.

37. Isley file memorandum, 11 December 1973.

CHAPTER NINE

Mastering in Old Masters
1972–1973

At a time when other people would be saying, "It's impossible to put a collection like that together," he actually did it.
—CHRISTOPHER BURGE[1]

RETURNING TO COLLECTING with renewed enthusiasm after the lull in 1970–1971, Norton Simon spent more in 1972 than in any previous year (see Appendix). While spending close to $6 million on South Asian art, he also acquired more than $12-million worth of European paintings and sculpture. Although he still bought works from all periods, he was clearly shifting his focus from nineteenth- and twentieth-century works (spending just $1.2 million) to old masters (more than $10.6 million).[2] Two old master paintings in particular, Francisco de Zurbarán's *Still Life with Lemons, Oranges, and a Rose* and Raphael's *Madonna and Child with Book*, were his most expensive paintings to date and certainly among the most noteworthy.

Before these two, however, in March 1972 Simon bought his fifth work by Peter Paul Rubens, *David Slaying Goliath* (fig. 1), from Frederick Mont in New York for $500,000. Simon directed Isley to solicit opinions from five different seventeenth-century Flemish specialists before finally deciding on its purchase.[3] Rubens has chosen the moment when David, having felled the giant and taken possession of his sword, is about to sever his head. The two monumental figures occupy nearly the entire painting, with only a fragment of the battle in the background.

OPPOSITE
Francisco de Zurbarán, *Still Life with Lemons, Oranges, and a Rose*, 1633 (detail), The Norton Simon Foundation. cat. 769

ABOVE LEFT
Norton Simon

LEFT
FIG. 1. Peter Paul Rubens, *David Slaying Goliath*, c. 1615–1617, The Norton Simon Foundation. CAT. 759

FIG. 2. Francisco de Zurbarán, *Still Life with Lemons, Oranges, and a Rose*, 1633, The Norton Simon Foundation. CAT. 769

The following month, Simon concluded the purchase of Zurbarán's *Still Life with Lemons, Oranges, and a Rose* (fig. 2) from Eugene Thaw for $2,725,000. From the Florentine Contini-Bonacossi collection, the austere and elegant painting was lauded by the former National Gallery of Art director J. Carter Brown as "arguably the greatest still life in America."[4] It is Zurbarán's only signed and dated still life. The artist carefully arranged three separate elements on a brown tabletop against a dark background. A basket of oranges, with a few leaves and blossoms still attached, is flanked by two silver dishes. Four citrons rest on one dish; in the other, a two-handled cup and a pink rose. The orange blossoms and water-filled cup symbolize chastity and purity, and the painting may be a devotional homage to the Virgin Mary. The former Princeton University Art Museum acting director and now Norton Simon Museum trustee David Steadman recalled a discussion about the Zurbarán that revealed Simon's deep understanding and appreciation of the painting:

> I remember him saying that wasn't it interesting that the artist wanted to show the kind of individuality of each one of these groups, as if it almost were like the individuality of a person, where one was connected compositionally with others, but each group contained within itself a composition unto itself, which had relationship with other units, but none was dominated by any of the others. I remember thinking, he's talking about the human condition; how a still life can talk about the human condition and what it's like for each one of us as individuals. I never forgot it.[5]

Simon had known about the still life since Barbara Roberts's first contact with the heirs of Count Alessandro Contini-Bonacossi in March 1969. For the next three years Simon played an impossible game of trying to keep his interest secret while simultaneously discussing the picture with dealers, art historians, and conservators. Eugene Thaw (fig. 3) later explained how he finally managed to push Simon to buy the painting:

> I did that together with Stanley Moss, who was in touch with the Contini-Bonacossi family. Stanley was having lunch with me one day and told me he thought that the curator of the Louvre was going to Zurich to make a deal for the *Still Life*. I called Mr. Simon while Stanley was there, and we all three got on the phone. I told him that it looked like the Louvre was going to move on that picture, which he had been toying with but hadn't done anything about. He told Stanley, "How soon can you get on a plane? I'll meet you in Zurich tomorrow." And so they met in Zurich, and the thing was bought overnight. But Mr. Simon needed the feeling of competition. In other words, as long as the thing wasn't competed for, he was taking his time. As soon as he heard that there was somebody else like the Louvre on top of it, he moved very quickly to beat them. That was a typical, very typical move, and of course the Zurbarán *Still Life* became, perhaps with the Raphael, the single most important object in the museum.[6]

FIG. 5. Guariento di Arpo, *Coronation of the Virgin*, 1344, Norton Simon Art Foundation. CAT. 815

After its April 1972 purchase, the Zurbarán received considerable publicity, because of both its beauty and its cost. It made a triumphal journey across the United States, with exhibitions at the Metropolitan Museum of Art, the Art Institute of Chicago, and San Francisco's M. H. de Young Memorial Museum, before coming to Los Angeles.

Returning briefly to the twentieth century, Simon bought the iconic *Bird in Space* by Constantin Brancusi (fig. 4) from the New York dealer Richard Feigen in April for $335,000. Brancusi worked on the theme of a bird in flight throughout the 1920s, making each iteration progressively more abstract.

OPPOSITE BELOW
FIG. 3. Eugene V. Thaw

LEFT
FIG. 4. Constantin Brancusi, *Bird in Space*, 1931, The Norton Simon Foundation. CAT. 774

The highly polished bronze embodies the artist's efforts to depict not the external form but its fundamental nature. The work, therefore, represents not a bird but the essence of flight. The Maharaja of Indore had purchased *Bird in Space* from the artist in about 1933. He also commissioned two additional birds, one in black marble and one in white. The three were to be the centerpiece of a proposed (but never completed) temple of meditation in Indore. The bronze stayed with the family until it was purchased by Simon.

In July Simon acquired Guariento di Arpo's fourteenth-century altarpiece, *Coronation of the Virgin* (fig. 5), considered the earliest Italian gold-ground altarpiece in the country. The work was commissioned for a convent in Padua and was later in the Tuscan grand ducal collections in Florence. The main panel depicts the Virgin's coronation as the Queen of Heaven. She is surrounded by thirty-one narrative scenes depicting saints and the life of Christ. The refined technique and detail anticipate the International Gothic style. Simon first learned of the work in May 1968 from the dealer Roderic Thesiger at Colnaghi's in London, who was selling it on behalf of the Czernin collection in Vienna. LACMA director Kenneth Donahue reported that Count Czernin had been "vaguely offering it around for years without naming a price."[7] On 8 November 1968 Simon cabled Colnaghi to reserve it for a week but then waited more than a month to notify the dealer that he was no longer interested.[8] However, six months later, Simon reversed his decision and asked that the enormous altarpiece be shipped on approval, agreeing in advance to the price of $575,000. It arrived in late November 1969 with the request that a decision be made in six weeks' time. Simon countered with a request for three months. The altarpiece was sent to LACMA's conservation laboratory for examination by Ben Johnson. More than three months passed before Simon's assistant Angelina Boaz was instructed to inform Thesiger that Simon was reluctant to spend that much money, since the painting would need a good deal of conservation.[9] Thesiger asked for either a firm offer or the immediate return of the picture. Further negotiations led to Czernin agreeing to $575,000 if the painting was paid for right away and $600,000 if spread out over two years, but he eventually agreed to $575,000 over two years.[10] Then in late May 1970 Simon instructed Boaz to write again to Thesiger with the excuse that he was sidetracked by his senate campaign, and

> In all fairness, because of the continual drastic drop in the stock market and grave economic conditions in this country I question whether he [Simon] can stand by the original offer. Unless Count Czernin is prepared to wait until after the primary election [on 1 June], we have no choice but to return the painting.[11]

Thesiger was furious. When he returned the altarpiece to the dealer, Simon wrote a letter defending his position based on his concern about the condition of the panels.[12] But when the owner, no longer trying to sell the altarpiece through Colnaghi's, put it in a July 1972 Christie's sale, Simon bought it for more than $630,000.[13] After the auction, Simon learned that he had been competing with the J. Paul Getty Museum. Getty's curator, Burton Fredericksen, told Isley that he assumed Simon was not interested in the painting since he had returned it to Colnaghi years earlier. Because of Fredericksen, Isley reported to Simon, "The Guariento cost about $100,000 more than it would have. He was *the* underbidder right to the end."[14] After that sale, the two institutions tried to coordinate their efforts to ensure that they no longer bid against each other. Simon's not buying the picture from Colnaghi for $575,000 earned the ill will of the dealer and cost him extra, but he would have argued that during that period he earned enough interest to more than make up the difference.

FIG. 6. Jean-Antoine Watteau, *Reclining Nude*, c. 1713–1717, The Norton Simon Foundation. cat. 819

Simon was buying not only religious imagery such as the Guariento but also distinctly secular works such as the exquisitely painted *Reclining Nude* by the eighteenth-century French master Jean-Antoine Watteau (fig. 6). Purchased from Thaw in July 1972, the tiny work depicts a nude woman reclining on a bed. The dark brown background emphasizes the curves of her body and contrasts superbly with the white of the sheets.[15] At one time Simon owned nine drawings by Watteau, but today only the painting remains in the collection.[16]

A few weeks after purchasing the Watteau, one of the smallest paintings in the collections, Simon bought one of the largest, Giovanni Battista Tiepolo's *The Triumph of Virtue and Nobility over Ignorance* (fig. 7), also from Thaw. Painted for a ceiling in the Palazzo Manin in Venice and later in the Contini-Bonacossi collection, the luminous composition depicts airborne personifications of Virtue and Nobility ruling the skies. At their command a figure of Ignorance is being

vanquished and banished from the heavens. At the time of its purchase, the painting suffered from a discolored varnish, which masked its subtle pastel shades. Simon arranged for the conservator Marco Grassi to clean it before it left New York. At more than ten feet high and nearly thirteen feet across, it was too large to fit in Grassi's studio, so he hired a garage in New York in which to store and work on the picture. Thaw recalled, "every time Norton came to New York, he observed the cleaning. He was fascinated by its appearance, and it's one of his great pictures."[17] It is indeed.

FIG. 7. Giovanni Battista Tiepolo, *The Triumph of Virtue and Nobility over Ignorance*, c. 1740–1750, The Norton Simon Foundation cat. 829

Perhaps even greater is Raphael's *Madonna and Child with Book* (fig. 8) that Simon acquired in November for $3 million. Painted when the artist was just nineteen years old, the work epitomizes the clarity and classical balance of High Renaissance paintings. Protected in the stable pyramid formed by the Madonna's head and shoulders, the Christ Child gazes at his mother while reaching for a book depicting the nones of the canonical offices. Since the nones commemorates Christ's Crucifixion and death, the Child is portrayed contemplating his own role as Savior. Simon first learned about the painting from Eugene Thaw.[18] It had been with Wildenstein for years at the asking price of $3.5 million. Sequestered at the dealer's storage facility at Iron Mountain, 125 miles north of New York City, the Raphael radiated an air of secrecy and exclusivity that Simon no doubt found tantalizingly appealing. On the basis of photographs, Simon asked Wildenstein in late 1969 or early 1970 to reserve the painting for him until he had an opportunity to see it in person. Shortly after he bought the Bassano *Flight into Egypt* in December 1969, in an effort to learn more about the comparative worth of the Raphael, Simon wrote to the former National Gallery of Art director John Walker, asking his opinion on the price:

> You know I always like to compare completely different objects and I wonder whether you would consider the Bassano, at $660,000 to be a more extravagant purchase than the Raphael would be for $3,500,000; or do you know of any other comparisons you might make in evaluating the price of the Raphael?[19]

There is no record of Walker's answer, and there were no further discussions with Wildenstein until the summer of 1972, when in consideration of a nonrefundable $100,000 deposit, the dealer agreed to grant Simon an option until the end of October to purchase the painting for $3 million. If Simon decided to exercise the option, he agreed to pay another $300,000 then and the $2.6 million balance by 13 December 1972.[20] The deposit was sent on 7 July. Toward the end of October, Simon asked for a short extension, and on 6 November the Norton Simon Art Foundation notified Wildenstein that it would purchase the painting.

As was so often the case, particularly with his largest purchases, Simon used the five-month option period to solicit opinions from experts. In the case of the Raphael, Simon contacted John Shearman of the Courtauld Institute, whom he flew to New York to examine the picture. He also queried Metropolitan Museum of Art curator Everett Fahy, who wrote, "When final arrangements are made about the Wildenstein Raphael, I hope Mr. Simon will consider lending it to the Metropolitan Museum, at least for awhile. I have no doubt that it is the single most important picture in his collection, and it would be wonderful to let the New York public have an opportunity to see it."[21]

ABOVE
FIG. 8. Raffaelo Sanzio, also called Raphael, *Madonna and Child with Book*, 1502–1503, Norton Simon Art Foundation. CAT. 885

The Raphael was not exhibited first at the Metropolitan, however, but at the Princeton University Art Museum as the centerpiece of a loan exhibition that opened 2 December.[22] Isley reported to Simon that Princeton's acting director David Steadman was thrilled: "David called and had just come back from Wildenstein's. He was ecstatic about the picture and said you made a real coup: 'I'm absolutely sailing in orbit.'"[23] Steadman had already installed the exhibition but was more than happy to make the changes necessary to accommodate the painting. In the process, he produced a serendipitous but brilliant installation design. He reported later:

> What did you do with this installation? The painting was not that big, but it had to hold a fairly large wall. It was clear that we had to get a big swatch of red behind it. So I went to New York to look for red velvet, and I'm finally talking to an art dealer [Wildenstein's Harry Brooks], and I said, "Harry, I'm just at my wit's end, I can't find a decent piece of old velvet to put the Raphael on." He said, "I have exactly what you want," and it was this fabulous piece of old velvet; it was one of the curtains that had been in his mother's drawing room when he was growing up, and had been kept. So off I go, back to Princeton with my old drapes under my arm; we redo the whole thing, and that became the focus. It was unveiled the day of the opening, and made the front page of the New York Times. It was a very nice way to begin an exhibition.[24]

The painting became the centerpiece of the exhibition. As visitors entered, they walked through a gallery flanked with sculptures and up a flight of stairs to be greeted by the Raphael (p. 151, fig. 1).

Simon expanded his collection of seventeenth-century Dutch and Flemish paintings in 1972, spending more than $2.2 million on twenty-one works. In addition to the Rubens *David Slaying Goliath*, they included still lifes by Jan Fyt, Pieter Claesz., and Balthasar van der Ast (cats. 844, 850, 858), landscapes by Aert van der Neer and Roelandt Savery (cats. 843, 846), and portraits by Nicholas Maes (cats. 790, 859). Finally, at the end of the year, Simon added Rubens's *The Holy Women at the Sepulchre* (fig. 9) for $520,000 from Thomas Agnew. As with the Guariento altarpiece, the Rubens came from the Czernin collection in Vienna. The painting portrays that moment recounted in Luke's gospel when the women visiting Christ's tomb were greeted by angels who deliver the news of the Resurrection. Though the exact identity of each person is unclear, the central figure in lavender is thought to be the Virgin Mary, while the woman to her left shielding her eyes with her veil is Mary Magdalene.

FIG. 9. Peter Paul Rubens, *The Holy Women at the Sepulchre*, c. 1617, The Norton Simon Foundation. CAT. 890

FIG. 10. Giovanni di Paolo, *Baptism of Christ*, early 1450s, The Norton Simon Foundation. CAT. 927

Considerably earlier than the Rubens are three Italian paintings Simon bought in March 1973. The first was Giovanni di Paolo's fifteenth-century *Baptism of Christ* (fig. 10), part of a narrative cycle on the life of Saint John the Baptist. The painting depicts Jesus standing in the Jordan River at the moment of baptism, surrounded by a host of angels. The dealer David Carritt discovered the panel in 1971 at a Paris auction and recognized it as the missing central panel from an important series on the life of Saint John the Baptist, then housed in several museums around the world.[25] Eugene Thaw offered the picture to Simon in May 1972 at $500,000 and sent it to Los Angeles for examination. Simon asked Kenneth Donahue to hang it at LACMA so he could judge how it looked in a gallery setting and to observe the public's reaction. He also requested a technical examination from the conservator Ben Johnson. No one doubted its authenticity and appeal, but everyone was flabbergasted by the extremely high price for the small panel. Simon learned, much to his consternation, that Thaw purchased the painting at the Paris auction just a year earlier for a little more than $40,000.[26] All the same, Thaw refused to reduce the price by any more than $25,000. Although the markup was more than ten times its cost to Thaw, Simon acquiesced and agreed to buy it for $475,000.

A week after buying the Giovanni di Paolo panel, Simon purchased two even earlier works, Pietro Lorenzetti's *Saint John the Baptist* and *The Prophet Elisha* (fig. 11). The full-length figures are fragments of a larger altarpiece commissioned in 1329 by the church of Santa Maria del Carmine in Siena, and they originally flanked a large panel depicting the Virgin and Child. The circumstances of its purchase offer another example of Simon's often tortuous negotiating techniques. The New York dealer Frederick Mont first offered the panels in November 1972. He asked $500,000 but, based on Simon's interest, dropped the price to $450,000.[27] Over the New Year's weekend, Mont agreed to drop it further to $400,000 for an immediate cash payment[28] and sent the panels to Los Angeles on approval. Many weeks ensued with Mont imploring Simon to pay and attempting new persuasive maneuvers, such as invoking his European partner, who was concerned about the dropping value of the dollar, as well as asking for the immediate return of the panels. Although the works came with recommendations from historians of Italian art such as Enzo Carli, Sir John Pope-Hennessy, Everett Fahy, and Federico Zeri,[29] Simon stalled by saying that he wanted to further confirm the paintings' authenticity and condition. Simultaneously, Simon was concerned about a portrait by the Flemish artist Bernaert

FIG. 11. Pietro Lorenzetti, *Saint John the Baptist* and *The Prophet Elisha*, c. 1329, The Norton Simon Foundation CAT. 928A-B

van Orley (cat. 714), purchased from Mont three years earlier, which he had just learned had been published as a copy.[30] Simon wrote to Mont, suggesting a dramatic reduction in the price of the Lorenzettis by trading back the van Orley:

> We recently discovered that the van Orley we purchased from you in 1969 for $85,000 has now been published in the new edition of Friedländer as a copy. In addition, we have learned that the picture was sold in the Paris auction where you purchased it as "attributed to van Orley" rather than by the master as you represented it to us. You told Darryl Isley that you believe that the van Orley is worth $150,000 in today's market. We believe that if the picture were in fact by van Orley, it should be worth $200,000, based upon the fact that you told us we were buying the picture at a special price and that the Old Master market has rapidly escalated in value. We will therefore return [it] to you to be credited against the $400,000 purchase price of the Lorenzettis. We believe the credit should be $175,000 but we will accept your valuation of $150,000 if you insist.[31]

Mont was not pleased and wrote a long letter reminding Simon that the price for the Lorenzettis had been lowered to $400,000, based on immediate cash payment and not a trade, and that in any case the deal had dragged on to the point that it was no longer immediate. He insisted on a decision by 5 March or the return of the panels. Mont added that he would take back the van Orley against the Lorenzettis only at its purchase price of $85,000.[32]

The dealer held his ground. Simon assented and sent a check for $315,000 plus the van Orley. He also agreed that after Mont cleaned the painting he would reconsider it at the original price,[33] but in June he decided he did not want it, in spite of favorable comments from experts.[34] Three years later Mont wrote to tell Simon that the van Orley had been acquired by the Musée de Brou in Bourg-en-Bresse, with help from the Louvre:

> The fact that you had returned this beautiful painting to us because you did not believe in the attribution hurt us deeply; you know how anxious we have always been to serve you well. We hope that this exonerates us completely.[35]

Simon wrote a conciliatory reply:

> Believe me it was never my lack of belief in the attribution that was the problem. I am not an

art historian and cannot pretend to know what I don't live and know by my own experience. I have never doubted your sincerity and believe you have never doubted mine. I am glad that it has turned out well.[36]

Sadly, Simon's pugnacious attitude soured a long and courteous relationship with another dealer, Arthur Tooth & Sons. In 1963 Simon purchased from Tooth a charming if somewhat sentimental portrait of an English urchin attributed to Théodore Géricault (cat. 151). Since Simon often asked Isley to elicit opinions from art historians about his artworks, in February 1969 Isley reported that the Géricault expert Lorenz Eitner said the painting had been passed around to a number of art dealers and declared that it was a "dull and stupid study" not by the artist.[37] Simon approached Dudley Tooth about a possible sale or trade, omitting his attribution concerns, but nothing transpired.[38]

Three years later, in September 1972, he discussed with Dudley's son Nicholas a possible trade of the Géricault for two landscape paintings by Eugène Boudin and Paul Guigou (cats. 943, 944) and arranged to have them sent on approval.[39] Simon was also interested in Tooth's painting by Alfred Sisley entitled *Port-Marly in the Snow*, and in early April 1973 he asked to have it also sent with the assurance that a decision would be made "within a reasonable period of time."[40] In late April Tooth wrote that he understood Simon was interested in negotiating a deal that included the Boudin and Guigou. Now aware of Simon's concerns about the Géricault's attribution problems, and the fact that Simon was, in effect, holding three of his pictures hostage, Tooth offered to take the Géricault back with what he considered generous terms:

Since we last talked the Géricault "Le Gamin" has been on my conscience and I hope very much that we can settle this unfortunate matter through this transaction. Our records show that you paid £12,000 for the Géricault which today (at 2.485) equals $29,820 but I think that I am correct in saying that when you purchased the picture the dollar stood to the pound at 2.80 which equals $33,600. Of course we are prepared to pay the latter figure. Vis-à-vis the prices of the Guigou and Boudin, you will remember that I have already reduced them from £16,000 to £13,500 and I can do no more. In view of the fact that we are buying the Géricault, the most I could do on the Sisley is to reduce it by $10,000 to $215,000.[41]

Unhappy with the offer, Simon wrote a note to Isley on Tooth's letter: "If you haven't talked yet do so, so that I can call and raise hell finally." Nicholas Tooth wrote again in May:

Mr. Isley spoke to me on the telephone yesterday afternoon and said "Mr. Simon wants $125,000 for the Géricault and will then return the three paintings." From this it is obvious that you do not intend to purchase the Boudin, Guigou, and Sisley, and I therefore insist that you return them to London *immediately*.[42]

He went on to say that he originally agreed to send the Sisley only on the condition that he received an answer as to its purchase within a reasonable period. "Two months have elapsed and our patience is being tried, as we cannot afford to have paintings of value under indefinite option. Please dispatch the three pictures at once to London." Simon finally returned the Sisley and, using the Géricault in trade, bought the Guigou and Boudin.[43] In 1976 Arthur Tooth & Sons was involved once more with Simon, in a three-way transaction over a Monet (cat. 1332), but the dealer never sold directly to Simon again.

FIG. 12. Filippino Lippi, *Saints Benedict and Apollonia* and *Saints Paul and Frediano*, c. 1483, The Norton Simon Foundation. CAT. 973A-B

Considering the negotiating turmoil with other picture dealers at this time, Simon's dealings with Wildenstein were comparatively placid. At the end of July he bought from the firm two late-fifteenth-century panels by Filippino Lippi, *Saints Benedict and Apollonia* and *Saints Paul and Frediano* (fig. 12). A student of Sandro Botticelli, Lippi painted the panels for the church of San Ponziano in Lucca, where they formed part of a triptych, flanking a statue of Saint Anthony. Wildenstein's Louis Goldenberg brought the panels to Simon's attention in May 1972. Simon spent a year investigating their attribution and condition but did not balk at the $1.5 million price, making it the most expensive purchase of 1973. The rest of Simon's old master purchases for the year included works by Paolo Veneziano (cat. 977), Bartolomé Esteban Murillo (cat. 1003), and Giovanni Francesco Barbieri, called Guercino, whose *Suicide of Cleopatra* (cat. 987) was also of interest to the National Gallery of Art in Washington. According to the gallery's director J. Carter Brown, "He picked off things that I

was rather interested in for the National Gallery, like the Guercino *Cleopatra* that we didn't move fast enough on."[44] Brown admired Simon's thoroughness when investigating works and appreciated his extraordinary love of the objects:

> He was one collector who really felt works of art and felt passionately about them. Simon was obsessively thorough about his purchasing and he would call you up and bend your ear and try to milk dry every bit of nuance that you might have about whether this object was the best of its kind. I think his eye was such that he knew darn well how good it was but he seemed to want to get this corroboration. And it was exactly the way we should operate in the museums. I wonder whether professional museum curators are as thorough as Norton was in vetting and checking out what he acquired.[45]

LEFT
FIG. 13. Claude Monet, *Mouth of the Seine,
Honfleur*, 1865, The Norton Simon Foundation.
CAT. 992

BELOW LEFT
FIG. 14. Pablo Picasso, *Women of Algiers, I*, 1955,
Norton Simon Art Foundation. CAT. 938

Even as he was spending large sums on old masters in 1973, Simon was equally active purchasing works by nineteenth- and twentieth-century artists, including a view of Venice by Jean-Baptiste Camille Corot (cat. 981), Édouard Vuillard's monumental *First Fruits* (cat. 994), and an early seascape by Claude Monet. The Monet, entitled *Mouth of the Seine, Honfleur* (fig. 13) and bought from Wildenstein for $850,000, is one of two that Monet exhibited in his Salon debut in 1865.[46] Monet flawlessly realized a formal arrangement in this large composition with its tilted masts and sails, mirrored in the perfect grouping of white gulls in the distance. Every detail in the sky and water speaks of a blustery day, with one band of sunlight on the horizon.

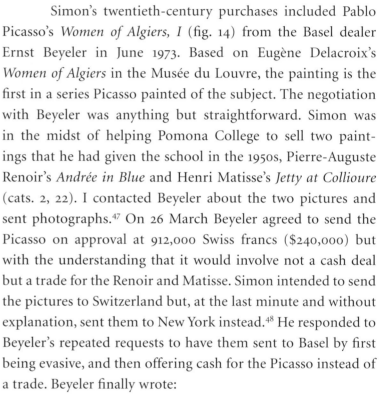

Simon's twentieth-century purchases included Pablo Picasso's *Women of Algiers, I* (fig. 14) from the Basel dealer Ernst Beyeler in June 1973. Based on Eugène Delacroix's *Women of Algiers* in the Musée du Louvre, the painting is the first in a series Picasso painted of the subject. The negotiation with Beyeler was anything but straightforward. Simon was in the midst of helping Pomona College to sell two paintings that he had given the school in the 1950s, Pierre-Auguste Renoir's *Andrée in Blue* and Henri Matisse's *Jetty at Collioure* (cats. 2, 22). I contacted Beyeler about the two pictures and sent photographs.[47] On 26 March Beyeler agreed to send the Picasso on approval at 912,000 Swiss francs ($240,000) but with the understanding that it would involve not a cash deal but a trade for the Renoir and Matisse. Simon intended to send the pictures to Switzerland but, at the last minute and without explanation, sent them to New York instead.[48] He responded to Beyeler's repeated requests to have them sent to Basel by first being evasive, and then offering cash for the Picasso instead of a trade. Beyeler finally wrote:

> From the beginning of our negotiations, it was understood that we were only interested to deal on a basis of a trade. You offered to us paintings by Matisse and Renoir. On this basis we would have agreed to make the trade. You answered us that you could not remove the works as they were in the hands of a museum which refused to let them go. Next, I find the two paintings with a dealer in New York. Your rather weak answer was that the museum did not allow them to go to Europe. Naturally the New York dealer can sell them to Europe any time. I am sorry, but I refuse to do business on this basis and manner. I expect the Picasso returned to Basel at once.[49]

Simon responded by simply wiring full payment (with no trades) on 6 June; in spite of Beyeler's earlier stipulations, the dealer accepted the money. Unfortunately, Simon's delaying tactics were costly, as the exchange rate on 912,000 Swiss francs had climbed to $296,217, or an extra $50,000. He never hesitated to engage in hard-hitting negotiations with dealers, believing they had (or should have) tough skin. Substantiating Simon's premise, a few months later Beyeler's assistant visited the Simon collection. Isley reported that although they had been very angry with Simon, "neither he nor Beyeler have bad feelings now and hope that you don't either. It's in the past and they look forward to doing something in the future."[50]

Norton Simon's intense 1972 and 1973 acquisition activity has been noted. Simultaneously he continued to deaccession artworks, though at a much less hectic pace in 1972 with just thirteen works being sold, including four sculptures in October through Parke-Bernet and nine others through private dealers. Sales in 1972 totaled almost $983,000, for a profit of more than $650,000.

Simon returned to significant auction sales in May 1973, maintaining his advantageous arrangements with Sotheby's and Parke-Bernet, and negotiating something even more favorable, a guarantee. Sotheby's representatives Peter Wilson, Peregrine Pollen, and David Nash reviewed a list of artworks and set a guaranteed price for each item. After deducting commission, they paid Simon $5,333,690.[51] The profit, based on the guarantees alone, was more than $2.75 million. Simon included additional unguaranteed paintings in the sale, increasing the profits from the full sale to more than $4 million. While several objects could be seen as expendable in the logic of upgrading the overall quality of the collections—works by Léon Lhermitte and Jules Dupré, for instance—others remain very regrettable losses, such as Degas's *Rehearsal of the Ballet* (p. 77), now in the Nelson-Atkins Museum of Art in Kansas City, and Cézanne's *Still Life with Kettle, Milk Pitcher, Sugar Bowl, and Seven Apples* (cat. 348), now in the J. Paul Getty Museum, Los Angeles. Fortunately, two other important pictures sold in this auction subsequently came back to the Simon collection: Édouard Manet's *Still Life with Fish and Shrimp* (p. 188) and Cézanne's *Tulips in a Vase* (p. 41).

The Manet still life (whose original purchase price was $110,000) did not meet its reserve at the sale and went unsold, but Simon still received the agreed-upon guarantee of $1.5 million. Parke-Bernet now owned the painting and tried unsuccessfully over the years to sell it privately. They approached Simon as well and in 1974 offered it back to him for $1,250,000 without success.[52] Simon finally reacquired the painting in 1978 for considerably less.[53]

Simon originally purchased Cézanne's *Tulips in a Vase* in 1962 for a little more than $400,000. Although the painting was a favorite, for more than six and a half years he apparently was unaware that its medium was oil on paper mounted on board rather than oil on canvas.[54] The paper conservator Francis Dolloff visited the collection in September 1968 and mentioned that the *Tulips* was painted on paper and mounted to panel.[55] An astonished Simon then learned that what appeared to be a crease was in fact a tear, and concern about condition haunted him to the point that he made overtures to sell the work to Lefevre Gallery in 1971.[56] He eventually consigned it to the May 1973 auction, with a guarantee of $1.4 million. Nevertheless, by the time of the sale, Simon again changed his mind, deciding to keep the picture and have it properly restored.[57] He therefore made a confidential arrangement with Louis Goldenberg of the Wildenstein gallery that it would buy back the painting for him at the guaranteed amount.[58] Simon kept the repurchase quiet for several months, but eventually he began to hear negative comments about Sotheby's guarantee provisions and his arrangement with Wildenstein. The dealer Eugene Thaw, for instance, told Isley:

> The general public thinks the sale was a great success. The trade knows it wasn't. The important collectors and the dealers are all very suspicious. There is a lot of talk about our having prearranged things with Wildenstein and having worked out a tricky arrangement with Sotheby's. Both the dealers and collectors were generally quiet at the auction because of all of the discussion about guarantees and sliding reserves. [You] suffer in the public marketplace by having a reputation for trickiness.[59]

FIG. 15. Arshile Gorky, *Plumage Landscape*, 1947, National Gallery of Australia, Canberra. CAT. 118

Thaw was not alone. This sentiment was held by others as well. While discussing the possibility of another sale, Isley learned from Sotheby's director Marcus Linnell, "He personally feels we would not do well to have another large auction at least for a while. The last sale made people think you are a dealer and not just a collector who was refining."[60]

Simon sold forty-nine artworks at auction in 1973, and he deaccessioned an additional fourteen paintings, drawings, and sculptures through sales and trades with private dealers. Two in particular were significant losses to the collection, Arshile Gorky's *Plumage Landscape* (fig. 15) and Cézanne's *Portrait of a Peasant* (p. 27). The Gorky (bought in 1962 for $25,000) was sold for $180,000 to the National Gallery of Australia in Canberra. *Portrait of a Peasant* (bought in 1956 for $70,000) was sold to Eugene Thaw for $1 million and is now in the Thyssen-Bornemisza Collection, Madrid.

In spite of the sales, it was clear by the end of 1973 that Simon had regained his former interest in collecting. In 1972 he bought 152 objects, spending more than $17.6 million. In 1973 he made 109 acquisitions and spent almost $9.5 million (see Appendix). Even after the sales from 1970–1973, the collections contained more than six hundred works of art of which one hundred were in Simon's private collection, either displayed at his home or kept in storage. The approximately five hundred works belonging to the two foundations, however, were available for public display, a circumstance that prompted a far-reaching series of loan exhibitions initiated in 1972 and 1973. ❧

1. Christopher Burge, undated [1996] interview by Davis Guggenheim.

2. Even so, his first purchase of the year was from the nineteenth century—his reacquisition of Edgar Degas's *Actress in Her Dressing Room* (cat. 221), recounted on p. 60.

3. The scholars were Julius Held, Jakob Rosenberg, Wolfgang Stechow, Seymour Slive, and Michael Jaffé.

4. J. Carter Brown, interview by Charles Guggenheim, 4 October 1996.

5. David Steadman, undated [1996] interview by Davis Guggenheim.

6. Eugene V. Thaw, interview by Anna Jhirad of Guggenheim Productions, 25 March 1997.

7. Reported in National Gallery, London director Cecil Gould to Kenneth Donahue, 2 July 1968.

8. Simon assistant Angelina Boaz to Roderic Thesiger, 11 December 1968.

9. Boaz, file memorandum, 12 March 1970.

10. Thesiger to Simon, 7 May 1970.

11. Boaz to Thesiger, 21 May 1970.

12. Simon to Thesiger, 10 June 1970.

13. London, Christie's, 7 July 1972, lot 14.

14. Isley to Simon, 24 August 1972.

15. A preparatory drawing for the picture is in the J. Paul Getty Museum, Los Angeles.

16. The drawings are cats. 97, 191, 197, 305–307, 549, 691, 718.

17. Eugene V. Thaw, interview by Anna Jhirad of Guggenheim Productions, 25 March 1997.

18. Thaw said that Simon would often ask his opinion of the best picture on the market. At one point Thaw asked the painting conservator Mario Modestini for suggestions and Modestini told him about the Raphael. Thaw immediately gave the information to Simon (Muchnic, 1998, p. 129).

19. Simon to John Walker, 8 January 1970.

20. Letter of Agreement between Wildenstein and Co. and The Norton Simon Foundation, 29 June 1972.

21. Everett Fahy to Norton Simon Foundation president Robert Macfarlane, 14 June 1972.

22. See chap. 10, pp. 151, 154–156. The painting was subsequently lent to the Metropolitan on two occasions. It was on loan from June to August 1973, and most recently for the exhibition *Raphael at the Metropolitan: The Colonna Altarpiece*, 20 June–3 September 2006.

23. Isley to Simon, 21 November 1972.

24. David Steadman, undated [1996] interview by Davis Guggenheim.

25. The painting sold at Paris, Palais Galliéra, 27 March 1971. Six panels from the series are in the Art Institute of Chicago; two are in the Westfälisches Landesmuseum, Münster; one is at the Metropolitan Museum of Art, New York; and one is in the Musée du Louvre, Paris. For a discussion of the Saint John narrative cycle, see Gordon, 2003, pp. 98–99.

26. Isley to Simon, 6 December 1972.

27. Frederick Mont to Simon, 27 February 1973.

28. Ibid.

29. Norton Simon Museum curatorial files.

30. Isley to Simon, 26 January 1973. The publication is Friedländer, 1967–1976, vol. 8, p. 116.

31. Simon to Mont, 22 February 1973.

32. Mont to Simon, 27 February 1973.

33. Simon to Mont, 8 March 1973.

34. Isley to Betty Mont, 14 June 1973.

35. Frederick Mont to Simon, 23 January 1976.

36. Simon to Mont, 10 February 1976.

37. Isley to Simon, 25 February 1969.

38. Reported in Tooth director Timothy Bathurst to Simon, 25 March 1969.

39. Isley to Nicholas Tooth, 27 September 1972. Dudley Tooth died in May 1972.

40. Reported in Tooth to Simon, 23 May 1973.

41. Tooth to Simon, 26 April 1973.

42. Tooth to Simon, 23 May 1973.

43. Tooth to Simon, 14 June 1973.

44. J. Carter Brown, interview by Charles Guggenheim, 4 October 1996.

45. Ibid.

46. The second seascape, *Pointe de la Hève at Low Tide*, is in the Kimbell Art Museum, Fort Worth.

47. Sara Campbell to Ernst Beyeler, 19 March 1973.

48. Shipping document, Cart and Crate, Inc., 16 April 1973.

49. Beyeler to Simon, 25 May 1973.

50. Isley to Simon, 13 October 1973.

51. In the 2 May 1973 sale at Sotheby Parke Bernet Simon sold artworks belonging to both his foundations and his private collection. The commission was 17 ½ percent.

52. Isley to Simon, 30 May 1974.

53. See pp. 180–181.

54. Most of the early literature makes no mention of the painting's support. Although Venturi, 1936 (vol. 1, no. 618) gives a slightly ambiguous description of "oil on panel and paper" [l'huile sur bois et papier] it is not clear that Simon knew about the entry or the medium. The dealer Dudley Tooth had referred to the picture only as a "painting"; shipping documents at the time of purchase said that it was a "painting on board"; and some earlier references (e.g., Lefevre Gallery, 1946) had described it as an oil on canvas.

55. Francis Dolloff to Hunt Museum director James Brown, 1 October 1968.

56. Isley to Simon, 5 November 1971.

57. See the Technical Notes for Cézanne's *Tulips in a Vase* in Brettell and Eisenman, 2006, p. 308.

58. Simon to Louis Goldenberg, 30 May 1973.

59. Isley to Simon, 10 May 1973.

60. Isley to Simon, 9 November 1973.

CHAPTER TEN

Museum without Walls II
1972–1973

We hope to fill a real gap in the cultural life of this country.
—NORTON SIMON[1]

THE RAPHAEL *Madonna and Child with Book*, purchased in late 1972 and lent to the Princeton University Art Museum at the last minute, joined one hundred other paintings and sculptures for an exhibition that opened on 3 December 1972 (fig. 1). The show was drawn from the collection of the corporate foundation, the Norton Simon, Inc. Museum of Art, and featured artworks from the Renaissance through the twentieth century.[2] The Princeton loan was, astonishingly, one of seven large long-term displays from the Simon collections that were organized in 1972–1973, in addition to the dozens of short-term loans that could be seen at other museums around the country (fig. 2).[3] This nationwide exhibition program was developed by the new president of the Norton Simon Foundation, Robert Macfarlane. A longtime family friend, Macfarlane remembers both Simon's request that he come to work for the foundation and his response: "If you're willing to work as hard in the foundation field as you've worked to make money, I'll come and work with you. His response was that yes, his life had taken a shift. He was looking to do other things."[4]

Macfarlane believed his role as president was to develop the assets of the foundations, in this case, the art collection. Foundation collections, as charitable assets held for the benefit of the public, were required to be available for public display. Showing as much of the collection as possible would fully exploit its educational and outreach potential. Given the size of the Simon foundations' collections, the exhibitions would have to be much larger than the small groups of artworks that were shown in Portland and Philadelphia in 1968. Simon had also become interested in broader statewide and national audiences than were afforded by the local visitorship of the Los Angeles County Museum of Art. Nevertheless, the first such presentation overseen by Macfarlane was the two-year installation at LACMA that opened in June 1972.

Notwithstanding the difficulties between Simon and LACMA, Macfarlane kept plans for an exhibition moving forward. As the board chairman Franklin Murphy reported to Simon, "Robbie's reports of the negotiations make me hopeful that we are

OPPOSITE
Raffaelo Sanzio, also called Raphael, *Madonna and Child with Book*, 1502–1503 (detail), Norton Simon Art Foundation. CAT. 885

ABOVE LEFT
Norton Simon

ABOVE
FIG. 1. Installation photograph, *Selections from the Norton Simon, Inc. Museum of Art*, Princeton University Art Museum, 1972

FIG. 2. Installation photograph, *Recent Acquisitions of the Norton Simon, Inc. Museum*, Virginia Museum of Fine Arts, Richmond, 1972

now on a constructive course for the museum and the foundations. I want you to know that I recognize and appreciate the strong and decisive role you have played throughout the discussions."[5] The museum, relying on the recently appointed curator Charles Millard, chose artworks from a list supplied by the foundation and requested a few others that were not on the list. Simon did not take a back seat, however. Although Millard was the curator in charge of the hanging, he cleared most details with Simon through Isley and Macfarlane, and gave Simon a large role in deciding where objects were placed. The exhibition, which opened on 16 June, spread over LACMA's entire plaza level, and included forty-six paintings, six Romanelli tapestry cartoons, eight tapestries, eleven sculptures, and the sixty Claude drawings.

In reporting the exhibition, the *Los Angeles Times* critic Henry Seldis wrote that it was the first time Simon had entered into a formal agreement with the museum, in spite of his fourteen years' involvement as founder and former trustee. Aside from its great artistic worth, Seldis wrote, "the exhibition marks the beginning of a steady, positive relationship between the museum and the mercurial collector who until very recently was seriously considering establishing his own museum."[6] The article discussed Simon's emerging program of long-term loans such as those to be held at the Princeton University Art Museum and San Francisco's California Palace of the Legion of Honor, saying that the LACMA showing was the first in this nationwide program. Putting a positive spin on the fact that the County Museum was not now the sole beneficiary of Simon loans, Seldis wrote:

> As long as the bulk of the most important Simon treasures rotate among a small group of important museums, including our own, the question of their eventual disposition becomes irrelevant and a pattern will have been established that might well be emulated by other foundation and corporate art collections. Meanwhile, a large and sometimes ominous question mark has been erased from the local art scene. By clarifying their relationship in such a positive manner both the Simon

foundation and the museum's trustees have rendered an important service to the increasingly art hungry Southern California public.[7]

Even though Simon believed LACMA was poorly managed, he often created the problems himself. The loan contract, for instance, stated that he could remove and substitute up to 10 percent of the objects during the exhibition's duration. Nevertheless, he exceeded the percentage and often asked to have artworks removed on short notice. The installation was slated to run for one year, but, with a number of substitutions, it was extended for an additional year, to June 1974. Further, the hangings were enhanced with two stars—the Raphael *Madonna and Child with Book* from August 1973 to October 1974 and the Zurbarán *Still Life* from January 1974 to March 1975.[8]

During negotiations with LACMA, Princeton, and San Francisco in the spring of 1972, Simon and his staff were working on yet another exhibition, this time in Pasadena, a precursor of momentous events that were to follow. Through his brother-in-law and Pasadena Art Museum board member Frederick Weisman, three trustees approached Simon in the fall of 1971 for financial help for the ailing institution.[9] Not interested in their proposal, which involved substantial monetary assistance and a permanent association with the institution, Simon instead suggested a loan of foundation artworks. Since the Pasadena Museum's focus was on modern art, he offered examples of twentieth-century sculpture, and Isley and I assembled a list of objects not committed to exhibitions elsewhere.[10] After a final selection by the Pasadena curators, Simon committed to a yearlong display, beginning 1 August 1972, of thirty-five sculptures by Henry Moore, Barbara Hepworth, Auguste Rodin, David Smith, Jacques Lipchitz, and others (figs. 3, 4).[11] It was further understood that there might be future loans akin to those at Princeton and San Francisco.[12] No further loans ensued, since by the end of 1973 it was clear that the museum (whose name was changed in March to the Pasadena Museum of Modern Art) had entered the deep financial distress[13] that would lead to Simon's foundations assuming fiscal responsibility for the institution in April 1974.

ABOVE
FIG. 3. Installation photograph, *Modern Sculpture from the Norton Simon, Inc. Museum of Art and The Norton Simon Foundation*, Pasadena Art Museum, 1972

BELOW
FIG. 4. Installation photograph, *Modern Sculpture from the Norton Simon, Inc. Museum of Art and The Norton Simon Foundation*, Pasadena Art Museum, 1972

Another major exhibition was being discussed in June 1972. Isley received a letter from Philippe de Montebello, director of the Museum of Fine Arts in Houston and later director of the Metropolitan Museum of Art for thirty years, asking that the foundation look favorably at a request from one of the museum's supporters (a department store owner) to lend to a display to be installed in one of the stores.[14] Isley understandably turned down the request, but with shows now scheduled on both coasts, exposure in Texas seemed a reasonable next step.

In late July Macfarlane flew to Houston, and by August discussions were under way about a large-scale exhibition at the Houston museum.[15] We on the curatorial staff suggested artworks not already at LACMA or committed to Princeton and San Francisco, and in early September Houston chose forty-eight paintings and sculptures from the Renaissance through the twentieth century. Some of the objects were in storage, and others were on short-term loans to museums such as the Metropolitan Museum of Art and the Nelson-Atkins Gallery. Everything was sent to Houston as soon as possible, and *Masterpieces of Five Centuries* (with Rembrandt's *Titus* as the featured painting) opened on 4 October 1972, just two months after talks began. Simon agreed to a one-year run and a possible second year. The museum's press release quoted Simon's feelings about his "museum without walls" program. He believed that too much attention was given to the construction of museum buildings to the detriment of art acquisitions:

> In deciding against a permanent museum building, we hoped to fill a real gap in the cultural life of this country and achieve maximum effectiveness out of the works of art. We may yet build, but there seemed to be some dynamic possibilities if we could develop long-term relationships with five or six museums.[16]

De Montebello called the exhibition "the single most important loan of Western European paintings ever to be seen at one time in Houston."[17] Planned construction of a new wing, however, required that the entire museum close from April to June 1973.

When it reopened, fewer Simon objects went back on display. The show ended after one year, in November 1973, although—probably owing to its massive size and resulting difficulty of moving it from place to place—Giovanni Battista Tiepolo's ceiling painting, *The Triumph of Virtue and Nobility over Ignorance* (p. 139), remained at the museum and was installed in the new galleries when they opened in January.

At the same time works were on display in Houston, the Norton Simon, Inc. Museum of Art opened the impressive exhibition at the Princeton University Art Museum (figs. 1, 5, 6). The genesis of the Princeton show can be traced back to Simon's visit in April 1971 to Princeton University while in town for a board meeting of the Institute for Advanced Study.[18] During his tour of the campus with development officer George Pequignot, Simon mentioned the possibility of a showing of his works in the University Art Museum. Pequignot discussed the conversation with Princeton president Robert Goheen, who alerted Wen C. Fong, chairman of the Department of Art and Archeology, and P. J. Kelleher, director of the art museum.[19]

By June, Kelleher and Isley had arranged for Princeton to borrow six Cubist paintings and one sculpture, whose loan to *The Cubist Epoch* at the Metropolitan Museum of Art was just concluding, and they were shipped to New Jersey from New York by the end of the month.[20] Three old master works followed.[21] Shortly after the Cubist works went on view, David Steadman, the newly appointed assistant director of the University Art Museum, was going through stacks of old paperwork. He came across a memorandum from Pequignot describing his conversation with Simon and specifically "a possible exhibition of some of the major works." Steadman believed that an exhibition could be much larger than the handful of paintings and sculpture lent piecemeal: "I was just transfixed because of course, I knew the collection, and I knew the quality of the collection, and I knew everything that this could mean if something happened."[22]

Steadman and Fong received Goheen's blessing to arrange a meeting with Simon, which occurred in Los Angeles in December. The next month Steadman and Fong met with

FIG. 5. Installation photograph, *Selections from the Norton Simon, Inc. Museum of Art*, Princeton University Art Museum, 1972

FIG. 6. Installation photograph, *Selections from the Norton Simon, Inc. Museum of Art*, Princeton University Art Museum, 1972

Macfarlane and Isley to discuss in depth the scope and size of the loan list and the details of a catalogue. Simon's staff completed the list of artworks in early March, and Steadman recruited scholars to write the entries. The date of the opening was to coincide with the publication of the catalogue, which was completed in the incredibly short span of eight months (fig. 7). During this same period, from December 1971 to March 1972, Simon was also considering the exhibition at LACMA to open that June, as well as beginning discussions with the California Palace of the Legion of Honor in San Francisco about a future showing there. However, Princeton offered him something even greater than either of these California institutions. Steadman believed that Simon's interest in education coupled with the venue at a major Ivy League university proved irresistible:

> I think there was a desire to have a large enough core of his collection on view in the East for a long enough period of time so the importance of that collection became very, very well known in the whole Eastern corridor. And that is precisely what happened with the exhibition. Everybody in the Eastern art world came to see the show while the exhibition was up, and it was there long enough so it was enormously useful to the university because they were able to plan two years of courses around that collection. So you had a very large proportion of Princeton undergraduates who were really looking at this collection. And so it became a major focus of all of the art training on the Princeton University campus—and in fact in all of New Jersey, because Rutgers was using it as well as Princeton.[23]

While Simon was interested in art education, especially at the university level, he was also interested in presenting the collection to the larger public. Princeton's proximity to New York meant that many East Coast museum visitors could finally see a large part of the collection firsthand:

FIG. 7.
Catalogue cover, *Selections from the Norton Simon, Inc. Museum of Art*, Princeton University Art Museum, 1972

The basic reaction to the exhibition was of surprise and delight. Surprise because this was a collection that everyone had heard about, but no one in the East had really seen. And it was the first time that you could get a sense of the scope and the quality of the Norton Simon collection. And it had that element of surprise—a lot of people heard that it was awfully good but hadn't seen it— and suddenly everyone realized this is truly a major collection.[24]

In an *Art News* article about the exhibition, Simon discussed his hope of building long-term loan relationships with museums in Princeton, San Francisco, Los Angeles, and elsewhere. He envisioned the establishment of a consortium of museums and university galleries that would circulate the loans among themselves, giving each museum's community an opportunity to see the entire traveling collection.[25] He held a deeply felt conviction about the power of art, which he hoped would be conveyed through his collection. He expressed this belief in his introduction to the Princeton exhibition catalogue:

One of the most profound means of human communication is the visual arts. By establishing a meaningful dialogue between an artist's vision of the world and our own perceptions, art can help us to understand ourselves more fully. Moreover, art at its finest gives us a deep sense of history, tradition and the true potentialities of man's creativity.[26]

LEFT

FIG. 8. Catalogue cover, *Three Centuries of French Art: Selections from The Norton Simon, Inc. Museum of Art and The Norton Simon Foundation*, California Palace of the Legion of Honor, San Francisco, 1973

OPPOSITE

FIGS. 9, 10. Installation photographs, *Henry Moore: Fifteen Bronzes from the Collections of The Norton Simon Foundation and the Norton Simon, Inc. Museum of Art*, New Orleans Museum of Art, 1974

Simon was so moved by his warm reception at the Princeton opening that, when he delivered remarks during the dinner festivities, he discarded his prepared text. He spoke off the cuff, expanding on the theme of art as communicator, saying, "Art, in the form of the paintings and sculpture in the museum, is to me only a basis for starting with the art of human relations. Tonight is the best example I've had of witnessing this in my life."[27] Despite his great satisfaction, however, the objects in the show were not exempt from Simon's active deaccessions during these years. Although Princeton asked for assurances that at least 90 percent of the display would remain intact for a year,[28] thirty-seven of the one hundred objects were pulled for the May 1973 Parke-Bernet sale, leading to multiple substitutions and rehangings.

While the Princeton discussions were under way, Isley was also making overtures in March 1972 for a one-year loan to San Francisco's California Palace of the Legion of Honor. Isley reported to Simon that the museum's director, Ian McKibbin White, was interested in the idea and suggested that since the museum had shifted its focus to French art, he would prefer French pictures.[29] White enthusiastically wrote to Macfarlane, "This concept is one of the most exciting ideas for developing the collections ever suggested for the museums in San Francisco."[30]

By May the museum and the foundation had reached an agreement on a schedule for the exhibition and catalogue (fig. 8).[31] The foundation submitted a list of French artworks not committed to LACMA and Princeton, and the museum selected sixty-three works by thirty-six French artists. Over the next few months, paintings and sculptures were transferred to San Francisco from museums around the country where they had been on temporary loan, such as the Toledo Museum of Art, the Art Institute of Chicago, the National Gallery of Art, the Phoenix Art Museum, the Metropolitan Museum of Art, and the Virginia Museum of Fine Arts, as well as from LACMA. Titled *Three Centuries of French Art: Selections from The Norton Simon, Inc. Museum of Art and The Norton Simon Foundation*, the exhibition opened on 2 May 1973, the same night as Simon's sale of forty-seven artworks at Parke-Bernet in New York.[32] The foundation eventually agreed to extend the show for a second year, adding enough artworks to merit a second catalogue.[33] The supplemental exhibition of another fifty-two artworks opened in October 1974. Since Simon had committed to a permanent relationship with the Pasadena Museum of Modern Art the previous April, the artworks moved to their new home in Pasadena when the Legion of Honor took down the display in June 1976.

In addition to the sculptures on loan at the Pasadena Museum in 1972–1973, the foundations arranged another exhibit of bronzes to be held at the New Orleans Museum of Art. In late 1973 Simon purchased Henry Moore's *Family Group*, an overlife-size depiction of a father and mother holding a child. Searching for a loan venue in another region of the country, Isley asked New Orleans Museum of Art director E. John Bullard to show the bronze for a few months. Bullard was receptive and suggested that New Orleans be considered as well for a more extensive loan on the order of San Francisco and Princeton. Fifteen Henry Moore bronzes were sent to the museum in December for a yearlong loan (figs. 9, 10), but another exhibition never materialized. Before New Orleans could take other, larger thematic loans, Simon was involved in Pasadena.

Before Pasadena was settled, however, a last major showing of Simon artworks was arranged at the Detroit Institute of Arts. Impressed with the Princeton and San Francisco displays, Detroit curator Ronald Winokur met with Isley in Los Angeles in October 1973 to discuss a possible loan to the institute.[34] Before the end of the year, I was in Detroit meeting the director, Frederick Cummings, and reviewing the museum. Two paintings that were bought at the end of December were shipped immediately to Detroit. There were many candidates for

a larger exhibition. Houston had just closed its show, LACMA's would end its two-year run in June, and Princeton's would close in July. After perusing art lists and available works, Isley assembled a group consisting of the two foundations' entire Italian holdings. Cummings's response was "immediate, enthusiastic, and excited," and he suggested publishing a catalogue.[35]

When the news broke in April 1974 about Simon's involvement with the Pasadena Museum of Modern Art, Macfarlane was quick to assure Detroit that the event "in no way alters our interest and desire to have the Italian exhibition at the Institute."[36] It was agreed that the foundations would lend about seventy-five objects for two years, with the option of extending for an additional two. As artworks arrived, a few, such as the Romanelli cartoons, were hung right away, and a gallery holding about thirty-five paintings and sculptures was opened in January 1975. Budget cuts imposed on the institute by the city of Detroit, however, delayed completion of the catalogue, and an official opening of the full exhibition continued to be postponed. By July 1975 Detroit pushed off the opening date by another year.[37] With a new permanent home for Simon's collections now secured in Pasadena,[38] Macfarlane was reluctant to extend the loan for an additional two years beyond the June 1976 closing date, and he informed Detroit of this in October 1975.[39] This led Cummings to conclude that it was in Detroit's best interests to terminate the loan rather than to complete a catalogue and installation by April to have it on view for only a month.[40] While catalogue work ceased and a portion of the artworks were shipped out, others, such as the Romanelli cartoons and the Tiepolo ceiling, remained in Detroit until the following spring, when the remaining pictures moved to their new quarters in Pasadena.

In addition to the seven exhibitions noted above, two more were under consideration by the Metropolitan Museum of Art. The first, discussed in detail with European paintings curator Everett Fahy, would mirror LACMA's show and those scheduled at Princeton, Houston, and San Francisco.[41] Ultimately, there were loans of a few individual pictures, but a larger installation never materialized. The second exhibition, a major showing of Asian art from the Simon collections, was in the planning stages for much of 1972 and 1973.

Discussions concerning an Asian art exhibition commenced when Princeton University Art Department chairman Wen C. Fong, who was also consultative chairman of the Metropolitan's Far Eastern Art Department, first met with Simon regarding the Princeton installation in late 1971. Simon was beginning to avidly collect Asian art, and the two discussed collections, museums, dealers, the relative merits of artworks, and, eventually, a loan of Asian sculpture to the Metropolitan. At the end of May 1972 Simon owned just twenty-three Asian sculptures, but his ambition for the collection was such that he and Macfarlane were already discussing a major exhibition with Thomas Hoving, director of the Metropolitan Museum.[42] In July of that year, Macfarlane supplied Hoving with a list of sixty-nine objects for consideration, even though some were not yet officially in the collection.[43] Curator Martin Lerner was to write the catalogue and advise on the selection of objects. In fall 1972 Simon began sending the sculptures to the museum so that Lerner would have them available while writing the catalogue, and the conservators Plowden and Smith made two trips to New York of several weeks' duration to treat objects and fabricate mounts. Preparing the catalogue and loan list was not easy, since Simon continued to buy objects every month. By the end of 1972 he had accumulated more than one hundred Indian, Himalayan, and Southeast Asian sculptures at a cost of more than $5.6 million. The most expensive piece was the Shivapuram *Nataraja* bought from Ben Heller in December. Simon expected this spectacular Chola bronze to be given preeminence in the installation and to grace the cover of the catalogue. Lerner strongly advised against this, citing the negative publicity surrounding the work, since in May the Indian government had declared it stolen. He believed its position on the cover was an affront that would bring even more harmful exposure.[44] Hoving and Lerner agreed to the bronze's inclusion, however, and plans continued throughout 1973. By the end of the year, the catalogue's colorplates and galleys had been proofed and were ready to go to press. Featuring seventy-five sculptures and titled *Images of Divinity*, the exhibition was scheduled to open on 28 March 1974.

Meanwhile, in the midst of the ongoing preparations, in late 1973 Hoving presented Simon with a plan considerably grander in scale than an Asian art exhibition. He proposed the creation of a Norton Simon Center at the Metropolitan Museum of Art.[45] The projected three-story, 28,000-square-foot center was to be housed in the museum's southeast corner. Simon was to bear the $2.2-million construction costs and salaries for his curatorial staff in exchange for the Metropolitan's providing support services. The building would house Simon's collection, and he would control its program. He could still lend elsewhere with no commitment to the Metropolitan regarding its ultimate disposition.[46] In spite of the optimistic spirit embodied in the proposal, plans for a Norton Simon Center soon evaporated, along with the *Images of Divinity* exhibition.

In December 1973, as the catalogue was headed to press, Hoving told the foundation that the Metropolitan wanted the Shivapuram *Nataraja* removed.[47] Macfarlane rejoined that the museum had a legal and moral obligation to show it.[48] Defending his stance, Hoving cited the American Association of Museum Directors' principle that member museums not display artworks that had been illegally exported from their country of origin.[49] Simon was furious, blaming the about-face on Hoving's public relations problems over the Metropolitan's 1972 purchase of a 2,500-year-old Greek vase by the painter Euphronios, reported to have been illegally removed from Italy. Simon believed it was a hypocritical attempt to turn potentially controversial attention away from the museum and instead to The Norton Simon Foundation.[50]

In days Simon had moved the sculptures out of the Metropolitan to a storage warehouse. Initially, it was publicized that the exhibition was simply postponed; in June 1974, however, it was announced that it was canceled altogether. Hoving was quoted as saying Simon withdrew the artworks after the museum agreed to abide by India's request that the *Nataraja* not be shown. Simon's attorney and spokesperson, Helen Buckley, put an unexpected spin on the news, stating instead that Simon was "disenchanted with the Met and the manner in which it is administered. This was to have been set up in honor of the 25th anniversary of the state of India in 1972 but the museum just couldn't seem to get the show together."[51] Needless to say, the ruptured agreement on the Asian sculpture display also ended any conceivable grander relationship between Simon and the Metropolitan.

A final potential collaboration during this period began in July 1973, when Simon asked Macfarlane to contact the J. Paul Getty Museum trustee Norris Bramlett to discuss a possible association between the two institutions. Getty Museum curator Burton Fredericksen followed up by reporting to Isley that Mr. Getty was interested in borrowing "a gallery full of Simon pictures" to be installed in his new museum in Malibu.[52] Built to resemble a villa from ancient Herculaneum and designed to house the Getty's Greek and Roman antiquities as well as its European paintings and decorative arts, the museum was scheduled to open on 15 January 1974. During a trip to England in the fall of 1973, Simon met with Getty to talk about the loan. Regrettably, there is no record of their meeting or what else these two great collectors might have discussed. Macfarlane and Isley continued talks with newly appointed Getty Museum director Stephen Garrett and Getty curators. After a meeting with Getty, Garrett reported that there was no urgency or necessity to reach an agreement before the opening in January 1974, but that he and Getty were interested in further considering a possible loan:

> Mr. Getty repeated to me that he would favor collaboration between Mr. Simon and this museum and could envisage an arrangement whereby some galleries were devoted to Mr. Simon's collection. Mr. Getty was very flexible concerning the period over which such an arrangement might span considering that any period between three and twenty years might be acceptable.[53]

After the opening, Garrett and Macfarlane conferred about a much more elaborate and permanent collaboration, beginning with the erection of a building to house the Simon collections on Getty property, built and administered by the Getty Museum:

> At the moment it is not easy to envisage what scale of building might be required. Certainly it would be very much smaller than the present museum. It is also possible that further investigation would suggest that rather than form a distinct division between the JPGM collection in our building and the NSF collection in a new building, an amalgamation of the two collections spread between the two buildings would be better.[54]

J. Paul Getty's reaction to the proposal is not known. It is unlikely that he was interested in paying for a building to house Simon art on Getty property. Unquestionably, Simon would have balked at subsuming his collection to that of Getty's. There is no record of further talks between the parties, and, in any event, within weeks Simon had made arrangements to bring his collections to the Pasadena Art Museum. ❧

1. Norton Simon, in The Museum of Fine Arts, Houston press release, 3 October 1972.

2. Princeton, 1972. Raphael's *Madonna and Child with Book* was added too late to be included in the catalogue (Steadman et al., 1972).

3. During this period works from the Simon collections were exhibited in cities such as Toledo, Chicago, Washington, D.C., Phoenix, New York, and Richmond, Va., as well as Los Angeles.

4. Robert Macfarlane, speaking at "Collector without Walls: A Symposium on Norton Simon," 27 October 2007.

5. Franklin Murphy to Simon, 31 March 1972.

6. Seldis, 1972a.

7. Ibid.

8. Although many of the artworks left LACMA in June 1974 to travel to Detroit, the Raphael did not move until October, when it was lent to the M. H. de Young Memorial Museum in San Francisco. The Zurbarán *Still Life* stayed at LACMA until Simon opened the museum in Pasadena.

9. Alfred M. Esberg to Simon, 9 December 1971. The trustees were Esberg, Coleman Morton, and Robert Rowan. For the history of Norton Simon–Pasadena Art Museum negotiations, see Muchnic, 1998, pp. 199–222, and chap. 11, below.

10. Sara Campbell to Macfarlane, 18 May 1972.

11. Simon to Esberg, 15 June 1972.

12. Macfarlane to Simon, 18 January 1973.

13. Macfarlane to Simon, 28 December 1973.

14. Philippe de Montebello to Darryl Isley, 22 June 1972.

15. The Museum of Fine Arts, Houston, curator Thomas P. Lee to Simon and MacFarlane, 11 August 1972.

16. The Museum of Fine Arts, Houston, press release, 3 October 1972.

17. *Southwest Art Gallery Magazine*, 1972, p. 36.

18. Simon was a member of the institute's board of trustees 1970–1980.

19. Robert Goheen to Simon, 11 June 1971.

20. Isley to P. J. Kelleher, 22 June 1971. *The Cubist Epoch* was held at the Los Angeles County Museum of Art 15 December 1970–21 February 1971, and at The Metropolitan Museum of Art 7 April–7 June 1971. The works lent were *Still Life with Musical Instruments* (cat. 232) and *Still Life with Pipe* (cat. 652) by Georges Braque, *Still Life with Poem* (cat. 435) by Juan Gris, *Bather III*

(cat. 446) by Jacques Lipchitz, *Open Window in Paris* (cat 327) and *Pointe de la Cité* (cat. 449) by Pablo Picasso, and *The Traveler* (cat. 349) by Liubov Popova.

21. In October the recently acquired *Three Great Trees in a Mountainous Landscape with a River* (cat. 743) by Jacob van Ruisdael was lent to Princeton to satisfy out-of-state exhibition requirements. In January two additional old masters from the Duveen collection followed, Jusepe de Ribera's *Sense of Touch* (D44) and Giambologna's *Rape of Proserpina* (cat. D74).

22. David Steadman, interview by Davis Guggenheim, n.d.

23. Ibid.

24. Ibid.

25. Seldis, 1972b, p. 26.

26. Simon, in Steadman et al., 1972, p. 11.

27. Simon, from a transcript of remarks delivered at Princeton University, 2 December 1972.

28. Simon to Fong, 23 February 1972.

29. Isley to Simon, 31 March 1972. In 1972 the collections of San Francisco's two art museums, the M. H. de Young Memorial Museum and the California Palace of the Legion of Honor, merged to form The Fine Arts Museums of San Francisco. The California Palace of the Legion of Honor became the home of the arts of France, while other national schools were to be housed at the M. H. de Young Memorial Museum.

30. Ian McKibbin White to Macfarlane, 10 April 1972.

31. Graham et al., 1973.

32. For more about the 2 May 1973 Parke-Bernet sale, see p. 147.

33. Graham et al., 1974; Macfarlane to White, 25 February 1974.

34. Ronald Winokur to Isley, 9 October 1973.

35. Isley to Simon, 1 February 1974.

36. Macfarlane to Detroit trustee Lee Hills, 26 April 1974.

37. As discussed in Macfarlane to Hills, 9 July 1975.

38. See chap. 11.

39. As discussed in Cummings to Macfarlane, 7 October 1975.

40. Ibid.

41. Isley to Simon, 18 August 1972.

42. Macfarlane to Simon, 24 May 1972.

43. Macfarlane to Thomas Hoving, 14 July 1972. At the time of the letter, Simon owned forty-four of the sixty-nine offered for loan. The rest were part of the Klejman package to be paid for in separate installments and other objects he expected to buy (see p. 125).

44. Isley to Simon, 9 October 1973. Instead of the *Nataraja*, a bronze from Nepal (cat. 878) was chosen for the cover.

45. Hoving to Simon, 13 October and 9 November 1973. While his essay in the *Los Angeles Times* (Hoving, 2008) suggests that Simon initiated the idea for the center, Hoving's October 1973 letter confirms that the director himself submitted the proposal.

46. Ibid.

47. As reported in Macfarlane to Hoving, 20 December 1973.

48. Ibid.

49. Hoving to Macfarlane, 11 January 1974.

50. On 7 March 1974 the Metropolitan issued a report to its members declaring that the vase had been lawfully purchased. Thirty-four years later, however, in January 2008, the museum returned it to Italy.

51. *Los Angeles Times*, 1974b.

52. Isley to Simon, 9 August 1973.

53. Stephen Garrett to Macfarlane, 12 December 1973.

54. Garrett to Macfarlane, 23 January 1974.

CHAPTER ELEVEN

A Museum with Walls
1974–1976

I have fifty people ready to jump down my neck, and it's going to be controversial, regardless of how good it is.—NORTON SIMON[1]

THE PASADENA ART MUSEUM (PAM) was founded in 1924 as the Pasadena Art Institute. For the first three decades, its reputation was that of a provincial art gallery with a small collection of European and American art. In 1953, however, the institute received a bequest of 450 artworks and extensive archives from the dealer and collector Galka E. Scheyer (fig. 1). Scheyer's collection of modernist works consisted chiefly of paintings and works on paper by the artists she dubbed the Blue Four—Lyonel Feininger, Alexei Jawlensky, Vasily Kandinsky, and Paul Klee. The enormously important gift completely changed the organization's collecting aims. The following year the institute changed its name to the Pasadena Art Museum and, using the Scheyer collection as its nucleus, shifted its acquisition and exhibition focus to modern art.

Over the next two decades, the Pasadena Art Museum earned an international reputation for organizing and presenting critically acclaimed exhibitions of twentieth-century art. The museum presented the first retrospective of the work of Marcel Duchamp, a landmark Bauhaus exhibition, and many others. Wanting to expand PAM's ambitious programs and believing it had outgrown its facilities in downtown Pasadena, the museum's supporters desired an equally worthy building. The PAM trustees decided to construct a new 85,000-square-foot building on former park land at the western edge of the city at the corner of Colorado and Orange Grove boulevards (fig. 2).[2] The staff moved into the newly completed structure in November 1969, but, plagued with unfulfilled fund-raising campaign pledges and skyrocketing expenses, the museum was soon on the verge of bankruptcy. The *Wall Street Journal* reported in August 1971 that after less than two years in the new facility, the operating debt forced the institution to cut back staff, services, and programs and to reduce its

hours to four days a week. According to the *Journal*, "Pasadena's problems generally spring from the incompatibility of grand ambitions and minimal endowment."[3]

OPPOSITE
Vincent van Gogh, *Portrait of a Peasant (Patience Escalier)*, 1888 (detail), Norton Simon Art Foundation. CAT. 1130

ABOVE LEFT
Norton Simon

ABOVE
FIG. 1. Galka Scheyer, 1940

LEFT
FIG. 2. Norton Simon Museum, c. 1976

After an unsuccessful bid for help from the county of Los Angeles, the museum, said the article, was "retrenching" and seeking new avenues of support. One of these avenues led in 1971 to Norton Simon. Three trustees (Alfred Esberg, Coleman Morton, and Robert Rowan) secretly approached him through fellow board member Frederick Weisman, Simon's brother-in-law. By the end of 1971 they had offered an extraordinary plan that would relieve them of their enormous construction debt and operating expenses and at the same time provide them with the funds to build a less expensive exhibition space. They proposed that Simon lease the present museum building to store and exhibit his own collection. In exchange, Simon would provide the Pasadena Art Museum with $1.5 million for construction of "a new contemporary art museum on a mutually agreed upon portion of the present building site."[4] Further, the Pasadena group asked for storage and office space in the existing building until the new museum was ready for occupancy. Areas for discussion included consideration of the possible sharing of entrance fee income, museum member-ships, and gifts, as well as other ways in which "two independently operating museum groups might work harmoniously."[5]

Discussions continued through January and February 1972, bringing rumors of a possible Simon bailout. Isley, for instance, reported that former Simon staffer Barbara Roberts told him, "The major rumor circulating at the College Art Association is that you have purchased the Pasadena Art Museum."[6] However, Simon was not interested in involving himself and the foundations in a complicated union of two independent institutions and instead suggested a loan of nineteenth- and twentieth-century sculpture, as previously noted.[7]

The sculpture loan did little to allay the financial woes at Pasadena, which only worsened as 1972 wore on. In an effort to make the museum more fully identified with its exhibitions and collection, in early 1973 the board changed the institution's name to the Pasadena Museum of Modern Art (PMMA), but this rebranding had no effect on the bottom line. In January and February 1974 the board's executive committee even briefly considered deaccessioning artworks to raise money to pay for operating expenses.[8] After struggling through another year, and citing the economic problems that continued to plague the museum, its then director William Agee left to assume the directorship of the Museum of Fine Arts in Houston in February 1974.[9]

Throughout this period, Simon maintained a clandestine interest in Pasadena, directing Robert Macfarlane to keep open a line of communication with the museum's trustees. Although Simon enjoyed the immense success of the several loan exhibitions around the country, the idea of gathering the collection under one roof was becoming more appealing. Even so, Pasadena was not the only option, and Simon instructed Macfarlane to pursue other possibilities as well. Macfarlane described Simon's philosophy as one of always having what Simon called a golden bridge of retreat:

> This was a common phrase, so that we were always having or constructing a golden bridge of retreat before anything was done. For example, with [the Pasadena museum], when I was the designated negotiator over three or four years, almost everything that we did in terms of offer and counter offer, we were also at the very same time in conversations with three or four other entities. So that if we were turned down here, we weren't in a corner or weren't in a box; there was always another possibility.[10]

The other sites were as disparate as property in Ojai, California; land adjacent to the California Institute of the Arts in Valencia; and what Macfarlane described as "perhaps the most impressive presentation...an incredible proposal," from

Thomas Hoving offering to create the Norton Simon Center at the Metropolitan Museum of Art.[11] In spite of Simon's keeping open other options, when Pasadena trustees approached him again in early 1974, he was ready to work toward an agreement.[12]

There were many reasons Simon at this stage was more interested in making an arrangement with the museum in Pasadena. In the intervening two years, he had seen the results of several exhibitions devoted to his artworks, with shows in Los Angeles, Pasadena, Houston, Princeton, and San Francisco, and another in the planning stages in Detroit. Aside from the accolades they received, these exhibitions offered Simon his first opportunity (aside from his loans to LACMA) to see major portions of his collections on view together in one location. Another major factor was undoubtedly the opening in January 1974 of the J. Paul Getty Museum in Malibu. The spectacular re-created Roman villa housed European paintings, decorative art and furniture, and Greek and Roman antiquities. Ever comparing his collection to others, Simon surely looked at the Getty works now on view and the worldwide publicity the new museum enjoyed with an eye to his own holdings and realized that for his to be seen at its best, it needed to be in one location. In addition, the collections had simply become too big to manage, store, lend, and conserve effectively when they were spread out across the country. In spite of the massive deaccessions over the previous four years, in April 1974 the collections contained more than 3,700 objects, which presented complicated logistical challenges and the constant threat of damage inherent in travel. Finally, with the collapse of the scheduled Asian sculpture exhibition at the Metropolitan Museum of Art, he needed to find a suitable home for close to 150 Indian, Himalayan, and Southeast Asian sculptures. All of these factors made Pasadena's renewed overture much more appealing the second time around. Within a few weeks, the parties had reached agreement.

In essence, Simon's foundations ("the Norton Simon group") would assume control of a newer and smaller board. The Pasadena board of trustees would be reduced from thirty-five members to ten, with four persons from the Simon group, three from the Pasadena museum, and three public members selected by the Simon group. In addition, "no less than 25 percent of the museum exhibition space over a three to five year average" would be devoted to Pasadena's permanent collection.[13] In April Simon wrote to the Pasadena board outlining the agreement under consideration, announcing the closure of the museum in June to allow time for repairs and the termination of some employees. He stated that once the Pasadena board had approved the proposal, he would present it to the boards of the Norton Simon foundations, adding optimistically:

> I personally look forward with great pleasure and anticipation to a joining of our various collections. I have great faith in the possibilities. I earnestly believe that each collection will be enhanced by the other by presenting to the general public an historic sweep of the evolution of art.[14]

At its April 1974 meeting, the PMMA board agreed to accept the proposal and voted itself out of office.[15] Shortly thereafter, the museum's name was changed back to the Pasadena Art Museum. The press described the entire process as a takeover,[16] which bothered Macfarlane: "The word 'takeover' was used repeatedly and that was not what we wanted to do. We were to assume the responsibilities, and believe me there was an enormous number of such responsibilities financial and otherwise."[17]

FIG. 3. Darryl Isley and George Peters, March 1975

For the next few months Simon and his staff were consumed with issues of management and staffing. I left the foundation offices on Wilshire Boulevard to assume overall curatorial responsibilities, and George Peters (fig. 3, *right*), director of the Princeton, New Jersey, United Way and long-time associate of Macfarlane's, became the museum's executive director. A handful of former PAM employees were kept on, including security staff, preparators, the registrar, and clerical support, but everyone else was terminated when the museum closed in June. Peters's first job was to attempt to recover outstanding contributions pledged to the old museum. His next was to oversee the remodeling of and repairs to the building. Windows at the end of corridors, for instance, needed to be walled over to provide backdrops for artworks, the building's perpetual leaks had to be stopped, buckling floors replaced, and the air-conditioning system repaired. The London conservators Anna Plowden and Peter Smith designed sculpture bases that harmonized with the museum's curved walls and spent several weeks at the museum, mounting both Asian and European pieces on new bases (fig. 4). Simon and his team had weekly meetings for months, in which they discussed every facet of the museum's operations.[18] These included the design and remodeling of the galleries; design and fabrication of sculpture bases; inventory and staffing of the bookstore; opening hours; a membership program and the relationship of the museum's current members to the new institution; timing of returns of the art on loan around the country; when to reopen; and, especially, the design and installation of the opening exhibition. Not completely comfortable with the idea of charging for admission, Simon instigated a policy whereby, in return for paying an admission fee, all visitors would receive a reproduction of one of the artworks on view, a tradition that continues today.

The move was not without controversy. Outrage in the modern art community was directed at the trustees who negotiated the agreement and even more at Simon. Museum sponsors were wounded in particular by Simon's elimination of support groups and the children's art workshops and the loss of the museum's focus on contemporary art. Thirty-five years later, one still occasionally hears echoes of regret in the community but now couched with great pride in what the Norton Simon Museum means for Pasadena. It is widely lauded as a boon to Southern California's cultural life.

FIG. 4. Anna Plowden, Peter Smith, and Erik Binas preparing a sculpture mount, March 1975

The Simon exhibitions at LACMA and Princeton ended in June and July 1974. Since the Pasadena Museum was temporarily closed, the artworks were instead placed on view elsewhere. French paintings traveled to San Francisco for the second installment of the Legion of Honor loan, and Italian objects went to Detroit. The Asian sculpture, however, was shipped to Pasadena from its New York warehouse, where it had been stored since the cancellation of the Metropolitan exhibition. Over the course of the year, artworks filtered in. After ten months of intense preparations, the museum reopened on 1 March 1975.

After seeing the fanfare accompanying the long-term loans at Princeton, San Francisco, and elsewhere, Simon's staff encouraged him to have a formal opening attended by art dealers, curators, directors, and others who knew and admired the collection. Simon, by contrast, insisted that the entire event be kept low-key. Since the best of his collections were on loan elsewhere, the majority of the space was devoted to Pasadena's twentieth-century art, and this first installation did not represent his ultimate intentions. Shortly before the opening, Simon explained his thinking:

> We're opening without any celebration, no formalities, just opening the doors, opening with twentieth-century art. I partially did this because we couldn't get ready in time, we had commitments in our Italian and French art, which are the two greatest parts of our collection, in other museums, and then I didn't want to get into the old masters at all because I wouldn't do a full job and a halfway job might demean the whole thing, so I wound up with twentieth century and Asian. The rationale was that I want to play it reasonably safe. I don't want an opening that is not going to work. I'm going on the basis of underkill rather than overkill. If we have an opening night, I can't expect the people from the east and Europe to come for that kind of an opening. The place isn't fixed up enough, a lot of important works won't be there, and if I have an opening that doesn't have that connotation, I'd rather just open the doors and let it happen and low-key it as much as possible. This is a new world to me and I want to be damn careful about it. I have fifty people ready to jump down my neck, and it's going to be controversial, regardless of how good it is.[19]

As loan commitments elsewhere ended, the Simon collections took up more and more of the galleries. In October 1975, believing that the museum's name no longer reflected its collections or management, the board of trustees changed the name of the institution to the Norton Simon Museum of Art at Pasadena. Simon later admitted that the name gave him great pleasure, confessing, "It would be foolish to say there wasn't some ego in it. In the end we decided to use my name because I had a personal art foundation known all over the world. And I thought, why not? The name tells it straight."[20]

Historically, because of the geographic dispersal of his collection, Simon's association with it was most often through photographs and typewritten lists. He had seen less than one-tenth of it together at any one time. As he finally began to observe the collection as a whole, he spent more and more time directing the display of the artworks and essentially performing the work of a curator. This experimentation became a never-ending process.

The dogged pursuit of an ideal, whether in business, creativity, or art collecting, was a hallmark of Simon's philosophy and what he often referred to as his "process of becoming."[21] Simon used the phrase in conversation with numerous individuals over the years.[22] It was a characteristic formulation that he used about psychology, business development, and the evolution of institutions. Most important, he used it when thinking about art and his own collection. In the Norton Simon Museum, he strived to attain the ideal hanging, which meant that an artwork—once comfortable in the best possible spot—would forever remain there so that visitors would always know where to find it. Paradoxically, his search for that perfection meant that he was continually changing the installations. In the first year the museum was open, for instance, each gallery was rehung on average six times. Some of this can be attributed to the fact that objects arrived almost daily. On the other hand, when things settled down the following year, the changes did not significantly abate, and we were often involved in the wholesale reshuffling of artworks and galleries.

This need to find an optimum solution was certainly not a new trait. In 1967 he discussed his penchant for constantly rehanging the art at his home with the *Los Angeles Times* writer Henry Seldis:

> We are constantly reshuffling things here because I am always looking for a better relationship between the picture or sculpture and me. Putting them in different positions gives new life to them and takes away any tendency to become static. As different pros and cons become evident in each work as it is moved around, I am better able to identify with a particular artist's vision. Each artist sees life in a different way and eventually you are able to share that vision to some extent. Looking out of the window one projects these personal manners of seeing even to nature, thinking of a "Sisley cloud" or a "van Gogh field."[23]

In addition to constantly rehanging the art, Simon had unorthodox ideas about installation design. In June 1974 he bought at Sotheby's a series of watercolors called *The Great Tulip Book* by an anonymous seventeenth-century Dutch artist (fig. 5). Originally the catalogue of a tulip dealer, the book features 158 detailed representations of tulips, with inscriptions that give the name of each variety and its cost. The book reflects the speculative market in tulips at the time and the phenomenon of tulipomania, seventeenth-century Holland's obsession with tulips that led ultimately to a financial meltdown. As an investor in the stock market as well as in art, Simon found both the series and the speculation in the tulip market extremely intriguing. Fascinated with the exhibition possibilities, Simon had the book unbound and the watercolors individually framed. He directed that when they were first exhibited, every tulip was to be on view and, in effect, curated the exhibition. They were hung floor to ceiling, almost as if they were wallpaper, with the top row tilted so that it could be more easily seen (fig. 6).

FIG. 5. Anonymous Dutch Artist, *The Great Tulip Book: Admirael Der Admiraels de Gouda*, c. 1640s, Norton Simon Art Foundation. CAT. 1060

FIG. 6. Installation photograph, *The Great Tulip Book*, Norton Simon Museum, 1978

Simon's desire to exhibit as much as possible to demonstrate a point was also in effect when he directed the installation of his hundreds of works on paper by Francisco de Goya. In this case we designed a gallery for each of Goya's four large suites of prints, *Los Caprichos*, *Los Desastres de la Guerra*, *Los Proverbios*, and *La Tauromaquia*. The *Caprichos* gallery, for instance (p. 179), exhibited examples of each of the suite's eighty plates, showing one or more first-edition sets alongside a second, fourth, and eighth edition, so that the viewer could compare the various plates. Goya prints provided Simon with endless opportunities for comparison. He enjoyed evaluating not only the same plate in different editions but also many examples of a plate in the same edition. In *Los Caprichos*, for instance, at some point during the printing of the first edition, plate number 45, titled *Mucho hay que chupar*, received a small scratch on the face of one figure. Simon owned first-edition sets that were pulled both before and after the scratch occurred and insisted that both be shown and discussed in explanatory labels.

He also had his own ideas about what constituted prominence in a display. If, for example, a hanging design called for one painting to be hung above another, Simon insisted that the top position was the more important, and therefore the more important artwork should be placed on top, regardless of its size relative to the one below.

In spite of the activity surrounding Simon's move to the museum in Pasadena and the interest he showed in its installations, he continued to define the character of his collection both by what he bought and by what he sold. In 1974 he bought 117 artworks for a little more than $2.6 million. He also sold close to one hundred for more than $5.9 million—a profit of about $3.8 million.[24] Put another way, with profits from his 1974 sales at more than $3.8 million, after he bought 117 artworks that year, he was still ahead more than $1 million. The works appeared in nine auctions in New York and London throughout 1974. Sotheby's in New York sold the lion's share, seventy-three objects, primarily works on paper, with sales that reached close to $1.4 million. As in the past, Simon and Sotheby's negotiated a guarantee. Another thirty-seven objects, including graphics, sculptures, and paintings, were sold or traded to dealers. The group consisted of some works that today would have little relevance in the collections—thirteen small Egyptian sculptures, for instance—but others would have added significantly to the quality of the present holdings, such as works by Picasso, Matisse, and Brancusi (cats. 327, 347, 525, 630).

The auction sales were planned before Simon made the agreement with Pasadena, and news articles explained that his reason for selling was a concern that fragile drawings and watercolors, unsuitable for constant travel and exhibition, did not fit his "museum without walls" concept.[25] This stated apprehension about fragile works on paper notwithstanding, Simon sold four paintings and a sculpture to private dealers for $3.2 million between January 1974 and the April agreement with Pasadena.[26] He spent significantly less on new acquisitions in 1974. Although he bought 117 artworks that year, he spent only a little more than $2.6 million, a striking drop, compared to the $27 million spent in both of the two previous years (see

RIGHT
FIG. 7. Thailand, Si Thep, Mon-Dvaravati Period, *Torso of a Hindu Deity*, 7th century, Norton Simon Art Foundation. CAT. 1012

BELOW
FIG. 8. Thailand, Si Thep, Mon-Dvaravati Period, *Hindu Deity*, 7th century, Norton Simon Art Foundation. CATS. 899, 1012

Appendix). Of the 117, eighty-four were Asian works. Knowing that in the auction salesroom he was competing with dealers for objects that they would later sell at marked-up prices, Simon broadened his access to Asian works by buying more than two-thirds of them at auction. The reduction in the amounts spent that year could be attributed in part to economic circumstances and to creative retrenching in light of his commitment to the Pasadena museum. Certainly the museum played a factor in his increased buying in the Asian field.

Simon's most important Asian acquisition in 1974 was a sandstone torso bought in April (fig. 7). In December 1972 he had purchased from Ben Heller a Thai bust of a Hindu deity (p. 130). The bust was exceptional, not only because of its extraordinary beauty but also because of its distinctive diagonal break from the right shoulder to the left armpit. In September 1973 Adrian Maynard of Spink & Son in London notified Simon that the firm recently received a torso they believed belonged with the bust.[27] The similarity of the stone and the style of the carving, along with the unique line of the break, left little doubt that the pieces had originally been joined. Maynard quoted the somewhat high price of $340,000.[28] It was obvious to Simon that the dealer would never ask such an elevated amount if he offered it to anyone other than the owner of the bust. He also knew that the bust by itself was the more desirable piece and that it would be difficult to sell the torso without it. Simon considered selling the bust to Spink or going into partnership with the firm on the joined body. He offered $100,000 for the torso, a price designed to diminish in their eyes his own interest in the piece. Spink dropped the price to $240,000 and then to $150,000. Simon said he would go no higher than $120,000.

Adrian Maynard of Spink accepted the offer, writing:

> I passed your offer back to the owner, with some trepidation, and to my great surprise and considerable embarrassment, I find that he is prepared to accept it. I would like you to realize that had this piece been mine I would not have asked you a figure anything like the amount that was originally asked. I would not like you to think that Spinks raised their prices in this manner.[29]

Heller remembered that during the negotiations both Simon and Spink repeatedly telephoned him to discuss the matter:

> I got phone calls from both sides, Norton complaining that the seller was asking too much money and the seller saying, he's giving me a hard time. So here are two people who had to reconcile their differences. Where else is the seller going to place it, and he got a good price. What else is Norton going to do but complete one of the great stone works of all time? They both won.[30]

The bust and torso were sent to London, where Plowden and Smith assembled the two sections into the magnificent standing figure we see today (fig. 8).

LEFT
FIG. 9. Gerolamo Savoldo, *Shepherd with Flute*, The J. Paul Getty Museum, Los Angeles. CAT. 1005

BELOW
FIG. 10. Tibet, *Future Buddha Maitreya Flanked by the Eighth Dalai Lama and His Tutor*, 1793–1794 (detail), Norton Simon Art Foundation. CAT. 1122

As mentioned above, Simon's 1974 purchases were predominantly Asian. Only about 25 percent were European paintings and sculpture, including marble sculptures by Henry Moore (cat. 1078) and Barbara Hepworth (cat. 1082) and Rubens's *Saint Ignatius of Loyola* (cat. 1119). He bought the Rubens, which had been at Warwick Castle since the late eighteenth century, for a little more than $330,000 in the Earl of Warwick's sale at Sotheby's in London. Simon's most expensive purchase, however, Gerolamo Savoldo's *Shepherd with Flute* (fig. 9), is one he did not keep. Wildenstein offered the Savoldo, from the Contini-Bonacossi collection, to Simon in late 1972.[31] It was offered again in March 1973 by the dealers Stanley Moss and Eugene Thaw, who sent it to Los Angeles for examination. Simon agreed to purchase the painting for $500,000, and Thaw agreed to buy it back in one year, or June 1974, if Simon changed his mind.[32] The painting was lent to the Princeton exhibition, replacing the Raphael *Madonna and Child with Book*. Simon kept the picture on exhibit at Princeton, where scholars and conservators examined it and sent him their opinions.[33] He eventually exercised his option to return the painting, and Thaw reimbursed the foundation $500,000. Simon's ambivalence resulted in the picture's appearance again in Pasadena from May to July 1980 and then again from March 1982 until April 1983. In spite of favorable opinions from all sides, Simon finally decided against it. Ultimately, the J. Paul Getty Museum bought it in 1985.

Indian and Southeast Asian artworks dominated Simon's purchases again in 1975. He had come to believe that Asian art offered him better value and great quality at less cost than Western art, and, not incidentally, more than 50,000 square feet of galleries needed to be filled. During this first year that the museum was open under his direction, he made 175 purchases, more than 80 percent of them Asian.[34] Two of the earliest examples are from ancient Gandhara, a *Bodhisattva Maitreya* and a *Buddha Shakyamuni* (cats. 1146, 1147), two over-life-size figures carved from dark gray schist. Simon had never shied away from buying large artworks, and his first purchase in 1975 had been a monumental Tibetan appliquéd silk thanka (fig. 10). As it turned out, the thanka proved to be too big even for the Pasadena museum's sixteen-foot-high walls. The work is thought to have been commissioned by the eighth Dalai Lama in honor of his tutor. Commanding a height of more than twenty-two feet, *Future Buddha Maitreya Flanked by the Eighth Dalai Lama and His Tutor*, 1793–1794, is considered the largest such thanka outside Tibet.[35] Simon was first informed

of the work in September 1974, saw it in Paris in October, and bought it in January 1975.[36] Simon vexed his staff with such suggestions as hanging the piece on the building's outside walls or suspending it in the middle of a two-storey circular staircase. The central panel, depicting the Maitreya Buddha, measures a little less than fourteen feet high, and the work was briefly exhibited in one of the large galleries with the upper and lower borders rolled so that only this center section was visible. To see the entire thanka fully unfurled, Simon asked that it be temporarily hung in the museum's auditorium, at that time closed to the public. It was not until a temporary exhibition in 2001 that the work was shown in its entirety, resting in a specially designed reclining display case.[37]

Simon also bought European art in 1975, thirty-two works by Edgar Degas, Francisco de Goya, Claude Monet, and others, at a cost of more than $4.3 million. In April, shortly after the museum's opening, he acquired his ninth work by Vincent van Gogh, *Portrait of a Peasant (Patience Escalier)* (fig. 11) for $1,250,000. Wildenstein sent the painting on approval in February, and it stayed at Simon's Malibu home for two months while he considered its purchase. During the time the painting was on approval, Simon was interviewed for a proposed biography. The unpublished transcripts record Simon's opinions about business, politics, and art, and about this painting in particular. These transcripts make it evident that Simon rigorously considered multiple factors when deciding whether to

LEFT
FIG. 11. Vincent van Gogh, *Portrait of a Peasant (Patience Escalier)*, 1888, Norton Simon Art Foundation. CAT. 1130

ABOVE
FIG. 12. Vincent van Gogh, *Patience Escalier*, 1888, oil on canvas, private collection, London

buy a picture. He believed that his first responsibility was to judge whether he or the foundations could afford it. Second, he compared the painting with works by other artists on the market, as well as its value compared with other works by the particular artist. While its beauty was a major consideration, it was also important to know if it was a crowd-pleaser:

> I feel comfortable that it is a very fine work by van Gogh. [Regarding] condition or authenticity, I have nominal questions, but I would reassure myself in any event because I never would fail to do that—that's almost routine. I would say the primary worry would be the economic conditions and the price of it in relationship to other paintings. Now I've got to watch out for my own subjectivity and bias— and I have a tremendous bias towards certain works by van Gogh, and little biases against other works of his. So I've got a bias for it and I've got to think, well it's an abstraction. What the hell, a painting is an abstraction.... How do you weigh that abstraction against economics? It's a painting, it's a precious object, it's a rare work by van Gogh, van Gogh's a good artist, great artist, there aren't going to be that many on the market where you're going to be able to buy a better one cheaper, there aren't many better ones, so it becomes difficult. But then again its rarity, and how far do you go on rarity? It's still an abstraction.[38]

At the time of the interview, thinking about the painting as a rarity was a fairly subjective exercise, as Simon was in fact considering a second van Gogh portrait of the same sitter, the two painted a few weeks apart. Offered by the Lefevre Gallery, the second is now in a London private collection (fig. 12). Characteristically, Simon intensively compared the two works. Here the same bearded, sun-baked farmer wearing a bright yellow straw hat looks pensively at the viewer. Yet the poses and color schemes are strikingly different. Simon ultimately preferred the Wildenstein version, citing the intensity of the sitter's eyes, which was magnified by the juxtaposition of the brilliant yellow hat against the bright blue background.

Simon's restless energy and quest for great pictures persisted through the summer, as he turned again to nineteenth-century works. In late June he bought from Wildenstein Pierre-Auguste Renoir's *Gabrielle with Jean and a Little Girl* (cat. 1164) for $340,000 and the next day from Sotheby's Claude Monet's *Rouen Cathedral, the Tour d'Albane, Morning* (cat. 1165) for close to $444,000. The two paintings did not stay in the collection, and their departure probably had more to do with the rising market for Impressionist works than it did with Simon's feelings about the objects. He sold the Renoir to Eugene Thaw after five years for more than twice its cost, and in 1982 he sold the Monet to the Galerie Beyeler in Basel for over three times its purchase price. In June 1975 he also bought another Monet that remains in the collection, *The Artist's Garden at Vétheuil* (cat. 1173), and he repurchased two paintings that he originally bought years before and lost: Amedeo Modigliani's *The Artist's Wife, Jeanne Hebuterne* (cat. 294) and Jean-Baptiste Camille Corot's *The Cicada* (cat. 390). Both were allotted to Lucille Simon in 1970. When she sold them to the dealer Alexandre Rosenberg in 1975, Simon was able to bring them back into the collection.

Simon bought close to one hundred artworks in 1976, spending about $4.4 million.[39] He had become engrossed with purchasing at auction, believing that many bargains were to be had there. In 1976 almost 50 percent of his purchases were from auction sales, but the cost of those works represented just 10 percent of the year's total expenditure on art. Except for the few occasions when he famously bid in person, Simon had no characteristic practice when bidding at auctions where he was not physically present. He might leave a maximum bid with the auction house before a sale, ask a dealer to bid on his behalf, or occasionally delegate staff to bid. For European sales, he often used the services of the Parisian dealer Sylvia Blatas.

Simon asked Blatas to bid for him at a Swedish auction in March 1976, and in what turned out to be one of his best auction bargains, he bought *Venus and Cupid in a Landscape* by Jacopo Palma il Vecchio (fig. 13) for about $19,500. The low price was based in part on its questionable condition, but also on its attribution in the catalogue as "School of Palma."[40] Simon saw the picture in an advertisement and asked the English conservator Lucilla Kingsbury to travel to Sweden to examine it. Kingsbury reported that the Cupid standing behind Venus was painted over and almost completely hidden by the landscape; only a faint outline of his head and a portion of the bow and arrow were visible (fig. 14). Otherwise, she believed it was in reasonable condition for a painting of its age.

Simon decided to bid on the picture. The chance of a good buy, the striking beauty of the nude, and the beautifully painted landscape, as well as the challenge of proving that it was a work by the master and not his school, considerably piqued Simon's interest. He was always intrigued with questions related to conservation and restoration because of his interest in the exploration and analysis of the issues as well as the opportunity to improve the quality and value of the artwork. Simon asked Kingsbury to clean away the landscape, fill in losses, and reconstruct the Cupid. This arduous process was fraught with questions, importantly, whether it should be restored at all. Was it the artist, for instance, or someone else who painted over the figure? After extensive examination and testing, Kingsbury confirmed that "Palma clearly intended the child to be there."[41] She was able to remove the overpainting and restore the Cupid (fig. 15). There was also the question of attribution. The painting had appeared in a 1962 exhibition as "School of Palma Vecchio,"[42] yet in a notice about that exhibition, the art historian Benedict Nicolson disagreed, saying that the figure of Venus was a Palma original.[43] While it is believed that the background was painted by an artist with stylistic leanings to northern landscape painting, the attribution of Venus herself to Palma is unquestioned,[44] and the painting is considered one of the jewels of Simon's sixteenth-century Italian collection, with a value today of one hundred times its purchase price.

ABOVE

FIG. 13. Jacopo Palma il Vecchio, *Venus and Cupid in a Landscape*, c. 1515, Norton Simon Art Foundation. CAT. 1308

RIGHT

FIGS. 14, 15. Detail of landscape before (*above*) and after (*below*) restoration

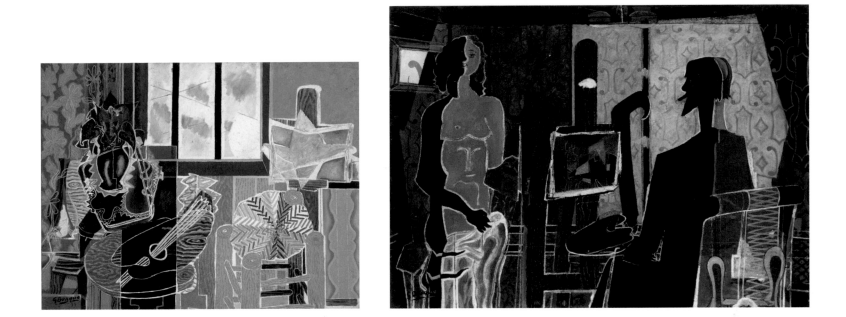

Simon was especially fond of Braque's *The Studio*, 1939 (fig. 16), purchased in 1968. Bought for his private collection, the large, colorful painting occupied an entire pull-out screen in the Simons' family room and was most often the screen on view. It went to Lucille Simon in the 1970 property settlement, and is now in the Metropolitan Museum of Art. As with Paul Gauguin's *Brittany Landscape with Swineherd*, this picture was particularly difficult for Simon to part with. He often brought it up when asking for comparisons with other works by the artist, and when M. Knoedler & Co. offered him a large Braque *Artist and Model* (fig. 17), also painted in 1939, he was fascinated with the possibility of replacing the one he lost.[45] The paintings are indeed very similar. Both depict the artist's studio, and each represents the artist at various stages of work. In *Artist and Model* the artist sits on the right in front of his painting resting on the easel and faces his subject, a nude model, who sits on the left. In the Metropolitan's picture, the subject, this time a still life, is again on the left, and although the artist has temporarily left the scene, his presence is manifest in the empty stool, the easel, and the unfinished painting. Simon frequently compared the two and asked his staff to weigh the advantages of each. He repeatedly pushed the merits of *Artist and Model*, yet I think he always regretted the loss of *The Studio*.

In addition to the buying and selling of artworks and managing the new museum, Simon was still dealing with complex and time-consuming issues surrounding the Shivapuram *Nataraja* (p. 130), which by late 1974 had evolved into a lawsuit with the government of India.[46] On 20 March 1974 Simon met with the Indian ambassador, T. N. Kaul, at the embassy in Washington. They discussed Simon's concern about his damaged reputation; a plan for Simon to be able to exhibit the bronze for a period of time; and India's insistence that it ultimately be returned.[47] He was especially interested in talking about the foundering Asian sculpture exhibition at the Metropolitan Museum of Art, soliciting the ambassador's assistance in dealing with the museum. After two more months of failed discussions with the Metropolitan, Simon officially canceled the exhibition in June. His negotiations with the Indian ambassador on that front proved fruitless, and in December

ABOVE LEFT
FIG. 16. Georges Braque, *The Studio*, 1939, The Metropolitan Museum of Art, New York. CAT. 406

ABOVE
FIG. 17. Georges Braque, *Artist and Model*, 1939, Norton Simon Art Foundation. CAT. 1319

FIG. 18. Asian galleries, Norton Simon Museum, c. 1977, with the Shivapuram *Nataraja* at center left

1974 India filed a $1.5-million lawsuit alleging that Simon bought the statue knowing it had been stolen. In February 1975 the Norton Simon Foundation countersued, arguing that the Indian government knew its whereabouts when it was in an Indian private collection and forfeited any rights to the bronze by not claiming it then. In May the parties reached an out-of-court settlement. In exchange for renouncing interest and title, the foundation would retain exclusive possession and control of the *Nataraja* for ten years, at the end of which time it would relinquish possession to a representative of the Union of India. Further, India would make no claims against the foundation for possessing any other Indian art object purchased before the settlement.[48] The agreement would take effect after the foundation settled its separate dispute with Ben Heller, the dealer from whom it bought the bronze. The foundation had sued Heller to recover the purchase price of the *Nataraja*. That claim was finally settled in April 1976, when Heller agreed to sell the foundation fifteen artworks at a discounted price.[49] As Heller described it, in spite of the litigation and years of uncertainty, in the end Simon won:

He ultimately got a clean bill of health from the Indian government on everything [else] he owned, keeping the Nataraja for ten years, and he got virtually his money back from me, and he got a lot of publicity, so by his standards, he came out pretty well. We never really found out at trial how the issues would've been solved. It would've been a fascinating trial.[50]

The bronze, up until that time stored in a bank vault in London, was brought to Pasadena, where it became the centerpiece of the opening exhibition of Simon's Asian collection (fig. 18) and, ironically, the occasion for a gala reception in August 1976 honoring the Indian ambassador. As stipulated in the settlement, the exhibition label read, "On loan from the Union of India to The Norton Simon Foundation for a period of ten years as part of an amicable resolution of a dispute as to title between the Union of India and The Norton Simon Foundation." The bronze was handed over to a representative of the Indian government on 5 May 1986. Its present whereabouts are not known.

By the end of 1976 Norton Simon had been overseeing the museum in Pasadena for almost three years. He had assembled for the first time hundreds of his artworks, returned from loans across the country. He had assumed responsibility for an institution on the verge of bankruptcy, and his foundations had spent $3.75 million to relieve its debts and renovate the building. None of his staff, including Simon himself, had any museum management or curatorial experience in a museum proper. Yet in nine months they had remodeled the building, hired staff, furnished and staffed a bookstore, supervised the design and fabrication of sculpture bases and exhibition cases, and installed an exhibition. Simon had not only continued to buy hundreds of art objects, but he had overseen dozens of installations. In spite of forgoing a formal opening in March 1975, he had celebrated his Asian collection in grand style with the reception for the Indian ambassador eighteen months later. In March 1976 Darryl Isley (fig. 3, *left*) was appointed director of the museum, replacing George Peters. It was clear to us all, however, that no matter who held the title, Simon was the de facto director. ✷

1. Norton Simon, referring to the reopening of the Pasadena Museum under his direction, in Berges, 1975.

2. For twenty-seven years the museum was at 46 North Los Robles Avenue in a building known as the Grace Nicholson Chinese House and Emporium. The building is now home to the Pacific Asia Museum.

3. Isenberg, 1971.

4. Robert Rowan to Norton Simon, 13 January 1972.

5. Ibid.

6. Darryl Isley to Simon, 28 January 1972.

7. Pasadena, 1972. See also p. 152.

8. Seldis, 1974.

9. Pardo, 1974, p. 1.

10. Robert Macfarlane, speaking at "Collector without Walls: A Symposium on Norton Simon," 27 October 2007.

11. Ibid. For more on the proposed Norton Simon Center at the Metropolitan Museum, see pp. 158–159. The Metropolitan was not the only suitor at the time. Keeping all options open, Macfarlane and Simon also discussed a "Norton Simon Center" with Princeton University (Princeton president William G. Bowen to Macfarlane, 1 October 1973; Dean of the College Neil L. Rudenstine to Macfarlane, 7 January 1974).

12. The trustees were Alfred Esberg, Coleman Morton, Robert Rowan, and board president Gifford Phillips.

13. Gifford Phillips to Macfarlane, 27 March 1974.

14. Simon to Pasadena Museum of Modern Art board of trustees, 22 April 1974.

15. Pasadena Museum of Modern Art, minutes of the board of trustees meeting, 26 April 1974.

16. See, for instance, Coplans, 1975.

17. Macfarlane, as in n. 10 above.

18. Aside from Simon, the group planning the reopening included, at the museum, George Peters and me, and from the foundations, Robert Macfarlane, Julia Mayer, Alvin Toffel, Darryl Isley, and George Abdo.

19. Berges, 1975.

20. Whitman, 1979, p. SC-31. Trustees Esberg, Phillips, and Rowan were so upset by the name change that they considered resigning from the board. They stayed another three years, , however, finally resigning in 1978 over the lack of interest in contemporary art and lending (Muchnic, 1998, p. 222).

21. Berges, 1975.

22. *Time*, 1963, p. 64; Whalen, 1965, p. 146; David Mahoney, interview by Charles Guggenheim, 29 October 1996; Michael Phelps, interview by Davis Guggenheim, 23 July 1996.

23. Seldis, 1967a.

24. The cost of the sold items was $2,056,643.

25. *Los Angeles Times*, 1974a.

26. Simon sold Pablo Picasso's *Open Window in Paris* (p. 85) and *Woman in an Armchair* (cat. 347); Henri Matisse's *Small Blue Dress before a Mirror* (cat. 525); Marc Chagall's *The Violinist* (cat. 583); and Constantin Brancusi's *Little Bird* (p. 230).

27. Adrian Maynard to Isley, 13 September 1973.

28. Maynard to Simon, 24 September 1973.

29. Maynard to Simon, 18 February 1974.

30. Ben Heller, interview by Davis Guggenheim, 31 October 1996.

31. As reported in Isley to Simon, 14 December 1973.

32. Eugene Thaw to Simon, 4 June 1973.

33. The painting was seen and commented on by the art historians David Steadman and Millard Meiss and the conservators Bernard Rabin and Marco Grassi, among others, Norton Simon Museum curatorial files.

34. Simon spent $6,760,100 in 1975 buying thirty-two European artworks, including paintings by Modigliani and Corot that he had previously owned (cats. 294, 390), for $4,348,159. He bought 143 Asian pieces for $2,411,931. Although he made 175 purchases this year, only a relative few were memorable—124, for instance, cost $10,000 or less. He sold just six objects in 1975 for $502,600. The most important works were by Henri de Toulouse-Lautrec (cat. 548) and Picasso (cat. 145).

35. Pal, 2003b, pp. 197–198.

36. Oliver Hoare to Isley, 9 September 1974; Isley to Simon, 7 October 1974.

37. Pasadena, Norton Simon Museum, *Creation, Constellations and the Cosmos*, 4 February–4 June 2001.

38. Berges, 1975.

39. He sold just nine objects in 1976 for $365,180. The most important were drawings by Rembrandt van Rijn (cat. 169) and Jean-Antoine Watteau (cat. 691), and a pre–first edition of Francisco de Goya's *Los Caprichos* (cat. 957).

40. Göteborg, Sweden, Göteborgs Auktionsverk, 24–26 March 1976, lot 334.

41. Lucilla Kingsbury to Simon, 4 October 1977.

42. Stockholm, Nationalmuseum, *Konstens Venedig*, 20 October 1962–10 February 1963, lot 86.

43. Nicolson, 1963, p. 32.

44. Seilern, 1959, p. 9 n. 2; Nicolson, 1963, p. 32; Mariacher, 1968, no. 83; Braham, 1981, p. 32; Rylands, 1989, p. 41.

45. *The Studio* is now in the collection of the Metropolitan Museum of Art, The Walter H. and Leonore Annenberg Collection, Gift of Walter H. and Leonore Annenberg, 1993.

46. See Muchnic, 1998, pp. 223–231.

47. Norton Simon Foundation president Alvin Toffel, memorandum, 25 March 1974.

48. Agreement, Stipulation and Order between The Norton Simon Foundation and the Union of India, 6 May 1975.

49. Settlement Agreement between The Norton Simon Foundation and Ben Heller, 29 April 1976. The artworks are cats. 1335–1349.

50. Ben Heller, interview by Davis Guggenheim, 31 October 1996.

CHAPTER TWELVE

The Opportune Moment
1977–1979

The richest museum in the world cannot make a list of pictures to acquire and then buy them, because 90 percent of them are not for sale and never will be. The life of a collector is one of reacting to opportunity. What comes on the market, for one reason or another, is what is available.—DAVID NASH[1]

NORTON SIMON HAD BEEN COLLECTING artworks by Edgar Degas, Pablo Picasso, and Rembrandt van Rijn since 1955, his first full year as a collector, and, in addition to paintings, owned many bronzes by Degas as well as prints by Picasso and Rembrandt. In 1977, however, three unique opportunities presented themselves and made it possible for Simon to expand his holdings of works by these three artists, vastly broadening the collection and influencing its final shape and character.

Simon had spent a good deal of the early and mid-1970s attending to his South and Southeast Asian acquisitions, but once the Asian galleries were installed, and especially after the Indian art opening in August 1976, he turned his attention again to European art. For the next three years, he spent most of his energy and money on the three above-mentioned artists, and in particular, he focused on their work in multiples. Simon was fascinated with serialized images and reproductions. He was intrigued by how images changed through the various stages of their making, and he studied the question at length as it applied to various editions of etchings and lithographs. He had collected works on paper by Francisco de Goya for many years, buying different states and editions of the same series for comparison. He relished showing the comparisons in Goya print exhibitions (fig. 1). He was equally curious about the subject of sculpture editions and fascinated with the process of bronze casting. When buying the work of Auguste Rodin and Aristide Maillol, he questioned the differences between artist's proofs and the number of casts in the editions.[2] Further, he was used to buying enormous quantities of art en bloc, such as the Duveen Brothers stock, for example, or the inventory of the Klejman galleries, so it was not unusual for him to consider compiling an abundance of works by three artists whom he clearly admired and who already figured strongly in the collection.

OPPOSITE
Rembrandt van Rijn, *The Three Trees*, 1643 (detail), Norton Simon Art Foundation. CAT. 1452

ABOVE LEFT
Norton Simon

ABOVE
FIG. 1. Installation photograph of Francisco de Goya print exhibition, Norton Simon Museum, 1977

DEGAS

Simon had an extraordinary interest in Edgar Degas. Works by the artist were among the first he bought in the 1950s, and by 1976 he had spent more than $4 million on twenty-six Degas paintings and drawings, and thirteen pieces of sculpture. In 1977 only two of the sculptures remained: eight had gone to Lucille Simon, and he had sold three. His long acquaintance with Degas and his sculptures, coupled with his fascination with bronze casting, led to his interest in a group of seventy Degas bronzes, known as the modèle set, from Reid & Lefèvre Gallery, and his purchase in January 1977 of the group for $1.8 million.[3]

Degas made sculptures throughout his career but exhibited only one, *The Little Dancer, Aged Fourteen*, at the sixth Impressionist exhibition in 1881.[4] He was often quoted as saying he was not interested in having his sculpture cast into bronze, which he considered "a medium for eternity."[5] At the time of Degas's death in 1917, he left more than 150 sculptures made of wax and modeling clay. Seventy-four of these figures were salvaged by the artist's dealers and heirs, who authorized their casting into bronze. In order not to destroy the originals during the arduous process of bronze casting, the Hébrard foundry made a set of bronze foundry models, or modèles.[6] Between 1919 and 1921 the foundry used this modèle set as the matrix from which to cast the many editions of Degas bronzes now populating the world's museums and private collections. Cast from molds of Degas's original sculptures, the works belonged to Nelly Hébrard, daughter of the founder A.-A. Hébrard. Virtually unknown to Degas scholars until 1976, these bronzes are closest to the wax originals and differ substantially from the serialized casts.[7]

Desmond Corcoran of Lefèvre Gallery had known of the set's existence for some years, but was mystified as to its place in the history of the bronze casts. In 1976 Michel Kellerman, agent for Mlle. Hébrard notified the gallery that she was prepared to sell the bronzes, and Corcoran traveled to Paris with Degas specialist John Rewald to examine them firsthand. As Corcoran later recounted, "We went together to the Hébrard home and examined the bronzes. John gave them his seal of approval and we agreed to buy them."[8]

Lefèvre Gallery first brought the set to Simon's attention in late 1976. In a 1996 interview, Lefèvre's Martin Summers explained that a complete set of Degas bronzes was such an unlikely thing to find:

There are only four complete sets in the world: one in Copenhagen, one in São Paulo, one in the Metropolitan, and one in Paris. So we examined them, and were just knocked out by the quality. So they weren't fakes, but what were they? What had happened was that when Hébrard made the first casting, using the waxes, he realized that the waxes were so fragile that by proceeding with an edition of twenty-two, he'd cause damage to these delicate objects. So he used the first set as the matrix—and we weren't sure about this. It was actually Norton, after he bought them, who did a lot more research and found more about this.[9] But we then agreed to buy them and we brought them back to London and polished them up, and had an exhibition of the complete set, which was a great coup, a great discovery. The art world was all agog.[10]

FIG. 2. Edgar Degas, *Grande arabesque, first time*, 1885–1890, Norton Simon Art Foundation. CAT. 1397

Summers related that Norton Simon was the first collector the gallery approached, but at the mention of a complete set of Degas bronzes, Simon laughed, declaring that there was no such thing. After hearing about Corcoran and Rewald's examination, he became intrigued and asked Summers to fly to Los Angeles and to bring one of the bronzes (*Grande arabesque, first time,* fig. 2) with him:

> We had a date to meet in the Polo Lounge of the Beverly Hills Hotel. I walked into the Polo Lounge, and there was Norton with Darryl Isley, and they were sitting in one of the booths with [an example of *Grande arabesque, first time*]. So I strolled in with my bronze and put it on the table, and he grabbed mine, and I grabbed his. Then he said, "Well, mine's much better than yours." So I said, "Well, I actually don't agree." He turned to Darryl and said, "What do you think?" Darryl said, "Well, frankly, Norton, I do think you've just got to trust your eyes. I mean, one can see the difference." So then we started to negotiate a bit and he eventually bought them. [We sold the entire set] for considerably less than you'd have to pay for the one piece [*Little Dancer, Aged Fourteen*] now, and made a profit. So Norton landed on his feet and has got the definitive set of bronzes.[11]

In keeping with his interest in sculpture editions, and the relative differences between the modèle bronzes and the casts made from them, Simon bought additional bronze casts so that museum visitors could draw comparisons between a serialized cast and the modèle example. In addition to the sculptures, Simon bought from Robert Schmit in Paris that February the elegant drawing *Dancer (Battement in Second Position)* (cat. 1408). This was followed in March by *Dancers in the Wings* (fig. 3), which he purchased from Wildenstein & Co. After his May purchase of a bronze horse, he waited a year to buy another Degas. Then, in the course of eighteen months, he acquired twelve more.

The first of these was a copy after Nicolas Poussin's *Rape of the Sabines* (fig. 4), a life-size replica that Degas made from the original in the Musée du Louvre, and the earliest and largest Degas painting in Simon's collection. Unlike Simon's other examples, it was on the whole not a painting or subject typically associated with Degas. Rather than a small depiction of dancers or bathers, the work is a large and precise copy of Poussin's seventeenth-century rendering of swirling, struggling figures and battling soldiers. The dealer Eugene Thaw

ABOVE LEFT
FIG. 3. Edgar Degas, *Dancers in the Wings,* c. 1876–1878, Norton Simon Art Foundation. CAT. 1409

ABOVE RIGHT
FIG. 4. Edgar Degas, *The Rape of the Sabines (after Nicolas Poussin),* c. 1861–1862, The Norton Simon Foundation. CAT. 1520

understood that this would be a bold and unusual purchase and patiently gave the collector more than a year to make up his mind. Simon had the painting on approval, which he hung in the museum for fifteen months before he decided to buy it in May 1978. During that time, he instructed his staff to record and send to him comments about the painting from any dealers, art historians, or museum curators we escorted through the galleries. At the end of 1978 Simon profitably purchased for the second time *Woman Drying Herself after the Bath* (p. 56). He had first bought the pastel in 1964 from Wildenstein for $210,000 and sold it back to the dealer in 1974 for $700,000. Almost five years later, in December 1978, he bought it back from Wildenstein for $660,000—$40,000 less than he sold it for in 1974.[12]

Norton Simon's level of interest in Degas is evident in a census of his collection. In less than three decades, Simon bought and sold 130 paintings, drawings, prints, and sculptures by Degas, spending more than $9 million in total. He collected examples in every medium attempted by the artist except photography. Obviously, the bronzes lead by the sheer number of objects in the modèle set, but even without the one acquisition of seventy modèles, one-third of his acquisitions were bronzes. Degas artworks had been among the first Simon collected, and they were also among his last, when in May 1983, toward the end of his collecting life, he purchased three Degas pastels at auction (cats. 1703–1705).

PICASSO

If Norton Simon accumulated a large number of artworks by Degas, he acquired even more works by Pablo Picasso. Although his first two Picasso acquisitions were minor works, his third, in 1960, was the vibrant 1932 oil painting *Woman with a Book* (p. 36). By 1964 he had decorated his home with four paintings and a set of one hundred linocuts by the artist. Over the next decade he added other suites of lithographs and etchings, including *The Vollard Suite* of one hundred prints (cat. 703), and 116 examples from the *347* series, etchings made by the eighty-seven-year-old artist in 1968 (cats. 609, 733). In early 1977 he became interested in the changing states Picasso achieved with the lithographic process and acquired at auction eleven plates from his series *The Bull* (figs. 5, 6, 7). Shortly after this, Simon decided to acquire an exceptional collection of 228 Picasso lithographs.

While in Paris in April, he visited the dealer Heinz Berggruen, who showed him a group of prints from the collection of Picasso's printer Fernand Mourlot. Berggruen arranged to have all of the prints shipped to Los Angeles for Simon's examination. By late June the dealer agreed to sell the entire group to Simon for $450,000, with half payable in July and half due in six months.[13] The collection comprised two sections. The first is a group of unsigned lithographs of progressive

states and artist's proofs. The second is the unique group of "bon à tirer" (good for printing) proofs that Picasso signed to authorize Mourlot to run the editions. When Picasso was pleased with a state, he would mark it *bon à tirer* (fig. 8, lower left). This print established the standard of quality for the rest of the edition. Picasso's prints in progressive states illustrate different stages of his inventive process. With each successive state, the composition is reduced from one of volume, shadow, and detail to a spare, almost abstract form, as seen in *The Bull* series. Picasso would draw his composition, and the printer would pull a series of proof prints. The artist might then develop the print in multiple states, simplifying the image with each state.

Simon was fascinated with the prints and the exhibition potential they provided and asked his staff to have all of the prints framed and placed on view as soon as possible. The installation, which took up seven galleries, opened in December 1977. Never content to sit back and wait for results, Simon advised on the exhibition design as well as the labels and the hanging of individual prints. One review called it an "exemplary selection and installation."[14]

By the beginning of 1977, Norton Simon had made 40 acquisitions of more than 500 paintings, sculptures, and works on paper by Pablo Picasso, spending more than $3.5 million. During the remainder of his collecting life, he spent another

OPPOSITE, FROM LEFT
FIG. 5. Pablo Picasso, *The Bull*, 1945, 1st state, Norton Simon Art Foundation. CAT. 1413

FIG. 6. Pablo Picasso, *The Bull*, 1945, 4th state, Norton Simon Art Foundation. CAT. 1413

FIG. 7. Pablo Picasso, *The Bull*, 1945, 9th state, Norton Simon Art Foundation. CAT. 1413

ABOVE RIGHT
FIG. 8. Pablo Picasso, *Jacqueline with Black Kerchief*, 1958, 2nd state, *bon à tirer* print. CAT. 1449

$3.2 million, adding 356 objects, primarily works on paper. They included etchings and linocuts as well as lithographs, and he pored over catalogues raisonnés of the graphic works, looking to fill gaps in the collection. This was not necessarily because he wanted to have a copy of every print Picasso made. The curatorial staff, for example, was never instructed to search for prints he did not yet own. Rather, it was a quest to accumulate all of the states of one print, such as *Two Nude Women*, of which he bought a range of states over several years (cats. 1435, 1517, 1652, 1670A, 1700).[15] Simon never tired of discussing Picasso's unceasing search for perfection, quoting the artist's statement that a picture was "a sum of destructions."[16] He compared it with his own quest, which he called "the process of becoming." Indeed, his friend Franklin Murphy, UCLA's chancellor, said of Simon, "I think of Norton as a Cézanne or Picasso, unconventional, constantly probing, testing, and continually dissatisfied."[17]

REMBRANDT

Until 1977 Simon did not collect works by Rembrandt with the same intensity that he brought to Degas and Picasso. During the previous twenty-four years of collecting, his eighteen purchases included four paintings and four drawings, and with the exception of one group of late prints (cat. 447), just nine etchings—a number that did not make him a serious collector of Rembrandt's graphic works. In the next three years, however, Simon acquired more than two hundred etchings by the Dutch master, spending almost $2.7 million.

The first and most significant purchase, bought in August 1977, was a collection of 118 etchings from the collection of Charles C. Cunningham Jr. Cunningham was a New England collector who, with the help of the Boston dealer Robert Light (fig. 9), put together an extraordinary group of Rembrandt etchings during the 1960s and 1970s.[18] Not only were there examples of almost all of Rembrandt's greatest works, such as *The Three Trees* (fig. 10), but the quality of the individual prints was exceptionally high. Simon learned in early 1974 that the collection might be for sale, but the owner eventually decided to wait.[19] Somewhat later, the Los Angeles County Museum of Art considered acquiring the prints but could not raise the money.[20] In March 1977 Light approached Simon again, and this time he described the collection in detail. In an effort to pique Simon's interest further, he reminded him of the paucity of Rembrandt prints available on the West Coast, saying, "It is really sad indeed to think that there is no major collection of Rembrandt etchings west of the Mississippi."[21] Light mailed a

list of the objects and—perhaps unaware of Simon's intense concentration on Picasso prints at the time—encouraged him to return to his earlier interest in works on paper. He pointed out that this large collection made it possible to "demonstrate convincingly and in detail the creative growth and process of development over an artist's career." The dealer continued:

> In other words, your collections chart the panorama of art history with telling examples from most schools and periods, whereas this collection would allow you to concentrate on one of the greatest artists of all time and show his development and powerful creativity during his entire artistic lifetime (and, all for a price which is less than a single important painting by the same artist).[22]

Light's observations were not an entirely accurate description of Simon's interests or methods of collecting. By this time, Simon owned large groups of drawings by Claude Lorrain and Jean-Honoré Fragonard, as well as numerous Goya prints (acquired from Light himself), to say nothing of the hundreds of Picassos in the collection (soon to be joined by the Mourlot lithographs). Yet Light was partially correct. He

RIGHT
FIG. 9. Robert M. Light

ABOVE RIGHT
FIG. 10. Rembrandt van Rijn, *The Three Trees*, 1643, Norton Simon Art Foundation. CAT. 1452

witnessed Simon's divesting works on paper in the early 1970s, for instance, and with the exception of Goya and Picasso, none of Simon's other examples could demonstrate an artist's creative growth as successfully as the Rembrandt etchings he offered.

While he was considering the set, Simon asked Light to rank each print, and Light suggested a scale of 1 to 5, ranging from the finest impression extant (1) to "less than satisfactory and should be upgraded when the opportunity arises" (5).[23] Light rated seventeen in the first category and only two in the last, and emphasized that if Simon bought this collection and found prints to fill in the few remaining gaps, he would have "one of the two or three finest collections of Rembrandt etchings in the country."[24]

Light quoted a lump sum of $1.9 million and reluctantly sent him a list with a price breakdown by print. As usual in such transactions, Simon wanted the opinion of every specialist, and he tirelessly studied the subject, reviewing past print auction results and comparing prices. He diligently went over the list and noted the measurements of each print in the margins. Light then had to defend the price of every print against Simon's complaints of excessive markups.[25] After weeks of haggling, they finally agreed on a price of $1.7 million for the group of 118, with $400,000 payable in trade for other artworks Simon owned.[26] In describing the process to an interviewer, Light characterized the experience as a "slightly torturous negotiation":

> The negotiations were very tough—it was a very sizable amount of money in the print area. I thought we had closed the transaction to our mutual satisfaction, and then I received a telephone call at one o'clock in the morning, and I suspect that this is one of Norton's ploys, catching people off balance. He woke me up out of a sound sleep and started to renegotiate the whole transaction, and I lost my cool and swore at him and hung up. And then of course went through hell because I thought I'd absolutely blown this extremely important

deal. And within five minutes he had called me back saying, "Bob, don't get so excited, we're only negotiating—you're getting too emotionally involved," which I thought was absolutely fascinating. When I hung up on him, I think he had two reactions: first of all, he might've blown the deal. In other words, I might've said, that's it, I'm not talking to you anymore, I'm going to offer them somewhere else. But I also think he felt that he had violated the trust of a friend, and that bothered him too, when he called me back and in effect almost apologized, and said, "You're getting too emotionally involved in this negotiation—we can do this, we can put it together."[27]

And in fact they not only put it together, Simon continued to work with Light for the remainder of his collecting life, spending more than $550,000 on another seven Rembrandt etchings and a drawing by van Gogh.

At the end of 1977 Simon added his last painting by Rembrandt when he bought from Eugene Thaw *Portrait of a Bearded Man in a Wide-Brimmed Hat* (cat. 1489) for $1,150,000. An oval panel painting at one time in the collection of Henry Clay Frick, the work is a striking example of Rembrandt's early portrait style.[28] This portrait was followed a few weeks later by *Young Man with Red Beret* (fig. 11), by Rembrandt's colleague

FIG. 11. Jan Lievens, *Young Man with Red Beret*, c. 1629–1630, Norton Simon Art Foundation. CAT. 1501

Jan Lievens, purchased at Christie's for $48,400. In the nineteenth and early twentieth century, the portrait was attributed to Rembrandt.[29] Hoping that the consensus might again return to Rembrandt, Simon wanted the opinion of every visiting scholar of Dutch art, although most agreed that it is probably by Lievens.[30] Simon liked to think that if it was again given to Rembrandt, the small price he paid made it an incredibly good buy. At the same time, with the help of Light and other dealers, he continued to fill gaps in his Rembrandt print collection. Over the next two years he bought more than thirty additional etchings, including two more landscape prints, and unusual examples such as the striking still life *The Shell (Conus Marmoreus)* (fig. 12) and *The Phoenix or the Statue Overthrown* (p. 225). Simon made only one more Rembrandt purchase after 1979—a group of eighty-seven posthumous prints that he bought at auction in 1980. The Rembrandt print collection today is considered one of the most impressive in the country, with more than three hundred examples representing most of the subjects and states from the artist's oeuvre.

FIG. 12. Rembrandt van Rijn, *The Shell (Conus Marmoreus)*, 1650, Norton Simon Art Foundation.
CAT. 1514

IN SPITE OF DARRYL ISLEY'S TITLE of director, it was no secret that Simon was in charge and inevitable that they would eventually clash. During one such argument in August 1977, Isley threatened to quit. Simon talked him into staying just long enough to call a staff meeting and publicly fire him.[31] In September Simon named himself director of the museum. He stated in a museum press release that he became director because of "my historic personal interest in art and my desire to devote myself to the creation of as fine an art museum as possible."[32] It was obvious, however, that he needed another curator to replace Isley and work with dealers. The J. Paul Getty Museum antiquities curator Jiří Frel introduced Simon to Selma Holo, an art historian who specialized in the graphic work of Francisco de Goya, and in October 1977 Simon hired her to work with art dealers on his acquisitions. Simon's interest in Degas, Picasso, and Rembrandt may have dominated his collecting during the last three years of the 1970s, but he still found time to acquire other works. The European examples ranged from a nineteenth-century wood cupboard designed and carved by Émile Bernard to an extraordinary fifteenth-century panel painting, the *Branchini Madonna*, by Giovanni di Paolo.

Bernard's massive cupboard (fig. 13), bought in 1978, is a two-tiered chest decorated with painted carvings and brass hardware. The carvings on the upper and lower registers illustrate Breton women in traditional dress who are picking and eating fruit. After reading the literature on the chest, Simon hoped to advocate a different attribution than that of Bernard. While the doors on the upper portion were credited to Bernard, two publications attributed the lower panel to Paul Gauguin.[33] The two artists briefly collaborated at Pont-Aven in 1888, and Simon believed that further research might prove that he had a unique cabinet partially carved by Gauguin himself. Although it is now agreed that a Gauguin attribution cannot be supported,[34] for many years after its purchase, Simon directed his staff to question any and all scholars of the period about the possibility.[35] Attributions to Gauguin were still on his mind the following year, when he bought at auction Georges Lacombe's *Autumn: The Chestnut Gatherers* (fig. 14). Lacombe, too, worked under the influence of Gauguin, and

FAR LEFT
FIG. 13. Émile Bernard,
Cupboard, 1891–1893,
Jennifer Jones Simon Art
Trust, Los Angeles. CAT. 1513

LEFT
FIG. 15. Giovanni di Paolo,
Branchini Madonna,
1427, The Norton Simon
Foundation. CAT. 1531

FIG. 14. Georges Lacombe, *Autumn: The Chestnut Gatherers*, 1894, Norton Simon Art Foundation. CAT. 1617.

Simon believed that the painting had enough in common with Gauguin's Brittany period that museum visitors walking by the painting (and not bothering to read the label) might assume that the painting was by that artist. He argued—somewhat but not entirely in jest—that this made the Lacombe's $90,000 price a bargain for a "Brittany Gauguin."

As mentioned above, Simon also added works from earlier centuries. Among the most important was a $1.1-million purchase at Sotheby's June 1978 sale, Giovanni di Paolo's stunning *Branchini Madonna* (fig. 15), so called because it was created for the Branchini family chapel in the church of San Domenico in Siena. The relatively low price was a result of questions about the painting's condition. A tempera and gold leaf work on panel, the picture suffered from some damage and heavy restoration, especially in the area of the Madonna's blue robe. Referring to it as one of the most important paintings of the early Renaissance in private hands, Sotheby's specialist

FIG. 16. Édouard Manet, *Still Life with Fish and Shrimp*,
1864, Norton Simon Art Foundation. CAT. 82

David Nash said, "This was a picture which Norton really got quite a good bargain on. There wasn't a lot of competition for this painting."[36] It has been suggested that if it had been cleaned before the sale, it would have fetched twice its hammer price.[37] Simon commissioned the conservator Marco Grassi to remove the old restoration and repair the damage, and the Madonna and Child are now seen in luxurious detail, held aloft by a host of angels' wings.

Simon's purchase of the *Branchini Madonna* paved the way for him to reacquire another painting, Manet's *Still Life with Fish and Shrimp* (fig. 16). Although the picture, which initially cost him $110,000, went unsold in his May 1973 sales, Simon received a $1.5-million guarantee. Yet in the intervening five years, Sotheby's was unable to sell the painting. According to Simon, he arranged with the auction house that if he was the winning bidder (or even the underbidder) on the *Branchini Madonna*, he could buy back the Manet for $400,000, or $1.1 million less than Sotheby's paid him in 1973.[38] Per his agreement, since he was the successful bidder on the *Madonna*, he repurchased the Manet. Simon was fond of relating this transaction, in which he made a profit of $990,000 and still owned the picture. Sotheby's Nash recalled, "Clearly, Norton was delighted and it was a great relief to him that he hadn't had to part with it."[39]

In the late 1970s Simon's attention to Asian art tapered off considerably. The number of acquisitions began to decline slightly after the Asian galleries opened in August 1976. By the end of that year, after four full years of collecting, he had purchased more than four hundred examples of South and Southeast Asian art. He added forty-one objects in 1977, but more than half were small figures from a November sale at Christie's. He bought just six in 1978 and seven in 1979, spending comparatively small amounts. His flagging interest could be attributable to the fact that the Asian galleries now had more objects than they could hold. But it was not entirely about gallery space being filled. When Simon first began to collect Asian art in the early 1970s, there was a tremendous amount of material available at prices that were relatively low compared to Western objects of the same quality. Not only had prices for the best works elevated—Simon's own entry into the field had a direct impact on the rise—but he believed the number of works of high quality had diminished. Whether or not that was true, by the end of the decade Simon could be confident that he had assembled one of the finest collections of Indian, Himalayan, and Southeast Asian art in the world.

The decade of the 1970s was for the Simon collection one of exceptional growth and change (see Appendix). He had spent an astonishing $62.2 million in more than one thousand transactions. In the 1970–1974 auctions, he sold two-thirds of the collection he had assembled in the 1950s and 1960s. He began collecting in the completely unfamiliar area of Indian and Southeast Asian art. By expanding his holdings in Degas sculpture and works on paper by Rembrandt, Goya, and Picasso, he became one of the world's foremost collectors of graphic art. Finally, he assumed control of a failing art museum and made it one of the finest small museums in the country. ❧

1. David Nash, interview by Davis Guggenheim, 14 July 1996.

2. See p. 86 for a discussion of the casting of Matisse's *The Back, I–IV*.

3. There are seventy-four bronzes by Degas. When Simon acquired the modèles from Lefevre, the set was missing four: *Arabesque over the right leg, left arm in front* (marked as bronze no. 1), *Horse at Trough* (no. 13), *Horse trotting, the feet not touching the ground* (no. 49), and *The Schoolgirl*. Norton Simon acquired the modèle cast of no. 49 in 1978 and another cast of *The Schoolgirl* in 1979. The Art Foundation is still without examples of casts 1 and 13.

4. Paris, 35 bd des Capucines, *6ème Exposition de peinture*, 2 April–1 May 1881, no. 12.

5. Vollard, 1924, p. 112.

6. The wax and clay originals were bought in 1956 by Mr. and Mrs. Paul Mellon. Many are now in the National Gallery of Art, Washington, D.C.

7. For a description and in-depth technical analysis of the bronzes, see Campbell et al., 2009.

8. Desmond Corcoran, e-mail message to Sara Campbell, 22 February 2010.

9. Summers was correct that Simon performed considerable research; he talked with many Degas art historians including John Rewald and Charles Millard and sent Millard to London to examine and approve the bronzes before he agreed to buy them. After their purchase they were lent to the Fogg Art Museum, where the conservator Arthur Beale performed extensive technical examinations. All of the specialists confirmed that this set, marked "modèle," is the original master set of bronzes from which all other casts were produced. For more on the technical aspects of the modèles, see Barbour and Sturman in Campbell et al., 2009.

10. Martin Summers, interview by Davis Guggenheim, 6 June 1996.

11. Ibid.

12. The $660,000 represented $310,000 in cash plus Monet's *Water Lilies* (cat. 1332) valued at $350,000.

13. Darryl Isley to Berggruen, 19 July 1977.

14. Seldis, 1977.

15. Mourlot, 1970, nos. 16 i–xviii.

16. Picasso to Christian Zervos, in Ashton, 1972, p. 38.

17. Berges, 1965, p. 75.

18. Cunningham was the son of Charles Cunningham Sr., the director, successively, of the Wadsworth Atheneum and the Art Institute of Chicago. Some of Cunningham's best prints came from the collection of Captain Gordon W. Nowell-Usticke, which was sold at Parke-Bernet Galleries in New York in 1967–1968.

19. Isley to Simon, 7 February 1974.

20. Isley to Simon, 19 January 1977.

21. Robert Light to Simon, 8 March 1977.

22. Ibid.

23. Light to Simon, 14 March 1977.

24. Ibid. Light thought perhaps only the Morgan Library's collection was superior, having been "put together many years ago and almost complete." Light originally offered ninety-seven prints. In a letter of 27 June 1977 he added another twenty-one.

25. Light to Simon, 13 May 1977.

26. Light to Simon, 29 July 1977. Along with $50,000 in cash, the Art Foundation traded to Light ten working proofs from Goya's *Disasters of War*, a first-edition set of Goya's *Los Caprichos*, and two drawings by Jean-Baptiste Greuze (cats. 958, 529, 684A-B).

27. Light, interview by Davis Guggenheim, 20 June 1996.

28. Rembrandt's companion portrait of the sitter's wife is in the Speed Art Museum, Louisville, KY.

29. See, for instance, Hofstede de Groot, 1916, vol. 6, no. 431.

30. Scholars attributing the painting to Lievens include Seymour Slive, Christopher Brown, Claus Grimm, and Arthur Wheelock.

31. Isley went into art dealing, working at first for Wildenstein and later as a private dealer. He and Simon patched up their differences and Isley returned to the museum as a consulting curator for a brief period in the early 1980s. He died in April 1990.

32. Simon, in Norton Simon Museum press release, 14 September 1977.

33. Jaworska, 1972, p. 26; Luthi, 1974, p. 15.

34. Eisenman, in Brettell and Eisenman, 2006, p. 478.

35. Selma Holo to Simon, 28 August 1979; Sara Campbell to Ronald de Leeuw, 6 June 1989; Campbell to Simon, 29 June 1989.

36. Nash, interview by Davis Guggenheim, 14 July 1996.

37. Edward Lucie-Smith, interview by Davis Guggenheim, 6 June 1996.

38. Conversation with the author, 30 May 1989.

39. Nash, as in n. 36 above.

CHAPTER THIRTEEN

Refining the Legacy
1980–1989

What was good about Norton, and what made everybody forgive him was his caring and passion about works of art.
—BEN HELLER[1]

AT THE BEGINNING OF THE 1980S, Norton Simon's enormous collections contained about 5,500 objects, representing almost 1,300 separate acquisitions. He managed a similar number of artworks from the former Pasadena Art Museum, now called the Norton Simon Museum. He was still actively acquiring objects and constantly on the telephone with his curator, Selma Holo, as they formulated various deals. Simon visited the museum frequently, often several times a week, but surprisingly he never had an office in the museum. He preferred to meet with the staff in their offices and to walk with them through the galleries. We would thrash out exhibition designs, which could and would change weekly, as he strove for the perfect hanging. Simon often portrayed the museum's management as one with a customary line of authority in decision making regarding the collection, but there was no question that he was the director.

A 1979 *New West* magazine article about the museum described Simon's hands-on supervision of the display of the collection, pointing out that his imprimatur was on the placement of every painting and every sculpture. *New West* quoted him as saying, "I pay a lot of attention to detail, to how paintings are displayed, to grouping them properly. We disagree at times. When we disagree, I prevail. But it's a happy relationship."[2] Nevertheless, he occasionally allowed his curators to prevail. We were encouraged to state our opinions, and he welcomed candor and disagreement. It was essentially a happy arrangement, undoubtedly because, as curators, we completely understood the line of authority. It was a more difficult situation for those designated as director, a position that at any other institution would imply a substantial degree of power and autonomy. Simon inevitably clashed with anyone in that role, which led to Isley's departure as director in 1977. After Isley, Simon brought in Alvin E. Toffel, whom he had met when Toffel was managing California congressman Paul "Pete" McCloskey's campaign to challenge President Nixon in the 1972 election. After the election, Toffel began working for Simon and the foundations as an advisor on business and government matters. In September 1977 Toffel became the museum's president and chief executive officer, while Simon retained the role of director. In

OPPOSITE
Guido Cagnacci, *Martha Rebuking Mary for Her Vanity*, after 1660 (detail), Norton Simon Art Foundation.
CAT. 1695

ABOVE LEFT
Norton Simon

the 1979 article mentioned above, Simon outlined the relationship, describing himself as the nominal art director who reported to the museum board and administration. When this was reported to Toffel, he joked, "If you believe Norton reports to me, you believe in Santa Claus."[3] While there was no question as to who was in charge, the curatorial staff nominally reported to Toffel, who handled the day-to-day museum and foundation administrative matters. In the late 1970s the curators—Selma Holo and I—were joined by David Steadman, who had left the Princeton University Art Museum in January 1974 and moved to Southern California to become an associate professor of art history and director of the art galleries of the Claremont Colleges.[4] Remembering the very successful Princeton exhibition, Simon invited Steadman to work one-quarter time at the museum to advise him concerning art acquisitions and displays. Toffel eventually became discontented with his role as administrator and left the museum in March 1980.

After Toffel's departure, Simon again decided to try a more traditional approach to museum management and, as he had done with James Brown in 1967 and Isley in 1976, hired an art historian in the role of museum director. David Bull, a former restorer at London's National Gallery and later in private practice, came to California in 1978 to head paintings conservation at the J. Paul Getty Museum. Intrigued with issues of conservation and restoration, Simon often invited Bull to his home to discuss the quality and condition of artworks, and early in 1980 he asked him to leave the Getty to take over as director of the Norton Simon Museum.

ABOVE
FIG. 1. Dieric Bouts, *Resurrection*, c. 1455, The Norton Simon Foundation. CAT. 1646

OPPOSITE
FIG. 2. Mr. and Mrs. Norton Simon at a press conference regarding the purchase of Dieric Bouts, *Resurrection*, April 1980

Undeterred by warnings from colleagues, Bull assumed the directorship on 1 April 1980 and found the experience of working with Simon exhilarating: "I had I think for the first six months the greatest time I have ever had in my life. Being with him, talking with him, trying to learn from him; it was absolutely magical."[5] Bull quickly became involved in the heady world of art acquisitions, when, two weeks after his arrival, he participated in an extraordinary and typically convoluted purchase at auction by Simon. Sotheby's had informed Simon in February that Dieric Bouts's *Resurrection* (fig. 1) would be sold on 16 April in London.[6] A fifteenth-century distemper painting on linen, the picture shows Christ triumphantly rising from the tomb, which is set in a vast landscape. The work was originally part of an altarpiece; other known panels are *The Annunciation* (J. Paul Getty Museum, Los Angeles), *The Adoration of the Magi* (private collection), and *The Entombment* (National Gallery, London). Interested in the picture, Simon decided not to bid in person or to ask an agent to bid on his behalf. Instead, he arranged for Mrs. Simon to travel to London, accompanied by Bull. Sotheby's originally estimated that the Bouts would fetch $400–500,000 but, based on the extraordinary interest shown by Simon and museums such as the National Gallery, London, which owned the *Entombment* panel, raised the figure to $1 million. When the hammer finally came down, the painting brought the remarkable sum of $4.2 million—the third-highest price ever paid at auction and the most expensive work of art to enter the Norton Simon collections.[7] The London dealer Geoffrey Agnew, bidding on behalf of the National Gallery, was the underbidder. In an elaborate plan reminiscent of the *Titus* auction, Simon was on the telephone giving instructions throughout the sale. David Bull later recounted the process:

> Norton said that he would be on the phone with [Sotheby's specialist] Tim Llewellyn while Derek Johns was the auctioneer. Norton told me to go out and buy three envelopes, seal them and label them A, B and C. When I asked him what I should do with them, he said, "We are going to have some fun." Then he said that he would be on the phone with Tim and that at any given time during the bidding he would ask, through Tim, for me to open envelope A, B or C. "Of course," he said, "there will be nothing in the envelopes." I arrived at Sotheby's and sat in the third row so that I could watch Sir Geoffrey Agnew in the front row. We had already worked out that he was going to bid. Derek Johns came up to me having had a call from Norton, red in the face, and said angrily, "It is hard enough to hold an auction, but playing games with envelopes is just too much." The arrangement with Tim was that if I were to continue bidding, he would hold the telephone to his left ear, and if I was to stop he would put it to his right ear. I also asked Derek, that if we made the winning bid, he would announce, "Bought by Jennifer Jones Simon on behalf of the Norton Simon Museum." When the hammer came down on our winning bid and Derek made his announcement, Jennifer turned to me and said, "I did not know we were bidding. Please come out to my car and tell me what was going on!" Just before I went out with her I gave the three empty envelopes to Derek. Afterwards, I realized that NS wanted publicity. If it went for a record price, he would get all the publicity, but if not, the envelope trick would catch the attention of every TV camera in the room.[8]

In just a week, the painting was in Los Angeles and hanging in the galleries, the subject of a press conference in the museum. Sitting in front of the painting, the Simons discussed its acquisition and its importance to the collections (fig. 2). It was an extraordinary public-relations move on many levels. A beautiful former movie star paying millions for a Renaissance picture made headlines, and the press conference ensured that the story appeared in dozens of newspapers and was discussed on radio and television. After a favorable review of the painting was printed in the *Los Angeles Times*,

Simon wrote an appreciative letter to the reporter, describing his own reaction to the Bouts:

> In these unsettling times, journalistic expression can inspire people in our community and can incite their desire to look, to see, and to feel. The profundity of the faith projected from mankind's creative endeavors through a sculpture of Buddha, a biblical painting, or an exquisite landscape should never be forgotten. I appreciate your sentiments and agree with you, the Bouts is priceless.[9]

At $4.2 million, the Bouts accounted for almost 64 percent of the $6.6 million Simon spent on artworks in 1980. After five years of relatively few deaccessions, Simon sold sixty artworks that year for $8.9 million. The sixty objects had originally cost a little over $2 million. In other words, his $6.8-million profit paid not only for the Bouts but for all of his purchases in 1980. Nonetheless, some of the works that were sold are unfortunate losses for the collection. Eugene Thaw bought three: Camille Pissarro's *Place du Théâtre Français, Afternoon Sun in Winter* (cat. 237), Jean-Auguste-Dominique Ingres's *Study for the "Odalisque and Slave"* (cat. 705), and Pierre-Auguste Renoir's *Gabrielle and Jean with a Little Girl* (cat. 1164). The two most profitable for Simon were sold at Christie's in October 1980. Simon bought Edvard Munch's *Three Girls on a Bridge* (fig. 3) from Marlborough Gallery in May 1963 for $130,000 and sold it at Christie's for $2 million. Picasso's *Woman with Guitar* (cat. 148), also from Marlborough, cost $125,000 and sold for $2.8 million. The Indian collection was not immune to deaccessions, and Simon sold to Spink & Son a Chola bronze Shiva for $800,000 that he had purchased eight years earlier for $340,000 (cat. 886).

Simon planned on selling not only personal and foundation art in 1980 but also a few contemporary works from the former Pasadena Art Museum at Christie's 16 May sale. These projected deaccessions unfortunately led to a lawsuit brought by three former museum trustees against the Norton Simon Museum. In looking through the Christie's auction catalogue before the sale, Robert Rowan noticed two works that he had

FIG. 3. Edvard Munch, *Three Girls on a Bridge*, 1902, private collection, Switzerland. CAT. 139

donated to the museum: Richard Diebenkorn's 1953 *Urbana I* and Franz Kline's *Composition 1948*. Rowan, along with two other former trustees, Alfred Esberg and Gifford Phillips,[10] sued to stop the sale, charging the museum with depleting its assets. The museum responded that the new board under Simon's leadership had acted responsibly by renovating the museum and eliminating its debts, actions the former trustees had not undertaken. Furthermore, the new board had adopted a formal deaccession policy declaring that any money realized from deaccessioning would be used to upgrade the collection. A legal battle ensued, and a temporary restraining order stopped the sale. A trial followed more than a year later, in September 1981, in which the court found that the claims against the Norton Simon Museum by former trustees were completely without merit, and the ruling was upheld on appeal.

While the case was pending, Simon was concerned that the court might actually assume control of the museum and thus of the pictures. He therefore directed his curatorial staff to hurriedly lend his most important and valuable artworks out of state. Along with many other paintings, the Raphael *Madonna and Child with Book* and Giovanni di Paolo's *Branchini Madonna* went to the Phoenix Art Museum. Degas's *Women Ironing* and Zurbarán's *Still Life with Lemons, Oranges, and a Rose* were lent to the Philadelphia Museum of Art.[11]

Although the museum ultimately prevailed in the lawsuit, Simon was angered that his management had been questioned, especially after the foundations had distributed $3.75 million creating what he believed was a better institution. Furthermore, he was genuinely surprised and hurt. Bull witnessed the striking alteration in Simon's attitude, noting, "He lost interest in his collection almost overnight. It was terrible. I was left sitting there basically doing nothing for months, trying to find something to do because he wasn't taking any interest in the museum at all."[12] The inactivity finally led to the resignation of both Holo and Bull in February 1981.[13] Even with the relative inactivity, however, Simon found it difficult to manage without a curator to work with dealers, and shortly after Holo's departure, he hired Tessa Helfet to fill the position. Helfet was another art historian with an interest

in prints and had been with Sotheby Parke Bernet in New York and most recently in its print department in Los Angeles. After David Bull left, Simon decided to return to a museum administrator with a background in business rather than art. He initially hired Jeffrey Rupp, Deputy Director of the California Department of Transportation, whom Simon knew through his position as chairman of the state transportation commission.[14] Rupp directed museum operations from June 1980 until the end of 1982. Walter Timoshuk, formerly with Hunt-Wesson Foods, was recommended to Simon by a former Hunt colleague. Timoshuk joined the staff in late 1982 to manage the day-to-day business of the museum and the foundations.

The distractions of the lawsuit may have been responsible for the fact that Simon made fewer than thirty acquisitions in 1980, and, aside from the Bouts, only a small number were noteworthy. One of these important acquisitions in 1980, the *Aldrovandi Dog* (fig. 4) exemplifies Norton Simon's

FIG. 4. Giovanni Francesco Barbieri, called Il Guercino, *Aldrovandi Dog*, c. 1625, The Norton Simon Foundation. LAI. 1654

ability to make bold purchases, but it also reflects his at times deep ambivalence about an artwork. An immense portrait of a dog by Giovanni Francesco Barbieri (called Guercino), the *Aldrovandi Dog* is a picture that Simon first knew about in 1972, bought eight years later in 1980 and returned after a year, only to reacquire it in 1984. Simon first became aware of the painting in May 1972, when Sotheby's Peter Wilson told him that it would be appearing in its July sale.[15] The mastiff fills the composition, looming over a landscape. The coat of arms on his collar indicates that he was a prized possession of the Bolognese Count Filippo Aldrovandi, whose castle is possibly the one depicted in the background. When he considered the purchase in 1972, Simon sent a color transparency to LACMA's Kenneth Donohue, who responded bluntly, "There are certainly more important and interesting Guercinos in private collections which may be on the market eventually. I would not recommend it."[16] Simon was still intrigued enough to ask the London conservator Herbert Lank to examine the picture, and Lank reported that it was "generally in good condition. On the whole the landscape is more interesting than the dog."[17] In the end, Simon decided not to bid on the work at auction and learned after the sale that it had been bought by the London dealer Leonard Koetser for £110,000, roughly 20 percent more than its presale estimate.[18]

Simon remained curious about the painting, and when Darryl Isley inquired about it the following year, he learned that Koetser owned the picture together with the Galerie Nathan in Zurich, and that the price was now double the hammer price.[19] Seven more years passed before Simon again showed an interest in the work, and in October 1980 he reached an agreement with the Galerie Nathan whereby the Norton Simon Art Foundation would buy the painting for two million Swiss francs ($1,153,600), with payment made no later than sixteen months after delivery. However, the foundation retained the right to return it at any time within the sixteen months.[20] As soon as the painting arrived at the museum and was uncrated, it was placed on exhibit, where it remained for the duration of the agreement period.[21] As with so many of his works, Simon wanted to know the opinion of every scholar, dealer, and auction specialist who visited the museum. One specialist, Christopher Burge of Christie's, later remembered:

> I always think of that Guercino Dog as one of the greatest masterpieces in the museum. But it's a tough picture, it's not everybody's picture at all. And it's not the sort of picture you'd expect to see in a collection by somebody who's just buying safe masterpieces, it's really an out of the ordinary picture—one of the three or four most fascinating Guercinos ever painted, and typical of Norton.[22]

During every visit to the museum Simon spent time in the Baroque gallery, watching visitors' reactions. As a former dog owner, he was attracted to the subject.[23] If someone complained about the dog's dominance, he pointed to the beauty of the landscape. Nevertheless, he was ambivalent enough that he returned the picture in 1982. Then, two years later, David Koetser (son of the 1972 auction buyer Leonard Koetser and Galerie Nathan's partner in the picture) asked Simon if he might be interested in the painting at a more agreeable price, this time 1.7 million Swiss francs (about $784,000).[24] Simon was tempted, and eventually Helfet was able to negotiate an amount of $600,000—almost half the $1,153,600 he had originally paid in 1980. Before its repurchase, Simon investigated the possibility of a joint acquisition with the Getty Museum and had a favorable response from the Getty's director, John Walsh.[25] However, once the sale was complete, Simon changed his mind, much to the consternation of the Getty staff. As Helfet reported, "Burton [Fredericksen] was *very* disconcerted—said that it was NS who had suggested it in the first place."[26]

The Guercino in 1984 was not the first time Simon and the Getty Museum conferred about a shared ownership. The first such conversation transpired in 1977, when Simon approached the Getty about jointly buying Lorenzo Lotto's *Madonna and Child with Two Donors*, to be sold at Christie's on 2 December. Stephen Garrett, director of the Getty, responded:

> In the available time I have not been able to get approval for this from my fellow Trustees. Thus, I have instructed Burton that he should proceed to bid solely on behalf of the Getty Museum. If we purchase the painting, I would be pleased to discuss with them whether they would like to make a joint acquisition between us. I know that a number of our Trustees favor such collaboration between us and I would very much like to put proposals to them for future joint acquisitions.[27]

The Getty was the successful bidder on the Lotto but decided to retain sole possession.

The two museums did eventually collaborate on purchases, first a Nicolas Poussin in 1981, and then a Degas in 1983. The joint acquisitions were aided by the recent appointment of Simon's friend and former Hunt Foods executive Harold Williams as head of the J. Paul Getty Trust. Simon and Williams agreed to bid jointly on Poussin's *The Holy Family with the Infant Saint John the Baptist and Saint Elizabeth* (fig. 5) at Christie's in April 1981. Purchased by Wildenstein on behalf of the Getty and Simon, the painting cost about $3.6 million.[28] At the time of the acquisition, Simon stressed the "new level of cooperation" between the two museums.[29] The export license was delayed until September to permit British museums the opportunity to raise the necessary funds to keep the picture in Britain, but when that proved unsuccessful, the painting traveled to California. The picture moves between the two museums every two years.

The Poussin purchase was Simon's first important acquisition in 1981.[30] The second was Francisco de Goya's portrait of Dona Francisca Vicenta Chollet y Caballero (fig. 6). The painting had appeared in a July 1981 sale at Christie's in London, where it was bought by the London dealer Thomas Agnew & Sons for £900,000 ($1,615,000). Shortly after the sale, Simon received an option from Julian Agnew to buy the painting for 25 percent over the hammer price if he were satisfied with its condition after cleaning and restoration. While

FAR LEFT
FIG. 5. Nicolas Poussin, *The Holy Family with the Infant Saint John the Baptist and Saint Elizabeth*, Norton Simon Art Foundation and The J. Paul Getty Museum, Los Angeles. CAT. 1671

LEFT
FIG. 6. Francisco de Goya y Lucientes, *Dona Francisca Vicenta Chollet y Caballero*, 1806, Norton Simon Art Foundation. CAT. 1684

the work was being performed by the restorer Mario Modestini, Simon's staff researched the painting's authenticity and quality. Simon was pleased with the restoration results and agreed in December to buy the picture at the established price of a little more than $2 million.

Aside from the Poussin and the Goya, Simon bought just a few other works on behalf of the foundations in 1981, including an architectural scene by Hubert Robert (cat. 1682) and a Degas drawing of a horse and jockey (cat. 1672). Most of his purchases that year were South Indian decorative bronzes and small pots for his private collection (cat. 1677). In addition, he deaccessioned twenty-two foundation and personal artworks that year for almost $3.2 million (and a profit of $2.3 million). Again, a few went to Eugene Thaw, including the lovely Paul Cézanne watercolor *Still Life with Pears and Apples, Covered Blue Jar, and a Bottle of Wine* (cat. 225), which is now in the Pierpont Morgan Library, New York, and Georges Braque's *Still Life with Pipe* (cat. 652), now in the Museum Berggruen, Berlin.

Simon's 1981 and 1982 deaccessions were not simply to refine the collections. He was investigating potential sales with an eye both to increasing the foundations' endowment and to have greater flexibility to build the old master collection. He often discussed with the staff the museum's long-term financial well-being and emphasized the need to boost the endowment.[31] He used several institutions as examples, but he most frequently cited the inadequate endowment left to San Marino's Huntington Library, Art Collections, and Botanical Gardens by its founder, Henry E. Huntington. Although the institution today enjoys greater economic security, in the 1980s it was known to be suffering financial hardships. Helfet recalled that Simon had a "very real concern that the foundations be left with a big enough endowment not only to survive but to prosper."[32] In addition, he wanted to have ready resources to make quick decisions. Helfet described one such discussion of possible deaccessions:

> Mr. Simon and I were discussing how to increase the war chest. Part of his motivation was the strong belief that great old masters were becoming harder to find—whereas there were

still opportunities to replace great moderns—and he wanted the flexibility to move quickly. He wanted to create a sum big enough so that the future of the museum, and the foundations' continued support of the museum, would not need to be dependent upon anyone/anything else.[33]

Whether through sales of objects or investments, Simon succeeded. To this day, the museum operates through a combination of its own assets, as well as grants from, and coordination of programming with, the Simon foundations.

With this concern about endowment in mind, Simon sold twenty-eight foundation artworks in 1982, and, compared to previous years, the prices were staggering. These sales amounted to almost $20 million, with a profit of almost $16 million. The losses to the foundation collections were equally stunning. A few were sold at auction, but the most important works were sold to private dealers. Eugene Thaw bought six oils, including the collection's only painting by Eugène Delacroix, *Abd Er Rahman, Sultan of Morocco Reviewing His Guard* (cat. 837), two paintings by Vasily Kandinsky (cats. 922, 923), and Piet Mondrian's *Composition with Red, Yellow, and Blue* (cat. 320). The Swiss dealer Ernst Beyeler acquired Claude Monet's *Rouen Cathedral, the Tour d'Albane, Morning* (fig. 7) and Henri Matisse's four bronze bas-reliefs, *The Back, I–IV* (p. 86). The Marlborough Gallery bought David Smith's *Cubi XXVIII* (p. 90). The most notable deaccession, however, was the sale in June 1982 of an early Picasso painting, *Nude Combing Her Hair* (fig. 8).

The Picasso was first discussed when Helfet and Simon brainstormed about works to sell. They both were against deaccessioning a work readily associated with the museum (such as Rembrandt's *Titus*). They also agreed that the object should be by an artist who was so well represented in the collection that its loss would not severely affect the overall presentation, and that the proceeds from the sale should be big enough to warrant the object's absence. Picasso was an obvious choice, and Simon suggested the artist's 1906 *Nude Combing Her Hair* (fig. 8).

TOP
FIG. 7. Claude Monet, *Rouen Cathedral, the Tour d'Albane, Morning*, 1894, Beyeler Foundation, Riehen, Switzerland. CAT. 1165

ABOVE
FIG. 8. Pablo Picasso, *Nude Combing Her Hair*, 1906, Kimbell Art Museum, Fort Worth. CAT. 558

Helfet had recently walked through the museum with Edmund Pillsbury Jr., then director of the Kimbell Art Museum in Fort Worth, and reported that he had been particularly enthralled with the *Nude*. Selling directly to a museum was unusual for the Norton Simon Art Foundation, but Simon believed the Kimbell had more financial and managerial flexibility than most institutions. In addition, he liked the idea of saving the commission one ordinarily pays to an agent. He suggested Helfet telephone Pillsbury to learn the extent of his interest:

> As Ted's comments to me had not been in terms of a purchase, I had to call him up and say that we were discussing a possible sale— that I wasn't at all persuaded that NS might consider the 1906 Picasso, but thought I would see *if* the Kimbell might be interested *if* indeed NS were to seriously consider, etc., etc.—very reluctant, but dangling a hook. I remember NS initially splitting the negotiation with me but finding Ted difficult and finally (to my eternal amusement) handing him over to me, saying "Why can't he just say what he means?"[34]

While Simon may have encountered difficulty with the negotiations, Pillsbury eventually agreed to purchase the Picasso for $4 million, an extraordinary sum in the early 1980s. When Simon told me about the deaccession, I replied that it was a terrible mistake, in spite of the impressive price (and a profit of more than $3.3 million on the painting's $680,000 original cost). I argued that this sale violated his proviso to sell only a work by an artist who was well represented in the collection. Although we had an extremely impressive number of graphic works by Picasso, the number of paintings left in the collection was very small, and the loss of one more would be significant. Of the nineteen Picasso paintings Simon had acquired by June 1982, he had sold fourteen—and *Nude Combing Her Hair* would be the fifteenth. That would leave just four, with none from the decades 1900–1920. Simon countered with his standard argument about relative value, asking what was more important for a museum collection, a Picasso or a Giovanni di Paolo, knowing that the preference would be for the older, presumably rarer object. He continued to buy in all areas, but in his last decade of collecting, he bought just one more painting by Picasso, *Woman with Mandolin* (cat. 1712). Dated 1925, it did not fill the 1900–1920 void.

Simon made even fewer purchases in 1982 than he had in 1981—just fifteen for $1.3 million. There were several interesting additions to the collections, including a study made by Georges Seurat when he was a student. Throughout his long buying career, Simon had always been fascinated with the work of young artists, their sketches, and their copies of the works of other artists. He had many early works that he believed presaged the artist's later achievements, such as an 1899 Mondrian pastel landscape (cat. 1120) or an ink drawing by Picasso from 1901 (cat. 1629). He enjoyed comparing Honoré Daumier's *Study for "Saltimbanques Resting"* (cat. 49) with the artist's final version (cat. 19). He had a number of examples by Picasso, including his painting *Women of Algiers, I* after Delacroix (p. 146), and many printed studies after Cranach and Rembrandt. In addition, Simon enjoyed comparing two still lifes in his collection, Cézanne's *Vase of Flowers* and the copy Odilon Redon made after it (cats. 403, 1001), and arguing about whether Redon had subjugated his own style in the process. A purchase in 1982 fell along these lines when he acquired for his private collection Seurat's *Angelica at the Rock (after Ingres)* (fig. 9) from Wildenstein. Simon appreciated the formalism and harmony manifest in the work of both artists. He liked not only to compare the Seurat with the version by Jean-Auguste-Dominique Ingres in the Musée du Louvre, but he often insisted that he could see evidence of Seurat's later work in this student copy.

Simon also took pleasure in comparing examples by the same artist, and in November he bought from Colnaghi in London Nicolas de Largillière's *Portrait of Lambert de Vermont* (fig. 10), his third work by this eighteenth-century French painter. The acquisition of a third, arguably unneeded Largillière, represents yet one more instance of what makes the Simon collection such a personal one. Two other Largillière portraits (cats. D30, D31) came with the Duveen collection and were fine examples of eighteenth-century French portraiture. Yet Simon rejected his curators' concerns about spending resources to add a third Largillière painting when there were gaps in the collection that could be filled instead. He rightly argued that the superb portrait was a bravado rendering of velvety blacks and intricate lace that would become a highlight of the eighteenth-century collection. Simon continued to listen to his tastes above all else. Scott Schaefer, senior curator of paintings at the J. Paul Getty Museum, admired Simon's methods, recalling, "He bought picture by picture, but he seemed to have some vision about how it all worked together. It wasn't about the history of art; it was about the individual great object."[35]

Along with the Largillière that November, Simon bought from Colnaghi the magnificent *Martha Rebuking Mary for Her Vanity* by Guido Cagnacci (fig. 11). Simon Dickinson, former old master painting specialist at Christie's, had found the picture "in a stable storeroom stacked up with dozens of paintings where it had been undiscovered for 100 years."[36] Christie's had mistakenly attributed the picture to Guido Cagnacci and assistants when it appeared in a December 1981 London auction with a presale estimate of £25–35,000. Simon investigated the painting before the sale and, along with others, surmised that while there were condition problems, the work was possibly not a studio effort but by the master alone. Competition brought the price up to £209,000 (about $400,000), with the London dealer Colnaghi the winning bidder. Afterward, Simon talked Colnaghi's Richard Herner into agreeing to an option of $600,000 good for two weeks after the painting had been restored. Colnaghi stressed that the painting's size and condition ruled out its traveling to Los Angeles for examination and requested that Simon journey to

ABOVE
FIG. 9. Georges Seurat, *Angelica at the Rock (after Ingres)*, 1878, Norton Simon Art Foundation. CAT. 1690

ABOVE RIGHT
FIG. 10. Nicolas de Largillière, *Portrait of Lambert de Vermont*, c. 1697, Norton Simon Art Foundation. CAT. 1696

RIGHT
FIG. 11. Guido Cagnacci, *Martha Rebuking Mary for Her Vanity*, after 1660, Norton Simon Art Foundation. CAT. 1695

London instead.[37] Simon prevailed, and in August, after restoration was completed, the picture was shipped to California. By agreeing to pay for part of the cost of restoration and transportation, as well as to purchase two additional paintings (the Largillière mentioned above and a portrait by Louis Tocqué, cat. 1697), Simon was able to have the price of the Cagnacci dropped to a little less than $525,000.

Simon bought only six objects in 1983, three of which were Degas pastels in Sotheby's May sale of the estate of Doris Dick Havemeyer, daughter-in-law of the collector Louisine Havemeyer. In addition to two monotype and pastel landscapes, Simon purchased *Waiting* (fig. 12), the second artwork bought in cooperation with the J. Paul Getty Museum. According to Helfet, who accompanied him to the sale, "the Getty had authorized the purchase, half share to a certain point, and Simon thought that if it went above that, he might even carry it on and buy it outright."[38] Helfet and Simon met before the sale with the auctioneer John Marion to discuss— yet again—a series of secret and complicated bidding signals. Simon worried that if he were seen bidding, it might drive up the price. Marion did not want to take the bid, because he was nervous that he would muddle the signals, but Simon insisted. As it turned out, the signals were so complicated that even Simon did not know what had happened. Helfet recalled:

> When the gavel came down I whispered to him, "Congratulations, you've got it." And Simon was nervous that he hadn't got it. He said to me "Are you quite sure?" Because no one could see he was bidding. It was all these signals going on. He was so anxious that he asked me to please go and speak to David Nash and confirm it. So in the middle of this black tie auction, I went to the rostrum in front of everybody, called David Nash down to the front of the stage, and whispered to him, "Can you please confirm that Simon has bought the thing," and went back to Simon and said, "Yes, you did buy it." I think it was just the excitement of the moment and it was such a convoluted bid that even he wasn't quite sure.[39]

ABOVE
FIG. 12. Edgar Degas, *Waiting*, c. 1879–1882, Norton Simon Art Foundation and The J. Paul Getty Museum, Los Angeles. CAT. 1704

OPPOSITE LEFT
FIG. 13. Jean-Auguste-Dominique Ingres, *Baron Joseph-Pierre Vialètes de Mortarieu*, 1805–1806, The Norton Simon Foundation. CAT. 1706

OPPOSITE RIGHT
FIG. 14. Vincent van Gogh, *Head of a Peasant Woman in a White Bonnet*, 1885, The Norton Simon Foundation. CAT. 1713

Aside from the three Degas pastels, Simon bought just two other paintings in 1983, an interior scene by Édouard Vuillard (cat. 1702) and, for $1.1 million, a portrait by Ingres of Baron Joseph-Pierre Vialètes de Mortarieu (fig. 13). Completed by the twenty-six-year-old Ingres in 1806, the portrait depicts in precise detail the young mayor of the artist's hometown of Montauban. The sitter displays a Romantic air, with dark curls and high collar framing his face. At various times Simon owned nine drawings by Ingres, all later sold, but this was his first and only painting by the master.

In May 1984 Simon was stricken with Guillain-Barré Syndrome, a disorder of the nervous system that usually progresses from weakness in the limbs to paralysis. He was in the hospital for several weeks, and when he was released, his home became an intensive care unit, with round-the-clock nursing care. Therapies may reduce the severity of Guillain-Barré and accelerate recovery for many, but the seventy-seven-year-old Simon never fully regained the use of his limbs and spent the rest of his life in a wheelchair. For some time the staff was not aware of the extent of his illness, or how it would affect his collecting and management of the museum. The most profound change was his physical absence from the museum. However, Simon had always very effectively conducted business by telephone, and he eventually adjusted to substituting telephone communication with his curators for museum visits.

Simon bought fourteen artworks in 1984, and the purchases occurred only in June and at the end of the year. Those in June were not undertaken while he was ill but merely concluded negotiations that had been under way for some time. The first, in June, was the completion of a commission begun in December 1982 from the Musée Rodin, Paris, for three full-scale studies of Auguste Rodin's *Burghers of Calais* (cats. 1709–1711).[40] Also in June he finally repurchased Guercino's *Aldrovandi Dog*. For the rest of the summer and fall his energies were dedicated to regaining his health. When he again began to communicate with the art staff, he felt a keen need to convince Helfet and others that he was still a player in the market, and in November he bought seven paintings in two days of auctions at Sotheby's in New York. The first, and most important, was Vincent van Gogh's *Head of a Peasant Woman in a White Bonnet* (fig. 14). The painting is a representation of the painter's mistress, Sien de Groot, and served as a preparation for one of the figures in van Gogh's important canvas *The Potato Eaters*.

Clearly Simon's illness affected his collecting, both physically and psychologically, but it could be argued that he had stopped collecting even earlier. He had, for instance, added nothing to the foundations' collections for almost a year in 1983 and 1984, well before he contracted Guillaume-Barré Syndrome. In fact, to all intents and purposes, Norton

Simon had stopped collecting in mid-1980. In May of that year (a month after Simon bought Dieric Bouts's *Resurrection*), the former Pasadena Museum trustees initiated legal actions that led to the lawsuit described earlier. The lawsuit almost completely curtailed Simon's interest in adding to the collection. He continued to buy artworks for the foundations during the next few years, including several important pictures, but he never again equaled, or even approached, the intense level of acquisitions of the 1960s and 1970s (see Appendix). Simon added a handful of objects from 1984 to 1989, but he reduced his acquisition level to the point that he was no longer a serious or active collector. Aside from his illness, the slowdown can be attributed to his concern about increasing the foundations' endowment to provide long-term financial security to support the proper display of the collections. Moreover, the galleries of the Norton Simon Museum were now brimming with artworks, and many more objects were in storage. Once he could see it all together and play with it, he did not have the urge to keep buying that had possessed him in the previous decade. Finally, by the late 1980s, his diminished vitality combined with his concern for the endowment made him unwilling to compete in what he saw as an unreasonably inflating art market.

FIG. 15. Pierre-Paul Prud'hon, *The Abduction of Psyche by Zephyrus to the Palace of Eros*, Norton Simon Art Foundation. CAT. 1722

In 1985 he bought only two objects, both from Alexandre Rosenberg in January. The first was a small *Fête Champêtre* by Jean-Baptiste Pater (cat. 1721), and the second was Pierre-Paul Prud'hon's *The Abduction of Psyche by Zephyrus to the Palace of Eros* (fig. 15), another painting with which he had had an on-again, off-again relationship for years. The painting was first offered by a Swiss dealer in 1972. It resurfaced with a London dealer in 1978 and traveled to Pasadena, where it hung in the galleries, on approval, for six months before it was returned. With a New York dealer the following year, it journeyed once more to Pasadena and was again in the galleries, this time for a year, until December 1980. Again it was returned. Alexandre Rosenberg bought it at a New York Sotheby's sale in May 1981 and sent it to Simon on approval from June until October 1983, when once more it was sent back. Finally, a year later in November 1984, Rosenberg again sent the painting. Simon's continued ambivalence about the work, a smaller version of Prud'hon's famous Salon painting *The Abduction of Psyche* in the Musée du Louvre, can be attributed in part to condition problems. There are also questions about its position vis-à-vis the larger work. Several possibilities presented themselves, ranging from its being a preparatory version for the Salon painting, to a reduced copy made by Prud'hon for an admirer, to a copy of the painting by another artist. It is now thought to be in all probability a collaborative work, begun by Prud'hon but worked on by his student, Constance Mayer.[41] Simon finally decided to buy it in January 1985.

Simon's inactivity with dealers and accessions meant that Tessa Helfet found herself with little to occupy her time, and in April 1985 she moved to Paris to become an art dealer.[42] After the purchase of the Prud'hon in January 1985, it was fifteen months before Simon bought anything else. The Zurich dealer Marianne Feilchenfeldt and her son, Walter, visited the museum in late 1985 and toured the galleries with Simon. While viewing the Degas collection, she told him that she had a 1907 bronze bust of Degas by Paul Paulin (cat. 1723). Simon was intrigued to have a portrait of one of his favorite artists, and after its purchase in April 1986, he placed it in the Degas galleries.

Even though Simon no longer actively collected, he still telephoned me every day, often several times, to discuss the state of the galleries and installation design. Still, Helfet's absence left a void, and he missed having someone on staff who would discuss the art market with him and interact with dealers. Although he relied on his curators to communicate with dealers and occasionally still talked with them himself, such activity was now more for his amusement than it was indicative of an active interest in purchasing artworks. In January 1986 he made his last hire of a curator, Paula Kendall. As with Helfet, who recommended her, Kendall came from the print department at Sotheby Parke Bernet in Los Angeles.[43]

Simon still wanted to know what works dealers had available and what people thought of the collection, but another year passed before he again became interested in buying anything. When he read the catalogue for a Sotheby's May 1987 sale of nineteenth- and twentieth-century Russian art, he decided that he could pick up great bargains on unrecognized artists. In spite of objections from his art staff, who worried that the works did not fit into the existing collection, Simon directed Kendall to buy six paintings and drawings by Russian artists (cats. 1724–1729). Although they have increased in value many times, they are seldom exhibited.

The last artwork to enter the Norton Simon collections during his lifetime was a painting by Gustave Courbet, entitled *Peasant Girl with a Scarf*, purchased at the end of 1989 (fig. 16). The portrait belonged to John T. Dorrance Jr., the son of the founder of Campbell Soup, and it was in the Dorrance sale at Sotheby's in New York in October. Sotheby's promoted the sale by exhibiting the paintings at its Beverly Hills showrooms, where Simon saw the Courbet and expressed an interest in it. He had acquired eight paintings by Courbet over the years, but never a female subject. Momentary ambivalence, or perhaps his failing health, made it difficult for him to make up his mind before the auction, and the picture went instead to the dealer William Acquavella for $550,000. Simon was no longer up to the rigors of negotiation and agreed to buy it from Acquavella three months after the sale for $900,000.

FIG. 16. Gustave Courbet, *Peasant Girl with a Scarf*, c. 1849, Norton Simon Art Foundation. CAT. 1732

In spite of Simon's diminished interest in new acquisitions, he continued to supervise the museum's curatorial staff and its programs. It was not until late 1986 that he distanced himself from exhibitions to the point of allowing me to independently organize temporary shows from the foundation and museum collections. Even so, he never stepped away from the management of publications, ranging from gallery brochures to museum catalogues. When a new collections handbook was planned in 1989,[44] Simon not only demanded final say in the artworks to be included but oversaw their placement, size, and the overall design of the book. His ability to supervise steadily diminished in his last years, but he continued to be interested in the collection. We would often converse about the artworks, their placement, and their relative value, and he never lost his curiosity about the opinions of every visiting specialist. His greatest concern, however, was about the ultimate disposition of the collection. ❧

1. Ben Heller, interview by Davis Guggenheim, 31 October 1996.

2. Whitman, 1979, p. SC-35.

3. Ibid. Toffel left the museum in 1980 to work for Frederick Weisman, Simon's brother-in-law, who controlled Mid-Atlantic Toyota Distributors, Inc. He died in 2005.

4. Steadman was later director of the Chrysler Museum, Norfolk, Virginia (1980–1989) and the Toledo Museum of Art (1989–1999).

5. David Bull, speaking at "Collector without Walls: A Symposium on Norton Simon," 27 October 2007. Bull was director of the Norton Simon Museum from April 1980 to February 1981.

6. Derek Johns to Selma Holo, 15 February 1980.

7. *Juan de Pareja* by Diego Velázquez was sold in 1970 to the Metropolitan Museum of Art for $5.5 million. Titian's *Death of Actaeon* brought $4.3 million in 1971, when it was sold to the J. Paul Getty Museum. The Titian, however, was refused an export license and now hangs in London's National Gallery. Simon's next most expensive pictures were the Raphael *Madonna and Child with Book* ($3 million), the Zurbarán *Still Life with Lemons, Oranges, and a Rose* ($2,725,000), and Rembrandt's *Titus* (a little more than $2.2 million).

8. Bull, e-mail message to Sara Campbell, 11 June 2008.

9. Simon to *Los Angeles Times* writer William Wilson, 29 April 1980.

10. Rowan, Esberg, and Phillips were the three Pasadena Museum of Modern Art trustees who invited Simon to manage the museum in 1974 and were the three Pasadena representatives who stayed on the board after Simon assumed control of the institution. They resigned from the board in June 1978 in protest over what they believed was the museum's lack of attention paid to the contemporary collection (Isenberg, 1978).

11. As Muchnic, 1998, p. 253, notes fifty-one artworks were sent on short notice to thirteen museums in the United States and Canada. For a thorough account of the lawsuit, see ibid., chap. 26.

12. Bull, as in n. 5 above.

13. Selma Holo left Simon to work for the University of Southern California, where she created USC's Museum Studies Program. She now directs the university's Fisher Museum of Art. David Bull became the chairman of painting conservation at the National Gallery of Art, Washington, D.C. He is now a freelance art conservator in New York.

14. Simon was chairman of the California Transportation Commission 1978–1982.

15. Peter Wilson to Simon, 15 May 1972. The painting was being sold in London, Sotheby's, 12 July 1972, lot 7.

16. Kenneth Donohue to Simon, 23 May 1972.

17. Herbert Lank to Simon, 1 July 1972.

18. Darryl Isley to Simon, 12 July 1972. Isley reported that the dealer Anthony Speelman thought the price was "ridiculous": "a nice picture, but a curiosity really and certainly not worth £110,000." According to Speelman, a deranged man in the saleroom bid indiscriminately and drove up the prices on a number of works to unreasonable levels. The man was eventually removed from the room, and the objects he had bought were put back on the block and resold. Speelman attributed the overly high price of the Guercino to the fact that the man had been the underbidder.

19. Isley memorandum, 21 September 1973. The price was now set at £225,000.

20. Agreement dated 8 October 1980.

21. The agreement had authorized the cleaning and restoration of the picture, and it was removed from exhibit only long enough for it to be cleaned and restored in February 1981.

22. Christopher Burge, undated [1996] interview by Davis Guggenheim.

23. In Conrad, 1968, Simon is asked to name the first thing he would save if his house were on fire. "That's easy," Simon replied, "Rex, our German Shepherd."

24. David Koetser to Simon, 27 March 1984.

25. Helfet to Simon, 17 May 1984.

26. Helfet to Walter Timoshuk, 12 June 1984.

27. As reported in a memorandum from Simon's administrative assistant Linda Traister to Norton Simon, 1 December 1977.

28. Each institution paid $1,716,947.

29. Wilson, 1981.

30. Simon made just twenty acquisitions in 1981, spending a little more than $4 million.

31. The Code of Ethics of the American Association of Museums states that the disposal of collections should be solely for the advancement of the museum's mission, and that sale proceeds should be used only for "acquisition or direct care of collections." Simon had no interest in AAM accreditation since he did not want to be bound by any rules that might accompany such endorsement. He believed that the foundations' collections were properly under the care and management of their respective boards of trustees and officers. In any event, his goal of amassing a sufficient endowment had no other purpose than guaranteeing the "direct care" of the collection.

32. Helfet, e-mail message to Campbell, 25 November 2008.

33. Ibid.

34. Ibid.

35. Scott Schaefer, speaking at "Collector without Walls: A Symposium on Norton Simon," 27 October 2007.

36. Campbell, memorandum of conversation with Simon Dickinson, 19 January 1994.

37. Richard Herner to Simon, 19 April 1982.

38. Helfet, interview by Davis Guggenheim, 6 June 1996.

39. Ibid.

40. Helfet to the Musée Rodin, 16 December 1982.

41. Brettell and Eisenman, 2006, p. 54.

42. Helfet now works for a private collector in England.

43. Kendall worked at the museum from January 1986 until October 1987. She was subsequently a curator for a private collector and taught in the Los Angeles public schools.

44. Campbell et al., 1989.

azzo Vecchia · Vienne

Courtships

Suddenly everyone realized this is truly a major collection.
—DAVID STEADMAN[1]

Simon's acclaimed success both as a collector and as steward
of the Norton Simon Museum led many other institutions
to propose partnerships with the Simon collections. I think
he entertained these offers for several reasons. He was always
thinking about alternatives and better options. Certainly he enjoyed the flattery. But
in large measure his interest related to what Simon's biographer Suzanne Muchnic
has called his "dancing with immortality."[2]

In late 1979, Simon, along with California Institute of Technology (Caltech)
president Marvin L. "Murph" Goldberger and Norton Simon Museum trustee John
G. Braun, began discussing ways that Caltech and the museum could work together.
The discussions evolved into a proposed "Project Medici," which would result in the
donation of the Norton Simon Museum and its collections to Caltech. The university
would use the Simon collections as the cornerstone of its Humanities Department,
and the museum would be guaranteed the resources of a renowned institute to ensure
its future. However, Goldberger eventually wrote to Simon that Caltech's faculty was
not completely enthusiastic:

> I am pleased that you appreciated the fact that the report from my
> faculty committee did not represent a final Caltech position. I have
> some concrete ideas about how we might approach what you had
> earlier called your ultimate fantasy in a more gradual and evolu-
> tionary fashion. I think that we have an opportunity to do some-
> thing truly unique in the academic world and something which the
> museum world has never seen.[3]

Whatever Goldberger meant by Simon's "ultimate fantasy," by February 1980 Simon
had decided against a connection. He declared that while he wanted to cooperate
with Caltech in improving its arts and humanities program, "It is my definitive intention to continue to build and expand and even more importantly, improve the operation of the museum."[4]

Notwithstanding his high hopes for the museum, the lawsuit filed by the
former Pasadena Museum trustees made him consider a move completely out of

OPPOSITE
Jean-Honoré Fragonard, *The Meeting of Anthony
and Cleopatra*, after Giovanni Battista Tiepolo,
1760–1761 (detail), The Norton Simon Foundation
CAT. 716

ABOVE LEFT
Norton Simon

the area. Aside from lending numerous paintings out of state during the litigation, he approached San Francisco's mayor Dianne Feinstein in July 1981 about moving his collection to one of that city's museums. Feinstein jumped at the idea, arranging a formal dinner for the Simons at the California Palace of the Legion of Honor and bringing officials to Pasadena to view the collection. However, after the museum prevailed in the lawsuit, he suspended the talks.

FIG. 1. Aerial view of Norton Simon's houses, Malibu, c. 1983

Again in early 1987 Simon explored the idea of merging with an institution of higher learning, this time the University of California, Los Angeles. Simon had long been a supporter of the university. In addition to serving as a regent, he had donated artworks to UCLA's Wight Art Gallery, Elmer Belt Library, and Franklin Murphy Sculpture Garden.[5] When the Simons moved to Beverly Hills in 1983, they gave their Malibu residence consisting of two adjoining houses (fig. 1) to UCLA to be used as a conference center.[6] The latest discussions in 1987 centered on dividing the art collection between the museum in Pasadena and a building constructed on prime university-owned Wilshire Boulevard property in Westwood. One of the many issues that disturbed Simon, however, was the university's plan to provide parking below ground. Simon believed that it was inconvenient and unattractive to approach an art museum from an underground parking lot.[7] The negotiations continued for a few months, but, as with Simon's other flirtations about the long-term disposition of his collection, the talks eventually came to an end. Alan Charles, UCLA's vice chancellor for university relations, who participated in the discussions, believed that Simon was a "reluctant debutante" who never completely expected the deal to be resolved, adding, "He may have meant it intellectually because he loved to negotiate, but on an emotional level I don't think he was ever really committed to UCLA or any other suitor that came along."[8] Norton Simon Museum trustee Frank Rothman, who was intensely involved in the UCLA negotiations, thought that Simon's reluctance stemmed from more serious concerns:

> What he was worried about, more than anything, was what would happen to his collection after he died. It was a very valuable collection; it needed care; it needed people who would worry about it, and he didn't trust everybody. Who was going to run it? I think there are a lot of people who care about the collection, and will care for it, but he worried.[9]

Another suitor was the National Gallery of Art in Washington, D.C. When the news first broke about a possible deal with UCLA, National Gallery director J. Carter Brown made overtures about a broader, more national merger, writing to Simon:

> I have been reading with great interest the accounts about the plans for UCLA. Anything that keeps the magic of [your] museum intact seems to me eminently worthwhile. My personal dream would be to have it rise from local to national status, and somehow be related to our National Gallery of Art. All my career here I have looked for ways to make that word national come true. My admiration for the Los Angeles area as a world-class art center is unbounded, and if you should ever think of us in this connection, I hope you will not be shy in letting us know.[10]

The Norton Simon Museum board concluded in June 1987 that an agreement with UCLA was unlikely, and that it was preferable "to pursue a course of independence for the museum."[11] However, another year passed before the termination of UCLA negotiations was publicly announced, and the Norton Simon Foundation and the university each issued press releases to that effect.[12]

Within days, a flurry of offers arrived from several other institutions. Martin Lerner, Indian and Southeast Asian art curator at the Metropolitan Museum of Art, proposed joining Simon's Indian and Southeast Asian art collections with that of the Metropolitan, and later its board chair Arthur Ochs Sulzberger urged Simon to reconsider the Norton Simon Center first suggested by director Thomas Hoving some fifteen years earlier.[13] The Fine Arts Museums of San Francisco director Harry S. Parker more boldly suggested collaboration along the lines of the UCLA proposal—a merger of the two collections: "I have followed with great interest the newspaper accounts of your discussions with UCLA," he wrote. "You will recall that we are underrepresented in first rate works of art of the type which you have been so skillful and fortunate in acquiring. There may be a natural match in our interests."[14] LACMA director Earl A. Powell was no doubt aware of Simon's tortured history with the Los Angeles County Museum of Art and perhaps for this reason did not solicit a permanent association. Instead, he continued ongoing discussions regarding collaborative loans.[15] Likewise, the Huntington Library, Art Collections, and Botanical Gardens in San Marino did not suggest a merger. Rather, board chairman Stanton Avery proposed an informal association between the administrators, curators, and staff of the Huntington, the Norton Simon Museum, and the J. Paul Getty Museum, "to build and maintain each in the premier positions they have attained."[16] Of all of the proposals, however, the most impressive came from J. Carter Brown:

> Predictable as it might be, I nonetheless do not hesitate to write you on learning of the recent pullback from the UCLA plans. I need not remind you that our National Gallery is unique in many ways. The faith and credit of the United States is pledged to maintain the Gallery and its collection in perpetuity. And, perpetuity, when you stop to think about it, is a big word. Now that the whole momentum of the United States is shifting to the Pacific Rim, I, for one, would very much like to see this institution have an opportunity to serve this nation on the west coast. Your collection is so superb, that it would be highly logical to have it on view in the west in any setting you wished. My own view is that it looks so beautiful in Pasadena, that one need not look further. Obviously, however, one would be open-minded.[17]

Simon talked with Brown in early September and again the following spring. After a visit to Los Angeles, Brown discussed the issue with his board: "The light was basically green to explore the possibilities with you. A national solution would seem an obvious and appropriate fit. They authorized me to take some judicious soundings on the Hill."[18]

In late July Brown wrote Simon an extraordinary letter offering preliminary ideas about forming the Norton Simon Museum as "America's national gallery in the west." He believed that "no private collection of old master art in America can rival the quality and range shown in the Norton Simon Museum," and he felt that the National Gallery, located as it is in Washington, was "hampered in making original works of art of great quality available to those in the West who find it difficult to get to Washington." Knowing that Simon wanted to keep his collection together, he added, "The quality of the selection in the Norton Simon Museum is such that its impact is greatly enhanced by keeping its installation together as a document of American collecting achievement." Brown believed the future of the Norton Simon Museum "could be assured as a federally supported, national museum in the same way that the collections of the National Gallery are in the two buildings on the Mall." He proposed that the art collections in the Norton Simon Museum, as well as (eventually) Simon's private collection, "come to the nation, to form part, technically and legally, of the collections of the National Gallery of Art." Unlike the present collections in the National Gallery, however, the Simon objects would remain on view in Pasadena, with expenses underwritten by the museum in Washington. Having no doubt discussed with Simon the collector's favorite museums, Brown summoned appropriate comparisons when he added, "The vision would be to present a facility of at least the quality of the Frick in New York, the Kimbell in Fort Worth, the Kröller-Müller in Otterlo, all of which present a unique kind of art experience by virtue of their scale and the attention to artistic quality that they embody." He ended by suggesting that the entity might be called "the Norton Simon Museum, National Gallery of Art."[19]

More proposals from Washington followed, including suggested bylaws for the new institution, but talks were finally suspended. Simon found it impossible to relinquish control of the collection he had worked so long and passionately to form. When asked for a reason, he blamed the breakdown on his distrust of the federal government. Eugene Thaw recalled his role in the negotiations and Simon's reasons for pulling back:

> Toward the very end of his life, the last time I went out to see him I had dinner with him; I was supposed to meet Carter Brown there and to talk about a merger of the Norton Simon Museum with the National Gallery in Washington, which I was promoting. I thought it would be a good idea to have it become the National Gallery West and he toyed with it for a while and then he dropped it. He said, "You talk about the full faith and credit of the U.S. government but I want to be independent. I don't want to depend on that because I don't believe in that." Sure enough, a couple of years later, the National Gallery shut down while the Vermeer show was on. So he was right in a way that even the full faith and credit of the U.S. government didn't keep the National Gallery open at a crucial period. He had these quirky ideas, but they always had a grain of truth in them.[20]

The J. Paul Getty Museum proved to be the final institution with which Simon conducted a short courtship. As early as 1973 he briefly considered a lending collaboration with the Getty similar to those he had arranged with other museums.[21] After Harold Williams assumed the presidency of the Getty Trust in 1981, rumors of a Getty-Simon association surfaced. Williams's long relationship with Simon, as well as the joint ownership of the Poussin and Degas paintings and Mrs. Simon's position on the Getty Museum board,[22] added some credence to the hearsay. In 1989–1990 the two institutions officially discussed the possibility of a merger, to be accomplished in part through a sale of the Simon collections to the Getty for $250 million.[23] Subjects included the makeup of a joint board, the name of the institution ("Getty-Simon" versus "Simon-Getty"), the future of the Pasadena site, the disposition of the Simon Museum staff, and the legal implications. The Getty wanted to merge its collection with the Simon collections, whereas Simon wanted them displayed separately. That, coupled with Simon's desire to control both institutions and his inability to let go of his collection, doomed the talks. At a symposium in honor of Simon's centennial year, Harold Williams addressed the issue:

> One frequent subject of discussion between Norton and me when I was at the Getty was the possibility of combining the Getty and the Simon. I wanted it for two reasons. I felt the resources of the Getty would be able to assure that the identity and integrity of the Simon collection would be best preserved. And I envisioned the ability to build on the complementary aspects of the two collections using the resources of the Getty. I made numerous proposals, and modified every response to Norton's negotiations. Several times I thought we were pretty close. Eventually I realized that this was not the Norton who could walk away from the company. This collection was Norton's immortality. I told him so and he didn't respond. And we never discussed it again.[24]

In a rare—and what proved to be his last—interview, Norton Simon spoke at length with *Los Angeles Times* writer Suzanne Muchnic in June 1990 about his art collection.[25] Citing rumors that Simon was seeking another museum to take charge of his collection, rumors often "ignited by Simon himself," Muchnic allowed that "Simon wouldn't be Simon if he weren't negotiating with someone somewhere." When she asked him directly about the future of his collection, Simon

FIG. 2. Pasadena Art Museum galleries, c. 1970

assured her that he wanted to keep the Norton Simon Museum independent. "Our desire is to keep going on our own, if we can, and we really think we can. I have a lot of faith in my wife, my board and our people, and the people of the United States who have supported the museum."[26]

The Norton Simon Museum, with ongoing support from The Norton Simon Foundation and the coordination of its programming with the Norton Simon Art Foundation, has continued as the independent institution Simon envisioned. In the mid-1990s, under the leadership of his widow, Jennifer Jones Simon, the board of trustees approved plans to upgrade the facility. Originally built to showcase the Pasadena Art Museum's mid-twentieth-century collection of large-scale paintings and sculpture, the design by Thornton Ladd and John Kelsey featured an open floor plan of curved walls and long corridors leading from one expansive gallery to the next (fig. 2). The arrangement was not as favorable to the multifaceted Simon collection, which covered more than two thousand years of art history from many cultures. Between 1996 and 1999 the architect Frank O. Gehry, a longtime friend of Mrs. Simon and at that time a Norton Simon Museum trustee, directed a remodeling of the building, which provided a design more suited to the collections. While the building's curved exterior walls remained unchanged, the interior was entirely renovated. The European collections benefited when long corridors became a series of independent rooms, ceilings were raised, and skylights brought filtered natural light into the galleries (fig. 3).

FIG. 3. Norton Simon Museum galleries, c. 1999

FIG. 4. Norton Simon Museum Asian galleries, c. 1999

FIG. 5. Norton Simon
Museum garden, c. 1980

FIG. 6. Norton Simon
Museum garden, c. 2002

Asian sculpture now occupies a separate level, enhanced by galleries lined in red sandstone. A sandstone colonnade provides a backdrop for hanging stone reliefs, suggesting Indian temple structures (fig. 4). The former garden, dominated by a large expanse of lawn and a tiled reflecting pool (fig. 5), has been replaced with a lush sculpture garden created by the landscape designer Nancy Goslee Power. The new garden (fig. 6) features a meandering pond filled with water lilies, a waterfall, and almost two hundred species of plants. The renovation was completed in 2000, when the museum's theater was remodeled by Arthur Gensler, Jr. & Associates.

Along with the facility's renewal, museum programming continues to promote Simon's appreciation of the myriad dialogues that exist between artist and viewer. In addition to the approximately one thousand works from the collection continually on view, each year the curatorial department mounts three to six temporary exhibitions centered on the collection. Both the permanent and temporary exhibitions are further explored through lectures and symposia, adult education courses, music and dance performances, and hands-on activities for children. In 1994 the Norton Simon Art Foundation undertook a massive program to produce a series of scholarly collection catalogues documenting segments of the holdings. There are now seven books in the series.[28]

In keeping with Simon's wish, the Norton Simon Museum successfully continues as an independent entity. The art collection remains his most enduring legacy. ❧

1. David Steadman, undated [1996] interview by Davis Guggenheim.

2. Muchnic, 1998, p. 264.

3. Marvin Goldberger to Simon, 13 December 1979.

4. Simon to Goldberger, 7 February 1980.

5. Cats. 216, 284, 302A–G, D139, D222. In 1967 Simon commissioned from the Musée Rodin a cast of Auguste Rodin's *Walking Man*, which he gave as an anonymous gift to UCLA in honor of Franklin Murphy.

6. UCLA sold the property in 1987.

7. Frank Rothman, interview by Davis Guggenheim, 19 June 1996. Rothman was a trustee of the Norton Simon Museum.

8. Alan Charles to Suzanne Muchnic, in Muchnic, 1998, p. 274.

9. Rothman, interview by Davis Guggenheim, 19 June 1996.

10. J. Carter Brown to Simon, 27 February 1987.

11. Minutes of the Norton Simon Museum of Art Board of Trustees meeting, 3 June 1987.

12. Minutes of the Norton Simon Museum of Art Board of Trustees meeting, 16 June 1988.

13. Martin Lerner to Simon, 24 June 1988; Arthur Ochs Sulzberger to Simon, 20 March 1989.

14. Harry S. Parker to Simon, 20 June 1988.

15. LACMA director Earl A. Powell to Simon, 27 June 1988. The Norton Simon Museum lent nineteen artworks to LACMA from 1988 to 1994 (Los Angeles, 1988a).

16. Huntington trustee Stanton Avery to Simon, 24 June 1988.

17. Brown to Simon, 20 June 1988.

18. Brown to Simon, 15 May 1989.

19. Brown to Simon, 27 July 1989.

20. Eugene V. Thaw, interview by Anna Jhirad of Guggenheim Productions, 25 March 1997.

21. See chap. 10.

22. Jennifer Jones Simon served on the J. Paul Getty Museum board from 1984 until 1992.

23.. Getty Trust executive vice president Stephen Rountree to Walter Timoshuk, 28 November 1989; undated memorandum (c. November 1989) from Harold Williams to Simon; Williams to Simon, 21 March 1990.

24. Williams, speaking at "Collector without Walls: A Symposium on Norton Simon," 27 October 2007.

25. Muchnic, 1990, pp. 9, 92–94, 95.

26. Ibid., p. 9.

27. Barnett, 2002; Pal, 2003a; Pal, 2003b; Pal, 2004; Brettell and Eisenman, 2006; Sander et al., 2006. Campbell et al., 2009.

CHAPTER FIFTEEN

The Collection

When you sum up who were the great American collectors of the nineteenth and twentieth century, the name of Norton Simon would have to be very near the top of that list.
—J. CARTER BROWN, 1996[1]

The Norton Simon collection stands as testimony to Simon's exceptional eye and his insistence on excellence. It is regarded as one of the finest in the United States, containing thousands of artworks spanning more than two thousand years of creative accomplishment. Its distinction is all the more stunning when one considers that Simon assembled it from nothing in the short span of three decades. Christie's Christopher Burge recognized Simon's achievement not only in terms of the collection's superiority and the short amount of time it took to form, but in light of the particular time in which he collected:

> It's one thing to do it in the 1920s or in the 1880s—when works of art were readily available and were not incredibly expensive in rela-tion to other things. But to do it in what was the 1960s and 1970s was phenomenal, because he went from scratch to building one of the great collections in America, either public or private. It's partly gut, it's partly nose, it's partly a visual instinct, and he had that in a very large degree.[2]

The collection's reputation eventually worked to its advantage. Its outstanding quality was itself the catalyst by which it became even greater as it attracted better and better objects. The dealer Eugene Thaw, for instance, has said that when he acquired a great artwork and thought about the collection into which it would best fit, Simon was the first client he would call.[3]

I am frequently asked if Norton Simon had a favorite dealer. In the course of the thirty-five years of his collecting from 1954 to 1989, he and his foundations spent more than $125 million, acquiring close to 8,000 artworks in more than 1,700 transactions.[4] The number and range of works coupled with Simon's probing and restless temperament naturally meant that he worked with a wide range of art dealers and auction houses. They were in constant communication with Simon, not only when they were offering objects or letting him know what was on the market but

OPPOSITE
Giovanni Battista Tiepolo, *The Triumph of Virtue and Nobility over Ignorance*, c. 1740–1750 (detail), The Norton Simon Foundation. CAT. 829

ABOVE
Norton Simon

RIGHT
FIG. 1. Peter Wilson, director of Sotheby's

BELOW RIGHT
FIG. 2. Dealers with twelve or more sales to Norton Simon

also just to keep in touch. Just as often, Simon called them to ask what was available or how the market was doing. He never hesitated to grill one dealer about another's inventory, always comparing quality and value. Even after he bought an artwork, he remained curious about how it compared with others on the market.

Simon bought from many sources in the United States and Europe. Although there was not one favorite dealer, several figured prominently in his transactions. The names of many of the dealers will be familiar to the reader from the preceding chapters. Geoffrey Agnew, Christopher Burge of Christie's, Ben Heller, Robert Light, David Nash of Sotheby's, Alexandre Rosenberg, Martin Summers and Desmond Corcoran of Lefevre Gallery, Eugene Thaw, Dudley Tooth, Doris Wiener, Peter Wilson of Sotheby's (fig. 1), and William Wolff were among those with whom Simon developed long-term relationships and on whom he relied for opinions.

The table to the right (fig. 2) lists the dealers and auction houses with which Simon conducted twelve or more transactions.[5] Six dealers in Asian art are represented, as Spink & Son, J. J. Klejman, Doris Wiener, William Wolff, Ben Heller, and Oriental Antiquities (along with Christie's and Sotheby's) are the primary sources for the Asian collection. With the exception of Spink (who sold Simon two Egyptian figures in the early 1960s before selling him Asian art in the 1970s), the Asian art dealers worked with him just nine years or less, underlining the fact that he formed the Asian collection in a remarkably short time.

Many dealers worked with Simon for twenty years or longer, including Eugene Thaw (twenty), M. Knoedler & Co. (twenty-one), Thomas Agnew & Sons (twenty-three), Drs. Fritz

and Peter Nathan (twenty-three), Wildenstein & Co. (twenty-seven), William Schab (twenty-eight), and Paul Rosenberg & Co. (twenty-eight). Simon bought objects at Sotheby's in London for more than thirty years. At first, the London dealers Geoffrey Agnew and Dudley Tooth alerted him to potential purchases and placed the bids on his behalf. As Simon familiarized himself with specialists and the auctioneers, he became more comfortable working directly with the auction houses in both London and New York.

Dealers with 12 or more sales to Norton Simon
Listed by number of sales

Dealer	No. Sales	No. Objects	Dates	No. Years	Total in dollars*
Reid & Lefevre	12	81	1968–1977	9	2,319,700
Speelman	12	13	1969–1976	7	1,504,200
Agnew	14	14	1958–1981	23	3,346,700
Klejman	14	68	1972–1977	5	840,000
Perls, New York	14	14	1955–1969	14	103,800
Musée Rodin	14	14	1966–1984	18	806,000
Slatkin	14	14	1958–1965	7	111,900
Schab	16	161	1961–1989	28	190,500
Spink	18	70	1960–1976	16	1,792,500
Hahn	19	19	1964–1972	8	1,796,400
Nathan	19	19	1957–1980	23	1,792,600
Schaeffer	19	30	1964–1976	12	336,000
Heller	26	26	1972–1976	4	2,750,000
Kantor	26	30	1957–1976	19	581,500
Tooth	28	28	1959–1973	14	1,702,200
Vierny	29	34	1967–1980	13	109,700
Knoedler	32	33	1955–1976	21	2,379,300
Oriental Antiquities	37	37	1972–1975	3	910,000
Wildenstein	40	102	1955–1982	27	13,809,300
Thaw	41	48	1963–1983	20	11,099,300
Wolff	41	74	1972–1981	9	1,076,100
Wiener	43	81	1971–1975	4	1,568,500
Colnaghi	45	375	1968–1982	14	2,205,700
Light	55	1,121	1963–1979	16	3,471,900
Marlborough	56	328	1961–1974	13	4,375,800
Rosenberg	63	63	1957–1985	28	7,447,300
Christie's	106	418	1964–1983	19	10,321,700
Sotheby's, New York	109	293	1974–1984	10	7,845,900
Sotheby's, London	203	1,574	1958–1988	30	10,200,500

to nearest 100

The table also illustrates that Christie's and Sotheby's accounted for considerably more transactions than any of the private dealers. In spite of his reputation after the *Titus* sale as an inexperienced, even naïve auction buyer, Simon dealt with a number of auction houses in several countries. He spent close to $28.6 million at auction, principally through Christie's and Sotheby's. Certainly Sotheby's director Peter Wilson (fig. 1) understood Simon's potential as a serious client and as early as 1956 assiduously nurtured the collector, even before he began to buy at auction.[6] Wilson kept Simon close to the vest, remaining not just the primary but for many years the only contact Simon had with the auction house. Wilson handled the inquiries about artworks, collectors, and the art market, as well as everything from insurance, billing, and catalogue transmittal to photography requests. Nothing was given to assistants or other departments. When, for instance, Simon wanted to be kept apprised of Egyptian art, Wilson was the one who took action. While he was probably relying on his antiquities expert for information, Wilson wrote to Simon's assistant, "Please tell Mr. Simon that I will keep my eyes open for a fine large Egyptian cat and let him know of anything I can find."[7] This kind of personal attention paid off. Whereas Simon spent more than $10.3 million on 106 transactions at Christie's, he made 311 purchases—more than three-quarters of his auction activity at a cost of more than $18 million—through Sotheby's in London and New York.[8] Further, when he consigned his own works to auction, he sold 18 works through Christie's and 259 through Sotheby's.

Among the private dealers, Simon spent the most money, $13.8 million, with Wildenstein & Co. in New York. The forty transactions amounted to 102 artworks, which included the album of sixty drawings by Claude Lorrain ($1 million). Simon initially worked with vice president E. J. "Mannie" Rousuck (p. 18), who sold him his first two important paintings, those by Paul Gauguin and Camille Pissarro. Later he most often dealt with Wildenstein's president Louis Goldenberg (fig. 3). Not only did Wildenstein & Co. do business with Simon for more than twenty-seven years, the firm sold him

FIG. 3. Louis Goldenberg, president of Wildenstein & Co.

some of his most expensive paintings, including Raphael's *Madonna and Child with Book* ($3 million), Filippino Lippi's magnificent pair of panels, *Benedict and Apollonia* and *Paul and Frediano* ($1.5 million), and Vincent van Gogh's *Portrait of a Peasant (Patience Escalier)* ($1.25 million).

Another dealer to whom Norton Simon returned often was Eugene Thaw (p. 136). During their twenty-year relationship, Thaw sold Simon close to $11.1 million worth of artworks.[9] Simon was nearly a decade into collecting when Thaw sold him the first painting, Jean-Baptiste Camille Corot's *Site in Italy* in 1963 for $70,000. As with those from Wildenstein, Thaw's artworks are among the most important (and most expensive) objects in the collection, including Francisco de Zurbarán's *Still Life with Lemons, Oranges, and a Rose* ($2,725,000), Rembrandt van Rijn's *Portrait of a Bearded Man in a Wide-Brimmed Hat* ($1,150,000), and Giovanni Battista Tiepolo's monumental ceiling painting, *The Triumph of Virtue and Nobility over Ignorance* ($975,000). Thaw appreciated the relationship, acknowledging, "I became the dealer I was because of one collector only—Norton Simon. He made me as a dealer and I owe him a lot."[10]

Prints account for the largest numbers of individual objects, since they were often sold in bound sets, and the print dealer Robert Light (p. 184) sold Simon more than one thousand works. Among these are several rare editions of Goya's *Los Caprichos* and *Disasters of War* and the set of 118 Rembrandt etchings (cat. 1452).[11] In addition, on many occasions Light acted as Simon's agent, bidding on his behalf at auction, including for the purchase of Rembrandt's *Self-Portrait* (cat. 654) at Christie's in 1969. Light first met Simon on a visit to his home in the early 1960s. He later remembered that he was intrigued by the fact that Simon began to test him almost at once by bringing out an assortment of artworks for him to compare:

> We sat down to have a drink and on the cock-
> tail table there were a half a dozen works of
> art. There was a little Daumier bronze, a
> Dürer engraving, a Vuillard drawing, a small
> painting. I remember him saying to me, "Let's
> assume for a moment these are all the same
> price, and I can only afford one, which one
> should I buy and why?" I'd never been in
> contact with a collector who in a way, turned
> the tables and said to the dealer, which of these
> various works, in different media—a number
> of these were not my field and he knew that.
> He was testing my eye and my sense of quality.
> I thought that was absolutely fascinating and
> well within his rights to do.[12]

In what certainly appealed to Simon's love of comparisons, Light brought out another example of the same Dürer
engraving that Simon had just shown him:

> By curious coincidence, I had another impres-
> sion in my portfolio which was better quality.
> So I pulled out my impression and pointed out
> why I thought the one on the table had short-
> comings. He very quickly perceived a differ-
> ence of the quality in printing, and a difference
> in the condition of the paper.[13]

Such comparisons as these may in fact have contributed to
Simon's later fascination with comparing various states of prints.

The dealer Alexandre Rosenberg (p. 37) sold Simon
artworks for twenty-eight years and concluded the largest
number of individual transactions with the collector. Son of
the legendary art dealer Paul Rosenberg, whose Paris art gallery

was established in 1878, Alexandre was founding president of
the Art Dealers Association of America. Simon acquired sixty-
three artworks from Rosenberg over the course of a business
and personal relationship that ended only with the dealer's
death in 1987. Simon was a notoriously challenging client and
sometimes cavalier in his treatment of dealers—including
Rosenberg—but he often told me how much he respected
Alexandre Rosenberg's integrity. Aside from Rosenberg's
expertise, fine inventory, and generosity,[14] I believe this may
have stemmed in part from his 1964 sale to Simon of a pastel
of a woman attributed to Henri de Toulouse-Lautrec (cat.
239) for $135,000. Rosenberg had assured Simon that while the
pastel did not appear in the 1926 catalogue raisonné, it would
certainly be in Madame M. G. Dortu's forthcoming updated
version.[15] In 1969, however, Madame Dortu confirmed that it
was not genuine.[16] The embarrassed dealer offered as compen-
sation Henri Fantin-Latour's *Asters and Fruit on a Table* (cat.
725) for $15,000—its $150,000 value less the $135,000 price for
the "Lautrec." He asked Simon to destroy or otherwise dispose
of the pastel, possibly by donating it to "a reliable educational
institution, as a specimen for study and training of young art
students."[17] Not surprisingly, however, Simon kept the picture,
storing it out of sight at home. He never gave it away and never
destroyed it, hoping perhaps that one day it might be proved
genuine.[18]

Did Norton Simon have a favorite artist? The collection itself is a testament to the fact that he was attracted to
numerous artists and cultures in all media. He mentioned on
many occasions that Titian's *Man with the Glove* in the Musée
du Louvre had been the first painting that captivated him. He
often discussed its beauty, comparing it with other Titians
and with other portraits, but there is no evidence that he ever
attempted to acquire any works by Titian.[19] I once tried to pin
him down about artworks in his own collection, and he told
me that Paul Cézanne's *Tulips in a Vase* was a favorite, but this
may have been an offhand comment, since he sold it at auction
in 1973 (only to have second thoughts and buy it back at the
sale).[20] He regretted the loss of several paintings that went to
Lucille Simon in their divorce settlement, including Georges

Braque's *The Studio* (which he replaced with another Braque that reminded him of the lost example),[21] as well as paintings by Amedeo Modigliani and Corot (cats. 294, 390) that he later reacquired. He was sorry to have missed Rembrandt's *Aristotle with a Bust of Homer*, and it is possible he bought *Titus* on the rebound. The same can be said for his acquisition of Pierre-Auguste Renoir's *The Pont des Arts, Paris* after losing out on Claude Monet's *Garden at Sainte-Adresse*. Simon never owned a painting by the Dutch artist Jan van Huysum, but on several occasions he unsuccessfully tried to buy a pair of van Huysum still lifes from a London dealer's private collection. Moreover, there were many times when he returned to dealers to learn if they still had a particular piece he had previously rejected. Near the end of his collecting life, for instance, he was fascinated with Nicolas Poussin's *Hannibal Crossing the Alps* and periodically instructed me to call the London dealer Julian Agnew to find out if it were still available. He never followed through, perhaps owing to his failing health, and the painting is now in the Frick Collection in New York.

Simon's interests were as changing as his nature; nonetheless, it is tempting to gauge them by the amount of money he spent or by the number of works by a particular artist he acquired. Although Simon spent a considerable amount on the collection, the table below (fig. 4) illustrates that he spent $1 million or more in just nineteen transactions. Three of those, the Degas modèles (cat. 1397), Rembrandt's group of etchings (cat. 1452), and the Claude Lorrain album of drawings (cat. 740), were for multiple artworks, and the fourth, Guercino's *Aldrovandi Dog* (cat. 1654), was returned to the dealer and later repurchased for $600,000. Thus, there are only fifteen single works that cost more than $1 million. Rembrandt's *Portrait of a Boy in Fancy Costume* (Titus) is the earliest $1-million-plus purchase on the list and is still Simon's fourth most expensive painting behind Zurbarán, Raphael, and Bouts. The high prices may reflect the art market at the time of purchase more accurately than what they reveal about Simon's favorites. On the other hand, more than half the transactions that cost more than one million dollars feature artists whom Simon collected in large numbers.

FIG. 4.
Art purchases of $1 million or more

List of artworks with a purchase price of $1 million or more

Cat. no.	Artist	Title	Dealer	Year	Price in dollars
740	Claude Lorrain	Album of 60 Drawings	Wildenstein	1970	1,000,000
1531	Giov. di Paolo	*Branchini Madonna*	Sotheby's	1978	1,098,707
1706	Ingres	*Baron Vialètes de Mortarieu*	Thaw	1983	1,100,000
1489	Rembrandt	*Portrait of a Bearded Man*	Thaw	1977	1,150,000
654	Rembrandt	*Self-Portrait*	Christie's	1969	1,150,486
1654	Guercino	*Aldrovandi Dog*	Nathan	1980	1,153,600
1130	van Gogh	*Portrait of a Peasant*	Wildenstein	1975	1,250,000
973	Lippi	*Four Saints*	Wildenstein	1973	1,500,000
531	Renoir	*The Pont des Arts, Paris*	Parke-Bernet	1968	1,550,000
1671	Poussin	*The Holy Family*	Wildenstein	1981	1,716,947 *
1452	Rembrandt	Group of 118 etchings	Light	1977	1,770,510
1397	Degas	70 modèle bronzes	Lefevre	1977	1,800,000
1704	Degas	*Waiting*	Sotheby's	1983	1,870,000 *
1711	Picasso	*Woman with Mandolin*	Christie's	1984	1,925,000
1684	Goya	*Portrait of Dona Francisca*	Agnew	1981	2,018,750
266	Rembrandt	*Portrait of a Boy (Titus)*	Christie's	1965	2,245,453
769	Zurbarán	*Still Life*	Thaw	1972	2,725,000
885	Raphael	*Madonna and Child with Book*	Wildenstein	1972	3,000,000
1646	Bouts	*Resurrection*	Sotheby's	1980	4,214,000

*One-half the total cost; owned jointly with the J. Paul Getty Museum, Los Angeles

Artists with ten or more works purchased by Norton Simon			
Artist	No. of Works	Total Purchase Price in dollars	No. of Deaccessions
Corot	10	1,463,714	4
Delacroix	10	452,466	9
Watteau	10	419,100	9
Boudin	11	479,107	9
Monet	11	3,014,515	8
Vuillard	11	550,083	6
van Gogh	12	2,862,854	4
Nolde	14	138,765	13
Pissarro	14	2,129,053	11
Renoir	22	4,411,008	15
Cézanne	23	2,650,363	19
Rodin	24	986,900	12
Daumier	24	303,218	20
Moore	27	1,648,744	11
Matisse	36	1,344,815	19
Maillol	51	1,684,085	24
Goya	103 *	4,541,204	27
Degas	130	10,107,124	30
Rembrandt	380 **	7,880,081	13
Picasso	885	6,781,173	24

*Includes forty-two complete sets of multiple images
**Includes three sets of Basan impressions

FIG. 5. Artists with ten or more works purchased by Norton Simon

The table at the left (fig. 5) lists artists whose works Simon purchased ten or more times. While the table is a sign of his interest at the time of purchase, the number of works does not necessarily represent a lasting favorite. As discussed earlier, Simon deaccessioned many objects beginning in 1970 with his divorce settlement and in his 1970–1974 sales. For example, although he bought twenty-two Renoirs, spending more than $4.4 million, he eventually donated or sold fifteen (recouping close to $4.2 million). Simon bought twenty-three works by Cézanne; he designated fifteen of these (including eight watercolors) for his private collection and displayed them in a separate room at his home. Today only four Cézannes remain. There were thirty-six acquisitions of works by Matisse, although Simon gave away ten.[22] In spite of the deaccessions, the number of purchases of these and the other listed artists indicates an extraordinary interest.

In addition to the twenty-four bronzes by Rodin that he purchased for his own collections (see, for example, fig. 6), Simon bought two additional Rodins to donate to universities.[23] He owned twenty-three marble and bronze sculptures by Henry Moore, as well as a watercolor and two sets of graphic works. He favored even more the works of the sculptor Aristide Maillol, buying forty-six figures in bronze, lead, and marble (fig. 7), as well as three paintings and two drawings by the artist.[24] With the help of Maillol's last muse and model, Dina Vierny, Simon assembled perhaps the largest Maillol sculpture collection outside France.

The largest numbers by far—in terms of works purchased, as well as works remaining in the collection—belong to Rembrandt van Rijn, Pablo Picasso, Francisco de Goya, and Edgar Degas, with an extraordinary number of printed works by the first three. Simon bought five paintings and five drawings by or attributed to Rembrandt and close to four hundred etchings (see, for example, fig. 8), spending close to $7.9 million.[25] Even considering these numbers, he did not collect the artist's prints with the zeal he reserved for Picasso and Goya.

ABOVE
FIG. 6. Auguste Rodin, *The Burghers of Calais*,
1884–1895, Norton Simon Art Foundation. CAT. 413

ABOVE RIGHT
FIG. 7. Aristide Maillol, *Standing Bather with
Raised Arms*, 1930, Norton Simon Art Foundation.
CAT. 410

RIGHT
FIG. 8. Rembrandt van Rijn, *The Phoenix or the
Statue Overthrown*, 1658, Norton Simon Art
Foundation. CAT. 1521

Simon was enthralled with the work of Picasso and owned 885 artworks by the Spanish artist. Between 1955 and 1984 he spent more than $6.7 million on 112 acquisitions. The artworks consisted of 20 paintings in oil and pastel, 9 bronzes, 6 drawings, and 850 prints. Among the prints were the 100 etchings and aquatints in *The Vollard Suite*, 100 linocuts, 116 etchings and aquatints from the *347* series, and the 228 lithographs from the Mourlot collection that included the set of *bon à tirer* proofs.[26]

Another Spaniard, Goya, is represented by the largest number of individual works. Simon spent more than $2.5 million on four paintings and two drawings. The remaining $2 million went toward 2,381 etchings and lithographs bought in 98 transactions. Goya's graphic works most often appeared as bound books.[27] There were thirteen complete sets of *Los Caprichos* in the collection, of which nine were first-edition sets or earlier (fig. 9). Simon bought seven complete sets of *The Disasters of War*, of which six were from the first edition or earlier. He acquired an astonishing fourteen first-edition sets of *La Tauromaquia* as well as two from the fourth edition, and there were four first-edition sets of *Los Proverbios*, along with a set of trial proofs, and a fifth edition. Simon also bought early etched portraits after Diego Velázquez, the *Bulls of Bordeaux* series, and other single works.

Simon was clearly attracted to works on paper, buying prints and drawings for his home from the mid-1950s until 1970. Although he sold most of those in his private collection in the early 1970s, he continued to buy prints for his two foundations, especially by the three great painter-printmakers mentioned above. He enjoyed discussing prints in all of their forms, the quality of an impression, its relative worth in the market, or how many examples might be available. He was not only fascinated with the differences between first, second, or later editions; he wanted to compare plates from the same edition.[28] Whenever he bought a new set, he instructed his curators to rate each plate, comparing it with corresponding plates in the other editions he owned. During one period of collecting first-edition sets of *La Tauromaquia*, he directed me to contact all the print departments in larger North American and European museums to discover the number of first-edition sets in their collections. He was pleased to discover that none had as many as he. It is not a coincidence that his last three curators were all trained in the print field. Selma Holo specialized in the works of Goya, and both Tessa Helfet and Paula Kendall had worked in the print department of Sotheby's. Holo understood Simon's attraction to Goya and believed there was a direct connection between the two:

> Goya did things that were so amazingly before their time—social commentary, a kind of realism that strikes the chord of the suffering of humanity—a kind of incisive look at the personalities that had the psychological acuity and truth that simply nobody else was able to do. Here we have Norton Simon, who was interested in psychology and how people thought, how they felt—how they came to decisions, and then you find Goya, who also obviously was looking at his society around him.[29]

Simon's Degas purchases represent an equally impressive number of works and the largest amount of money spent. Simon owned several monotypes, etchings, and lithographs, as well as pastels over monotypes, but Degas's graphic works were for him secondary to the artist's paintings and sculpture (fig. 10). Degas was an enduring favorite for almost thirty years. His work was among the first Simon collected in 1955 and among the last in 1983.[30] Simon spent more than $10 million on 62 transactions amounting to 130 artworks, including two paintings that were sold and later repurchased. In the course of his collecting, he bought 89 bronzes, 30 paintings in oil and pastel, 5 drawings, and 6 graphics. Although his two foundations bought many Degas examples intended for public exhibition, he purchased 28 from 1955 to 1969 for his private collection.

Why did Simon buy so many works by Degas? As someone who continually challenged himself in his business and personal life, he was fascinated with Degas's technical brilliance and difficult compositions. Further, his appreciation of sculptural works, ranging from Indian bronzes and Cambodian stones to Rodin and Moore, was certainly a factor in his attraction to Degas's bronzes. Because Eugene Thaw had a long and close association with Norton Simon, he knew the collector and the collection perhaps better than any other dealer. Thaw believed that Simon and Degas were very much alike, in that both of them loved and understood modern paintings but "learned to look backwards and see the great masters of the past," and that this attribute explained why Simon reacted so favorably to Degas, an artist who represented the transition between the old masters and the modern era.[31]

OPPOSITE
FIG. 9. Francisco de Goya y Lucientes, *Pretty Teacher!* plate 68 of *Los Caprichos*, working proof before letters and numbers, c. 1796–1798, The Norton Simon Foundation. CAT. 956

RIGHT
FIG. 10. Norton Simon Museum, gallery with sculptures by Edgar Degas

As NORTON SIMON'S TASTE, knowledge, and connoisseurship changed, his collection evolved. This history of his acquisitions and sales illustrates that evolution. It also sadly points to some of the wonderful masterpieces that got away. He sold objects because he worried about their condition or because he grew to doubt an object's staying power, authenticity, or inherent value. Most often, however, he sold artworks simply because he could turn a profitable deal. His art staff deeply regretted the sales and lost many arguments trying to prevent them. When Simon told Darryl Isley he was selling Constantin Brancusi's *Little Bird* (fig. 13) in 1974 to Marlborough Gallery for $850,000 (a $600,000 profit), Isley stormed out of Simon's office, slamming the door. More often, of course, we tried to use logic instead of temper, but Simon's argument that the realized profits made new acquisitions possible usually carried the day.

At the outset, Norton Simon's reputation as a collector rested chiefly on his nineteenth- and twentieth-century art—an area in which he collected early and well and continued to buy over the years. These objects also increased in value at a greater rate than old masters. He did sell old master drawings by such artists as Jean-Antoine Watteau, Rembrandt, Claude Lorrain, and François Boucher, but because of the lively market for nineteenth- and twentieth-century items, most of his deaccessioned paintings and sculpture were from later periods. Simon considered old masters in general to be undervalued and a better buy, and as he continued to collect, he more often than not replaced a later work with an earlier one. Thus, the old master painting collection is now larger and increasingly well known. Yet, while he reaped enormous profits from the hundreds of deaccessions, it is difficult to justify the loss of so many remarkable masterpieces—paintings by Picasso, Degas, Edvard Munch, Piet Mondrian, Cézanne, and Vincent van Gogh, as well as sculptures by Henri Matisse, David Smith, and Brancusi—which have found their way into some of the world's great museums and private collections. Yet without the extraordinary sales proceeds, subsequent purchases of equally great works may not have been possible, and we would not have the unparalleled collection we have today. ✸

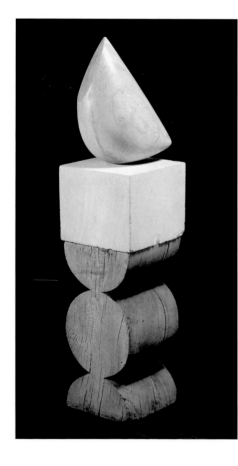

FIG. 13. Constantin Brancusi, *Little Bird*, 1927, private collection, New York. CAT. 630

1. J. Carter Brown, interview by Charles Guggenheim, 4 October 1996.

2. Christopher Burge, undated [1996] interview by Davis Guggenheim.

3. Eugene V. Thaw, interview by Anna Jhirad of Guggenheim Productions, 25 March 1997.

4. One transaction might represent multiple artworks. The Duveen purchase, for instance, represented more than seven hundred objects.

5. The table does not take into account the numerous instances when works were owned jointly by several dealers and reflects only the dealer who issued the invoice.

6. See chap. 2, n. 57.

7. Peter Wilson to Angelina Boaz, 21 July 1967.

8. Until 1972 Parke-Bernet Galleries in New York was a separate business. In mid-1972 the company merged with Sotheby & Co. and became Sotheby, Parke Bernet Inc. Now both the New York and London branches are known as Sotheby's.

9. Works sold by Eugene Thaw were occasionally owned jointly by Thaw and other dealers. Simon also sold forty-one artworks to Thaw for more than $17 million.

10. Thaw, conversation with the author, 11 August 2003.

11. See chap. 12.

12. Robert Light, interview by Davis Guggenheim, 20 June 1996.

13. Ibid.

14. In 1978 Rosenberg gave to the Norton Simon Museum Picasso's 1925 still life, *The Ram's Head* (P.1978.6).

15. Joyant, 1926; Dortu, 1971.

16. Dortu to Rosenberg, 6 May 1969.

17. Rosenberg to Simon, 23 January 1970.

18. Rosenberg's letter and Dortu's opinion were never part of the curatorial file for this painting; instead, they were kept by Simon in his personal files at his home and found only after his death. Recent scholarship continues to doubt the attribution (author's discussions with Richard Thomson, September 1993, and Richard Brettell and Stephen Eisenman, February 2004).

19. Four paintings attributed to followers of Titian were part of the Duveen inventory (cats. D53–D56); they are still in the collection but rarely exhibited.

20. See p. 147.

21. See p. 175.

22. Simon donated Matisse's *Jetty at Collioure* (cat. 22) to Pomona College in 1957 and nine works on paper (cats. 216, 284, 302A-G) to the University of California, Los Angeles in 1966.

23. See chap. 6, n. 10.

24. In addition to the forty-six Maillol sculptures Simon bought for his collection, he donated the artist's bronze entitled *Sorrow* to the University of California, Berkeley in 1968.

25. Simon spent about $4.8 million on five paintings and some $3.1 million for the works on paper.

26. See pp. 182–183.

27. *Los Caprichos* and *The Disasters of War* were published with eighty plates each, *Los Proverbios* with eighteen plates, and *La Tauromaquia* with between thirty-three and forty.

28. See p. 169 for a discussion of Simon's interest in exhibiting plates from various editions.

29. Selma Holo, interview by Davis Guggenheim, 20 June 1996.

30. See Campbell et al., 2009.

31. Thaw, interview by Anna Jhirad of Guggenheim Productions, 25 March 1997.

32. Pratapaditya Pal, interview by Davis Guggenheim, 20 June 1996; Pal, 2003a. See also chap. 8 for a discussion of Simon's attraction to Chola bronzes.

33. Simon, 1974.

34. Thaw, interview by Anna Jhirad of Guggenheim Productions, 25 March 1997. In September 1973 Ben Heller sold Pollock's *Blue Poles: Number 11, 1952* to the National Gallery of Australia for $2 million.

35. Campbell, 1976.

CHAPTER SIXTEEN

The Collector

He was a heroic buyer. He kept the art market perky for a long time.—MARTIN SUMMERS[1]

WHEN NORTON SIMON'S CURATOR Darryl Isley invited me to interview with the Norton Simon, Inc. Museum of Art in 1969, I asked him what it was like to work for Simon. Isley said that Simon gave 150 percent and expected the same from everyone else; that he wanted your opinion even if you disagreed—especially if you disagreed; and that he hated to hear that something was done a certain way because it always had been done that way. Over the twenty-four years that I worked directly with him, I learned that Simon was multifaceted, difficult, and brilliant. He was a complex thinker who was impossible to pigeonhole. He had a restless but cautious nature and investigated every aspect of a subject before reaching a conclusion. He was a tough negotiator and a perfectionist. He was a relentless questioner and a good teacher.

This narrative has traced the development of Simon's collections through his acquisitions and deaccessions. The account of those transactions often portrays a collector given to tough or tortured negotiations, a hard-hitting and sometimes stubborn individual. This chapter will point out other facets of Simon's character and relationships, seen through the perspective of those who knew him. Evident in all of these recollections is that as time went by, old antagonisms gave way to a profound (if sometimes grudging) admiration for Simon's achievements. Moreover, when people talk about Simon and his collection they often describe the same character traits, time and again using the same language.

Simon's colleagues agree that he was an extremely intricate thinker. It was also a given that it was difficult to follow his conversation and thoughts. A 1953 article cited his conversation as convoluted but lauded his ability to juggle several unrelated, complex business problems at the same time "without confusing himself or others."[2] In business meetings he would often keep an associate present to serve as a translator of sorts—to restate his intentions if they became unclear—and to get him back on track if necessary. I performed this service on several occasions during discussions with conservators and dealers.

OPPOSITE AND ABOVE LEFT
Norton Simon

The former television newsman and Norton Simon Museum trustee Tom Brokaw understood that what was often perceived as inarticulateness was in fact Simon's restless nature and ability to think about a subject's many nuances at the same time. Brokaw thought the reason Simon could never give a straight answer was because he saw so many dimensions to a subject. When he pursued an idea or carried on a conversation, he took "detours along the way because he wanted to examine everything":

> It was from Norton that I began to understand
> the real meaning of deconstruction. Whether
> it was art or politics or personal relationships,
> he was always taking them apart, putting them
> back together again, kind of all at once. I never
> met anybody as complex as he was.[3]

Former Norton Simon Foundation president Robert Macfarlane described working with Simon as "creative chaos": he was "a captain who sailed with the wind constantly changing."[4] Simon's friend and Norton Simon Art Foundation trustee Michael Phelps compared the impossibility of pinning him down to "nailing Jell-O on the wall."[5]

Simon had his own opinion about the best description of his restlessness, pointing to a 1965 *Fortune* article that stated in part:

> He is a study in dissatisfaction. Restlessly and
> intuitively, he seeks the stimulation of new
> involvements, preferably in troubled situations,
> and craves the feeling of "creativity" he gets
> from straightening them out…. He describes
> himself as an "abstract businessman," governed
> by a personal "philosophy of change."[6]

In discussing Simon's interest in art and in the formation of his collection, people who knew him were unanimous in their conviction that he was more interested in pursuing an artwork than in keeping it (fig. 1). Robert Light believed that "the search, the chase, and the negotiations that led to an acquisition were almost as rewarding to him as the possession of the work of art."[7] Eugene Thaw agreed that "Norton Simon knows art and really loves art. But I think he loves the chase—and if it's complicated so much the better—as much as he loves the prize."[8] This might explain in part why Simon was content to lend the collection for years before finding for it a permanent home. He often spent more time studying an object and working through the negotiations for its purchase than he did looking at it after its acquisition. Many objects, in fact, never came to California before they were bought and went straight to museums in other states for loan. The art historian Pratapaditya Pal gave the most colorful description of Simon's proclivity:

> I don't think it's hooking the fish that he liked,
> I think it was the reeling it in. The longer the
> better. He would love to cogitate. I could see
> him thinking, "Is this a good deal? Am I getting
> the best thing?" He liked to, not demoralize,
> but sort of desensitize his opponent or deflate
> them, and then pounce.[9]

This is just one aspect of his personality, of course, and one he perfected during negotiations. There is no question that Simon loved art, as evidenced by the collection he formed. Ben Heller believed that Simon's deep affection for art was foremost, and that it excused some of his behavior: "Everybody forgave him [because of] his caring and passion about works of art."[10]

Simon was famous for asking everyone for an opinion about the artwork he was considering. He asked not only the experts; he was curious about what everyone thought of a potential purchase, whether the person was a member of his household staff or the director of a museum. Former J. Paul Getty Museum director John Walsh remembered Simon as a "great brain picker," who would telephone ostensibly to discuss a particular artwork but end up talking about every aspect of the artist and period.[11] This was a trait that applied not only to art but to any subject that interested him, from politics and business to psychology and medicine. Former Norton Simon Inc. president David Mahoney described Simon as an "insatiable sponge" that was always dry and needed to be filled up with answers to "a million and one questions."[12] When Simon was criticized for asking questions but never answering them, he responded, "My philosophy is when you are asked a question, ask a question back and keep asking questions until you run out. From my standpoint that doesn't happen very often. It sure frustrates a lot of people, but better that they are frustrated than I."[13]

Simon's telephone calls (figs. 2, 3) were infamous, often inconvenient, and frequently interminable, yet dealers rarely complained. As Lefevre Gallery's Martin Summers recalled, "He just adored the telephone, and he wouldn't let you get off. Of course, as a young man, here's the biggest buyer in town ringing you up. You think it's Christmas."[14] Christie's specialist and veteran auctioneer Christopher Burge concurred, adding that since it was the job of the art dealer and auction house to develop and encourage passionate collectors, "Here was the epitome of that in action, so we could hardly complain when we were on the receiving end of it."[15] While some dealers begrudged the telephone calls, the potential financial gain made the interruptions tolerable. Museum directors and curators obliged him as well, trusting that their advice would lead to loans for their institutions and, before Simon controlled his own museum in Pasadena, to gifts.

Many, however, grew to resent what they saw as Simon's exploiting their knowledge for his personal gain. This was especially true at the Los Angeles County Museum of Art, where members of the staff, from the director and curators to the conservator, were repeatedly called on for advice with little reciprocity. After Simon began selling works on paper in the early 1970s, Ebria Feinblatt, curator of prints and drawings at LACMA, told Isley that the sales, coupled with the absence of gifts to the museum, the removal of loans, and no commitment to the museum about his collection, disturbed her to the point that she was no longer willing to advise Simon on his collection.[16] The resentment was still strong after Simon moved the collection to Pasadena. Pal, then senior curator of Indian and Southeast Asian art, complained that he disliked giving Simon opinions because he felt used, that for years it had been a one-way street with neither funds for the museum nor loans to his exhibitions: "I have made it a policy here not to give my time freely unless the museum gets something in return, and I prefer not to make any exceptions. I have talked to Mr. Simon about this in great detail but it obviously doesn't matter."[17]

While some enjoyed the conversations, many independent art historians felt equally exploited. John Rewald, for instance, complained to Isley that he had given Simon years of free advice without receiving "even a bottle of catsup."[18] All the same, the telephone calls continued.

OPPOSITE
FIG. 1. Norton Simon
examining a painting at
the Los Angeles County
Museum of Art, c. 1970

LEFT, FAR LEFT
FIGS. 2, 3. Norton
Simon, May 1970

In my own experience of working with Simon for more than two decades, time spent on the telephone significantly exceeded time spent face to face. Since he worked from his home in Malibu while his staff was in Pasadena, telephone meetings were more convenient for him. He also loved to talk in the evenings and on weekends, which may have been tolerated by dealers but was not always welcomed by others. When Princeton University Art Museum assistant director David Steadman was preparing the exhibition of Simon artworks in 1972, Simon inundated him with telephone calls. To ensure uninterrupted time with his family, Steadman hired an answering service to take messages during the dinner hour. Simon accepted the maneuver with no comment, but at Princeton's opening festivities, he good-naturedly told Steadman's wife that the family no longer needed the answering service.[19]

Because it was faster than mail and less expensive than travel, Simon encouraged his staff to conduct business by telephone. Selma Holo, his curator in the late 1970s, recalled that the essence of her relationship with dealers was almost exclusively telephonic. She commented one day to Simon that it was often difficult to discern reactions without being face to face. Holo reported that he responded, "That's pretty easy, looking into people's eyes. Reading voices takes real talent. You've got to learn to read voices."[20] Ben Heller agreed, saying about Simon, "He believed that his telephone ear, unimpeded by sight, by physical manifestations, was much more perceptive."[21]

Norton Simon loved negotiating, not just in business and art, but in everything. If you told him a project would take a week, he would ask you to finish it in three days. If you said you could arrive for a meeting at 10, he wanted you there at 9 or 11. Every negotiation, not only with dealers but with framers and base makers, involved days of bargaining.

He not only enjoyed the game, especially with dealers, but he was extremely good at it, and I believe this was primarily due to his ability to remain impartial and dispassionate enough to walk away from a deal. In fact, he was wary of craving ownership of any work, stating, "I'm always bothered by the idea of being possessed by that which I possess. I think out why a possession is important, and when it becomes too important, I try to dispossess."[22] He asserted that after living with a work of art for a certain length of time, he could let it go, "and in a spiritual sense, still own it."[23] He worried that collecting for its own sake was a slippery slope, which he tried to avoid:

> You have to fight the lure of becoming an acquisitive collector—when you become acquisitive about art, which I think every collector does at some time, it's the same as chasing mirages that you chase in business—more, more, and more. And when this happens to me, I cut off the art. I get back to my business. If I'm going to chase something, I might as well chase it there.[24]

As this account has demonstrated, however, Simon was unsuccessful in controlling his acquisitive nature, eventually owning thousands of artworks, and he collected examples by several artists in vast numbers. Moreover, while he may have declared that he returned to business to stem his passion about art, in 1969 he walked away with seeming ease from the company that bore his name.

For dealers, he was certainly a difficult customer, since he took a long time to conclude a deal. Negotiations played out over months and even years. Eugene Thaw spoke for many dealers when he bemoaned Simon's habit of reserving works and keeping them on approval for months without an answer: "God forbid you sold it to somebody else, and ignored his reserve; he would be furious and wouldn't buy from you. But sometimes he abused you in the sense of taking an awfully long time to make up his mind."[25]

OPPOSITE
FIG. 4. Anna Plowden and
Peter Smith with Norton
Simon, 1975

The London art restorers Anna Plowden and Peter Smith (fig. 4) had watched Simon's assertive negotiating tactics and, with some trepidation, decided to put them to the test against Simon himself. As part of their arrangement with Simon, they periodically made monthlong trips to Los Angeles to inspect and repair the Asian sculpture collection. They had not increased their prices in several years and notified Isley that they would raise their fees before making their next trip. When Isley tried to negotiate, they held their ground, insisting that if Simon did not agree to the raise, they would no longer go to Los Angeles. Weeks passed with no reply. Smith later described their anxiety about taking a hard line and Simon's response to it:

> We felt that we should make a stand, so we said to him, "Unless we hear by so-and-so date, we're terribly sorry but we can't come." Then we shook. We thought, "Oh, God, what have we done? We've got this wonderful customer that we've been working with for years and having these wonderful trips to California and we've killed the whole thing." And the day before we were due to leave, Darryl Isley rung us up and said, "Okay, your figures have been accepted." We went there and when we saw Mr. Simon, the first thing he said was, "You're learning."[26]

Coupled with his reputation as a shrewd negotiator, Simon had a cautious nature, which he admitted was based in part on watching his father go through the 1920–1921 depression as well as living himself through the depression of the early 1930s. While he thought it made him skeptical, he believed that, all in all, it was better to be overcautious, giving rise to what he called his "golden bridge of retreat":

> I have a natural intuitive sense of where I am anchored and where wind is and how I'm going to run. I try to watch for that golden bridge of retreat anytime I look forward. Sometimes I don't judge the bridge of retreat well enough. But it's kind of where I live, to have an anchor windward, to have a bridge of retreat.[27]

This cautiousness, he felt, worked in his favor. When asked if he ever regretted decisions or asked himself, "Why didn't I?" he replied, "Not very often any more, because I know why I didn't." When discussing his success in investing, he added, "I've never done too badly in the market. I've had my times when I've taken some losses, but generally I guess I've never had a year where I've personally actually lost money."[28]

Was Norton Simon an investor or an obsessed collector? He was probably both, and at various times when he was selling art, he was derisively labeled a dealer who sold art off the museum's walls. He justified all of his sales to his staff by asking us to compare the departing work with one he had just acquired. It goes without saying that he used profits from sales to buy other great works. He clearly was obsessed with art, but as Eugene Thaw observed, because of Simon's nature, business experience, and his incredible mind for figures, he could never completely separate his collecting from monetary considerations. Thaw believed that Simon made mistakes in selling but conceded that the collection grew in the process:

> The collection might not have been able to be as good as it is if he hadn't sold at one point or another and been able to reinvest. He was calculating about the value all the time and he always questioned me as a dealer as to whether this was worth more than that. There was no question that his mind was on both subjects— on the value of the art and the quality of it. He never separated the two because they were both there in his mind together.[29]

His ability to detach himself from the possession of artworks—or at least his desire not to be possessed by them; his ability to walk away from a deal; and his many sales might suggest an intensely unsentimental view of ownership, but Simon was deeply concerned about his art and about the process of collecting (figs. 5, 7, 8). He loved to talk about art and to discuss what an artwork could teach one about the artist and his culture—but especially about oneself. Tom Brokaw remembered Simon not only as a passionate student but as a thoughtful teacher:

> I remember going with him to a restorer who was doing a Renaissance painting he had, and they stalked that painting and argued about it for half an hour. I sat quietly off to the side watching them talking about the folds in the garment and talking about what the artist had in mind. Norton said, "You know Tom, don't look at the whole picture. Just look at this part of it, for example, the garments and how wonderfully well it's painted. That's as contemporary as anything you'll ever see when you think about it." He always had to raise my consciousness about what I was looking at.[30]

In the same way that he quizzed dealers, Norton Simon probed curators, museum directors, and scholars for information about art, both his and others', but he especially enjoyed discussing the condition of artworks and issues surrounding restoration and preservation. He took pleasure in the company of restorers and in discussing how the process of creating artworks was revealed through technical analysis. The condition of an object weighed heavily in Simon's decision to buy or sell. He used the services of independent conservators, as well as those associated with the museums to which he lent his collection. In the late 1960s and early 1970s, because the bulk of his collection was at the Los Angeles County Museum of Art, he depended almost exclusively on LACMA's Ben Johnson for both condition consultation and treatment and for advice on acquisitions.

After Simon moved his collection to Pasadena, he decided not to construct and furnish a conservation laboratory on-site. On two occasions he employed trained conservators to oversee the care of the collection, but they were equipped with minimal examination equipment and performed only minor treatments. He preferred instead to send works to New York and London to the care of such restorers as Mario Modestini or Lucilla Kingsbury, or to invite independent restorers to visit the museum for extended periods of time to conduct condition surveys and treat the artworks. These included, among others, paintings conservators Marco Grassi and Bernard Rabin and sculpture restorers Anna Plowden and Peter Smith. At the same time, he often relied on the advice of Andrea Rothe, the J. Paul Getty Museum's affable and knowledgeable head of paintings conservation.

FIG. 5. Norton Simon in his den, Malibu, c. 1978

Simon especially enjoyed working with the conservator Bernard Rabin (fig. 6), whose irreverence and refreshing frankness endeared him to the collector.[31] Rabin's forthrightness and Simon's reaction to it were evident during one of their first excursions together, when they went to see an old master painting at a prominent New York gallery, which Rabin described as a "high-class joint."[32] In a 1996 interview, Rabin remembered that the painting looked extremely fresh and very well preserved. On examination, however, he determined that restorations had been masked by an ultraviolet-inhibiting varnish that prevented easy discovery of repairs. With the aid of an instrument that could see through the varnish, Rabin concluded that the work was not in as unspoiled a state as advertised:

> I would say that 95% of the painting had been gone over, repainted; actually reinforced. Mr. Simon says, "Well, what do you think?" I said, "You know what, Mr. Simon? This reminds me of a very high class whorehouse, and up on the balcony is a 40-year-old whore and the madam down here is swearing on a stack of bibles that she's a virgin." Well the dealer, he got as red as the red carpet and he walked out in a huff. Mr. Simon leans over and says, "Bernie, next time wait 'til we get outside."[33]

In spite of his fascination with problems of condition, on the whole Simon was remarkably restrained in his approach to restoration. If an object was not in imminent danger he would put off having it worked on for years or decide not to have it treated at all. He took a cautious and skeptical approach, asking how one could be certain that the advice being given was right, or whether it would hold up to scrutiny in later years. He knew from firsthand experience that paintings restored in the 1930s were treated with methods that were later deemed outdated or inappropriate. He would say, "How do I know that in fifty years they're not going to say the same thing about what we've just done? So let's don't do it."[34] On the other hand, he often arranged with dealers to have works cleaned or repaired before he acquired them, thereby leaving the risk (and expense) in the hands of others.

ABOVE LEFT
FIG. 6. Bernard Rabin in the rotunda of the U.S. Capitol with a fresco by Constantino Brumidi in the background, c. 1988

ABOVE
FIG. 7. Norton Simon in his den, Malibu, c. 1972

AFTER THIS LENGTHY INVESTIGATION, the question remains: Why art? What was it about art that so captured Simon's imagination and resources? His friend and fellow University of California regent Frederick Dutton thought that art challenged Simon because it was an area of intangibles with conventional standards as well as breakthroughs and new styles:

> I think from his background in the business community, it was a raging new frontier that really engrossed him. I've always assumed that he also had conquered the business world as much as he really wanted. He was playing that piano with his left hand by then. He was looking for new challenges. Norton was a terribly restless person. I don't think his soul ever rested really. This was not just a rich man who was buying well-known paintings. This was a guy who saw it as a learning experience.[35]

Michael Phelps believed that the reason went even deeper than that, that Simon collected art as part of an exploration of himself, explaining, "Norton was always trying to figure out who the hell he was, what his place was in life, and the art provides a fresh way for him to explore many different things about himself. He was enormously studious about it."[36]

In 1974 Simon wrote an essay he intended to submit to the *New York Times*. Titled "Musings of an Art Collector," it mirrors Phelps's view that art was a process whereby Simon could examine himself:

When I first started collecting art, my thoughts were essentially inwardly directed. What does this picture tell me about me? The more I looked, the more I felt my perceptions sharpening, the more I felt the nurturing aspect of art, the more I became convinced that art is the major form of human communication—crossing the years—crossing cultures—crossing all political considerations. Through art we see the history of man and we see man's creativity bursting forth. It is this pushing away at frontiers, this removing of artificial boundaries, whether they are visual or audible that increases our fundamental capacities as human beings. Art is our touchstone with the past and present, and our bridge to the future.[37]

Later in life Simon came to be closely identified with his art collection, much as he was associated with his companies from the 1940s through the 1960s. At the same time, his self-examination moved from the general subject of man's creativity to a more tightly focused view of his own collection. Ultimately, Simon used his extraordinarily creative eye and shrewd business judgment to become one of the greatest American collectors of his day. Simon's wonderful legacy is the collection displayed at the Norton Simon Museum. Ben Heller perhaps said it best:

> In the course of a lifetime, a privilege happened to him that doesn't happen to many people. He was able to exercise his skills to acquire a number of works of art where the resonance, given off by individual works, as they bounce back and forth between one another, makes an experience when you go to that museum quite rare. As long as it's alive and as long as we look at these things, there's going to be splendor. Just plain old splendor.[38] ❦

1. Martin Summers, interview by Davis Guggenheim, 6 June 1996.

2. Lincoln, 1953, p. 180.

3. Tom Brokaw, interview by Charles Guggenheim, 29 October 1996.

4. Robert Macfarlane, speaking at "Collector without Walls: A Symposium on Norton Simon," 27 October 2007.

5. Michael Phelps, interview by Davis Guggenheim, 23 July 1996.

6. Whalen, 1965, pp. 146–147, as discussed by Simon in Berges, 1975.

7. Robert Light, interview by Davis Guggenheim, 20 June 1996.

8. Whitman, 1979, p. SC-30.

9. Pratapaditya Pal, interview by Davis Guggenheim, 20 June 1996.

10. Ben Heller, interview by Davis Guggenheim, 31 October 1996.

11. John Walsh, interview by Anna Jhirad of Guggenheim Productions, 29 March 1997.

12. David Mahoney, interview by Charles Guggenheim, 29 October 1996.

13. Norton Simon, conversation with the author, May 1990.

14. Summers, interview by Davis Guggenheim, 6 June 1996.

15. Christopher Burge, undated [1996] interview by Davis Guggenheim.

16. Darryl Isley to Simon, 13 January 1972.

17. As reported in Sara Campbell to Simon, 5 September 1978.

18. As reported to Campbell, April 1977. Rewald was alluding to Simon's largest company, Hunt Foods and Industries, a major producer of tomato products.

19. David Steadman, speaking at "Collector without Walls: A Symposium on Norton Simon," 27 October 2007.

20. Selma Holo, interview by Davis Guggenheim, 20 June 1996.

21. Heller, interview by Davis Guggenheim, 31 October 1996.

22. Berges, 1974, p. 61.

23. Ibid., p. 60.

24. Conrad, 1968.

25. Eugene V. Thaw, interview by Anna Jhirad of Guggenheim Productions, 25 March 1997.

26. Anna Plowden and Peter Smith, interview by Davis Guggenheim, 6 June 1996.

27. Berges, 1975.

28. Ibid.

29. Thaw, interview by Anna Jhirad of Guggenheim Productions, 25 March 1997.

30. Brokaw, interview by Charles Guggenheim, 29 October 1996.

31. Rabin recalled that at their first meeting, Simon asked him if he ever made mistakes: "I said, 'Yes, I make mistakes but I try not to repeat them.' 'Fine,' Simon said, 'you're hired.' Just like that." Bernard Rabin, undated [1996] interview by Davis Guggenheim.

32. Ibid.

33. Ibid. Bernard Rabin led a group of American restorers in Florence, Italy after the November 1966 floods. He was in charge of restoration of the Constantino Brumidi frescoes in the Capitol dome, Washington, D. C., completed in 1988. He died in 2003.

34. Conversations with the author. This reticence was conspicuously lacking, however, when he directed that his Degas *Three Dancers* (cat. 686) be folded to hide half the picture (see pp. 96–97).

35. Frederick Dutton, interview by Charles Guggenheim, 2 October 1996.

36. Phelps, speaking at "Collector without Walls: A Symposium on Norton Simon," 27 October 2007.

37. Simon, 1974.

38. Heller, interview by Davis Guggenheim, 31 October 1996.

OPPOSITE
FIG. 8. Norton Simon in his living room, Malibu, c. 1972

Artworks Purchased by Norton Simon
1954–1989

THE ENTRIES FOR THE ARTWORKS in the following checklist contain no provenance information before their sale to Norton Simon; thereafter, ownership is listed in chronological order. To distinguish them from private owners, dealers are enclosed in brackets, and auction sales, in parentheses. Connections between owners are indicated by punctuation: a semicolon indicates that the work passed directly from one owner to the next; a period separates two owners if a direct transfer did not occur or if the means of transfer is not known. For works that Simon deaccessioned, the sales information is given and, whenever possible, their later history and present locations. A catalogue number in **bold** indicates the work is still in the collections. The Duveen inventory, purchased 18 April 1964, begins on page 441. Although the Norton Simon Art Foundation has operated under multiple prior legal names, for the reader's ease, I have consistently used its current appellation. Those wishing to pursue detailed provenance research should refer to the foundation's history and list of name changes in the Note to the Reader on page 4.

1

2

4

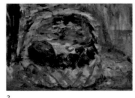

3

6

7

8

1954

Cat. 1
Dan Lutz (American, 1906–1978)
Bass Section, 1949
Oil on canvas, 11 ⅞ x 16 in. (30.2 x 40.6 cm)
[Dalzell Hatfield Gallery, Los Angeles, sold 22 December 1954 for $300 to]; Norton Simon, sold 22 December 1966 to; Norton Simon Art Foundation (sale, Los Angeles, Sotheby Parke Bernet, 23 June 1980, lot 511, for $550).

Cat. 2
Pierre-Auguste Renoir (French, 1841–1919)
Andrée in Blue, 1916–1918
Oil on canvas, 15 ¾ x 19 ⅞ in. (40 x 50.5 cm)
[Dalzell Hatfield Gallery, Los Angeles, sold 22 December 1954 for $16,000 to]; Norton Simon, gift 27 December 1956 to; Pomona College, Claremont, Calif., sold 1973 to; [the trade, New York, sold 1973 to]; private collection, Japan. Mr. Charmers, Houston; Herbert L. Kramer (sale, New York, Sotheby's, 18 November 1986, lot 27, for $572,000 to); private collection, U.S.A. (sale, New York, Sotheby's, 10 November 1992, lot 19, unsold).

1955

Cat. 3
Pierre Bonnard (French, 1867–1947)
Basket of Fruit
Oil on canvas, 9 ½ x 13 in. (24.1 x 33 cm)
[Dalzell Hatfield Gallery, Los Angeles, sold 14 January 1955 for $3,500 to]; Norton Simon, used in trade 10 September 1969 with a value of $3,500 as partial payment for Georges Braque, *Still Life with Napkin* (cat. 681) to; [Paul Kantor, Beverly Hills, Calif.].

Cat. 4
Amedeo Modigliani (Italian, 1884–1920)
Man with a Cigarette
Pencil, 15 ¾ x 9 ¼ in. (40 x 23.5 cm)
[James Vigeveno Gallery, Los Angeles, sold 17 January 1955 for $600 to]; Norton Simon (sale, New York, Parke-Bernet Galleries, 5 May 1971, lot 66, for $4,500).

Cat. 5
Dietz Edzard (French, 1893–1963)
Young Woman
Oil on canvas, 14 x 9 ½ in. (35.6 x 24.1 cm)
[James Vigeveno Gallery, Los Angeles, sold 20 January 1955 for $700 to]; Norton Simon, used in trade 13 October 1955 as partial payment for Edgar Degas, *Dancer in Green* (cat. 18) to; [Dalzell Hatfield Gallery, Los Angeles].

Cat. 6
Hans Hofmann (American, 1880–1966)
Floral Composition, 1954
Oil on canvas, 48 x 36 in. (121.9 x 91.4 cm)
[Samuel M. Kootz Gallery, New York, sold 7 March 1955 for $1,200 to]; Norton Simon (sale, New York, Parke-Bernet Galleries, 17 November 1971, lot 10, for $15,000).

Cat. 7
Paul Gauguin (French, 1848–1903)
Brittany Landscape with Swineherd, 1888
Oil on canvas, 28 ¾ x 36 ⅝ in. (73 x 93 cm)
[Wildenstein & Co., New York, sold 22 March 1955 for $60,000 to]; Norton Simon, transferred 24 July 1970 to; Lucille Ellis Simon, gift 1991 to; Los Angeles County Museum of Art.

Cat. 8
Camille Pissarro (French, 1830–1903)
Banks of the River at Pontoise, 1872
Oil on canvas, 21 ⅝ x 35 ¾ in. (54.9 x 90.8 cm)
[Wildenstein & Co., New York, sold 22 March 1955 for $28,000 to]; Norton Simon, transferred 24 July 1970 to; Lucille Ellis Simon, sold 1997 through [Lionel Pissarro, Paris] to; private collection, Chicago.

Cat. 9
Attributed to Pablo Picasso
(Spanish, 1881–1973)
Portrait of a Young Woman, 1954
Ink, 12 x 9 ½ in. (30.5 x 24.1 cm)
[French dealer, Paris, sold 1 July 1955 for
$1,000 to]; Norton Simon, used in trade
11 May 1966 with a value of $1,000 as
payment for Honoré Daumier, *Amateur in
Contemplation* and *Surprised Amateur*
(cat. 309, 310) to; [Paul Kantor, Beverly
Hills, Calif.].

Cat. 10
Pierre-Auguste Renoir (French, 1841–1919)
Woman in a Corset
Oil on canvas, 12 ⅝ x 10 in. (32 x 25.5 cm)
[Paul Petrides, Paris, sold 1 July 1955 for
$13,000 to]; Norton Simon, used in trade
4 June 1956 with a value of $14,400 as
partial payment for Honoré Daumier,
The Studio (cat. 29) to; [Wildenstein &
Co., New York, sold to]; Mimi de Herrera
Uslar, New York. (sale, New York, Christie's,
10 November 1987, lot 24, for $660,000
to); private collection (sale, New York,
Sotheby's, 8 November 2006, lot 171).

Cat. 11
Henri Matisse (French, 1869–1954)
Woman Leaning on Her Hands
Bronze, 5 ¼ x 9 ½ in. (13.3 x 24.1 cm)
[M. Knoedler & Co., New York, sold
8 July 1955 for $1,800 to]; Norton Simon,
transferred 24 July 1970 to; Lucille Ellis
Simon (estate sale, New York, Christie's,
9 November 2000, lot 148, for $85,000 to);
[Jeffrey H. Loria & Co., New York].

Cat. 12
Bernard Lorjou (French, 1908–1986)
White Flowers on a Yellow Background
Oil on panel, 25 ⅝ x 21 ¼ in. (65.1 x 54 cm)
[Galerie Charpentier, Paris, sold 9 July 1955
for $2,300 to]; Norton Simon, used in trade

18 July 1956 with a value of $2,850 as partial
payment for Édouard Manet, *Madame Manet*
(cat. 30) to; [Wildenstein & Co., New York].

Cat. 13
Angna Enters (American, 1897–1989)
Child Playing in the Bois de Boulogne
Oil on canvasboard, 8 x 10 in. (20.3 x 25.4 cm)
[James Vigeveno Gallery, Los Angeles,
sold 9 September 1955 for $125 to]; Norton
Simon, sold 22 December 1966 to; Norton
Simon Art Foundation (sale, Los Angeles,
Sotheby Parke Bernet, 15 September 1980,
lot 460, for $125).

Cat. 14
Arshile Gorky
(American, b. Armenia, 1904–1948)
Housatonic, 1943
Ink and crayon, 19 x 24 ¾ in. (48.3 x 62.9 cm)
[Sidney Janis Gallery, New York, sold
26 September 1955 for $750 to]; Norton
Simon, gift 15 March 1967 to; Norton Simon
Art Foundation (sale, New York, Sotheby
Parke Bernet, 3 May 1974, lot 505, for
$55,000 to); [Alan Stone Gallery, New York].
Estate of private collection, Memphis.

Cat. 15
Edgar Degas (French, 1834–1917)
Dancer in the role of Harlequin
(formerly *Dancer rubbing her knee*)
Bronze, cast no. 39/HER.D, 12 ³/₁₆ in. (31 cm)
[M. Knoedler & Co., New York, sold
27 September 1955 for $1,800 to]; Norton
Simon (sale, New York, Sotheby Parke
Bernet, 2 May 1973, lot 3, for $24,000).
[Waddington Galleries, London]. (sale,
London, Sotheby Parke Bernet & Co.,
29 June 1983). [Maxwell Davidson Gallery,
New York]. [Achim Moeller, London, sold
c. 1984 to]; private collection, New York
(sale, New York, Christie's, 12 November
1997 to); [Browse & Darby, London].

9

13

10

15

11

20

17

21

18

22

19

23

Cat. 16
Attributed to Pablo Picasso
(Spanish, 1881–1973)
Classic Model
Oil on canvas, 7 ⅞ x 3 ⅝ in. (20 x 9.2 cm)
[Perls Galleries, New York, sold 3 October
1955 for $2,070 to]; Norton Simon, used in
trade 11 May 1966 with a value of $2,070
as payment for Honoré Daumier, *In the
Courtroom* (cat. 311) to; [Paul Kantor,
Beverly Hills, Calif.].

Cat. 17
Georges Braque (French, 1882–1963)
Mandolin (formerly *Still Life with Guitar
[Oval Cubist]*), 1911
Oil on canvas, 9 ½ x 13 ¾ in. (24.1 x 34.9 cm)
[Sidney Janis Gallery, New York, sold
6 October 1955 for $8,000 to]; Norton
Simon (sale, New York, Parke-Bernet
Galleries, 21 October 1971, lot 121, for
$70,000). [Minami Gallery, Tokyo, sold
June 1973 to]; Kawamura Memorial
Museum of Art, Sakura, Japan.

Cat. 18
Edgar Degas (French, 1834–1917)
Dancer in Green, c. 1897–1901
Pastel mounted on board, 25 ¼ x 19 ¼ in.
(64.1 x 48.9 cm)
[Dalzell Hatfield Gallery, Los Angeles, sold
12 October 1955 for $20,850 to]; Norton
Simon, gift 18 October 1983 to; The Norton
Simon Foundation (F.1983.18).

Cat. 19
Honoré Daumier (French, 1808–1879)
Saltimbanques Resting, 1870
Oil on canvas, 21 ½ x 25 ¾ in.
(54.6 x 65.4 cm)
[Wildenstein & Co., New York, sold
20 December 1955 for $85,000 to]; Norton
Simon, gift 29 June 1976 to; Norton Simon
Art Foundation (M.1976.6).

1956

Cat. 20
Fritz Winter (German, 1905–1976)
Tensions, 1952
Oil on canvas, 43 ¼ x 45 ¼ in.
(109.9 x 114.9 cm)
[Galerie Ferdinand Möller, Cologne, sold
3 January 1956 for $571 to]; Norton Simon,
gift 24 December 1957 to; Pomona College,
Claremont, Calif., used in trade 4 April 1974
with a value of $1,500 as partial payment for
Francisco de Goya, *Los Caprichos* (cat. 419)
to; The Norton Simon Foundation (sale,
Los Angeles, Sotheby Parke Bernet, 23 June
1980, lot 262, for $3,750).

Cat. 21
Georges Rouault (French, 1871–1958)
Sea and Sky
Glazed ceramic vase, 16 in. (40.6 cm)
[Dalzell Hatfield Gallery, Los Angeles,
sold 23 March 1956 for $5,500 to]; Norton
Simon, transferred 24 July 1970 to; Lucille
Ellis Simon.

Cat. 22
Henri Matisse (French, 1869–1954)
Jetty at Collioure
Oil on canvas, 24 ¼ x 25 ½ in. (61.6 x 64.8 cm)
[Pierre Matisse Gallery, New York, sold
21 April 1956 for $18,000 to]; Norton Simon,
gift (one-half interest 24 December 1957;
remaining one-half interest 7 March 1958
to); Pomona College, Claremont, Calif.,
sold 1973 to; [the trade, New York, sold 1973
to]; private collection, Japan. [Acquavella
Galleries, New York, 2008].

Cat. 23
Henri Matisse (French, 1869–1954)
Woman Sleeping, c. 1931
Pencil, 9 ½ x 12 ⅜ in. (24.1 x 31.4 cm)
[Pierre Matisse Gallery, New York, sold
21 April 1956 for $700 to]; Norton Simon
(sale, New York, Parke-Bernet Galleries,

5 May 1971, lot 63, for $7,000 to); Kasser Art
Foundation, Montclair, N.J.

Cat. 24
Edgar Degas (French, 1834–1917)
Portrait of a Man, c. 1868–1869
Oil on canvas, 13 ⅝ x 7 ⅞ in. (34.6 x 20 cm)
[Sam Salz, New York, sold 23 April 1956 for
$17,150 to]; Norton Simon (sale, New York,
Parke-Bernet Galleries, 5 May 1971, lot 32,
for $100,000). private collection.

Cat. 25A-B
Edgar Degas (French, 1834–1917)
Study of a Man (recto), 1874; *Sketch for
Dante and Beatrice* (verso), 1856–1858
Pencil, 14 ½ x 8 ½ in. (36.8 x 21.6 cm)
[Sam Salz, New York, sold 23 April 1956 for
$850 to]; Norton Simon, sold 4 January 1974
for $22,500 to; [E. V. Thaw & Co., New York,
sold to]; Leonardo Mondadori, Milan, by
inheritance to; private collection, Milan.

Cat. 26
Formerly attributed to Rembrandt van Rijn
(Dutch, 1606–1669)
*Portrait of a Lady, Traditionally Said to Be
Hendrickje Stoeffels*
Oil on canvas, 26 x 21 ½ in. (66 x 54.6 cm)
[Duveen Brothers, New York, sold 28 May
1956 for $133,500 to]; Norton Simon,
transferred 24 July 1970 to; Lucille Ellis
Simon (estate sale, New York, Christie's,
7 June 2002, lot 24, for $130,000, as Studio
of Rembrandt, *Portrait of a Lady* to); [a
consortium of dealers, sold to]; Alfred and
Isabel Bader, Milwaukee.

Cat. 27
Georges Braque (French, 1882–1963)
Carafe, Grapes, and Lemons, 1924
Oil on canvas, 12 x 25 in. (30.5 x 63.5 cm)
[Dalzell Hatfield Gallery, Los Angeles,
sold 1 June 1956 for $16,500 to]; Norton
Simon (sale, New York, Sotheby Parke
Bernet, 2 May 1973, lot 10, for $100,000 to);

[Waddington Galleries, London, sold 1973
to]; private collection, consigned, 1974 to;
[Waddington Galleries, London, sold 1974
to]; [Galerie Rosengart, Lucerne, sold 1975
to]; Dr. Bernhard Sprengel, Hanover.

Cat. 28
Formerly attributed to Rembrandt van Rijn
(Dutch, 1606–1669)
A Jewish Philosopher, c. 1656
Oil on canvas, 26 ⅜ x 23 ¼ in. (67 x 59.1 cm)
[Duveen Brothers, New York, sold 1 June
1956 for $100,000 to]; Norton Simon,
returned June 1959 for full purchase price
to; [Duveen Brothers, New York].

Cat. 29
Honoré Daumier (French, 1808–1879)
The Studio, 1870
Oil on canvas, 15 ¾ x 12 ⅝ in. (40 x 32.1 cm)
[Wildenstein & Co., New York, sold
4 June 1956 for $50,000 to]; Norton Simon,
transferred 24 July 1970 to; Lucille Ellis
Simon, sold 1985 to; The J. Paul Getty
Museum, Los Angeles.

Cat. 30
Édouard Manet (French, 1832–1883)
Madame Manet, 1874–1876
Oil on canvas, 23 ⅞ x 20 in. (60.6 x 50.8 cm)
[Wildenstein & Co., New York, sold
18 July 1956 for $55,000 ($52,150 and
Bernard Lorjou, *White Flowers on a Yellow
Background* [cat. 12] valued at $2,850)
to]; Norton Simon, gift 16 August 1973 to;
Norton Simon Art Foundation (M.1973.4).

Cat. 31
Paul Cézanne (French, 1839–1906)
Portrait of a Peasant, c. 1900–1906
Oil on canvas, 21 x 26 in. (53.3 x 66 cm)
[Rosenberg & Stiebel, New York, sold
1 August 1956 for $70,000 to]; Norton
Simon, sold 16 August 1973 for $1,000,000
to; [E. V. Thaw & Co., New York]; Thyssen-
Bornemisza Collection, Madrid

24

28

25B

29

26

30

27

31

32

33

34

35

36

37

38

39

Cat. 32
Rembrandt van Rijn (Dutch, 1606–1669)
Abraham Francken, the Art Dealer, 1657
Etching, 6 ¼ x 8 ¼ in. (15.9 x 21 cm)
[Ernest Raboff, Los Angeles, sold 30 August
1956 for $45 to]; Norton Simon, gift 11 March
1958 to; Pomona College, Claremont, Calif.

Cat. 33
Rembrandt van Rijn (Dutch, 1606–1669)
Diana at the Bath
Etching, 6 ⅞ x 6 ⅜ in. (17.5 x 16.2 cm)
[Ernest Raboff, Los Angeles, sold 30 August
1956 for $75 to]; Norton Simon, gift 11 March
1958 to; Pomona College, Claremont, Calif.

Cat. 34
Jules Pascin (French, 1885–1930)
The Model, c. 1923
Oil over charcoal on canvas, 37 x 28 ½ in.
(94 x 72.4 cm)
[Dalzell Hatfield Gallery, Los Angeles,
sold 31 August 1956 for $4,000 to]; Norton
Simon (sale, New York, Parke-Bernet
Galleries, 5 May 1971, lot 67, for $36,000).
private collection (sale, New York,
Christie's, 13 May 1999, lot 200, for $118,000
to); private collection, California.

Cat. 35
Edgar Degas (French, 1834–1917)
Woman arranging her hair
Bronze, cast no. 50/C, 18 ¼ in. (46.4 cm)
[Otto Gerson Fine Arts Associates, New
York, 28 September 1956 for $4,800 to];
Norton Simon, transferred 24 July 1970 to;
Lucille Ellis Simon; private collection,
Los Angeles.

Cat. 36
Jacques Lipchitz (French, 1891–1973)
Flight, 1940
Bronze, 15 in. (38.1 cm)
[Otto Gerson Fine Arts Associates, New
York, sold 28 September 1956 for $2,200
to]; Norton Simon, transferred 24 July 1970

to; Lucille Ellis Simon. (sale, New York,
Christie's, 25 February 2004, lot 71, for
$22,000 to); [Michelle Rosenfeld Gallery,
New York].

Cat. 37
Jules Pascin (French, 1885–1930)
The Coach with Pink Umbrella, 1917
Watercolor, 7 x 9 ⅝ in. (17.8 x 24.5 cm)
[Perls Galleries, New York, sold 27 October
1956 for $600 to]; Norton Simon, sold
22 December 1966 to; Norton Simon Art
Foundation (sale, New York, Parke-Bernet
Galleries, 13 May 1970, lot 4, for $1,500).

Cat. 38
Jules Pascin (French, 1885–1930)
Young Country Girls, 1917
Watercolor, 8 ¼ x 10 ¼ in. (21 x 26 cm)
[Perls Galleries, New York, sold 27 October
1956 for $520 to]; Norton Simon, sold
22 December 1966 to; Norton Simon Art
Foundation (sale, New York, Parke-Bernet
Galleries, 13 May 1970, lot 5, for $1,500).
[Arthur James Galleries, Delray Beach,
Florida]. (sale, New York, Sotheby's, 12 June
1997, lot 41, for $3,000).

Cat. 39
Jean Dubuffet (French, 1901–1985)
Garden of Bibi Trompette, 1955
Butterfly wings collage, 9 x 12 ½ in.
(22.9 x 31.8 cm)
[Samuel M. Kootz Gallery, New York, sold
2 November 1956 for $400 to]; Norton
Simon, gift 24 December 1957 to; Pomona
College, Claremont, Calif., used in trade
4 April 1974, with a value of $8,500 as
partial payment for Francisco de Goya,
Los Caprichos (cat. 419) to; The Norton
Simon Foundation, sold 2 December 1974
for $15,000 to; [Stephen Hahn Gallery,
New York, promised gift 1995 to]; National
Gallery of Art, Washington, D.C.

Cat. 40
Jean Dubuffet (French, 1901–1985)
Garden of Islands, 1955
Butterfly wings collage, 9 x 12 ½ in.
(22.9 x 31.8 cm)
[Samuel M. Kootz Gallery, New York, sold
2 November 1956 for $400 to]; Norton
Simon, gift 24 December 1957 to; Pomona
College, Claremont, Calif., used in trade
4 April 1974, with a value of $8,500 as
partial payment for Francisco de Goya, *Los
Caprichos* (cat. 419) to; The Norton Simon
Foundation (sale, New York, Sotheby Parke
Bernet, 18 May 1978, lot 183, for $15,000).

Cat. 41
Alfred Sisley (French, 1839–1899)
The Seine at Bougival, 1873
Oil on canvas, 15 x 24 in. (38.1 x 61 cm)
[Wildenstein & Co., New York, sold
18 November 1956 for $15,000 to]; Norton
Simon, sold October 1972 for $160,000 to;
[E. V. Thaw & Co., New York]. [Arthur
Tooth & Sons, London]. (sale, New York,
Christie's, 13 May 1980, lot 19, unsold). (sale,
New York, Christie's, 17 May 1983, lot 11, for
$280,000, to); private collection, Germany.

Cat. 42
Thomas Gainsborough (English, 1727–1788)
Lady Mendip, 1787
Oil on canvas, 28 x 23 in. (71.1 x 58.4 cm)
[Newhouse Galleries, New York, sold
13 December 1956 for $10,000 to]; Norton
Simon, sold August 1967 to; Robert Ellis
Simon, bequest 29 October 1969 to; private
collection.

1957

Cat. 43
Paul Cézanne (French, 1839–1906)
Mont Sainte Victoire, c. 1895
Watercolor, 11 x 17 ½ in. (27.9 x 44.5 cm)
[Dalzell Hatfield Gallery, Los Angeles, sold
3 January 1957 for $8,000 to]; Norton Simon

(sale, New York, Parke-Bernet Galleries,
21 October 1971, lot 74, unsold), sold
15 April 1974 for $125,000 to; [E. V. Thaw &
Co., New York]. (sale, New York, Christie's,
15 April 1975, lot 27). private collection,
Europe.

Cat. 44A-B
Paul Cézanne (French, 1839–1906)
Wooded Road (recto); *Mont Sainte Victoire*
(verso)
Watercolor, 18 ⅞ x 12 ¼ in. (47.9 x 31.1 cm)
[Paul Rosenberg & Co., New York, sold
30 January 1957 for $15,000 to]; Norton
Simon, transferred 24 July 1970 to; Lucille
Ellis Simon, sold by her estate in 2000 to;
Donald B. Marron, New York (sale, New
York, Christie's, 6 November 2007, lot
32, for $6,760,000 to); private collection,
Switzerland.

Cat. 45
Edgar Degas (French, 1834–1917)
Madame Dietz-Monnin, 1879
Pastel on brown paper, 18 ½ x 12 ¼ in.
(47 x 31.1 cm)
[Paul Rosenberg & Co., New York, sold
30 January 1957 for $45,000 to]; Norton
Simon, gift 29 June 1976 to; Norton Simon
Art Foundation (M.1976.7).

Cat. 46
Henri de Toulouse-Lautrec
(French, 1864–1901)
The Streetwalker (formerly *Portrait of a
Prostitute*), 1892–1894
Oil on cardboard, 24 ¾ x 19 ⅛ in.
(62.9 x 48.6 cm)
[Paul Rosenberg & Co., New York, sold
25 February 1957 for $67,000 to]; Robert
Ellis Simon, bequest 29 October 1969 to;
The Norton Simon Foundation, transferred
27 November 2000 to; Norton Simon Art
Foundation (M.2000.1.3).

40

44A

41

45

42

46

43

47

51

48   52

49   53

50

54

Cat. 47

Camille Pissarro (French, 1830–1903)
Boulevard des Fossés, Pontoise, 1872
Oil on canvas, 18 ¼ x 21 ⅞ in. (46.4 x 55.6 cm)
[M. Knoedler & Co., New York, sold
13 March 1957 for $34,000 to]; Norton
Simon, gift 30 December 1975 to; Norton
Simon Art Foundation (M.1975.20).

Cat. 48

Ernst Ludwig Kirchner
(German, 1880–1938)
The Deciduous Forest, 1904
Oil on canvas, 24 x 35 ¾ in. (61 x 90.8 cm)
[Paul Kantor, Beverly Hills, Calif., sold
19 April 1957 for $6,500 to]; Norton Simon,
gift 7 February 1964 to; private collection,
Los Angeles.

Cat. 49

Honoré Daumier (French, 1808–1879)
Study for "Saltimbanques Resting,"
c. 1865–1866
Oil on panel, 11 ¾ x 14 ¾ in. (29.9 x 37.5 cm)
[Sam Salz, New York, sold 2 May 1957 for
$15,000 to]; Robert Ellis Simon, bequest
29 October 1969 to; The Norton Simon
Foundation, transferred 27 November
1985 to; Norton Simon Art Foundation
(M.1985.2).

Cat. 50

After Honoré Daumier (French, 1808–1879)
Study of Two Figures
Oil on board, 13 ⅞ x 10 ⅝ in. (35.2 x 27 cm)
[Sam Salz, New York, sold 2 May 1957 for
$1,000 to]; Norton Simon, gift 15 March
1967 to; Norton Simon Art Foundation
(sale, New York, Sotheby Parke Bernet,
2 May 1973, lot 26, for $3,500 to); Ian
Woodner, New York, by inheritance 1990 to;
Ian Woodner Family Collection, sold July
1999 to; [Daniel Barr, New York]; Daniel
Barr estate, New York.

Cat. 51

Helen Frankenthaler (American, b. 1928)
Untitled, 1955
Collage: oil on papers and cloth on
cardboard, 19 ½ x 12 ⅛ in. (49.5 x 30.8 cm)
[Tibor de Nagy Gallery, New York, 9 May
1957 for $150 to]; Norton Simon, sold
22 December 1966 to; Norton Simon Art
Foundation (M.1966.10.3).

Cat. 52

Leonard Edmondson
(American, 1916–2002)
Untitled, 1957
Gouache and crayon, 14 x 20 in.
(35.6 x 50.8 cm)
Leonard Edmondson, sold 22 May 1957 for
$250 to; Norton Simon, sold 22 December
1966 to; Norton Simon Art Foundation
(sale, Los Angeles, Sotheby Parke Bernet, 23
June 1980, unsold, sold privately 15 August
1980 for $50).

Cat. 53

Édouard Vuillard (French, 1868–1940)
Green Hillside at L'Étang-la-Ville (formerly
Landscape in the Île-de-France), c. 1900
Oil on board, 30 ¾ x 41 ½ in. (78.1 x 105.4 cm)
[Sam Salz, New York, sold 29 May 1957 for
$10,000 to]; Donald Ellis Simon, gift 1971
to; The Norton Simon Foundation, used in
trade 9 May 1970 with a value of $60,000
as partial payment for Lucas Cranach the
Elder, *Eve* (cat. 734) to; [Spencer A. Samuels
& Co., New York]. [Thomas Gibson Fine
Art, London, 1979]. (sale, New York,
Christie's, 3 November 1981, lot 26, unsold).
private collection, Switzerland

Cat. 54

Paul Cézanne (French, 1839–1906)
Group of Trees beside a Stream, c. 1895–1900
Pencil and watercolor, 12 x 18 ½ in.
(30.5 x 47 cm)
[Paul Rosenberg & Co., New York, sold

13 August 1957 for $10,000 to]; Norton Simon (private sale, New York, Christie's, 31 January 1983 for $82,000). Yayoi Museum, Tokyo.

Cat. 55
Paul Cézanne (French, 1839–1906)
Farmhouse and Chestnut Trees at Jas de Bouffan, 1884–1885
Oil on canvas, 36 ⅛ x 28 ¹¹/₁₆ in. (91.8 x 72.9 cm)
[Paul Rosenberg & Co., New York, sold 1 October 1957 for $87,500 to]; Robert Ellis Simon, bequest 29 October 1969 to; The Norton Simon Foundation, transferred 29 November 1995 to; Norton Simon Art Foundation (M.1995.1).

Cat. 56
Edgar Degas (French, 1834–1917)
Young Girls beside the Sea (formerly *Nursemaids on the Beach*), c. 1869
Essence on mauve laid paper, 17 ¾ x 23 ¾ in. (45.1 x 60.3 cm)
[Paul Rosenberg & Co., New York, sold 1 October 1957 for $30,000 to]; Robert Ellis Simon, bequest 29 October 1969 to; The Norton Simon Foundation, transferred 31 October 1996 to; Norton Simon Art Foundation (M.1996.2).

Cat. 57
Édouard Vuillard (French, 1868–1940)
The Artist's Mother
Black chalk, 25 x 18 in. (63.5 x 45.7 cm)
[Sam Salz, New York, sold 3 October 1957 for $3,500 to]; Norton Simon, transferred 24 July 1970 to; Lucille Ellis Simon (estate sale, New York, Christie's, 9 November 2000, lot 408, for $100,000 to); private collection, New York.

Cat. 58
Paul Cézanne (French, 1839–1906)
Crouching Venus, c. 1879–1882

Pencil, 18 ½ x 11 ¹³/₁₆ in. (47 x 30 cm)
[Drs. Fritz and Peter Nathan, Zurich, sold 26 November 1957 for $5,000 to]; Norton Simon (sale, New York, Parke-Bernet Galleries, 5 May 1971, lot 26, for $9,500 to); Kasser Art Foundation, Montclair, N.J.

Cat. 59
Hans Hofmann (American, 1880–1966)
Abstraction, 1956
Gouache, 10 ⁷/₁₆ x 8 in. (26.5 x 20.3 cm)
[Dealer, date of purchase, and price unknown, by 31 December 1957 to]; Norton Simon, gift 11 March 1958 to; Pomona College, Claremont, Calif.

1958

Cat. 60
Attributed to Alexis Grimou (French, 1678–1733) (formerly attributed to Jean-Honoré Fragonard [French, 1732–1806])
Self-Portrait(?) (formerly *Portrait of the Artist's Cook*)
Oil on canvas, 21 ¾ x 18 ¼ in. (55.3 x 46.4 cm)
[Wildenstein & Co., New York, sold 13 January 1958 for $10,000 to]; Norton Simon (sale, New York, Parke-Bernet Galleries, 8 May 1971, lot 215A, for $8,200). [Michael Drinkhouse, New York]. [William Kennedy, New York, sold 1972 to]; Helen Clay Frick, bequest 1984 to; The Frick Art Museum, Pittsburgh.

Cat. 61A-B
Jean-Siméon Chardin (French, 1699–1779)
Still Life with Cooking Utensils and *Still Life with Fowl*, c. 1728–1730
Oil on canvas, each 15 ¾ x 12 ⅜ in. (40 x 31.4 cm)
[Wildenstein & Co., New York, sold 14 January 1958 for $23,500 to]; Robert Ellis Simon, bequest 29 October 1969 to; The Norton Simon Foundation (F.1969.38.3.1–2).

55

59

56

60

57

61A

58

61B

62

66

63

67

68

65

69

Cat. 62
Greece: Attic
Lekythos, 440–430 B.C.
Painted pottery, 13 x 3 ½ in. (33 x 8.9 cm)
[Charles L. Morley, New York, sold 10 February 1958 for $2,000 to]; Norton Simon, by inheritance 2 June 1993 to; Jennifer Jones Simon Art Trust, Los Angeles (N.1958.1).

Cat. 63
Jean-François Millet (French, 1814–1875)
Peasants Resting (formerly *Le Briquet*), c. 1866
Pastel, 16 ¾ x 20 ¼ in. (42.6 x 51.4 cm)
(Sale, London, Sotheby & Co., through [Thomas Agnew & Sons], 9 July 1958 for $2,128 to); Norton Simon (sale, New York, Parke-Bernet Galleries, 5 May 1971, lot 23, for $36,000 to); The Armand Hammer Foundation, Los Angeles, gift 1990 to; Armand Hammer Museum of Art and Culture Center, Los Angeles.

Cat. 64
Leonard Kaplan (American, b. 1922)
Untitled
Drawing (medium and dimensions unknown)
Leonard Kaplan, sold 18 August 1958 for $100 to; Norton Simon, gift 31 December 1966 to R. Siegel, Los Angeles.

Cat. 65
Georg Kolbe (German, 1877–1947)
Kneeling Girl, 1926
Bronze, edition of 30, unnumbered cast, 21 in. (53.3 cm)
[Dalzell Hatfield Gallery, Los Angeles, sold 18 September 1958 for $3,000 to]; Norton Simon, transferred 24 July 1970 to; Lucille Ellis Simon (estate sale, New York, Christie's, 7 November 2002, lot 271, for $15,000).

Cat. 66
Marcel Gromaire (French, 1872–1971)
Head of a Woman, 1937
Black ink, 12 ½ x 9 ⅝ in. (31.8 x 24.5 cm)
[Charles E. Slatkin, New York, sold 2 October 1958 for $450 to]; Norton Simon, sold 22 December 1966 to; Norton Simon Art Foundation (sale, New York, Parke-Bernet Galleries, 13 May 1970, lot 58, for $700). [R. S. Johnson Fine Art, Chicago, 2006].

Cat. 67
Louis-Eugène Boudin (French, 1824–1898)
Antwerp Harbor, 1872
Oil on panel, 10 ½ x 13 ¾ in. (26.7 x 34.9 cm)
(Sale, London, Sotheby & Co., through [Thomas Agnew & Sons], 3 December 1958 for $7,289 to); Robert Ellis Simon, bequest 29 October 1969 to; The Norton Simon Foundation (sale, New York, Sotheby Parke Bernet, 2 May 1973, lot 164, for $40,000 to); private collection, Texas.

Cat. 68
Jules Dupré (French, 1811–1889)
Farmyard
Oil on canvas, 8 ½ x 12 ½ in. (21.6 x 31.8 cm)
(Sale, London, Sotheby & Co., through [Thomas Agnew & Sons], 3 December 1958 for $534 to); Robert Ellis Simon, bequest 29 October 1969 to; The Norton Simon Foundation (sale, New York, Sotheby Parke Bernet, 2 May 1973, lot 17, for $2,800 to); [Maurice Rheims, Paris].

Cat. 69
Henri Fantin-Latour (French, 1836–1904)
A Bunch of Mixed Zinnias, 1881
Oil on canvas, 10 x 13 ½ in. (25.4 x 34.3 cm)
(Sale, London, Sotheby & Co., through [Thomas Agnew & Sons], 3 December 1958 for $11,385 to); Robert Ellis Simon, bequest

29 October 1969 to; The Norton Simon Foundation (sale, New York, Parke-Bernet Galleries, 13 May 1970, lot 7, unsold), (sale, New York, Sotheby Parke Bernet, 1 November 1978, lot 18A, for $55,000 to); private collection, New York.

Cat. 70
Henri Fantin-Latour (French, 1836–1904)
Madame Fantin-Latour, 1876
Oil on canvas, 10 x 8 ⅛ in. (25.5 x 20.5 cm)
(Sale, London, Sotheby & Co., through [Thomas Agnew & Sons], 3 December 1958 for $3,665 to); Robert Ellis Simon, bequest 29 October 1969 to; The Norton Simon Foundation (sale, New York, Parke-Bernet Galleries, 13 May 1970, lot 14, for $7,000). (sale, New York, Christie's, 6 May 1999, lot 105, for $20,000 to); private collection, New York.

Cat. 71
Henri-Joseph Harpignies
(French, 1819–1916)
A Farmhouse, 1875
Oil on canvas, 11 x 16 ¼ in. (28 x 41.2 cm)
(Sale, London, Sotheby & Co., through [Thomas Agnew & Sons], 3 December 1958 for $6,364 to); Robert Ellis Simon, bequest 29 October 1969 to; The Norton Simon Foundation (F.1969.38.8).

Cat. 72
Johan Barthold Jongkind (Dutch, 1819–1891)
Notre Dame and the Île de la Cité at Sunset
Pen, ink, and watercolor, 9 ½ x 15 ½ in. (24.1 x 39.4 cm)
(Sale, London, Sotheby & Co., through [Thomas Agnew & Sons], 3 December 1958 for $1,320 to); Robert Ellis Simon, bequest 29 October 1969 to; The Norton Simon Foundation, (sale, New York, Parke-Bernet Galleries, 13 May 1970, lot 1, for $3,750 to); private collection.

Cat. 73
Paul Signac (French, 1863–1935)
Bourg-Argental
Black chalk and watercolor, 8 ¼ x 10 ½ in. (21 x 26.7 cm)
(Sale, London, Sotheby & Co., through [Thomas Agnew & Sons], 3 December 1958 for $1,455 to); Robert Ellis Simon, bequest 29 October 1969 to; The Norton Simon Foundation (sale, New York, Sotheby Parke Bernet, 2 May 1973, lot 29, for $9,000 to); private collection.

Cat. 74
Hilda Levy (American, 1908–2001)
Abstract
Mixed media, 11 ¾ x 16 in. (29.9 x 40.6 cm)
[Dealer and date of purchase unknown, by 31 December 1958 for $60 to]; Norton Simon, gift 17 May 1977 to; Norton Simon Museum (P.1977.8).

Cat. 75
John McLaughlin (American, 1898–1976)
Untitled, c. 1946
Acrylic on board, 10 ¾ x 12 ¹⁵/₁₆ in. (27.3 x 32.9 cm)
[Dixie Hall Studio, Laguna Beach, Calif., by 31 December 1958 for $60 to]; Norton Simon, gift 17 May 1977 to; Norton Simon Museum (P.1977.3).

1959

Cat. 76
Henri Fantin-Latour (French, 1836–1904)
Vase of Chrysanthemums
Oil on canvas, 21 ⅞ x 18 ⅛ in. (55.6 x 46 cm)
[Wildenstein & Co., New York, sold 9 February 1959 for $22,500 to]; Norton Simon (sale, New York, Parke-Bernet Galleries, 5 May 1971, lot 39, for $40,000 to); private collection, Texas.

73

70

74

71

75

72

76

77

78

79

80

81

82

83A

83B

83C

Cat. 77

Jacob van Ruisdael (Dutch, 1628/1629–1682)
Landscape with Church and Windmill,
c. 1665
Oil on canvas, 15 x 15 ¾ in. (38.1 x 40 cm)
[Thomas Agnew & Sons, London, sold
17 March 1959 for $40,000 to]; Norton
Simon, sold 16 June 1972 for $150,000 to;
[Edward Speelman, London].

Cat. 78

Edgar Degas (French, 1834–1917)
Women Ironing, begun c. 1875–1876;
reworked c. 1882–1886
Oil on canvas, 32 ¼ x 29 ¾ in. (81.9 x 75.6 cm)
[Arthur Tooth & Sons, London, sold
7 April 1959 for $260,000 to]; Norton
Simon (one-quarter interest), Lucille
Simon (one-quarter interest), and Robert
Simon (one-half interest); bequest of
Robert's one-half interest 29 October
1969 to; The Norton Simon Foundation;
transfer of Lucille's one-quarter interest
24 July 1970 to; Norton Simon, gift of
one-half interest 30 December 1971 to;
Norton Simon Art Foundation; The Norton
Simon Foundation sold its half-interest
28 February 1979 to; Norton Simon Art
Foundation (M.1979.17).

Cat. 79

Roman, mid- to late 2nd century A.D.
Head of a Hero
Marble, 13 ⅜ x 9 ⅝ x 7 in. (34 x 24.5 x 17.8 cm)
(Sale, Lucerne, Ars Antiqua, 2 May 1959,
through [William Schab, New York] for
$6,917 to); Norton Simon, by inheritance
2 June 1993 to; Jennifer Jones Simon Art
Trust, Los Angeles (N.1959.1).

Cat. 80

Peter Paul Rubens (Flemish, 1577–1640)
and Workshop

*Isabella Clara Eugenia, Governor of the
Spanish Netherlands, as a Poor Clare*, 1625
Oil on canvas, 45 ⅝ x 35 ¼ in. (115.9 x 89.5 cm)
[Rosenberg & Stiebel, New York, sold 17
June 1959 for $30,000 to]; Norton Simon,
sold 22 December 1966 to; Norton Simon
Art Foundation (M.1966.10.10).

1960

Cat. 81

Odilon Redon (French, 1840–1916)
Trees, 1890s
Charcoal, 19 ¾ x 14 ¾ in. (50.2 x 37.5 cm)
[Walter Goetz, France, sold 8 January 1960
for $3,000 to]; Norton Simon (sale, New
York, Parke-Bernet Galleries, 5 May 1971, lot
57, for $16,000). The Museum of Fine Arts,
Houston.

Cat. 82

Édouard Manet (French, 1832–1883)
Still Life with Fish and Shrimp, 1864
Oil on canvas, 17 ⅝ x 28 ¾ in. (44.8 x 73 cm)
[Paul Rosenberg & Co., New York, sold
29 January 1960 for $110,000 to]; Donald
Ellis Simon, gift 1971 to; The Norton Simon
Foundation (sale, New York, Sotheby Parke
Bernet 2 May 1973, lot 28, for $1,500,000
to); [Sotheby Parke Bernet & Co., London,
sold privately 21 May 1978 for $400,000 to];
Norton Simon Art Foundation (M.1978.25).

Cat. 83A-C

Marsden Hartley (American, 1877–1943)
Central Park No. 3, Central Park No. 4, and
Rocks on the Maine Coast
Charcoal, each 17 x 14 in. (43.2 x 35.6 cm)
[Paul Rosenberg & Co., New York, sold
28 March 1960 for $750 to]; Norton Simon,
sold 22 December 1966 to; Norton Simon
Art Foundation (sale, New York, Sotheby
Parke Bernet, 12 December 1974, lot 67,
for $800).

Cat. 84
Georg Kolbe (German, 1877–1947)
Large Kneeling Girl, 1943
Bronze, edition of 3, cast no. 2,
40 in. (101.6 cm)
[Dalzell Hatfield Gallery, Los Angeles, sold
18 April 1960 for $7,000 to]; Robert Ellis
Simon, bequest 29 October 1969 to; The
Norton Simon Foundation (sale, New York,
Sotheby Parke Bernet, 2 May 1973, lot 42, for
$20,000 to); private collection, U.K.

Cat. 85
Honoré Daumier (French, 1808–1879)
Undecided, 1830–1832
Bronze, edition of 30, cast no. 11,
5 ¾ in. (14.6 cm)
[M. Knoedler & Co., New York, sold 18
April 1960 for $2,500 to]; Robert Ellis
Simon, bequest 29 October 1969 to; The
Norton Simon Foundation (sale, New York,
Sotheby Parke Bernet, 14 May 1980, lot 102,
for $5,750).

Cat. 86
Henri Matisse (French, 1869–1954)
Jeanette III
Bronze, edition of 10, cast no. 2, 24 in. (61 cm)
[M. Knoedler & Co., New York, sold
18 April 1960 for $16,500 to]; Robert Ellis
Simon, bequest 29 October 1969 to; The
Norton Simon Foundation (sale, New York,
Sotheby Parke Bernet, 2 May 1973, lot 39, for
$160,000 to); [Forum Gallery, New York].

Cat. 87
Greece
Draped Female Figure
Bronze, 13 in. (33 cm)
[Walter Goetz, Paris, sold 1 September 1960
for $3,500 to]; Norton Simon, transferred
24 July 1970 to; Lucille Ellis Simon.

Cat. 88
Egypt
Cat, c. 600 B.C.
Bronze, 9 ½ in. (24.1 cm)

[Spink & Son, London, sold 6 September
1960 for $6,204 to]; Norton Simon, trans-
ferred 24 July 1970 to; Lucille Ellis Simon.

Cat. 89
Greece
Venus
Marble, 16 in. (40.6 cm)
[Otto Wertheimer, sold through Walter
Goetz, Paris, 26 September 1960 for $3,120
to]; Norton Simon, transferred 24 July 1970
to; Lucille Ellis Simon.

Cat. 90
Pablo Picasso (Spanish, 1881–1973)
Woman with a Book, 1932
Oil on canvas, 51 ⅜ x 38 ½ in.
(130.5 x 97.8 cm)
[Paul Rosenberg & Co., New York, sold 19
December 1960 for $115,000 to]; Robert Ellis
Simon, bequest 29 October 1969 to; The
Norton Simon Foundation (F.69.38.10).

1961

Cat. 91
Wilhelm Lehmbruck (German, 1881–1919)
Climbing Girl (formerly *Young Bather*)
Bronze, 24 ¾ in. (62.9 cm)
(Sale, London, Sotheby's, 6 July 1961
through [Arthur Tooth & Sons] for $5,000
to); Norton Simon, transferred 24 July 1970
to; Lucille Ellis Simon (estate sale, London,
Christie's, 26 June 2002, lot 114, for $18,109).

Cat. 92
Honoré Daumier (French, 1808–1879)
The Reader
Ink wash, 9 ½ x 11 ⅞ in. (24.1 x 30.2 cm)
[Wildenstein & Co., New York, sold 28
August 1961 for $14,000 to]; Norton Simon,
sold 14 March 1973 for $75,000 to; [E. V.
Thaw & Co., New York]; Eugene V. and
Clare E. Thaw, New York, promised gift to;
The Pierpont Morgan Library, New York.

84

89

85

90

86

87

91

88

92

93

94

97

95

99

96

Cat. 93
Frans Hals (Dutch, 1581–1666)
Portrait of a Young Man (formerly *Jan van de Cappelle*), 1650–1655
Oil on canvas, 26 ⅝ x 20 in. (67.6 x 50.8 cm)
[Wildenstein & Co., New York, sold
28 August 1961 for $142,500 (plus $42,180
interest) to]; Norton Simon, gift
22 December 1972 to; Norton Simon
Art Foundation (M.1972.4).

Cat. 94
Paul Cézanne (French, 1839–1906)
Bathers, c. 1895–1898
Oil on canvas, 13 ¾ x 8 ¾ in. (34.9 x 22.2 cm)
[Sam Salz, New York, sold 20 November
1961 for $52,500 to]; Norton Simon (sale,
New York, Parke-Bernet Galleries, 5 May
1971, lot 23, for $120,000). [Galerie Beyeler,
Basel, sold to]; private collection.

Cat. 95
Édouard Vuillard (French, 1868–1940)
The Open Door (formerly *Interior*), 1898
Oil on canvas, 15 ¾ x 16 ¼ in. (40 x 41.3 cm)
[Sam Salz, New York, sold 20 November
1961 for $16,500 to]; Norton Simon, sold
22 December 1966 to; Norton Simon Art
Foundation, used in trade 13 January 1971
with a value of $45,000 as partial payment
for Lucas Cranach the Elder, *Adam* (cat.
742) to; [Spencer A. Samuels & Co., New
York]. [O'Hana, London]. (sale, Geneva,
Galerie Motte, 29 June 1973, lot 47, unsold)
(sale, London, Christie's, 4 December 1973,
lot 27, withdrawn).

Cat. 96
Paul Cézanne (French, 1839–1906)
The Gardener Vallier
Pencil and watercolor, 18 ¾ x 12 ¼ in.
(47.6 x 31.1 cm)
[Rosenberg & Stiebel, New York, sold
20 November 1961 for $45,000 to]; Norton

Simon, transferred 24 July 1970 to; Lucille
Ellis Simon, sold by her estate in 2000 to;
Donald B. Marron, New York (sale, New
York, Christie's, 6 November 2007, lot 31,
for $17,400,000 to); private collection.

Cat. 97
Jean-Antoine Watteau (French, 1684–1721)
Seated Young Woman
Black, red, and white chalk, 6 ⅞ x 8 ⅛ in.
(17.4 x 20.6 cm)
[Rosenberg & Stiebel, New York, sold
20 November 1961 for $35,000 to]; Norton
Simon, sold 18 December 1973 for $205,000
to; [E. V. Thaw & Co., New York]; Eugene V.
and Clare E. Thaw, New York, gift 2000 to;
The Pierpont Morgan Library, New York.

Cat. 98
Jean-Auguste-Dominique Ingres
(French, 1780–1867)
The Banker Laffitt, 1819
Pencil, 9 ½ x 7 ½ in. (24.1 x 19.1 cm)
[Paul Rosenberg & Co., New York, sold
21 November 1961 for $16,000 to]; Norton
Simon, returned to dealer 15 May 1962 and
used as partial credit against Vincent van
Gogh, *St. Paul's Hospital at St. Rémy* (cat. 99).

Cat. 99
Vincent van Gogh (Dutch, 1853–1890)
St. Paul's Hospital at St. Rémy, 1889
Oil on canvas, 35 ½ x 28 in. (90.2 x 71.1 cm)
[Paul Rosenberg & Co., New York, sold
1 December 1961 for $380,000 ($364,000
and $16,000 credit for returned Ingres
The Banker Laffitt [cat. 98] plus $18,050
interest) to]; Norton Simon (sale, New
York, Parke-Bernet Galleries, 5 May 1971,
lot 48, for $1,200,000, to); The Armand
Hammer Foundation, Los Angeles, gift 1990
to; Armand Hammer Museum of Art and
Culture Center, Los Angeles.

Cat. 100
Georges Rouault (French, 1871–1958)
Illustrations for Baudelaire's "Flowers of Evil"
Color etchings with aquatint, group of
twelve, 12 x 8 ½ in. (30.5 x 21.6 cm)
[William Schab, New York, sold
13 December 1961 for $1,800 to]; Hunt
Foods and Industries, Fullerton, Calif.,
gift 19 December 1969 to; Norton Simon
Art Foundation (M.1970.5.18).

Cat. 101
Vincent van Gogh (Dutch, 1853–1890)
The Mulberry Tree, 1889
Oil on canvas, 21 ¼ x 25 ½ in. (54 x 64.8 cm)
[Marlborough Fine Art, London, sold
20 December 1961 for $300,000 to]; Norton
Simon, gift 29 June 1976 to; Norton Simon
Art Foundation (M.1976.9).

1962

Cat. 102
Paul Signac (French, 1863–1935)
The Port of Collioure, 1887
Oil on canvas, 35 ¼ x 22 ¾ in. (89.5 x 57.8 cm)
[Rosenberg & Stiebel, New York, sold
5 January 1962 for $54,000 to]; Norton
Simon (sale, New York, Parke-Bernet
Galleries, 5 May 1971, lot 56, for $250,000
to); [Acquavella Galleries, New York, sold
to]; private collection, Europe.

Cat. 103
Paul Cézanne (French, 1839–1906)
Tulips in a Vase, 1888–1890
Oil on paper, mounted on board,
28 ½ x 16 ½ in. (72.4 x 41.9 cm)
[Arthur Tooth & Sons, London, sold
15 January 1962 for $404,472 to]; Norton
Simon (sale, New York, Sotheby Parke
Bernet, 2 May 1973, lot 8, to); [Wildenstein
& Co., New York, on behalf of] Norton
Simon, gift 22 December 1976 to; Norton
Simon Art Foundation (M.1976.12).

Cat. 104
Edgar Degas (French, 1834–1917)
After the Bath, Woman Drying Herself,
1888–1892
Pastel, 24 x 19 in. (61 x 48.3 cm)
[M. Knoedler & Co., New York, sold
29 January 1962 for $70,000 to]; Norton
Simon (sale, New York, Parke-Bernet
Galleries, 5 May 1971, lot 35, for $145,000
to); private collection, Miami (sale, New
York, Sotheby's, 13 November 1990, lot
23, for $990,000 to); Harmon Fine Arts/
Leonard Stern, New York.

Cat. 105
Claude Monet (French, 1840–1926)
Sailboat at Argenteuil, 1874
Oil on canvas, 21 x 28 ⅞ in. (53.3 x 73.3 cm)
[Arthur Tooth & Sons, London, sold
1 March 1962 for $125,000 to]; Norton
Simon, transferred 24 July 1970 to; Lucille
Ellis Simon; sold by her estate 2001 through
[Giraud-Pissarro-Segalot, Paris, to]; private
collection, U.S.A.

Cat. 106
Pierre-Auguste Renoir (French, 1841–1919)
Seated Nude, c. 1872
Oil on canvas, 14 ¾ x 10 in. (37.5 x 25.4 cm)
[Paul Rosenberg & Co., New York, sold
19 March 1962 for $45,000 to]; Norton
Simon, gift 21 June 1982 to; The Norton
Simon Foundation (F.1982.1).

Cat. 107
Wilhelm Lehmbruck (German, 1881–1919)
Female Torso
Bronze, edition of 3, unnumbered cast,
27 in. (68.6 cm)
(Sale, London, Sotheby & Co., 11 April 1962
through [Arthur Tooth & Sons] for $5,000
to); Norton Simon, gift 5 December 1963 to;
private collection, Los Angeles.

104

100

105

101

106

102

103

108

109

110

111

112

113

114

115

Cat. 108
Pierre Bonnard (French, 1867–1947)
The Lessons (formerly *Interior*), c. 1898
Oil on canvas, 20 ½ x 13 ¾ in.
(52.1 x 34.9 cm)
[Arthur Tooth & Sons, London, sold
16 April 1962 for $53,496 to]; Norton Simon
(sale, New York, Parke-Bernet Galleries,
5 May 1971, lot 60, for $42,000). [Olivier
Bernier, New York, sold 1972 to]; North
Carolina Museum of Art, Raleigh.

Cat. 109
Édouard Vuillard (French, 1868–1940)
Woman Lighting a Stove, 1910
Oil on canvas, 22 ¼ x 27 ¼ in. (56.5 x 69.2 cm)
[Arthur Tooth & Sons, London, sold
16 April 1962 for $43,640 to]; Norton Simon
(sale, New York, Parke-Bernet Galleries, 5
May 1971, lot 69, for $54,000). Flint Institute
of Arts, Flint, Mich., 1972.

Cat. 110
Paul Cézanne (French, 1839–1906)
Mont Sainte Victoire
Watercolor, 16 ⅞ x 20 ¼ in. (42.9 x 51.4 cm)
[Paul Rosenberg & Co., New York, sold
15 May 1962 for $48,000 (plus $2,880
interest) to]; Norton Simon, transferred
24 July 1970 to; Lucille Ellis Simon, sold by
her estate in 2000 to; Donald B. Marron,
New York (sale, New York, Christie's, 6
November 2007, lot 33, for $4,520,000 to);
private collection, Russia.

Cat. 111
Edgar Degas (French, 1834–1917)
*Horse galloping, turning the head to the
right, the feet not touching the ground*
Bronze, cast no. 32/B, 11 ¹/₁₆ in. (28.1 cm)
[Paul Rosenberg & Co., New York, sold
15 May 1962 for $14,500 to]; Norton Simon,
transferred 24 July 1970 to; Lucille Ellis
Simon, by inheritance to; private collection.

Cat. 112
Peter Paul Rubens (Flemish, 1577–1640)
*Meleager and Atalanta and the Hunt of the
Calydonian Boar*, c. 1618–1619
Oil on panel, 18 ¾ x 29 ⅛ in. (47.6 x 74 cm)
[Rosenberg & Stiebel, New York, sold 25
June 1962 for $118,750 to]; Norton Simon,
gift 30 December 1975 to; Norton Simon Art
Foundation (M.1975.21).

Cat. 113
Edgar Degas (French, 1834–1917)
Arabesque over the right leg, left arm in line
Bronze, cast no. 3/I, 11 ¾ in. (29.9 cm)
[M. Knoedler & Co., New York, sold
3 July 1962 for $15,500 to]; Norton Simon,
transferred 24 July 1970 to; Lucille Ellis
Simon (estate sale, New York, Christie's,
8 November 2000, lot 6, for $666,000 to);
private collection, New York.

Cat. 114
Amedeo Modigliani (Italian, 1884–1920)
A Young Italian Girl, 1918
Oil on canvas, 23 ¾ x 17 ½ in. (60.3 x 44.5 cm)
(Sale, London, Sotheby & Co., 4 July
1962 for $53,042 to); Norton Simon (sale,
New York, Parke-Bernet Galleries, 13 May
1970, lot 36, unsold), sold 17 April 1971 for
$60,000 to; [Paul Kantor, Beverly Hills,
Calif.]. Elliot and Ruth Handler, Los
Angeles (sale, New York, Sotheby's,
13 November 1985, lot 54, for $407,000).

Cat. 115
Egypt, 12th Dynasty
Statuette of a Priest
Carved wood, 13 ½ in. (34.3 cm)
(Sale, London, Sotheby & Co., 16 July 1962
for $1,913 to); Norton Simon (private sale,
New York, Sotheby Parke Bernet, 22 May
1974, for $24,000 for this work and *Horus
Falcon*, cat. 244).

Cat. 116
Edgar Degas (French, 1834–1917)
Grande arabesque, second time
Bronze, cast no. 15/F, 17 in. (43.2 cm)
[Edgardo Acosta Gallery, Beverly Hills,
Calif., sold 19 July 1962 for $20,800 to];
Norton Simon, transferred 24 July 1970
to; Lucille Ellis Simon, by inheritance
to; private collection (sale, New York,
Christie's, 6 November 2001, lot 29, unsold)
private collection, Los Angeles.

Cat. 117
Gustave Courbet (French, 1819–1877)
The Forest Pool
Oil on canvas, 30 x 36 in. (76.2 x 91.4 cm)
[Paul Kantor, Beverly Hills, Calif., sold
1 August 1962 for $25,000 to]; Norton
Simon, gift 15 March 1967 to; Norton Simon
Art Foundation, sold 16 December 1981 for
$140,000 to; [E. V. Thaw & Co., New York,
sold 1985 to]; private collection.

Cat. 118
Arshile Gorky (American, b. Armenia,
1904–1948)
Plumage Landscape, 1947
Oil on canvas, 38 x 51 in. (96.5 x 129.5 cm)
[Paul Kantor, Beverly Hills, Calif., sold
1 August 1962 for $25,000 to]; Norton
Simon, sold 22 December 1966 to; Norton
Simon Art Foundation, sold [through
Fourcade, Droll, New York] 16 August
1973 for $180,000 to; National Gallery of
Australia, Canberra.

Cat. 119
Pablo Picasso (Spanish, 1881–1973)
Still Life with Guitar and Clarinet, 1915
Pencil, charcoal, and watercolor,
7 ½ x 5 ⅞ in. (19.1 x 14.9 cm)
[Paul Kantor, Beverly Hills, Calif., sold
1 August 1962 for $8,333 to]; Norton Simon
(sale, New York, Parke-Bernet Galleries,

5 May 1971, lot 73, for $20,000 to); [Spencer
A. Samuels & Co., New York, for]; Fletcher
Jones, Los Angeles (estate sale, 2 December
1975, lot 188, for $34,950). [Janie C. Lee
Gallery, Houston, 1982]. (sale, London,
Christie's, 27 June 2002, lot 386, for $244,670
to); [the trade, Germany].

Cat. 120
Pablo Picasso (Spanish, 1881–1973)
Still Life with Table, 1922
Gouache and watercolor, 6 ½ x 4 ⅛ in.
(16.5 x 10.5 cm)
[Paul Kantor, Beverly Hills, Calif., sold
1 August 1962 for $8,333 to]; Norton Simon
(sale, New York, Parke-Bernet Galleries,
5 May 1971, lot 74, for $21,000 to); [Spencer
A. Samuels & Co., New York, for]; Fletcher
Jones, Los Angeles (estate sale, 2 December
1975, lot 190, for $23,300).

Cat. 121
Pablo Picasso (Spanish, 1881–1973)
Still Life with Palette, 1915
Pencil and watercolor, 5 ¾ x 4 ¾ in.
(14.6 x 12.1 cm)
[Paul Kantor, Beverly Hills, Calif., sold 1
August 1962 for $8,333 to]; Norton Simon
(sale, New York, Parke-Bernet Galleries,
5 May 1971, lot 72, for $16,000 to); [Spencer
A. Samuels & Co., New York, for]; Fletcher
Jones, Los Angeles (estate sale, 2 December
1975, lot 189, for $23,300).

Cat. 122
Odilon Redon (French, 1840–1916)
Woman with Flowers
Pastel, 24 ½ x 19 in. (62.2 x 48.3 cm)
[World Arts Establishment, Vaduz,
Liechtenstein, sold 1 August 1962 for
$40,000 to]; Norton Simon (sale, New York,
Parke-Bernet Galleries, 5 May 1971, lot 58,
for $30,000 to); [Jan Krugier, Geneva].

116

120

117

121

118

122

119

123

127

124

128

125

129

130

Cat. 123
Edgar Degas (French, 1834–1917)
At the Stock Exchange, 1878–1879
Pastel, 28 ⅜ x 22 ⅞ in. (72.1 x 58.1 cm)
[Rosenberg & Stiebel, New York, sold
6 September 1962 for $60,000 to]; Norton
Simon (sale, New York, Parke-Bernet
Galleries, 5 May 1971, lot 36, for $185,000
to); Philip and Janice H. Levin, New York,
gift 1991 to; The Metropolitan Museum of
Art, New York.

Cat. 124
Lorenzo Monaco (Piero di Giovanni)
(Italian, c. 1370–1425)
Virgin Annunciate, c. 1410–1415
Tempera and gold leaf on panel,
31 ⅝ x 17 ½ in. (80.3 x 44.5 cm)
[Thomas Agnew & Sons, London, sold
13 December 1962 for $115,000 to]; Norton
Simon, gift 20 November 1973 to; Norton
Simon Art Foundation (M.1973.5)

1963

Cat. 125
Jean Metzinger (French, 1883–1956)
Woman with Grapes, 1917
Oil on canvas, 32 x 39 ½ in. (81.3 x 100.3 cm)
[Dalzell Hatfield Gallery, Los Angeles, sold
14 January 1963 for $7,800 to]; Norton
Simon, sold 22 December 1966 to; Norton
Simon Art Foundation (sale, New York,
Parke-Bernet Galleries, 13 May 1970, lot 70,
for $14,500 to); private collection, Texas.

Cat. 126
China, Late Chou Period
Wine Jar
Bronze, 12 in. (30.5 cm)
(Sale, London, Sotheby & Co., 5 March 1963
for $3,857 to); Norton Simon, transferred
24 July 1970 to; Lucille Ellis Simon.

Cat. 127
Camille Pissarro (French, 1830–1903)
The Market at Pontoise, 1887
Gouache, 12 ¼ x 9 ¼ in. (31.1 x 23.5 cm)
[Paul Kantor, Beverly Hills, Calif., sold
15 April 1963 for $22,500 to]; Norton Simon
(sale, New York, Parke-Bernet Galleries,
21 October 1971, lot 73, unsold), sold
7 January 1974 for $70,000
to; [E. V. Thaw & Co., New York].

Cat. 128
Jean-Baptiste Camille Corot (French,
1796–1875)
*Marino, Rider and Peasant Woman in a
Valley*, 1827
Pencil, 11 x 17 in. (27.9 x 43.2 cm)
[Robert M. Light, Boston, sold 18 April 1963
for $4,500 to]; Norton Simon (sale, New
York, Parke-Bernet Galleries, 5 May 1971,
lot 1, for $10,000 to); Samuel J. LeFrak,
New York, by inheritance to; LeFrak Family
Collection, New York.

Cat. 129
Édouard Manet (French, 1832–1883)
The Little Cavaliers, 1860
Etching heightened with watercolor,
9 ½ x 15 ¼ in. (24.1 x 38.7 cm)
[Robert M. Light, Boston, sold 18 April 1963
for $6,750 to]; Norton Simon (sale, London,
Sotheby & Co., 4 November 1971, lot 81,
unsold, sold privately for $3,000 to); private
collection.

Cat. 130
Lucas Cranach the Elder (German,
1472–1553)
Christ and the Twelve Apostles
Woodcuts, set of 13 prints
[William Schab, New York, sold 29 April
1963 for $12,031 to]; Norton Simon, gift
31 December 1979 to; Norton Simon Art
Foundation (M.1979.63.1–13).

Cat. 131
Albrecht Dürer (German, 1471–1528)
Madonna by the Wall, 1514
Engraving, 5 ¾ x 4 in. (14.6 x 10.2 cm)
[William Schab, New York, sold 29 April
1963 for $2,074 to]; Norton Simon (sale,
London, Christie's, 1 December 1971, lot 21,
for $4,112).

Cat. 132
Hans Holbein the Younger (German,
1497–1543)
Erasmus of Rotterdam
Engraving, 11 ¼ x 6 ⅝ in. (28.6 x 16.8 cm)
[William Schab, New York, sold 29 April
1963 for $622 to]; Norton Simon (sale,
London, Christie's, 1 December 1971, lot 24,
for $1,079).

Cat. 133
Jean-Auguste-Dominique Ingres (French,
1780–1867)
Lady and Lord Glenbrevie, 1815
Lithograph, 12 x 17 ¼ in. (30.5 x 43.8 cm)
[William Schab, New York, sold 29 April
1963 for $622 to]; Norton Simon, gift 1965
to; Robert Ellis Simon, bequest 29 October
1969 to; private collection.

Cat. 134
Rembrandt van Rijn (Dutch, 1606–1669)
Jan Lutma
Etching on Japan paper, 1st state
[William Schab, New York, sold 29 April
1963 for $8,400 to]; Norton Simon, returned
to Schab 13 February 1964 in exchange for
another copy of the same print (cat. 178);
purchase price given in credit toward the
second *Lutma*, along with Rembrandt van
Rijn, *Woman at the Bath, with a Hat beside
Her* (cat. 179) and Luca Signorelli, *Seated
Female Saint* (cat. 180).

Cat. 135
Honoré Daumier (French, 1808–1879)
Third-Class Carriage
Pen and ink over charcoal and washed with
watercolor, 13 ½ x 9 ⅜ in. (34.3 x 23.9 cm)
[Paul Kantor, Beverly Hills, Calif., sold
17 May 1963 for $14,000 to]; Norton Simon
(sale, New York, Parke-Bernet Galleries,
21 October 1971, unsold), sold 18 December
1973 for $40,000 to; [E. V. Thaw & Co.,
New York, and Robert M. Light, Boston,
consigned 1973 to]; [Kornfeld & Klipstein,
Bern].

Cat. 136
Louis-Eugène Boudin (French, 1824–1898)
Beach Scene at Trouville, 1865
Watercolor, 6 ⅞ x 10 ⅛ in. (17.5 x 25.7 cm)
[Wildenstein & Co., New York, sold
17 May 1963 for $10,000 to]; Norton Simon
(sale, New York, Parke-Bernet Galleries,
5 May 1971, lot 9, for $16,000 to); Abraham
Bersohn, New York.

Cat. 137
Georges-Pierre Seurat (French, 1859–1891)
The Model
Crayon and ink, 10 ¼ x 6 ½ in. (26 x 16.5 cm)
[Wildenstein & Co., New York, sold 17 May
1963 for $27,000 to]; Norton Simon (sale,
New York, Parke-Bernet Galleries, 5 May
1971, lot 46, for $33,000 to); The Armand
Hammer Foundation, Los Angeles, gift 1991
to; National Gallery of Art, Washington, D.C.

Cat. 138
Louis-Eugène Boudin (French, 1824–1898)
Beach Scene with Crinolines
Oil on canvas, 13 ½ x 22 ½ in. (34.3 x 57.2 cm)
[Galerie des Arts Anciens et Modernes,
Schaan, Liechtenstein, sold 21 May 1963 for
$100,000 to]; Norton Simon (sale, New York,
Parke-Bernet Galleries, 5 May 1971, lot 10, for
$160,000). private collection, Mexico City.

131

135

136

134

137

138

139

143

140

144

145

141

146

142

Cat. 139
Edvard Munch (Norwegian, 1863–1944)
Three Girls on a Bridge, 1902
Oil on canvas, 39 ¾ x 39 ½ in. (101 x 100.3 cm)
[Galerie des Arts Anciens et Modernes,
Schaan, Liechtenstein, sold 21 May 1963
for $130,000 to]; Norton Simon (sale, New
York, Christie's, 21 October 1980, lot 201,
for $2,000,000 to); Wendell and Dorothy
Cherry (sale, New York, Sotheby's,
12 November 1996 to); private collection,
Europe (sale, New York, Sotheby's, 7 May
2008, lot 25, for $30,841,000). private
collection, Switzerland.

Cat. 140
Edgar Degas (French, 1834–1917)
Dancer Bowing (Green Dancer), c. 1879
Pastel, 26 x 14 ¼ in. (66 x 36.2 cm)
(Sale, London, Sotheby & Co., through
[Arthur Tooth & Sons], 11 June 1963 for
$303,165 to); Norton Simon (sale, New
York, Parke-Bernet Galleries, 5 May 1971, lot
30, for $530,000 to); Thyssen-Bornemisza
Collection, Madrid.

Cat. 141
Edgar Degas (French, 1834–1917)
Portrait of a Polytechnician, c. 1865–1868
Oil on canvas, 13 ¾ x 11 in. (34.9 x 28 cm)
(Sale, London, Sotheby & Co., through
[Arthur Tooth & Sons], 11 June 1963 for
$29,266 to); Norton Simon (sale, London,
Christie's, 30 November 1971, unsold),
sold privately after the sale for $60,000 to;
private collection. Murauchi Art Museum,
Tokyo.

Cat. 142
Pierre-Auguste Renoir (French, 1841–1919)
Young Woman in Black, c. 1875–1877
Oil on canvas, 13 ⅛ x 10 in. (33.2 x 25.5 cm)
(Sale, London, Sotheby & Co., through
[Arthur Tooth & Sons], 11 June 1963 for
$132,048 to); Norton Simon (sale, London,
Christie's, 30 November 1971, unsold), by

inheritance 2 June 1993 to; Jennifer Jones
Simon Art Trust, Los Angeles (N.1963.5).

Cat. 143
Francisco de Goya y Lucientes
(Spanish, 1746–1828)
Bien tirada está (It Fits Perfectly), plate 17 of
Los Caprichos, working proof, c. 1796–1798
Etching, burnished aquatint, and burin,
working proof before letters and number:
plate, 9 ⅞ x 5 ⅞ in. (25 x 15 cm); sheet,
12 ⅝ x 8 ½ in. (32.1 x 21.6 cm)
[William Schab, New York, sold 28 June
1963 for $3,840 to]; Donald Ellis Simon,
gift 30 June 1971 to; The Norton Simon
Foundation (F.1971.1.1).

Cat. 144
Claude Monet (French, 1840–1926)
Argenteuil, 1875–1877
Oil on canvas, 22 x 29 ¼ in. (55.9 x 74.3 cm)
[Wildenstein & Co., New York, sold 28 June
1963 for $85,000 to]; Norton Simon (sale,
New York, Parke-Bernet Galleries, 5 May
1971, lot 40, for $200,000). Pola Museum of
Art, Hakone, Japan.

Cat. 145
Pablo Picasso (Spanish, 1881–1973)
Head of a Young Woman
Oil on canvas, 22 x 17 in. (55.9 x 43.2 cm)
[M. Knoedler & Co., New York, sold 28 June
1963 for $125,000 to]; Norton Simon (sale,
New York, Parke-Bernet Galleries, 5 May
1971, lot 70, unsold), sold 28 November 1973
for $377,500 to; [Marlborough Gallery, New
York].

Cat. 146
Henri Matisse (French, 1869–1954)
Odalisque with Striped Dress, 1937
Oil on canvas, 15 x 18 in. (38.1 x 45.7 cm)
[Paul Rosenberg & Co., New York, sold
8 July 1963 for $75,000 to]; Norton Simon,
sold 23 February 1982 for $450,000 to; [E. V.
Thaw & Co., New York]; William Acquavella
collection, New York.

Cat. 147
Francisco de Goya y Lucientes
(Spanish, 1746–1828)
The Water Carrier
Oil on canvas, 22 x 16 ⅝ in. (55.9 x 42.2 cm)
[Galerie des Arts Anciens et Modernes,
Schaan, Liechtenstein, sold 10 July 1963
for $250,000 to]; Norton Simon, sold
12 September 1973 for $250,000 to;
[Marlborough Gallery, New York].

Cat. 148
Pablo Picasso (Spanish, 1881–1973)
Woman with Guitar, 1915
Oil on canvas, 72 ¾ x 29 ½ in.
(184.8 x 74.9 cm)
[Galerie des Arts Anciens et Modernes,
Schaan, Liechtenstein, sold 10 July 1963
for $125,000 to]; Norton Simon (sale, New
York, Christie's, 21 October 1980, lot 203, for
$2,800,000). private collection, New York,
1997.

Cat. 149A-D
Jean-Auguste-Dominique Ingres
(French, 1780–1867)
The Bartolini Family
Pencil, four drawings, each 8 ¼ x 6 ¹/₁₆ in.
(21 x 15.4 cm)
[Paul Kantor, Beverly Hills, Calif., sold 11
July 1963 for $21,000 to]; Norton Simon
(sale, New York, Christie's, 23 November
1971, lots 146–149, unsold), sold 7 January
1974 for $150,000 to; [Wildenstein & Co.,
New York. The drawings (Naef 37–40) were
separated and sold to]; private collection,
Switzerland (Naef 37), Fine Arts Museums
of San Francisco, Achenbach Foundation
for Graphic Arts (Naef 38), Esmond B.
Martin, 2006 (Naef 39), and [Jan Krugier,
Geneva, 1988 (Naef 40).

Cat. 150
Jean-Baptiste Camille Corot (French,
1796–1875)
Site in Italy, 1839

Oil on canvas, 21 ¼ x 32 in. (54 x 81.3 cm)
[E. V. Thaw & Co., New York, sold 19 July
1963 for $70,000 to]; Donald Ellis Simon,
gift 30 June 1971 to; The Norton Simon
Foundation (F.1971.1.2).

Cat. 151
Théodore Géricault (French, 1791–1824)
The English Urchin
Oil on paper on canvas, 18 x 13 ½ in.
(45.7 x 34.3 cm)
[Arthur Tooth & Sons, London, sold
2 August 1963 for $33,600 to]; Norton
Simon, gift 15 March 1967 to; Norton Simon
Art Foundation, used in trade 21 June
1973 with a value of $33,000 as payment
for Louis-Eugène Boudin, *Cottage and
Pasture on the Banks of the Touques* (cat.
943) and Paul-Camille Guigou, *Landscape
in Martigues* (cat. 944) to; [Arthur Tooth &
Sons, London].

Cat. 152
Attributed to Giorgione (Italian,
1477/1478–1510)
Bust Portrait of a Courtesan
Oil on panel, transferred to canvas,
12 ½ x 9 ⅜ in. (31.8 x 23.9 cm)
[Duveen Brothers, sold 10 September 1963
for $192,500 to]; Norton Simon, returned
29 September 1964 with initial payment of
$20,000 to; [Duveen Brothers, sold along
with the entire Duveen stock 18 April
1964 to]; The Norton Simon Foundation
(F.1965.1.28).

Cat. 153
Théodore Chassériau (French, 1819–1856)
Othello and Desdemona, 1847
Watercolor, 8 ¼ x 6 ⁵/₁₆ in. (21 x 16 cm)
[William Schab, New York, sold
18 September 1963 for $3,200 to]; Norton
Simon (sale, New York, Parke-Bernet
Galleries, 5 May 1971, lot 8, for $1,700 to];
John Katopis, New Jersey. (sale, Monaco,
3 December 1989, lot 525).

147

151

148

152

153

149A

150

154

157

155

158

156

159

160

Cat. 154
Albrecht Dürer (German, 1471–1528)
Melancholia, 1514
Etching 2nd state, 9 ½ x 7 ⅜ in.
(24.1 x 18.7 cm)
[William Schab, New York, sold
18 September 1963 for $8,750 to]; Norton
Simon, sold 18 October 1972 for a total of
$82,000 for this print, Pieter Brueghel the
Elder, *Landscape with Rabbit Hunters* (cat.
496) and Rembrandt van Rijn, *Jan Lutma*
(cat. 178) to; [E. V. Thaw & Co., New York].

Cat. 155
Francisco de Goya y Lucientes
(Spanish, 1746–1828)
Carnival Folly, plate 14 of *Los Proverbios*,
working proof, 1819–1820, printed c. 1848
Etching and aquatint: plate, 8 ¼ x 12 ½ in.
(21 x 31.8 cm); sheet, 9 ⁹/₁₆ x 13 ¾ in.
(24.3 x 34.9 cm)
[William Schab, New York, sold 26
September 1963 for $900 to]; Hunt Foods
and Industries, Fullerton, Calif., gift 19
December 1969 to; Norton Simon Art
Foundation (sale, London, Sotheby Parke
Bernet & Co., 16 May 1980, lot 235, for
$6,500).

Cat. 156
Francisco de Goya y Lucientes
(Spanish, 1746–1828)
Poor Folly, plate 11 of *Los Proverbios*,
working proof, 1819–1820, printed c. 1848
Etching and aquatint: plate, 8 ¼ x 12 ½ in.
(21 x 31.8 cm); sheet, 9 ⁹/₁₆ x 13 ¾ in.
(24.3 x 34.9 cm)
[William Schab, New York, sold 26
September 1963 for $900 to]; Hunt Foods
and Industries, Fullerton, Calif., gift 19
December 1969 to; Norton Simon Art
Foundation (sale, London, Sotheby Parke
Bernet & Co., 16 May 1980, lot 236, for
$8,400).

Cat. 157
Albert Pinkham Ryder
(American, 1847–1917)
Autumn Landscape
Oil on canvas, 6 x 8 ½ in. (15.2 x 21.6 cm)
[Wildenstein & Co., New York, sold
27 September 1963 for $3,750 to]; Norton
Simon, sold 22 December 1966 to; Norton
Simon Art Foundation (sale, New York,
Parke-Bernet Galleries, 21 May 1970, lot 39,
for $4,500).

Cat. 158
Mary Cassatt (American, 1845–1926)
Afternoon Tea Party
Color aquatint with drypoint, 13 ½ x 10 ½ in.
(34.3 x 26.7 cm)
[Robert M. Light, Boston, sold 8 October
1963 for $1,275 to]; Hunt Foods and
Industries, Fullerton, Calif., gift
19 December 1969 to; Norton Simon Art
Foundation, sold 13 February 1974 for
$10,000 to; [Robert M. Light, Boston,
consigned to]; [Thomas Agnew & Sons,
London].

Cat. 159
Paul Cézanne (French, 1839–1906)
The Bathers, Large Plate, 1899
Lithograph, 15 ¾ x 19 ¾ in. (40 x 50.2 cm)
[Robert M. Light, Boston, sold 8 October
1963 for $2,500 to]; Hunt Foods and
Industries, Fullerton, Calif., gift
19 December 1969 to; Norton Simon Art
Foundation, sold 17 April 1974 for $11,000
to; [Robert M. Light, Boston, consigned to];
[Thomas Agnew & Sons, London].

Cat. 160
Édouard Manet (French, 1832–1883)
The Boy with a Dog, 1861
Etching, 7 ⅞ x 5 ½ in. (20 x 14 cm)
[Robert M. Light, Boston, sold 8 October
1963 for $390 to]; Hunt Foods and

Industries, Fullerton, Calif., gift
19 December 1969 to; Norton Simon Art
Foundation, sold 2 June 1975 for $2,250 to;
[Robert M. Light, Boston, sold 1975 to];
National Gallery of Canada, Ottawa.

Cat. 161
Rembrandt van Rijn (Dutch, 1606–1669)
Old Man with Divided Fur Cap, 1640
Etching, 6 x 5 ½ in. (15.2 x 14 cm)
[Robert M. Light, Boston, sold 8 October
1963 for $435 to]; Hunt Foods and
Industries, Fullerton, Calif., gift
19 December 1969 to; Norton Simon Art
Foundation, sold 17 April 1974 for $5,500
to; [Robert M. Light, Boston, sold 1974 to];
[Greater India Co., New York].

Cat. 162
Attributed to Peter Paul Rubens (Flemish,
1577–1640)
Portrait of a Young Lady
Red and black chalk, 7 ¹¹⁄₁₆ x 10 ⅛ in.
(19.5 x 25.7 cm)
(Sale, London, Sotheby & Co., through
[Arthur Tooth & Sons], 21 October 1963 for
$12,500 to); Norton Simon (sale, New York,
Parke-Bernet Galleries, 8 May 1971, lot 200a,
for $1,750).

Cat. 163A-B
China
Two Bowls, 18th century
Jade, diameter, 5 ¾ in. (14.6 cm)
(Sale, London, Sotheby & Co., through
[Arthur Tooth & Sons], 22 October 1963
for $2,347 to); Norton Simon, transferred
24 July 1970 to; Lucille Ellis Simon.

Cat. 164
Théodore Géricault (French, 1791–1824)
The Kiss
Sepia and black chalk heightened with
white, 8 x 10 ½ in. (20.3 x 26.7 cm)

(Sale, London, Sotheby & Co., through
[Arthur Tooth & Sons], 23 October 1963
for $21,153 to); Norton Simon (sale, New
York, Sotheby Parke Bernet, 2 May 1973, lot
4, for $160,000 to); Thyssen-Bornemisza
Collection, Madrid.

Cat. 165
Willem de Kooning (American, b. the
Netherlands, 1904–1997)
Two Standing Women, 1949
Oil, charcoal, and enamel on paper,
mounted on board, 29 ½ x 26 ¼ in. (74.9 x
66.7 cm)
(Sale, New York, Parke-Bernet Galleries,
30 October 1963 for $27,000 to); Norton
Simon, sold 22 December 1966 to; Norton
Simon Art Foundation (sale, New York,
Parke-Bernet Galleries, 14 May 1970, lot 19,
for $47,500). (sale, New York, Christie's, 18
November 1997 to); [L & M Arts, New York,
sold to]; private collection.

Cat. 166
Eugène Delacroix (French, 1798–1863)
Iago, c. 1825
Pen and sepia wash, 9 ½ x 6 ¾ in. (24.1 x
17.2 cm)
[Gerhard Pinkus, Beverly Hills, Calif., sold
6 November 1963 for $4,150 to]; Norton
Simon (sale, New York, Parke-Bernet
Galleries, 5 May 1971, lot 3, for $6,000 to);
Samuel J. LeFrak, New York, by inheritance
to; LeFrak Family Collection, New York.

Cat. 167
Ernst Barlach (German, 1870–1938)
Singing Man, 1930
Bronze, 19 ¾ in. (50.2 cm)
[Jules Bar, Zurich, sold 26 November 1963
for $12,275 to]; Norton Simon, transferred
24 July 1970 to; Lucille Ellis Simon (estate
sale, London, Christie's, 17 October 2000,
lot 16, for $482,269).

161

165

162

166

164

167

168

171

169

170

172

173

Cat. 168

Walter Richard Sickert (English, 1860–1942)
*A View of the Basilica of St. Mark's and the
Torre del Orologio, Venice*, c. 1903
Oil on canvas, 14 ½ x 17 ½ in. (36.8 x 44.5 cm)
(Sale, London, Christie's, 6 December 1963,
lot 60, for $9,000 to); Norton Simon (sale,
New York, Parke-Bernet Galleries,
5 May 1971, lot 49, for $10,000 to); private
collection, Texas.

1964

Cat. 169

Rembrandt van Rijn (Dutch, 1606–1669)
Rest on the Flight into Egypt, c. 1655
Ink and wash, 6 ¹³/₁₆ x 9 ³/₁₆ in. (17.3 x 23.4 cm)
[Simpson, Thatcher & Bartlett, New York
(through M. Knoedler & Co., New York),
sold 14 January 1964 for $40,000 to]; The
Norton Simon Foundation, sold 7 May
1976 for $110,000 to; [E. V. Thaw & Co.,
New York]; Eugene V. and Clare E. Thaw,
New York, promised gift to; The Pierpont
Morgan Library, New York.

Cat. 170

Rembrandt van Rijn (Dutch, 1606–1669)
Three Studies for a Descent from the Cross,
c. 1653/54
Ink, 7 ½ x 8 ¹/₁₆ in. (19 x 20.5 cm)
[Simpson, Thatcher & Bartlett, New York
(through M. Knoedler & Co., New York),
sold 14 January 1964 for $40,000 to]; The
Norton Simon Foundation, used in trade
31 January 1974 with a value of $120,000
as payment for Francisco de Goya, *Los
Caprichos* (cat. 1006) to; [Robert M. Light,
Boston, and E. V. Thaw & Co., New York];
Eugene V. and Clare E. Thaw, New York,
promised gift to; The Pierpont Morgan
Library, New York.

Cat. 171

Pablo Picasso (Spanish, 1881–1973)
Linocuts, group of 100
[Marlborough-Gerson Gallery, New
York, sold 15 January 1964 for $66,500 to];
Norton Simon. Fifty transferred 24 July
1970 to; Lucille Ellis Simon. Of the fifty
remaining, twenty were deaccessioned
(sales, Los Angeles, Sotheby Parke Bernet,
25 September 1974, New York, Sotheby
Parke Bernet, 18 February 1975, Los
Angeles, Sotheby Parke Bernet, 10 March
1976, used in trade 14 December 1979 for
Daniel de Monfreid, *The Blue Coffee Pot*
(cat. 545), and Attributed to Philippe de
Champaigne, *Abbess of the Trinitarians,
Caen* (cat. 616) to; Norton Simon Inc., New
York, and thirty were donated to Norton
Simon Art Foundation (30 December 1975
[M.1975.26.1–7] and 31 December 1979
[M.1979.69.1–23]).

Cat. 172

Edgar Degas (French, 1834–1917)
Woman Drying Herself after the Bath,
1876–1877
Pastel over monotype, 18 x 23 ¾ in.
(45.7 x 60.3 cm)
[Wildenstein & Co., New York, sold
26 January 1964 for $210,000 to]; Norton
Simon, sold 7 January 1974 for $700,000 to;
[Wildenstein & Co., New York], sold
27 December 1978 for $660,000 ($310,000
plus Claude Monet *Water Lilies* [cat. 1332],
with a value of $350,000) to; The Norton
Simon Foundation (F.1978.4).

Cat. 173

Jan van der Heyden (Dutch, 1637–1712)
Square in Utrecht, 1676
Oil on panel, 18 x 23 ¾ in. (45.7 x 60.3 cm)
[Wildenstein & Co., New York, sold
26 January 1964 for $80,000 to]; Norton
Simon, sold 3 April 1972 for $225,000 to;

[Frederick Mont, New York]. (sale, London, Christie's, 7 July 1978, lot 181). (sale, London, Christie's, 9 July 1993, lot 25). (sale, Zurich, Koller Galerie, 20 March 1996, lot 22, to); private collection.

Cat. 174
Édouard Vuillard (French, 1868–1940)
Landscapes and Interiors, 1899
Lithographs, group of thirteen
[Marlborough-Gerson Gallery, New York, sold 26 January 1964 for $10,000 to]; Norton Simon, transferred 24 July 1970 to; Lucille Ellis Simon.

Cat. 175
Formerly attributed to Juan Gris (Spanish, 1887–1927)
Still Life with Grapes, 1914
Collage, oil, watercolor, crayon, and pencil on cardboard, 10 x 13 in. (25.4 x 33 cm)
[Paul Kantor, Beverly Hills, Calif., sold 6 February 1964 for $15,000 to]; Norton Simon, sold 22 December 1966 to; Norton Simon Art Foundation (sale, New York, Parke-Bernet Galleries, 13 May 1970, lot 69, for $41,000 to); private collection, Peru, returned to [Sotheby Parke Bernet, New York].

Cat. 176
Aristide Maillol (French, 1861–1944)
Young Girl with Arm over Her Eyes
Bronze, 8 ¾ in. (22.2 cm)
[Paul Kantor, Beverly Hills, Calif., sold 6 February 1964 for $2,000 to]; Norton Simon (sale, New York, Parke-Bernet Galleries, 13 May 1970, lot 18, for $5,500).

Cat. 177
Rembrandt van Rijn (Dutch, 1606–1669)
Mercury, Argus, and Io, c. 1645
Ink, 6 ½ x 8 in. (16.5 x 20.3 cm)
[Paul Kantor, Beverly Hills, Calif., sold 6 February 1964 for $13,000 to]; Norton

Simon (sale, New York, Parke-Bernet Galleries, 8 May 1971, lot 201A, unsold, sold privately 1 June 1971 for $2,500).

Cat. 178
Rembrandt van Rijn (Dutch, 1606–1669)
Jan Lutma
Etching, 1st state
[William Schab, New York, sold 13 February 1964 for $8,400 to]; Norton Simon, sold 18 October 1972 for $82,000 for this print, Pieter Brueghel the Elder, *Landscape with Rabbit Hunters* (cat. 496), and Albrecht Dürer, *Melancholia* (cat. 154) to; [E. V. Thaw & Co., New York].

Cat. 179
Rembrandt van Rijn (Dutch, 1606–1669)
Woman at the Bath, with a Hat beside Her
Etching on Japan paper, 2nd state
[William Schab, New York, sold 13 February 1964 for $6,100 to]; Norton Simon (sale, London, Christie's, 1 December 1971 for $12,348).

Cat. 180
Luca Signorelli (Italian, c. 1445–1523)
Seated Female Saint
Black chalk, 8 ⅝ x 6 ¹¹/₁₆ in. (22 x 17 cm)
[William Schab, New York, sold 13 February 1964 for $4,000 to]; Norton Simon, used in trade 14 June 1973 with a value of $5,500, plus $15,000 as payment for 1st-edition set of Francisco de Goya, *Los Caprichos* (cat. 940) to; [William Schab, New York].

Cat. 181
Anthony van Dyck (Flemish, 1599–1641)
Oriental on Horseback
Oil on paper, mounted on canvas, 16 ¼ x 13 ⅛ in. (41.3 x 33.3 cm)
[Paul Kantor, Beverly Hills, Calif., sold 13 February 1964 for $15,000 to]; Norton Simon (sale, New York, Parke-Bernet Galleries, 8 May 1971, lot 212A, for $4,900).

174

178

175

179

176

180

177

181

182

183

184

185

186

187

188

189

190

Cat. 182
Eugène Delacroix (French, 1798–1863)
Jewish Bride of Tangier, 1832
Oil on canvas, 18 ⅝ x 15 ¾ in. (47.3 x 40 cm)
[E. V. Thaw & Co., New York, sold 17
February 1964 for $34,000 to]; Norton
Simon (sale, New York, Parke-Bernet
Galleries, 5 May 1971, lot 4, for $50,000 to);
Samuel J. LeFrak, New York, by inheritance
to; LeFrak Family Collection, New York.

Cat. 183
Peru, Mochica culture
Stirrup-Spout Vessel, c. 200–700
Ceramic, 14 in. (35.6 cm)
[Ralph C. Altman, Los Angeles, sold
21 February 1964 for $85 to]; Norton Simon,
gift 28 December 1978 to; The Norton
Simon Foundation (F.1978.6).

Cat. 184
Edgar Degas (French, 1834–1917)
Horse standing (Horse at rest)
Bronze, cast no. 38/HER.D, 11 ⅜ in. (28.9 cm)
[Paul Rosenberg & Co., New York, sold
25 February 1964 for $21,000 to]; Norton
Simon, transferred 24 July 1970 to; Lucille
Ellis Simon, by inheritance to; private
collection, Los Angeles (sale, New York,
Christie's, 6 November 2001, lot 30, unsold,
sale, New York, Christies, 6 May 2009, lot 17,
unsold).

Cat. 185
Aristide Maillol (French, 1861–1944)
Crouching Bather
Bronze, 8 ¼ in. (21 cm)
[Paul Rosenberg & Co., New York, sold
25 February 1964 for $7,000 to]; Norton
Simon, transferred 24 July 1970 to; Lucille
Ellis Simon.

Cat. 186
Pieter Brueghel the Elder (Flemish,
1525–1569)
Alpine Landscape with a Deep Valley
Etching

(Sale, London, Sotheby & Co., 10 March
1964, lot 18, for $3,123 to); Norton Simon
(sale, London, Sotheby & Co., 23 November
1971, lot 73, for $1,600 to); [Baskett & Day,
London].

Cat. 187
Pieter Brueghel the Elder (Flemish,
1525–1569)
Insidiousus Auceps
Etching
(Sale, London, Sotheby & Co., 10 March
1964, lot 19, for $2,563 to); Norton Simon
(sale, London, Sotheby & Co., 23 November
1971, lot 74, for $1,215 to); [Baskett & Day,
London].

Cat. 188
Pieter Brueghel the Elder
(Flemish, 1525–1569)
The Resurrection
Etching
(Sale, London, Sotheby & Co., 10 March
1964, lot 53, for $9,840 to); Norton Simon
(sale, London, Sotheby & Co., 23 November
1971, lot 75, for $8,262 to); [William Schab,
New York].

Cat. 189
Jan van der Heyden (Dutch, 1637–1712)
The Ship of Depravity (after Bosch)
Engraving, 9 ¹/₁₆ x 11 ⅞ in. (23 x 30.2 cm)
(Sale, London, Sotheby & Co., 10 March
1964 for $771 to); Norton Simon (sale,
London, Christie's, 1 December 1971, lot 22,
for $3,341).

Cat. 190
Jean-Honoré Fragonard (French, 1732–1806)
Danae Visited by Jupiter
Brush and brown wash, 10 ⅝ x 15 ½ in.
(27 x 39.4 cm)
[Charles Slatkin, New York, sold 20 March
1964 for $15,000 to]; Norton Simon (sale,
New York, Parke-Bernet Galleries, 8 May
1971, lot 208, for $22,000).

Cat. 191
Jean-Antoine Watteau (French, 1684–1721)
Portrait of an Artist
Black chalk with sanguine, 8 ½ x 6 in.
(21.6 x 15.2 cm)
[Charles Slatkin, New York, sold 20 March
1964 for $12,000 to]; Norton Simon (sale,
New York, Parke-Bernet Galleries, 8 May
1971, lot 205).

Cat. 192
Henry Moore (English, 1898–1986)
Family Group, 1945–1946
Bronze, 10 in. (25.4 cm)
[Marlborough-Gerson Gallery, New York,
sold 27 March 1964 for $22,450 to]; Norton
Simon, transferred 24 July 1970 to; Lucille
Ellis Simon.

Cat. 193
Follower of Giovanni Francesco Barbieri,
called Il Guercino (Italian, 1591–1666)
Heads of Two Young Girls
Ink, 5 x 7 ⅞ in. (12.7 x 20 cm)
[Schaeffer Galleries, New York, sold 7 April
1964 for $680 to]; Norton Simon (sale, New
York, Parke-Bernet Galleries, 8 May 1971, lot
200, for $1,000). (sale, London, Sotheby's,
11 July 2001, lot 84, for £14,300).

Cat. 194
Nicolas Lancret (French, 1690–1743)
Fête Champêtre
Sanguine, 12 ½ x 15 ⅜ in. (31.8 x 39.1 cm)
[Schaeffer Galleries, New York, sold 7 April
1964 for $2,000 to]; Norton Simon (sale,
New York, Sotheby Parke Bernet, 8 May
1973, lot 204A, for $1,100).

Cat. 195
Hubert Robert (French, 1733–1808)
The Ruined Temple of the Sybil at Tivoli
Watercolor and gouache over black chalk,
13 ½ x 17 ⅝ in. (34.3 x 44.8 cm)
[Schaeffer Galleries, New York, sold 7 April
1964 for $2,400 to]; Norton Simon (sale,
New York, Parke-Bernet Galleries, 8 May
1971, lot 212, for $8,500).

Cat. 196
Jacopo Robusti, called Tintoretto (Italian,
1518–1594)
Study after an Antique Bust
Black chalk heightened with white,
11 x 7 ¼ in. (27.9 x 18.4 cm)
[Schaeffer Galleries, New York, sold 7 April
1964 for $7,200 to]; Norton Simon (sale,
New York, Parke-Bernet Galleries, 8 May
1971, lot 199, for $3,000).

Cat. 197
Jean-Antoine Watteau (French, 1684–1721)
Study of a Tree in a Landscape
Red chalk, 16 ½ x 11 ¾ in. (41.9 x 29.9 cm)
[Schaeffer Galleries, New York, sold 7 April
1964 for $9,600 to]; Norton Simon, sold
22 December 1966 to; Norton Simon Art
Foundation (sale, London, Sotheby & Co.,
27 June 1974, lot 49, for $8,160).

Cat. 198
François Boucher (French, 1703–1770)
Landscape with Rustic Bridge
Black chalk heightened with white, 8 x 11 in.
(20.3 x 27.9 cm)
[Charles E. Slatkin, New York, sold 13 April
1964 for $6,500 to]; Norton Simon (sale, New
York, Parke-Bernet Galleries, 7 May 1971, lot
207, for $6,000 to); The Armand Hammer
Foundation, Los Angeles, gift 1991 to;
National Gallery of Art, Washington, D.C.

Cat. 199
François Boucher (French, 1703–1770)
Reclining Venus with Dolphin
Black chalk heightened with white,
8 ¹¹/₁₆ x 13 ¼ in. (22.1 x 33.7 cm)
[Charles E. Slatkin, New York, sold 13 April
1964 for $10,000 to]; Norton Simon (sale,
New York, Parke-Bernet Galleries, 7 May
1971, lot 206, for $19,000 to); The Armand
Hammer Foundation, Los Angeles, gift 1991
to; National Gallery of Art, Washington, D.C.

191

196

192

197

193

194

198

199

195

200

205

201

206

202

207

203

204

Cat. 200
Follower of Giovanni Francesco Barbieri,
called Il Guercino (Italian, 1591–1666)
Landscape with Soldiers in the Foreground
Brown ink, 14 x 19 in. (35.6 x 48.3 cm)
[Charles E. Slatkin, New York, sold
13 April 1964 for $2,500 to]; Norton Simon,
gift 16 March 1967 to; Norton Simon Art
Foundation (M.1967.5).

Cat. 201
Jean-Baptiste Pater (French, 1695–1736)
Seated Gallant Seen from Behind
Red chalk, 5 ¼ x 8 in. (13.3 x 20.3 cm)
[Charles E. Slatkin, New York, sold 13 April
1964 for $3,000 to]; Norton Simon (sale,
New York, Parke-Bernet Galleries, 8 May
1971, lot 203, for $2,800). private collection
(sale, London, Sotheby's, 6 July 2004, lot
125, for £7,200).

Cat. 202
Lorenzo Tiepolo (Italian, 1736–1772)
Head of a Young Boy
Black and white chalk, 20 x 16 in.
(50.8 x 40.6 cm)
[Charles E. Slatkin, New York, sold 13 April
1964 for $5,250 to]; Norton Simon, sold
22 December 1966 to; Norton Simon Art
Foundation (sale, London, Sotheby & Co.,
27 June 1974, lot 65, for $3,600).

Cat. 203
Giovanni Battista Tiepolo (Italian,
1696–1770)
Punchinellos
Ink wash, 9 ⅛ x 8 in. (23.2 x 20.3 cm)
[Charles E. Slatkin, New York, sold 13 April
1964 for $6,500 to]; Norton Simon, sold
22 December 1966 to; Norton Simon Art
Foundation (sale, London, Sotheby & Co.,
27 June 1974, lot 64, for $7,440).

Cat. 204
Giovanni Battista Tiepolo (Italian,
1696–1770)

Young Man in Flat Cap
Ink wash, 9 ½ x 6 ⅛ in. (24.1 x 15.6 cm)
[Charles E. Slatkin, New York, sold 13 April
1964 for $2,250 to]; Norton Simon, sold
22 December 1966 to; Norton Simon Art
Foundation (sale, London, Sotheby & Co.,
27 June 1974, lot 63, for $5,040).

Cat. 205
Hendrick van Balen the Elder
(Flemish, 1575–1632)
Mythological Scene
Pen and sepia with wash, 8 ½ x 11 ½ in.
(21.6 x 29.2 cm)
[Mortimer Brandt Galleries, New York, sold
17 April 1964 for $743 to]; Norton Simon
(sale, New York, Parke-Bernet Galleries,
8 May 1971, lot 201, for $700).

Cat. 206
Baccio Bandinelli (Italian, 1488–1560)
Hercules, c. 1548
Brown ink, 13 ¼ x 8 ¾ in. (33.7 x 22.2 cm)
[Mortimer Brandt Galleries, New York, sold
17 April 1964 for $1,530 to]; Norton Simon
(sale, New York, Parke-Bernet Galleries, 8
May 1971, lot 198, for $2,000). (sale, New
York, William Doyle, 14 May 2008, lot 1001,
unsold).

Cat. 207
Bartolommeo Passarotti (Italian, 1529–1592)
Crouching Male Nude
Brown ink, 17 ¼ x 14 in. (43.8 x 35.6 cm)
[Mortimer Brandt Galleries, New York, sold
17 April 1964 for $1,530 to]; Norton Simon,
gift 30 December 1975 to; Norton Simon Art
Foundation (sale, London, Christie's,
9 December 1980, lot 33, for $6,353).

The Duveen Purchase
[Duveen Brothers, New York, sold 18 April
1964 for $4,000,000 to]; The Norton Simon
Foundation
Please see The Duveen Inventory,
beginning p. 441

Cat. 208
Aristide Maillol (French, 1861–1944)
Kneeling Girl, c. 1900
Bronze, artist's proof, 7 in. (17.8 cm)
[Paul Kantor, Beverly Hills, Calif., sold
21 April 1964 for $2,250 to]; Norton Simon
(sale, New York, Parke-Bernet Galleries,
13 May 1970, lot 27, for $4,500).

Cat. 209
Aristide Maillol (French, 1861–1944)
Woman Arranging Her Hair, c. 1898
Bronze, 10 ¾ in. (27.3 cm)
[Paul Kantor, Beverly Hills, Calif., sold
21 April 1964 for $3,250 to]; Norton Simon
(sale, New York, Parke-Bernet Galleries,
5 May 1971, lot 54, for $11,000).

Cat. 210
Hans Memling (Netherlandish, c.
1430/1440–1494)
Christ Giving His Blessing, 1478
Oil on panel, 15 ⅛ x 11 ¼ in. (38.4 x 28.6 cm)
[M. Knoedler & Co., New York, sold
21 April 1964 for $225,000 to]; Norton
Simon, gift 30 December 1974 to; Norton
Simon Art Foundation (M.1974.17).

Cat. 211
Anthony van Dyck (Flemish, 1599–1641)
Portrait of a Woman (formerly *Marchesa
Lomellini Durazzo*)
Oil on canvas, 39 ½ x 29 ½ in.
(100.3 x 74.9 cm)
[M. Knoedler & Co., New York, sold 21 April
1964 for $175,000 to]; Norton Simon, gift
28 December 1967 to; Norton Simon Art
Foundation (sale, London, Sotheby & Co.,
11 July 1973, lot 20, for $450,000).

Cat. 212
Jean-Baptiste Camille Corot (French,
1796–1875)
Study of Medieval Ruins (formerly
*Pierrefonds, Glacis of the Château Fort in
Ruins*), c. 1829–1834
Oil on canvas, laid down on board,
9 ⅜ x 12 ¾ in. (23.9 x 32.4 cm)

(Sale, London, Sotheby & Co., 29 April
1964 for $13,482 to); Norton Simon (sale,
New York, Parke-Bernet Galleries, 5 May
1971, lot 2, for $26,000 to); The Armand
Hammer Foundation, Los Angeles, gift 1990
to; Armand Hammer Museum of Art and
Culture Center, Los Angeles.

Cat. 213
Claude Monet (French, 1840–1926)
The Wooden Bridge at Argenteuil, 1872
Oil on canvas, 21 x 28 ¾ in. (53.3 x 73 cm)
(Sale, London, Sotheby & Co., 29 April
1964 for $135,222 to); Norton Simon (sale,
London, Christie's, 30 November 1971, lot
24, for $411,000). Fondation Rau, Zurich.

Cat. 214
Pierre Bonnard (French, 1867–1947)
Les Pastorales de Longus or *Daphnis and
Chloe*, 1902
Illustrated book, 13 x 10 ⁵⁄₁₆ in. (33 x 26.2 cm)
(Sale, London, Sotheby & Co., 12 May 1964
for $2,098 to); Norton Simon (sale, New
York, Parke-Bernet Galleries, 11 May 1971,
lot 76, for $3,400).

Cat. 215
Honoré Daumier (French, 1808–1879)
Bohemians of Paris
Lithographs, group of twenty-eight,
each 9 ¼ x 7 ½ in. (23.5 x 19.1 cm)
(Sale, London, Sotheby & Co., 12 May 1964
for $757 to); Norton Simon, gift
17 May 1977, of two to; Norton Simon Inc.,
and twenty-six to; Norton Simon Museum
(P.1977.11.1–26).

Cat. 216
Henri Matisse (French, 1869–1954)
Illustrations to "Ulysses"
Etchings, group of six, each 11 x 8 ⅝ in.
(27.9 x 22 cm)
(Sale, London, Sotheby & Co., 12 May 1964
for $379 to); Norton Simon, gift 1966 to;
University of California, Los Angeles.

208

213

209

214

210

215

211

212

216

221

217

218

219

220

222

223

224

Cat. 217

Pablo Picasso (Spanish, 1881–1973)
Painter at Work, Observed by a Model, plate
8 of *Balzac's "Chef d'oeuvre inconnu"*
Etching, 7 ¾ x 11 in. (19.7 x 27.9 cm)
(Sale, London, Sotheby & Co., 12 May
1964 for $292 to); Norton Simon, gift 31
December 1979 to; Norton Simon Art
Foundation (M.1979.70).

Cat. 218

Henri Matisse (French, 1869–1954)
Woman Leaning on Her Elbows on a Table
Lithograph on Japan paper: image,
12 x 9 ½ in. (30.5 x 24.1 cm); sheet,
17 ½ x 16 ⅝ in. (44.5 x 42.2 cm)
(Sale, London, Sotheby & Co., 13 May
1964 for $379 to); Norton Simon, gift 31
December 1979 to; Norton Simon Art
Foundation (M.1979.68).

Cat. 219

Edgar Degas (French, 1834–1917)
Horse with head lowered
Bronze, cast no. 22/H, 7 ⅛ in. (18.1 cm)
[M. Knoedler & Co., New York, sold
14 May 1964 for $16,000 to]; Norton Simon,
transferred 24 July 1970 to; Lucille Ellis
Simon (estate sale, New York, Christie's,
8 November 2000, lot 7, for $556,000 to);
private collection, Washington, D.C.

Cat. 220

Edgar Degas (French, 1834–1917)
Rearing horse
Bronze, cast no. 4/L, 12 ⅛ in. (30.8 cm)
[M. Knoedler & Co., New York, sold
14 May 1964 for $27,000 to]; Norton Simon,
transferred 24 July 1970 to; Lucille Ellis
Simon (estate sale, New York, Christie's,
8 November 2000, lot 5, for $1,051,000 to);
private collection, U.K.

Cat. 221

Edgar Degas (French, 1834–1917)
Actress in Her Dressing Room, c. 1875–1880
and c. 1895–1905
Oil on canvas, 33 ⅝ x 29 ¾ in. (85.4 x 75.6 cm)
[Arthur Tooth & Sons, London, sold
8 June 1964 for $122,973 to]; Norton Simon
(sale, New York, Parke-Bernet Galleries,
5 May 1971, lot 33, for $100,000 to);
[Michael F. Drinkhouse, New York];
[Stephen Hahn Gallery, New York, sold
20 January 1972 for $135,000 to]; The
Norton Simon Foundation (F.1972.3).

Cat. 222

Claude Monet (French, 1840–1926)
Water Lilies, Giverny, 1919
Oil on canvas, 39 ⅜ x 79 ⅛ in. (100 x 201 cm)
[Sam Salz, New York, sold 8 June 1964 for
$240,000 to]; Norton Simon (sale, New
York, Parke-Bernet Galleries, 5 May 1971,
lot 41, for $320,000 to); Mrs. Elizabeth C.
Miller Tangeman, Columbus, Ind., sold 1993
to; J. Irwin and Xenia S. Miller, Columbus,
Ind. (estate sale, London, Christie's, 24 June
2008, lot 16, for $80 million to); private
collection.

Cat. 223

Edgar Degas (French, 1834–1917)
*Arabesque over the right leg, right hand
near the ground, left arm outstretched*
Bronze, cast no. 2/HER.D, 10 ¾ in. (27.3 cm)
[Paul Rosenberg & Co., New York, sold
9 June 1964 for $16,000 to]; Norton Simon,
transferred 24 July 1970 to; Lucille Ellis
Simon (estate sale, New York, Christie's,
8 November 2000, lot 4, for $391,000 to);
private collection, Florida.

Cat. 224

Aristide Maillol (French, 1861–1944)
Young Girl with Arm over Her Eyes
Bronze, edition of 6, cast no. 2,
8 ¾ in. (22.2 cm)
[Paul Rosenberg & Co., New York, sold
9 June 1964 for $6,500 to]; Norton Simon,
transferred 24 July 1970 to; Lucille Ellis Simon.

Cat. 225
Paul Cézanne (French, 1839–1906)
Still Life with Pears and Apples, Covered Blue Jar, and a Bottle of Wine
Watercolor, 18 ¾ x 24 ¼ in. (47.6 x 61.6 cm)
[A. Martinais (Galerie de Paris), sold 29 June 1964 for $90,000 to]; Norton Simon, gift 22 December 1976 to; Norton Simon Art Foundation, sold 17 March 1981 for $500,000 to; [E. V. Thaw & Co., New York]; Eugene V. and Clare E. Thaw, New York, gift 2002 to; The Pierpont Morgan Library, New York.

Cat. 226
Paul-Camille Guigou (French, 1834–1871)
The Banks of the River Durance at Saint-Paul, 1864
Oil on canvas, 24 ⅜ x 58 ¼ in. (62 x 148 cm)
(Sale, London, Sotheby & Co., 1 July 1964 for $12,509 to); Norton Simon (sale, New York, Sotheby Parke Bernet, 11 May 1978, lot 179, for $60,000). The Art Institute of Chicago.

Cat. 227
Auguste Rodin (French, 1840–1917)
Eve
Marble, 30 ½ in. (77.5 cm)
(Sale, London, Sotheby & Co., 1 July 1964 for $36,600 to); Norton Simon (sale, New York, Parke-Bernet Galleries, 13 May 1970, lot 23, for $30,000).

Cat. 228
Raymond Duchamp-Villon (French, 1876–1918)
Baudelaire, 1911
Bronze, 15 ⅞ in. (40.3 cm)
[E. V. Thaw & Co., New York, sold 14 August 1964 for $25,000 to]; Norton Simon, transferred 24 July 1970 to; Lucille Ellis Simon (estate sale, New York, Christie's, 9 November 2000, lot 243, for $99,500).

Cat. 229
Giovanni Antonio Canal, called Canaletto (Italian, 1697–1768)
The Piazzetta, Venice, Looking North, early 1730s
Oil on canvas, 29 ⅞ x 47 ⅛ in. (75.9 x 119.7 cm)
[Arthur Tooth & Sons, London, sold 1 September 1964 for $139,202 to]; The Norton Simon Foundation (F.1964.2).

Cat. 230
Albert Lebourg (French, 1849–1928)
Bridge at Neuilly, 1888
Oil on canvas, 16 x 25 ¾ in. (40.6 x 65.4 cm)
[Arthur Tooth & Sons, London, sold 1 September 1964 for $13,084 to]; Norton Simon, gift 15 March 1967 to; Norton Simon Art Foundation (sale, New York, Sotheby Parke Bernet, 2 May 1973, lot 21, for $16,000 to); [Galerie Hervé Odermatt, Paris]. (sale, London, Sotheby's, 4 December 1991, lot 124).

Cat. 231
Albert Marquet (French, 1875–1947)
Bay of Audierne, 1928
Oil on canvas, 18 x 24 in. (45.7 x 61 cm)
[Arthur Tooth & Sons, London, sold 1 September 1964 for $16,147 to]; Norton Simon, gift 15 March 1967 to; Norton Simon Art Foundation, used in trade 13 January 1971 with a value of $35,000 as partial payment for Lucas Cranach the Elder, *Adam* (cat. 742) to; [Spencer A. Samuels & Co., New York]. (sale, Paris, Calmels-Chambre-Cohen, 28 June 1999, lot 22, for $101,120).

Cat. 232
Georges Braque (French, 1882–1963)
Still Life with Musical Instruments, 1918
Oil on canvas, 25 ½ x 36 ¼ in. (64.8 x 92.1 cm)
[E. V. Thaw & Co., New York, sold 4 September 1964 for $117,314 to]; The Norton Simon Foundation, transferred 26 November 1986 to; Norton Simon Art Foundation (M.1986.2).

225

229

226

227

230

231

228

232

233

237

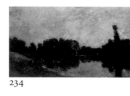

234

238

235

239

236

240

241

Cat. 233
Jacques Villon (French, 1875–1963)
Baudelaire on a Base, 1920
Etching, 2nd state, 16 ⅜ x 11 ⅛ in.
(41.6 x 28.3 cm)
[Robert M. Light, Boston, sold 8 September 1964 for $1,800 to]; Norton Simon, gift 22 December 1976 to; Norton Simon Art Foundation (M.1976.19).

Cat. 234
Charles François Daubigny
(French, 1817–1878)
Daybreak
Oil on canvas, 31 ½ x 56 ½ in. (80 x 143.5 cm)
[Arthur Tooth & Sons, London, sold 15 October 1964 for $8,353 to]; The Norton Simon Foundation (sale, New York, Sotheby Parke Bernet, 25 January 1980, lot 224, for $36,000).

Cat. 235
Nicolas de Staël (Russian, 1914–1955)
Still Life with Decanter, 1953
Oil on canvas, 32 x 25 ¾ in. (81.3 x 65.4 cm)
(Sale, New York, Parke Bernet Galleries, 21 October 1964 for $33,000 to); Norton Simon, gift 15 March 1967 to; Norton Simon Art Foundation (sale, New York, Parke-Bernet Galleries, 13 May 1970, lot 75, for $72,500). Lucia Moreira Salles (estate sale, London, Sotheby's, 25 June 2009, lot 5, for $1,427.230).

Cat. 236
Maurice Prendergast
(American, b. Canada, 1858–1924)
Beach at St. Malo, 1907
Oil on canvas, 17 ½ x 21 in. (44.5 x 53.3 cm)
(Sale, New York, Parke-Bernet Galleries, 21 October 1964 for $21,000 to); Norton Simon, sold 11 January 1966 [through Paul Kantor, Beverly Hills, Calif., for $25,000 to]; Justin Dart. Taubman Museum of Art, Roanoke, Va.

Cat. 237
Camille Pissarro (French, 1830–1903)
The Place du Théâtre Français, Afternoon Sun in Winter, 1898
Oil on canvas, 29 x 36 ½ in. (73.7 x 92.7 cm)
[Stephen Hahn Gallery, New York, sold 30 October 1964 for $155,000 to]; Norton Simon, sold 5 April 1980 for $500,000 to; [E. V. Thaw & Co., New York]; private collection.

Cat. 238
Honoré Daumier (French, 1808–1879)
Before the Hearing, c. 1860–1865
Watercolor, 9 x 9 in. (22.9 x 22.9 cm)
[Paul Rosenberg & Co., New York, sold 2 November 1964 for $70,000 to]; Norton Simon (sale, New York, Parke-Bernet Galleries, 5 May 1971, lot 14, for $85,000 to); private collection.

Cat. 239
Formerly attributed to Henri de Toulouse-Lautrec (French, 1864–1901)
Young Girl in Profile
Pastel on cardboard, 17 ⅝ x 15 ¼ in.
(44.8 x 38.7 cm)
[Paul Rosenberg & Co., New York, sold 2 November 1964 for $135,000 to]; Norton Simon, by inheritance 2 June 1993 to; Jennifer Jones Simon Art Trust, Los Angeles (N.1964.13).

Cat. 240
Honoré Daumier (French, 1808–1879)
The Bon Vivant
Bronze, edition of 30, cast no. 8,
6 ½ in. (16.5 cm)
[M. Knoedler & Co., New York, sold 6 November 1964 for $3,750 to]; Norton Simon (sale, New York, Parke-Bernet Galleries, 5 May 1971, lot 21, for $5,500)

Cat. 241
Honoré Daumier (French, 1808–1879)
The Lawyer Waving

Bronze, edition of 30, cast no. 4, 6 in. (15.2 cm)
[M. Knoedler & Co., New York, sold
6 November 1964 for $3,750 to]; Norton
Simon (sale, New York, Parke-Bernet
Galleries, 5 May 1971, lot 16, for $6,000).

Cat. 242
Honoré Daumier (French, 1808–1879)
The Reader
Bronze, edition of 30, cast no. 16, 6 ¼ in.
(15.9 cm)
[M. Knoedler & Co., New York, sold
6 November 1964 for $3,750 to]; Norton
Simon, gift of unknown date to; Franklin
Murphy, Los Angeles.

Cat. 243
Honoré Daumier (French, 1808–1879)
The Waiting Bourgeois
Bronze, edition of 30, cast no. 29, 6 ¼ in.
(15.9 cm)
[M. Knoedler & Co., New York, sold
6 November 1964 for $3,750 to]; Norton
Simon (sale, New York, Parke-Bernet
Galleries, 5 May 1971, lot 17, for $4,500).

Cat. 244
Egypt
Horus Falcon, c. 30th Dynasty
Bronze, 8 ½ in. (21.6 cm)
(Sale, London, Sotheby & Co., 17 November
1964 for $3,997 to); Norton Simon (private
sale, New York, Sotheby Parke Bernet,
22 May 1974, for $24,000 for this work and
Statuette of a Priest, cat. 115).

Cat. 245
Egypt, Coptic
Vase and Cover
Glazed faience, 6 ¾ in. (17.2 cm)
(Sale, London, Sotheby & Co.,
17 November 1964 for $2,320 to); Norton
Simon, transferred 24 July 1970 to; Lucille
Ellis Simon.

Cat. 246
Georg Kolbe (German, 1877–1947)
Falling Woman
Bronze, edition of 6, cast no. IV,
15 in. (38.1 cm)
(Sale, New York, Parke-Bernet Galleries,
18 November 1964 for $5,250 to); Norton
Simon (sale, New York, Parke-Bernet
Galleries, 5 May 1971, lot 65, for $9,500).
[Possibly Marlborough Fine Art, London,
(described as "cast no. 4") sold, 1981 to];
?private collection (sale, New York, Phillips,
De Pury & Luxembourg, 5 November 2002,
lot 122, for $80,000).

Cat. 247
François Pompon (French, 1856–1933)
Duck, c. 1932
Bronze, edition of 8, unnumbered cast,
7 ¼ in. (18.4 cm)
(Sale, New York, Parke-Bernet Galleries,
18 November 1964 for $2,122 to); Norton
Simon (sale, New York, Parke-Bernet
Galleries, 13 May 1970, lot 24, for $3,500).

Cat. 248
William Etty (English, 1787–1849)
Study for "Leda and the Swan," c. 1840
Oil on canvas, 16 ¾ x 21 in. (42.6 x 53.3 cm)
(Sale, London, Christie's, 20 November
1964 for $10,800 to); Norton Simon, by
inheritance 2 June 1993 to; Jennifer Jones
Simon Art Trust, Los Angeles (N.1964.14).

Cat. 249
Joseph Mallord William Turner
(English, 1775–1851)
Great Yarmouth Fishing Boats
Gouache on blue paper, 9 ¼ x 7 in.
(23.5 x 17.8 cm)
(Sale, London, Christie's, 20 November 1964
for $5,850 to); Norton Simon (sale, New
York, Parke-Bernet Galleries, 8 May 1971, lot
216A, for $10,500).

243

242

246

247

244

248

249

250

254

251

255

252

256

253

257

258

Cat. 250
Henri-Joseph Harpignies
(French, 1819–1916)
Trees by the Seashore, 1899
Watercolor, 12 x 9 in. (30.5 x 22.9 cm)
(Sale, London, Sotheby & Co., 25 November
1964 for $560 to); Norton Simon (sale, New
York, Parke-Bernet Galleries, 21 October
1971 lot 70, for $1,350 to); private collection.

Cat. 251
Ernst Barlach (German, 1870–1938)
The Avenger, 1914, cast in 1945
Bronze, edition of 10 not realized,
unnumbered cast, 17 ¼ x 22 ⅞ in.
(43.8 x 58.1 cm)
[Marlborough-Gerson Gallery, New
York, sold 3 December 1964 for $15,000
to]; Norton Simon, gift 15 March 1967 to;
Norton Simon Art Foundation (sale, New
York, Parke-Bernet Galleries, 13 May 1970,
lot 79, unsold), (M.1967.4).

Cat. 252
Georg Kolbe (German, 1877–1947)
Dancer, 1922
Bronze, 27 ⅛ in. (69 cm)
[Marlborough-Gerson, Gallery, New York,
sold 3 December 1964 for $6,000 to];
Norton Simon, transferred 24 July 1970 to;
Lucille Ellis Simon (estate sale, New York,
Christie's, 5 November 2003, lot 295, for
$55,000).

Cat. 253
Francisco de Goya y Lucientes
(Spanish, 1746–1828)
Los Proverbios, 1st edition, 1819–1820,
printed 1864
Etching, aquatint, and drypoint, 18 plates
[Zeitlin & Ver Brugge, Los Angeles, sold
7 December 1964 for $3,150 to]; Norton
Simon, gift 22 December 1976 to; Norton
Simon Art Foundation (M.1976.17.1–18).

Cat. 254
Jacques Villon (French, 1875–1963)
Bucoliques de Virgile
Color lithographs, set of 27
[Zeitlin & Ver Brugge, Los Angeles, sold
7 December 1964 for $1,500 to]; Norton
Simon, gift 17 May 1977 to; Norton Simon
Museum (P.1977.12.1–27).

Cat. 255
Bernardo Bellotto (Italian, c. 1721–1780)
A Capriccio of Padua
Pen and brown ink, 7 ½ x 12 ¾ in.
(19.1 x 32.4 cm)
[Mortimer Brandt Galleries, New York, sold
15 December 1964 for $2,640 to]; Norton
Simon (sale, New York, Parke-Bernet
Galleries, 8 May 1971, lot 209, for $1,000).

Cat. 256
Louis-Léopold Boilly (French, 1761–1845)
Portrait of a Woman
Pencil, 7 ¾ x 5 ¼ in. (19.7 x 13.3 cm)
[Mortimer Brandt Galleries, New York,
sold 15 December 1964 for $800 to]; Norton
Simon (sale, New York, Parke-Bernet
Galleries, 8 May 1971, lot 210, for $4,100).

Cat. 257
Francesco Guardi (Italian, 1712–1793)
*A View of the Rialto, Venice,
from the Grand Canal*
Oil on canvas, 17 x 24 ¾ in. (43.2 x 62.9 cm)
[Thomas Agnew & Sons, London, sold
28 December 1964 for $58,000 to]; Norton
Simon, sold 22 December 1966 to; Norton
Simon Art Foundation (M.1966.10.5).

Cat. 258
Paul Gauguin (French, 1848–1903)
Self-Portrait with Palette, 1893–1894
Oil on canvas, 21 ½ x 18 in. (54.6 x 45.7 cm)
[Paul Rosenberg & Co., New York, sold
29 December 1964 for $275,000 to]; Norton
Simon (sale, New York, Parke-Bernet
Galleries, 5 May 1971, lot 45, for $420,000
to); private collection, New York.

1965

Cat. 259
Ernst Barlach (German, 1870–1938)
Reading Monks III, 1939
Bronze, 22 ⅞ in. (58.1 cm)
[Marlborough-Gerson Gallery, New York, sold 4 January 1965 for $13,000 to]; Norton Simon (sale, New York, Parke-Bernet Galleries, 5 May 1971, lot 64, for $18,500 to); B. Gerald Cantor, Los Angeles. private collection, Los Angeles.

Cat. 260
Pierre-Auguste Renoir (French, 1841–1919)
The Source (Woman at the Fountain), 1910
Oil on canvas, 36 x 29 in. (91.4 x 73.7 cm)
[Marguerite Rosenberg, New York, sold 4 January 1965 for $225,000 to]; Norton Simon (sale, New York, Parke-Bernet Galleries, 5 May 1971, lot 44, for $230,000 to); [Claus Virch, Paris]. [Acquavella Galleries, New York, sold 1973 to]; [Art Salon Takahata, Osaka, sold 1979 to]; private collection, Japan.

Cat. 261
Pierre-Auguste Renoir (French, 1841–1919)
Dance in the Country, 1883
Pen, ink, and wash, 18 ¾ x 11 ⅞ in. (47.6 x 30.2 cm)
[Schaeffer Galleries, New York, sold 4 January 1965 for $30,000 to]; Norton Simon, sold 14 March 1973 for $100,000 to [E. V. Thaw & Co., New York, sold to]; Mr. and Mrs. Paul Mellon, gift 1995 to; National Gallery of Art, Washington, D.C.

Cat. 262
Paul Gauguin (French, 1848–1903)
Tahitian Woman and Boy, 1899
Oil on canvas, 37 ¼ x 24 ⅜ in. (94.6 x 61.9 cm)

[Hammer Galleries, New York, sold 5 January 1965 for $365,000 to]; Norton Simon, gift 29 June 1976 to; Norton Simon Art Foundation (M.1976.8).

Cat. 263
Honoré Daumier (French, 1808–1879)
Le Ratapoil
Bronze, edition of 20, cast no. 17, 17 ½ in. (44.5 cm)
[E. V. Thaw & Co., New York, sold 1 February 1965 for $17,000 to]; Norton Simon (sale, New York, Parke-Bernet Galleries, 5 May 1971, lot 15, for $20,000).

Cat. 264
Egypt
Cat
Bronze with gold fur, 3 ¼ in. (8.3 cm)
[Spink & Son, London, sold 18 February 1965 for $3,900 to]; Norton Simon, gift 18 October 1983 to; The Norton Simon Foundation (F.1983.36).

Cat. 265A-B
Louis-Léopold Boilly (French, 1761–1845)
The Interrupted Supper
Oil on canvas, a pair, each 15 x 18 in. (38.1 x 45.7 cm)
(Sale, London, Christie's, 19 March 1965 for $13,960 to); Norton Simon, gift 28 December 1967 to; Norton Simon Art Foundation (M.1967.23.1–2).

Cat. 266
Rembrandt van Rijn (Dutch, 1606–1669)
Portrait of a Boy in Fancy Costume (formerly *Portrait of a Boy, Presumed to Be the Artist's Son, Titus*), c. 1655–1660
Oil on canvas, 25 ½ x 22 in. (64.8 x 55.9 cm)
(Sale, London, Christie's, 19 March 1965 for $2,243,653 to); The Norton Simon Foundation (F.1965.2).

259

263

260

264

261

265A

265B

262

266

267

268

269

270

271

272

273

274

Cat. 267

Kees van Dongen (Dutch, 1877–1968)
Bar in Cairo, 1920
Oil on canvas, 25 ½ x 21 ¼ in. (64.8 x 54 cm)
(Sale, London, Sotheby & Co., 31 March
1965 for $28,776 to); Norton Simon, sold
22 December 1966 to; Norton Simon Art
Foundation, sold 28 October 1969 for
$33,750 to; [Stephen Hahn Gallery, New
York]. [Waddington Galleries, London,
on consignment 1984 to]; [Galerie Daniel
Malingue, Paris, sold 1985 to]; private
collection, France.

Cat. 268

Gustave Courbet (French, 1819–1877)
Stream of the Puits-Noir at Ornans,
c. 1867–1868
Oil on canvas, 39 ⅜ x 59 ¼ in.
(100 x 150.5 cm)
[Paul Kantor, Beverly Hills, Calif., sold
7 April 1965 for $65,000 to]; Norton Simon,
gift 22 December 1976 to; Norton Simon
Art Foundation (M.1976.13).

Cat. 269

Edgar Degas (French, 1834–1917)
Little Dancer, Aged Fourteen
Bronze, cast no. HER, 37 ½ in. (95.3 cm)
[Marlborough-Gerson Gallery, New
York, sold 12 April 1965 for $115,000 to];
Norton Simon (sale, New York, Parke-
Bernet Galleries, 5 May 1971, lot 29, for
$380,000 to); Mr. and Mrs. Jack Linsky, by
inheritance to; Mrs. Belle Linsky (sale, New
York, Sotheby's, 10 May 1988, for $10 million
to); private collection, Brunei.

Cat. 270

Louis-Eugène Boudin (French, 1824–1898)
The Beach at Trouville, 1874
Oil on panel, 6 ½ x 11 ¾ in. (16.5 x 29.9 cm)
[Schoneman Galleries, New York, sold
14 April 1965 for $40,000 to]; Norton Simon
(sale, New York, Parke-Bernet Galleries,
5 May 1971, lot 11, for $50,000 to); private
collection, New York.

Cat. 271

Edgar Degas (French, 1834–1917)
Rehearsal of the Ballet, c. 1876
Gouache and pastel over monotype,
21 ¾ x 26 ¾ in. (55.3 x 68 cm)
(Sale, New York, Parke-Bernet Galleries,
14 April 1965 for $410,000 to); Norton
Simon (sale, New York, Sotheby Parke
Bernet, 2 May 1973, lot 7, for $780,000 to);
[Marlborough Gallery, New York, for]; Mrs.
Kenneth Spencer, gift 1973 to; The Nelson-
Atkins Museum of Art, Kansas
City, Mo.

Cat. 272

Henri Le Sidaner (French, 1862–1939)
Small Village: Gerberoy, 1937
Oil on canvas, 49 ⅜ x 59 in.
(125.4 x 149.9 cm)
[Arthur Tooth & Sons, London, sold
20 April 1965 for $4,196 to]; Norton Simon,
gift 31 December 1979 to; Norton Simon Art
Foundation (M.1979.53).

Cat. 273

Attributed to Édouard Manet (French,
1832–1883)
Woman in a Hat, Turned to the Left
Charcoal, 13 x 9 ¾ in. (33 x 24.8 cm)
[Arthur Tooth & Sons, London, sold 20
April 1965 for $8,393 to]; Norton Simon,
sold 22 December 1966 to; Norton Simon
Art Foundation, used in trade 15 May 1969
with a value of $8,400 as partial payment
for Richard Parkes Bonington, *The Visit,
or the Use of Tears* (cat. 625).

Cat. 274

Aristide Maillol (French, 1861–1944)
Torso of Venus, 1918–1928
Bronze, edition of 6, cast no. 3,
45 x 14 in. (114.3 x 35.6 cm)
[Paul Rosenberg & Co., New York, sold
21 April 1965 for $54,000 to]; Norton Simon,
by inheritance 2 June 1993 to; Jennifer Jones
Simon Art Trust, Los Angeles (N.1965.6).

Cat. 275
Auguste Rodin (French, 1840–1917)
Burgher of Calais, 1895
Bronze, 18 ½ in. (47 cm)
[Paul Rosenberg & Co., New York, sold
21 April 1965 for $6,000 to]; Norton Simon
(sale, New York, Parke-Bernet Galleries,
5 May 1971, lot 38, for $13,000).

Cat. 276
Pierre Bonnard (French, 1867–1947)
Madame Lucienne Dupuy de Frenelle, 1916
Oil on canvas, 14 ⅜ x 16 ½ in.
(36.5 x 41.9 cm)
[M. Knoedler & Co., New York, sold 5
May 1965 for $33,600 to]; Norton Simon
(sale, New York, Parke-Bernet Galleries, 5
May 1971, lot 61, for $37,000 to); [Richard
Feigen, New York for]; Viviane Woodward
Cosmetics Corp. (sale, London, Sotheby
Parke Bernet & Co., 30 June 1981, lot 46).

Cat. 277
Henry Moore (English, 1898–1986)
Maquette for Reclining Figure, 1946
Bronze, 8 in. (20.3 cm)
(Sale, London, Christie's, 21 May 1965
through [Arthur Tooth & Sons] for $7,395
to); Norton Simon (sale, New York, Sotheby
Parke Bernet, 25 October 1972, lot 45, for
$17,500).

Cat. 278
Henry Moore (English, 1898–1986)
Maquette for Reclining Figure, 1956
Bronze, 7 in. (17.8 cm)
(Sale, London, Christie's, 21 May 1965
through [Arthur Tooth & Sons] for $5,846
to); Norton Simon, transferred 24 July 1970
to; Lucille Ellis Simon (estate sale, New
York, Christie's, 7 November 2002, lot 346,
for $55,000).

Cat. 279
Auguste Rodin (French, 1840–1917)
Torso of Adèle, 1882
Bronze, 17 ½ in. (44.5 cm)
[Charles E. Slatkin, New York, sold
24 May 1965 for $9,000 to]; Norton Simon,
transferred 24 July 1970 to; Lucille Ellis
Simon (estate sale, New York, Christie's,
9 November 2000, lot 121, for $70,500 to);
[Jan Krugier, Geneva].

Cat. 280
Auguste Rodin (French, 1840–1917)
Despair, 1890
Bronze, 11 x 13 ½ in. (27.9 x 34.3 cm)
[Charles E. Slatkin, New York, sold
24 May 1965 for $10,800 to]; Norton
Simon, transferred 24 July 1970 to;
Lucille Ellis Simon.

Cat. 281
Auguste Rodin (French, 1840–1917)
Fatigue, 1887
Bronze, 6 ¾ x 19 ¾ x 7 ¾ in.
(17.2 x 50.2 x 19.7 cm)
[Charles E. Slatkin, New York, sold 24 May
1965 for $6,140 to]; Norton Simon (sale,
New York, Parke-Bernet Galleries, 13 May
1970, lot 26, for $6,000).

Cat. 282
Auguste Rodin (French, 1840–1917)
The Kiss, 1884–1886
Bronze, 35 ½ in. (90.2 cm)
[Charles E. Slatkin, New York, sold 24 May
1965 for $26,500 to]; Norton Simon (sale,
New York, Parke-Bernet Galleries,
5 May 1971, lot 37, for $37,000 to); Pamela
Harriman, by inheritance to; private
collection (sale, New York, Christie's,
11 May 1995, lot 115, for $855,000 to); Iris
and B. Gerald Cantor Foundation, Los
Angeles, gift 2 September 2009 to; North
Carolina Museum of Art, Raleigh.

275

279

276

280

277

281

278

282

283

287

285

286

288

290, 289

Cat. 283
Henry Moore (English, 1898–1986)
Reclining Figure, 1956
Bronze, edition of 8, cast no. 8, length,
96 in. (243.8 cm)
[Marlborough-Gerson Gallery, New York,
sold 27 May 1965 for $42,000 to]; Hunt
Foods and Industries, Fullerton, Calif., gift
19 December 1969 to; Norton Simon Art
Foundation (M.1970.5.14).

Cat. 284
Henri Matisse (French, 1869–1954)
Charles d'Orléans
Book of 54 color lithographs and decorated
pages: sheets, 16 ⅛ x 10 ½ in. (41 x 26.5 cm)
(Sale, London, Sotheby & Co., 1 June 1965
for $130 to); Norton Simon, gift 11 October
1966 to; University of California,
Los Angeles

Cat. 285
Henri Matisse (French, 1869–1954)
*Illustrations for "Florilege des Amours"
by Pierre de Ronsard*, 1947–1950
Lithographs, set of 126,
15 x 11 in. (38.1 x 27.9 cm)
(Sale, London, Sotheby & Co., 1 June
1965 for $2,120 to); Norton Simon, by
inheritance 2 June 1993 to; Jennifer
Jones Simon Art Trust, Los Angeles
(N.1965.8.1–126).

Cat. 286
Johan Barthold Jongkind (Dutch, 1819–1891)
La Chapelle de Grâce
Watercolor and gouache, 14 x 20 in.
(35.6 x 50.8 cm)
[Sarec S.A., Geneva, sold 3 June 1965 for
$10,000 to]; Norton Simon (sale, New York,
Parke-Bernet Galleries, 21 October 1971,
lot 71, unsold), sold 8 November 1972 for
$13,000 to; [E. V. Thaw & Co., New York];
Eugene V. and Clare E. Thaw, New York,
gift 1998 to; The Pierpont Morgan Library,
New York.

Cat. 287
Henri Matisse (French, 1869–1954)
The Venetian Dress, c. 1922
Charcoal, 17 x 21 ½ in. (43.2 x 54.6 cm)
(Sale, London, Sotheby & Co., 23 June 1965,
for $6,985 to); Norton Simon (sale, New
York, Parke-Bernet Galleries, 13 May 1970, lot
64, for $10, 500 to); [Jan Krugier, Geneva].

Cat. 288
Auguste Rodin (French, 1840–1917)
Dance Movement A
Bronze, 12 ½ in. (31.8 cm)
(Sale, London, Sotheby & Co., 24 June 1965,
for $6,300 to); Norton Simon, transferred
24 July 1970 to; Lucille Ellis Simon (estate
sale, New York, Christie's, 9 November
2000, lot 147, for $259,000).

Cat. 289
Alberto Giacometti (Swiss, 1901–1966)
Standing Woman I, 1960
Bronze, edition of 6, cast no. 5,
105 ½ in. (268 cm)
[Pierre Matisse Gallery, New York, sold
12 July 1965 for $32,000 to]; Norton Simon
Art Foundation (sale, New York, Parke-
Bernet Galleries, 13 May 1970, lot 77 [cited
in error as *Standing Woman IV*, cast 1 of 6],
for $130,000 to]; [Sidney Janis Gallery, New
York, sold to]; [Ronald Feldman Fine Arts,
New York, sold to]; private collection (sale,
New York, Christie's, 14 November 1990, lot
37 [as *Standing Woman IV*], for $3,600,000
to]; [Thomas Ammann Fine Art, Zurich,
sold to]; [Jan Krugier, Geneva, sold to];
private collection, Switzerland (sale, New
York, Christie's, 8 November 2000, lot 63,
for $14,206,000).

Cat. 290
Alberto Giacometti (Swiss, 1901–1966)
Standing Woman IV, 1960

Bronze, edition of 6, cast no. 1, 106 ½ in.
(270.5 cm)
[Pierre Matisse Gallery, New York, sold
12 July 1965 for $32,000 to]; Norton Simon
Art Foundation (M.1965.1).

Cat. 291
Aristide Maillol (French, 1861–1944)
Night, 1902–1909, cast after 1944
Bronze, edition of 6, cast no. 5,
41 x 42 ½ x 25 in. (104.1 x 108 x 63.5 cm)
[Marlborough-Gerson Gallery, New
York, sold 23 July 1965 for $42,500 to];
Norton Simon, transferred 24 July 1970 to;
Lucille Ellis Simon (estate sale, New York,
Christie's, 8 November 2000, lot 8, for
$2,096,000 to]; private collection, U.S.A.
(sale, New York, Sotheby's, 2 November
2005, lot 8, for $2,816,000).

Cat. 292
Ernst Barlach (German, 1870–1938)
Der Tote Tag
Lithographs, set of 27
[Arnold Luyken, Pacific Palisades, Calif.,
sold 11 August 1965 for $500 to]; Hunt
Foods and Industries, Fullerton, Calif.,
gift 31 August 1970 to; Norton Simon Art
Foundation (sale, Los Angeles, Sotheby
Parke Bernet, 16 June 1980, lot 636, for
$7,750).

Cat. 293
Aristide Maillol (French, 1861–1944)
Torso of One of the Three Graces, 1936 1938
Bronze, edition of 6, cast no. 1,
52 in. (132.1 cm)
[Marlborough-Gerson Gallery, New York,
sold 20 September 1965 for $27,000 to];
Norton Simon (sale, New York, Parke-Bernet
Galleries, 5 May 1971, lot 55, for $51,000 to);
private collection, Los Angeles, on loan to
Yale University Art Gallery, New Haven.

1966

Cat. 294
Amedeo Modigliani (Italian, 1884–1920)
The Artist's Wife, Jeanne Hebuterne, 1918
Oil on canvas, 39 ¾ x 25 ⅞ in. (101 x 65.7 cm)
[Marlborough-Gerson Gallery, New York,
sold 11 January 1966 for $250,000 to];
Norton Simon, transferred 24 July 1970
to; Lucille Ellis Simon, sold 14 August 1975
to; [Paul Rosenberg & Co., New York, sold
14 August 1975 for $480,000 to]; Norton
Simon Art Foundation (M.1975.13.2).

Cat. 295
Henri de Toulouse-Lautrec
(French, 1864–1901)
Girl on a Galloping Horse, 1899
Pastel, 8 x 12 in. (20.3 x 30.5 cm)
[Rosenberg & Stiebel, New York, sold
12 January 1966 for $85,000 to]; Norton
Simon, sold 18 October 1972 for $120,000 to;
[E. V. Thaw & Co., New York, sold 1972 to];
Mr. and Mrs. B. Edward Bensinger, Chicago,
gift 1972 to; The Art Institute of Chicago.

Cat. 296
Honoré Daumier (French, 1808–1879)
The Scavenger, 1852
Bronze, edition of 30, cast no. 1, 5 ¾ in.
(14.6 cm)
[Paul Kantor, Beverly Hills, Calif., sold 18
January 1966 for $2,250 to]; Norton Simon
(sale, New York, Parke-Bernet Galleries, 5
May 1971, lot 20, for $5,500).

Cat. 297
Henry Moore (English, 1898–1986)
Standing Figure: Knife Edge, 1961
Bronze, edition of 7, cast no. 4,
117 x 46 x 43 in. (297.2 x 116.8 x 109.2 cm)
[Marlborough-Gerson Gallery, New York,
sold 28 January 1966 for $60,000 to]; Hunt
Foods and Industries, Fullerton, Calif., gift
19 December 1969 to; Norton Simon Art
Foundation (M.1970.5.15).

291

294

295

293

296

297

298

303

299

304

300

305

301

Cat. 298
Georg Kolbe (German, 1877–1947)
Young Woman, 1926
Bronze, 50 ⅛ in. (127.3 cm)
[Marlborough-Gerson Gallery, New York,
sold 5 February 1966 for $12,150 to]; Hunt
Foods and Industries, Fullerton, Calif., gift
19 December 1969 to; Norton Simon Art
Foundation (sale, New York, Parke-Bernet
Galleries, 13 May 1970, lot 30, unsold) (sale,
New York, Sotheby Parke Bernet,
14 May 1980, lot 133, for $32,000).

Cat. 299
Aristide Maillol (French, 1861–1944)
Debussy Monument, 1930
Bronze, edition of 6, cast no. 6,
36 ¼ in. (92.1 cm)
[Marlborough-Gerson Gallery, New York,
sold 5 February 1966 for $55,000 to]; Hunt
Foods and Industries, Fullerton, Calif.,
gift 31 December 1969 to; Norton Simon
Art Foundation, sold 22 February 1982 for
$220,000 to; [Perls Galleries, New York].

Cat. 300
Jacques Lipchitz (French, 1891–1973)
Bather, 1923–1925
Bronze, edition of 7, cast no. 7,
77 x 31 ¾ x 27 ½ in. (195.6 x 80.6 x 69.9 cm)
[Marlborough-Gerson Gallery, New York,
sold 10 February 1966 for $55,000 to];
Norton Simon Art Foundation (M.1966.1).

Cat. 301
Giacomo Manzu (Italian, 1908–1991)
Dance Step, 1959
Bronze, unique cast, 82 in. (208.3 cm)
[Paul Rosenberg & Co., New York, sold
17 February 1966 for $52,000 to]; Hunt
Foods and Industries, Fullerton, Calif., gift
31 December 1969 to; Norton Simon Art
Foundation (sale, New York, Sotheby Parke
Bernet, 2 May 1973, lot 40, for $135,000 to);
[Forum Gallery, New York]. (sale, London,
Christie's, 2 December 1975, lot 48).

Cat. 302A-G
Henri Matisse (French, 1869–1954)
Seated Odalisque, 1929, lithograph,
17 ¼ x 12 ¼ in. (44 x 31 cm)
Decency, 1903, etching, 5 ½ x 3 ½ in.
(14 x 9 cm)
Head of a Woman, 1952, aquatint,
21 ¼ x 16 ½ in. (54 x 42 cm)
*Seated Nude Resting Her Elbows on her
Knees*, 1929, etching, 6 x 3 ¾ in. (15 x 9.5 cm)
Nude on Her Knees, Arms behind Her Head,
1930, etching, 7 x 5 ¼ in. (18 x 13 cm)
Seated Figure, Three-Quarter Profile, 1929,
etching, 5 x 6 ¼ in. (12.5 x 15.5 cm)
Seated Figure, 1929, etching, 6 ¼ x 4 ¾ in.
(15.5 x 12 cm)
(Sale, New York, Parke-Bernet Galleries,
29 March 1966 for $3,725 to); The Norton
Simon Foundation, gift 22 December 1966
to; University of California, Los Angeles.

Cat. 303
Alberto Giacometti (Swiss, 1901–1966)
Seated Nude, 1965
Lithograph, 31/100, 30 x 22 ¼ in.
(76.2 x 56.5 cm)
Graphic Arts Council, Los Angeles County
Museum of Art, sold April 1966 for $200 to;
Norton Simon, gift 17 May 1977 to; Norton
Simon Museum (P.1977.14).

Cat. 304
Charles-François Daubigny
(French, 1817–1878)
Village on the Seine near Vernon, 1872
Oil on canvas, 33 ⅝ x 57 ⅝ in.
(85.4 x 146.4 cm)
[E. V. Thaw & Co., New York, sold 2 May
1966 for $28,000 to]; Norton Simon Art
Foundation (M.1966.2.4).

Cat. 305
Jean-Antoine Watteau (French, 1684–1721)
Actress Dressed as Folly
Red chalk, 11 ½ x 8 in. (29.2 x 20.3 cm)
[E. V. Thaw & Co., New York, sold 2 May
1966 for $7,500 to]; Norton Simon Art

Foundation (sale, London, Sotheby & Co., 27 June 1974, lot 41, for $6,240).

Cat. 306
Jean-Antoine Watteau (French, 1684–1721)
Actor of the Comedie Français
Red chalk, 10 ½ x 7 in. (26.6 x 17.3 cm)
[E. V. Thaw & Co., New York, sold 2 May 1966 for $7,500 to]; Norton Simon Art Foundation (sale, London, Sotheby & Co., 27 June 1974, lot 44, for $6,240).

Cat. 307
Jean-Antoine Watteau (French, 1684–1721)
Actor in Sixteenth-Century Court Costume, Looking to His Left
Red chalk, 11 x 7 ½ in. (27.9 x 19.1 cm)
[E. V. Thaw & Co., New York, sold 2 May 1966 for $7,500 to]; Norton Simon Art Foundation (sale, London, Sotheby & Co., 27 June 1974, lot 42, for $5,040).

Cat. 308
Egypt
Vase, 7th c. B.C.
Faience, 5 ½ in. (14 cm)
[M. Costeletos, Athens, sold 4 May 1966 for $1,000 to]; Norton Simon, transferred 24 July 1970 to; Lucille Ellis Simon.

Cat. 309
Honoré Daumier (French, 1808–1879)
Amateur in Contemplation
Bronze, edition of 30, cast no. 21, 7 ¼ in. (18.4 cm)
[Paul Kantor, Beverly Hills, Calif., sold 11 May 1966 for $500 and Pablo Picasso, *Portrait of a Young Woman* (cat. 9) to]; Norton Simon (sale, New York, Parke-Bernet Galleries, 5 May 1971, lot 18, for $6,300).

Cat. 310
Honoré Daumier (French, 1808–1879)
Surprised Amateur
Bronze, edition of 30, cast no. 21, 7 ¼ in. (18.4 cm)

[Paul Kantor, Beverly Hills, Calif., sold 11 May 1966 for $500 and Pablo Picasso, *Portrait of a Young Woman* (cat. 9) to]; Norton Simon (sale, New York, Parke-Bernet Galleries, 5 May 1971, lot 19, for $6,600).

Cat. 311
Honoré Daumier (French, 1808–1879)
In the Courtroom, c. 1855
Ink, charcoal, and watercolor, 8 ¾ x 9 in. (22.2 x 22.9 cm)
[Paul Kantor, Beverly Hills, Calif., traded 11 May 1966 with a value of $2,070 for Pablo Picasso, *Classic Model* (cat. 16) to]; Norton Simon (sale, New York, Sotheby Parke Bernet, 2 May 1973, lot 1, for $24,000 to); Samuel J. LeFrak, New York, by inheritance to; LeFrak Family Collection, New York.

Cat. 312
Egypt
Head of a King
Faience, dimensions unknown
[C. Dikran Kelekian, New York, sold 31 May 1966 for $300 to]; Norton Simon, transferred 24 July 1970 to; Lucille Ellis Simon.

Cat. 313
Egypt
Fragment of a Head, c. 650 B.C.
Limestone, 3 ¼ x 2 ¼ in. (8.3 x 5.7 cm)
[C. Dikran Kelekian, New York, sold 31 May 1966 for $300 to]; Norton Simon, gift 28 December 1978 to; The Norton Simon Foundation (F.1978.16).

Cat. 314
Louis-Eugène Boudin (French, 1824–1898)
The Valley, 1881
Oil on canvas, 26 x 36 in. (66 x 91.4 cm)
[Stephen Hahn Gallery, New York, sold 1 June 1966 for $10,780 to]; Norton Simon (sale, New York, Parke-Bernet Galleries, 5 May 1971, lot 12, for $15,000). (sale, New York, Christie's, 11 May 1994, lot 108, for $65,000 to); private collection, Italy.

306

311

312

307

308

313

314

309, 310

315

316

317

319B

320

321

322

318

323

Cat. 315A-K
Egypt and Greece
Small sculptures, set of 11
Bronze, stone, and wood
[M. Costeletos, Athens, sold 12 June 1966 for $21,016 to]; The Norton Simon Foundation (sale, New York, Sotheby Parke Bernet, 4 May 1974, lots 155, 192, 203, for $8,700, and sale, New York, Sotheby Parke Bernet, 24 September 1974, lots 226–233, for $1,210).

Cat. 316
Egypt
Goddess Maat
Bronze, 3 in. (7.6 cm)
[M. Costeletos, Athens, sold 13 June 1966 for $1,000 to]; Norton Simon, sold 13 February 1979 for $1,200 to; [Superior Stamp and Coin Co., Beverly Hills, Calif.]

Cat. 317
Egypt
Ibis of Thoth, 7th–6th cent. B.C.
Bronze, 6 ½ in. (16.5 cm)
[M. Costeletos, Athens, sold 13 June 1966 for $3,000 to]; Norton Simon, transferred 24 July 1970 to; Lucille Ellis Simon.

Cat. 318
Egypt, New Kingdom
Head
Limestone, 7 ¼ in. (18.4 cm)
[M. Costeletos, Athens, sold 13 June 1966 for $3,000 to]; Norton Simon, gift 28 December 1978 to; The Norton Simon Foundation (F.1978.18).

Cat. 319A-B
Egypt
Portrait of a Man
Quartzite, 7 in. (17.8 cm)
Head, New Kingdom
5 ½ in. (14 cm)
[M. Costeletos, Athens, sold 13 June 1966 for $3,000 to]; Norton Simon, sold 9 August 1978 for $5,000 to; [Superior Stamp and Coin Co., Beverly Hills].

Cat. 320
Piet Mondrian (Dutch, 1872–1944)
Composition No. 10 with Blue, Yellow and Red, 1938–1942
Oil on canvas, 31 ¼ x 28 ¾ in. (79.4 x 73 cm)
© 2010 Mondrian/Holtzman Trust c/o HCR International, Virginia, USA
[Galerie des Arts Anciens et Modernes, Schaan, Liechtenstein, sold 5 July 1966 for $88,000 to]; Norton Simon Art Foundation, sold 11 March 1982 for $1,500,000 to; [E. V. Thaw & Co., New York, sold to]; private collection, New York.

Cat. 321
Auguste Rodin (French, 1840–1917)
Monument to Balzac, 1897
Bronze, edition of 12, cast no. 8, 107 in. (271.8 cm)
Musée Rodin, sold 11 July 1966 for $73,693 to; Norton Simon Art Foundation (M.1966.9).

Cat. 322
Maurice Vlaminck (French, 1876–1958)
Still Life with Lemons, 1907
Oil on board, 19 ¾ x 25 ¼ in. (50.2 x 64.1 cm)
[Galerie des Arts Anciens et Modernes, Schaan, Liechtenstein, sold 18 July 1966 for $85,000 to]; Norton Simon Art Foundation, sold 5 February 1982 for $250,000 to; [Alex Reid & Lefevre, London, sold to]; private collection, London.

Cat. 323
Auguste Rodin (French, 1840–1917)
The Walking Man
Bronze, edition of 12, cast no. 7, 83 ¾ in. (212.7 cm)
[Pierre Matisse Gallery, New York, sold 20 July 1966 for $55,000 to]; Norton Simon Art Foundation (M.1966.5).

Cat. 324
Pablo Picasso (Spanish, 1881–1973)
Lithographs and etchings, group of 54
[Marlborough-Gerson Gallery, New York,

works from this group have been sold at various auctions for a total of $62,369. Fourteen remain.

Cat. 325
Aristide Maillol (French, 1861–1944)
Air, 1938
Lead, edition of 6, cast no. 4, 52 x 97 x 32 in. (132.1 x 246.4 x 81.3 cm)
[Galerie des Arts Anciens et Modernes, Schaan, Liechtenstein, sold 4 August 1966 for $85,000 to]; Hunt Foods and Industries, Fullerton, Calif., gift 31 August 1970 to; Norton Simon Art Foundation (M.1970.5.9).

Cat. 326
Henri Matisse (French, 1869–1954)
Odalisque with Tambourine, 1926
Oil on canvas, 36 ¼ x 25 ⅝ in. (92.1 x 65.1 cm)
[Paul Rosenberg & Co. (Marguerite Rosenberg), New York, sold 2 September 1966 for $150,000 to]; Norton Simon Art Foundation (M.1966.7).

Cat. 327
Pablo Picasso (Spanish, 1881–1973)
Open Window in Paris, 1920
Oil on canvas, 64 ½ x 43 in. (163.8 x 109.2 cm)
[Paul Rosenberg & Co., New York, sold 14 October 1966 for $225,000 to]; Norton Simon Art Foundation, sold 21 January 1974 for $1 million to; [E. V. Thaw & Co., New York, sold to]; Empress Farah Pahlavi; Museum of Modern Art, Tehran.

1967

Cat. 328A–D
Henri Matisse (French, 1869–1954)
The Back, I–IV, c. 1904–1929
Bronze, edition of 10, erroneously marked as cast no. 10,
each 74 x 45 ¾ x 8 in. (188 x 116.2 x 20.3 cm)
[Pierre Matisse Gallery, New York, sold

3 January 1967 for $190,000 to]; Norton Simon Art Foundation, sold 24 March 1982 for $1,750,000 to; [Ernst Beyeler, Basel]. The Burnett Foundation, Fort Worth.

Cat. 329
Jacques Lipchitz (French, 1891–1973)
The Dance, 1936
Bronze, edition of 7, cast no. 5,
43 ¼ in. (109.9 cm)
[Marlborough-Gerson Gallery, New York, sold 8 February 1967 for $25,000 to]; Norton Simon Art Foundation (M.1967.2.1).

Cat. 330
Aristide Maillol (French, 1861–1944)
Kneeling Girl, 1922
Bronze, edition of 4, cast no. 4,
39 ⅜ in. (100 cm)
[Marlborough-Gerson Gallery, New York, sold 8 February 1967 for $30,000 to]; Norton Simon Art Foundation (sale, London, Sotheby Parke Bernet & Co., 5 December 1979, lot 29, for $29,000).

Cat. 331
Achille-Jacques-Jean-Marie Devéria (French, 1800–1857)
Odalisque, c. 1830–1835
Oil on panel, 9 x 12 ½ in. (22.9 x 31.8 cm)
(Sale, New York, Parke-Bernet Galleries, 2 March 1967 for $2,400 to); Norton Simon Art Foundation (M.1967.6).

Cat. 332
Aristide Maillol (French, 1861–1944)
The Nymph, 1930
Bronze, edition of 6, cast no. 3,
61 ½ in. (156.2 cm)
[Dina Vierny, Paris, sold 13 March 1967 for $35,000 to]; Hunt Foods and Industries, Fullerton, Calif., gift 19 December 1969 to; Norton Simon Art Foundation (sale, London, Sotheby Parke Bernet & Co., 5 December 1979, lot 30, for $58,000).

325

329

330

327

331

326

328D

332

333

338

334

335

339

336

340

337

341

Cat. 333
John Constable (English, 1776–1837)
John Charles Constable
Oil on board, 15 ¼ x 12 in. (38.7 x 30.5 cm)
(Sale, London, Sotheby & Co., 15 March
1967 for $5,051 to); Norton Simon Art
Foundation (sale, London, Sotheby & Co.,
27 June 1973, lot 24, for $4,900). private
collection, U.K. (sale, London, Sotheby's,
8 April 1992, lot 59, for $30,960).

Cat. 334
Erich Heckel (German, 1883–1970)
Landscape with a Pond, 1911
Drypoint, 7 ¾ x 9 ¾ in. (19.7 x 24.8 cm)
(Sale, London, Sotheby & Co., 16 March
1967 for $150 to); Norton Simon Art
Foundation (sale, Los Angeles, Sotheby
Parke Bernet, 16 June 1980, lot 685, for
$2,300).

Cat. 335
Erich Heckel (German, 1883–1970)
Man Harpooning, 1909
Drypoint, 5 ⅜ x 9 (13.7 x 22.9 cm)
(Sale, London, Sotheby & Co., 16 March
1967 for $150 to); Norton Simon Art
Foundation (sale, Los Angeles, Sotheby
Parke Bernet, 16 June 1980, lot 684, for
$4,200).

Cat. 336
André Dunoyer de Segonzac
(French, 1884–1974)
Nude Reading a Newspaper, 1924
Etching, 6 ⅝ x 4 ¾ in. (16.8 x 12.1 cm)
(Sale, London, Sotheby & Co., 16 March
1967 for $89 to); Norton Simon Art
Foundation (sale, Los Angeles, Sotheby
Parke Bernet, 16 June 1980, lot 779,
for $325).

Cat. 337
James McNeill Whistler
(American, 1834–1903)

The Rag Gatherers, 1858
Etching, 6 x 3 ¼ in. (15.2 x 8.3 cm)
(Sale, London, Sotheby & Co., 16 March
1967 for $98 to); Norton Simon Art
Foundation (sale, Los Angeles, Sotheby
Parke Bernet, 16 June 1980, lot 791, for $350).

Cat. 338
James McNeill Whistler
(American, 1834–1903)
Robert de Montesquiou-Fezenzac, 1895
Lithograph, 8 x 3 ¾ in. (20.3 x 9.5 cm)
(Sale, London, Sotheby & Co., 16 March
1967 for $294 to); Norton Simon Art
Foundation (sale, Los Angeles, Sotheby
Parke Bernet, 16 June 1980, lot 797, for
$1,100).

Cat. 339
Aristide Maillol (French, 1861–1944)
The River, 1939–1943
Lead, one of two artist's proofs,
52 x 91 x 65 in. (132.1 x 231.1 x 165.1 cm)
[SAREC S.A., Geneva, sold 29 March 1967
for $92,000 to]; Hunt Foods and Industries,
Fullerton, Calif., gift 19 December 1969
to; Norton Simon Art Foundation
(M.1970.5.12).

Cat. 340
Jean-Baptiste Carpeaux (French, 1827–1875)
Louis Bonaparte, the Prince Imperial, c. 1867
Bronze, 12 ¾ in. (32.4 cm)
(Sale, New York, Parke-Bernet Galleries,
5 April 1967 for $1,100 to); Norton Simon
Art Foundation (M.1967.12).

Cat. 341
Barbara Hepworth (English, 1903–1975)
Oread, 1958
Bronze, with stone base, edition of seven,
27 ¼ in. (69.2 cm)
(Sale, New York, Parke-Bernet Galleries,
5 April 1967 for $3,000 to); Norton Simon
Art Foundation (M.1967.8.1).

Cat. 342
Georg Kolbe (German, 1877–1947)
Mother and Child, c. 1905
Bronze, 12 x 7 ½ x 9 in. (30.5 x 19.1 x 22.9 cm)
(Sale, New York, Parke-Bernet Galleries,
5 April 1967 for $5,250 to); Norton Simon
Art Foundation (sale, New York, Sotheby
Parke Bernet, 14 May 1980, lot 131, for
$10,000).

Cat. 343
Aristide Maillol (French, 1861–1944)
Head of Venus
Bronze; edition of 6, cast no. 5,
16 in. (40.6 cm)
(Sale, New York, Parke-Bernet Galleries,
5 April 1967 for $7,000 to); Norton Simon
Art Foundation (sale, New York, Parke-
Bernet Galleries, 13 May 1970, lot 22, for
$5,000).

Cat. 344
Fernand Léger (French, 1881–1955)
Mechanical Elements, 1918
Oil on canvas, 27 ½ x 19 ½ in.
(69.9 x 49.5 cm)
[Galerie d'Art Moderne, Basel, 11 April
1967 for $45,000 to]; Norton Simon Art
Foundation (sale, New York, Parke-Bernet
Galleries, 13 May 1970, lot 33, for $55,000
to); [Perls Galleries, New York, sold
to]; [Stephen Hahn, New York]. private
collection.

Cat. 345
Auguste Rodin (French, 1840–1917)
Pas de Deux B, c. 1910–1913
Bronze, edition of 12, cast no.
12, 13 in. (33 cm)
Musée Rodin, Paris, sold 14 April 1967 for
$4,048 to; Norton Simon Art Foundation
(M.1967.10).

Cat. 346
Auguste Rodin (French, 1840–1917)
Pas de Deux G
Bronze, edition of 12, cast no. 4, 13 in. (33 cm)
Musée Rodin, Paris, sold 17 April 1967 for

$4,048 to; Norton Simon, by inheritance
2 June 1993 to; Jennifer Jones Simon Art
Trust, Los Angeles (N.1967.2).

Cat. 347
Pablo Picasso (Spanish, 1881–1973)
Woman in an Armchair, 1922–1923
Oil on canvas, 31 ¾ x 25 ¼ in.
(80.7 x 64.1 cm)
[Paul Rosenberg & Co., New York, sold
20 April 1967 for $215,000 to]; Norton
Simon, sold 9 January 1974 for $697,500
to; [E. V. Thaw & Co., New York, sold to];
[Stephen Hahn, Santa Barbara, Calif., sold
to]; Michael and Judy Steinhardt, New York.

Cat. 348
Paul Cézanne (French, 1839–1906)
*Still Life with Kettle, Milk Pitcher, Sugar
Bowl, and Seven Apples*, c. 1895–1900
Watercolor, 18 ¼ x 24 ¼ in. (46.4 x 61.6 cm)
(Sale, London, Sotheby & Co., 26 April 1967
for $405,391 to); Norton Simon (sale, New
York, Sotheby Parke Bernet, 2 May 1973, lot
9, for $620,000 to); Alain Delon. The J. Paul
Getty Museum, Los Angeles, 1983.

Cat. 349
Liubov Popova (Russian, 1889–1924)
The Traveler, 1915
Oil on canvas, 56 x 41 ½ in. (142.2 x 105.4 cm)
(Sale, London, Sotheby & Co., 26 April
1967 for $25,162 to); Norton Simon Art
Foundation (M.1967.11).

Cat. 350
Pierre-Auguste Renoir (French, 1841–1919)
Young Woman (Gabrielle), 1902
Oil on canvas, 19 x 14 ½ in. (48.3 x 36.8 cm)
[Paul Kantor, Beverly Hills, Calif., sold
20 June 1967 for $80,000 to]; Norton Simon
Art Foundation (sale, New York, Parke-
Bernet Galleries, 13 May 1970, lot 9, for
$125,000 to); [Spencer A. Samuels & Co.,
New York, for]; Fletcher Jones, Los Angeles
(estate sale, 2 December 1975, lot 29, for
$139,800).

342

343

344

347

348

349

345

346

350

351

353

352

354

355

356

357A

358

359

Cat. 351
Aristide Maillol (French, 1861–1944)
Torso of Venus, 1918
Bronze, edition of 6, cast no. 4,
45 x 14 in. (114.3 x 35.6 cm)
[Dina Vierny, Paris, sold 26 June 1967 for
$45,000 to]; Norton Simon Art Foundation
(sale, New York, Sotheby Parke Bernet,
14 May 1980, lot 226, for $150,000). [Achim
Moeller Fine Art, New York, March 2005].

Cat. 352
Honoré Daumier (French, 1808–1879)
Amateur in Contemplation
Bronze, edition of 30, cast no. 28,
7 ¼ in. (18.4 cm)
(Sale, London, Sotheby & Co., 28 June
1967 for $3,900 to); The Norton Simon
Foundation (sale, New York, Sotheby Parke
Bernet, 25 October 1972, lot 43c, for $5,000).

Cat. 353
Honoré Daumier (French, 1808–1879)
The Lawyer Waving
Bronze, edition of 30, cast no. 27,
6 in. (15.2 cm)
(Sale, London, Sotheby & Co., 28 June
1967 for $4,000 to); The Norton Simon
Foundation (sale, New York, Sotheby Parke
Bernet, 25 October 1972, lot 43a, for $5,000).

Cat. 354
Honoré Daumier (French, 1808–1879)
The Scoffer
Bronze, edition of 30, cast no. 8,
7 in. (17.8 cm)
(Sale, London, Sotheby & Co., 28 June 1967
for $3,900 to); Norton Simon (sale, New
York, Parke-Bernet Galleries, 5 May 1971, lot
22, for $7,000).

Cat. 355
Stanislas-Victor-Édouard Lépine
(French, 1836–1892)
A Courtyard on the rue de la Fontenelle
(formerly *Figures in a Courtyard of a
Château*), 1874–1878

Oil on canvas, 17 ½ x 12 ½ in. (44.5 x 31.8 cm)
(Sale, London, Sotheby & Co., 28 June
1967 for $18,114 to); The Norton Simon
Foundation (F.1967.1).

Cat. 356
Camille Pissarro (French, 1830–1903)
View of Berneval, 1900
Oil on canvas, 28 ¾ x 36 ¼ in. (73 x 92.1 cm)
(Sale, London, Sotheby & Co., 28 June
1967 for $66,880 to); Norton Simon, by
inheritance 2 June 1993 to; Jennifer Jones
Simon Art Trust, Los Angeles (N.1967.4).

Cat. 357A–B
Auguste Rodin (French, 1840–1917)
Figure Studies for a Vase
Terracotta, 10 in. (25.4 cm) and
12 in. (30.4 cm)
(Sale, London, Sotheby & Co., 28 June 1967
for $5,700 to); Norton Simon, transferred
24 July 1970 to; Lucille Ellis Simon.

Cat. 358
Louis-Eugène Boudin (French, 1824–1898)
The Beach at Trouville, 1868
Oil on panel, 8 x 13 ⅞ in. (20.3 x 35.2 cm)
[Galerie Schmit, Paris, sold 30 June 1967 for
$62,700 to]; Norton Simon (sale, New York,
Parke-Bernet Galleries, 5 May 1971, lot 13,
for $75,000). (sale, New York, Sotheby's,
11 November 1988, lot 2, for $357,500).

Cat. 359
Louis-Eugène Boudin (French, 1824–1898)
The Port of Bordeaux, 1874
Oil on canvas, 14 ⅛ x 23 in. (35.9 x 58.4 cm)
[Galerie Schmit, Paris, sold 30 June 1967 for
$28,500 to]; Norton Simon Art Foundation,
returned 1 April 1968 as partial credit
($28,500) toward Camille Pissarro, *Poultry
Market at Pontoise* (cat. 397).

Cat. 360
Honoré Daumier (French, 1808–1879)
Fishing, 1840
Lithographs, set of 7

(Sale, London, Sotheby & Co., 4 July 1967 for $336 to); Hunt Foods and Industries, Fullerton, Calif., gift 19 December 1969 to; Norton Simon Art Foundation (sale, Los Angeles, Sotheby Parke Bernet, 16 June 1980, lot 664, for $850).

Cat. 361
Oskar Kokoschka (Austrian, 1886–1980)
Oh Eternity, You Thunderous Word
Lithographs, set of 11
(Sale, London, Sotheby & Co., 4 July 1967 for $1,820 to); Hunt Foods and Industries, Fullerton, Calif., gift 19 December 1969 to; Norton Simon Art Foundation (sales, Los Angeles, Sotheby Parke Bernet, 7 March 1976, five prints, lots 271–275, for $895, and Los Angeles, Sotheby Parke Bernet, 16 June 1980, six prints, lots 698–701, for $3,900).

Cat. 362
Salvatore Rosa (Italian, 1615–1673)
The Works of Salvatore Rosa
Etchings, group of 87
(Sale, London, Sotheby & Co., 4 July 1967 for $700 to); Hunt Foods and Industries, Fullerton, Calif., gift 19 December 1969 to; Norton Simon Art Foundation (M.1970.6.1–87), three given to Norton Simon Museum in order to be sold in the Museum store; 84 remain.

Cat. 363
Maurice-Quentin de La Tour
(French, 1704–1788)
Self-Portrait, 1764
Pastel, 18 x 15 in. (45.7 x 38.1 cm)
(Sale, London, Sotheby & Co., 5 July 1967 for $55,700 to); Robert Ellis Simon, bequest 29 October 1969 to; The Norton Simon Foundation (F.1969.38.9).

Cat. 364
Jean-Baptiste Monnoyer
(French, 1636–1699)
A Flower Piece
Oil on canvas, 29 ¼ x 36 in. (74.3 x 91.4 cm)

(Sale, London, Sotheby & Co., 5 July 1967 for $2,230 to); Norton Simon Art Foundation (sale, London, Sotheby Parke Bernet & Co., 6 July 1980, lot 80, for $14,280).

Cat. 365
Bartolomé Esteban Murillo
(Spanish, 1617–1682)
Madonna and Child, c. 1660–1675
Oil on canvas, 40 x 30 in. (101.6 x 76.2 cm)
(Sale, London, Sotheby & Co., 5 July 1967 for $20,915 to); Norton Simon Art Foundation (sale, London, Sotheby Parke Bernet & Co., 16 April 1980, lot 90, for $59,967). [Harari and Johns, London, sold to]; private collection, San Francisco.

Cat. 366
Barent Averkamp (Dutch, 1612–1679)
Family Group, 1650
Watercolor, 7 ¼ x 10 ⅞ in. (18.4 x 27.6 cm)
[Schaeffer Galleries, New York, sold 19 July 1967 for $2,400 to]; Norton Simon Art Foundation (sale, London, Sotheby & Co., 27 June 1974, lot 120, for $1,000).

Cat. 367
Louis-Eugène Boudin (French, 1824–1898)
Low Tide, Berck, 1886
Oil on canvas, 19 ¾ x 24 ⅛ in.
(50.2 x 61.3 cm)
[Stephen Hahn Gallery, New York, sold 19 July 1967 for $50,000 to]; The Norton Simon Foundation, transferred 16 November 1992 to); Norton Simon Art Foundation (M.1992.1).

Cat. 368
Eugène Delacroix (French, 1798–1863)
Sketches
Brown ink wash, 7 ¾ x 11 ¾ in.
(19.7 x 29.9 cm)
[Schaeffer Galleries, New York, sold 19 July 1967 for $2,600 to]; Norton Simon Art Foundation, returned 12 June 1969 for $2,600 credit to; [Schaeffer Galleries, New York].

365

361

366

363

367

368

362

364

369

373

370

374

371

375

372

376

Cat. 369
Jean-Auguste-Dominique Ingres
(French, 1780–1867)
Scipio and His Son with the Envoys of Antiochus, 1800
Pencil, 9 ½ x 14 ½ in. (24.1 x 36.8 cm)
[Schaeffer Galleries, New York, sold 19 July 1967 for $15,500 to]; Norton Simon Art Foundation (sale, London, Sotheby & Co., 27 June 1974, lot 53, for $48,000); private collection, Paris.

Cat. 370
Jean-Michel Moreau (French, 1741–1814)
Studies of Young Women, group of 12
Black and red pencil, each 1 ⅞ x 1 ⅞ in. (4.8 x 4.8 cm)
[Schaeffer Galleries, New York, sold 19 July 1967 for $2,040 to]; Norton Simon Art Foundation (sale, London, Sotheby & Co., 27 June 1974, lot 46, for $360).

Cat. 371
Aristide Maillol (French, 1861–1944)
Seated Nude
Marble, 12 ½ x 11 x 5 ⅛ in.
(31.8 x 27.9 x 13 cm)
[Hirschl & Adler Galleries, New York, sold 24 July 1967 for $25,000 to]; Norton Simon, by inheritance 2 June 1993 to; Jennifer Jones Simon Art Trust, Los Angeles, gift 12 February 2009 to; Norton Simon Art Foundation (M.2009.1).

Cat. 372
Pierre Bonnard (French, 1867–1947)
Leila Claude Anet, 1930
Oil on canvas, 49 x 32 ⅝ in. (124.5 x 82.9 cm)
Leila Claude Anet Mabilleau, sold 31 July 1967 for $85,000 to; Robert Ellis Simon, bequest 29 October 1969 to; The Norton Simon Foundation, transferred 23 November 1993 to; Norton Simon Art Foundation (M.1993.1).

Cat. 373
Wilhelm Lehmbruck (German, 1881–1919)
Inclined Head of Kneeling Woman, 1911
Plaster, 18 ½ x 17 ½ x 11 ½ in.
(47 x 44.5 x 29.2 cm)
[Roman Norbert Ketterer, Lake Lugano, Switzerland, sold 31 July 1967 for $6,300 to]; Norton Simon Art Foundation (M.1967.15).

Cat. 374
Wilhelm Lehmbruck (German, 1881–1919)
Small Reflective Girl, 1911
Plaster with coat of shellac,
21 ¼ x 6 ¼ x 5 ¾ in. (54 x 15.9 x 14.6 cm)
[Roman Norbert Ketterer, Lake Lugano, Switzerland, sold 31 July 1967 for $5,625 to]; Norton Simon Art Foundation (sale, New York, Sotheby Parke Bernet, 2 May 1973, lot 43, for $5,000 to); Joseph Hirshhorn.

Cat. 375
Auguste Rodin (French, 1840–1917)
Adam, 1880
Bronze, edition of 12, cast no. 5,
77 in. (195.6 cm)
Musée Rodin, Paris, sold 3 August 1967 for $31,218 to; Norton Simon Art Foundation (sale, New York, Parke-Bernet Galleries, 13 May 1970, lot 19, for $37,500 to); B. Gerald Cantor, Los Angeles, sold 1972 to; [Paul Kantor, Beverly Hills, Calif.].

Cat. 376
Aristide Maillol (French, 1861–1944)
The Three Nymphs, 1937
Lead, artist's proof, 62 x 56 ⅞ x 31 in.
(157.5 x 144.5 x 78.7 cm)
[Marlborough-Gerson Gallery, New York, sold 1 September 1967 for $120,000 to]; Norton Simon, transferred 24 July 1970 to; Lucille Ellis Simon, gift 1991 to; National Gallery of Art, Washington, D.C.

Cat. 377
Pablo Picasso (Spanish, 1881–1973)
Bust of a Woman, 1923
Oil with fixed black chalk on canvas,
39 ¼ x 32 in. (99.7 x 81.3 cm)
[Paul Rosenberg & Co., New York, sold
20 September 1967 for $175,000 to]; Hunt
Foods and Industries, Fullerton, Calif., gift
19 December 1969 to; Norton Simon Art
Foundation (M.1970.5.16).

Cat. 378
Aristide Maillol (French, 1861–1944)
Venus, 1918–1928
Bronze, edition of 12, unnumbered cast,
68 ½ in. (174 cm)
[Dina Vierny, Paris, sold 2 October 1967 for
$72,000 to]; Norton Simon Art Foundation
(sale, New York, Sotheby Parke Bernet,
20 May 1982, lot 210, for $210,000). (sale,
New York, Sotheby's, 5 November 2002,
lot 47, to); Sidney E. Frank (estate sale,
London, Sotheby's, 19 June 2006, lot 50,
for $797,824).

Cat. 379A-D
Aristide Maillol (French, 1861–1944)
Bather Fixing Her Hair
Bronze, artist's proof, 14 in. (35.6 cm)
Draped Woman, 1920
Bronze, artist's proof, 12 in. (30.5 cm)
Seated Woman Holding Her Leg, 1900
Bronze, 8 ½ in. (21.6 cm)
Young Bather, 1920
Bronze, artist's proof, 13 in. (33 cm)
[Dina Vierny, Paris, sold 16 October 1967 for
$29,700 to]; Norton Simon Art Foundation,
returned 31 October 1967 to; [Dina Vierny,
Paris].

Cat. 380
Aristide Maillol (French, 1861–1944)
Draped Torso, 1900
Bronze, edition of 4, cast no. 1,
8 ¼ in. (21 cm)
[Dina Vierny, Paris, sold 16 October 1967 for
$6,300 to]; Norton Simon Art Foundation,

sold 31 October 1968 for $6,300 to; Gustave
Levy, Los Angeles.

Cat. 381
Aristide Maillol (French, 1861–1944)
Bather with a Scarf, 1919
Bronze, artist's proof, 13 ¼ in. (33.7 cm)
[Dina Vierny, Paris, sold 16 October 1967 for
$8,100 to]; Norton Simon Art Foundation
(M.1967.19.1).

Cat. 382
Aristide Maillol (French, 1861–1944)
Crouched Bather, Head Lowered, 1930
Bronze, artist's proof, 4 ¾ x 6 ½ in.
(12.1 x 16.5 cm)
[Dina Vierny, Paris, sold 16 October 1967 for
$9,000 to]; Norton Simon Art Foundation
(M.1967.19.2).

Cat. 383
Aristide Maillol (French, 1861–1944)
The Washerwoman
Bronze, edition of 6, cast no. 3,
4 ½ x 10 ½ in. (11.4 x 26.7 cm)
[Dina Vierny, Paris, sold 16 October 1967 for
$7,200 to]; Norton Simon Art Foundation
(M.1967.19.5).

Cat. 384
Aristide Maillol (French, 1861–1944)
Woman Holding Her Foot, 1920
Bronze, edition of 6, cast no. 6, 8 in.
(20.3 cm)
[Dina Vierny, Paris, sold 16 October 1967 for
$9,000 to]; Norton Simon Art Foundation
(M.1967.19.6).

Cat. 385
Aristide Maillol (French, 1861–1944)
Crouching Woman, 1920
Bronze, edition of 6, cast no. 2, 6 ⅞ in.
(17.5 cm)
[Perls Galleries, New York, sold 17 October
1967 for $7,700 to]; Norton Simon Art
Foundation (M.1967.20.3).

377

381

378

382

383

384

385

380

386

391

387

388

389

390

394

392

393

Cat. 386

Aristide Maillol (French, 1861–1944)
Seated Woman Arranging Her Hair, 1936
Bronze, edition of 6, cast no. 4,
9 ¾ in. (24.8 cm)
[Perls Galleries, New York, sold 17 October 1967 for $7,700 to]; Norton Simon Art Foundation (M.1967.20.2).

Cat. 387

Aristide Maillol (French, 1861–1944)
Seated Woman, 1902
Bronze, edition of 6, cast no. 1,
10 ⅞ in. (27.6 cm)
[Perls Galleries, New York, sold 17 October 1967 for $8,900 to]; Norton Simon Art Foundation (M.1967.20.1).

Cat. 388

Aristide Maillol (French, 1861–1944)
Woman Holding Her Feet, c. 1920
Bronze, edition of 6, cast no. 4,
7 ½ in. (19.1 cm)
[Perls Galleries, New York, sold 17 October 1967 for $7,700 to]; Norton Simon Art Foundation (M.1967.20.4).

Cat. 389

Pablo Picasso (Spanish, 1881–1973)
The Cock, 1932
Bronze, edition of 6, cast no. 2, 26 in. (66 cm)
[Perls Galleries, New York, sold 19 October 1967 for $60,000 to]; Norton Simon, transferred 24 July 1970 to; Lucille Ellis Simon, gift 1982 to; Los Angeles County Museum of Art.

Cat. 390

Jean-Baptiste Camille Corot
(French, 1796–1875)
The Cicada, 1865–1875
Oil on panel, 18 ¼ x 14 ½ in. (46.4 x 36.8 cm)

(Sale, New York, Parke-Bernet Galleries, 26 October 1967 for $310,000 to); Norton Simon, transferred 24 July 1970 to; Lucille Ellis Simon, sold 14 August 1975 to; [Paul Rosenberg & Co., New York, sold 14 August 1975 for $370,000 to]; Norton Simon Art Foundation (M.1975.13.1).

Cat. 391

Henri Laurens (French, 1885–1954)
The Ondines, 1934
Bronze, edition of 6, cast no. 4,
29 ⅛ x 64 ½ x 20 in. (74 x 163.8 x 50.8 cm)
[Marlborough-Gerson Gallery, New York, sold 26 October 1967 for $39,000 to]; Norton Simon Art Foundation (M.1967.21).

Cat. 392

Aristide Maillol (French, 1861–1944)
Head of Harmony
Bronze, edition of 6, cast no. 5,
10 in. (25.4 cm)
[Dina Vierny, Paris, sold 31 October 1967 for $5,400 to]; Norton Simon Art Foundation (sale, New York, Parke-Bernet Galleries, 13 May 1970, lot 25, for $5,000).

Cat. 393

Aristide Maillol (French, 1861–1944)
Night, 1905
Bronze, artist's proof, 7 in. (17.8 cm)
[Dina Vierny, Paris, sold 31 October 1967 for $9,000 to]; Norton Simon Art Foundation (M.1967.19.3).

Cat. 394

Aristide Maillol (French, 1861–1944)
Study for "Thought," 1902
Bronze, edition of 6, cast no. 4,
7 in. (17.8 cm)
[Dina Vierny, Paris, sold 31 October 1967 for $6,300 to]; Norton Simon Art Foundation (M.1967.19.4).

Cat. 395
Aristide Maillol (French, 1861–1944)
Woman with a Dove, 1905
Bronze, artist's proof, 9 in. (22.9 cm)
[Dina Vierny, Paris, sold 31 October 1967 for $9,000 to]; Norton Simon Art Foundation (M.1967.19.7).

Cat. 396
Jacques Lipchitz (French, 1891–1973)
The Figure, 1926–1930
Bronze, edition of 7, cast no. 2,
83 ¼ in. (211.5 cm)
[Marlborough-Gerson Gallery, New York, sold 3 November 1967 for $99,127 to];
Norton Simon Art Foundation (M.1967.22).

Cat. 397
Camille Pissarro (French, 1830–1903)
Poultry Market at Pontoise, 1882
Oil on canvas, 31 ⅞ x 25 ⅝ in. (81 x 65 cm)
[Galerie Schmit, Paris, sold 9 November 1967 for $140,000 to]; Norton Simon, sold 29 January 1981 for $950,000 to;
[E. V. Thaw & Co., New York]; [Acquavella Galleries, New York, sold 3 December 1984 for $750,000 to]; Norton Simon Art Foundation (M.1984.2).

Cat. 398
Henri Fantin-Latour (French, 1836–1904)
White and Pink Mallows in a Vase, 1895
Oil on canvas, 21 x 19 ½ in. (53.3 x 49.5 cm)
On 15 November 1967 Acquavella Galleries, New York, purchased the building at 18 East Seventy-ninth Street, New York (formerly the Duveen Brothers Gallery, belonging to The Norton Simon Foundation) for $425,000. This painting was valued at $75,000 and used as partial payment (along with Pierre-Auguste Renoir, cat. 399) to; The Norton Simon Foundation, transferred 24 November 2003 to; Norton Simon Art Foundation (M.2003.1).

Cat. 399
Pierre-Auguste Renoir (French, 1841–1919)
Woman with a Rose, 1915
Oil on canvas, 25 ½ x 32 in. (64.8 x 81.3 cm)
On 15 November 1967 Acquavella Galleries, New York, purchased the building at 18 East Seventy-ninth Street, New York (formerly the Duveen Brothers Gallery, belonging to The Norton Simon Foundation) for $425,000. This painting was valued at $175,000 and used as partial payment (along with Henri Fantin-Latour, cat. 398) to; The Norton Simon Foundation (sale, New York, Parke-Bernet Galleries, 13 May 1970, lot 16, unsold), sold 13 February 1981 for $526,750 to; [William Beadleston, New York]. (sale, New York, Sotheby's, 16 November 1983, lot 38, unsold).

Cat. 400
Francisco de Goya y Lucientes
(Spanish, 1746–1828)
The Disasters of War (*Los Desastres de la Guerra*), 1st edition, 1814–1820, printed 1863
Etching, aquatint, and drypoint, 80 plates
(Sale, London, Christie's, 28 November 1967 for $6,600 to); The Norton Simon Foundation (F.1968.3.1–80).

Cat. 401
Auguste Rodin (French, 1840–1917)
Bust of Balzac, Arms Crossed, c. 1895
Bronze, 11 /2 in. (29.2 cm)
(Sale, London, Sotheby & Co., 29 November 1967 for $10,850 to); Norton Simon Art Foundation (sale, New York, Parke-Bernet Galleries, 13 May 1970, lot 20, for $10,000).

Cat. 402
Oskar Kokoschka (Austrian, 1886–1980)
Frau Reuther, c. 1921
Oil on canvas, 37 ½ x 26 ⅛ in.
(95.3 x 66.4 cm)
[Jane Wade, New York, sold 18 December 1967 for $50,000 to]; The Norton Simon Foundation (F.1967.4).

395

399

400

396

401

397

402

398

403

408A 408B

404

408C 408D

405

406

409

407 410

1968

Cat. 403
Paul Cézanne (French, 1839–1906)
Vase of Flowers, 1880–1881
Oil on canvas, 18 ½ x 21 ¾ in. (47 x 55.2 cm)
[Paul Rosenberg & Co., New York, sold
2 January 1968 for $360,000 to]; The
Norton Simon Foundation (F.1968.1).

Cat. 404
Camille Pissarro (French, 1830–1903)
Pontoise, Banks of the Oise River, 1872
Oil on canvas, 21 ¼ x 28 ¾ in. (54 x 73 cm)
[Lock Galleries, New York, sold 5 January
1968 for $160,000 to]; The Norton Simon
Foundation, sold 18 February 1982 for
$325,000 to; [Alex Reid & Lefevre, London,
sold to]; private collection, Germany.

Cat. 405
Henri-Joseph Harpignies
(French, 1819–1916)
Landscape in Auvergne, 1870
Oil on canvas, 21 x 31 ¾ in. (53.3 x 80.7 cm)
(Sale, London, Sotheby & Co., 8 January
1968 for $9,644 to); The Norton Simon
Foundation (sale, New York, Sotheby Parke
Bernet, 2 May 1973, lot 18, for $36,000).

Cat. 406
Georges Braque (French, 1882–1963)
The Studio, 1939
Oil on canvas, 44 ½ x 57 ½ in.
(113 x 146.1 cm)
[Paul Rosenberg & Co., New York, sold
16 January 1968 for $235,000 to]; Norton
Simon, transferred 24 July 1970 to; Lucille
Ellis Simon. Walter H. and Leonore
Annenberg, gift 1993 to; The Metropolitan
Museum of Art, New York.

Cat. 407
Henri Matisse (French, 1869–1954)
Woman in an Armchair (Antoinette), c. 1919
Oil on canvas, 20 ¾ x 14 ¼ in.
(52.7 x 36.2 cm)

[Stephen Hahn Gallery, New York, sold
16 January 1968 for $55,000 to]; Norton
Simon Art Foundation (sale, New York,
Sotheby Parke Bernet, 2 May 1973, lot 45, for
$140,000). [Galerie Daniel Malingue, Paris,
sold, 1995 to]; private collection, France.

Cat. 408A-E
Pablo Picasso (Spanish, 1881–1973)
Woman I, 1945
Bronze, edition of 10, cast no. 3, 8 ¾ in.
(22.2 cm)
Woman II
Bronze, edition of 10, cast no. 3, 8 ¼ in.
(21 cm)
Woman III, 1945
Bronze, edition of 10, cast no. 4, 7 ⅛ in.
(18.1 cm)
Woman IV, 1947
Bronze, edition of 10, cast no. 3, 7 ⅞ in.
(20 cm)
Woman V, 1947
Bronze, edition of 10, cast no. 3, 3 ⅜ in.
(8.6 cm)
[Berggruen, Paris, sold 16 January 1968 for
$14,000 to]; Norton Simon Art Foundation
(M.1968.1.1–5).

Cat. 409
Aristide Maillol (French, 1861–1944)
Flora
Bronze, edition of 6, unnumbered cast,
66 in. (167.6 cm)
[Dina Vierny, Paris, sold 17 January 1968 for
$54,000 to]; Norton Simon Art Foundation
(sale, New York, Parke-Bernet Galleries,
13 May 1970, lot 21, unsold) sold 31 October
1971 for $90,000 through [William Kennedy,
New York].

Cat. 410
Aristide Maillol (French, 1861–1944)
Standing Bather with Raised Arms, 1930
Marble, 62 ½ in. (158.8 cm)
[Dina Vierny, Paris, sold 17 January 1968 for
$90,739 to]; Norton Simon Art Foundation
(M.1968.2).

Cat. 411

Edgar Degas (French, 1834–1917)
Woman Combing Her Hair before a Mirror,
c. 1870–1875
Oil on canvas, 18 ¼ x 12 ¾ in.
(46.4 x 32.4 cm)
[M. Knoedler & Co., New York, sold
23 January 1968 for $90,000 to]; Norton
Simon Art Foundation (M.1968.3).

Cat. 412

Henry Moore (English, 1898–1986)
Maquette for Rocking Chair No. 3, 1950
Bronze, edition of 9, unnumbered cast,
6 in. (15.2 cm)
[M. Knoedler & Co., New York, sold 23
January 1968 for $8,400 to]; The Norton
Simon Foundation, sold 22 February 1982
for $45,000 to; [Jeffrey H. Loria & Co.,
New York].

Cat. 413

Auguste Rodin (French, 1840–1917)
The Burghers of Calais, 1884–1895
Bronze, edition of 12, cast no. 10,
82 ½ x 93 ½ x 70 ¾ in.
(209.6 x 237.5 x 179.7 cm)
Musée Rodin, Paris, sold 6 February
1968 for $267,660 to; Norton Simon Art
Foundation (M.1968.4).

Cat. 414

Pierre-Auguste Renoir (French, 1841–1919)
Couple Reading
Oil on canvas, 12 ⅞ x 9 ¾ in. (32.7 x 24.8 cm)
[Lock Galleries, New York, sold 16 February
1968 for $215,000 to]; Norton Simon
(sale, New York, Sotheby Parke Bernet,
2 May 1973, lot 6, for $290,000). (sale,
New York, Sotheby's, 9 May 1989, lot 6,
for $2,800,000). Museum of Modern Art,
Gunma, Japan.

Cat. 415

Jean-Baptiste Camille Corot (French,
1796–1875)

Thatched Cottage in Normandy, c. 1872
Oil on canvas, 17 ¾ x 24 ¹/₁₆ in.
(45.1 x 61.2 cm)
[Stephen Hahn Gallery, New York, sold
23 February 1968 for $95,000 to]; Norton
Simon, by inheritance 2 June 1993 to;
Jennifer Jones Simon Art Trust, Los Angeles,
gift 12 February 2002 to; Norton Simon Art
Foundation (M.2002.1).

Cat. 416

Edgar Degas (French, 1834–1917)
Grande arabesque, first time
Bronze, cast no. 18/HER, 19 in. (48.3 cm)
[Stephen Hahn Gallery, New York, sold
23 February 1968 for $55,000 to]; Norton
Simon Art Foundation, even trade 16
November 1977 for Edgar Degas, *Grande
arabesque, first time*, cast no. 18/M (cat. 1464)
to; [Stephen Hahn Gallery, New York].

Cat. 417

Paul Cézanne (French, 1839–1906)
Park of the Château Noir, c. 1900–1906
Watercolor, 18 ¼ x 12 in. (46.4 x 30.5 cm)
[Paul Rosenberg & Co., New York, sold
11 March 1968 for $65,000 to]; Norton
Simon (sale, New York, Parke-Bernet
Galleries, 5 May 1971, lot 28, for $85,000).
The Henry and Rose Pearlman Foundation,
on long-term loan to the Princeton
University Art Museum.

Cat. 418

Henri Matisse (French, 1869–1954)
The Serpentine, 1909
Bronze, edition of 10, cast no. 9,
22 ⅜ in. (56.8 cm)
[Frank Perls, Beverly Hills, Calif. (on behalf
of Jean Matisse), sold 11 March 1968 for
$63,000 to]; Norton Simon (sale, New York,
Parke-Bernet Galleries, 5 May 1971, lot 62,
for $94,000 to); private collection (sale,
New York, Sotheby's, 10 May 2000, lot 25,
for $12,750,000).

411

412

416

413

414

417

415

418

419

420

421

422

426

423

424

425

Cat. 419
Francisco de Goya y Lucientes
(Spanish, 1746–1828)
Los Caprichos, 1st edition, c. 1797–1799
Etching, aquatint, and drypoint, 80 plates
[Robert M. Light, Boston, sold 14 March
1968 for $18,000 to]; The Norton Simon
Foundation, sold 4 April 1974 for $40,000
($21,500 cash and Fritz Winter, *Tensions*
[cat. 20], valued at $1,500; Jean Dubuffet,
Garden of Bibi Trompette [cat. 39], valued
at $8,500; Dubuffet, *Garden of Islands* [cat.
40], valued at $8,500) to; Pomona College,
Claremont, Calif.

Cat. 420
Chaim Soutine (French, 1893–1943)
Woman Knitting, c. 1925
Oil on canvas, 32 ½ x 23 ½ in.
(82.6 x 59.7 cm)
[Frank Perls, Beverly Hills, Calif. (on behalf
of J. Spreiregen), sold 14 March 1968 for
$93,500 to]; The Norton Simon Foundation
(F.1968.7).

Cat. 421
Camille Pissarro (French, 1830–1903)
Boulevard Montmartre, Mardi-Gras, 1897
Oil on canvas, 25 ⅝ x 31 ⅞ in. (65.1 x 81 cm)
[Marlborough Alte und Moderne Kunst,
Zurich, sold 15 March 1968 for $235,000
to]; Norton Simon (sale, New York,
Parke-Bernet Galleries, 5 May 1971, lot 24,
for $230,000 to); The Armand Hammer
Foundation, Los Angeles, gift 1990 to;
Armand Hammer Museum of Art and
Culture Center, Los Angeles.

Cat. 422
Mary Cassatt (American, 1845–1926)
Woman Reading, 1878
Oil on canvas, 31 x 24 ¾ in. (78.7 x 62.9 cm)
[Galerie des Arts Anciens et Modernes,
Schaan, Liechtenstein, sold 18 March
1968 for $250,000 to]; The Norton Simon
Foundation (sale, New York, Christie's,
19 May 1982, lot 14, for $700,000).

Cat. 423
Henri Matisse (French, 1869–1954)
Reclining Odalisque, 1925
Pencil, 11 ¹/₁₆ x 15 in. (28 x 38 cm)
[Dina Vierny, Paris, sold 18 March 1968 for
$4,000 to]; Norton Simon Art Foundation
(sale, New York, Sotheby Parke Bernet, 2
May 1973, lot 35, for $13,000 to); Mrs. Phyllis
Mailman, New York.

Cat. 424
Henri Matisse (French, 1869–1954)
Two Women, 1938
Ink, 15 x 23 ⅝ in. (38 x 60 cm)
[Dina Vierny, Paris, sold 18 March 1968 for
$6,300 to]; Norton Simon Art Foundation
(sale, New York, Sotheby Parke Bernet,
2 May 1973, lot 34, for $19,000 to);
[Waddington Galleries, London, sold 1973
to]; private collection, returned 1973 to;
[Waddington Galleries, London, sold to];
private collection.

Cat. 425
Henri Matisse (French, 1869–1954)
Woman Resting Her Head on Her Hand, 1936
Ink, 15 x 10 ⅝ in. (38 x 27 cm)
[Dina Vierny, Paris, sold 18 March 1968 for
$4,000 to]; Norton Simon Art Foundation
(sale, New York, Sotheby Parke Bernet,
2 May 1973, lot 36, for $14,500).

Cat. 426
Paul-Camille Guigou (French, 1834–1871)
*The Village of Saint-Paul on the Banks of
the Durance*, 1865
Oil on canvas, 25 ½ x 59 ¼ in.
(64.8 x 150.5 cm)
[Arthur Tooth & Sons, London, sold
19 March 1968 for $46,887 to]; The Norton
Simon Foundation (F. 1968.8).

Cat. 427
Aristide Maillol (French, 1861–1944)
The Tree, 1928
Charcoal on gray paper, 17 ¾ x 8 ½ in.
(45.1 x 21.6 cm)

[Dina Vierny, Paris, sold 19 March 1968 for $3,600 to]; Norton Simon Art Foundation (sale, London, Sotheby & Co., 2 April 1974, lot 51, for $7,680 to); private collection, Peru.

Cat. 428
Jackson Pollock (American, 1912–1956)
Composition No. 13, 1950
Oil on canvas, 22 ¼ x 22 ¼ in.
(56.5 x 56.5 cm)
[Galerie Beyeler, Basel, sold 19 March 1968 for $30,000 to]; Norton Simon Art Foundation (salc, New York, Parke-Bernet Galleries, 14 May 1970, lot 42, for $30,000 to); [Waddington Galleries, London, to]; Basil Goulandris, Lausanne, Switzerland and Andros, Greece.

Cat. 429
Aristide Maillol (French, 1861–1944)
The American Woman, 1935
Pastel on gray paper, 14 ³/₁₆ x 8 ⅝ in.
(36 x 22 cm)
[Dina Vierny, Paris, sold 20 March 1968 for $4,500 to]; Norton Simon (sale, New York, Parke-Bernet Galleries, 5 May 1971, lot 52, for $5,300 to); Evelyn Sharp, New York and Los Angeles.

Cat. 430
Aristide Maillol (French, 1861–1944)
Dina, 1939
Pastel, 42 ½ x 28 in. (108 x 71.1 cm)
[Dina Vierny, Paris, sold 20 March 1968 for $31,500 to]; Norton Simon (sale, New York, Parke-Bernet Galleries, 5 May 1971, lot 51, for $26,000 to); private collection.

Cat. 431
Aristide Maillol (French, 1861–1944)
Reclining Nude from the Back, 1940
Sanguine and pencil, 8 ¾ x 14 ¾ in.
(22.2 x 37.5 cm)
[Dina Vierny, Paris, gift 20 March 1968 to]; Norton Simon (sale, New York, Parke-Bernet Galleries, 5 May 1971, lot 53, for $5,200 to); private collection, Montecito, Calif.

Cat. 432
William Hogarth (English, 1697–1764)
The Works of William Hogarth
Engravings, group of 83
(Sale, London, Sotheby & Co., 21 March 1968 for $2,112 to); Norton Simon, gift 31 December 1969 to; Norton Simon Art Foundation (M.1979.67.1–83).

Cat. 433
Édouard Manet (French, 1832–1883)
The Ragpicker, c. 1865–1870
Oil on canvas, 76 ¾ x 51 ½ in.
(195 x 130.8 cm)
[Wildenstein & Co., New York, sold 21 March 1968 for $850,000 to]; The Norton Simon Foundation (F.1968.9).

Cat. 434
Pierre-Auguste Renoir (French, 1841–1919)
Jacques Eugène Spuller, 1877
Oil on canvas, 18 ¼ x 15 in. (46.4 x 38.1 cm)
[Arthur Tooth & Sons, London, sold 2 April 1968 for $60,200 to]; Norton Simon (sale, New York, Parke-Bernet Galleries, 5 May 1971, lot 43, for $60,000 to); Reed Erickson, (sale, New York, Sotheby Parke Bernet, 1 November 1978, lot 10, to); Krishna Foundation (sale, New York, Christie's, 15 November 1983, lot 49, to); Charles and Rose Wohlstetter, New York (sale, New York, Sotheby's, 8 November 2006, lot 116, for $744,000).

Cat. 435
Juan Gris (Spanish, 1887–1927)
Still Life with a Poem, 1915
Oil on canvas, 31 ¾ x 25 ½ in.
(80.7 x 64.8 cm)
(Sale, New York, Parke-Bernet Galleries, 3 April 1968 for $120,000 to); Norton Simon Art Foundation (M.1968.8.1).

427

432

428

433

429

434

430

431

435

436

441

437

438

442

443

439

440

444

Cat. 436
Jacques Lipchitz (French, 1891–1973)
Mother and Child, 1914/15
Bronze, edition of 7, cast no. 3,
23 ¼ in. (59.1 cm)
(Sale, New York, Parke-Bernet Galleries,
3 April 1968 for $22,000 to); Norton Simon
Art Foundation (sale, New York, Parke-
Bernet Galleries, 13 May 1970, lot 82, for
$19,000 to); private collection, New York.

Cat. 437
Georges Rouault (French, 1871–1958)
The Chinese Man, 1937
Oil on canvas, 41 x 28 ½ in. (104.1 x 72.4 cm)
(Sale, New York, Parke-Bernet Galleries,
3 April 1968 for $92,500 to); Norton Simon
Art Foundation (M.1968.8.3).

Cat. 438
Marino Marini (Italian, 1901–1980)
The Horseman, 1947
Bronze, 39 ½ x 18 ½ x 25 in.
(100.3 x 47 x 63.5 cm)
(Sale, New York, Parke-Bernet Galleries,
4 April 1968 for $39,434 to); Norton Simon
Art Foundation (M.1968.8.2).

Cat. 439
Paul Cézanne (French, 1839–1906)
On the Flanks of Mont Sainte Victoire
Watercolor, 21 x 14 in. (53.3 x 35.6 cm)
[Drs. Fritz and Peter Nathan, Zurich, sold
8 April 1968 for $85,500 to]; Norton Simon
(sale, New York, Parke-Bernet Galleries,
5 May 1971, unsold, sold privately after the
sale for $85,300); private collection.

Cat. 440
Eugène Delacroix (French, 1798–1863)
Othello and Desdemona, c. 1835
Watercolor, 5 ¼ x 8 in. (13.3 x 20.3 cm)
[Drs. Fritz and Peter Nathan, Zurich, sold
8 April 1968 for $7,650 to]; Norton Simon
Art Foundation, returned to dealer 18 July
1969 for purchase price, as partial payment

for Alessandro Magnasco, *Mountain
Landscape* (cat. 667) and Henri Matisse,
Seated Nude (cat. 668).

Cat. 441
Johan Barthold Jongkind (Dutch, 1819–1891)
*The Church of St.-Médard on the Rue
Mouffetard*, 1871
Oil on canvas, 17 x 22 ¹/₁₆ in. (43.2 x 56 cm)
[Drs. Fritz and Peter Nathan, Zurich, sold
8 April 1968 for $36,036 to]; Norton Simon
Art Foundation (M.1968.7).

Cat. 442
Gustave Moreau (French, 1826–1898)
The Poet and the Saint, 1869
Watercolor, 11 ⅜ x 6 ½ in. (28.9 x 16.5 cm)
[Drs. Fritz and Peter Nathan, Zurich, sold
8 April 1968 for $8,100 to]; Norton Simon
Art Foundation (sale, New York, Sotheby
Parke Bernet, 2 May 1973, lot 14, for
$45,000).

Cat. 443
Pierre Puvis de Chavannes
(French, 1824–1898)
The Sacred Grove, 1844
Watercolor, 11 x 16 in. (27.9 x 40.6 cm)
[Drs. Fritz and Peter Nathan, Zurich, sold
8 April 1968 for $4,050 to]; Norton Simon
Art Foundation (sale, New York, Sotheby
Parke Bernet, 2 May 1973, lot 15, for $30,000
to); [Maurice Rheims, Paris].

Cat. 444
Pierre Bonnard (French, 1867–1947)
Nude against the Light, 1909
Oil on canvas, 48 ½ x 21 ½ in.
(123.2 x 54.6 cm)
[Alex Reid & Lefevre, London, sold 12 April
1968 for $120,000 to]; Norton Simon (sale,
New York, Parke-Bernet Galleries, 5 May
1971, lot 59, for $100,000 to); The Armand
Hammer Foundation, Los Angeles, gift 1990
to; Armand Hammer Museum of Art and
Culture Center, Los Angeles, returned 2007
to; The Armand Hammer Foundation.

Cat. 445
Théodore Rousseau (French, 1812–1867)
Country Scene with Cows
Oil on canvas, 9 ½ x 15 ¼ in. (24.1 x 38.7 cm)
Jeanne Ruddy, Los Angeles, sold 12 April
1968 for $1,800 to; Norton Simon (sale, New
York, Sotheby Parke Bernet, 12 May 1978, lot
183, for $15,000).

Cat. 446
Jacques Lipchitz (French, 1891–1973)
Bather III, 1917
Bronze, edition of 7, cast no. 6,
28 in. (71.1 cm)
[Marlborough-Gerson Gallery, New York,
sold 17 April 1968 for $20,400 to]; Norton
Simon Art Foundation (M.1968.9).

Cat. 447
Rembrandt van Rijn (Dutch, 1606–1669)
The Basan Recueil
Etchings, group of 77
[Robert M. Light, Boston, sold 18 April
1968 for $18,216 to]; Norton Simon Art
Foundation (M.1968.10.1–77) (34 sold in
several auctions between 1974 and 1977),
gift of 43 remaining prints 27 June 1977
to; Norton Simon Museum (25 sold in the
Museum store and at auction between 1977
and 1980), 18 remain in the collection of the
Norton Simon Museum.

Cat. 448
Jacques Lipchitz (French, 1891–1973)
Seated Woman (Cubist Figure), 1916
Stone, 42 ½ x 11 ¼ x 12 ¼ in.
(108 x 28.6 x 31.1 cm)
[Marlborough-Gerson Gallery, New York,
sold 22 April 1968 for $42,500 to]; Norton
Simon Art Foundation (sale, New York,
Sotheby Parke Bernet, 2 May 1973, lot 38, for
$70,000 to); [Modarco, Switzerland].
M. Knoedler & Company, New York, sold
1977 to]; Raymond and Patsy Nasher,
Dallas; Nasher Sculpture Center, Dallas.

Cat. 449
Pablo Picasso (Spanish, 1881–1973)
Pointe de la Cité, 1912
Oil on canvas, oval, 35 ½ x 28 in.
(90.2 x 71.1 cm)
(Sale, London, Sotheby & Co., 23 April
1968 for $298,300 to); Norton Simon
Art Foundation, sold 21 January 1982 for
$3,050,000 ($2,600,000 cash and two
paintings: Francesco Guardi, *Venetian
Capriccio* [cat. 1687] valued at $200,000
and Jan van der Heyden, *Townscape* [cat.
1688] valued at $250,000) to; [E. V. Thaw &
Co., New York, sold to]; Emilio Azcárraga,
Mexico City, bequest 1997 to; private
collection, Mérida.

Cat. 450
Jean-Baptiste Armand Guillaumin
(French, 1841–1927)
The Seine at Charenton
(formerly *The Break of Day*), 1874
Oil on canvas, 21 ¼ x 25 ⅜ in. (54 x 64.5 cm)
(Sale, London, Sotheby & Co., 24 April
1968 for $45,342 to); Norton Simon Art
Foundation (M.1968.16.2).

Cat. 451
Stanislas-Victor-Édouard Lépine
(French, 1836–1892)
The Bridge at Bercy
Oil on canvas, 14 ½ x 23 ½ in.
(36.8 x 59.7 cm)
(Sale, London, Sotheby & Co., 24 April
1968 for $20,525 to); Norton Simon Art
Foundation (sale, New York, Parke-Bernet
Galleries, 13 May 1970, lot 11, for $26,000).
[Stephen Hahn Gallery, New York].
[Michael Drinkhouse, New York (sale, New
York, Sotheby Parke Bernet, 17 May 1978,
lot 2, for $24,000)].

445

449

446

450

451

448

452

453

454

455

456

457

458

459

460

461

Cat. 452
Rembrandt van Rijn (Dutch, 1606–1669)
Peter and John at the Gate of the Temple,
1659
Etching, 2nd state: plate, 7 ⅛ x 8 ½ in. (18.1 x
21.6 cm); sheet, 7 ¼ x 8 ¾ in. (18.4 x 22.2 cm)
(Sale, New York, Parke-Bernet Galleries,
1 May 1968 for $2,400 to); Norton Simon
Art Foundation (M.1968.13.1).

Cat. 453
Rembrandt van Rijn (Dutch, 1606–1669)
Peter and John at the Gate of the Temple,
1659
Etching, drypoint, burin, state IV, plate,
7 ⅛ x 8 ½ in. (18.1 x 21.6 cm); sheet,
7 ⅜ x 8 ⁹/₁₆ in. (18.7 x 21.7 cm)
(Sale, New York, Parke-Bernet Galleries,
1 May 1968 for $900 to); Norton Simon Art
Foundation (M.1968.13.2).

Cat. 454
Franz Marc (German, 1880–1916)
Bathing Girls, 1910
Oil on canvas, 43 x 56 in. (109.2 x 142.2 cm)
[Marlborough-Gerson Gallery, New York,
sold 8 May 1968 for $70,000 to]; Norton
Simon Art Foundation (M.1968.11).

Cat. 455
Aristide Maillol (French, 1861–1944)
Crouching Woman, 1920
Bronze, artist's proof, 6 ⅞ in. (17.5 cm)
[Dina Vierny, Paris, sold 13 May 1968 for
$9,000 to]; Norton Simon Art Foundation
(M.1968.12.3).

Cat. 456
Aristide Maillol (French, 1861–1944)
Draped Torso, 1900
Bronze, artist's proof, 8 ¼ in. (21 cm)
[Dina Vierny, Paris, sold 13 May 1968 for
$6,300 to]; Norton Simon Art Foundation
(M.1968.12.1).

Cat. 457
Aristide Maillol (French, 1861–1944)
Leda, 1900
Bronze, artist's proof, 11 ½ in. (29.2 cm)
[Dina Vierny, Paris, sold 13 May 1968 for
$9,000 to]; Norton Simon Art Foundation
(M.1968.12.2).

Cat. 458
Aristide Maillol (French, 1861–1944)
Young Man Standing, 1930
Bronze, artist's proof, 12 ¼ in. (31.1 cm)
[Dina Vierny, Paris, sold 13 May 1968 for
$9,000 to]; Norton Simon Art Foundation
(M.1968.12.4).

Cat. 459
Odilon Redon (French, 1840–1916)
Vase of Flowers, c. 1912–1916
Pastel, 25 ½ x 20 in. (64.8 x 50.8 cm)
[Marlborough Alte und Moderne Kunst,
Schellenberg, Switzerland, sold 16 May
1968 for $120,000 to]; Norton Simon Art
Foundation (sale, New York, Sotheby Parke
Bernet, 2 May 1973, lot 32, for $225,000
to); [Reid & Lefevre, London for]; [Fuji
International Art Company, Tokyo, sold to];
private collection, Japan. private collection,
U. S. A.

Cat. 460
Théodore Rousseau (French, 1812–1867)
Landscape with a Road, 1829
Oil on paper, mounted on canvas,
6 ¾ x 13 ⅝ in. (17.2 x 34.6 cm)
[Stephen Hahn Gallery, New York, sold
20 May 1968 for $6,000 to]; Norton Simon
Art Foundation (sale, New York, Sotheby
Parke Bernet, 2 May 1973, lot 20, for $14,000
to); private collection.

Cat. 461
Paul Cézanne (French, 1839–1906)
Rock Quarry at Bibemus
Oil on canvas, 25 ⅝ x 21 ¼ in. (65.1 x 54 cm)

[Galerie des Arts Anciens et Modernes, Schaan, Liechtenstein, sold 22 May 1968 for $500,000 to]; Norton Simon, transferred 24 July 1970 to; Lucille Ellis Simon (sale, New York, Sotheby's, 15 November 1989, lot 25, for $6,000,000 to); [Stephen Hahn Gallery, New York]. private collection.

Cat. 462A-B
Georges-Pierre Seurat (French, 1859–1891)
Corn and Trees (recto), *Félix Fénéon* (verso)
Conté crayon, 9 5/16 x 12 3/16 in. (23.7 x 31 cm)
[Drs. Fritz and Peter Nathan, Zurich, sold 22 May 1968 for $20,000 to]; Norton Simon (sale, New York, Parke-Bernet Galleries, 5 May 1971, lot 47, for $12,000). [Jan Krugier, Geneva, 2006].

Cat. 463
Edgar Degas (French, 1834–1917)
Arabesque over the right leg, left arm in front
Bronze, cast no. 1/HER, 11 ½ in. (29.2 cm)
[Paul Rosenberg & Co., New York, sold 24 May 1968 for $21,000 to]; Norton Simon (sale, New York, Parke-Bernet Galleries, 5 May 1971, lot 31, for $32,000). [Wildenstein & Co., New York]. [Alex Reid & Lefevre, London]. John T. Dorrance Jr. (sale, New York, Sotheby's, 18 October 1989).

Cat. 464
Edgar Degas (French, 1834–1917)
Woman rubbing her back with a sponge, torso
Bronze, cast no. 28/HER.D, 17 in. (43.2 cm)
[Paul Rosenberg & Co., New York, sold 24 May 1968 for $56,000 to]; Norton Simon Art Foundation (sale, New York, Sotheby Parke Bernet, 14 May 1980, lot 203, for $40,000). (sale, New York, Sotheby's, 19 November 1986, lot 125).

Cat. 465
Jean-Auguste-Dominique Ingres (French, 1780–1867)
Madame de Lavalette, 1817

Pencil, 6 ¼ x 4 ½ in. (15.9 x 11.4 cm)
[Paul Rosenberg & Co., New York, sold 24 May 1968 for $32,000 to]; Norton Simon (sale, New York, Parke-Bernet Galleries, 8 May 1971, lot 211, for $25,000).

Cat. 466
Camille Pissarro (French, 1830–1903)
The Woods at Marly, 1871
Oil on canvas, 17 ¾ x 21 ¾ in. (45.1 x 55.3 cm)
[Paul Rosenberg & Co., New York, sold 24 May 1968 for $82,000 to]; Norton Simon Art Foundation (sale, New York, Parke-Bernet Galleries, 13 May 1970, lot 13, for $95,000 to); Baron Hans Heinrich Thyssen-Bornemisza, Lugano, sold 1993 to; Museo Thyssen-Bornemisza, Madrid.

Cat. 467
Pierre-Auguste Renoir (French, 1841–1919)
Young Woman with Flowered Hat, 1882
Pen and ink, 19 ¼ x 11 ¼ in. (48.9 x 28.6 cm)
[Paul Rosenberg & Co., New York, sold 24 May 1968 for $16,000 to]; Norton Simon (sale, New York, Sotheby Parke Bernet, 2 May 1973, lot 2, for $38,000 to); [Stephen Hahn, New York].

Cat. 468
Georges-Pierre Seurat (French, 1859–1891)
The Embroideress, 1883
Conté crayon, 11 13/16 x 9 5/16 in. (30 x 23.7 cm)
[Paul Rosenberg & Co., New York, sold 24 May 1968 for $42,000 to]; Norton Simon Art Foundation (sale, London, Sotheby & Co., 2 April 1974, lot 45, for $57,600 to); [Jan Krugier, Geneva]. On loan to the Kunsthalle, Hamburg.

Cat. 469
Louis-Eugène Boudin (French, 1824–1898)
The Beach at Trouville, 1873
Oil on panel, 8 ¼ x 16 ¼ in. (21 x 41.3 cm)
[M. Knoedler & Co., New York, sold 11 June 1968 for $120,000 to]; The Norton Simon Foundation (F.1968.10).

462A

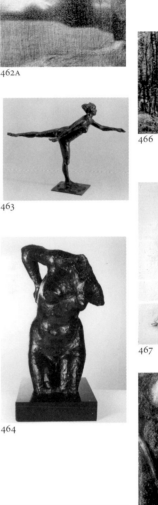
466

463

467

464

468

465

469

470

471

472

473

475 CENTER PANEL

476

477

478

474

Cat. 470
School of Bergamo (Italian, 16th century)
Portrait of a Young Man
Oil on canvas, 34 ½ x 26 ½ in.
(87.6 x 67.3 cm)
(Sale, London, Sotheby & Co., 12 June
1968 for $1,911 to); The Norton Simon
Foundation (F.1968.11.1).

Cat. 471
Orazio Borgianni (Italian, c. 1575–1616)
Saint Bonaventure, 1610
Oil on canvas, 34 ½ x 29 ½ in.
(87.6 x 74.9 cm)
(Sale, London, Sotheby & Co., 12 June
1968 for $4,300 to); The Norton Simon
Foundation (F.1968.11.2).

Cat. 472
School of Caravaggio (Italian, 17th century)
A Geographer
Oil on canvas, 51 ¾ x 39 ¼ in.
(131.5 x 99.7 cm)
(Sale, London, Sotheby & Co., 12 June
1968 for $5,974 to); The Norton Simon
Foundation (F.1968.11.3).

Cat. 473
Attributed to Nicolas Henry Jeurat de
Bertry (French, 1728 – after 1796) (formerly
attributed to Jean-Siméon Chardin [French,
1699–1779])
Still Life
Oil on canvas, 36 ¾ x 53 ½ in.
(93.4 x 135.9 cm)
(Sale, London, Sotheby & Co., 12 June
1968 for $9,559 to); The Norton Simon
Foundation (sale, London, Sotheby Parke
Bernet & Co., 16 July 1980, lot 86, for
$20,230). private collection (sale, London,
Christie's, 7 July 2009, lot 51

Cat. 474
Thomas de Keyser (Dutch, 1596/97–1667)
Portrait of a Father and His Son, 1631

Oil on canvas, 25 ⅛ x 19 ¼ in.
(63.8 x 48.9 cm)
(Sale, London, Sotheby & Co., 12 June
1968 for $15,533 to); The Norton Simon
Foundation (F.1968.11.9).

Cat. 475
Workshop of Cornelis Engebrechtsz.
(Dutch, c. 1465–1527)
The Adoration of the Magi, c. 1520
Oil on panel, triptych: center panel,
18 ¾ x 13 ¼ in. (47.6 x 33.7 cm); left panel,
18 ¾ x 6 ½ in. (47.6 x 16.5 cm); right panel,
18 ¾ x 6 ⅝ in. (47.6 x 16.8 cm)
(Sale, London, Sotheby & Co., 12 June
1968 for $11,949 to); The Norton Simon
Foundation (F.1968.11.5).

Cat. 476
Prospero Fontana (Italian, 1512–1597)
Portrait of a Cardinal
Oil on canvas, 48 ½ x 43 in. (123.2 x 109.2 cm)
(Sale, London, Sotheby & Co., 12 June
1968 for $6,691 to); The Norton Simon
Foundation (F.1968.11.7).

Cat. 477
Abraham Janssens (Flemish, c. 1573–1632)
An Allegory of Winter, c. 1623
Oil on canvas, 47 x 38 ½ in. (119.4 x 97.8 cm)
(Sale, London, Sotheby & Co., 12 June
1968 for $3,585 to); The Norton Simon
Foundation (sale, London, Sotheby Parke
Bernet & Co., 16 April 1980, lot 52, for
$5,330).

Cat. 478
Andrea Locatelli (Italian, 1695–1741)
Landscape with Figures by a River
Oil on canvas, 22 ½ x 30 ½ in.
(57.2 x 77.5 cm)
(Sale, London, Sotheby & Co., 12 June
1968 for $7,169 to); The Norton Simon
Foundation (F.1968.11.10).

Cat. 479
Juan Bautista del Mazo
(Spanish, c. 1612–1667)
Philip IV of Spain, c. 1650
Oil on canvas, 25 ¾ x 21 ½ in.
(65.4 x 54.6 cm)
(Sale, London, Sotheby & Co., 12 June
1968 for $2,868 to); The Norton Simon
Foundation, sold along with Dosso Dossi
Man with a Large Hat (cat. D123) 21
February 1975 for $45,000 to; [Dino Fabbri,
New York].

Cat. 480
Francesco de Mura (Italian, 1696–1782)
Christ and the Adulteress
Oil on canvas, 39 x 49 in. (99.1 x 124.5 cm)
(Sale, London, Sotheby & Co., 12 June
1968 for $5,974 to); The Norton Simon
Foundation (sale, London, Sotheby Parke
Bernet & Co., 16 April 1980, lot 79, for
$6,663). (sale, London, Bonhams, 9 July
2003, lot 28, unsold).

Cat. 481
Attributed to Guido Reni
(Italian, 1575–1642)
Saint Joseph and the Infant Christ
Oil on canvas, 32 x 25 ½ in. (81.3 x 64.8 cm)
(Sale, London, Sotheby & Co., 12 June
1968 for $1,434 to); The Norton Simon
Foundation (sale, London, Sotheby Parke
Bernet & Co., 16 April 1980, lot 66, for
$8,439).

Cat. 482
Peter Paul Rubens (Flemish, 1577–1640)
Portrait of an Elderly Man,
after a sixteenth-century portrait attributed
to Joos van Cleve, c. 1616
Oil on panel, 26 ¹/₁₆ x 20 ⁵/₁₆ in.
(66.2 x 51.6 cm)

(Sale, London, Sotheby & Co., 12 June
1968 for $8,519 to); The Norton Simon
Foundation (F.1968.11.14).

Cat. 483
Attributed to Eusebio da San Giorgio
(Italian, c. 1470–c. 1550)
Madonna (copy after Raphael)
Oil on panel, 15 ¾ x 14 ½ in. (40 x 36.8 cm)
(Sale, London, Sotheby & Co., 12 June
1968 for $1,000 to); The Norton Simon
Foundation (sale, London, Sotheby Parke
Bernet & Co., 16 July 1980, lot 24, for
$3,800).

Cat. 484
Francesco Solimena (Italian, 1657–1747)
The Garden of Eden
Oil on metal, 18 ¼ x 14 ½ in. (46.4 x 36.8 cm)
(Sale, London, Sotheby & Co., 12 June
1968 for $4,780 to); The Norton Simon
Foundation (F.1968.11.15).

Cat. 485
Francesco Trevisani (Italian, 1656–1746)
Apelles Painting Campaspe, 1720
Oil on canvas, 19 ½ x 23 ¾ in.
(49.5 x 60.3 cm)
(Sale, London, Sotheby & Co., 12 June
1968 for $6,207 to); The Norton Simon
Foundation (F.1968.11.16).

Cat. 486
Francisco de Goya y Lucientes
(Spanish, 1746–1828)
La Tauromaquia, 1st edition, 1816
Etching, aquatint, and drypoint, 33 plates
[Robert M. Light, Boston, sold 13 June
1968 for $14,500 to]; Norton Simon Art
Foundation, sold 23 April 1981 for $80,000
to; [William Schab, New York].

479

483

480

484

481

485

486

482

487

491

488

492

489

493

490

494

495

Cat. 487
Paul Cézanne (French, 1839–1906)
Afternoon in Naples, 1870
Pencil overlaid with watercolor on white
paper, 4 ¼ x 6 ¼ in. (10.8 x 15.9 cm)
[Drs. Fritz and Peter Nathan, Zurich, sold
24 June 1968 for $13,000 to]; Norton Simon
Art Foundation (sale, London, Sotheby &
Co., 2 April 1974, lot 41, for $26,400 to);
[Jan Krugier, Geneva]; [Galerie Krugier
& Geoffroy, Geneva]. [Barbara Divver
Fine Arts, New York, 1986]. (sale, London,
Christie's, 9 February 2006, lot 514, for
$423,898 to); private collection, Delaware.

Cat. 488
Théodore Géricault (French, 1791–1824)
Lion
Pencil, 4 x 4 ¾ in. (10.2 x 12.1 cm)
[Drs. Fritz and Peter Nathan, Zurich, sold
24 June 1968 for $2,000 to]; Norton Simon
Art Foundation (sale, New York, Sotheby
Parke Bernet, 2 May 1973, lot 12, for $4,800
to); [Jan Krugier, Geneva].

Cat. 489
Constantin Guys (French, 1802–1892)
Pierreuse
Watercolor, 6 ½ x 4 ⅛ in. (16.5 x 10.5 cm)
[Drs. Fritz and Peter Nathan, Zurich, sold
24 June 1968 for $3,000 to]; Norton Simon
Art Foundation (sale, New York, Parke-
Bernet Galleries, 13 May 1970, lot 3, for
$2,000 to); [Daniel Varenne, Geneva].

Cat. 490
Constantin Guys (French, 1802–1892)
Woman, Seen from the Front
Ink, pen, and brush, 8 ¾ x 5 ½ in.
(22.2 x 14 cm)
[Drs. Fritz and Peter Nathan, Zurich, sold
24 June 1968 for $3,000 to]; Norton Simon
Art Foundation (sale, New York, Parke-
Bernet Galleries, 13 May 1970, lot 2, for $850
to); [Daniel Varenne, Geneva].

Cat. 491
Henri Matisse (French, 1869–1954)
Seated Nude in the Studio, 1917–1918
Oil on canvas, 16 ¼ x 13 in. (41.3 x 33 cm)
[Drs. Fritz and Peter Nathan, Zurich,
sold 24 June 1968 for $56,700 to]; Norton
Simon Art Foundation (sale, New York,
Parke-Bernet Galleries, 13 May 1970, lot 38,
unsold), sold 14 July 1971 for $55,000 to; [
Drs. Fritz and Peter Nathan, Zurich].

Cat. 492
Maurice Utrillo (French, 1883–1955)
The Basilica of Saint Denis, 1909
Oil on canvas, 27 x 19 in. (68.6 x 48.3 cm)
[Drs. Fritz and Peter Nathan, Zurich, sold
24 June 1968 for $85,500 to]; Norton Simon
Art Foundation (M.1968.18).

Cat. 493
Edgar Degas (French, 1834–1917)
*Nude Woman in Her Room, Seen from
Behind*, c. 1879
Monotype, 6 ¼ x 8 ½ in. (15.9 x 21.6 cm)
[Alex Reid & Lefevre, London, sold 24 June
1968 for $1,910 to]; Norton Simon (private
sale, New York, Sotheby Parke Bernet,
23 October 1974, with Edgar Degas,
The Earring [cat. 518] for $17,000).

Cat. 494
Constantin Guys (French, 1802–1892)
Loges and Spectators at the Theater
Pen, ink, and wash, 8 x 12 ½ in.
(20.3 x 31.8 cm)
[Alex Reid & Lefevre, London, sold 24 June
1968 for $2,269 to]; Norton Simon (sale,
New York, Parke-Bernet Galleries, 5 May
1971, lot 7, for $1,600 to); private collection,
New York, by descent to; private collection.

Cat. 495
Aristide Maillol (French, 1861–1944)
Mountain, 1937
Lead, edition of 6, cast no. 2,

65 ½ x 75 ½ x 36 in. (166.4 x 191.8 x 91.4 cm)
[Dina Vierny, Paris, sold 25 June 1968 for
$54,000 to]; Norton Simon Art Foundation
(M.1968.17).

Cat. 496
Pieter Brueghel the Elder
(Flemish, 1525–1569)
Landscape with Rabbit Hunters
Etching, 8 ⁷/₁₆ x 11 ⅜ in. (21.4 x 28.9 cm)
[P. & D. Colnaghi, London, sold 26 June
1968 for $18,753 to]; Norton Simon,
sold 18 October 1972 for $82,000 with
Albrecht Dürer, *Melancholia* (cat. 154) and
Rembrandt van Rijn, *Jan Lutma* (cat. 178)
to; [E. V. Thaw & Co., New York].

Cat. 497
Francisco de Goya y Lucientes
(Spanish, 1746–1828)
La Tauromaquia, 1st edition, 1816
Etching, aquatint, and drypoint, 33 plates
[P. & D. Colnaghi, London, sold 26 June
1968 for $14,343 to]; Norton Simon, gift
22 December 1976 to; Norton Simon Art
Foundation (M.1976.18.1–33).

Cat. 498
Formerly attributed to Eugène Delacroix
(French, 1798–1863)
Lion
Pencil, 8 ½ x 10 ½ in. (21.6 x 26.7 cm)
[Alex Reid & Lefevre, London, sold 28 June
1968 for $2,866 to]; Norton Simon (sale,
New York, Parke-Bernet Galleries, 5 May
1971, lot 5, unsold; sold after the sale to);
[the trade, London].

Cat. 499
Vincent van Gogh (Dutch, 1853–1890)
The Artist's Mother, 1888
Oil on canvas, 16 x 12 ¾ in. (40.6 x 32.4 cm)
(Sale, London, Christie's, 28 June 1968 for
$275,354 to); Norton Simon Art Foundation
(M.1968.32).

Cat. 500
Maurice Utrillo (French, 1883–1955)
Place du Tertre in Montmartre, c. 1911
Oil on canvas, 21 x 28 ½ in. (53.3 x 72.4 cm)
(Sale, London, Christie's, 28 June 1968 for
$52,845 to); Norton Simon Art Foundation
(M.1968.24).

Cat. 501
Jean-Auguste-Dominique Ingres
(French, 1780–1867)
Prosper Debia, 1828
Pencil, 8 ½ x 6 ½ in. (21.6 x 16.5 cm)
[Paul Rosenberg & Co., New York, sold
1 July 1968 for $16,000 to]; Norton Simon
Art Foundation (sale, London, Sotheby &
Co., 27 June 1974, lot 52, for $26,400).

Cat. 502
Édouard Vuillard (French, 1868–1940)
The Sunlit Path (formerly *The Garden*),
1908–1910
Drained oil on paper, 15 ¾ x 14 in.
(40 x 35.6 cm)
[Arthur Tooth & Sons, London, sold 1 July
1968 for $20,000 to]; Norton Simon Art
Foundation, used in trade 13 January 1971
with a value of $40,000 as partial payment
for Lucas Cranach the Elder, *Adam* (cat.
742) to; [Spencer A. Samuels & Co., New
York]. [O'Hana, London, 1973].

Cat. 503
Jean-Louis Forain (French, 1852–1931)
Dancer Retying Her Slipper
Oil on panel, 10 ½ x 8 ¼ in. (26.7 x 21 cm)
(Sale, London, Sotheby & Co., 3 July
1968 for $12,937 to); Norton Simon Art
Foundation (sale, New York, Sotheby Parke
Bernet, 2 May 1973, lot 25, for $24,000 to);
[Peter Matthews, London], sold 1973 to;
Mrs. Frederick J. Hellman, California.

500

496

498

501

502

499

503

508

504

505

506

509

510

511

507

Cat. 504
Roger de La Fresnaye (French, 1885–1925)
Eve and the Apple
Bronze, edition of 10, cast no. 3,
12 ½ x 17 ½ in. (31.8 x 44.5 cm)
(Sale, London, Sotheby & Co., 3 July
1968 for $10,780 to); Norton Simon Art
Foundation (sale, New York, Parke-Bernet
Galleries, 13 May 1970, lot 28, unsold)
(M.1968.26).

Cat. 505
Marino Marini (Italian, 1901–1980)
Miracolo
Bronze, edition of 6, cast no. 6, 55 ¾ in.
(141.6 cm)
(Sale, London, Sotheby & Co., 3 July
1968 for $15,812 to); Norton Simon Art
Foundation (sale, New York, Sotheby Parke
Bernet, 2 May 1973, lot 41, for $24,000 to);
[Galerie Hervé Odermatt, Paris].

Cat. 506
Constantin Guys (French, 1802–1892)
The Washerwoman
Pencil and watercolor, 11 x 9 in.
(27.9 x 22.9 cm)
(Sale, London, Sotheby & Co., 4 July 1968
for $2,000 to); Norton Simon (sale, New
York, Parke-Bernet Galleries, 5 May 1971,
lot 6, for $2,200 to); [Weintraub Gallery,
New York].

Cat. 507
Wilhelm Lehmbruck (German, 1881–1919)
Inclined Head of the Kneeling Woman
Bronze, edition of 3, unnumbered cast,
18 ¹⁵/₁₆ in. (48 cm)
[Roman Norbert Ketterer, Lugano, sold
5 July 1968 for $13,050 to); Norton Simon,
transferred 24 July 1970 to; Lucille Ellis
Simon (estate sale, New York, Christie's,
17 October 2000, lot 74, for $148, 474 to);
[Achim Moeller, New York].

Cat. 508
Pierre Puvis de Chavannes
(French, 1824–1898)
The Pastoral Life of Saint Geneviève, 1879
Oil on canvas, triptych: left panel,
53 x 32 ¼ in. (134.5 x 81.9 cm); center panel,
53 x 35 ⅛ in. (134.5 x 89.1 cm); right panel,
52 ¾ x 32 ¼ in. (134 x 81.9 cm)
[Hirschl & Adler Galleries, New York, sold
10 July 1968 for $55,000 to); Norton Simon
Art Foundation (M.1968.49).

Cat. 509
Pierre-Auguste Renoir (French, 1841–1919)
Mme Henriot, c. 1871
Oil on canvas, 18 x 15 in. (45.7 x 38.1 cm)
[Arthur Tooth & Sons, London, sold 10 July
1968 for $105,260 to]; Norton Simon (sale,
New York, Parke-Bernet Galleries, 5 May
1971, lot 42, for $130,000). (sale, New York,
Sotheby Parke Bernet, 17 May 1978, lot 36,
for $125,000 to); [Waddington Galleries and
Arthur Tooth and Son, London].

Cat. 510
Antoine Vestier (French, 1740–1824)
Portrait of a Lady, 1763
Oil on canvas, 31 x 26 ¾ in. (78.7 x 68 cm)
[Arthur Tooth & Sons, London, sold 16 July
1968 for $24,421 to]; Norton Simon Art
Foundation (M.1968.20).

Cat. 511
Louis-Eugène Boudin (French, 1824–1898)
The Old Fish Market in Brussels, 1871
Oil on panel, 9 ½ x 13 ¼ in. (24.1 x 33.7 cm)
[Marlborough Alte und Moderne Kunst,
Schellenberg, Switzerland, sold 17 July
1968 for $18,900 to]; Norton Simon Art
Foundation (sale, New York, Sotheby
Parke Bernet, 7 November 1979, lot 538, for
$55,000).

Cat. 512
Barbara Hepworth (English, 1903–1975)
Rock Form (Porthcurno), 1964
Bronze, edition of 6, cast no. 3, 99 ¾ x 42 in.
(253.4 x 106.7 cm)
[Marlborough-Gerson Gallery, New York,
sold 24 July 1968 for $40,000 to]; Norton
Simon Art Foundation (M.1968.22.1).

Cat. 513
Henri Laurens (French, 1885–1954)
Small Seated Woman
Bronze, edition of 6, cast no. 2,
27 x 20 ½ x 13 in. (68.6 x 52.1 x 33 cm)
[Marlborough-Gerson Gallery, New York,
sold 24 July 1968 for $22,500 to]; Norton
Simon Art Foundation (M.1968.22.2).

Cat. 514
Gerhard Marcks (German, 1889–1981)
Dancer, 1947
Bronze, 42 x 13 x 12 in. (106.7 x 33 x 30.5 cm)
[Marlborough-Gerson Gallery, New York,
sold 24 July 1968 for $6,750 to]; Norton
Simon Art Foundation (sale, New York,
Sotheby Parke Bernet, 14 May 1980, lot 132,
for $18,000).

Cat. 515
David Smith (American, 1906–1965)
Cubi XXVIII, 1965
Stainless steel,
108 x 112 ⅛ x 40 in. (274.3 x 284.8 x 101.6 cm)
[Marlborough-Gerson Gallery, New York,
sold 24 July 1968 for $65,000 to]; Norton
Simon Art Foundation, sold 14 July 1982 for
$1,100,000 to; [Marlborough Gallery, New
York, for]; Sid W. Richardson Foundation,
Fort Worth (sale, New York, Sotheby's, 9
November 2005, lot 23, for $23, 800,000 to);
The Broad Art Foundation, Los Angeles.

Cat. 516
Gustave Courbet (French, 1819–1877)
Cliffs by the Sea in the Snow, 1870

Oil on canvas,
21 ½ x 25 ¾ in. (54.6 x 65.4 cm)
[Drs. Fritz and Peter Nathan, Zurich, sold
25 July 1968 for $35,000 to]; Norton Simon
Art Foundation, sold 14 January 1975 for
$58,500 to; [Stephen Hahn Gallery, New
York]. private collection (sale, New York,
Sotheby Parke Bernet, 29 October 1981, lot
33a, to); private collection, Japan. (sale, New
York, Sotheby's, 23 October 2008, lot 140,
unsold).

Cat. 517
Edgar Degas (French, 1834–1917)
Dancer at the Barre, 1875–1876
Charcoal and white pastel on gray paper,
18 ⅛ x 11 ⅛ in. (46 x 28.3 cm)
[Drs. Fritz and Peter Nathan, Zurich, sold
25 July 1968 for $22,000 to]; Norton Simon
Art Foundation (sale, London, Sotheby
& Co., 2 April 1974, lot 43, for $60,000).
private collection, Germany, 1996.

Cat. 518
Edgar Degas (French, 1834–1917)
The Earring
Monotype, 6 ¼ x 4 ¾ in. (15.9 x 12 cm)
[Alex Reid & Lefevre, London, sold 25 July
1968 for $2,600 to]; Norton Simon (private
sale, New York, Sotheby Parke Bernet,
23 October 1974, with Edgar Degas, *Nude
Woman in Her Room, Seen from Behind*
[cat. 493] for $17,000).

Cat. 519
Edgar Degas (French, 1834–1917)
In the Salon of a Brothel
Monotype, 8 ½ x 6 ¾ in. (21.6 x 17.1 cm)
[Alex Reid & Lefevre, London, sold 25
July 1968 for $4,553 to]; Norton Simon
[on consignment with E. V. Thaw & Co.,
December 1972]; [Robert M. Light, Boston,
sold March 1973 to]; Iris and B. Gerald
Cantor Center for Visual Arts at Stanford
University, Stanford, Calif.

512

517

513

518

514

519

515

516

520

521

525

522

526

523

527

524

528

Cat. 520
Constantin Guys (French, 1802–1892)
Promenade at the Music Hall
Ink wash, 7 ¼ x 9 ⅝ in. (18.4 x 24.5 cm)
[Alex Reid & Lefevre, London, sold 25 July
1968 for $2,042 to]; Norton Simon Art
Foundation (sale, London, Sotheby & Co.,
3 July 1974, lot 126, for $936).

Cat. 521
Edgar Degas (French, 1834–1917)
Dancers in the Rotunda of the Paris Opéra,
c. 1875–1878 and c. 1894
Oil on canvas, 34 ⅞ x 37 ¾ in.
(88.6 x 95.9 cm)
[Patricia Kane Matisse, New York, sold
30 July 1968 for $200,000 to]; Norton
Simon Art Foundation (M.1968.25).

Cat. 522
Henri Matisse (French, 1869–1954)
The Black Shawl (Lorette VII), 1918
Oil on canvas, 27 x 52 in. (68.6 x 132.1 cm)
[Stephen Hahn Gallery, New York, sold
4 August 1968 for $275,000 to]; Norton
Simon, gift 13 March 1982 to; Norton Simon
Art Foundation (M.1982.3).

Cat. 523
Paul Signac (French, 1863–1935)
The Seine at Les Andelys, 1886
Oil on canvas, 18 x 25 ½ in. (45.7 x 64.8 cm)
[Stephen Hahn Gallery, New York, sold 20
August 1968 for $63,000 to]; Norton Simon
Art Foundation (M.1968.27).

Cat. 524
Georges-Pierre Seurat (French, 1859–1891)
The Stone Breakers, Le Raincy, c. 1882
Oil on canvas, 14 ¾ x 17 ⅞ in. (37.5 x 45.4 cm)
[Stephen Hahn Gallery, New York, sold
4 September 1968 for $280,000 to]; Norton
Simon Art Foundation (M.1968.28).

Cat. 525
Henri Matisse (French, 1869–1954)
The Small Blue Dress, before a Mirror, 1937
Oil on canvas, 25 ½ x 19 ½ in.
(64.8 x 49.5 cm)
[Paul Rosenberg & Co., New York, sold
5 September 1968 for $130,000 to]; Norton
Simon Art Foundation, sold 22 April 1974
for $350,000 to; [E. V. Thaw & Co., New
York, sold to]; [Stephen Hahn Gallery, New
York, sold to]; The National Museum of
Modern Art, Kyoto.

Cat. 526
Alfred Sisley (French, 1839–1899)
Louveciennes in the Snow, 1872
Oil on canvas, 20 x 28 ¾ in. (50.8 x 73 cm)
[David Gibbs, New York, sold 24 September
1968 for $160,000 to]; The Norton Simon
Foundation, transferred 31 October 1996 to;
Norton Simon Art Foundation (M.1996.3).

Cat. 527
Paul Cézanne (French, 1839–1906)
Uncle Dominique, c. 1865–1867
Oil on canvas, 18 ⅛ x 15 in. (46 x 38.1 cm)
[Jane Wade, New York, sold 25 September
1968 for $167,500 to]; Norton Simon Art
Foundation (M.1968.31).

Cat. 528
Aristide Maillol (French, 1861–1944)
Summer, 1910–1911
Bronze, edition of 6, unnumbered cast,
64 in. (162.6 cm)
[Dina Vierny, Paris, sold 30 September
1968 for $54,000 to]; Norton Simon Art
Foundation (M.1968.33).

Cat. 529
Francisco de Goya y Lucientes
(Spanish, 1746–1828)
Los Caprichos, 1st edition, c. 1797–1799
Etching, aquatint, and drypoint, 80 plates

(Sale, London, Sotheby & Co., 8 October 1968 for $25,119 to); Norton Simon Art Foundation, used in trade 2 August 1977 as part of a settlement agreement for the purchase of 118 Rembrandt etchings (cat. 1452) to; [Greater India Co. (Robert M. Light), Boston].

Cat. 530
Camille Pissarro (French, 1830–1903)
Bouquet of Flowers, 1876
Oil on canvas, 28 x 23 in. (71.1 x 58.4 cm)
(Sale, New York, Parke-Bernet Galleries, 9 October 1968 for $90,000 to); Norton Simon Art Foundation (sale, New York, Sotheby Parke Bernet, 2 May 1973, lot 24, for $150,000 to); [Marlborough Gallery, New York, sold 1974 to]; private collection, Madrid. private collection (sale, New York, Christie's, 2 May 2006, lot 3, unsold).

Cat. 531
Pierre-Auguste Renoir (French, 1841–1919)
The Pont des Arts, Paris, 1867–1868
Oil on canvas, 24 x 39 ½ in. (61 x 100.3 cm)
(Sale, New York, Parke-Bernet Galleries, 9 October 1968 for $1,550,000 to); The Norton Simon Foundation (F.1968.13).

Cat. 532
Pierre Bonnard (French, 1867–1947)
Views of Paris Life, 1899
Color lithographs, group of 13, each 21 x 16 in. (53.3 x 40.6 cm)
[Robert M. Light, Boston, sold 10 October 1968 for $16,704 to]; Norton Simon Art Foundation (M.1968.34.1.1–13).

Cat. 533
Pablo Picasso (Spanish, 1881–1973)
Balzac's "Le chef-d'oeuvre inconnu," 1927
Etchings, group of 13, each 9 ¾ x 13 in. (24.8 x 33 cm)
[Robert M. Light, Boston, sold 10 October 1968 for $4,305 to]; Norton Simon Art Foundation (M.1968.34.3.1–13).

Cat. 534
Pablo Picasso (Spanish, 1881–1973)
Ovid's "Metamorphoses," 1931
Etchings, group of 30,
each 13 x 10 in. (33 x 25.4 cm)
[Robert M. Light, Boston, sold 10 October 1968 for $8,908 to]; Norton Simon Art Foundation (M.1968.34.2.1–30).

Cat. 535
Giovanni Battista Piranesi
(Italian, 1720–1778)
Collected Etchings, c. 1750
Etchings, 97 on 91 plates,
each 21 ¾ x 16 ½ in. (55.3 x 41.9 cm)
[Robert M. Light, Boston, sold 10 October 1968 for $9,300 to]; Norton Simon Art Foundation (sale, New York, Sotheby Parke Bernet, 15 February 1979, lot 689, for $21,000).

Cat. 536
Walter Richard Sickert (English, 1860–1942)
Mornington Crescent Nude, 1907
Oil on canvas, 18 x 20 in. (45.7 x 50.8 cm)
[Arthur Tooth & Sons, London, sold 11 October 1968 for $8,000 to]; Norton Simon (sale, New York, Parke-Bernet Galleries, 5 May 1971, lot 50, for $8,500). [Thomas Agnew & Sons, London, sold to]; Mrs. Maurice Hill, U.K., gift, 1990 to; The Fitzwilliam Museum, Cambridge.

Cat. 537
Gerhard Marcks (German, 1889–1981)
Little Fiddler, 1962
Bronze, 7 in. (17.8 cm)
[Gallery Masters, New York, sold 14 October 1968 for $900 to]; Hunt Foods and Industries, Fullerton, gift 22 December 2009 by ConAgra Grocery Products LLC, (successor to Hunt Foods) to; Norton Simon Art Foundation (M.2009.3.1).

530

534

531

532

536

533

537

538A

543

544

545

546

Cat. 538A-B
Pierre Bonnard (French, 1867–1947)
Nudes
Lithographs, group of 2,
each 7 ⅞ x 5 ¾ in. (20 x 14.6 cm)
[Paul Prouté, Paris, sold 31 October 1968
for $98 to]; Norton Simon Art Foundation
(M.1968.50.3.1–2).

Cat. 539
Honoré Daumier (French, 1808–1879)
Lithographs, group of 11
[Paul Prouté, Paris, sold 31 October 1968 for
$1,078 to]; Norton Simon Art Foundation,
gift 30 November 1976 and 27 June 1977 to;
Norton Simon Museum in order to be sold
in the Museum store.

Cat. 540A-B
Maurice Denis (French, 1870–1943)
Madonna and Child, 1922
Etching, 10 x 13 ½ in. (25.4 x 34.3 cm)
Nativity, 1907
Color lithograph, 7 x 5 ½ in. (17.8 x 14 cm)
[Paul Prouté, Paris, sold 31 October 1968
for $196 to]; Norton Simon Art Foundation
(sale, Los Angeles, Sotheby Parke Bernet, 23
September 1980, lot 261a, for $400).

Cat. 541A-B
Maurice Denis (French, 1870–1943)
Nativity, 1907
Color lithograph, 7 x 5 ½ in. (17.8 x 14 cm)
Saint Geneviève of Paris, 1931
Color lithograph, 14 ¼ x 21 in.
(36.2 x 53.3 cm)
[Paul Prouté, Paris, sold 31 October 1968
for $196 to]; Norton Simon Art Foundation
(M.1968.50.1.1, 4).

Cat. 542A-B
Jean-Louis Forain (French, 1852–1931)
Man with Top Hat and Bouquet and *Two
Men in Tuxedos*
Lithographs, 10 ⅞ x 7 ¾ in. (27.6 x 19.7 cm)
and 6 ⅛ x 4 ⅜ in. (15.6 x 11.1 cm)

[Paul Prouté, Paris, sold 31 October 1968
for $196 to]; Norton Simon Art Foundation
(sale, Los Angeles, Sotheby Parke Bernet, 23
September 1980, for $200).

Cat. 543
Pablo Picasso (Spanish, 1881–1973)
Head of Fernande, 1905
Bronze, edition of 9, cast no. 7,
14 in. (35.6 cm)
[Stephen Hahn Gallery, New York, sold
31 October 1968 for $32,000 to]; Norton
Simon Art Foundation (M.1968.36).

Cat. 544
Pablo Picasso (Spanish, 1881–1973)
*Illustrations for "La Tauromaquia"
by Jose Delgado, Alias Pepe Illo*
Aquatints, group of 26, each 13 ¾ x 19 ¾ in.
(34.9 x 50.2 cm)
[Robert M. Light, Boston, sold 31 October
1968 for $5,846 to]; Norton Simon Art
Foundation (sale, Los Angeles, Sotheby
Parke Bernet, 23 September 1980, lot 396a,
for $15,000).

Cat. 545
Daniel de Monfreid (French, 1856–1929)
The Blue Coffee Pot, 1910
Oil on board, 25 ½ x 21 ½ in. (64.8 x 54.6 cm)
[Arthur Tooth & Sons, London, sold
31 October 1968 for $4,200 to]; Hunt Foods
and Industries, Fullerton, Calif., used in
trade 14 December 1979 as payment for
Josef Albers *Centennial Print–1* (cat. 744),
and two Pablo Picasso linocuts, *Dancers and
Musician* and *Still Life with a Bottle* (cat.
171) to, Norton Simon Inc. (sale, New York,
Sotheby Parke Bernet, 21 May 1981, lot 658,
for $19,000).

Cat. 546
Jean Arp (French, 1887–1966)
Classical Sculpture, 1960
Bronze, edition of 5, cast no. 2,
50 ⅝ in. (128.6 cm)

[Weintraub Gallery, New York, sold
31 October 1968 for $45,000 to]; Norton
Simon Art Foundation (M.1968.38).

Cat. 547
Claude Monet (French, 1840–1926)
The Coast of Normandy, 1882
Oil on canvas, 23 x 31 in. (58.5 x 78.7 cm)
[Stephen Hahn Gallery, New York, sold
1 November 1968 for $150,000 to]; Norton
Simon Art Foundation (sale, New York,
Sotheby Parke Bernet, 7 November 1979,
lot 544, for $180,000). [Yamaso Art Gallery,
Kyoto, 1987].

Cat. 548
Henri de Toulouse-Lautrec
(French, 1864–1901)
Elles
Color lithographs, set of 12, each 16 x 21 in.
(40.6 x 53.3 cm)
[Robert M. Light, Boston, sold 1 November
1968 for $22,000 to]; Norton Simon Art
Foundation, sold 9 July 1975 for $90,000 to;
[Robert M. Light, Boston, consigned 1975
to]; [Thomas Agnew & Sons, London].

Cat. 549
Jean-Antoine Watteau (French, 1684–1721)
Head of a Man, Two Studies of Hands
Black and red chalk, 9 ⅞ x 6 ⅞ in.
(25.1 x 17.5 cm)
[M. Knoedler & Co., New York, sold
1 November 1968 for $50,000 to]; Norton
Simon Art Foundation, used in trade
30 December 1977 with a value of $85,000
as partial payment for Rembrandt van
Rijn, *Portrait of a Bearded Man in a Wide-
Brimmed Hat* (cat. 1489) to]; [E. V. Thaw &
Co., New York, sold to]; private collection,
New York.

Cat. 550
Emil Nolde (German, 1867–1956)
Lonesome Couple
Watercolor, 10 ¼ x 9 ⅛ in. (26 x 23.2 cm)
[M. Knoedler & Co., New York, sold

14 November 1968 for $3,800 to]; Norton
Simon Art Foundation (sale, New York,
Sotheby Parke Bernet, 2 May 1974, lot 137,
for $17,500).

Cat. 551
Emil Nolde (German, 1867–1956)
Portrait of a Gentleman
Watercolor, 7 ⅞ x 6 in. (20 x 15.2 cm)
[M. Knoedler & Co., New York, sold
14 November 1968 for $3,400 to]; Norton
Simon Art Foundation (sale, New York,
Sotheby Parke Bernet, 2 May 1974, lot 142,
for $9,000 to); [Serge Sabarsky, New York].

Cat. 552
Emil Nolde (German, 1867–1956)
Woman's Head with Red Hair
Watercolor, 19 x 14 in. (48.3 x 35.6 cm)
[M. Knoedler & Co., New York, sold 14
November 1968 for $6,000 to]; Norton
Simon Art Foundation (sale, London,
Sotheby & Co., 2 April 1974, lot 57, unsold;
later sold for $15,120 to); [Kende Gallery,
New York].

Cat. 553
David Smith (American, 1906–1965)
Zig II, 1961
Steel, painted black with three reds,
100 ⅝ in. (255.6 cm)
[Marlborough-Gerson Gallery, New York,
sold 14 November 1968 for $35,000 to];
Norton Simon Art Foundation (sale, New
York, Sotheby Parke Bernet, 26 October
1972, lot 16, for $80,000 to); Des Moines Art
Center.

Cat. 554
Auguste Rodin (French, 1840–1917)
Large Torso of a Man, c. 1898
Bronze, edition of 12, cast no. 1,
36 in. (91.4 cm)
Musée Rodin, Paris, sold 18 November
1968 for $16,147 to; Norton Simon Art
Foundation (sale, New York, Parke-Bernet
Galleries, 13 May 1970, lot 29, for $11,000).

547

551

548

552

549

553

550

554

555

560

556

557

561

558

562

559

Cat. 555
Adolphe-Joseph-Thomas Monticelli
(French, 1824–1886)
Flowers, 1870–1880
Oil on panel, 24 ¼ x 19 in. (61.6 x 48.3 cm)
[Alex Reid & Lefevre, London, sold
20 November 1968 for $30,000 to]; Norton
Simon Art Foundation (M.1968.45).

Cat. 556
Robert Clark (American, 1920–1997)
Richard, 1968
Egg tempera on panel, 24 x 32 in.
(61 x 81.3 cm)
[Zantman Art Galleries, Carmel, Calif., sold
20 November 1968 for $3,675 to]; Norton
Simon Art Foundation, sold 18 July 1980
for $3,300 through [Zantman Art Galleries,
Carmel, Calif.] to; private collection.

Cat. 557
Robert Clark (American, 1920–1997)
Studies of a Young Man
Egg tempera on panel, 24 x 36 in.
(61 x 91.4 cm)
[Zantman Art Galleries, Carmel, Calif., sold
20 November 1968 for $1,575 to]; Norton
Simon Art Foundation, sold 18 July 1980
for $1,500 through [Zantman Art Galleries,
Carmel, Calif.] to; private collection.

Cat. 558
Pablo Picasso (Spanish, 1881–1973)
Nude Combing Her Hair, 1906
Oil on canvas, 41 x 31 ½ in. (104.1 x 80 cm)
[Paul Rosenberg & Co., New York, sold
25 November 1968 for $680,000 to]; Norton
Simon Art Foundation, sold 1 June 1982
for $4 million to; Kimbell Art Museum,
Fort Worth.

Cat. 559
Paul Cézanne (French, 1839–1906)
Temptation of Saint Anthony, 1872–1877
Watercolor, 3 ½ x 5 ⅛ in. (8.9 x 13 cm)
[Hirschl & Adler Galleries, New York, sold

11 December 1968 for $13,000 to]; Norton
Simon Art Foundation (sale, London,
Sotheby & Co., 2 April 1974, lot 40, for
$19,200 to); [Jan Krugier, Geneva]. (sale,
London, Sotheby's, 3 December 1991, lot 16,
for £45,000).

Cat. 560
Pablo Picasso (Spanish, 1881–1973)
Two Heads of Women, 1906
Gouache on brown paper,
17 x 23 in. (43.2 x 58.4 cm)
[Hirschl & Adler Galleries, New York, sold
11 December 1968 for $165,000 to]; Norton
Simon Art Foundation (sale, New York,
Sotheby Parke Bernet, 2 May 1973, lot 44,
for $250,000). Hakone Open Air Museum,
Japan.

Cat. 561
Henri-Horace Roland de la Porte
(French, c. 1724–1793)
Still Life, c. 1765
Oil on canvas, 20 ⅞ x 25 ½ in.
(53 x 64.8 cm)
[Old Masters Galleries, London (Herner
& Wengraf), sold 17 December 1968 for
$14,000 to]; Norton Simon Art Foundation
(M.1968.48).

1969

Cat. 562
Henry Moore (English, 1898–1986)
Upright Motive No. 8, 1955–1956
Bronze, edition of 7, unnumbered cast,
84 ½ x 24 x 21 in. (214.6 x 61 x 53.3 cm)
Mary Moore, Much Hadham, England, sold
2 January 1969 for $20,200 to; The Norton
Simon Foundation (F.1969.1).

Cat. 563
Honoré Daumier (French, 1808–1879)
Croquis du jour
Lithograph, 3rd state, 13 ½ x 10 ³/₁₆ in.
(34.3 x 25.9 cm)

[P. & D. Colnaghi, London, sold 6 January 1969 for $22 to]; Norton Simon Art Foundation (sale, Los Angeles, Sotheby Parke Bernet, 16 June 1980, lot 668, for $125).

Cat. 564
Pierre-Auguste Renoir (French, 1841–1919)
Reclining Nude, c. 1892
Oil on canvas, 13 x 16 ⅜ in. (33 x 41.6 cm)
[Stephen Hahn Gallery, New York, sold 9 January 1969 for $110,000 to]; Norton Simon Art Foundation (M.1969.2).

Cat. 565
Pierre-Auguste Renoir (French, 1841–1919)
Girl in a Yellow Hat, 1885
Oil on canvas, 26 ¼ x 21 ⅝ in. (66.7 x 54.9 cm)
[Wildenstein & Co., New York, sold 9 January 1969 for $425,000 to]; Norton Simon Art Foundation, sold 5 February 1982 for $1 million to; [E. V. Thaw & Co., New York, sold to]; [Acquavella Galleries, New York] (sale, New York, Sotheby's, 14 November 1984, lot 21, for $1,900,000 to); private collection.

Cat. 566A–F
Jean-Louis Forain (French, 1852–1931)
The Miracle at Lourdes
Etching with drypoint, 2nd state, 10 ³/₁₆ x 13 ⅝ in. (25.9 x 34.6 cm)
Study of a Nude Woman, Her head on a Pillow; *Before the Supper at Emmaus*; *After the Execution*; *The Miracle at Lourdes*; and *Three drawings on one sheet*
Six etchings and lithographs
[P. & D. Colnaghi, London, sold 16 January 1969 for $650 to]; Norton Simon Art Foundation (cat. 566a: sale, Los Angeles, Sotheby Parke Bernet, 23 September 1980, lot 268a, for $200); (cat. 566b–f: sale, Los Angeles, Sotheby Parke Bernet, 16 June 1980, for $1,000).

Cat. 567
Marie-Louise-Élisabeth Vigée-Lebrun (French, 1755–1842)
Theresa, Countess Kinsky, 1793
Oil on canvas, 54 ⅛ x 39 ⅜ in. (137.5 x 100 cm)
[Schaeffer Galleries, New York, sold 16 January 1969 for $50,000 to]; Norton Simon Art Foundation (M.1969.3).

Cat. 568
Wilhelm Lehmbruck (German, 1881–1919)
Head of a Woman, 1913–1914
Plaster, 17 ¼ x 13 ¾ x 8 ¼ in. (43.8 x 34.9 x 21 cm)
[Jane Wade, New York, sold 20 January 1969 for $12,500 to]; Norton Simon Art Foundation (M.1969.8).

Cat. 569
Jan Steen (Dutch, 1626–1679)
Wine Is a Mocker, c. 1668–1670
Oil on canvas, 34 ⅜ x 41 ¼ in. (87.3 x 104.8 cm)
[G. Cramer, The Hague, sold 5 February 1969 for $46,779 to]; Norton Simon Art Foundation (M.1969.5).

Cat. 570
Edgar Degas (French, 1834–1917)
Woman Drying Her Hair, c. 1900–1908
Pastel, 28 x 24 ½ in. (71.1 x 62.2 cm)
[Alex Reid & Lefevre, London, sold 6 February 1969 for $240,000 to]; Norton Simon Art Foundation (sale, New York, Christie's, 19 May 1982, lot 15, unsold) (M.1969.6).

Cat. 571
Studio of Pierre-Paul Prud'hon (French, 1758–1823)
Study of a Male Nude
Black chalk on gray-blue paper, 24 x 18 ¼ in. (61 x 46.4 cm)
[Paul Botte, Paris, sold 10 February 1969 for $500 to]; Norton Simon, gift 30 December 1975 to; Norton Simon Art Foundation (M.1975.22).

567

564

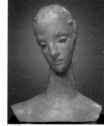
568

569

570

571

565

572

576

573

577

574

578

575

579

Cat. 572
Pablo Picasso (Spanish, 1881–1973)
Head of a Woman, 1909
Bronze, edition of 9, cast no. 3,
16 ¼ in. (41.3 cm)
[Stephen Hahn Gallery, New York, sold
19 February 1969 for $66,000 to]; Norton
Simon Art Foundation (M.1969.7).

Cat. 573
Emil Nolde (German, 1867–1956)
Couple (Violet and Blue), c. 1941–1945
Watercolor, 7 ⅜ x 5 ⅜ in. (18.7 x 13.7 cm)
Stiftung Seebull Ada und Emil Nolde,
Seebull, sold 26 February 1969 for $5,470
to; Norton Simon Art Foundation (sale,
London, Sotheby & Co., 3 July 1974, lot 164,
for $7,020 to); [Kende Gallery, New York].

Cat. 574
Emil Nolde (German, 1867–1956)
Red Poppies, c. 1925–1930
Watercolor, 13 ½ x 18 ¾ in. (34.3 x 47.6 cm)
Stiftung Seebull Ada und Emil Nolde,
Seebull, sold 26 February 1969 for $10,440
to; Norton Simon Art Foundation (sale,
London, Sotheby & Co., 3 July 1974, lot 163,
for $25,740 to); [Achim Moeller, New York].
[Roman Norbert Ketterer, Lugano, sold to];
private collection, Germany (sale, Cologne,
Van Ham Kunstauktionen, 9 June 2005, lot
555, for $207,842).

Cat. 575
Emil Nolde (German, 1867–1956)
Two Farmhouses under Red Skies,
c. 1920–1925
Watercolor, 8 ⅞ x 10 ¾ in. (22.5 x 27.3 cm)
Stiftung Seebull Ada und Emil Nolde,
Seebull, sold 26 February 1969 for $6,200 to;
Norton Simon Art Foundation (M.69.9.3)
(sale, New York, Sotheby Parke Bernet, 2
April 1974, lot 55, for $25,200 to); Thyssen-
Bornemisza Collection, Madrid.

Cat. 576
Emil Nolde (German, 1867–1956)
*Woman's Portrait (Red-Brown and Blue
Hair)*, c. 1920–1925
Watercolor, 18 ¾ x 13 ¾ in. (47.6 x 34.9 cm)
Stiftung Seebull Ada und Emil Nolde,
Seebull, sold 26 February 1969 for $7,455 to;
Norton Simon Art Foundation (sale, New
York, Sotheby Parke Bernet, 2 May 1974, lot
138, for $38,000).

Cat. 577
Wilhelm Lehmbruck (German, 1881–1919)
Standing Woman, 1910
Bronze, 75 ¾ in. (192.4 cm)
[Guido Lehmbruck, sold 28 February
1969 for $119,763 to]; Norton Simon Art
Foundation (M.1969.10).

Cat. 578
Georges Rouault (French, 1871–1958)
Miserere, 1922–1927
Etchings, set of 58, 34/450,
each 25 ¾ x 20 in. (65.4 x 50.8 cm)
(Sale, New York, Parke-Bernet Galleries, 5
March 1969 for $12,075 to); Norton Simon
Art Foundation (M.1969.12.4.1–58).

Cat. 579
Pablo Picasso (Spanish, 1881–1973)
Head of a Jester, 1905
Bronze, unnumbered edition, Vollard cast,
15 ¾ x 14 ½ x 9 ½ in. (40 x 36.8 x 24.1 cm)
[Stephen Hahn Gallery, New York, sold 10
March 1969 for $67,029 to]; Norton Simon
Art Foundation (M.1969.11).

Cat. 580
Max Beckmann (German, 1884–1950)
Jahrmarkt (The Fair), 1922
Drypoint, portfolio of 10,
each 12 ⅝ x 9 ⅞ in. (32 x 25 cm)
[Robert M. Light, Boston, sold 11 March
1969 for $4,500 to]; Norton Simon Art

Foundation, sold 13 February 1974 for
$5,500 to; [Robert M. Light, Boston, to];
[Karl & Faber, Munich].

Cat. 581
Eugène Delacroix (French, 1798–1863)
Hamlet, 1834–1843
Lithographs, set of 14
[Robert M. Light, Boston, sold 11 March
1969 for $3,700 to]; Norton Simon Art
Foundation (M.1969.12.2.1–14).

Cat. 582
Francisco de Goya y Lucientes
(Spanish, 1746–1828)
Spanish Entertainment from *The Bulls of
Bordeaux*, 1825
Lithograph, proof: image, 11 ⅞ x 16 ¼ in.
(30.2 x 41.3 cm); sheet, 18 ¼ x 21 ¹/₁₆ in.
(46.4 x 53.5 cm)
[Robert M. Light, Boston, sold 11 March
1969 for $15,750 to]; Norton Simon Art
Foundation (M.1969.12.3).

Cat. 583
Marc Chagall (French, b. Russia, 1887–1985)
The Violinist, 1911
Oil on canvas, 37 x 27 ½ in. (94 x 69.9 cm)
R. Sturgis Ingersoll, sold through [Jane
Wade Ltd., New York] 11 March 1969 for
$120,000 to; Norton Simon Art Foundation,
sold 10 April 1974 for $425,000 to;
[Marlborough A.G., Vaduz, Liechtenstein,
sold 1975 to]; Kunstsammlung Nordrhein-
Westfalen, Düsseldorf.

Cat. 584
Giovanni Bellini (Italian, c. 1430–1516)
Joerg Fugger, 1474
Oil on panel, 10 ¼ x 7 ⅞ in. (26 x 20 cm)
Lorenzo Papi, Florence [through Stanley
Moss], sold 11 March 1969 for $220,000 to;
Norton Simon Art Foundation (M.1969.13).

Cat. 585
Jean-Baptiste Camille Corot (French,
1796–1875)
Peasant at Prayer, c. 1840–1845
Oil on canvas, 19 ½ x 14 ¼ in.
(49.5 x 36.2 cm)
[Galerie Claude Bernard, Paris, sold
12 March 1969 for $26,500 to]; Norton
Simon Art Foundation (sale, New York,
Parke-Bernet Galleries, 13 May 1970, lot 10,
for $10,000). (sale, New York, Christie's,
27 May 1992, lot 143 to); private collection,
Japan.

Cat. 586
Barbara Hepworth (English, 1903–1975)
Four Square: Walk Through, 1966
Bronze, edition of 3, cast no. 1,
169 x 88 x 78 ½ in. (429.3 x 223.5 x 199.4 cm)
[Marlborough Alte und Moderne Kunst,
Schellenberg, Switzerland, sold 13 March
1969 for $45,000 to]; Norton Simon Art
Foundation (M.1969.15).

Cat. 587
Pierre-Auguste Renoir (French, 1841–1919)
Venus Victorious, 1914
Bronze, edition of 5, cast E, 70 in. (177.8 cm)
Mr. and Mrs. Jean Renoir, Los Angeles,
sold 20 March 1969 for $60,000 to; Norton
Simon Art Foundation (M.1969.16).

Cat. 588
Richard Earlom (English, 1743–1822)
Liber Veritatis
Mezzotints after Claude Lorrain,
group of 200
(Sale, London, Sotheby & Co., 25 March
1969 for $905 to); Norton Simon Art
Foundation, gift 27 June 1977 to; Norton
Simon Museum in order to be sold in the
Museum store.

581

585

582

586

583

587

584

589

594

590

595

596

592

593

Cat. 589
Hendrik Goltzius (Dutch, 1558–1617)
Hercules Slaying Cacus
Woodcut, 16 ½ x 13 in. (41.9 x 33 cm)
(Sale, London, Sotheby & Co., 25 March
1969 for $2,025 to); Norton Simon Art
Foundation, sold 14 April 1974 for $5,500 to;
[Robert M. Light, Boston, consigned to];
[August Laube, Zurich].

Cat. 590
Henri Matisse (French, 1869–1954)
Reclining Nude
Pen and ink, 11 x 15 ½ in. (27.9 x 39.4 cm)
[Galerie Claude Bernard, Paris, sold
25 March 1969 for $16,500 to]; Norton Simon
Art Foundation (sale, New York, Sotheby
Parke Bernet, 2 May 1973, lot 33, for $31,000
to); [Frank Perls, Beverly Hills, Calif.].

Cat. 591
Giovanni Francesco Romanelli
(Italian, 1610–1662)
Dido's Banquet, c. 1630–1635
Gouache and black chalk on paper, laid
down on linen, 111 x 231 in. (281.9 x 586.7 cm)
(Sale, London, Sotheby & Co., 26 March
1969 for $14,400 to); Norton Simon Art
Foundation (M.1969.26.2).

Cat. 592
Giovanni Francesco Romanelli
(Italian, 1610–1662)
Dido's Sacrifice to Juno, c. 1630–1635
Gouache and black chalk on paper,
laid down on linen, 109 x 166 in.
(276.9 x 421.6 cm)
(Sale, London, Sotheby & Co., 26 March
1969 for $16,800 to); Norton Simon Art
Foundation (M.1969.26.1).

Cat. 593
Giovanni Francesco Romanelli
(Italian, 1610–1662)
Death of Dido, c. 1630–1635
Gouache and black chalk on paper,

laid down on linen, 109 x 166 in.
(276.9 x 421.6 cm)
(Sale, London, Sotheby & Co., 26 March
1969 for $9,600 to); Norton Simon Art
Foundation (M.1969.27).

Cat. 594
Follower of William van de Velde the
Younger (1633–1707), formerly attributed to
Abraham Storck (1644–1708)
Vessels Offshore in a Calm, c. 1670
Oil on canvas, 15 ½ x 20 in. (39.4 x 50.8 cm)
(Sale, London, Sotheby & Co., 26 March
1969 for $11,202 to); Norton Simon Art
Foundation (M.1969.24.5).

Cat. 595
Annibale Carracci (Italian, 1560–1609)
A Study of the Head of a Young Man, c. 1590
Red chalk, 8 ⅝ x 7 ¼ in. (22 x 18.4 cm)
(Sale, London, Sotheby & Co., 27 March
1969 for $7,865 to); Norton Simon Art
Foundation (sale, London, Sotheby & Co.,
27 June 1974, lot 25, for $10,080).

Cat. 596
Rembrandt van Rijn (Dutch, 1606–1669)
Dido Divides the Ox Hide (also known as
King Solomon and the Queen of Sheba),
1640–1641
Pen and ink with wash, 8 x 11 in.
(20.3 x 27.9 cm)
(Sale, London, Sotheby & Co., 27 March
1969 for $75,080 to); Norton Simon Art
Foundation, used in trade 30 December
1977 with a value of $200,000 as partial
payment for Rembrandt, *Portrait of a Man
in a Wide-Brimmed Hat* (cat. 1489) to; [E.
V. Thaw & Co., New York, sold 1987 to];
Leonardo Mondadori, Milan, by descent to;
private collection, Milan.

Cat. 597
Hubert Robert (French, 1733–1808)
A View of Tivoli
Red chalk, 11 ½ x 16 ½ in. (29.2 x 41.9 cm)

(Sale, London, Sotheby & Co., 27 March 1969 for $2,264 to); Norton Simon Art Foundation (sale, London, Sotheby & Co., 27 June 1974, lot 39, for $5,040).

Cat. 598
Eugène Delacroix (French, 1798–1863)
Wounded Arab at the Feet of His Horse
Watercolor, 10 ⅛ x 13 ½ in. (25.7 x 34.3 cm)
[André Lorenceau, Allschwil, Switzerland, sold 2 April 1969 for $37,500 to]; Norton Simon Art Foundation (sale, London, Sotheby & Co., 2 April 1974, lot 38, for $72,000 to); [David Ellis-Jones, New York].

Cat. 599
Georges Rouault (French, 1871–1958)
Three Women, c. 1930
Oil on paper on canvas, 20 ⅞ x 16 ¹⁵/₁₆ in. (53 x 43 cm)
[Stephen Hahn Gallery, New York, sold 14 April 1969 for $41,150 to]; Norton Simon Art Foundation, used in trade 13 January 1971 with a value of $70,000 as partial payment for Lucas Cranach, *Adam* (cat. 742) to; [Spencer A. Samuels & Co., New York].

Cat. 600
Jan van Goyen (Dutch, 1596–1656)
Winter Scene with Skaters, 1640
Oil on panel, 15 ¼ x 21 ¾ in. (38.7 x 55.3 cm)
[Société pour le Commerce des Tableaux, S.A., Geneva (Heim Gallery, Paris), sold 17 April 1969 for $60,000 to]; Norton Simon Art Foundation, sold 6 June 1978 for $138,540 to; [Robert Noortman, London].

Cat. 601
Stanislas-Victor-Édouard Lépine (French, 1836–1892)
The Pont de l'Estacade, Paris, c. 1880–1884
Oil on canvas, 10 ⅝ x 16 ⅛ in. (27 x 41 cm)
[Robert Schmit, Paris, sold 17 April 1969 for $22,182 to]; Norton Simon Art Foundation (M.1969.19).

Cat. 602
Edvard Munch (Norwegian, 1863–1944)
The Death Chamber, c. 1896
Lithograph, 15 ¼ x 23 ⅛ in. (38.7 x 58.7 cm)
[Frank Perls, Beverly Hills, Calif., sold 17 April 1969 for $6,000 to]; Norton Simon Art Foundation, sold 25 February 1980 for $6,000 to; [Margo P. Schab, New York].

Cat. 603
Edvard Munch (Norwegian, 1863–1944)
Jealousy II, 1896
Lithograph, 18 ⅞ x 22 ⅞ in. (47.9 x 58.1 cm)
[Frank Perls, Beverly Hills, Calif., sold 17 April 1969 for $5,500 to]; Norton Simon Art Foundation, sold 1 September 1974 for $5,500 to; [Margo P. Schab, New York].

Cat. 604
Edvard Munch (Norwegian, 1863–1944)
Madonna, 1895–1902
Lithograph, 23 ⅞ x 17 ½ in. (60.6 x 44.5 cm)
[Frank Perls, Beverly Hills, Calif., sold 17 April 1969 for $28,000 to]; Norton Simon Art Foundation, sold 23 September 1974 for $55,000 to; [Fischer Fine Art, London].

Cat. 605
Edvard Munch (Norwegian, 1863–1944)
Self-Portrait, 1895
Lithograph, 18 ¼ x 12 ¾ in. (46.4 x 32.4 cm)
[Frank Perls, Beverly Hills, Calif., sold 17 April 1969 for $5,500 to]; Norton Simon Art Foundation, sold 1 September 1974 for $5,500 to; [Margo P. Schab, New York].

Cat. 606
Pierre-Auguste Renoir (French, 1841–1919)
Madame Renoir Nursing Her Baby, 1886
Oil on canvas, 31 ½ x 25 ½ in. (80 x 64.8 cm)
[M. Knoedler & Co., New York, sold one-half interest 17 April 1969 for $240,000 to; The Norton Simon Foundation [other one-half interest owned by Acquavella Galleries, New York, who sold the one-half interest November 1972 to Marlborough

597

602

598

603

599

604

600

605

601

606

607

611

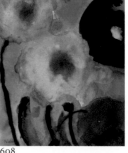

612

608

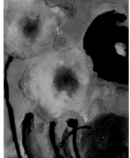

609

613

610

614

Gallery, New York], foundation's one-half interest sold 16 April 1973 for $400,000 to; [Marlborough A.G., Vaduz, Liechtenstein]; (sale, New York, Sotheby Parke Bernet, 20 October 1976, lot 15, for $600,000 to); private collection, Japan (sale, New York, Christie's, 5 May 1998, lot 32, unsold).

Cat. 607
Emil Nolde (German, 1867–1956)
Man and Nude Woman
Watercolor, 5 ½ x 8 ¾ in. (14 x 22.2 cm)
[Galerie des Arts Anciens et Modernes, Schaan, Liechtenstein, sold 23 April 1969 for $7,500 to]; Norton Simon Art Foundation (sale, London, Sotheby's, 3 July 1974, lot 165, for $7,020 to); [Kende Gallery, New York].

Cat. 608
Emil Nolde (German, 1867–1956)
Red, Yellow, and Blue Flowers
Watercolor, 9 ¼ x 6 ⅞ in. (23.5 x 17.5 cm)
[Galerie des Arts Anciens et Modernes, Schaan, Liechtenstein, sold 23 April 1969 for $7,500 to; Norton Simon Art Foundation (sale, London, Sotheby & Co., 2 April 1974, lot 56, for $21,600 to); [Fischer Fine Art, London].

Cat. 609
Pablo Picasso (Spanish, 1881–1973)
Prints from the series *347*, 1968
Etchings and aquatints, group of 29, 44/50
[Galerie des Arts Anciens et Modernes, Schaan, Liechtenstein, sold 23 April 1969 for $50,000 to]; Norton Simon Art Foundation (M.1969.21.2.1–29).

Cat. 610
Jackson Pollock (American, 1912–1956)
Etchings, 1944/1945
Etchings, group of 7
[Galerie des Arts Anciens et Modernes, Schaan, Liechtenstein, sold 23 April 1969 for $5,000 to]; Norton Simon Art Foundation (sale, Los Angeles, Sotheby Parke Bernet, 16 June 1980, lots 761–767, for $19,350).

Cat. 611
Käthe Kollwitz (German, 1867–1945)
Self-Portrait, Turned to the Left, 1901
Lithograph, working proof, 16 ⅛ x 13 ⅛ in. (41 x 33.3 cm)
[Marlborough-Gerson Gallery, New York, sold 29 April 1969 for $4,350 to]; Norton Simon Art Foundation (M.1969.22).

Cat. 612
Johan Barthold Jongkind (Dutch, 1819–1891)
The Farmhouse
Pencil and watercolor, 8 ½ x 11 ¼ in. (21.6 x 28.6 cm)
(Sale, London, Sotheby & Co., 1 May 1969 for $2,000 to); The Norton Simon Foundation (sale, New York, Sotheby Parke Bernet, 2 May 1973, lot 16, for $4,000 to); Samuel J. LeFrak, New York, by inheritance to; LeFrak Family Collection, New York.

Cat. 613
Henry Moore (English, 1898–1986)
Family Group, 1944
Bronze, edition of 9, unnumbered cast, 6 in. (15.2 cm)
[M. Knoedler & Co., New York, sold 1 May 1969 for $18,000 to]; The Norton Simon Foundation, sold 22 February 1982 for $75,000 to; [Jeffrey H. Loria & Co., New York].

Cat. 614
Camille Pissarro (French, 1830–1903)
View of Pontoise, 1873
Oil on canvas, 20 ⅞ x 31 ⅞ in. (53 x 81 cm)
(Sale, London, Christie's, 2 May 1969 for $213,269 to); The Norton Simon Foundation, used in trade 19 December 1969 with a value of $229,340 as payment for Claude Monet, *Entrance to the Port of Le Havre* (cat. 708) to; [Galerie Castiglione, Schaan, Liechtenstein (Alex Reid & Lefevre), sold one-half interest 15 December 1976 for $83,504 to]; Norton Simon, traded one-half interest 5 January 1979 with a

value of $83,504 as payment for Francois Boucher, *The Beautiful Country Woman* (cat. 1565), Paul-Camille Guigou, *Landscape in Southern France* (cat. 1566), and Joseph Werner, *Louis XIV* and *Mlle de la Valliere in Costume* (cat. 1567) to; [Wildenstein & Co., New York, sold 1980 to]; private collection, Dallas.

Cat. 615
Georges Rouault (French, 1871–1958)
Two Nudes (The Sirens), 1906
Gouache, 27 x 21 ½ in. (68.6 x 54.6 cm)
[Jane Wade, New York, sold 5 May 1969 for $70,000 to]; Norton Simon Art Foundation (M.1969.25).

Cat. 616
Attributed to Philippe de Champaigne (French, 1602–1674)
Abbess of the Trinitarians, Caen
Oil on canvas, 39 x 31 in. (99.1 x 78.7 cm)
[Paul Botte, Paris, sold 7 May 1969 for $10,000 to]; Hunt Foods and Industries, Fullerton, Calif., gift 14 December 1979 to; Norton Simon, by inheritance 2 June 1993 to; Jennifer Jones Simon Art Trust, Los Angeles (N.1979.20).

Cat. 617
Nicolas Lancret (French, 1690–1743)
Standing Woman
Red chalk, 9 ¼ x 5 ⅞ in. (23.5 x 14.9 cm)
[Paul Botte, Paris, gift 7 May 1969 to]; Norton Simon (sale, New York, Parke-Bernet Galleries, 8 May 1971, lot 204, for $350).

Cat. 618
Alexander Calder (American, 1898–1976)
Black Saucers, 1968
Gouache, 43 x 29 ⅜ in. (109.2 x 74.6 cm)
[Perls Galleries, New York, sold 14 May 1969 for $1,350 to]; Hunt Foods & Industries, Fullerton, Calif., gift 5 January 1983 to; Norton Simon Museum (P.1984.1.1).

Cat. 619
Alexander Calder (American, 1898–1976)
Black Sun and Fern, 1967
Gouache, 29 ⅜ x 43 in. (74.6 x 109.2 cm)
[Perls Galleries, New York, sold 14 May 1969 for $1,350 to]; Hunt Foods & Industries, Fullerton, Calif., sold 29 May 1981 for $1,350 to; William H. Hinkle, Los Angeles.

Cat. 620
Alexander Calder (American, 1898–1976)
Hovering Bowties
Gouache, 22 ¾ x 30 ¾ in. (57.8 x 78.1 cm)
[Perls Galleries, New York, sold 14 May 1969 for $1,080 to]; Hunt Foods & Industries, Fullerton, Calif., sold 29 May 1981 for $1,080 to; William H. Hinkle, Los Angeles.

Cat. 621
Alexander Calder (American, 1898–1976)
Maelstrom with Blue, 1967
Gouache, 43 x 29 ⅛ in. (109.2 x 74 cm)
[Perls Galleries, New York, sold 14 May 1969 for $1,350 to]; Hunt Foods & Industries, Fullerton, Calif., sold 29 May 1981 for $1,350 to; William H. Hinkle, Los Angeles, gift 29 December 1986 to; Norton Simon Museum (P.1986.1).

Cat. 622
Alexander Calder (American, 1898–1976)
On the Blue, 1944
Gouache, 22 ½ x 30 ½ in. (57.2 x 77.5 cm)
[Perls Galleries, New York, sold 14 May 1969 for $2,160 to]; Hunt Foods & Industries, Fullerton, Calif., gift 5 January 1983 to; Norton Simon Museum (P.1984.1.2).

Cat. 623
Alexander Calder (American, 1898–1976)
The Triangular Maze, 1967
Gouache, 29 ¼ x 43 in. (74.3 x 109.2 cm)
[Perls Galleries, New York, sold 14 May 1969 for $1,350 to]; Hunt Foods & Industries, Fullerton, Calif., gift 5 January 1983 to; Norton Simon Museum (P.1984.1.3).

615

616

617

618

619

620

621

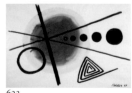
622

623

624

628

625

629

626

630

627

631

Cat. 624
Léon Lhermitte (French, 1844–1925)
View of Chateau-Thierry
Pastel, 25 ¼ x 33 ¼ in. (64.1 x 84.5 cm)
[Bernard Lorenceau, Paris, sold 14 May
1969 for $2,500 to]; Norton Simon Art
Foundation (sale, New York, Sotheby Parke
Bernet, 2 May 1973, lot 22, for $3,500 to);
[Ira Spanierman, New York].

Cat. 625
Richard Parkes Bonington (1802–1828)
The Visit, or the Use of Tears, 1827
Watercolor, 9 ¾ x 6 ¾ in. (24.8 x 17.2 cm)
[Arthur Tooth & Sons, London, sold 15 May
1969 for $12,000 ($3,600 plus $8,400 credit
on trade of Édouard Manet, *Woman in a
Hat, Turned to the Left* [cat. 273]) to; Norton
Simon Art Foundation (sale, London,
Sotheby Parke Bernet & Co., 10 July 1980,
lot 145, for $37,950).

Cat. 626
Pietro Longhi (Italian, 1702–1785)
Artist Sketching an Elegant Company, c. 1760
Oil on canvas, 24 ⅛ x 19 ½ in.
(61.3 x 49.5 cm)
[Hallsborough Gallery, London, sold
16 May 1969 for $120,000 to]; The Norton
Simon Foundation (F.1969.3).

Cat. 627
Francisco de Goya y Lucientes (Spanish,
1746–1828)
Los Caprichos, 1st edition, c. 1797–1799
Etching, aquatint, and drypoint with hand
coloring, 80 plates
[Robert M. Light, Boston, sold 20 May
1969 for $10,500 to]; The Norton Simon
Foundation (F.1969.4.1–80).

Cat. 628
Edgar Degas (French, 1834–1917)
Dancers in Pink, c. 1883
Pastel on paper, mounted on board,

28 ½ x 15 ¼ in. (72.4 x 38.7 cm)
[E. V. Thaw & Co., New York, sold 20 May
1969 for $230,000 to]; The Norton Simon
Foundation (sale, London, Sotheby Parke
Bernet & Co., 1 July 1980, lot 32a, unsold)
(F.1969.5.1).

Cat. 629
Francesco Guardi (Italian, 1712–1793)
Venetian Courtyard
Watercolor, pen and bistre, 7 x 7 ⅞ in.
(17.8 x 20 cm)
[E. V. Thaw & Co., New York, sold 20 May
1969 for $42,000 to]; The Norton Simon
Foundation, used in trade with a value of
$50,000 as partial payment for Giovanni
Paolo Pannini, *Interior of Saint Peter's,
Rome* (cat. 1009) to; [E. V. Thaw & Co.,
New York]; Eugene V. and Clare E. Thaw,
promised gift to; The Pierpont Morgan
Library, New York.

Cat. 630
Constantin Brancusi (Romanian, 1876–1957)
Little Bird, 1927
Marble on limestone base, 49 ¾ in.
(126.4 cm)
[Jane Wade, New York, sold 28 May 1969
for $200,000 to]; The Norton Simon
Foundation, sold 16 April 1974 for $850,000
to; [Marlborough Gallery, New York].
[Thomas Ammann Fine Art, Zurich, sold
to]; private collection, Switzerland. [Jason
McCoy, New York, sold 1997 to]; private
collection, New York.

Cat. 631
Henry Moore (English, 1898–1986)
*Working Model for Three-Way Piece No. 1:
Points*, 1964
Bronze, edition of 7, cast no. 5,
25 x 27 x 28 in. (63.5 x 68.6 x 71.1 cm)
[M. Knoedler & Co., New York, sold 28 May
1969 for $25,000 to]; The Norton Simon
Foundation (F.1969.7).

Cat. 632
Gustave Courbet (French, 1819–1877)
Cliffs at Étretat, the Porte d'Aval, 1869
Oil on canvas, 25 ¾ x 32 in. (65.4 x 81.3 cm)
R. Sturgis Ingersoll through [Jane Wade,
New York], sold 29 May 1969 for $69,500 to;
The Norton Simon Foundation (F.1969.6.2).

Cat. 633
Pierre Bonnard (French, 1867–1947)
The Place Clichy, Paris, 1900
Oil on cardboard, triptych: left panel,
13 ¾ x 9 ½ in. (34.9 x 24.1 cm); center panel,
13 ¼ x 20 ½ in. (33.7 x 52.2 cm); right panel,
13 ½ x 8 ¾ in. (34.3 x 22.2 cm)
[Hirschl & Adler Galleries, New York, sold
6 June 1969 for $200,000 to]; The Norton
Simon Foundation (F.1969.9).

Cat. 634
Johan Barthold Jongkind (Dutch, 1819–1891)
View of Harfleur, 1852
Oil on canvas, 17 x 23 ½ in. (43.2 x 59.5 cm)
[Robert Schmit, Paris, sold 6 June 1969 for
$22,000 to]; The Norton Simon Foundation
(F.1969.8.2).

Cat. 635
Stanislas-Victor-Édouard Lépine (French,
1836–1892)
The Pont Neuf, Paris, c. 1875–1879
Oil on canvas, 9 x 13 in. (22.9 x 33 cm)
[Robert Schmit, Paris, sold 6 June 1969 for
$21,000 to]; The Norton Simon Foundation
(F.1969.8.1).

Cat. 636
Jan Massys (Flemish, c. 1509–1575)
Susanna and the Elders, 1564
Oil on panel, 42 x 77 ½ in.
(106.7 x 196.9 cm)
(Sale, Paris, Galerie René Drouet, through
[Sylvia Blatas, Paris], 11 June 1969 for
$36,892 to); The Norton Simon Foundation,
transferred 23 November 2005 to; Norton
Simon Art Foundation (M.2005.2).

Cat. 637
Georges Rouault (French, 1871–1958)
At the Café, 1905
Watercolor and gouache, 9 ¾ x 8 in.
(24.8 x 20.3 cm)
[Stephen Hahn Gallery, New York, sold
11 June 1969 for $13,000 to]; The Norton
Simon Foundation (sale, London, Sotheby
& Co., 2 April 1974, lot 50, for $36,000).

Cat. 638
Claude Gellée, called Claude Lorrain
(French, 1600–1682)
Landscape with a Piping Shepherd, 1629–1632
Oil on canvas, 25 ¾ x 37 ½ in.
(65.4 x 95.3 cm)
[Newhouse Galleries, New York, sold 11 June
1969 for $115,000 to]; The Norton Simon
Foundation, transferred 26 November
2007 to; Norton Simon Art Foundation
(M.2007.3).

Cat. 639
Eugène Delacroix (French, 1798–1863)
*Studies after Rubens: Saint John the
Evangelist and Saint John the Baptist*, c. 1850
Pen and ink with wash, 5 x 7 ¾ in.
(12.7 x 19.7 cm)
[Schaeffer Galleries, New York, sold 11 June
1969 for $2,500 to]; The Norton Simon
Foundation (sale, New York, Sotheby Parke
Bernet, 2 May 1973, lot 13, for $2,800 to);
[Franz Bader, New York].

Cat. 640
Constantin Guys (French, 1802–1892)
She Flies to a Rendezvous
Pen and ink with wash, 9 ¾ x 7 in.
(24.8 x 17.8 cm)
[Schaeffer Galleries, New York, sold 11 June
1969 for $7,500 to]; The Norton Simon
Foundation (sale, London, Sotheby &
Co., 2 April 1974, lot 36, for $9,120 to);
Georg Waechter Memorial Foundation,
Switzerland (sale, New York, Sotheby's,
23 May 1996, lot 300a, for $4,000).

632

637

633

638

634

639

635

640

636

641

642

643

646

647

644

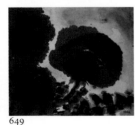
648

645

649

Cat. 641

Jan Steen (Dutch, c. 1626–1679)
Jacob Confronting Laban (formerly *Antiochus and Stratonice*), c. 1667–1668
Oil on panel, 18 ¾ x 23 ¼ in. (47.6 x 59.1 cm)
[Schaeffer Galleries, New York, sold 11 June 1969 for $30,000 to]; The Norton Simon Foundation (F.1969.10.1).

Cat. 642

Jacob Ochtervelt (Dutch, 1634–1682)
Family Portrait, c. 1672
Oil on canvas, 36 ⅛ x 31 ⅛ in. (91.8 x 79.1 cm)
[H. Shickman Gallery, New York, sold 11 June 1969 for $50,000 to]; The Norton Simon Foundation (F.1969.12).

Cat. 643

Domenikos Theotokopoulos, called El Greco (Spanish, b. Greece, 1541–1614)
Portrait of an Old Man with Fur, c. 1590–1600
Oil on canvas, 18 ½ x 15 ¼ in. (47 x 38.7 cm)
[E. V. Thaw & Co., New York, sold 16 June 1969 for $320,000 to]; The Norton Simon Foundation (F.1969.15).

Cat. 644

Lyonel Feininger (American, 1871–1956)
Near the Palace, 1915
Oil on canvas, 39 ½ x 31 ½ in. (100.3 x 80 cm)
[Roman Norbert Ketterer, Lake Lugano, sold 19 June 1969 for $92,500 to]; The Norton Simon Foundation, transferred 27 November 2000 to; Norton Simon Art Foundation (M.2000.1.1).

Cat. 645

Ernst Ludwig Kirchner (German, 1880–1938)
Bathers beneath the Trees, Fehmarn, 1913
Oil on canvas, 59 ½ x 47 ½ in. (151.1 x 120.7 cm)
[Roman Norbert Ketterer, Lake Lugano, sold 19 June 1969 for $60,000 to]; The Norton Simon Foundation, transferred

16 November 1994 to; Norton Simon Art Foundation (M.1994.1).

Cat. 646

Oskar Kokoschka (Austrian, 1886–1980)
Alma Mahler, 1913
Oil on canvas, 24 ¼ x 22 in. (61.6 x 55.9 cm)
[Roman Norbert Ketterer, Lake Lugano, Switzerland, sold 19 June 1969 for $87,570 to]; The Norton Simon Foundation (sale, New York, Sotheby Parke Bernet, 2 May 1973, lot 47, unsold, sold privately 7 June 1973 for $110,000 to); [Marlborough Gallery, New York, 1981]. National Museum of Modern Art, Tokyo.

Cat. 647

Emil Nolde (German, 1867–1956)
Native's Head: Profile in Mauve, c. 1913
Watercolor on buff paper, 13 ¾ x 10 ½ in. (34.9 x 26.7 cm)
[Roman Norbert Ketterer, Lake Lugano, sold 19 June 1969 for $4,500 to]; The Norton Simon Foundation (sale, London, Sotheby & Co., 2 April 1974, lot 54, for $12,000 to); private collection.

Cat. 648

Emil Nolde (German, 1867–1956)
Red Dahlias, c. 1935
Watercolor, 9 x 11 in. (22.9 x 27.9 cm)
[Roman Norbert Ketterer, Lake Lugano, sold 19 June 1969 for $7,000 to]; The Norton Simon Foundation (sale, London, Sotheby & Co., 2 April 1974, lot 53, for $21,600 to); [Fischer Fine Art, London].

Cat. 649

Emil Nolde (German, 1867–1956)
Red Poppies and Larkspur, c. 1935
Watercolor, 10 ⅜ x 9 in. (26.4 x 22.9 cm)
[Roman Norbert Ketterer, Lake Lugano, sold 19 June 1969 for $7,500 to]; The Norton Simon Foundation (sale, New York, Sotheby Parke Bernet, 2 May 1974, lot 147, for $22,000 to); private collection.

Cat. 650
Emil Nolde (German, 1867–1956)
Yellow Sunflower and Red Poppies, c. 1945
Watercolor, 10 ¾ x 13 in. (27.3 x 33 cm)
[Roman Norbert Ketterer, Lake Lugano,
sold 19 June 1969 for $7,000 to]; The
Norton Simon Foundation (sale, New York,
Sotheby Parke Bernet, 2 May 1974, lot 153,
for $24,000 to); private collection.

Cat. 651
Emil Nolde (German, 1867–1956)
The Sea I, 1912
Oil on canvas, 29 x 35 in. (73.7 x 88.9 cm)
[Roman Norbert Ketterer, Lake Lugano,
sold 19 June 1969 for $55,000 to]; The
Norton Simon Foundation, transferred
27 November 2000 to; Norton Simon Art
Foundation (M.2000.1.2).

Cat. 652
Georges Braque (French, 1882–1963)
Still Life with Pipe, 1912
Oil on canvas, 13 ⅜ x 16 ⅜ in. (34 x 41.6 cm)
[Hirschl & Adler Galleries, New York, sold
24 June 1969 for $160,000 to]; The Norton
Simon Foundation, sold 10 December 1981
for $525,000 to; [E. V. Thaw & Co., New
York]. Museum Berggruen, Berlin.

Cat. 653
Constantin Brancusi (Romanian, 1876–1957)
The Muse, 1912
Polished bronze, edition of 5 posthumous
casts from plaster original, cast no. 1, 1969,
17 ½ in. (44.5 cm)
Alexander Istrate, Paris, through [Sylvia
Blatas], sold 26 June 1969 for $57,936 to];
Norton Simon Art Foundation (M.1969.28).

Cat. 654
Rembrandt van Rijn (Dutch, 1606–1669)
Self-Portrait, late 1630s
Oil on panel, original panel: 24 ⅞ x 19 ⅞ in.
(63.2 x 50.5 cm); with additions: 25 ¾ x 20
¾ in. (65.4 x 52.7 cm)

(Sale, London, Christie's, 27 June 1969
for $1,150,486 to); The Norton Simon
Foundation (F.1969.18).

Cat. 655
Edgar Degas (French, 1834–1917)
Nude Women, 1879
Pastel over monotype, 5 ½ x 8 in.
(14 x 20.3 cm)
(Sale, London, Sotheby & Co., 2 July
1969 for $42,574 to); The Norton Simon
Foundation (sale, London, Sotheby & Co.,
2 April 1974, lot 44, for $52,800 to); Ronald
Segal, Surrey; Michael Stakol, South Africa
(sale, London, Sotheby's, 4 April 1989, lot
38, to); private collection (sale, London,
Sotheby's, 22 June 2004, lot 413, unsold).

Cat. 656
Edgar Degas (French, 1834–1917)
Two Dancers in the Foyer
(The Dance School), c. 1875
Pastel and gouache, 11 ¹³/₁₆ x 8 ¼ in.
(30 x 21 cm)
(Sale, London, Sotheby & Co., 2 July 1969
for $148,285 to); Norton Simon, transferred
24 July 1970 to; Lucille Ellis Simon, Los
Angeles. (sale, New York, Sotheby's, 13
November 1985, lot 42, for $520,000 to);
private collection, U.S.A. (sale, New
York, Sotheby's, 1 May 1996, lot 26, for
$1,700,000). [the trade, New York, 2007].
[Halcyon Gallery, London, 2010].

Cat. 657
Giovanni Francesco Romanelli (Italian,
1610–1662)
Dido Showing Aeneas Her Plans for
Carthage, c. 1630–1635
Gouache and black chalk on paper,
laid down on linen, 109 x 192 in.
(276.9 x 487.7 cm)
[Thomas Agnew & Sons, London, sold
3 July 1969 for $35,865 to]; The Norton
Simon Foundation (F.1969.19).

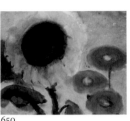
650

654

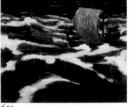
651

655

652

656

657

653

658

659

660

661

662

663

664

665

662   666

Cat. 658
Attributed to Albrecht Bouts
(Flemish, c. 1452/55–1549)
Saint Jerome in Penitence, c. 1520
Oil on panel, 16 ⅛ x 17 ¾ in. (41 x 45.1 cm)
[Hallsborough Gallery, London, sold 3 July
1969 for $60,000 to]; The Norton Simon
Foundation, transferred 19 November
2009 to; Norton Simon Art Foundation
(M.2009.2).

Cat. 659
Georges Michel (French, 1763–1843)
Landscape with Windmill
Oil on canvas, 19 ¼ x 26 in. (48.9 x 66 cm)
[Arthur Tooth & Sons, London, sold 3 July
1969 for $4,200 to]; The Norton Simon
Foundation (sale, New York, Sotheby Parke
Bernet, 2 May 1973, lot 19, for $7,000).

Cat. 660
Jan Steen (Dutch, c. 1626–1679)
Marriage at Cana, 1676
Oil on canvas, 31 ⅜ x 43 in. (79.7 x 109.2 cm)
[Frederick Mont, New York, sold 8 July
1969 for $70,000 to]; The Norton Simon
Foundation (F.1969.21).

Cat. 661
Henri Matisse (French, 1869–1954)
Nude on a Sofa, 1923
Oil on canvas, 20 x 24 in. (50.8 x 61 cm)
[Paul Petrides, Paris, sold 9 July 1969
for $210,000 to]; The Norton Simon
Foundation, transferred 18 November
1998 to; Norton Simon Art Foundation
(M.1998.2).

Cat. 662
Henry Moore (English, 1898–1986)
Relief No. 1, 1959
Bronze, edition of 6, cast no. 1,
87 ⅛ x 50 ½ x 21 in. (221.3 x 128.3 x 53.3 cm)
[M. Knoedler & Co., New York, sold 14 July

1969 for $31,000 to]; Norton Simon Art
Foundation (M.1969.29).

Cat. 663
Paul Cézanne (French, 1839–1906)
The Card Player
Pencil, 21 ¾ x 17 ⅛ in. (55.3 x 43.5 cm)
[E. V. Thaw & Co., New York, sold 14 July
1969 for $65,000 to]; The Norton Simon
Foundation, sold 25 March 1974 for $115,000
as partial payment for Giovanni Paolo
Pannini, *Interior of Saint Peter's, Rome* (cat.
1009) to; [E. V. Thaw & Co., New York];
Eugene V. and Clare E. Thaw, New York, gift
1975 to; The Pierpont Morgan Library,
New York.

Cat. 664
Eugène Delacroix (French, 1798–1863)
Arab on a Galloping Horse, 1838
Watercolor, 10 ⅛ x 13 ½ in. (25.7 x 34.3 cm)
[E. V. Thaw & Co., New York, sold 14 July
1969 for $27,500 to]; The Norton Simon
Foundation (sale, London, Sotheby & Co.,
2 April 1974, lot 37, for $62,400 to); private
collection, London, by inheritance 2000 to;
private collection, London.

Cat. 665
Edvard Munch (Norwegian, 1863–1944)
Girls on a Bridge, 1903
Etching, 7 ¼ x 10 ⅜ in. (18.4 x 26.4 cm)
[Robert M. Light, Boston, sold 16 July
1969 for $7,090 to]; Norton Simon Art
Foundation, sold 23 November 1976 for
$7,148 to; [Margo P. Schab, New York].

Cat. 666
Henry Moore (English, 1898–1986)
Upright Motive No. 5, 1955–1956
Bronze, edition of 5, unnumbered cast,
89 in. (226.1 cm)
Mary Moore, Much Hadham, England,
sold 18 July 1969 for $20,125 to; The Norton
Simon Foundation (F.1969.25).

Cat. 667
Circle of Alessandro Magnasco
(Italian, 1667–1749)
A Valley with Washerwomen in the
Foreground (formerly *Mountain Landscape*)
Oil on canvas, 32 ½ x 44 ¼ in.
(82.6 x 112.4 cm)
[Drs. Fritz and Peter Nathan, Zurich, sold
18 July 1969 for $26,000 to]; The Norton
Simon Foundation (sale, London, Sotheby
Parke Bernet & Co., 16 April 1980, lot 85,
for $71,072). (sale, New York, Christie's, 15
January 1985, lot 58 to); private collection
(sale, London, Christie's, 10 December 1993,
lot 350, for $30,936).

Cat. 668
Henri Matisse (French, 1869–1954)
Seated Nude, 1919
Pencil, 14 ¼ x 9 ½ in. (36.2 x 24.1 cm)
[Drs. Fritz and Peter Nathan, Zurich, sold
18 July 1969 for $6,500 to]; The Norton
Simon Foundation (sale, New York, Sotheby
Parke Bernet, 2 May 1973, lot 37, for $16,000
to); [Grace Borgenicht, New York].

Cat. 669
Jean-Honoré Fragonard (French, 1732–1806)
Music, c. 1760–1765
Oil on canvas, 30 ¾ x 52 in. (78.1 x 132.1 cm)
[Galerie André Weil, Paris, sold 29 July
1969 for $99,500 to]; The Norton Simon
Foundation (F.1969.28.1).

Cat. 670
Jean-Honoré Fragonard (French, 1732–1806)
Venus Binding Cupid's Wings, c. 1760–1765
Oil on canvas, 30 ¾ x 52 in. (78.1 x 132.1 cm)
[Galerie André Weil, Paris, sold 29 July
1969 for $100,000 to]; The Norton Simon
Foundation (sale, London, Sotheby Parke
Bernet & Co., 16 April 1980, lot 97, for
$71,072); private collection, Japan (sale,
New York, Christie's, 25 May 1999, lot 71,
for $300,000).

Cat. 671
Giovanni Battista Moroni
(Italian, c. 1525–1578)
Portrait of an Elderly Man, c. 1575
Oil on canvas, 20 x 16 ½ in. (50.8 x 41.9 cm)
Donatella and Lorenzo Papi, Florence, sold
31 July 1969 for $70,000 to; The Norton
Simon Foundation (F.1969.29).

Cat. 672
Vincent van Gogh (Dutch, 1853–1890)
The Park at St. Paul's Hospital, St. Rémy,
1889
Pen and charcoal, 18 ½ x 24 in. (47 x 61 cm)
[Feilchenfeldt, Zurich, sold 6 August
1969 for $115,000 to]; The Norton Simon
Foundation (sale, London, Sotheby & Co.,
2 April 1974, lot 46, for $160,800 to); private
collection, London. private collection,
Switzerland, 1991.

Cat. 673
Pablo Picasso (Spanish, 1881–1973)
Still Life with Fruit Dish, 6 November 1945
Lithograph, 9 ¼ x 13 ¼ in. (23.5 x 33.7 cm)
[Harold Diamond, New York, sold
14 August 1969 for $8,500 to]; The Norton
Simon Foundation (F.1969.31).

Cat. 674
Pablo Picasso (Spanish, 1881–1973)
Nude Woman, Legs Crossed, c. 1902–1903
Pen and ink with colored pencil on
postcard, 5 ¼ x 3 ⅝ in. (13.3 x 9.2 cm)
[Richard Feigen, Chicago, sold 21 August
1969 for $11,000 to]; The Norton Simon
Foundation (sale, London, Sotheby & Co.,
2 April 1974, lot 49, for $19,200); (sale, New
York, Sotheby Parke Bernet, 21 May 1975,
lot 15). [Rachel Adler Fine Art, New York,
November 2005, sold 2006 to]; [Leo Malca
Fine Art, New York].

667

671

668

672

673

669

670

674

675

678

676

679

677A

680

677B

681

677C

677D

Cat. 675
Pablo Picasso (Spanish, 1881–1973)
Seated Woman Combing Her Hair
Pen and ink with colored pencil on
postcard, 5 ¼ x 3 ⅝ in. (13.3 x 9.2 cm)
[Richard Feigen, Chicago, sold 21 August
1969 for $14,000 to]; The Norton Simon
Foundation (sale, London, Sotheby & Co.,
2 April 1974, lot 48, for $26,400 to);
[O'Hana, London].

Cat. 676
Pablo Picasso (Spanish, 1881–1973)
Three Women at the Fountain, 1921
Oil on canvas, 7 ½ x 9 ½ in. (19.1 x 24.1 cm)
[Richard Feigen, New York, sold 21 August
1969 for $80,000 to]; The Norton Simon
Foundation (sale, New York, Sotheby Parke
Bernet, 2 May 1973, lot 46, unsold, private
sale, 13 July 1973 for $130,000). [Acquavella
Galleries, New York, sold 2003 to]; private
collection, Singapore (sale, New York,
Christie's, 6 November 2007, lot 52, for
$1,945,000 to); private collection, Italy.

Cat. 677A–D
Giovanni Domenico Tiepolo
(Italian, 1727–1804)
A Session of the Magistrates, 1791
Ink, 11 ⅜ x 16 ¼ in. (28.9 x 41.3 cm)
Dancing Dogs
Ink, 11 ⅜ x 16 ⅜ in. (28.9 x 41.6 cm)
The Peep Show
Ink, 11 ⅝ x 16 ⅛ in. (29.5 x 41 cm)
*Scene of Contemporary Life: The Picture
Show*, 1790
Ink, 11 ⁵/₁₆ x 16 ⅜ in. (28.7 x 41.6 cm)
[Pittura Establishment, Vaduz,
Liechtenstein, sold 4 September 1969 for
$48,000 to]; Norton Simon Art Foundation,
sold 1 February 1974 for $80,000 to; [E. V.
Thaw & Co., New York]; Eugene V. and
Clare E. Thaw, New York, promised gifts to;
The Pierpont Morgan Library, New York.

Cat. 678
Luca Giordano (Italian, 1632–1705)
Sacrifice of Elias, c. 1650–1660
Pen and brown ink with gray wash,
7 ⅞ x 10 ⅝ in. (20 x 27cm)
[William Kennedy Gallery, New York, sold
9 September 1969 for $1,080 to]; Norton
Simon Art Foundation (M.1969.32.2).

Cat. 679
Claude Monet (French, 1840–1926)
Fishing Boats at Low Tide, c. 1868
Pen and ink with wash, 4 ½ x 8 ½ in.
(11.4 x 21.6 cm)
[William Kennedy Gallery, New York, sold
9 September 1969 for $6,200 to]; Norton
Simon Art Foundation (sale, London,
Sotheby & Co., 2 April 1974, lot 39, for
$12,000); (sale, New York, Sotheby Parke
Bernet, 21 May 1975, lot 5).

Cat. 680
Jacob van Ruisdael (Dutch, 1628/29–1682)
and Nicolaes Berchem (Dutch, 1620–1683)
Wooded Landscape with a Pool and Figures,
c. 1655
Oil on panel, 27 ⅝ x 36 ¼ in. (70.2 x 92.1 cm)
[P. & D. Colnaghi, London, sold 10
September 1969 for $75,211 to]; Norton
Simon Art Foundation (M.1969.33).

Cat. 681
Georges Braque (French, 1882–1963)
Still Life with Napkin, 1926
Oil on canvas, 21 ¼ x 25 ½ in. (54 x 64.8 cm)
[Paul Kantor, Beverly Hills, Calif., sold 10
September 1969 for $37,100 ($33,600 plus
Pierre Bonnard *Basket of Fruit* (cat. 3), used
in trade with a value of $3,500 to]; Norton
Simon (sale, New York, Parke-Bernet
Galleries, 5 May 1971, lot 68, for $63,000).
[Sári Heller Gallery, Beverly Hills]. (sale,
New York, Sotheby's, 14 May 1997, lot 372,
for $260,000).

Cat. 682

Giovanni Francesco Romanelli
(Italian, 1610–1662)
Aeneas Leaving Dido, c. 1630–1635
Gouache and black chalk on paper,
laid down on linen,
109 x 138 in. (276.9 x 350.5 cm)
[Thomas Agnew & Sons, London, sold
23 September 1969 for $14,293 to]; The
Norton Simon Foundation (F.1969.33.1).

Cat. 683

Giovanni Francesco Romanelli
(Italian, 1610–1662)
Royal Hunt and Storm, c. 1630–1635
Gouache and black chalk on paper,
laid down on linen, 109 x 138 in.
(276.9 x 350.5 cm)
[Thomas Agnew & Sons, London, sold
23 September 1969 for $21,440 to]; The
Norton Simon Foundation (F.1969.33.2).

Cat. 684A-B

Jean-Baptiste Greuze (French, 1725–1805)
The Departure of the Wet Nurse, and
The Return of the Wet Nurse
Black chalk with gray wash, 12 ¾ x 10 ¹³/₁₆ in.
(32.4 x 27.5 cm)
[Paul Drey Gallery, New York, sold
14 October 1969 for $11,875 to]; The Norton
Simon Foundation, used in trade 21 March
1978 as part of settlement agreement for
purchase of 118 Rembrandt etchings (cat.
1452 to); [Greater India Co. (Robert M. Light),
Boston]; private collection, Los Angeles.

Cat. 685

Gustave Courbet (French, 1819–1877)
Apples, Pears, and Primroses on a Table,
1871–1872
Oil on canvas, 23 ½ x 28 ¾ in. (59.7 x 73 cm)
[Paul Rosenberg & Co., New York, sold
14 October 1969 for $447,000 to]; The
Norton Simon Foundation, transferred
23 November 1999 to; Norton Simon Art
Foundation (M.1999.2.1).

Cat. 686

Edgar Degas (French, 1834–1917)
Three Dancers, c. 1872–1874
Essence and gouache on wove paper,
mounted on silk, 18 ¼ x 24 ½ in.
(46.4 x 62.2 cm)
[Paul Rosenberg & Co., New York, sold
14 October 1969 for $45,000 to]; The
Norton Simon Foundation (F.1969.35.1).

Cat. 687

Edgar Degas (French, 1834–1917)
The Star: Dancer on Pointe, c. 1878–1880
Gouache and pastel on paper, mounted on
board, 22 ¼ x 29 ¾ in. (56.5 x 75.6 cm)
(Sale, New York, Parke-Bernet Galleries,
15 October 1969 for $550,000 to); The
Norton Simon Foundation (F.1969.40).

Cat. 688

Henry Moore (English, 1898–1986)
Reclining Figure, Draped, 1957
Bronze, edition of 11, unnumbered cast,
12 in. (30.5 cm)
[Jeffrey H. Loria & Co., New York,
sold 20 October 1969 for $50,000 to];
The Norton Simon Foundation, sold
22 February 1982 for $120,000 to;
[Jeffrey H. Loria & Co., New York].

Cat. 689

Paul Cézanne (French, 1839–1906)
Seated Woman, c. 1895
Oil on canvas, 25 ¼ x 20 ¾ in.
(64.1 x 52.7 cm)
[Anne Johnson, Los Angeles, sold
28 October 1969 for $90,000 to]; The
Norton Simon Foundation (sale, New York,
Sotheby Parke Bernet, 2 May 1973, lot 27, for
$110,000). [Michael Drinkhouse, New York
(sale, New York, Sotheby Parke Bernet, 17
May 1978, lot 18, unsold)]. Stephen Mazoh,
Rhinebeck, New York.

682

683

684A

686

687

684B

688

685

689

690A

690B

691

692

693

694

695

696

697

698

Cat. 690A-B
Francesco Guardi (Italian, 1712–1793)
Ruins with Couple Walking and *Ruins with Workers*
Oil on panel, each 7 ⅜ x 5 ⅞ in. (18.7 x 14.9 cm)
[Anne Johnson, Los Angeles, sold 28 October 1969 for $40,000 to]; The Norton Simon Foundation, used in trade 4 March 1974 at a value of $43,333 as partial payment for Jan Lievens, *Panoramic Landscape* (cat. 1007) to; [Newhouse Galleries, New York].

Cat. 691
Jean-Antoine Watteau (French, 1684–1721)
A Woman Lying on a Chaise Longue
Red, black, and white chalk, 7 ⅝ x 9 ⅛ in. (19.4 x 23.2 cm)
[Anne M. Johnson, Los Angeles, sold 28 October 1969 for $50,000 to]; The Norton Simon Foundation, sold 26 March 1976 for $90,000 to; [Walter Feilchenfeldt, Zurich].

Cat. 692
Pierre-Auguste Renoir (French, 1841–1919)
Young Woman Seated, Décolleté, 1890
Oil on canvas, 13 ¼ x 8 ⅜ in. (33.7 x 21.3 cm)
[Stephen Hahn Gallery, New York, sold 29 October 1969 for $137,500 to]; The Norton Simon Foundation, sold 31 July 1973 for $137,500 to; [Stephen Hahn Gallery, New York].

Cat. 693
Vincent van Gogh (Dutch, 1853–1890)
Head of a Fisherman
Pencil, 17 ¼ x 10 ¾ in. (43.8 x 27.3 cm)
[E. J. van Wisselingh, Amsterdam, sold 4 November 1969 for $13,500 to]; The Norton Simon Foundation (sale, New York, Sotheby Parke Bernet, 2 May 1973, lot 30, for $28,000 to); private collection.

Cat. 694
Vincent van Gogh (Dutch, 1853–1890)
Winter (The Vicarage Garden under Snow), 1885

Oil on canvas, mounted on panel, 23 x 31 ⅛ in. (58.4 x 79.1 cm)
[E. J. van Wisselingh, Amsterdam, sold 4 November 1969 for $70,000 to]; The Norton Simon Foundation (F.1969.39.2).

Cat. 695
Camille Pissarro (French, 1830–1903)
Woman Breaking Wood
Gouache, 23 ¼ x 18 ¼ in. (59.1 x 46.4 cm)
[E. J. van Wisselingh, Amsterdam, sold 4 November 1969 for $68,000 to]; The Norton Simon Foundation (sale, London, Sotheby & Co., 2 April 1974, lot 47, for $108,000). (sale, London, Sotheby's, 1 December 1982, lot 10, unsold) (sale, New York, Sotheby's, 19 May 1983, lot 207).

Cat. 696
Dirck Hals (Dutch, 1591–1656)
A Fiddler, c. 1630
Oil on panel, 14 ¾ x 12 in. (37.5 x 30.5 cm.)
[A. van der Meer, Amsterdam, sold 17 November 1969 for $8,334 to]; The Norton Simon Foundation (F.1969.42.1).

Cat. 697
Workshop of Jan van Kessel (Dutch, 1626–1679)
Still Life with Fruit
Oil on copper, 5 ¼ x 6 ½ in. (13.3 x 16.5 cm)
[A. van der Meer, Amsterdam, sold 17 November 1969 for $5,000 to]; The Norton Simon Foundation (F.1969.42.2).

Cat. 698
Gerrit Dou (Dutch, 1613–1675)
Portrait of a Lady, c. 1640–1644
Oil on panel, oval, 19 ⅜ x 15 ¼ in. (49.2 x 38.7 cm)
[Newhouse Galleries, New York, sold 19 November 1969 for $20,000 to]; The Norton Simon Foundation (F.1969.43).

Cat. 699
Constantin Brancusi (Romanian, 1876–1957)
Head of a Woman, 1925
Marble, 20 ½ in. (52.1 cm)
[Jane Wade, New York, sold 21 November
1969 for $150,000 to]; The Norton Simon
Foundation (sale, New York, Christie's,
19 May 1982, lot 34, for $700,000). private
collection, New York.

Cat. 700
Isaak van Ostade (Dutch, 1621–1649)
*Peasants Outside a Farmhouse Butchering
a Pig*, 1641
Oil on panel, 19 ⅛ x 25 ½ in. (48.6 x 64.8 cm)
[A. van der Meer, Amsterdam, sold
21 November 1969 for $23,615 to];
The Norton Simon Foundation (F.1969.44).

Cat. 701
Attributed to Cornelis Bisschop
(Dutch, 1630–1674)
Bathsheba, early 1660s
Oil on panel, 15 ½ x 13 ¼ in. (39.4 x 33.7 cm)
[Gebr. Douwes, Amsterdam, sold
26 November 1969 for $30,000 to];
The Norton Simon Foundation (F.1969.45).

Cat. 702
Jacopo da Ponte, called Jacopo Bassano
(Italian, 1510–1592)
The Flight into Egypt, c. 1544–1545
Oil on canvas,
48 ½ x 77 ¼ in. (123.2 x 196.2 cm)
(Sale, London, Christie's, 5 December
1969 for $655,118 to); Norton Simon Art
Foundation (M.1969.35).

Cat. 703
Pablo Picasso (Spanish, 1881–1973)
The Vollard Suite, 1939
Drypoint, set of 100, 11 ¾ x 14 ¼ in.
(29.9 x 36.2 cm)
[Robert M. Light, Boston, sold 9 December
1969 for $147,000 to]; The Norton Simon
Foundation (F.1969.46.1–100).

Cat. 704
Henry Moore (English, 1898–1986)
Three Standing Figures, 1953
Bronze, 30 ½ x 28 x 12 ½ in.
(77.5 x 71.1 x 31.8 cm)
[Jeffrey H. Loria & Co., New York, sold
12 December 1969 for $55,000 to]; Norton
Simon Art Foundation (M.1969.34.1).

Cat. 705
Jean-Auguste-Dominique Ingres
(French, 1780–1867)
Study for "Odalisque and Slave," c. 1841
Pencil, black chalk and white gouache,
13 ⅛ x 18 ¼ in. (33.3 x 46.4 cm)
[E. V. Thaw & Co., New York, sold
16 December 1969 for $187,000 to];
The Norton Simon Foundation, sold
7 August 1980 for $200,000 to; [E. V. Thaw
& Co., New York]; Eugene V. and
Clare E. Thaw, New York, promised gift to;
The Pierpont Morgan Library, New York.

Cat. 706
Henry Moore (English, 1898–1986)
Mother and Child against an Open Wall, 1956
Bronze, edition of 12, unnumbered cast,
9 in. (22.9 cm)
[Jeffrey H. Loria & Co., New York, sold
16 December 1969 for $27,500 to]; Norton
Simon Art Foundation, sold 22 February
1982 for $60,000 to; [Jeffrey H. Loria & Co.,
New York].

Cat. 707A-C
Pierre Puvis de Chavannes
(French, 1824–1898)
The Legendary Saints of France, c. 1877–1878
Gouache on paper, mounted on canvas,
three panels: panel A, 86 ¼ x 110 ⅛ in.
(219 x 279.7 cm); panel B, 86 ¼ x 142 in.
(219 x 360.7 cm); panel C, 86 ¼ x 110 ½ in.
(219 x 280.7 cm)
[Hirschl & Adler Galleries, New York, gift
c. 18 December 1969 to]; Norton Simon, gift
28 December 1978 to; The Norton Simon
Foundation (F.78.38.1–3).

699

704

700

705

701

706

702

703

707B

708

709

710

711A   711B

712

713

714

715

Cat. 708

Claude Monet (French, 1840–1926)
The Entrance to the Port of Le Havre
(formerly *The Entrance to the Port of Honfleur*), c. 1867–1868
Oil on canvas, 19 ¾ x 24 ⅛ in.
(50.2 x 61.3 cm)
[Galerie Castiglione, Schaan, Lichtenstein
(Alex Reid & Lefevre), traded Camille
Pissarro, *View of Pontoise* (cat. 614)
19 December 1969 with a value of $229,340
to]; The Norton Simon Foundation,
transferred 23 November 1999 to; Norton
Simon Art Foundation (M.1999.2.2).

Cat. 709

Jean-Frédéric Bazille (French, 1841–1870)
Woman in a Moorish Costume, 1869
Oil on canvas, 39 ¼ x 23 ¼ in. (99.7 x 59 cm)
[E. V. Thaw & Co., New York, sold
23 December 1969 for $70,000 to];
The Norton Simon Foundation, transferred
25 November 1997 to; Norton Simon Art
Foundation (M.1997.2).

Cat. 710

Jan van Goyen (Dutch, 1596–1656)
River Landscape with a Village Church, 1642
Oil on panel, 12 x 15 ⅛ in. (30.5 x 38.4 cm)
[Edward Speelman, London, sold
23 December 1969 for $70,000 to];
The Norton Simon Foundation (F.1969.49).

Cat. 711A-B

Mourijn Simonsz. van Waterlant (active
c. 1475–c. 1515) and Claas van Waterlant
(active c. 1481–d. 1533/1534), also known as
the Master of Alkmaar
The Flagellation of Christ and *Christ
Carrying the Cross*, c.1500–1510
Oil on panel, 18 ⅝ x 9 ¾ in. (47.3 x 24.8 cm)
and 18 ⅝ x 9 ⅜ in. (47.3 x 23.9 cm)
[M. Knoedler & Co., New York, sold
31 December 1969 for $35,000 to]; Norton
Simon Art Foundation (M.1969.36.1–2).

1970

Cat. 712

Jean-Baptiste Pater (French, 1695–1736)
Fête Champêtre
Oil on panel, 7 ⅞ x 10 ¾ in. (20 x 27.3 cm)
[Richard Feigen, New York, sold 5 January
1970 for $20,500 to]; The Norton Simon
Foundation (F.1970.1).

Cat. 713

Rembrandt van Rijn (Dutch, 1606–1669)
*Christ with the Sick around Him, Receiving
the Children* (*The Hundred Guilder Print*)
Etching and drypoint, 2nd state,
11 ¾ x 16 in. (29.9 x 40.6 cm)
[Robert M. Light, Boston, sold 6 January
1970 for $75,000 to]; The Norton Simon
Foundation, transferred 27 November
1985 to; Norton Simon Art Foundation
(M.1985.3).

Cat. 714

Bernaert van Orley (Dutch, 1488–1541)
Margaret of Austria
Oil on panel, 14 ⅜ x 10 ¼ in. (36.5 x 26 cm)
[Frederick Mont, New York, sold 6 January
1970 for $85,000 to]; The Norton Simon
Foundation, returned 5 March 1973 for
$85,000 in partial payment for Pietro
Lorenzetti, *Saint John the Baptist* and *The
Prophet Elisha* (cat. 928A-B) to; [Frederick
Mont, New York, sold 1976 to]; Musée de
Brou, Bourg-en-Bresse, France.

Cat. 715

Jean-Baptiste Deshays de Colleville
(French, 1729–1765) formerly attributed to
François Boucher (French, 1703–1770)
Jupiter and Semele (formerly *Vertumnus and
Pomona*), c. 1760
Oil on canvas, 62 ¾ x 66 ⅜ in.
(159.4 x 168.6 cm)
[Ira Spanierman, New York, sold 6 January
1970 for $175,000 to]; The Norton Simon
Foundation (F.1970.4).

Cat. 716
Jean-Honoré Fragonard (French, 1732–1806)
Drawings after the Masters
Black chalk, group of 139, each 17 ¾ x 13 in.
(45.1 x 33 cm)
[Tulkens Bookseller, Brussels (through
Zeitlin and Ver Brugge, Los Angeles), sold
6 January 1970 for $100,000 to]; The Norton
Simon Foundation (F.1970.3.1–139).

Cat. 717
Paul Cézanne (French, 1839–1906)
Self-Portrait, c. 1875
Pencil, 5 ⅞ x 4 ¾ in. (14.9 x 12.1 cm)
[Wildenstein & Co., New York, sold
6 January 1970 for $48,000 to]; The Norton
Simon Foundation (sale, London, Sotheby
& Co., 2 April 1974, lot 42, unsold, later sold
in private sale for $91,200).

Cat. 718
Jean-Antoine Watteau (French, 1684–1721)
*Actor in Sixteenth-Century Court Costume,
Looking to His Right*
Red chalk, 9 ⅝ x 5 ⅞ in. (24.5 x 14.9 cm)
[E. V. Thaw & Co., New York, gift 13 January
1970 to]; Norton Simon Art Foundation
(sale, London, Sotheby & Co., 27 June 1974,
lot 43, for $4,560).

Cat. 719
Bernardo Daddi (Italian, c. 1280–1348)
*Madonna and Child Enthroned with Saints
John Gualbertus, John the Baptist, Francis,
and Nicholas*, c. 1330–1336
Tempera and gold leaf on panel,
18 x 9 ⅝ in. (45.7 x 24.4 cm)
[M. Knoedler & Co., New York, sold
14 January 1970 for $25,000 to]; The Norton
Simon Foundation (F.1970.6.2).

Cat. 720
Francisco de Zurbarán (Spanish, 1598–1664)
Fray Diego Deza, c. 1630
Oil on canvas, 65 ½ x 54 ¼ in.
(166.4 x 137.8 cm)
[M. Knoedler & Co., New York, sold

14 January 1970 for $65,000 to]; The Norton
Simon Foundation (F.1970.6.1).

Cat. 721
Aristide Maillol (French, 1861–1944)
Chained Action, 1906
Bronze, edition of 6, cast no. 5, 84 ⅝ in.
(215 cm)
[Dina Vierny, Paris, sold 20 January 1970 for
$90,000 to]; Norton Simon Art Foundation,
sold 18 May 1979 for $350,000 to; Ivan F.
Boesky, New York, by descent to; private
collection, New York.

Cat. 722
Henry Moore (English, 1898–1986)
Draped Seated Figure (Headless), 1961
Bronze, edition of 9, cast no. 3,
8 in. (20.3 cm)
[Paul Rosenberg & Co., New York, sold
27 January 1970 for $4,000 to]; Norton
Simon, sold 13 December 1973 for $11,500 to;
Mickleton Trading Corp., New York.

Cat. 723
Henry Moore (English, 1898–1986)
Maquette for Two-Piece Reclining Figure,
1960
Bronze, edition of 12, cast no. 9,
9 ½ x 5 ¼ in. (24.1 x 13.3 cm)
[Paul Rosenberg & Co., New York, sold
27 January 1970 for $4,000 to]; Norton
Simon, sold 13 December 1973 for $11,500 to;
Mickleton Trading Corp., New York.

Cat. 724
Pablo Picasso (Spanish, 1881–1973)
Bottle, Playing Card, Tobacco, and Pipe, 1919
Oil on canvas, 19 ¾ x 24 in. (50.2 x 61 cm)
[Paul Rosenberg & Co., New York, sold
27 January 1970 for $30,000 to]; Norton
Simon (sale, New York, Parke-Bernet
Galleries, 5 May 1971, lot 71, for $65,000).
(sale, London, Sotheby's, 31 March 1987, lot
52, for £341,000 to); [Waddington Galleries,
London, sold 1987 to]; Japanese corporate
collection.

716

721

717

722

718

723

719

724

720

725

729

726

730

727

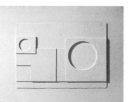
731

732

728

Cat. 725
Henri Fantin-Latour (French, 1836–1904)
Asters and Fruit on a Table, 1868
Oil on canvas, 22 ⅜ x 21 ⅝ in. (56.8 x 54.9 cm)
[Paul Rosenberg & Co., New York, sold
29 January 1970 for $15,000 to]; Norton
Simon (sale, New York, Parke-Bernet
Galleries, 21 October 1971, unsold), sold
16 March 1972 for $150,000 through [Alex
Reid & Lefevre, London to]; private
collection, Switzerland; Jaime Ortiz-Patiño,
Vandoeuvres, Switzerland (sale, Sotheby's,
New York, 9 May 1989, lot 3, for $1,870,000
to); [Acquavella Galleries, New York, sold
to]; Walter H. and Leonore Annenberg,
Rancho Mirage, Calif., gift 2001 to; The
Metropolitan Museum of Art, New York.

Cat. 726
Aelbert Cuyp (Dutch, 1620–1691)
Evening in the Meadows, c. 1650
Oil on canvas, 41 ½ x 54 ⅝ in.
(105.4 x 138.8 cm)
[G. Cramer, The Hague, sold 2 March
1970 for $140,000 to]; The Norton Simon
Foundation (F.1970.7).

Cat. 727
Auguste Rodin (French, 1840–1917)
The Thinker, 1880
Bronze, edition of 12, cast no. 11,
79 in. (200.7 cm)
Musée Rodin, Paris, sold 2 March 1970 for
$49,610 to; Norton Simon Art Foundation
(M.1970.2).

Cat. 728
Francisco de Goya y Lucientes
(Spanish, 1746–1828)
Saint Jerome in Penitence, 1796–1798
Oil on canvas, 75 ⅛ x 45 in. (190.8 x 114.3 cm)
[Spencer A. Samuels & Co., New York, sold
3 March 1970 for $275,000 ($237,500 plus
Peter Paul Rubens, cat. D165), to];
The Norton Simon Foundation (F.1970.8).

Cat. 729
Salomon van Ruysdael (Dutch, 1602/3–1670)
Halt in Front of an Inn, 1643
Oil on panel, 24 ⅛ x 36 ½ in. (61.3 x 92.7 cm)
[Rosenberg & Stiebel, New York, sold
31 March 1970 for $60,000 to]; The Norton
Simon Foundation (F.1970.9).

Cat. 730
Pierre-Auguste Renoir (French, 1841–1919)
The Washerwoman, 1917
Bronze, 48 ½ in. (123.2 cm)
Mr. and Mrs. Jean Renoir, Beverly Hills,
Calif., sold 16 April 1970 for $60,000 to;
Norton Simon Art Foundation (sale, New
York, Sotheby Parke Bernet, 20 May 1982,
lot 206, for $140,000 to); The Fran and
Ray Stark Foundation (sale, New York,
Sotheby's, 3 November 2005, lot 184, unsold,
sale, New York, Sotheby's, 8 November
2006, lot 161).

Cat. 731
Henry Moore (English, 1898–1986)
Two-Piece Reclining Figure, No. 9, 1968
Bronze, edition of 7, cast no. 2,
56 ½ x 96 x 52 in. (143.5 x 243.8 x 132.1 cm)
[Galerie des Arts Anciens et Modernes,
Schaan, Liechtenstein, sold 24 April 1970 for
$105,000 to]; Norton Simon Art Foundation
(M.1970.4.1).

Cat. 732
Ben Nicholson (English, 1894–1982)
*1939 (white relief—version 2: décor for
Beethoven 7th Symphony Ballet—4th
movement)*
Oil on carved board, 15 ¼ x 19 ½ in.
(38.7 x 49.5 cm)
[Galerie des Arts Anciens et Modernes,
Schaan, Liechtenstein, sold 24 April 1970 for
$27,500 to]; Norton Simon Art Foundation
(M.1970.4.2).

Cat. 733

Pablo Picasso (Spanish, 1881–1973)

Prints from the series *347*, 1968

Etchings and aquatints, 44/50, group of 87

[Galerie des Arts Anciens et Modernes, Schaan, Liechtenstein, sold 24 April 1970 for $163,400 to]; Norton Simon Art Foundation (M.1970.4.3.1–87).

Cat. 734

Lucas Cranach the Elder
(German, 1472–1553)

Eve, c. 1530

Oil on panel, 74 ¼ x 27 ¼ in.
(188.6 x 69.2 cm)

[Spencer A. Samuels & Co., New York, sold 9 May 1970 for $450,000 ($390,000 cash and $60,000 value in trade for Édouard Vuillard, *Green Hillside at L'Étang-la-Ville* [cat. 53]) to]; The Norton Simon Foundation, transferred 27 November 1991 to; Norton Simon Art Foundation (M.1991.1).

Cat. 735

Auguste Rodin (French, 1840–1917)

Saint John the Baptist, 1878–80

Bronze, edition of 12, cast no. 7,
78 ¾ in. (200 cm)

Musée Rodin, Paris, sold 5 June 1970 for $30,400 to; The Norton Simon Foundation (F.1970.11).

Cat. 736

Auguste Rodin (French, 1840–1917)

Eve, 1881

Bronze, edition of 12, cast no. 8,
68 in. (172.7 cm)

Musée Rodin, Paris, sold 27 July 1970 for $23,600 to; The Norton Simon Foundation, sold 22 March 1973 for $100,000 to; [Paul Kantor, Beverly Hills, Calif.]. Iris & B. Gerald Cantor Center for Visual Arts at Stanford University, Stanford, Calif.

Cat. 737

Gustave Courbet (French, 1819–1877)

Marine, c. 1865–1866

Oil on canvas, 19 ¾ x 24 in. (50.2 x 61 cm)

[E. V. Thaw & Co., New York, sold 28 July 1970 for $35,000 to]; The Norton Simon Foundation (F.1970.12).

Cat. 738

Francisco de Zurbarán (Spanish, 1598–1664)

The Birth of the Virgin, c. 1627

Oil on canvas, 55 ½ x 42 ¾ in.
(141 x 108.6 cm)

[E. V. Thaw & Co., New York, sold 10 September 1970 for $720,000 to]; The Norton Simon Foundation (F.1970.13).

Cat. 739

Nicolas Poussin (French, 1594–1665)

Camillus and the Schoolmaster of Falerii,
c. 1635–1640

Oil on canvas, 39 ⅝ x 54 in. (100.7 x 137.2 cm)

Kenneth Walker, New York (acting as agent for owners), sold 29 December 1970 for $500,000 to; The Norton Simon Foundation (F.1970.14).

Cat. 740

Claude Gellée, called Claude Lorrain
(French, 1600–1682)

An Album of Sixty Drawings, 1630–1677

Ink and pencil

[Wildenstein & Co., New York, sold 31 December 1970 for $1 million to]; Norton Simon Art Foundation, 53 drawings sold 30 July 1980 for $4,420,000 to; [Thomas Agnew & Sons, London, and E. V. Thaw & Co., New York]; three drawings promised gifts from Eugene V. and Clare E. Thaw to; The Pierpont Morgan Library. Three sold 1982 to; The Frick Collection, New York. Sixteen acquired in 2007 by the Sterling and Francine Clark Art Institute, Williamstown, Mass. Seven drawings remain (M.1970.7.11, 22, 41, 42, 44, 51, 56).

733

738

734

739

740

735

736

737

741

745

746

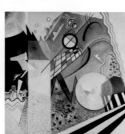

747

743

748

744C

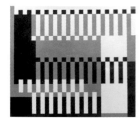

744D

Cat. 741

Salomon van Ruysdael (Dutch, 1602/3–1670)
Landscape with Sandy Road, 1628
Oil on panel, 11 ¼ x 15 ½ in. (28.6 x 39.4 cm)
[E. J. van Wisselingh, Amsterdam, sold 31
December 1970 for $20,000 to]; The Norton
Simon Foundation (F.1970.15).

1971

Cat. 742

Lucas Cranach the Elder
(German, 1472–1553)
Adam, c. 1530
Oil on panel, 74 x 27 ½ in. (188 x 69.9 cm)
[Spencer A. Samuels & Co., New York, sold
13 January 1971 for $350,000 ($160,000
cash and $190,000 value in trade for four
paintings: Georges Rouault, *Three Women*
[cat. 599]; Édouard Vuillard, *The Garden*
[cat. 502]; Édouard Vuillard, *Interior* [cat.
95]; Albert Marquet, *Bay of Audierne* [cat.
231]) to]; Norton Simon Art Foundation
(M.1971.1).

Cat. 743

Jacob van Ruisdael (Dutch, 1628/29–1682)
*Three Great Trees in a Mountainous
Landscape with a River*, late 1660s
Oil on canvas, 54 ⅜ x 68 ⅛ in.
(138.1 x 173 cm)
[Drs. Fritz and Peter Nathan, Zurich, sold
14 July 1971 for $220,000 to]; The Norton
Simon Foundation (F.1971.20).

Cat. 744A-D

Josef Albers (American, 1888–1976)
Set of Four Centennial Prints
Lithographs, 24 ⅝ x 26 ⅝ in. (62.6 x 67.6 cm)
The Metropolitan Museum of Art, New
York, sold 31 August 1971 for $1,340 to;
Norton Simon; *Centennial Print–1*, partial
trade 14 December 1979 for Philippe de
Champaigne, *Abbess of the Trinitarians,
Caen* (cat. 616) and Daniel de Monfreid,

The Blue Coffee Pot (cat. 545) to; Norton
Simon Inc.; *Centennial Print–2* and
Centennial Print–4 donated 17 May 1977
to; Norton Simon Museum (P.1977.9–10);
Centennial Print–3, by inheritance 2 June
1993 to; Jennifer Jones Simon Art Trust, Los
Angeles (N.1971.1.3).

Cat. 745

India, Delhi Region
Chess Set and Board, c. 1850
Ivory pieces, wood board inlaid with ivory:
pieces, 3–6 in. (7.6–15.2 cm); board,
29 ¾ x 29 ¾ x 2 ¼ in. (75.6 x 75.6 x 5.7 cm)
[The Ivory Palace, New Delhi, sold
5 October 1971 for $3,000 to]; Norton
Simon, gift 28 December 1978 to; The
Norton Simon Foundation (F.1978.20.1–33).

Cat. 746
India
Shiva and Parvati
Ivory, 13 ¼ x 3 ¾ in. (33.7 x 9.5 cm)
[Indian Handicrafts Emporium, New Delhi,
sold 5 October 1971 for $2,153 to]; Norton
Simon (sale, Los Angeles, Sotheby Parke
Bernet, 13 December 1977, for $475).

Cat. 747

Vasily Kandinsky (Russian, 1866–1944)
Open Green, 1923
Oil on canvas, 38 ¼ x 38 ¼ in.
(97.2 x 97.2 cm)
(Sale, New York, Parke-Bernet Galleries,
20 October 1971 for $155,000 to); The
Norton Simon Foundation (F.1971.4).

Cat. 748

Henri Rousseau (French, 1844–1910)
Exotic Landscape, 1910
Oil on canvas, 51 ¼ x 64 in. (130.2 x 162.6 cm)
(Sale, New York, Parke-Bernet Galleries, 21
October 1971 for $775,000 to); The Norton
Simon Foundation (F.1971.3).

Cat. 749

Henry Moore (English, 1898–1986)
Draped Reclining Woman, 1957–1958
Bronze, edition of 7, cast no. 6,
55 x 87 x 45 in. (139.7 x 221 x 114.3 cm)
[Jeffrey H. Loria & Co., New York, sold 8
November 1971 for $145,000 to]; Norton
Simon Art Foundation (M.1971.2).

Cat. 750

Vasily Kandinsky (Russian, 1866–1944)
On the Theme of the Last Judgment
Oil on canvas, 18 ⅝ x 20 ⅝ in.
(47.3 x 52.4 cm)
[Leonard Hutton Galleries, New York,
sold 16 December 1971 for $187,500 to];
The Norton Simon Foundation, sold
12 January 1973 for $225,000 to; [Leonard
Hutton Galleries, New York]. Fridart
Foundation, on loan to the Courtauld
Gallery, London.

Cat. 751

India, Madhya Pradesh
A Dejected Heroine(?), 11th century
Sandstone, 40 in. (101.6 cm)
[Doris Wiener, New York, sold 20 December
1971 for $45,000 to]; The Norton Simon
Foundation (F.1971.5).

1972

Cat. 752

Henry Moore (English, 1898–1986)
Girl Seated against a Square Wall
Bronze, artist's proof, 42 x 33 ⅝ x 28 ⅛ in.
(106.7 x 85.4 x 71.4 cm)
[Jeffrey H. Loria & Co., New York, sold 17
January 1972 for $70,000 to]; The Norton
Simon Foundation (F.1972.2.2).

Cat. 753

Henry Moore (English, 1898–1986)
Reclining Figure, 1957
Bronze, 13 x 28 in. (33 x 71.1 cm)
[Jeffrey H. Loria & Co., New York,
sold 17 January 1972 for $40,000 to];
The Norton Simon Foundation (sale, New

York, Christie's, 19 May 1982, lot 45, for
$130,000).

Cat. 754

India, Bihar, Gupta Period
Buddha Shakyamuni, c. 550
Bronze, 16 ½ in. (41.9 cm)
[Doris Wiener, New York, sold 17 January
1972 for $300,000 to]; The Norton Simon
Foundation (F.1972.1).

Cat. 755

India, Orissa, Tangi
Celestial Musician, early 12th century
Sandstone, 39 ¾ in. (101 cm)
[Doris Wiener, New York, sold 17 January
1972 for $15,000 to]; Norton Simon, by
inheritance 2 June 1993 to; Jennifer Jones
Simon Art Trust, Los Angeles (N.1972.1).

Cat. 756

India, Tamil Nadu
Parvati, c. 1000
Bronze, 34 ½ in. (87.6 cm)
[Doris Wiener, New York, sold 24 January
1972 for $100,000 to]; Norton Simon, gift
31 December 1982 to; The Norton Simon
Foundation (F.1982.2.2).

Cat. 757

Egypt
Cat, c. 600 B.C.
Bronze with gold earring, 6 ⅝ in. (16.8 cm)
[J. J. Klejman, New York, sold 28 January
1972 for $6,000 to]; Norton Simon, gift
18 October 1983 to; The Norton Simon
Foundation (F.1983.37).

Cat. 758

Henry Moore (English, 1898–1986)
Studies for Sculpture, 1944
Watercolor, 21 x 16 in. (53.3 x 40.6 cm)
[Jeffrey H. Loria & Co., New York, sold 24
February 1972 for $11,500 to]; The Norton
Simon Foundation (sale, New York, Sotheby
Parke Bernet, 2 May 1974, lot 179, for
$26,000 to); private collection.

749

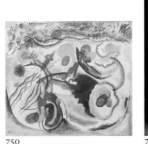

750   754

751   755   756

752

757

758

753

759

760

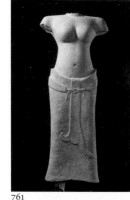
761

762

763

764

765

766

767

768

Cat. 759
Peter Paul Rubens (Flemish, 1577–1640)
David Slaying Goliath, c. 1615–1617
Oil on canvas, 48 ⅜ x 39 ⅛ in.
(122.9 x 99.4 cm)
[Frederick Mont, New York, sold 4 March
1972 for $500,000 to]; The Norton Simon
Foundation (F.1972.5).

Cat. 760
Africa, Nigeria, Ogboni
Seated Queen, 17th–18th century
Bronze, 32 ½ in. (82.6 cm)
[J. J. Klejman, New York, sold 4 April 1972
for $57,000 to]; Norton Simon, gift
28 December 1978 to; The Norton Simon
Foundation (F.1978.15).

Cat. 761
Cambodia, Angkor Period
Female Torso, 950–1000
Sandstone, 34 ½ in. (87.6 cm)
[J. J. Klejman, New York, sold 4 April
1972 for $9,500 to]; Norton Simon, gift
28 December 1978 to; The Norton Simon
Foundation (F.1978.25).

Cat. 762
Egypt
Head, 4th century B.C.
Diorite, 7 in. (17.8 cm)
[J. J. Klejman, New York, sold 4 April
1972 for $14,250 to]; Norton Simon, gift
18 December 1978 to; The Norton Simon
Foundation (F.1978.17).

Cat. 763
India, Kashmir
Bodhisattva Manjusri, 9th century
Bronze, 20 ⅛ in. (51.5 cm)
[J. J. Klejman, New York, sold 4 April
1972 for $33,250 to]; Norton Simon, gift
28 December 1978 to; The Norton Simon
Foundation (F.1978.27).

Cat. 764
India, Orissa
Furniture Leg, 17th century
Ivory, 15 ¾ in. (40 cm)
[J. J. Klejman, New York, sold 4 April
1972 for $4,750 to]; Norton Simon, gift
28 December 1978 to; The Norton Simon
Foundation (F.1978.21).

Cat. 765
India, Tamil Nadu
Ganesha, c. 1000–1050
Bronze, 14 in. (35.6 cm)
[J. J. Klejman, New York, sold 4 April
1972 for $40,000 to]; Norton Simon, by
inheritance 2 June 1993 to; Jennifer Jones
Simon Art Trust, Los Angeles (N.1972.3.2).

Cat. 766
India, Uttar Pradesh or Madhya Pradesh
Dancing Ganesha, 10th century
Sandstone, 23 in. (58.4 cm)
[J. J. Klejman, New York, sold 4 April
1972 for $8,000 to]; Norton Simon, by
inheritance 2 June 1993 to; Jennifer Jones
Simon Art Trust, Los Angeles (N.1972.3.3).

Cat. 767
Syrian, Byzantine
Architectural Subject, late 4th century
Mosaic, 54 ½ x 39 ½ in. (138.4 x 100.3 cm)
[J. J. Klejman, New York, sold 4 April
1972 for $7,000 to]; Norton Simon, by
inheritance 2 June 1993 to; Jennifer Jones
Simon Art Trust, Los Angeles (N.1972.3.60).

Cat. 768
Thailand
Torso of Buddha, 8th–9th century
Sandstone, 32 ½ in. (82.6 cm)
[J. J. Klejman, New York, sold 4 April
1972 for $10,450 to]; Norton Simon, gift
28 December 1978 to; The Norton Simon
Foundation (F.1978.24).

Cat. 769
Francisco de Zurbarán (Spanish, 1598–1664)
Still Life with Lemons, Oranges, and a Rose,
1633
Oil on canvas, 24 ½ x 43 ⅛ in.
(62.2 x 109.5 cm)
[Sea-Art Zurich (E. V. Thaw), sold 4 April
1972 for $2,725,000 to]; The Norton Simon
Foundation (F.1972.6).

Cat. 770
Cambodia, Angkor Period
Cosmic Deity or *Hari-Hara*, c. 1050
Sandstone, 41 ½ in. (105.4 cm)
[William Wolff, New York, sold 5 April
1972 for $86,500 to]; Norton Simon,
by inheritance 2 June 1993 to; Jennifer
Jones Simon Art Trust, Los Angeles, gift
6 February 2004 to; Norton Simon Art
Foundation (M.2004.1).

Cat. 771
India, Rajasthan
Door Jamb with Amorous Couples, c. 850
Sandstone, 51 in. (129.5 cm)
[William Wolff, New York, sold 5 April
1972 for $5,000 to]; Norton Simon, gift
18 October 1983 to; The Norton Simon
Foundation (F.1983.25).

Cat. 772
India, Uttar Pradesh
Celestial Dancer, 11th century
Sandstone, 36 x 19 in. (91.4 x 48.3 cm)
[William Wolff, New York, sold 5 April
1972 for $300,000 to]; Norton Simon, by
inheritance 2 June 1993 to; Jennifer Jones
Simon Art Trust, Los Angeles (N.1972.4.2).

Cat. 773
Augustus John (English, 1878–1961)
Head of a Child
Pen and ink, 8 ⅜ x 8 in. (21.3 x 20.3 cm)
[Francart S.A., Zug, Switzerland, sold 21

April 1972 for $5,917 to]; The Norton Simon
Foundation (sale, London, Christie's,
13 March 1981, lot 52, for $472).

Cat. 774
Constantin Brancusi (Romanian, 1876–1957)
Bird in Space, 1931
Polished bronze, 73 in. (185.4 cm)
[Richard Feigen, New York, sold 28 April
1972 for $335,000 to]; The Norton Simon
Foundation (F.1972.8).

Cat. 775
Jan Steen (Dutch, c. 1626–1679)
Bathsheba, late 1660s
Oil on panel, 15 x 12 ⅜ in. (38.1 x 31.4 cm)
[G. Cramer, Amsterdam, sold 28 April
1972 for $30,000 to]; The Norton Simon
Foundation (F.1972.9).

Cat. 776
Henri Matisse
Nude on Blue Cushion beside a Fireplace
(formerly titled *Seated Nude with Raised
Arms*), 1925
Lithograph, no. 4 of 10 artist's proofs:
image, 25 x 18 ⅞ in. (63.5 x 47.9 cm); sheet,
29 ¼ x 22 ⅛ in. (74.3 x 56.2 cm)
[Robert M. Light, Boston, sold 1 May 1972
for $2,000 to]; Norton Simon, gift 12 March
1982 to; Norton Simon Art Foundation
(M.1982.2).

Cat. 777
Greece, Attic
Grave Stele with Three Figures,
c. 360–350 B.C.
Marble, 38 ¾ x 23 ¾ in. (98.4 x 60.3 cm)
(Sale, New York, Sotheby, Parke-Bernet,
4 May 1972 for $155,000 to); Norton Simon,
by inheritance 2 June 1993 to; Jennifer
Jones Simon Art Trust, Los Angeles, gift
21 January 2005 to; Norton Simon Art
Foundation (M.2005.1).

769

770
774
771
772
775
776

773
777

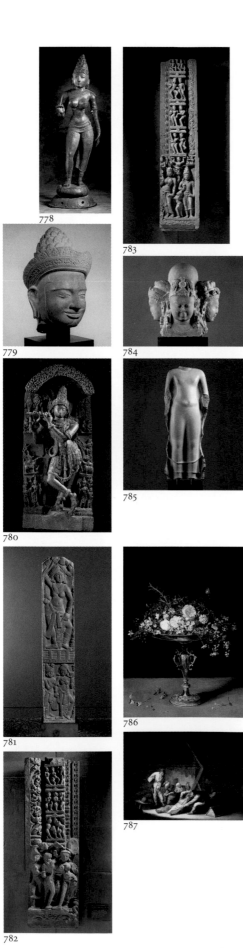

778

783

779

784

780

785

781

786

782

787

Cat. 778
India, Tamil Nadu
Parvati, c. 1000
Bronze, 32 ½ in. (82.6 cm)
[Doris Wiener, New York, sold 12 May
1972 for $80,000 to]; The Norton Simon
Foundation (F.1972.10).

Cat. 779
Cambodia, Angkor Period
Head of Shiva, c. 925
Sandstone, 18 ½ in. (47 cm)
[William Wolff, New York, sold 15 May
1972 for $49,700 to]; The Norton Simon
Foundation, combined with *Torso of Shiva*
(cat. 903) to become
Shiva, c. 925 (fig. 18, p. 132)
Sandstone, 72 ½ in. (184.2 cm)
The Norton Simon Foundation; transferred
28 November 1980 to; Norton Simon Art
Foundation (M.1980.19).

Cat. 780
India, Karnataka
Krishna Fluting in Brindavan, 1100–1150
Schist, 63 in. (160 cm)
[William Wolff, New York, sold 15 May
1972 for $39,800 to]; The Norton Simon
Foundation (F.1972.11.3).

Cat. 781
India, Madhya Pradesh, Bharhut
*Railing Pillar: Goddess and an Amorous
Couple*, c. 100 B.C.
Sandstone, 58 in. (147.3 cm)
[William Wolff, New York, sold 15 May
1972 for $149,200 to]; The Norton Simon
Foundation (F.1972.11.1).

Cat. 782
India, Rajasthan or Madhya Pradesh
*Doorjamb with River Goddess and Amorous
Scenes*, c. 1100
Sandstone, 41 ½ in. (105.4 cm)
[William Wolff, New York, sold 15 May
1972 for $5,000 to]; The Norton Simon
Foundation (F.1972.11.6).

Cat. 783
India, Uttar Pradesh or Madhya Pradesh
Doorjamb with River Goddess, 9th century
Sandstone, 43 ¾ in. (111.1 cm)
[William Wolff, New York, sold 15 May
1972 for $5,000 to]; The Norton Simon
Foundation (F.1972.11.5).

Cat. 784
India, Uttar Pradesh
Shivalingam with Four Faces, c. 900
Sandstone, 17 ½ x 17 x 17 in.
(44.5 x 43.2 x 43.2 cm)
[William Wolff, New York, sold 15 May
1972 for $16,600 to]; The Norton Simon
Foundation (F.1972.11.2).

Cat. 785
Thailand, Mon-Dvaravati Period
Torso of Buddha Shakyamuni,
7th–8th century
Sandstone, 36 ½ in. (92.7 cm)
[William Wolff, New York, sold 15 May
1972 for $13,200 to]; The Norton Simon
Foundation (F.1972.11.4).

Cat. 786
Jan Brueghel the Younger
(Flemish, 1601–1678)
Flowers in a Gilt Tazza, c. 1620
Oil on panel, 21 ¾ x 16 ¾ in.
(55.3 x 42.6 cm)
[Newhouse Galleries, New York, sold
19 May 1972 for $100,000 to]; The Norton
Simon Foundation (F.1972.13).

Cat. 787
Adriaen van Ostade (Dutch, 1610–1685)
Carousing Peasants, c. 1636
Oil on panel, 16 ½ x 23 ⅛ in. (41.9 x 58.7 cm)
[Schaeffer Galleries, New York, sold 30 May
1972 for $31,000 to]; The Norton Simon
Foundation (F.1972.14).

Cat. 788

Nicolaes Berchem (Dutch, 1620–1683)
Pastoral Scene, 1679
Oil on panel, 26 ¾ x 25 ¼ in. (68 x 64.1 cm)
[Edward Speelman, London, sold 31 May 1972 for $31,360 to]; The Norton Simon Foundation (F.1972.15.4).

Cat. 789A-B

Follower of Thomas de Keyser
(Dutch, 1596/97–1667)
Portrait of a Man and *Portrait of a Woman*, c. 1637
Oil on panel, 18 ⅜ x 15 ⅞ in.
(46.7 x 40.3 cm) and
18 x 15 ½ in. (45.7 x 39.4 cm)
[Edward Speelman, London, sold 31 May 1972 for $39,200 to]; The Norton Simon Foundation (F.1972.15.3.1–2).

Cat. 790

Nicolaes Maes (Dutch, 1634–1693)
Dordrecht Family in an Interior, c. 1656
Oil on canvas, 44 ¼ x 47 ⅝ in.
(112.4 x 121 cm)
[Edward Speelman, London, sold 31 May 1972 for $78,400 to]; The Norton Simon Foundation (F.1972.15.2).

Cat. 791

Gabriel Metsu (Dutch, 1629–1667)
Woman at Her Toilette, c. 1659
Oil on panel, 25 ½ x 22 ¾ in. (64.8 x 57.8 cm)
[Edward Speelman, London, sold 31 May 1972 for $209,000 to]; The Norton Simon Foundation (F.1972.15.1).

Cat. 792

Cambodia or Thailand, Angkor Period
Shiva, late 11th–early 12th century
Sandstone, 46 in. (116.8 cm)
[J. J. Klejman, New York, sold 1 June 1972 for $31,350 to]; The Norton Simon Foundation (F.1972.16.2).

Cat. 793

Cambodia, Angkor Period

Vishnu Riding on Garuda, c. 1200
Bronze, 3 ⅞ in. (9.8 cm)
[J. J. Klejman, New York, sold 1 June 1972 for $1,330 to]; The Norton Simon Foundation (F.1972.16.1).

Cat. 794

India, Bihar, Gaya Region
Future Buddha Maitreya, 12th century
Bronze inlaid with silver, 3 ½ in. (8.9 cm)
[J. J. Klejman, New York, sold 1 June 1972 for $1,520 to]; The Norton Simon Foundation (F.1972.16.4).

Cat. 795

India, Kashmir
Buddha Shakyamuni, c. 850
Brass with silver inlay and pigment,
5 ¼ in. (13.3 cm)
[J. J. Klejman, New York, sold 1 June 1972 for $3,325 to]; The Norton Simon Foundation (F.1972.16.5).

Cat. 796

India, Uttar Pradesh, Mathura
Lingam with Shiva's Face, c. 200
Sandstone, 8 ½ in. (21.6 cm)
[J. J. Klejman, New York, sold 1 June 1972 for $1,140 to]; The Norton Simon Foundation (F.1972.16.6).

Cat. 797

India, West Bengal or Bangladesh
Tara, 12th century
Brass, 4 ⅝ in. (11.7 cm)
[J. J. Klejman, New York, sold 1 June 1972 for $3,325 to]; The Norton Simon Foundation (F.1972.16.8).

Cat. 798

India, West Bengal or Bangladesh
Tara, 12th century
Brass inlaid with silver, 4 ⅝ in. (11.7 cm)
[J. J. Klejman, New York, sold 1 June 1972 for $2,850 to]; The Norton Simon Foundation (F.1972.16.3).

788

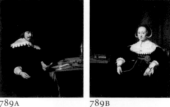
789A   789B

790

791

792

793

794

795

796

797

798

799

804

800

805

801

806

802

807

803

808

Cat. 799
India, West Bengal or Bangladesh
Buddhist Triad of Shadakshari Deities,
Late 11th century
Bronze inlaid with silver, 8 ¼ in. (21 cm)
[J. J. Klejman, New York, sold 1 June 1972 for
$2,660 to]; The Norton Simon Foundation
(F.1972.16.7).

Cat. 800
Jan van der Heyden (Dutch, 1637–1712)
Library Interior with Still Life, c. 1710–1712
Oil on canvas, 26 ¾ x 22 ½ in. (68 x 57.2 cm)
[Walter Feilchenfeldt, Zurich, sold 6 June
1972 for $34,210 to]; The Norton Simon
Foundation (F.1972.17).

Cat. 801
Gustave Courbet (French, 1819–1877)
Henri Rochefort, 1874
Oil on canvas, 25 ½ x 21 ¼ in. (64.8 x 54 cm)
[Paul Rosenberg & Co., New York, sold
7 June 1972 for $40,000 to]; The Norton
Simon Foundation (F.1972.18.1).

Cat. 802
Sebastian Stoskopff (German, 1597–1657)
Still Life with Empty Glasses, c. 1640
Oil on canvas, 34 x 43 ¼ in. (86.4 x 109.9 cm)
[Paul Rosenberg & Co., New York, sold
7 June 1972 for $80,000 to]; The Norton
Simon Foundation (F.1972.18.2).

Cat. 803
India, Orissa
Furniture Leg, 17th century
Ivory, 5 ⅝ in. (14.3 cm)
[J. J. Klejman, New York, sold 20 June
1972 for $6,000 to]; Norton Simon, by
inheritance 2 June 1993 to; Jennifer Jones
Simon Art Trust, Los Angeles (N.1972.14).

Cat. 804
Nepal, Kathmandu
Mandala of Chakrasamvara, dated 1648
Opaque watercolor on cotton,
43 ½ x 33 ½ in. (110.5 x 85.1 cm)
[Doris Wiener, New York, sold 20 June
1972 for $25,000 to]; Norton Simon, by
inheritance 2 June 1993 to; Jennifer Jones
Simon Art Trust, Los Angeles (N.1972.7).

Cat. 805
Cambodia, Angkor Period
Prajnaparamita, c. 1225
Bronze, 15 ¼ in. (38.7 cm)
[J. J. Klejman, New York, sold 1 July 1972 for
$9,500 to]; The Norton Simon Foundation
(F.1972.19.1).

Cat. 806
India, Andhra Pradesh
Shiva with Uma and Skanda, 11th century
Bronze, 16 ³/₁₆ x 18 ½ in. (41.1 x 21.6 cm)
[J. J. Klejman, New York, sold 1 July 1972 for
$95,000 to]; The Norton Simon Foundation
(F.1972.19.3).

Cat. 807
India, Madhya Pradesh
Amorous Couple, late 11th century
Sandstone, 26 1/6 x 14 in. (66.5 x 35.6 cm)
[J. J. Klejman, New York, sold 1 July 1972 for
$3,325 to]; The Norton Simon Foundation
(F.1972.19.4).

Cat. 808
India, Tamil Nadu
Cosmic Form of Krishna, 15th century
Bronze, 19 ⅜ in. (49.2 cm)
[J. J. Klejman, New York, sold 1 July 1972 for
$7,600 to]; The Norton Simon Foundation
(F.1972.19.7).

Cat. 809
India, Uttar Pradesh
Kumara, 8th–9th century
Sandstone, 25 ½ x 15 x 6 ½ in.
(64.8 x 38.1 x 16.5 cm)
[J. J. Klejman, New York, sold 1 July 1972 for
$4,275 to]; The Norton Simon Foundation
(F.1972.19.5).

Cat. 810
India, Tamil Nadu
Shaiva Saint Sundarar, 15th century
Bronze, 32 in. (81.3 cm)
[J. J. Klejman, New York, sold 1 July 1972 for
$11,400 to]; The Norton Simon Foundation
(F.1972.19.6).

Cat. 811
Thailand, Si Thep(?), Mon-Dvaravati
Period
Plaque with Vishnu with Attendant, c. 700
Gold repoussé, 11 ⅞ x 6 ⅜ in.
(30.2 x 16.2 cm)
[J. J. Klejman, New York, sold 1 July 1972 for
$24,000 to]; The Norton Simon Foundation
(F.1972.19.2).

Cat. 812A-B
Umbrian School
Saints, 1350–1360
Pen and ink, recto/verso, 5 ½ x 7 ⁹/₁₆ in.
(14 x 19.2 cm)
[Schaeffer Galleries, New York, sold 1 July
1972 for $4,000 to]; Norton Simon, gift
30 December 1975 to; Norton Simon Art
Foundation (M.1975.25).

Cat. 813
Cambodia, Khmer, Bakheng style
Vishnu, 9th–10th century
Stone, 39 in. (99.1 cm)
[Spink & Son, London, sold 5 July 1972
for $160,000 to]; The Norton Simon
Foundation, sold 29 January 1980 for
$340,000 to; [Spink & Son, London].

Cat. 814
Jean-Baptiste Camille Corot
(French, 1796–1875)
Rebecca at the Well, 1838–1839
Oil on canvas, 19 ¾ x 29 ¼ in. (50.2 x 74.3 cm)
[Galerie Schmit, Paris, sold 6 July 1972
for $200,000 to]; The Norton Simon
Foundation (F.1972.21).

Cat. 815
Guariento di Arpo (Italian, c. 1310–c. 1370)
Coronation of the Virgin, 1344
Tempera and gold leaf on panels, polyptych:
overall, 86 x 104 ⅜ in. (218.4 x 265.1 cm)
(Sale, London, Christie's, 7 July 1972
for $631,214 to); The Norton Simon
Foundation, transferred 27 November
1987 to; Norton Simon Art Foundation
(M.1987.3.1–32).

Cat. 816
India, Bihar, Kurkihar
Buddha in His Body of Bliss, 1050–1100
Bronze inlaid with silver, copper, and
turquoise, 7 in. (17.8 cm)
(Sale, London, Sotheby & Co., 11 July
1972 for $7,871 to); The Norton Simon
Foundation (F.1972.30.2).

Cat. 817
India, Tamil Nadu
Shiva as the Supreme Teacher, c. 1100
Granite, 16 in. (40.6 cm)
(Sale, London, Sotheby & Co., 11 July
1972 for $1,845 to); The Norton Simon
Foundation (F.1972.30.3).

Cat. 818
India, Tamil Nadu
Shiva and Parvati Embracing, 12th century
Bronze, 15 ⅝ in. (39.7 cm)
(Sale, London, Sotheby & Co., 11 July
1972 for $3,936 to); The Norton Simon
Foundation (F.1972.30.1).

809

814

810

815

811

816

812A

813

817

818

819

820

821

822   824

823

825

826

827

828

829

Cat. 819
Jean-Antoine Watteau (French, 1684–1721)
Reclining Nude, c. 1713–1717
Oil on panel, 6 x 6 ⅞ in. (15.2 x 17.5 cm)
[E. V. Thaw & Co., New York, sold 16 July 1972 for $240,000 to]; The Norton Simon Foundation (F.1972.12).

Cat. 820
Cambodia, Angkor Period
Bodhisattva Avalokiteshvara, 1000–1050
Sandstone, 44 in. (111.8 cm)
[Ben Heller, New York, sold 26 July 1972 for $50,000 to]; The Norton Simon Foundation (F.1972.22.1).

Cat. 821
India, Uttar Pradesh, Mathura
Serpent Deity, 100–150
Sandstone, 78 ¼ in. (198.8 cm)
[Ben Heller, New York, sold 26 July 1972 for $75,000 to]; The Norton Simon Foundation (F.1972.22.2).

Cat. 822
India, Tamil Nadu
Parvati, c. 975
Bronze, 30 in. (76.2 cm)
[Ben Heller, New York, sold 27 July 1972 for $150,000 to]; The Norton Simon Foundation (F.1972.23.2).

Cat. 823
India, Tamil Nadu, Shivapuram
Shiva with Uma and Skanda, 950–975
Bronze, 23 x 27 ½ x 14 in.
(58.4 x 69.8 x 35.6 cm)
[Ben Heller, New York, sold 27 July 1972 for $225,000 to]; The Norton Simon Foundation (F.1972.23.1).

Cat. 824
India, Tamil Nadu
Shiva the Bull-Rider, c. 1000
Bronze, 39 ½ in. (100.3 cm)
[E. V. Thaw & Co., New York, sold 27 July 1972 for $360,000 to]; The Norton Simon Foundation (F.1972.24).

Cat. 825
India, Tamil Nadu
Shaiva Saint Sambandar, 15th century
Bronze, 20 ½ in. (52.1 cm)
[J. J. Klejman, New York, sold 1 August 1972 for $14,250 to]; The Norton Simon Foundation (F.1972.25.3).

Cat. 826
India, Tamil Nadu
Shiva as Lord of Music, 1100
Bronze, 29 in. (73.7 cm)
[J. J. Klejman, New York, sold 1 August 1972 for $31,350 to]; The Norton Simon Foundation (F.1972.25.2).

Cat. 827
India, Tamil Nadu
Terrifying Form of Shiva, c. 1000
Bronze, 9 in. (22.9 cm)
[J. J. Klejman, New York, sold 1 August 1972 for $9,500 to]; The Norton Simon Foundation (F.1972.25.1).

Cat. 828
India, Uttar Pradesh
Stele with Shiva, Parvati and Ganesha, 9th century
Sandstone, 27 x 13 in. (68.6 x 33 cm)
[J. J. Klejman, New York, sold 1 August 1972 for $4,275 to]; The Norton Simon Foundation (F.1972.25.4).

Cat. 829
Giovanni Battista Tiepolo
(Italian, 1696–1770)
The Triumph of Virtue and Nobility over Ignorance, c. 1740–1750
Oil on canvas, 126 x 154 ½ in.
(320 x 392.4 cm)
[E. V. Thaw & Co., New York, sold 2 August 1972 for $975,000 to]; The Norton Simon Foundation (F.1972.26).

Cat. 830
India, Tamil Nadu
Ganesha, c. 950–1000
Bronze, 16 in. (40.6 cm)
[Ben Heller, New York, sold 3 August
1972 for $20,000 to]; The Norton Simon
Foundation (F.1972.28).

Cat. 831
Nepal
Indra, 13th century
Gilt bronze, 16 ⅛ in. (41 cm)
[Jitendra Wankaner, Los Angeles, sold
3 August 1972 for $80,000 to]; The Norton
Simon Foundation (F.1972.27).

Cat. 832
Thailand, Buriram Province, Prakhon Chai
Bodhisattva Avalokiteshvara, 8th century
Bronze, 36 in. (91.4 cm)
[Ben Heller, New York, sold 3 August
1972 for $220,000 to]; The Norton Simon
Foundation, transferred 28 November
1980 to; Norton Simon Art Foundation
(M.1980.14).

Cat. 833
Cambodia or Thailand, Angkor Period
Bodhisattva Avalokiteshvara, 1150–1175
Sandstone, 40 in. (101.6 cm)
[Robert Ellsworth, New York, sold
16 August 1972 for $30,000 to]; The Norton
Simon Foundation (F.1972.31.1).

Cat. 834
India, Tamil Nadu, Nagapattinam
Buddha Shakyamuni, late 11th century
Bronze, 29 ¾ in. (75.6 cm)
[Robert Ellsworth, New York, sold
16 August 1972 for $120,000 to]; The Norton
Simon Foundation (F.1972.31.2).

Cat. 835
India, Tamil Nadu
Vishnu, c. 875
Granite, 63 ½ in. (161.3 cm)
[Robert Ellsworth, New York, sold 16
August 1972 for $45,000 to]; The Norton
Simon Foundation (F.1972.31.3).

Cat. 836
India, Tamil Nadu
Vishnu, c. 1000
Granite, 70 ½ in. (179.1 cm)
[Robert Ellsworth, New York, sold
16 August 1972 for $45,000 to]; The Norton
Simon Foundation (F.1972.31.4).

Cat. 837
Eugène Delacroix (French, 1798–1863)
*Abd Er Rahman, Sultan of Morocco
Reviewing His Guard*, 1856
Oil on canvas, 25 ⅝ x 21 ⅝ in.
(65.1 x 54.9 cm)
[Hector Brame, Paris, sold 24 August
1972 for $330,000 to]; The Norton Simon
Foundation, sold 10 February 1982 for
$900,000 to; [E. V. Thaw & Co. and
Acquavella Galleries, New York, sold to];
private collection.

Cat. 838
India, Bihar, Kurkihar
Buddha in His Body of Bliss, 1050–1100
Bronze inlaid with silver, 6 ⅜ in. (16.2 cm)
[J. J. Klejman, New York, sold 1 September
1972 for $2,660 to]; The Norton Simon
Foundation (F.1972.34.3).

Cat. 839
India, Kashmir
Bodhisattva Vajrasatva, c. 1000
Bronze with silver inlay, 9 ⅛ in. (23.2 cm)
[J. J. Klejman, New York, sold 1 September
1972 for $3,800 to]; The Norton Simon
Foundation (F.1972.34.2).

830

835

831

836

832

837

833

838   839

834

840

841

842

843

844

845

846

848

849

Cat. 840
India, Tamil Nadu
Shiva with Uma and Skanda, 1250–1350
Bronze, 24 x 27 x 13 ¾ in.
(61 x 68.6 x 34.9 cm)
[J. J. Klejman, New York, sold 1 September
1972 for $14,250 to]; The Norton Simon
Foundation (F.1972.34.4).

Cat. 841
India, West Bengal or Bangladesh
*Bodhisattva Avalokiteshvara with Female
Devotee*, 12th century
Brass inlaid with silver and copper,
5 ½ in. (14 cm)
[J. J. Klejman, New York, sold 1 September
1972 for $2,375 to]; The Norton Simon
Foundation (F.1972.34.1).

Cat. 842
Thailand, Mon-Dvaravati Period
Head of Buddha Shakyamuni, 8th century
Bronze, 6 ½ in. (16.5 cm)
[J. J. Klejman, New York, sold 1 September
1972 for $31,350 to]; The Norton Simon
Foundation (F.1972.34.5).

Cat. 843
Aert van der Neer (Dutch, 1603–1677)
Winter Scene with Figures Playing Kolf,
1650–1655
Oil on canvas, 22 ¾ x 30 ⅞ in.
(57.8 x 78.4 cm)
[Edward Speelman, London, sold 1
September 1972 for $244,860 to]; The
Norton Simon Foundation (F.1972.35).

Cat. 844
Jan Fyt (Flemish, 1611–1661)
Still Life with Red Curtain, c. 1660
Oil on canvas, 43 x 62 ⅞ in. (109.2 x 159.7 cm)
[Edward Speelman, London, sold
5 September 1972 for $93,864 to]; The
Norton Simon Foundation (F.1972.36.3).

Cat. 845
Louise Moillon (French, 1610–1696)
*Still Life with Cherries, Strawberries, and
Gooseberries*, 1630
Oil on panel, 12 ⅝ x 19 ⅛ in. (32.1 x 48.6 cm)
[Edward Speelman, London, sold
5 September 1972 for $83,433 to]; The
Norton Simon Foundation (F.1972.36.2).

Cat. 846
Roelandt Savery (Dutch, 1576–1639)
Landscape with Ruins and Animals, 1624
Oil on panel, 20 ⅞ x 29 ⅞ in. (53 x 75.9 cm)
[Edward Speelman, London, sold
5 September 1972 for $104,290 to]; The
Norton Simon Foundation (F.1972.36.1).

Cat. 847
Francisco de Goya y Lucientes
(Spanish, 1746–1828)
The Disasters of War (*Los Desastres de la
Guerra*), 1st edition, 1814–1820, printed 1863
Etching, aquatint, and drypoint, 80 plates
[Robert M. Light, Boston, sold 6 September
1972 for $25,600 to]; Norton Simon Art
Foundation, sold 23 April 1981 for $50,000
to; [William Schab, New York]; Arthur Ross
Foundation, New York.

Cat. 848
India, Uttar Pradesh, Mathura,
Gupta Period
Serpent Goddess or *Revati*, 4th century
Sandstone, 66 in. (167.6 cm)
[Walter Randel, New York, sold 6 September
1972 for $50,000 to]; The Norton Simon
Foundation (F.1972.37).

Cat. 849
Louise Moillon (French, 1610–1696)
Still Life with Bowl of Curaçao Oranges, 1634
Oil on panel, 18 ¼ x 25 ½ in. (46.4 x 64.8 cm)
[Herner Wengraf, London, sold
7 September 1972 for $36,751 to]; The
Norton Simon Foundation (F.1972.38).

Cat. 850
Pieter Claesz. (Dutch, 1597/98–1660)
Still Life with Rummer, 1645 or 1648
Oil on panel, 12 ¼ x 15 ¾ in. (31.1 x 40 cm)
[Gebr. Douwes, Amsterdam, sold
19 September 1972 for $25,000 to];
The Norton Simon Foundation (F.1972.39).

Cat. 851
Thailand, Si Thep, Mon-Dvaravati Period
Buddha Shakyamuni, 9th century
Sandstone, 88 in. (223.5 cm)
[Spink & Son, Zurich, sold 19 September
1972 for $210,000 to]; The Norton Simon
Foundation (F.1972.40.1).

Cat. 852
Cambodia, Pre-Angkor Period
Hari-Hara, 8th century
Sandstone, 26 in. (66 cm)
[Spink & Son, Zurich, sold 19 September
1972 for $32,000 to]; The Norton Simon
Foundation (F.1972.40.2).

Cat. 853
India, West Bengal or Bangladesh
*Stele with Transcendental Buddhas and
Goddesses*, c. 1050–1100
Chlorite, 27 ⅞ x 15 ½ in. (70.8 x 39.4 cm)
[Spink & Son, Zurich, sold 19 September
1972 for $23,000 to]; The Norton Simon
Foundation (F.1972.41).

Cat. 854
India, Madhya Pradesh or Rajasthan
Woman with Lamp, 11th century
Sandstone, 26 ¾ in. (67.9 cm)
[J. J. Klejman, New York, sold 1 October
1972 for $3,800 to]; The Norton Simon
Foundation (F.1972.42.1).

Cat. 855
Nepal
Bodhisattva, c. 900
Gilt bronze, 9 ⅞ in. (25.1 cm)
[J. J. Klejman, New York, sold 1 October
1972 for $15,200 to]; The Norton Simon
Foundation (F.1972.42.2).

Cat. 856
Nepal or Tibet
Bodhisattva Avalokiteshvara(?), 10th century
Gilt bronze, 13 ½ in. (34.3 cm)
[J. J. Klejman, New York, sold 1 October
1972 for $17,100 to]; The Norton Simon
Foundation (F.1972.42.3).

Cat. 857
Attributed to Ambrosius Bosschaert the
Younger (Dutch, 1609–1645)
*Large Bouquet in a Gilt-Mounted Wan-Li
Vase*, c. 1628
Oil on panel, 31 ½ x 21 ½ in. (80 x 54.6 cm)
[Gebr. Douwes, Amsterdam, sold
18 October 1972 for $80,000 to]; Norton
Simon, gift 22 December 1976 to; Norton
Simon Art Foundation (M.1976.10).

Cat. 858
Balthasar van der Ast (Dutch, c. 1593–1657)
Still Life with Fruits and Flowers, c. 1630
Oil on panel, 16 ⁹/₁₆ x 30 ¼ in. (42.1 x 76.8 cm)
[G. Cramer, Amsterdam, sold 19 October
1972 for $59,328 to]; The Norton Simon
Foundation (F.1972.43.4).

Cat. 859A-B
Nicolaes Maes (Dutch, 1634–1693)
Dirck Frederiksz. Alewijn and *Agatha Bicker*,
c. mid-1670s
Oil on panel, 17 ½ x 12 ½ in. (44.5 x 31.8 cm)
and 17 ⅜ x 12 ½ in. (44.1 x 31.8 cm)
[G. Cramer, Amsterdam, sold 19 October
1972 for $12,360 to]; The Norton Simon
Foundation (F.1972.43.3.1–2).

Cat. 860
Master of the Mansi-Magdalena
(Dutch, active c. 1510–1525)
The Lamentation of Christ
Oil on panel, 21 ¼ x 25 ½ in. (54 x 64.8 cm)
[G. Cramer, Amsterdam, sold 19 October
1972 for $20,090 to]; The Norton Simon
Foundation (F.1972.43.2).

850

856

851

857

858

852

859A   859B

853

860

854   855

861

866A–C

862

867

863

868

864

865

869

870

Cat. 861

Rachel Ruysch (Dutch, 1664/65–1750)
Nosegay on a Marble Plinth, c. 1695
Oil on canvas, 15 x 12 in. (38.1 x 30.5 cm)
[G. Cramer, Amsterdam, sold 19 October
1972 for $26,264 to]; The Norton Simon
Foundation (F.1972.43.1).

Cat. 862

Jean-Louis Forain (French, 1852–1931)
Head of a Woman with Veil, c. 1878–1880
Oil on canvas, 13 ⅞ x 10 ⅞ in. (35.2 x 27.7 cm)
[E. J. van Wisselingh, Amsterdam, sold
19 October 1972 for $5,000 to]; Norton
Simon (sale, New York, Sotheby Parke
Bernet, 2 May 1973, lot 5, for $22,000).
private collection (sale, London, Sotheby
Parke Bernet & Co., 4 December 1980 for
$24,814 to); Norton Simon, by inheritance
2 June 1993 to; Jennifer Jones Simon Art
Trust, Los Angeles, gift 12 August 1997 to;
Norton Simon Art Foundation (M.1997.1.3).

Cat. 863

Vincent van Gogh (Dutch, 1853–1890)
Still Life, 1884
Oil on canvas, 15 ¾ x 22 ¼ in. (40 x 56.5 cm)
[E. J. van Wisselingh, Amsterdam, sold 19
October 1972 for $62,500 to]; The Norton
Simon Foundation (F.1972.44).

Cat. 864

Vincent van Gogh
The Mill, 1882
Black chalk, 11 ¾ x 14 ¾ in. (29.9 x 37.5 cm)
[E. J. van Wisselingh, Amsterdam, sold
19 October 1972 for $16,500 to]; The
Norton Simon Foundation (sale, New York,
Sotheby Parke Bernet, 2 May 1973, lot 31,
for $22,000). private collection, Memphis,
Tenn., 1992.

Cat. 865

India, Kerala
Vishnu, c. 1550
Bronze, 15 in. (38.1 cm)

[Oriental Antiquities, London, sold
26 October 1972 for $10,000 to]; The
Norton Simon Foundation (F.1972.45.10).

Cat. 866A-C

India, Tamil Nadu
Aiyanar with Two Consorts, 13th century
Bronze: Aiyanar, 11 ¾ in. (29.8 cm);
consorts, 7 in. (17.8 cm) and 6 ½ in. (16.5 cm)
[Oriental Antiquities, London, sold
26 October 1972 for $65,000 to]; The
Norton Simon Foundation (F.1972.45.1.1–3).

Cat. 867

India, Tamil Nadu
Shaiva Saint Appar, 13th–15th century
Bronze, 20 ¼ in. (51.4 cm)
[Oriental Antiquities, London, sold
26 October 1972 for $20,000 to]; The
Norton Simon Foundation (F.1972.45.2).

Cat. 868

India, Tamil Nadu
Krishna the Regal Cowherd with Consorts,
12th century
Bronze, 15 ¾ in. (40 cm)
[Oriental Antiquities, London, sold
26 October 1972 for $20,000 to]; The
Norton Simon Foundation (F.1972.45.3).

Cat. 869

India, Tamil Nadu
Dancing Krishna
Bronze, 21 ¾ in. (55.3 cm)
[Oriental Antiquities, London, sold
26 October 1972 for $15,000 to]; The Norton
Simon Foundation, sold 20 May 1981 for
$25,000 to; [Peter Marks, New York].

Cat. 870

India, Tamil Nadu
Hanuman, 13th century
Bronze, 19 ¼ x 6 ½ in. (48.9 x 16.5 cm)
[Oriental Antiquities, London, sold
26 October 1972 for $20,000 to]; The
Norton Simon Foundation (F.1972.45.5).

Cat. 871
India, Tamil Nadu
Shiva as Lord of Music, 11th century
Bronze, 16 ⅝ in. (42.2 cm)
[Oriental Antiquities, London, sold
26 October 1972 for $20,000 to]; The
Norton Simon Foundation (F.1972.45.6).

Cat. 872
India, Tamil Nadu
Shiva as Lord of Music, c. 1150–1200
Bronze, 23 ⅝ in. (60 cm)
[Oriental Antiquities, London, sold
26 October 1972 for $40,000 to]; The
Norton Simon Foundation (F.1972.45.8).

Cat. 873
India, Tamil Nadu
Shiva as the Beggar, c. 1600
Bronze, 22 in. (55.9 cm)
[Oriental Antiquities, London, sold
26 October 1972 for $40,000 to]; The
Norton Simon Foundation (F.1972.45.9).

Cat. 874
India, Tamil Nadu, Tandantottam
Shiva as Destroyer of Three Cities, c. 925
Bronze, 30 ½ in. (77.5 cm)
[Oriental Antiquities, London, sold
26 October 1972 for $65,000 to]; The
Norton Simon Foundation (F.1972.45.7).

Cat. 875
Nepal
Bodhisattva Ratnapani(?), 10th century
Gilt bronze, 8 in. (20.3 cm)
[Oriental Antiquities, London, sold
26 October 1972 for $20,000 to]; The
Norton Simon Foundation (F.1972.45.13).

Cat. 876
Nepal or Tibet
Buddha Shakyamuni, 12th century
Gilt bronze with traces of pigment,
27 ½ in. (69.9 cm)
[Oriental Antiquities, London, sold
26 October 1972 for $50,000 to]; The
Norton Simon Foundation (F.1972.45.12).

Cat. 877
Tibet
*Bodhisattva Avalokiteshvara with Eleven
Heads*, c. 1500
Gilt bronze with copper, gold and silver
inlay, and pigment, 17 in. (43.2 cm)
[Oriental Antiquities, London, sold
26 October 1972 for $15,000 to]; The Norton
Simon Foundation (F.1972.45.11).

Cat. 878
Nepal
Bodhisattva, 12th century
Gilt bronze inlaid with semiprecious stones,
23 ¾ in. (60.3 cm)
[Doris Wiener, New York, sold 31 October
1972 for $40,000 to]; Norton Simon,
gift 18 October 1983 to; The Norton Simon
Foundation (F.1983.28).

Cat. 879
Thailand, Mon-Dvaravati Period
Head of Buddha Shakyamuni, 8th century
Limestone, 13 in. (33.2 cm)
[J. J. Klejman, New York, sold 1 November
1972 for $33,250 to]; The Norton Simon
Foundation (F.1972.46.1).

Cat. 880
Thailand, Mon-Dvaravati Period
Head of Buddha Shakyamuni, 8th century
Limestone, 11 ½ in. (29.2 cm)
[J. J. Klejman, New York, sold 1 November
1972 for $31,350 to]; The Norton Simon
Foundation (F.1972.46.2).

Cat. 881
Francesco Guardi (Italian, 1712–1793)
*View of the Santa Maria della Salute with
the Dogana di Mare*
Oil on canvas, 16 ¾ x 20 ⅜ in.
(42.5 x 51.8 cm)
[Frederick Mont, New York, sold
7 November 1972 for $200,000 to]; The
Norton Simon Foundation (F.1972.47.1).

871

877

872

878

873

879

874

875

880

876

881

882

883

884

885

886

887

888

890

891

Cat. 882

Bartolomé Esteban Murillo (Spanish, 1617–1682)

Saint Thomas of Villanueva Giving Alms to the Poor, c. 1678

Oil on canvas, 52 ⅛ x 30 in. (132.4 x 76.2 cm)

[Frederick Mont, New York, sold 7 November 1972 for $125,000 to]; The Norton Simon Foundation (F.1972.47.2).

Cat. 883

India, Himachal Pradesh

Vishnu and Lakshmi with Avatars, 11th century

Bronze, 23 ¼ x 16 ¾ in. (59.1 x 42.5 cm)

[Doris Wiener, New York, sold 8 November 1972 for $40,000 to]; The Norton Simon Foundation (F.1972.48.1).

Cat. 884

India, Kashmir

Buddha and Adorants on the Cosmic Mountain, c. 700

Bronze with silver and copper inlay, 13 ¼ x 9 ½ x 4 ¾ in. (33.7 x 24.1 x 12.1 cm)

[Doris Wiener, New York, sold 8 November 1972 for $225,000 to]; The Norton Simon Foundation (F.1972.48.2).

Cat. 885

Raffaello Sanzio, also called Raphael (Italian, 1483–1520)

Madonna and Child with Book, 1502–1503

Oil on panel, 21 ¾ x 15 ¾ in. (55.2 x 40 cm)

[Wildenstein & Co., London, sold 8 November 1972 for $3 million to]; Norton Simon Art Foundation (M.1972.2).

Cat. 886

India, Tamil Nadu

Shiva as the Handsome Bridegroom, 11th century

Bronze, 41 ½ in. (105.4 cm)

[Spink & Son, London, sold 10 November 1972 for $340,000 to]; The Norton Simon

Foundation, sold 14 March 1980 for $800,000 to; [Spink & Son, London].

Cat. 887

Tibet

Vajradakini

Bronze inlaid with copper and silver, 4 ½ in. (11.4 cm)

(Sale, London, Christie's, 14 November 1972 for $793 to); Norton Simon, gift 28 December 1978 to; The Norton Simon Foundation (F.1978.11).

Cat. 888

India, West Bengal

Vishnu with Retinue

Chlorite, 46 ½ in. (118.1 cm)

(Sale, London, Christie's, 14 November 1972 for $5,200 to); Norton Simon, gift 28 December 1978 to; The Norton Simon Foundation (F.1978.22).

Cat. 889A-B

Cornelis de Visscher (Dutch, 1629–1658)

Portrait of a Man and *Portrait of a Woman*

Black chalk on parchment, each 12 ⅜ x 9 ⅜ in. (31.4 x 23.9 cm)

[Bernard Houthakker, Amsterdam, sold 22 November 1972 for $2,788 to]; The Norton Simon Foundation (sale, London, Sotheby & Co., 27 June 1974, lots 121 and 122, for $3,880).

Cat. 890

Peter Paul Rubens (Flemish, 1577–1640)

The Holy Women at the Sepulchre, c. 1617

Oil on panel, 34 ⅝ x 42 ⅜ in. (88 x 107.6 cm)

[Thomas Agnew & Sons, London, sold 4 December 1972 for $520,000 to]; The Norton Simon Foundation (F.1972.51).

Cat. 891

Nepal

Mahakala with Retinue and Lamas, c. 1470

Opaque watercolor on cotton, 18 x 14 ¼ in. (45.7 x 36.2 cm)

(Sale, London, Sotheby & Co., 5 December 1972 for $2,220 to); Norton Simon, gift, 18 October 1983 to; The Norton Simon Foundation (F.1983.26).

Cat. 892
Jan Miense Molenaer (Dutch, c. 1610–1668)
Portrait of a Gentleman, late 1630s
Oil on panel, 32 ¾ x 23 in. (83.2 x 58.4 cm)
[Shaeffer Galleries, New York, sold 7 December 1972 for $24,000 to]; The Norton Simon Foundation (F.1972.52).

Cat. 893
After Giovanni Francesco Romanelli (Italian, 1610–1662)
Death of Dido, c. 1620–1640
Wool and silk tapestry (woven by Michel Wauters after Romanelli cartoon), 158 ½ x 224 ¾ in. (402.6 x 570.9 cm)
[Galleria Luigi Bellini, Florence, sold 8 December 1972 for $11,000 to]; The Norton Simon Foundation (F.1972.53).

Cat. 894
Jean-Siméon Chardin (French, 1699–1779)
Dog and Game, 1730
Oil on canvas, 75 ¾ x 54 ¾ in. (192.4 x 139.1 cm)
[Galerie Schmit, Paris, sold 13 December 1972 for $162,798 to]; The Norton Simon Foundation (F.1972.56).

Cat. 895
India, Madhya Pradesh, Bharhut
Railing Pillar: The Great Departure of Siddhartha, c. 100 B.C.
Sandstone, 54 in. (137.2 cm)
[Ben Heller, New York, sold 13 December 1972 for $120,000 to]; The Norton Simon Foundation (F.1972.55).

Cat. 896
India, Tamil Nadu, Shivapuram
Shiva as King of Dance, c. 950
Bronze, 43 in. (109.2 cm)

[Ben Heller, New York, sold 13 December 1972 for $900,000 to]; The Norton Simon Foundation, returned 5 May 1986 to; the Government of India, location unknown.

Cat. 897
India, Uttar Pradesh, Mathura
Railing Pillar with Yakshi, 2nd century
Sandstone, 28 ½ in. (72.4 cm)
[Ben Heller, New York, sold 13 December 1972 for $50,000 to]; Norton Simon, by inheritance 2 June 1993 to; Jennifer Jones Simon Art Trust, Los Angeles (N.1972.12.1).

Cat. 898
India, Uttar Pradesh, Mathura
Head of Vishnu, c. 325
Sandstone, 9 ½ in. (21.6 cm)
[Ben Heller, New York, sold 13 December 1972 for $15,000 to]; Norton Simon, by inheritance 2 June 1993 to; Jennifer Jones Simon Art Trust, Los Angeles (N.1972.12.2).

Cat. 899
Thailand, Si Thep, Mon-Dvaravati Period
Bust of a Hindu Deity, 7th century
Sandstone, 22 in. (55.9 cm)
[Ben Heller, New York, sold 13 December 1972 for $175,000 to]; The Norton Simon Foundation, combined with *Torso of a Hindu Deity* (cat. 1012) to become *Hindu Deity* (fig. 8, p. 170)
Sandstone, 45 in. (114.3 cm)
Transferred 28 November 1980 to; Norton Simon Art Foundation (M.1980.13).

Cat. 900
Albrecht Dürer (German, 1471–1528)
Adam and Eve
Engraving, 9 ¾ x 7 ½ in. (24.8 x 19.1 cm)
[Robert M. Light, Boston, sold 21 December 1972 for $30,000 to]; Norton Simon Art Foundation, sold 8 October 1980 for $62,000 to; [Robert M. Light, Boston, sold 1980 to]; private collection, New York.

892

897

893

894

898

895

899

896

900

901

905

902

906

903

907

904

908

909

910

1973

Cat. 901

Cambodia, Angkor Wat
Bodhisattva Avalokiteshvara, 12th century
Gilt bronze, 4 in. (10.2 cm)
[Robert Ellsworth, New York, gift 2 January 1973 to]; Norton Simon, by inheritance 2 June 1993 to; Jennifer Jones Simon Art Trust, Los Angeles (N.1973.21).

Cat. 902

Africa, Benin
Melon-shaped Cover, 16th century
Bronze, 10 x 18 in. (25.4 x 45.7 cm)
[J. J. Klejman, New York, sold 5 January 1973 for $14,000 to]; Norton Simon, gift 1983 to; The Norton Simon Foundation (F.1983.34).

Cat. 903

Cambodia, Angkor Period
Torso of Shiva, c. 925
Sandstone, 53 in. (134.6 cm)
[Doris Wiener, New York, sold 5 January 1973 for $35,000 to]; The Norton Simon Foundation; combined with *Head of Shiva* (cat. 779) to become
Shiva, c. 925 (fig. 18, p. 132)
Sandstone, 72 ½ in. (184.2 cm)
The Norton Simon Foundation; transferred 28 November 1980 to; Norton Simon Art Foundation (M.1980.19).

Cat. 904

Cambodia, Angkor Period
Vishnu, c. 950
Sandstone, 72 in. (182.9 cm)
[Doris Wiener, New York, sold 5 January 1973 for $187,500 to]; The Norton Simon Foundation, transferred 28 November 1980 to; Norton Simon Art Foundation (M.1980.16).

Cat. 905

India, Bihar
Frieze with Seven Buddhas, 10th century

Chlorite, 8 ½ x 24 ½ in. (21.6 x 62.2 cm)
[J. J. Klejman, New York, sold 5 January 1973 for $4,500 to]; The Norton Simon Foundation (F.1973.1.9).

Cat. 906

India, Bihar, Gaya Region
Buddhist Triad with Shakyamuni, c. 1000
Schist, 26 ¾ x 17 ⅛ in. (67.9 x 43.5 cm)
[J. J. Klejman, New York, sold 5 January 1973 for $5,000 to]; The Norton Simon Foundation (F.1973.1.1).

Cat. 907

India, Madhya Pradesh or Uttar Pradesh
Vishnu and the Creation Myth,
11th century
Sandstone, 18 ¼ x 25 ½ x 6 in.
(46.4 x 64.8 x 15.2 cm)
[J. J. Klejman, New York, sold 5 January 1973 for $4,000 to]; Norton Simon, gift 28 December 1978 to; The Norton Simon Foundation (F.1978.30).

Cat. 908

India, Tamil Nadu
Devasena(?), 13th century
Bronze, 13 ¼ x 5 x 4 ¾ in.
(33.7 x 12.7 x 12.1 cm)
[J. J. Klejman, New York, sold 5 January 1973 for $18,000 to]; The Norton Simon Foundation (F.1973.1.13).

Cat. 909

India, Tamil Nadu
Parvati, 14th century
Bronze, 33 ½ in. (85.1 cm)
[J. J. Klejman, New York, sold 5 January 1973 for $6,000 to]; The Norton Simon Foundation (F.1973.1.2).

Cat. 910

India, Tamil Nadu
Shaiva Saint Sambandar, 13th century
Bronze, 20 ½ in. (52.1 cm)
[J. J. Klejman, New York, sold 5 January

1973 for $8,000 to]; The Norton Simon
Foundation (F.1973.1.12).

Cat. 911

India, Tamil Nadu
Shaiva Saint Sambandar, 12th century
Bronze, 9 ⁹/₁₆ in. (24.3 cm)
[J. J. Klejman, New York, sold 5 January
1973 for $3,500 to]; The Norton Simon
Foundation (F.1973.1.3).

Cat. 912

India, Tamil Nadu
Sri-Lakshmi, 15th century
Granite, 41 ½ in. (105.4 cm)
[J. J. Klejman, New York, sold 5 January
1973 for $5,000 to]; Norton Simon Art
Foundation (M.1973.1.2).

Cat. 913

India, Tamil Nadu
Vishnu, Late 13th century
Bronze, 32 ½ in. (82.6 cm)
[J. J. Klejman, New York, sold 5 January
1973 for $8,000 to]; The Norton Simon
Foundation (F.1973.1.4).

Cat. 914

India, Tamil Nadu
Vishnu, 15th century
Bronze, 23 ¼ in. (59.1 cm)
[J. J. Klejman, New York, sold 5 January
1973 for $12,000 to]; The Norton Simon
Foundation (F.1973.1.11).

Cat. 915

India, Tamil Nadu
Vishnu, 1000–1025
Bronze, 19 ⅛ in. (48.6 cm)
[J. J. Klejman, New York, sold 5 January
1973 for $18,000 to]; Norton Simon Art
Foundation (M.1973.1.1).

Cat. 916

Nepal
Hindu Goddess, c. 1700

Gilt bronze, 7 in. (17.8 cm)
[J. J. Klejman, New York, sold 5 January
1973 for $4,667 to]; The Norton Simon
Foundation (F.1973.1.7).

Cat. 917

Nepal
Shiva and Parvati, c. 1700
Gilt bronze, 8 ¼ in. (21 cm)
[J. J. Klejman, New York, sold 5 January
1973 for $4,667 to]; The Norton Simon
Foundation (F.1973.1.5).

Cat. 918

Nepal
Vaishnavi, c. 1700
Gilt bronze, 6 ⅜ in. (16.2 cm)
[J. J. Klejman, New York, sold 5 January
1973 for $4,667 to]; The Norton Simon
Foundation (F.1973.1.6).

Cat. 919

Pakistan, Ancient Gandhara
Seven Buddhas of the Past, 2nd–3rd century
Schist, 5 x 19 in. (12.7 x 48.3 cm)
[J. J. Klejman, New York, sold 5 January
1973 for $2,500 to]; The Norton Simon
Foundation (F.1973.1.10).

Cat. 920

Thailand, Lop Buri(?)
Reliquary with Multiple Buddhas,
13th–14th century
Bronze, 9 ¼ in. (23.5 cm)
[J. J. Klejman, New York, sold 5 January
1973 for $4,000 to]; The Norton Simon
Foundation (F.1973.1.14).

Cat. 921

Tibet
Tara, 18th century
Lacquered and gilt bronze, 5 ⅝ in. (14.3 cm)
[J. J. Klejman, New York, sold 5 January
1973 for $500 to]; The Norton Simon
Foundation (F.1973.1.8).

911

916

912

917

918

913

919

914

920

915

921

922

923

927

924

928A   928B

925

929

926

Cat. 922
Vasily Kandinsky (Russian, 1866–1944)
Improvisation No. 24
Oil on board, 19 ⅛ x 25 ⅝ in. (48.6 x 65.1 cm)
[Leonard Hutton, New York, sold 12 January 1973 for $230,000 to]; The Norton Simon Foundation, sale 11 February 1982 for $783,333 to; [E. V. Thaw & Co., New York, sold to]; Emilio Azcárraga, Mexico City, bequest 1997 to; private collection, Mérida.

Cat. 923
Vasily Kandinsky (Russian, 1866–1944)
Street in Murnau with Women, 1908
Oil on board, 28 x 38 ½ in. (71.1 x 97.8 cm)
[Leonard Hutton, New York, sold 12 January 1973 for $230,000 to]; The Norton Simon Foundation, sale 8 June 1982 for $900,000 to; [E. V. Thaw & Co., New York, sold to]; private collection, New York.

Cat. 924
Nepal, Bhaktapur(?)
Ragamala Album, c. 1625
Opaque watercolor and gold, 7 x 5 ½ in. (17.8 x 14 cm)
[Doris Wiener, New York, sold 12 January 1973 for $30,000 to]; Norton Simon; gifts 28 December 1978 to; The Norton Simon Foundation (F.1978.32.1–3), 27 June 1979 to; Norton Simon Museum (P.1979.3.1–2), 31 December 1979 to; Norton Simon Art Foundation (M.1979.92.1–31).

Cat. 925
India, Tamil Nadu
Shiva as King of Dance, c. 1000
Bronze, 31 ¾ x 24 in. (80.6 x 61 cm)
[Doris Wiener, New York, sold 6 February 1973 for $260,000 to]; The Norton Simon Foundation (F.1973.5).

Cat. 926
Jan Davidz. de Heem (Dutch, 1606–1683/84)
Vase of Flowers, mid-1670s

Oil on canvas, 26 ¼ x 21 ¾ in. (66.7 x 55.2 cm)
[Paul Rosenberg & Co., New York, sold 7 February 1973 for $85,000 to]; The Norton Simon Foundation (F.1973.6).

Cat. 927
Giovanni di Paolo (Italian, 1403–1482)
Baptism of Christ, early 1450s
Tempera and gold leaf on panel, 30 x 13 ⅜ in. (76.2 x 34 cm)
[E. V. Thaw & Co., New York, sold 7 March 1973 for $475,000 to]; The Norton Simon Foundation (F.1973.7).

Cat. 928A-B
Pietro Lorenzetti
(Italian, active c. 1306–1348?)
Saint John the Baptist and *The Prophet Elisha*, c. 1329
Tempera and gold leaf on panel: John, 49 ¾ x 18 ⅜ in. (126.4 x 46.7 cm); Elisha, 49 ½ x 18 ½ in. (125.7 x 47 cm)
[Frederick Mont, New York, sold 12 March 1973 for $400,000 to]; The Norton Simon Foundation (F.1973.8.1–2).

Cat. 929
Nepal
Buddha Shakyamuni or *Akshobhya*, 13th century
Gilt bronze, 13 ¾ in. (34.9 cm)
(Sale, London, Christie's, 19 March 1973 for $27,705 to); Norton Simon Art Foundation (M.1973.2).

Cat. 930
Francisco de Goya y Lucientes
(Spanish, 1746–1828)
Los Proverbios, 1st edition, 1819–1820, printed 1864
Etching, aquatint, and drypoint, 18 plates
(Sale, London, Sotheby & Co., 14 May 1973 for $20,600 to); The Norton Simon Foundation, sold 4 April 1974 for $30,000 to; Pomona College, Claremont, Calif.

Cat. 931

India, Imperial Mughal

Camp Scene with a Feast, c. 1610–1620

Watercolor, 21 x 13 ¼ in. (53.3 x 33.7 cm)

(Sale, London, Sotheby & Co., 26 March
1973 for $5,529 to); Norton Simon, by
inheritance 2 June 1993 to; Jennifer Jones
Simon Art Trust, Los Angeles (N.1973.4).

Cat. 932

Henry Fonda (American, 1903–1982)

Ripening, 1973

Gouache, 17 ⅜ x 24 in. (44.8 x 61 cm)

Neighbors of Watts, sold 29 March 1973 for
$24,115 to; Norton Simon, by inheritance
2 June 1993 to; Jennifer Jones Simon Art
Trust, Los Angeles, gift 3 January 1994 to;
Hollywood Entertainment Museum.

Cat. 933A-C

Egypt, 1126–525 B.C.

*Three Cases Comprising the Coffin of Tarutu,
Singer in the Temple of Amun*

Polychromed wood and gold leaf: box
coffin, 73 in. (185.4 cm); second coffin,
70 in. (177.8 cm); and inner coffin, 66 ¼ in.
(168.3 cm)

(Sale, New York, Sotheby Parke Bernet,
4 May 1973 for $28,000 to); Norton Simon,
two outer cases sold 9 August 1978 for
$7,500 to; Superior Stamp Co., Beverly
Hills. The inner case given 12 August
1997 to; Norton Simon Art Foundation
(M.1997.1.5).

Cat. 934

Francisco de Goya y Lucientes
(Spanish, 1746–1828)

Los Caprichos, 2nd edition, printed c. 1855

Etching, aquatint, and drypoint, 80 plates

(Sale, London, Sotheby & Co., 11 May 1973 for
$10,050 to); The Norton Simon Foundation
(F.1973.9.1.1–80); gift, 1979 of two plates
(1 and 44) to; the Norton Simon Museum in
order to be sold in the Museum store.

Cat. 935

Francisco de Goya y Lucientes
(Spanish, 1746–1828)

Late Caprichos, printed 1973

Folio of 6 etchings: two of each, plate,
7 ½ x 4 ¾ in. (19.1 x 12.1 cm); sheet, 11 ¼ x 8 in.
(28.6 x 20.3 cm)

[Walker & Co., New York, sold 15 May
1973 for $900 to]; Norton Simon, gift
17 May 1977 to; Norton Simon Museum
(P.1977.13.1–12).

Cat. 936

Georg Pencz (German, c. 1500–1550)

A Sleeping Female Nude (Vanitas), 1544

Oil on canvas, 36 ⅞ x 68 ⅞ in.
(93.7 x 174.9 cm)

[Schaeffer Galleries, New York, sold 1 June
1973 for $55,000 to]; Norton Simon, gift
31 December 1982 to; The Norton Simon
Foundation (F.1982.2.1).

Cat. 937A-D

Pablo Picasso (Spanish, 1881–1973)

David and Bathsheba, 1947

Four lithographs: 1st state, 29/50,
25 ⅛ x 19 ½ in. (63.8 x 49.5 cm); 1st state,
30/50, 27 x 19 ¾ in. (68.6 x 50.2 cm); 2nd
state, 19/50, 25 ½ x 19 ½ in. (64.8 x 49.5 cm);
4th state, 5/50, 25 ½ x 19 ½ in. (64.8 x 49.5 cm)

[Margo P. Schab, New York, sold 1 June
1973 for $19,000 to]; Norton Simon,
by inheritance 2 June 1993 to; Jennifer
Jones Simon Art Trust, Los Angeles, gift
4 February 2006 to; Norton Simon Art
Foundation (M.2006.2.1–4).

Cat. 938

Pablo Picasso (Spanish, 1881–1973)

Women of Algiers, I, 1955

Oil on canvas, 38 ⅛ x 51 ⅛ in.
(96.8 x 129.9 cm)

[Galerie Beyeler, Basel, sold 6 June 1973
for $296,217 to]; The Norton Simon
Foundation, transferred 26 November
1986 to; Norton Simon Art Foundation
(M.1986.3).

931

935

932

936

933 C

938

934

939

944

941

942

945A

945B

946

947

943

948

Cat. 939
Jacques Bellange (French, c. 1575–1616)
The Annunciation
Etching, 11 x 14 in. (27.9 x 35.6 cm)
[William Schab, New York, sold 14 June 1973 for $11,400 to]; The Norton Simon Foundation, sold 5 September 1975 for $10,350 to; [Robert M. Light, Boston, sold 1975 to]; Cabinet des estampes, Musées d'art et de l'histoire, Geneva.

Cat. 940
Francisco de Goya y Lucientes
(Spanish, 1746–1828)
Los Caprichos, 1st edition, c. 1797–1799
Etching, aquatint, and drypoint, 80 plates
[William Schab, New York, sold 14 June 1973 for $20,500 ($15,000 plus Luca Signorelli, *Seated Female Saint* [cat. 180] with a value of $5,500) to]; Norton Simon, gift 22 December 1976 to; Norton Simon Art Foundation (sale, London, Sotheby Parke Bernet & Co., 16 May 1980 for $118,846).

Cat. 941
Thailand, Mon-Dvaravati Period
Bust of Buddha Shakyamuni, 8th century
Sandstone, 21 ½ in. (54.6 cm)
[Robert Ellsworth, New York, sold 14 June 1973 for $15,000 to]; Norton Simon, by inheritance, 2 June 1993 to; Jennifer Jones Simon Art Trust, Los Angeles (N.1973.8).

Cat. 942
Thailand, Mon-Dvaravati Period
Buddha Shakyamuni, 8th–9th century
Bronze, 22 ½ in. (57.2 cm)
[Robert Ellsworth, New York, sold 18 June 1973 for $78,600 to]; The Norton Simon Foundation (F.1973.12).

Cat. 943
Louis-Eugène Boudin (French, 1824–1898)
Cottage and Pasture on the Banks of the Touques, 1860–1865
Oil on canvas, 15 ½ x 21 ¼ in. (39.4 x 54 cm)

[Arthur Tooth & Sons, London, sold 21 June 1973 for $30,938 to]; Norton Simon Art Foundation (sale, New York, Sotheby Parke Bernet, 1 November 1978, lot 9a, for $15,000 to); private collection.

Cat. 944
Paul-Camille Guigou (French, 1834–1871)
Landscape in Martigues, 1869
Oil on canvas, 11 x 18 ¼ in. (27.9 x 46.4 cm)
[Arthur Tooth & Sons, London, sold 21 June 1973 for $37,813 to]; Norton Simon Art Foundation (M.1973.3.1).

Cat. 945A-B
Pablo Picasso (Spanish, 1881–1973)
Illustrations for "La Tauromaquia" by Jose Delgado, Alias Pepe Illo
Two complete sets of 26, one bound
Aquatints, 13 ¾ x 19 ⅞ in. (34.9 x 50.5 cm)
[Robert M. Light, Boston, sold 21 June 1973 for $19,103 to]; The Norton Simon Foundation (F.1973.15.1.1–26; F.1973.15.2.1–26).

Cat. 946
Cambodia, Angkor Period
Pedestal with the Scene of Mara's Army, c. 1100–1150
Bronze, 3 ¼ x 11 ¾ x 7 ½ in.
(8.3 x 29.8 x 19.1 cm)
[J. J. Klejman, New York, sold 25 June 1973 for $4,500 to]; The Norton Simon Foundation (F.1973.13.7).

Cat. 947
India, Rajasthan or Madhya Pradesh
Shiva and Parvati, 11th century
Sandstone, 31 x 18 ½ in. (78.7 x 26.7 cm)
[J. J. Klejman, New York, sold 25 June 1973 for $2,280 to]; Norton Simon, gift 28 December 1978 to; The Norton Simon Foundation (F.1978.23).

Cat. 948
India, Uttar Pradesh, Gupta Period

Bust within a Lotiform Niche, 6th century
Terracotta, 8 ¾ x 9 in. (22.2 x 22.9 cm)
[J. J. Klejman, New York, sold 25 June
1973 for $6,000 to]; The Norton Simon
Foundation (F.1973.13.4).

Cat. 949
India, Tamil Nadu
Ganesha, c. 1050–1100
Bronze, 12 ⅞ x 8 in. (32.7 x 20.3 cm)
[J. J. Klejman, New York, sold 25 June
1973 for $14,250 to]; The Norton Simon
Foundation (F.1973.13.5)

949

Cat. 950
India, Tamil Nadu
Sridevi, 11th century
Bronze, 16 ⅜ in. (41.6 cm)
[J. J. Klejman, New York, sold 25 June
1973 for $24,000 to]; The Norton Simon
Foundation (F.1973.13.6).

950

Cat. 951
Nepal
Bodhisattva, 11th century
Gilt bronze, 17 in. (43.2 cm)
[J. J. Klejman, New York, sold 25 June
1973 for $29,000 to]; The Norton Simon
Foundation (F.1973.13.1).

951

Cat. 952
Nepal
Vajrapurusha, 10th century
Gilt bronze, 11 ¾ in. (29.8 cm)
[J. J. Klejman, New York, sold 25 June
1973 for $17,100 to]; The Norton Simon
Foundation (F.1973.13.3).

952

Cat. 953
Thailand, Mon-Dvaravati Period
Buddha Shakyamuni in Meditation,
7th–8th century
Stucco, 8 ½ x 5 ½ in. (21.6 x 14 cm)
[J. J. Klejman, New York, sold 25 June
1973 for $1,900 to]; Norton Simon, gift
18 October 1983 to; The Norton Simon
Foundation (F.1983.32).

Cat. 954
Thailand, Mon-Dvaravati Period
Buddha Shakyamuni in Meditation,
9th century
Bronze, 5 ½ in. (14 cm)
[J. J. Klejman, New York, sold 25 June
1973 for $8,750 to]; The Norton Simon
Foundation (F.1973.13.2).

953

Cat. 955
Francisco de Goya y Lucientes
(Spanish, 1746–1828)
Late Caprichos, printed 1973
Folio of 6 etchings: plate, 7 ½ x 4 ¾ in.
(19.1 x 12.1 cm); sheet, 11 ¼ x 8 in.
(28.6 x 20.3 cm)
[Robert M. Light, Boston, sold 28 June
1973 for $300 to]; The Norton Simon
Foundation (sale, London, Sotheby Parke
Bernet & Co., 16 May 1980, lot 232, for
$686).

954

Cat. 956
Francisco de Goya y Lucientes
(Spanish, 1746–1828)
Los Caprichos, working proofs before letters
and numbers, c. 1796–1798
Etching, aquatint, and drypoint,
plates 6, 7, 9, 14, 16, 20, 27, 63, 68, 69
[Robert M. Light, Boston, sold 28 June
1973 for $100,000 to]; The Norton Simon
Foundation; proofs of plates 27 and 63
sold 8 August 1981 for $35,000 to; [P. & D.
Colnaghi, London]; eight proofs remain in
the collection (F.1973.14.2.1–6, 9, 10).

956

Cat. 957
Francisco de Goya y Lucientes
(Spanish, 1746–1828)
Los Caprichos, pre-1st edition, c. 1797–1799
Etching, aquatint, and drypoint, 80 plates
[Robert M. Light, Boston, sold 28 June
1973 for $90,000 to]; The Norton Simon
Foundation, sold 10 May 1976 for $115,000
to; [H. Shickman Gallery, New York].

957

958

959

960A

960B

964A

964B

965C

965D

Cat. 958

Francisco de Goya y Lucientes
(Spanish, 1746–1828)
The Disasters of War (*Los Desastres de la Guerra*), working proofs, 1814–1820
Etching, aquatint, and drypoint, group of 20
[Robert M. Light, Boston, sold 28 June 1973 for $140,000 to]; The Norton Simon Foundation, (F.1973.14.4.1–20). Ten plates (nos. 16, 18, 20, 24, 31, 32, 34, 43, 57, and 61) used in trade 21 March 1978 to; [Greater India Co. (Robert M. Light), Boston] as part of settlement agreement for the purchase of 118 Rembrandt etchings (cat. 1452); plates 26 and 58 (sale, New York, Sotheby Parke Bernet, 15 February 1980, lot 933 [26], for $13,000; lot 934 [58], for $12,000); plate 15 (sale, London, Sotheby Parke Bernet & Co., 16 May 1980, lot 228, for $13,713); plate 44 sold 8 October 1980 for $13,000 to; [Robert M. Light, Santa Barbara, Calif.] (six plates remain in the collection: plates 5, 11, 21, 54, 55, 60).

Cat. 959

Francisco de Goya y Lucientes
(Spanish, 1746–1828)
The Disasters of War (*Los Desastres de la Guerra*), 1st edition, 1814–1820, printed 1863
Etching, aquatint, and drypoint, 80 plates in original wrappers
[Robert M. Light, Boston, sold 28 June 1973 for $20,000 to]; The Norton Simon Foundation (F.1973.14.5.1–80).

Cat. 960A-B

Francisco de Goya y Lucientes
(Spanish, 1746–1828)
Fierce Monster and *This Is The Truth*, plates 81 and 82 from *The Disasters of War* (*Los Desastres de la Guerra*), 2nd edition, printed 1959
Etching, aquatint, and drypoint:

plate, 6 ⅞ x 8 ½ in. (17.5 x 21.6 cm); sheet, 12 ¾ x 19 ¾ in. (32.4 x 50.2 cm) [Robert M. Light, Boston, sold 28 June 1973 for $1,000 to]; The Norton Simon Foundation (F.1973.14.6.1–2).

Cat. 961

Francisco de Goya y Lucientes
(Spanish, 1746–1828)
May God Repay You, post-edition impression, before 1804
Etching, aquatint, and drypoint: plate, 6 ⅞ x 8 ½ in. (17.5 x 21.6 cm); sheet, 8 x 11 ⅜ in. (20.3 x 28.9 cm) [Robert M. Light, Boston, sold 28 June 1973 for $200 to]; The Norton Simon Foundation, sold 23 April 1981 for $10,000 to; [William Schab, New York].

Cat. 962

Francisco de Goya y Lucientes
(Spanish, 1746–1828)
Los Proverbios, 1st edition, 1819–1820, printed 1864
Etching, aquatint, and drypoint, 18 plates
[Robert M. Light, Boston, sold 28 June 1973 for $15,000 to]; The Norton Simon Foundation (F.1973.14.7.1–18).

Cat. 963

Francisco de Goya y Lucientes
(Spanish, 1746–1828)
Los Proverbios, 5th edition, printed 1904
Etching, aquatint, and drypoint, 18 plates
[Robert M. Light, Boston, sold 28 June 1973 for $3,000 to]; The Norton Simon Foundation (F.1973.14.8.1–18).

Cat. 964A-B

Francisco de Goya y Lucientes
(Spanish, 1746–1828)
Punctual Folly and *Animal Folly*, two additional plates from *Los Proverbios*,

trial proofs, 1819–1820, printed before 1877
Etching, aquatint, and drypoint:
plate, 8 ¼ x 12 ½ in. (21 x 31.8 cm);
sheet, 9 ⁹/₁₆ x 13 ¾ in. (24.3 x 34.9 cm)
[Robert M. Light, Boston, sold 28 June
1973 for $3,000 to]; The Norton Simon
Foundation (F.1973.14.9.1–2).

Cat. 965A-D
Francisco de Goya y Lucientes
(Spanish, 1746–1828)
Punctual Folly, *Animal Folly*, *Little Bulls'
Folly*, and an engraving by F. Milius after
Goya, *Self-Portrait*, 4 additional plates from
Los Proverbios: two volumes of *L'Art*, vol. 2,
1877
Etching, aquatint, and drypoint
[Robert M. Light, Boston, sold 28 June
1973 for $3,000 to]; The Norton Simon
Foundation (F.1973.14.10.1–4).

Cat. 966
Francisco de Goya y Lucientes
(Spanish, 1746–1828)
La Tauromaquia, 1st edition, 1816
Etching, aquatint, and drypoint, 33 plates
[Robert M. Light, Boston, sold 28 June
1973 for $30,000 to]; The Norton Simon
Foundation (sale, New York, Sotheby
Parke Bernet, 15 February 1980, lot 946, for
$65,000).

Cat. 967
Francisco de Goya y Lucientes
(Spanish, 1746–1828)
La Tauromaquia, Loizelet edition, printed
1876
Etching, aquatint, and drypoint, 7 plates
lettered a–g
[Robert M. Light, Boston, sold 28 June
1973 for $3,500 to]; The Norton Simon
Foundation (F.1973.14.12.1–7).

Cat. 968
Frans Snyders (1579–1657) and Cornelis de
Vos (c. 1584/1585–1651)
Still Life with Fruit and Vegetables,
c. 1625–1635
Oil on canvas, 68 ¼ x 101 in.
(173.4 x 256.5 cm)
(Sale, London, Christie's, sold 29 June
1973, for $98,567 to); The Norton Simon
Foundation (F.1973.16).

968

Cat. 969
Pablo Picasso (Spanish, 1881–1973)
Three Ballet Dancers
Chinese ink, 13 ¾ x 9 ⅞ in. (34.9 x 25.1 cm)
[Paul Kantor, Beverly Hills, Calif., sold
17 July 1973 for $29,000 to]; The Norton
Simon Foundation (sale, London, Sotheby
& Co., 2 April 1974, lot 52, for $33,600 to);
[David Ellis-Jones, New York].

969

Cat. 970
Philips Koninck (Dutch, 1619–1688)
An Extensive River Landscape, 1651
Oil on canvas, 22 x 33 in. (55.9 x 83.8 cm)
[Thomas Agnew & Sons, London, sold
24 July 1973 for $129,247 to]; The Norton
Simon Foundation, sold 30 December
1977 for $350,000 to; Norton Simon Art
Foundation, used in trade the same day
with a value of $350,000 as partial payment
for Rembrandt van Rijn, *Portrait of a
Bearded Man in a Wide-Brimmed Hat* (cat.
1489) to; [E. V. Thaw & Co., New York, sold
1985 to]; [Artemis, London].

970

Cat. 971
Maerten van Heemskerck
(Dutch, 1498–1574)
Allegory of Nature, 1567
Oil on panel, 14 ⅜ x 63 in. (36.5 x 160 cm)
[Cyril Humphris, London, sold 25 July
1973 for $237,795 to]; The Norton Simon
Foundation (F.1973.20).

971

972E　　　　976

973A 　　　　973B

974

978A

975

979

Cat. 972A-G
Francisco de Goya y Lucientes
(Spanish, 1746–1828)
Seven Etchings after Velázquez: Philip IV,
14 ⁹/₁₆ x 12 ³/₁₆ in. (37 x 31 cm); *Dona Isabel*,
1st edition, 14 ⁹/₁₆ x 12 ³/₁₆ in. (37 x 31 cm);
Balthasar Carlos, 1st edition, 13 ¾ x 8 ⅝ in.
(34.9 x 21.9 cm); *Gaspar de Guzman*, 14 ⁹/₁₆
x 12 ³/₁₆ in. (37 x 31 cm); *Aesop*, 1st edition,
11 ¾ x 8 ½ in. (29.9 x 21.6 cm); *Sebastian de
Morra*, 2nd edition, 8 1/6 x 6 ⅛ in. (20.5 x 15.6
cm); *El Primo*, 8 ½ x 6 ⅛ in. (21.6 x 15.6 cm)
Museum of Fine Arts, Boston, sold 25
July 1973 for $8,100 to; The Norton Simon
Foundation (F.1973.19.1–7).

Cat. 973A-B
Filippino Lippi (Italian, 1457–1504)
Saints Benedict and Apollonia and *Saints
Paul and Frediano*, c. 1483
Tempera glazed with oil on panel: Benedict
and Apollonia, 62 x 23 ⅝ in. (157.5 x 60 cm);
Paul and Frediano, 62 ⅛ x 23 ½ in.
(157.8 x 59.7 cm)
[Wildenstein & Co., New York, sold 25 July
1973 for $1,5 million to]; The Norton Simon
Foundation (F.1973.21.1–2).

Cat. 974
Cambodia, Angkor Period
Goddess, c. 1050–1100
Sandstone, 28 ½ in. (72.4 cm)
[Robert Ellsworth, New York, sold 1 August
1973 for $26,400 to]; Norton Simon, gift
28 December 1978 to; The Norton Simon
Foundation, transferred 28 November
1980 to; Norton Simon Art Foundation
(M.1980.17).

Cat. 975
Francisco de Goya y Lucientes
(Spanish, 1746–1828)
Woman Reading to Two Children

Lithograph, 4 ½ x 4 ⅞ in. (11.4 x 12.4 cm)
[Robert M. Light, Boston, sold 15 August
1973 for $35,000 to]; The Norton Simon
Foundation (F.1973.22).

Cat. 976
Guido Reni (Italian, 1575–1642)
Saint Cecilia, 1606
Oil on canvas, 37 ¾ x 29 ½ in.
(95.9 x 74.9 cm)
[Wildenstein & Co., New York, sold
20 August 1973 for $165,000 to]; The Norton
Simon Foundation (F.1973.23).

Cat. 977
Paolo Veneziano (Italian, active 1333–1358)
Madonna and Child, c. 1340
Tempera and gold leaf on panel,
43 ⅝ x 24 ⅜ in. (110.8 x 61.9 cm)
[Thomas Agnew & Sons, London, sold
24 August 1973 for $123,035 to]; The Norton
Simon Foundation (F.1973.24).

Cat. 978A-D
Francisco de Goya y Lucientes
(Spanish, 1746–1828)
Feminine Folly, Flying Folly, Disorderly Folly,
and *Wounds Heal Quicker than Hasty Words*,
plates 1, 5, 7, and 16 from *Los Proverbios*,
trial proofs, 1819–1820, printed before 1877
Etching with aquatint: plate, 8 ¼ x 12 ½ in.
(21 x 31.8 cm); sheet, 9 ⁹/₁₆ x 13 ¾ in.
(24.3 x 34.9 cm)
Museum of Fine Arts, Boston, sold
28 August 1973 for $12,000 to; The Norton
Simon Foundation (F.1973.25.1–4).

Cat. 979
Nese Erdok (Turkish, b. 1940)
Portrait of a Lady, 1970
Oil on canvas, 35 ½ x 28 in. ((90.2 x 71.1 cm)
Nese Erdok, Istanbul, sold 19 September
1973 for $900 to; Norton Simon, gift 17 May
1977 to; Norton Simon Museum (P.1977.1).

Cat. 980

Attributed to Peter Binoit
(German, 1593–1632), formerly attributed to
Ambrosius Bosschaert the Elder
(Dutch, 1573–1621)
Flowers in a Glass Beaker, c. 1620
Oil on copper, 12 ½ x 9 ⅛ in. (31.8 x 23.2 cm)
[G. Cramer, Amsterdam, sold 27 September
1973 for $130,290 to]; The Norton Simon
Foundation (F.1973.26).

Cat. 981

Jean-Baptiste Camille Corot
(French, 1796–1875)
*View of Venice: The Piazzetta Seen from the
Riva degli Schiavoni*, 1835–1845
Oil on canvas, 18 ⅜ x 27 in. (46.7 x 68.6 cm)
[Paul Rosenberg & Co., New York, sold
27 September 1973 for $350,000 to];
The Norton Simon Foundation (F.1973.27).

Cat. 982

Cornelis Cornelisz. van Haarlem
(Dutch, 1562–1638)
Mars and Venus, 1599
Oil on copper, 22 ¹/₁₆ x 17 ⅝ in.
(56 cm x 44.8 cm)
[G. Cramer, Amsterdam, sold 27 September
1973 for $43,368 to]; Norton Simon, by
inheritance 2 June 1993 to; Jennifer Jones
Simon Art Trust, Los Angeles (N.1973.12).

Cat. 983

Pablo Picasso (Spanish, 1881–1973)
Circus Performers, 1905
Etching with drypoint: plate, 11 ¾ x 13 in.
(29.8 x 33 cm); sheet, 14 ¼ x 16 in.
(36.2 x 40.6 cm)
[Paul Kantor Gallery, Beverly Hills, Calif.,
sold 12 October 1973 for $6,000 to]; The
Norton Simon Foundation (F.1973.28.2).

Cat. 984

Pablo Picasso (Spanish, 1881–1973)
Salome, 1905
Drypoint: plate, 15 ¾ x 13 ¾ in.
(40 x 34.9 cm); sheet, 18 ⅞ x 16 ⅝ in.
(47.9 x 42.2 cm)
[Paul Kantor Gallery, Beverly Hills, Calif.,
sold 12 October 1973 for $9,000 to]; The
Norton Simon Foundation (F.1973.28.1).

Cat. 985

Luca Carlevarijs (Italian, 1665–1731)
*An Extensive View of the Molo, Venice,
Looking towards the Riva degli Schiavoni*
Oil on canvas, 33 ¼ x 64 ¼ in.
(84.5 x 163.2 cm)
[Herner Wengraf, London, sold 16 October
1973 for $91,467 to]; The Norton Simon
Foundation (F.1973.31).

Cat. 986A-D
Francisco de Goya y Lucientes
(Spanish, 1746–1828)
The Bulls of Bordeaux, 1825
Lithographic crayon and scraper: image,
11 ⅞ x 16 ¼ in. (30.2 x 41.3 cm);
sheet, 18 ¼ x 21 ¹/₁₆ in. (46.4 x 53.5 cm)
[Robert M. Light, Boston, sold 16 October
1973 for $60,000 to]; Norton Simon, gift
22 December 1976 to; Norton Simon Art
Foundation (M.1976.14.1–4); *Spanish
Entertainment* (M.1976.14.3) sold 23 April
1981 for $60,000 to; [William Schab,
New York].

Cat. 987

Giovanni Francesco Barbieri,
called Il Guercino (Italian, 1591–1666)
Suicide of Cleopatra, c. 1621
Oil on canvas, 46 x 36 ¾ in. (116.8 x 93.3 cm)
[Thomas Agnew & Sons, London, sold
16 October 1973 for $170,734 to]; The
Norton Simon Foundation (F.1973.30).

980

985

981

986

982

987

983

984

988

993

994

989

990

995

996

991A

997

992

Cat. 988
India, Kashmir
Preaching Buddha, dated 694(?)
Bronze with silver inlay and black pigment,
14 ½ in. (36.8 cm)
[Wilhelm Vader, Delft, sold 16 October
1973 for $45,000 to]; The Norton Simon
Foundation (F.1973.29).

Cat. 989
Chaim Soutine (Russian, 1894–1943)
Landscape at Cagnes, 1923–1924
Oil on paper, mounted on canvas,
21 ½ x 25 ¾ in. (54.6 x 65.4 cm)
[Martin Stone, Los Angeles, sold 16 October
1973 for $100,000 to]; Norton Simon, by
inheritance 2 June 1993 to; Jennifer Jones
Simon Art Trust, Los Angeles (N.1973.15).

Cat. 990
Henry Moore (English, 1898–1986)
Six Reclining Figures, 1973
Lithograph, 20 x 25 ¾ in. (50.8 x 65.4 cm)
Los Angeles County Museum of Art, sold
30 October 1973 for $448 to; Norton Simon
Inc., gift 22 Dec. 2009 by ConAgra Grocery
Prod. LLC (successor to Norton Simon
Inc.) to; Norton Simon Art Foundation
(M.2009.3.2).

Cat. 991A-D
Francisco de Goya y Lucientes (Spanish,
1746–1828)
Four Etchings after Velázquez, 1st edition:
Bacchus (or the Drunkards), 12 ⁵/₁₆ x 16 ¹⁵/₁₆
in. (31.3 x 43 cm); *Felipe III*, 14 ½ x 12 ³/₁₆ in.
(36.8 x 31 cm); *Margarita de Austria*, 14 ½ x
12 ³/₁₆ in. (36.8 x 31 cm); *Moenippvs-Menipo
Filosofo*, 11 ¾ x 8 ⅝ in. (29.8 x 21.9 cm)
[Robert M. Light, Boston, sold 31 October
1973 for $5,200 to]; The Norton Simon
Foundation (F.1973.32.1–4).

Cat. 992
Claude Monet (French, 1840–1926)
Mouth of the Seine, Honfleur, 1865

Oil on canvas, 35 ¼ x 59 ¼ in.
(89.5 x 150.5 cm)
[Wildenstein & Co., New York, sold
5 November 1973 for $850,000 to]; The
Norton Simon Foundation (F.1973.33.2).

Cat. 993
Henry Moore (English, 1898–1986)
Family Group No. 1, 1948–1949
Bronze, edition of 4, 60 x 44 ½ x 30 ¼ in.
(152.4 x 113 x 76.8 cm)
[Forum Gallery, New York, sold
5 November 1973 for $263,000 to]; Norton
Simon, gift 12 March 1982 to; Norton Simon
Art Foundation (M.1982.4).

Cat. 994
Édouard Vuillard (French, 1868–1940)
The First Fruits, 1899
Oil on canvas, 96 x 170 in. (243.8 x 431.8 cm)
[Wildenstein & Co., New York, sold
5 November 1973 for $200,000 to]; The
Norton Simon Foundation (F.1973.33.1).

Cat. 995
Alessandro Magnasco (Italian, 1667–1749)
Interior with Monks, c. 1725
Oil on canvas, 36 ¾ x 52 ¼ in.
(93.3 x 132.7 cm)
[Edward Speelman, London, sold
6 November 1973 for $213,064 to]; The
Norton Simon Foundation (F.1973.34.1).

Cat. 996
Johannes Cornelisz. Verspronck
(Dutch, 1606/1607–1662)
Portrait of a Woman, 1641
Oil on canvas, 31 x 26 in. (78.7 x 66 cm)
[Edward Speelman, London, sold
6 November 1973 for $106,756 to]; The
Norton Simon Foundation (F.1973.34.2).

Cat. 997
Nese Erdok (Turkish, b. 1940)
Portrait of Issabaye Wachill
Oil on canvas, 32 x 25 ½ in. (81.3 x 64.8 cm)

Nese Erdok, Istanbul, sold 29 November 1973 for $350 to; The Norton Simon Foundation (F.1973.35.1).

Cat. 998
Nese Erdok (Turkish, b. 1940)
Womb and Tomb
Oil on canvas, 63 ½ x 44 ½ in.
(161.3 x 113 cm)
Nese Erdok, Istanbul, sold 29 November 1973 for $630 to; The Norton Simon Foundation (F.1973.35.2).

Cat. 999
India, Tamil Nadu
Shiva as King of Dance, 11th century
Bronze, 32 ¾ in. (83.2 cm)
(Sale, London, Christie's, 11 December 1973 for $105,672 to); Norton Simon Art Foundation (M.1974.1.1).

Cat. 1000
Thailand, Buriram Province, Prakhon Chai
Bodhisattva Maitreya, 8th century
Bronze, 21 ½ in. (54.6 cm)
(Sale, London, Christie's, 11 December 1973 for $44,619 to); Norton Simon Art Foundation (M.1974.1.2).

Cat. 1001
Odilon Redon (French, 1840–1916)
Vase of Flowers, after Cézanne, 1896
Oil on canvas, 18 ¼ x 21 ¾ in. (46.4 x 55.2 cm)
Neison Harris, Chicago, gift 21 December 1973 to; Norton Simon Art Foundation (M.1973.7).

Cat. 1002
Giovanni Battista Gaulli,
also known as Baciccio (Italian, 1639–1709)
Saint Joseph and the Infant Christ,
c. 1670–1685
Oil on canvas, 50 x 38 ¼ in. (127 x 97.2 cm)
[Heim, London, sold 26 December 1973 for $27,760 to]; The Norton Simon Foundation (F.1973.36).

Cat. 1003
Bartolomé Esteban Murillo
(Spanish, 1617–1682)
The Birth of Saint John the Baptist, c. 1655
Oil on canvas, 57 ¾ x 74 ⅛ in.
(146.7 x 188.3 cm)
[Wildenstein & Co., New York, sold 31 December 1973 for $250,000 to]; The Norton Simon Foundation (F.1973.38).

Cat. 1004
Henri de Toulouse-Lautrec
(French, 1864–1901)
Red-Headed Woman in the Garden of M. Foret, 1887
Oil on cardboard, 28 ⅛ x 22 ⅞ in.
(71.4 x 58.1 cm)
[Wildenstein & Co., New York, sold 31 December 1973 for $750,000 to]; The Norton Simon Foundation (F.1973.37).

1974

Cat. 1005
Gerolamo Savoldo (Italian, 1480–1548)
Shepherd with Flute
Oil on canvas, 38 ¼ x 30 ⅝ in.
(97.2 x 77.8 cm)
[E. V. Thaw & Co., New York, sold 21 January 1974 for $500,000 to]; Norton Simon Art Foundation, returned 6 January 1975 for purchase price to; [E. V. Thaw & Co., New York]. The J. Paul Getty Museum, Los Angeles, 1985.

Cat. 1006
Francisco de Goya y Lucientes
(Spanish, 1746–1828)
Los Caprichos, pre-1st edition, c. 1797–1799
Etching, aquatint, and drypoint, trial proof set with 20 errors in the engraved titles, 80 plates
[Robert M. Light, Boston, sold 31 January 1974 for $120,000 to]; The Norton Simon Foundation (F.1974.1.1–80).

998

1003

999

1004

1000

1005

1001

1006

1002

1007

1008

1009

1010

1011A

1011B

1012

1012 after restoration

1013A–B

Cat. 1007

Jan Lievens (Dutch, 1607–1674)
Panoramic Landscape, 1640
Oil on panel, 15 ¼ x 19 5½ in. (38.7 x 49.5 cm)
[Newhouse Galleries, New York, sold
4 March 1974 for $150,000 ($85,000 plus
Francesco Guardi, *Ruins with Couple
Walking* and *Ruins with Workers* [cat. 690A-B]
and Francesco Granacci, *Madonna and
Child Enthroned* [cat. D133], at a combined
value of $65,000) to]; The Norton Simon
Foundation (F.1974.2).

Cat. 1008

Giovanni Boldini (Italian, 1842–1931)
Portrait of a Dandy (formerly *Portrait of
Toulouse-Lautrec*), 1880–1890
Pastel, 25 x 16 ¼ in. (62.9 x 41 cm)
[E. V. Thaw & Co., New York, sold 18 March
1974 for $49,000 (received in trade four
Giovanni Domenico Tiepolo drawings
(cat. 677A-D) with a value of $80,000;
remaining credit of $31,000) to]; Norton
Simon Art Foundation (M.1974.3).

Cat. 1009

Giovanni Paolo Pannini (Italian, 1691–1765)
Interior of Saint Peter's, Rome, 1735
Oil on canvas, 60 ¼ x 86 ½ in.
(153 x 219.7 cm)
[E. V. Thaw & Co., New York, sold 25 March
1974 for $250,000 to]; The Norton Simon
Foundation (F.1974.3).

Cat. 1010

Francisco de Goya y Lucientes
(Spanish, 1746–1828)
Los Caprichos, 1st edition, c. 1797–1799
Etching, aquatint, and drypoint, 80 plates;
plate 35 working proof
[R. E. Lewis, Larkspur, Calif., sold 8 April
1974 for $60,000 to]; Norton Simon Art
Foundation (M.1974.4.1.1–80).

Cat. 1011A-B

Francisco de Goya y Lucientes
(Spanish, 1746–1828)
She Is Bashful about Undressing (recto), and
Masquerades of Holy Week in the Year '94
(verso), 1796–1797
India ink wash, with sepia ink pen
inscription: image, 7 ⅝ x 5 in. (19.5 x 12.7
cm); sheet, 9 ⅛ x 5 ⅝ in. (23.2 x 14.2 cm)
[R. E. Lewis, Larkspur, Calif., sold 8 April
1974 for $70,000 to]; Norton Simon Art
Foundation (M.1974.4.2a–b).

Cat. 1012

Thailand, Si Thep, Mon-Dvaravati Period
Torso of a Hindu Deity, 7th century
Sandstone, 32 ¾ in. (83.2 cm)
[Spink & Son, London, sold 16 April 1974
for $120,000 to]; The Norton Simon
Foundation (F.1974.5); combined with *Bust
of a Hindu Deity* (cat. 899) to become
Hindu Deity
Sandstone, 45 in. (114.3 cm)
Transferred, 28 November 1980 to; Norton
Simon Art Foundation (M.1980.13).

Cat. 1013A-B

Southeast Asia, 19th century
Two Drums
Bronze, 21 ¾ x 25 ⅝ in. (55.3 x 65.1 cm) and
21 ¾ x 26 ¾ in. (55.3 x 68 cm)
(Sale, Los Angeles, Sotheby Parke Bernet,
21 April 1974 for $1,855 to); Norton Simon,
by inheritance 2 June 1993 to; Jennifer Jones
Simon Art Trust, Los Angeles (N.1974.3.1–2).

Cat. 1014
Francisco de Goya y Lucientes
(Spanish, 1746–1828)
Five Plates from Los Caprichos, 1st edition,
c. 1797–1799
Etching, aquatint, and drypoint, plates 20,
30, 33, 57, 69
[R. E. Lewis, Larkspur, Calif., sold 24 April
1974 for $1,500 to]; Norton Simon, gifts to
friends, 1975–1977.

Cat. 1015
India, Karnataka
The Holy Family of Shiva, c. 1200
Schist, 34 x 19 in. (86.4 x 48.3 cm)
(Sale, Paris, Ader-Picard-Tajan, 24 April
1974 for $5,400 to); Norton Simon, gift
28 December 1978 to; The Norton Simon
Foundation (F.1978.29).

Cat. 1016
India, Uttar Pradesh
Surya with Retinue, 9th century
Sandstone, 44 ½ x 23 ½ in. (113 x 59.7 cm)
(Sale, Paris, Ader-Picard-Tajan, 24 April
1974 for $9,628 to); Norton Simon, by
inheritance 2 June 1993 to; Jennifer Jones
Simon Art Trust, Los Angeles (N.1974.6.2).

Cat. 1017
Francisco de Goya y Lucientes
(Spanish, 1746–1828)
Los Caprichos, 4th edition, printed 1878
Etching, aquatint, and drypoint, 80 plates
[R. E. Lewis, Larkspur, Calif., sold 26
April 1974 for $4,000 to]; Norton Simon
(N.1974.2.1–80); miscellaneous gifts,
1976–1995; after gifts, 29 plates remain.

Cat. 1018
Francisco de Goya y Lucientes
(Spanish, 1746–1828)
Los Caprichos, 8th edition, printed c. 1905
Etching, aquatint, and drypoint, 80 plates
[R. E. Lewis, Larkspur, Calif., sold 26 April
1974 for $2,500 to]; The Norton Simon
Foundation, gift 27 June 1977 to; Norton
Simon Museum in order to be sold in
the Museum store. Twelve plates remain
(P.1979.5.1–12).

Cat. 1019
India, Karnataka
Jain Divine Couple, c. 900
Bronze, 6 ½ in. (16.5 cm)
(Sale, London, Sotheby & Co., 29 April

1974 for $1,500 to); Norton Simon, gift
28 December 1978 to; The Norton Simon
Foundation (F.1978.8).

Cat. 1020
Nepal
Cosmic Forms of Shiva and Parvati,
17th century
Gilt copper, 7 ½ in. (19.1 cm)
(Sale, London, Sotheby & Co., 29 April
1974 for $760 to); Norton Simon, gift 31
December 1979 to; Norton Simon Art
Foundation (M.1979.91).

Cat. 1021
Nepal
Jambhala, 10th century
Bronze, 4 in. (10.2 cm)
(Sale, London, Sotheby & Co., 29 April
1974 for $435 to); Norton Simon, gift 28
December 1978 to; The Norton Simon
Foundation (F.1978.35).

Cat. 1022
South-Central Tibet
Padmasambhava with Divine Companions,
late 18th century
Opaque watercolor and gold on cotton,
16 ¼ x 12 in. (41.3 x 30.5 cm)
(Sale, London, Sotheby & Co., 29 April
1974 for $243 to); Norton Simon, gift 31
December 1979 to; Norton Simon Art
Foundation (M.1979.97).

Cat. 1023
Tibet
*Padmasambhava with Wives and
Emanations*, 18th century
Opaque watercolor and gold on cotton,
19 ⅛ x 14 ½ in. (48.6 x 36.8 cm)
(Sale, London, Sotheby & Co., 29 April
1974 for $243 to); Norton Simon, gift 31
December 1979 to; Norton Simon Art
Foundation (M.1979.96).

1015

1020

1021

1016

1022

1023

1018

1019

1029

1024

1025

1026

1030A

1030B

1027

1031

Cat. 1024
India, Himachal Pradesh
Folio from a *Gitagovinda*: *Krishna Seated by a Riverbank*, 1780
Opaque watercolor, 6 ½ x 10 ½ in.
(16.5 x 26.7 cm)
[Doris Wiener, New York, sold 21 May 1974 for $8,500 to]; Norton Simon, by inheritance 2 June 1993 to; Jennifer Jones Simon Art Trust, Los Angeles (N.1974.4.1).

Cat. 1025
India, Himachal Pradesh
Folio from a *Gitagovinda*: *Balarama Diverting the River Jamuna*, 1780
Opaque watercolor, 6 ½ x 10 ½ in.
(16.5 x 26.7 cm)
[Doris Wiener, New York, sold 21 May 1974 for $8,500 to]; Norton Simon, by inheritance 2 June 1993 to; Jennifer Jones Simon Art Trust, Los Angeles (N.1974.4.2).

Cat. 1026
India, Himachal Pradesh
Folio from a *Bhagavatapurana*: *Krishna, Balarama, and Villagers Pay Homage to Vishnu*, 17th century
Opaque watercolor, 8 ¾ x 12 in.
(22.2 x 30.5 cm)
[Doris Wiener, New York, sold 21 May 1974 for $12,500 to]; Norton Simon, by inheritance 2 June 1993 to; Jennifer Jones Simon Art Trust, Los Angeles (N.1974.4.3).

Cat. 1027
Nepal
Buddhist Goddess, c. 1450
Gilt bronze with semiprecious stones, 12 x 7 ½ x 7 ½ in. (30.5 x 19.1 x 19.1 cm)
[Doris Wiener, New York, sold 21 May 1974 for $12,500 to]; Norton Simon, by inheritance 2 June 1993 to; Jennifer Jones Simon Art Trust, Los Angeles (N.1974.4.4).

Cat. 1028
Francisco de Goya y Lucientes
(Spanish, 1746–1828)
La Tauromaquia, 1st edition, 1816
Etching, aquatint, and drypoint, 33 plates
[H. P. Kraus, New York, sold 22 May 1974 for $43,000 to]; Norton Simon Art Foundation, sold 3 November 1981 for $75,000 to; [C. G. Boerner, Düsseldorf].

Cat. 1029
India, Bihar
Tara, late 9th century
Schist, 37 x 18 ¾ x 8 ½ in.
(94 x 47.6 x 21.6 cm)
[Doris Wiener, New York, sold 28 May 1974 for $22,500 to]; Norton Simon Art Foundation (M.1974.6).

Cat. 1030A-B
Cambodia, Angkor Period, 9th–12th century
Two Lingams
Sandstone, each 27 in. (68.6 cm)
[Doris Wiener, New York, sold 31 May 1974 for $3,500 to]; Norton Simon, by inheritance 2 June 1993 to; Jennifer Jones Simon Art Trust, Los Angeles (N.1974.05.10–11).

Cat. 1031
Cambodia or Thailand, Angkor Period
Buddha Sheltered by the Serpent, 12th century
Sandstone, 24 ½ in. (62.2 cm)
[Doris Wiener, New York, sold 31 May 1974 for $4,500 to]; Norton Simon, by inheritance 2 June 1993 to; Jennifer Jones Simon Art Trust, Los Angeles (N.1974.05.09).

Cat. 1032
China, Qing Dynasty (1644–1911)
Arhat, 18th century

Gilt bronze, 6 ¼ in. (15.9 cm)
[Doris Wiener, New York, sold 31 May
1974 for $1,200 to]; Norton Simon, by
inheritance 2 June 1993 to; Jennifer
Jones Simon Art Trust, Los Angeles
(N.1974.05.20).

Cat. 1033
China, Qing Dynasty (1644–1911)
Chakrasamvara and Vajravarahi,
late 18th century
Gilt bronze inlaid with gemstones and
pigments, 13 ⅞ in. (35.2 cm)
[Doris Wiener, New York, sold 31 May
1974 for $2,000 to]; Norton Simon, by
inheritance 2 June 1993 to; Jennifer Jones
Simon Art Trust, Los Angeles (N.1974.05.18).

Cat. 1034
India, Himachal Pradesh
Mohra with Shiva, 15th century
Brass, 8 ⅝ x 5 ⅛ in. (21.9 x 13 cm)
[Doris Wiener, New York, sold 31 May
1974 for $150 to]; Norton Simon, gift 31
December 1979 to; Norton Simon Art
Foundation (M.1979.77)

Cat. 1035
India, Himachal Pradesh
Uma-Maheshvara, c. 1050–1100
Brass, 13 in. (33 cm)
[Doris Wiener, New York, sold 31 May
1974 for $1,750 to]; Norton Simon, gift
28 December 1978 to; The Norton Simon
Foundation (F.1978.13)

Cat. 1036
India, Himachal Pradesh, Chamba
Vishnu and Lakshmi on Garuda, 1450–1500
Bronze, 6 ½ in. (16.5 cm)
[Doris Wiener, New York, sold 31 May 1974
for $350 to]; Norton Simon, by inheritance
2 June 1993 to; Jennifer Jones Simon Art
Trust, Los Angeles (N.1974.5.2).

Cat. 1037
India, Karnataka
Jina Suparsvanatha with Attending Deities,
15th century
Bronze, 11 ½ in. (29.2 cm)
[Doris Wiener, New York, sold 31 May
1974 for $1,100 to]; Norton Simon, gift
31 December 1979 to; Norton Simon Art
Foundation (M.1979.84)

Cat. 1038
India, Kashmir
Bodhisattva Avalokiteshvara, c. 1000
Bronze, 8 ¼ in. (21 cm)
[Doris Wiener, New York, sold 31 May
1974 for $1,500 to]; Norton Simon, by
inheritance 2 June 1993 to; Jennifer Jones
Simon Art Trust, Los Angeles (N.1974.05.1).

Cat. 1039
India, Kashmir or Ladakh
Bodhisattva Vajrasatva, 11th century
Bronze, 5 ¾ x 2 ⅞ x 2 in. (14.6 x 7.3 x 5.1 cm)
[Doris Wiener, New York, sold 31 May
1974 for $1,750 to]; Norton Simon, by
inheritance 2 June 1993 to; Jennifer Jones
Simon Art Trust, Los Angeles (N.1974.5.5).

Cat. 1040
India, Kerala
Ganesha, 17th century
Bronze, 5 ¾ in. (14.6 cm)
[Doris Wiener, New York, sold 31 May
1974 for $1,200 to]; Norton Simon, by
inheritance 2 June 1993 to; Jennifer Jones
Simon Art Trust, Los Angeles (N.1974.5.6).

Cat. 1041
India, Tamil Nadu
Kumara, late 13th century
Bronze, 6 x 4 ¼ in. (15.2 x 10.8 cm)
[Doris Wiener, New York, sold 31 May
1974 for $1,200 to]; Norton Simon, gift
31 December 1979 to; Norton Simon Art
Foundation (M.1979.74)

1032

1037

1033

1038

1034

1039

1035

1040

1036

1041

1042

1047

1043

1048

1044

1049

1045

1050

1046

1051

Cat. 1042

Nepal

Altarpiece with Tripura, dated 1620

Copper with vermilion powder, 8 ½ in.

(21.6 cm)

[Doris Wiener, New York, sold 31 May

1974 for $1,000 to]; Norton Simon, gift

31 December 1979 to; Norton Simon Art

Foundation (M.1979.88)

Cat. 1043

Nepal

Bodhisattva Manjusri and Prajnaparamita,

c. 1575

Gilt bronze, 10 ⅝ x 10 ⅜ x 5 ¾ in.

(27 x 26.4 x 14.6 cm)

[Doris Wiener, New York, sold 31 May

1974 for $1,200 to]; Norton Simon, by

inheritance 2 June 1993 to; Jennifer Jones

Simon Art Trust, Los Angeles (N.1974.05.12).

Cat. 1044

Nepal

Mahalakshmi with Kaumari and Chamunda,

c. 1700

Bronze, 4 ⅝ x 6 ¼ in. (11.7 x 15.9 cm)

[Doris Wiener, New York, sold 31 May

1974 for $350 to]; Norton Simon, gift 31

December 1979 to; Norton Simon Art

Foundation (M.1979.90)

Cat. 1045

Nepal

Mahasahasrapramardini, 1575–1600

Gilt bronze, 5 x 4 ¾ x 2 ¼ in.

(12.7 x 12.1 x 5.7 cm)

[Doris Wiener, New York, sold 31 May 1974

for $100 to]; Norton Simon, by inheritance

2 June 1993 to; Jennifer Jones Simon Art

Trust, Los Angeles (N.1974.05.13).

Cat. 1046

Nepal

Shaiva Guardian Deity, c. 1700

Iron, 4 in. (10.2 cm)

[Doris Wiener, New York, sold 31 May

1974 for $100 to]; Norton Simon, gift 31

December 1979 to; Norton Simon Art

Foundation (M.1979.95)

Cat. 1047

Nepal

Mahishasuramarddani, 16–17th century

Bronze, 8 ⅜ in. (21.3 cm)

[Doris Wiener, New York, sold 31 May

1974 for $400 to]; Norton Simon, gift 25

December 1982 to; private collection, Calif.

Cat. 1048

Nepal

Vishnu with Serpents, c. 1700

Gilt bronze, 8 in. (20.3 cm)

[Doris Wiener, New York, sold 31 May 1974

for $900 to]; Norton Simon, gift 18 October

1983 to; The Norton Simon Foundation

(F.1983.29)

Cat. 1049

Central Tibet

Mahakala of 'Tshal, 15th century

Bronze inlaid with turquoise, 6 ¾ in. (17.1 cm)

[Doris Wiener, New York, sold 31 May 1974

for $500 to]; Norton Simon, by inheritance

2 June 1993 to; Jennifer Jones Simon Art

Trust, Los Angeles (N.1974.05.22).

Cat. 1050

South Central Tibet

Bodhisattva Shadakshari Lokeshvara,

16th century

Gilt bronze inlaid with turquoise, lapis and

coral, 12 in. (30.5 cm)

[Doris Wiener, New York, sold 31 May 1974

for $750 to]; Norton Simon, by inheritance

2 June 1993 to; Jennifer Jones Simon Art

Trust, Los Angeles (N.1974.05.19).

Cat. 1051

India, Himachal Pradesh, Chamba

Composite Deity with Two Dogs,

19th century(?)

Bronze, 11 in. (27.9 cm)

(Sale, London, Christie's, 4 June 1974 for $477 to); Norton Simon, gift 18 October 1983 to; The Norton Simon Foundation (F.1983.24).

Cat. 1052
India, Himachal Pradesh, Chamba
Shiva, 19th century
Bronze, 10 ¾ in. (27.3 cm)
(Sale, London, Christie's, 4 June 1974 for $477 to); Norton Simon, gift 31 December 1979 to; Norton Simon Art Foundation (M.1979.82).

Cat. 1053
India, Himachal Pradesh, Chamba
Vishnu Reclining on the Serpent, 19th century(?)
Bronze, 7 ½ x 8 in. (19.1 x 20.3 cm)
(Sale, London, Christie's, 4 June 1974 for $351 to); Norton Simon, gift 31 December 1979 to; Norton Simon Art Foundation (M.1979.83).

Cat. 1054
Nepal
Bodhisattva Avalokiteshvara, 14th century
Gilt bronze with semiprecious stones, 6 in. (15.2 cm)
(Sale, London, Christie's, 4 June 1974 for $1,882 to); Norton Simon, gift 31 December 1979 to; Norton Simon Art Foundation (M.1979.87).

Cat. 1055
Nepal
Buddha Shakyamuni, c. 600–800
Bronze, 2 ¾ in. (7 cm)
(Sale, London, Christie's, 4 June 1974 for $753 to); Norton Simon, gift 28 December 1978 to; The Norton Simon Foundation (F.1978.10).

Cat. 1056
South-Central Tibet
Primordial Buddha Vajradhara, 15th century

Bronze with copper and silver inlay, 13 in. (33 cm)
(Sale, London, Christie's, 4 June 1974 for $3,513 to); Norton Simon, gift 28 December 1978 to; The Norton Simon Foundation (F.1978.12).

Cat. 1057
Tibet
Spiritual Lineage Tree, 17th century
Bronze with pigment, 12 ¼ x 6 ¾ x 4 in. (31.1 x 17.1 x 10.2 cm)
(Sale, London, Christie's, 4 June 1974 for $2,133 to); Norton Simon, gift 18 October 1983 to; The Norton Simon Foundation (F.1983.33).

Cat. 1058
Tibet or Mongolia(?)
Hayagriva, 17th century
Gilt bronze with pigment, 12 in. (30.5 cm)
[Doris Wiener, New York, sold 7 June 1974 for $10,000 to]; Norton Simon, by inheritance 2 June 1993 to; Jennifer Jones Simon Art Trust, Los Angeles (N.1974.7).

Cat. 1059
Francisco de Goya y Lucientes (Spanish, 1746–1828)
La Tauromaquia, 1st edition, 1816
Etching, aquatint, and drypoint, 33 plates
(Sale, Bern, Kornfeld & Klipstein, 13 June 1974, lot 333 through [Robert M. Light, Boston], for $60,560 to); Norton Simon Art Foundation (M.1974.11.1–33).

Cat. 1060
Anonymous Dutch Artist
The Great Tulip Book, c. 1640s
Opaque watercolor, 158 images: each 12 ⅛ x 7 ⅞ in. (30.8 x 20 cm)
(Sale, London, Sotheby & Co., 27 June 1974 for $59,355 to); Norton Simon Art Foundation (M.1974.8.1–158).

1052

1057

1053

1058

1054

1059

1055

1060

1056

1061

1066c

1062

1063

1067

1064

1068

1065

1069

Cat. 1061
Maerten van Heemskerck
(Dutch, 1498–1574)
Boaz and His Kinsmen at the Gate, 1549
Pen and ink over black chalk,
11 ¼ x 16 ¹⁵/₁₆ in. (28.6 x 43 cm)
(Sale, London, Sotheby & Co., 27 June
1974 for $4,748 to); Norton Simon, gift
30 December 1975 to; Norton Simon Art
Foundation (M.1975.24).

Cat. 1062
Francisco de Goya y Lucientes
(Spanish, 1746–1828)
La Tauromaquia, 1st edition, 1816
Etching, aquatint, and drypoint, 33 plates
(Sale, London, Christie's, 3 July 1974,
lot 117, for $48,861 to); Norton Simon Art
Foundation (M.1974.10.1–33).

Cat. 1063
India, Gujarat, Ahmedabad
*Jain Altarpiece with Kumthanatha and
Retinue*, 1468
Brass inlaid with silver and copper,
7 ¾ in. (19.7 cm)
(Sale, London, Sotheby & Co., 8 July 1974
for $304 to); Norton Simon, by inheritance
2 June 1993 to; Jennifer Jones Simon Art
Trust, Los Angeles (N.1974.13.6).

Cat. 1064
India, Gujarat
Jina Ajitanatha and His Divine Assembly,
1062
White marble with traces of pigment,
59 x 20 x 6 in. (149.9 x 50.8 x 15.2 cm)
(Sale, London, Sotheby & Co., 8 July
1974 for $7,493 to); Norton Simon, by
inheritance 2 June 1993 to; Jennifer Jones
Simon Art Trust, Los Angeles, gift 17 July
1998 to; Norton Simon Art Foundation
(M.1998.1).

Cat. 1065
India, Himachal Pradesh

Uma-Maheshvara, c. 1150–1200
Brass, 7 ¾ in. (19.7 cm)
(Sale, London, Sotheby & Co., 8 July 1974
for $234 to); Norton Simon, by inheritance
2 June 1993 to; Jennifer Jones Simon Art
Trust, Los Angeles (N.1974.13.4).

Cat. 1066A-C
India, Narmada River
Three Lingams
Stone: 9 in. (22.8 cm); 8 in. (20.3 cm);
11 ¼ in. (28.6 cm)
(Sale, London, Sotheby & Co., 8 July
1974 for $562 to); Norton Simon, gift 31
December 1979 to; Norton Simon Art
Foundation (M.1979.71–73).

Cat. 1067
Nepal
Bodhisattva Vajrapani, dated 1731
Gilt bronze with traces of pigment,
10 ⅜ x 7 ¼ x 5 ¼ in. (26.4 x 18.4 x 13.3 cm)
(Sale, London, Sotheby & Co., 8 July 1974
for $562 to); Norton Simon, by inheritance
2 June 1993 to; Jennifer Jones Simon Art
Trust, Los Angeles, gift 31 December 1979 to;
Norton Simon Art Foundation (M.1979.89).

Cat. 1068
Tibet
Bodhisattva Manjusri, 18th century
Gilt bronze, 3 ⅜ in. (8.6 cm)
(Sale, London, Sotheby & Co., 8 July 1974
for $234 to); Norton Simon, gift
28 December 1978 to; The Norton Simon
Foundation (F.1978.34).

Cat. 1069
Gerard Hoet (Dutch, 1648–1733)
Mercury and Herse, c. 1710
Oil on copper, 22 ⅝ x 27 ¼ in.
(57.5 x 69.2 cm)
(Sale, London, Sotheby & Co., 10 July
1974 for $6,640 to); Norton Simon, gift
31 December 1979 to; Norton Simon Art
Foundation (M.1979.51).

Cat. 1070
Francesco dei Rossi Salviati
(Italian, 1510–1563)
Portrait of a Young Man
Oil on panel, 15 ⅞ x 11 ¾ in. (40.3 x 29.9 cm)
(Sale, London, Sotheby & Co., 10 July
1974 for $3,557 to); Norton Simon, gift
31 December 1979 to; Norton Simon Art
Foundation (M.1979.56).

Cat. 1071
Hendrick van Steenwijck the Younger
(Dutch, 1580–c. 1648)
The Liberation of Saint Peter, 1618
Oil on panel, 19 ⅞ x 25 ½ in. (50.5 x 64.8 cm)
(Sale, London, Sotheby & Co., 10 July
1974 for $15,418 to); Norton Simon, gift
31 December 1979 to; Norton Simon Art
Foundation (M.1979.58).

Cat. 1072
India, West Bengal or Bangladesh
Cosmic Vishnu with Spouses, 11th century
Chlorite, 57 x 28 in. (144.8 x 71.1 cm)
(Sale, London, Christie's, 18 July 1974 for
$13,518 to); Norton Simon, by inheritance
2 June 1993 to; Jennifer Jones Simon Art
Trust, Los Angeles (N.1974.14.4).

Cat. 1073
India, West Bengal or Bangladesh
Stele with Buddhas and Bodhisattvas, c. 1100
Chlorite, 42 x 20 ¾ in. (106.7 x 52.7 cm)
(Sale, London, Christie's, 18 July 1974 for
$7,371 to); Norton Simon, by inheritance
2 June 1993 to; Jennifer Jones Simon Art
Trust, Los Angeles (N.1974.14.3).

Cat. 1074
India, Bihar, Nalanda
Bodhisattva Avalokiteshvara,
mid-9th century
Bronze, 6 ½ in. (16.5 cm)
(Sale, London, Christie's, 18 July 1974 for
$4,668 to); Norton Simon Art Foundation
(M.1974.9.1).

Cat. 1075
India, Himachal Pradesh, Chamba
Durga, 14th century
Bronze, 7 in. (17.8 cm)
(Sale, London, Christie's, 18 July 1974 for
$786 to); Norton Simon, gift 31 December
1979 to; Norton Simon Art Foundation
(M.1979.85).

Cat. 1076
India, Himachal Pradesh, Kulu
Garuda, dated 1521
Bronze, 5 ½ in. (14 cm)
(Sale, London, Christie's, 18 July 1974 for
$221 to); Norton Simon, by inheritance
2 June 1993 to; Jennifer Jones Simon Art
Trust, Los Angeles (N.1974.14.1).

Cat. 1077
Nepal
Dipankara Buddha, c. 1600–1650
Gilt and enameled copper with
semiprecious stones and pigments,
32 ½ in. (82.6 cm)
(Sale, London, Christie's, 18 July 1974 for
$11,793 to); Norton Simon Art Foundation
(M.1974.13).

Cat. 1078
Henry Moore (English, 1898–1986)
Reclining Form, 1966
Marble, two pieces, 15 x 44 ¾ in.
(38.1 x 113.7 cm)
[Wildenstein & Co., New York, sold 29 July
1974 for $119,000 to]; Norton Simon Art
Foundation (M.1974.7).

Cat. 1079
Francisco de Goya y Lucientes
(Spanish, 1746–1828)
Dona Isabel de Borbon, Queen of Spain,
after Velázquez, 1st edition, 1778
Etching: plate, 14 ⅝ x 12 ¼ in. (37.1 x 31.1
cm); sheet, 19 ¾ x 15 ¾ in. (50.2 x 40 cm)
[H. P. Kraus, New York, sold 1 August 1974
for $585 to]; Norton Simon, gift
22 December 1976 to; Norton Simon Art
Foundation (M.1976.15).

1070

1075

1071

1076

1072

1077

1073

1078

1074

1079

1080

1084

1085

1081

1086

1082

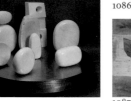

1087

1083

1088A

1088B

Cat. 1080

Henri Matisse (French, 1869–1954)
Jazz, 1947
Color stencil after collage and cut paper,
twenty plates, each 16 ½ x 12 ¾ in.
(41.9 x 32.4 cm)
[Robert M. Light, Boston, sold 20
September 1974 for $27,597 to]; Norton
Simon Art Foundation (M.1974.11.2.1–20),
9 prints: sold between 1978 and 1980 in the
Norton Simon Museum store; 5 prints:
gift 30 November 1981 to; The Hereditary
Disease Foundation, Beverly Hills, Calif.
Six prints remain.

Cat. 1081

Édouard Vuillard (French, 1868–1940)
Landscapes and Interiors, 1899
Color lithographs, group of 13: 12, 16 x 13 in.
(40.6 x 33cm); 1, 22 ¾ x 17 ¾ in.
(57.8 x 45.1 cm)
[Robert M. Light, Boston, sold 20
September 1974 for $62,000 to]; Norton
Simon Art Foundation (M.1974.11.3.1–13).

Cat. 1082

Barbara Hepworth (English, 1903–1975)
Assembly of Sea Forms, 1972
White marble, mounted on stainless steel
base, overall: 42 ½ x 72 in. (108 x 182.9 cm)
[Marlborough Gallery, New York, sold
23 September 1974 for $128,000 to]; Norton
Simon Art Foundation (M.1974.12.1a–h).

Cat. 1083

Barbara Hepworth (English, 1903–1975)
Duo, 1973
Marble, a: 20 x 9 ¼ x 5 ½ in.
(50.8 x 23.5 x 14 cm); b: 14 x 6 x 8 ½ in.
(35.6 x 15.2 x 21.6 cm)
[Marlborough Gallery, New York, sold
23 September 1974 for $25,600 to]; Norton
Simon Art Foundation (M.1974.12.2a–b).

Cat. 1084

Barbara Hepworth (English, 1903–1975)
Horizontal Vertical, 1972
Marble and slate, 25 in. (63.5 cm)
[Marlborough Gallery, New York, sold
23 September 1974 for $22,000 to]; Norton
Simon Art Foundation, sold 10 July 1981 for
$28,000 to; [Jeffrey H. Loria & Co., New
York].

Cat. 1085

Barbara Hepworth (English, 1903–1975)
Two Forms (Green and Green), 1973
Marble, 11 in. (27.9 cm)
[Marlborough Gallery, New York, sold
23 September 1974 for $22,400 to]; Norton
Simon Art Foundation (M.1974.12.3a–b).

Cat. 1086

Cambodia, Angkor Period
Lingam, 9th–12th century
Sandstone, 18 ½ in. (47 cm)
[William Wolff, New York, sold
24 September 1974 for $2,500 to]; Norton
Simon, by inheritance, 2 June 1993 to;
Jennifer Jones Simon Art Trust, Los Angeles
(N.1974.16.1).

Cat. 1087

Ronald Davis (American, b. 1937)
Wyoming Slab, 1974
Vinyl-acrylic copolymer and dry pigment
on canvas, 108 x 174 in. (274.3 x 442 cm)
[Nicholas Wilder, Los Angeles, sold
24 September 1974 for $7,420 to]; Norton
Simon, gift 31 December 1979 to; Norton
Simon Art Foundation (M.1979.44).

Cat. 1088A-B

Southeast Asia
Drums, 19th century or earlier
Bronze, 18 in. (45.7 cm) and 19 ½ in. (49.5 cm)
[William Wolff, New York, sold
24 September 1974 for $2,400 to];
Norton Simon, by inheritance, 2 June

1993 to; Jennifer Jones Simon Art Trust
(N.1974.16.2.1–2).

Cat. 1089
Cambodia, Angkor Period
Hook with Ring, 13th century
Bronze, 4 ¾ in. (12.1 cm)
(Sale, New York, Sotheby Parke Bernet,
26 October 1974 for $50 to); Norton Simon
Art Foundation (M.1974.16.7).

Cat. 1090
Cambodia, Angkor Period
Palanquin Ring, 13th century
Bronze, 4 ¾ in. (12.1 cm)
(Sale, New York, Sotheby Parke Bernet,
26 October 1974 for $150 to); Norton Simon
Art Foundation (M.1974.16.9).

Cat. 1091
Cambodia or Thailand, Angkor Period
Terminal with Garuda, c. 1200
Bronze, 11 ¼ in. (28.6 cm)
(Sale, New York, Sotheby Parke Bernet,
26 October 1974 for $250 to); Norton Simon
Art Foundation (M.1974.16.8).

Cat. 1092
Cambodia, Angkor Period
Vishnu, 12th century
Bronze, 11 ¼ in. (28.6 cm)
(Sale, New York, Sotheby Parke Bernet,
26 October 1974 for $550 to); Norton Simon
Art Foundation (M.1974.16.10).

Cat. 1093
Cambodia or Thailand, Angkor Period
Buddha Sheltered by the Serpent,
13th century
Bronze, 7 ¼ in. (18.4 cm)
(Sale, New York, Sotheby Parke Bernet,
26 October 1974 for $650 to); Norton Simon
Art Foundation (M.1974.16.12).

Cat. 1094
India, Bihar

Jain Family Group, 9th century
Copper alloy, 5 ¾ in. (14.6 cm)
(Sale, New York, Sotheby Parke Bernet,
26 October 1974 for $400 to); Norton Simon
Art Foundation (M.1974.16.4).

Cat. 1095
India, Himachal Pradesh, Kulu
Goddess, 18th century
Brass, 4 ¾ in. (12.1 cm)
(Sale, New York, Sotheby Parke Bernet,
26 October 1974 for $150 to); Norton Simon
Art Foundation (M.1974.16.5).

Cat. 1096
India, Karnataka
Folk Deity Virabhadra, 18th century
Brass, 9 ¾ in. (24.8 cm)
(Sale, New York, Sotheby Parke Bernet,
26 October 1974 for $400 to); Norton Simon
Art Foundation (M.1974.16.6).

Cat. 1097
Nepal
Bodhisattva Amoghapasa Lokeshvara, c. 1550
Bronze, 6 ⅜ in. (16.2 cm)
(Sale, New York, Sotheby Parke Bernet,
26 October 1974 for $400 to); Norton Simon
Art Foundation (M.1974.16.3).

Cat. 1098
Nepal
Vasudhara, 11th century
Gilt-copper alloy with traces of pigment,
4 ¼ in. (10.8 cm)
(Sale, New York, Sotheby Parke Bernet,
26 October 1974 for $400 to); Norton Simon
Art Foundation (M.1974.16.2).

Cat. 1099
Thailand
Buddha Shakyamuni, 13th century
Bronze, 10 ½ in. (26.7 cm)
(Sale, New York, Sotheby Parke Bernet,
26 October 1974 for $500 to); Norton Simon
Art Foundation (M.1974.16.11).

1089

1090

1095

1096

1091

1092   1093

1097

1094

1098

1099

1100

1105

1101

1106

1107

1102

1103

1108

1104

1109

Cat. 1100
Thailand, Ayutthaya Period
Finial in the Shape of a Chaitya,
16th century
Gold and crystal, 6 ½ in. (16.5 cm)
(Sale, New York, Sotheby Parke Bernet,
26 October 1974 for $250 to); Norton Simon
Art Foundation (M.1974.16.13).

Cat. 1101
Tibet
Bodhisattva Avalokiteshvara, 16th century
Bronze with pigment and gold paint, 10 in.
(25.4 cm)
(Sale, New York, Sotheby Parke Bernet,
26 October 1974 for $1,200 to); Norton
Simon Art Foundation (M.1974.16.1).

Cat. 1102
Giovanni Antonio Pellegrini (Italian,
1675–1741)
Christ on the Hill at Calvary, c. 1720
Oil on canvas, 32 ⅜ x 46 ¾ in. (82.2 x 118.7 cm)
[Hazlitt Gallery, London, sold 30 October
1974 for $28,560 to]; Norton Simon Art
Foundation (M.1974.14).

Cat. 1103
Thailand
Drum, 19th century
Bronze, 19 ½ in.
[William Wolff, New York, sold 30 October
1974 for $1,500 to]; Norton Simon, by
inheritance 2 June 1993 to; Jennifer Jones
Simon Art Trust, Los Angeles (N.1974.17.2).

Cat. 1104
Thailand
Drum, 19th century
Bronze, 19 ½ in.
[William Wolff, New York, sold 30 October
1974 for $1,500 to]; Norton Simon, gift
23 December 1991 to; private collection,
Los Angeles.

Cat. 1105
Francisco de Goya y Lucientes
(Spanish, 1746–1828)
La Tauromaquia, 4th edition, printed 1905
Etching with aquatint, 40 plates
(plates 1–33 and a–g)
(Sale, New York, Sotheby Parke Bernet,
7 November 1974 for $10,000 to); Norton
Simon Art Foundation (M.1975.8.1–40).

Cat. 1106
India, Madhya Pradesh
Head of Shiva, late 11th century
Sandstone, 31 in. (78.7 cm)
[William Wolff, New York, sold
12 November 1974 for $34,000 to]; Norton
Simon, by inheritance 2 June 1993 to;
Jennifer Jones Simon Art Trust, Los Angeles
(N.1974.18).

Cat. 1107
Francisco de Goya y Lucientes
(Spanish, 1746–1828)
Los Proverbios, 1st edition, 1819–1820,
printed 1864
Etching, aquatint, and drypoint, 18 plates
[Hugh Moss, London, sold 6 December
1974 for $15,208 to]; Norton Simon Art
Foundation (M.1974.15.1–18).

Cat. 1108
China, Qing Dynasty (1644–1911)
Arhat Gopaka, 18th century
Gilt bronze, 6 ¼ in. (15.9 cm)
(Sale, London, Christie's, 9 December 1974
for $812 to); Norton Simon Art Foundation
(M.1975.14.7).

Cat. 1109
China, Qing Dynasty (1644–1911)
Simhavaktra, c. 1700
Lacquered wood with traces of gold,
14 ½ in. (36.8 cm)
(Sale, London, Christie's, 9 December
1974 for $2,785 to); Norton Simon Art
Foundation (M.1975.14.9).

Cat. 1110
India, Bihar
Hunting Party with Revanta, 10th century
Chlorite, 13 ¼ x 9 x 2 ½ in.
(33.7 x 22.9 x 6.4 cm)
(Sale, London, Christie's, 9 December
1974 for $1,045 to); Norton Simon Art
Foundation (M.1975.14.14).

Cat. 1111
India, Himachal Pradesh
Mohra with Shiva, late 14th century
Brass, 7 ¾ in. (19.7 cm)
(Sale, London, Christie's, 9 December 1974
for $111 to); Norton Simon Art
Foundation (M.1975.14.12).

Cat. 1112A-D
India, Narmada River
Four Lingams
Stone: 21 in. (53.5 cm); 7 ¼ in. (18.5 cm);
5 ½ in. (14 cm); and 4 in. (10 cm)
(Sale, London, Christie's, 9 December
1974 for $1,745 to); Norton Simon Art
Foundation (M.1975.14.2–5).

Cat. 1113
India, Tamil Nadu
Kali, c. 1200
Bronze, 16 ½ x 10 ½ in. (41.9 x 26.7 cm)
(Sale, London, Christie's, 9 December
1974 for $6,500 to); Norton Simon Art
Foundation (M.1975.14.13).

Cat. 1114
Central Tibet
Mandala of Dorje Phurba, mid-18th century
Opaque watercolor on cotton with silk
border: image, 31 x 22 ½ in. (78.7 x 57.2 cm);
mount, 60 ½ x 37 ¼ in. (153.7 x 94.6 cm)
(Sale, London, Christie's, 9 December
1974 for $11,142 to); Norton Simon Art
Foundation (M.1975.14.11).

Cat. 1115A-B
Eastern Tibet or China
Ritual Daggers, c. 1700
Bronze with semiprecious stones and
pigment, each in 2 pieces, each 9 ¼ in.
(23.5 cm)
(Sale, London, Christie's, 9 December 1974
for $510 to); Norton Simon Art Foundation
(M.1975.14.1.1–2).

Cat. 1116
Tibet
Mahakala, 15th century
Bronze with pigment, 6 in. (15.2 cm)
(Sale, London, Christie's, 9 December
1974 for $2,321 to); Norton Simon Art
Foundation (M.1975.14.10).

Cat. 1117
Tibet
Padmasambhava, 15th–16th century
Gilt bronze, 6 ¼ in. (15.9 cm)
(Sale, London, Christie's, 9 December 1974
for $975 to); Norton Simon Art Foundation
(M.1975.14.8).

Cat. 1118
Western Tibet (?)
Jambhala, late 13th century
Brass and gilt copper with semiprecious
stones and pigment, 8 ¼ in. (21 cm)
(Sale, London, Christie's, 9 December
1974 for $3,482 to); Norton Simon Art
Foundation (M.1975.14.6).

Cat. 1119
Peter Paul Rubens (Flemish, 1577–1640)
Saint Ignatius of Loyola, c. 1616
Oil on canvas, 88 ¼ x 54 ¼ in.
(224.2 x 137.8 cm)
(Sale, London, Sotheby & Co., 11 December
1974 for $332,993 to); Norton Simon Art
Foundation (M.1975.3).

1110

1115A–B

1111

1116

1112B

1117

1113

1118

1114

1119

1120

1125

1121

1122

1127

1126

1128

1123

1124

Cat. 1120

Piet Mondrian (Dutch, 1872–1944)
*View near the Weesperzijde, Tower of Blooker
Chocolate Factory in the Distance*, 1899
Pastel, 18 x 25 ¾ in. (45.5 x 65.5 cm)
© 2010 Mondrian/Holtzman Trust c/o HCR
International, Virginia, USA
[E. J. van Wisselingh, Amsterdam, sold
23 December 1974 for $6,482 to]; Norton
Simon, gift 28 December 1978 to; The
Norton Simon Foundation (F.1978.37).

Cat. 1121

Constant Troyon (French, 1810–1865)
Bull and Chickens, 1850–1860
Oil on panel, 23 ¾ x 17 ¾ in.
(60.3 x 45.1 cm)
[E. J. van Wisselingh, Amsterdam, sold
23 December 1974 for $11,523 to]; Norton
Simon, gift 31 December 1979 to; Norton
Simon Art Foundation (M.1979.60).

1975

Cat. 1122

Tibet
*Future Buddha Maitreya Flanked by the
Eighth Dalai Lama and His Tutor*, 1793–1794
Appliquéd silk: image, 165 x 125 in.
(419.1 x 317.5 cm); overall, 268 x 177 in.
(680.7 x 449.6 cm)
[Elaine Hamilton, Baltimore, sold 2 January
1975 for $60,000 to]; Norton Simon Art
Foundation (M.1975.1).

Cat. 1123

Henry Moore (English, 1898–1986)
Elephant Skull Album, 1969–1970
Etchings, group of 33, 14/15, plates 1–28, A–E
[Comsky Gallery, Beverly Hills, Calif., sold
8 January 1975 for $9,900 to]; Norton
Simon Art Foundation (M.1975.2.1–33).

Cat. 1124

Émile Bernard (French, 1868–1941)

Brittany Landscape, c. 1888–1889
Oil on canvas, 28 ⅞ x 39 ½ in.
(73.3 x 100.3 cm)
[Hirschl & Adler Galleries, New York, sold
10 January 1975 for $40,000 to]; Norton
Simon, by inheritance 2 June 1993 to;
Jennifer Jones Simon Art Trust, Los Angeles,
gift 11 April 2008 to; Norton Simon Art
Foundation (M.2008.1.1).

Cat. 1125

Anselm Feuerbach (German, 1829–1880)
Old Woman Seated, 1853
Oil on linen, 43 x 33 ⅝ in. (109.2 x 85.4 cm)
Mrs. William Dieterle, Vogging, Germany,
sold 12 February 1975 for $4,000 to; The
Norton Simon Foundation (F.1975.1).

Cat. 1126

Francisco de Goya y Lucientes
(Spanish, 1746–1828)
The Garroted Man, 1st edition, c. 1778–1780
Etching: plate, 12 ⅞ x 8 ¼ in. (32.7 x 21 cm);
sheet, 16 ⅜ x 11 ¼ in. (41.6 x 28.6 cm)
[Huguette Beres, Paris, sold 25 February
1975 for $4,274 to]; Norton Simon Art
Foundation (M.1975.5).

Cat. 1127

Henry Moore (English, 1898–1986)
The Stonehenge Suite, 1972–1973
Lithographs, group of 16; etchings,
group of 3, 18 x 23 in. (45.7 x 58.4 cm)
[Ganymed Original, London, sold
25 February 1975 for $9,180 to]; Norton
Simon Art Foundation (M.1975.4.1–19).

Cat. 1128

Paul Sérusier (French, 1864–1927)
Still Life with Apples and Violets, 1890–1891
Oil on canvas, 15 x 18 ⅛ in. (38.1 x 46 cm)
[Paul Kantor Gallery, Beverly Hills, Calif.,
sold 21 March 1975 for $13,220 to]; Norton
Simon, gift 18 October 1983 to; The Norton
Simon Foundation (F.1983.14).

Cat. 1129
Cambodia, Angkor Period
Lingam, 9th–12th century
Sandstone, 38 ¾ in. (98.4 cm)
[Daniel Brooks, New York, sold 27 March
1975 for $8,500 to]; Norton Simon, gift
18 October 1983 to; The Norton Simon
Foundation (F.1983.21).

Cat. 1130
Vincent van Gogh (Dutch, 1853–1890)
Portrait of a Peasant (Patience Escalier), 1888
Oil on canvas, 25 ¼ x 21 ½ in. (64.1 x 54.6 cm)
[Wildenstein & Co., New York, sold 4 April
1975 for $1,250,000 to]; Norton Simon Art
Foundation (M.1975.6).

Cat. 1131
Edgar Degas (French, 1834–1917)
After the Bath, c. 1890–1893
(dated by another hand, "85")
Pastel on paper, mounted on cardboard,
26 x 20 ¾ in. (66 x 52.7 cm)
(Sale, London, Christie's, 15 April 1975
for $335,000 to); The Norton Simon
Foundation (F.1975.2).

Cat. 1132
Luca Giordano (Italian, 1632–1705)
Birth of the Virgin, c. 1696–1698
Oil on canvas, 40 x 102 in. (101.6 x 259.1 cm)
[Trafalgar Galleries, London, sold 30 April
1975 for $70,000 to]; The Norton Simon
Foundation (F.1975.4).

Cat. 1133
Francisco de Goya y Lucientes
(Spanish, 1746–1828)
La Tauromaquia, 1st edition, 1816
Etching, aquatint, and drypoint, 33 plates
[Margo P. Schab, New York, sold 30 April
1975 for $40,000 to]; Norton Simon Art
Foundation (M.1975.1.1–33) (sale, London,
Sotheby Parke Bernet & Co., 16 May 1980,
lot 224, for $68,565).

Cat. 1134
Francisco de Zurbarán (Spanish, 1598–1664)
Saint Francis in Prayer, c. 1638–1639
Oil on canvas, 46 ¼ x 35 ½ in.
(117.5 x 90.2 cm)
[Trafalgar Galleries, London, sold 30 April
1975 for $150,000 to]; The Norton Simon
Foundation (F.1975.3).

Cat. 1135
Francisco de Goya y Lucientes
(Spanish, 1746–1828)
Infante of Spain, after Velázquez
Etching, 11 x 6 ⅝ in. (27.9 x 16.8 cm)
(Sale, New York, Sotheby Parke Bernet,
6 May 1975 for $300 to); Norton Simon Art
Foundation (M.1975.10.1.4).

Cat. 1136A–C
Francisco de Goya y Lucientes
(Spanish, 1746–1828)
Three Etchings after Velázquez: Felipe III,
14 ½ x 12 ³/₁₆ in. (36.8 x 31 cm); *Margarita
of Austria*, 14 ½ x 12 ³/₁₆ in. (36.8 x 31 cm);
Balthasar Carlos, 13 ¾ x 8 ⅝ in.
(34.9 x 21.9 cm)
(Sale, New York, Sotheby Parke Bernet,
6 May 1975 for $750 to); Norton Simon Art
Foundation, sold 23 April 1981 for $10,500
to; [William Schab, New York, for]; Arthur
Ross Foundation, New York.

Cat. 1137
Francisco de Goya y Lucientes
(Spanish, 1746–1828)
Well-Known Folly, additional plate from
Los Proverbios, 1819–1820, trial proof before
letters, printed before 1877
Etching with aquatint: plate, 8 ¼ x 12 ½ in.
(21 x 31.8 cm); sheet, 9 ⁹/₁₆ x 13 ¾ in.
(24.3 x 34.9 cm)
(Sale, New York, Sotheby Parke Bernet, 6
May 1975 for $1,350 to); Norton Simon Art
Foundation (M.1975.10.2).

1129

1134

1130

1137

1131

1132

1139

1143

1140

1144

1145

1141

1146

1142

1147

Cat. 1138
Francisco de Goya y Lucientes
(Spanish, 1746–1828)
La Tauromaquia, 4th edition, printed 1905
Etching, aquatint, and drypoint, 40 plates
(Sale, New York, Sotheby Parke Bernet, 6
May 1975 for $6,000 to); The Norton Simon
Foundation, gift 27 June 1977 to; Norton
Simon Museum in order to be sold in the
Museum store.

Cat. 1139
India, Madhya Pradesh
Kubera, 11th century
Sandstone, 30 ¾ x 16 ¼ in. (78.1 x 41.3 cm)
(Sale, London, Christie's, 6 May 1975 for
$3,942 to); Norton Simon, by inheritance
2 June 1993 to; Jennifer Jones Simon Art
Trust, Los Angeles (N.1975.4.1).

Cat. 1140
India, Madhya Pradesh
*Lintel with Gajalakshmi and Other Hindu
Deities*, late 10th century
Sandstone, 16 ¼ x 65 ¾ in. (41.3 x 167cm)
(Sale, London, Christie's, 6 May 1975 for
$2,957 to); Norton Simon, by inheritance
2 June 1993 to; Jennifer Jones Simon Art
Trust, Los Angeles (N.1975.4.3).

Cat. 1141
India, Uttar Pradesh or Madhya Pradesh
Dancing Ganesha, c. 1000
Sandstone, 21 ¾ x 17 ½ x 7 in.
(55.2 x 44.5 x 17.8 cm)
(Sale, London, Christie's, 6 May 1975 for
$2,464 to); Norton Simon, by inheritance
2 June 1993 to; Jennifer Jones Simon Art
Trust, Los Angeles (N.1975.4.2).

Cat. 1142
India, Karnataka
Digambara Jina with Celestial Attendants,
c. 1000
Greenstone, 26 x 18 ¾ in. (66 x 47.6 cm)

(Sale, London, Sotheby & Co., 19 May
1975 for $4,428 to); Norton Simon, gift
28 December 1978 to; The Norton Simon
Foundation (F.1978.26).

Cat. 1143
India, Rajasthan
Chamunda, 9th century
Marble, 38 x 19 in. (96.5 x 48.3 cm)
(Sale, London, Sotheby & Co., 19 May
1975 for $2,214 to); Norton Simon, gift
28 December 1978 to; The Norton Simon
Foundation (F.1978.7).

Cat. 1144
Nepal
Avalokitesvara, 20th century(?)
Bronze, 6 ¾ in. (17.1 cm)
(Sale, London, Sotheby & Co., 19 May
1975 for $2,098 to); Norton Simon, gift
28 December 1978 to; The Norton Simon
Foundation (F.1978.9).

Cat. 1145
Auguste Rodin (French, 1840–1917)
Mouvement de Danse G, c. 1910–1911
Bronze, 13 in. (33 cm)
(Sale, London, Sotheby & Co., 19 May
1975 for $8,074 to); Norton Simon Art
Foundation (M.1975.9).

Cat. 1146
Pakistan, Ancient Gandhara
Bodhisattva Maitreya, 2nd–3rd century
Schist, 69 x 28 in. (175.3 x 71.1 cm)
[Ulrich von Schroeder, Zurich, sold 4 June
1975 for $129,870 to]; The Norton Simon
Foundation (F.1975.4.1).

Cat. 1147
Pakistan, Ancient Gandhara
Buddha Shakyamuni, c. 200
Schist, 75 x 28 in. (190.5 x 71.1 cm)
[Ulrich von Schroeder, Zurich, sold 4 June
1975 for $22,924 to]; The Norton Simon
Foundation (F.1975.4.2).

Cat. 1148
Francisco de Goya y Lucientes
(Spanish, 1746–1828)
La Tauromaquia, 1st edition, 1816
Etching, aquatint, and drypoint, 33 plates
[Sylvia Blatas, Paris, sold 5 June 1975 for
$18,832 to]; Norton Simon, gift 31 December
1979 to; Norton Simon Art Foundation
(M.1979.64.1–33).

Cat. 1149
Cambodia, Angkor Period
Goddess, 1100–1150
Sandstone, 51 in. (129.5 cm)
[William Wolff, New York, sold 9 June
1975 for $20,000 to]; Norton Simon Art
Foundation (M.1975.11.10).

Cat. 1150A-B
Cambodia, Angkor Period
Shiva and Uma, c. 1200–1250
Bronze, 19 in. (48.3 cm) and
17 ¼ in. (43.8 cm)
[William Wolff, New York, sold 9 June
1975 for $150,000 to]; The Norton Simon
Foundation (F.1975.5.1–2).

Cat. 1151
India, Uttar Pradesh
Kumara, c. 150–200
Sandstone, 23 ½ in. (59.7 cm)
[William Wolff, New York, sold 9 June
1975 for $2,000 to]; Norton Simon Art
Foundation (M.1975.11.3).

Cat. 1152
India, Uttar Pradesh
Mother Goddess, 2nd–1st century B.C.
Terracotta, 5 ¾ in. (14.6 cm)
[William Wolff, New York, sold 9 June 1975
for $500 to]; Norton Simon Art Foundation
(M.1975.11.7).

Cat. 1153
India, Uttar Pradesh
Stele with Vishnu and Other Hindu Deities,
c. 1100

Sandstone with indigo pigments,
36 x 26 in. (91.4 x 66 cm)
[William Wolff, New York, sold 9 June
1975 for $9,000 to]; Norton Simon Art
Foundation (M.1975.11.11).

Cat. 1154
India, Gujarat or Rajasthan
Male Torso, 11th–12th century
Sandstone, 25 in. (63.5 cm)
[William Wolff, New York, sold 9 June
1975 for $3,500 to]; Norton Simon Art
Foundation (M.1975.11.2).

Cat. 1155
India, Gujarat or Rajasthan
Torso of a Deity, 11th–12th century
Sandstone, 30 in. (76.2 cm)
[William Wolff, New York, sold 9 June
1975 for $7,500 to]; Norton Simon Art
Foundation (M.1975.11.1).

Cat. 1156
India, Uttar Pradesh, Gupta Period
Kubera, 4th century
Sandstone, 20 ⅛ x 13 ¾ in. (51.1 x 34.9 cm)
[William Wolff, New York, sold 9 June
1975 for $4,000 to]; Norton Simon Art
Foundation (M.1975.11.4).

Cat. 1157
India, Uttar Pradesh, Gupta Period
Mother Goddess with Child, c. 600
Sandstone, 29 ½ in. (74.9 cm)
[William Wolff, New York, sold 9 June
1975 for $4,500 to]; Norton Simon Art
Foundation (M.1975.11.5).

Cat. 1158A-B
India, Uttar Pradesh, Mathura
Heads of Two Female Fertility Figures,
c. 200 B.C.
Terracotta, 2 ¾ in. (7 cm) and 2 in. (5.1 cm)
[William Wolff, New York, sold 9 June 1975
for $500 to]; Norton Simon Art Foundation
(M.1975.11.8–9).

1148

1154

1155

1149

1150A–B

1156

1152

1151

1157

1153

1158A

1158B

1159

1160

1161

1162

1163

1164

1165

1167

Cat. 1159

India, Uttar Pradesh, Mathura
Lion Protoma, c. 200
Sandstone, 15 ¼ x 5 x 6 ¾ in.
(38.7 x 12.7 x 17.1 cm)
[William Wolff, New York, sold 9 June
1975 for $1,500 to]; Norton Simon Art
Foundation (M.1975.11.6).

Cat. 1160

India, Gujarat
Jain Triad with Parsvanatha and Retinue,
1004
Bronze, 8 ⅜ x 7 ½ x 3 ⅜ in.
(21.3 x 19.1 x 8.6 cm)
[William Wolff, New York, sold 12 June
1975 for $4,000 to]; The Norton Simon
Foundation (F.1975.6).

Cat. 1161

India, Rajasthan, Harshagiri(?)
Pandava Hero Bhima(?), c. 956
Sandstone, 66 in. (167.6 cm)
(Sale, New York, Sotheby Parke Bernet,
16 June 1975 for $34,000 to); Norton Simon,
by inheritance 2 June 1993 to; Jennifer Jones
Simon Art Trust, Los Angeles (N.1975.11.1).

Cat. 1162

India, Rajasthan, Harshagiri(?)
Pandava Hero(?), c. 956
Sandstone, 86 ¼ in. (218.8 cm)
(Sale, New York, Sotheby Parke Bernet,
16 June 1975 for $28,000 to); Norton Simon,
gift 12 April 1976 to; The Norton Simon
Foundation (F.1976.7).

Cat. 1163

India, Rajasthan, Harshagiri(?)
Pandava Hero(?), c. 956
Sandstone, 66 ½ in. (168.9 cm)
(Sale, New York, Sotheby Parke Bernet,
16 June 1975 for $42,000 to); Norton Simon,
by inheritance 2 June 1993 to; Jennifer Jones
Simon Art Trust, Los Angeles (N.1975.11.3).

Cat. 1164

Pierre-Auguste Renoir (French, 1840–1919)
Gabrielle with Jean and a Little Girl, c. 1895
Oil on canvas, 25 ⅜ x 31 ½ in. (65 x 80 cm)
[Wildenstein & Co., New York, sold 30 June
1975 for $340,000 to]; Norton Simon, sold 4
February 1980 for $980,000 to; [E. V. Thaw
& Co. and Acquavella Galleries, New York,
sold 1980 to]; private collection, Greece.
(sale, New York, Sotheby's, 10 May 2001, lot
215, unsold). Murauchi Art Museum, Tokyo.

Cat. 1165

Claude Monet (French, 1840–1926)
*Rouen Cathedral, the Tour d'Albane,
Morning*, 1894
Oil on canvas, 41 ¾ x 29 in. (106 x 73.7 cm)
(Sale, London, Sotheby & Co., 1 July
1975 for $443,753 to); The Norton Simon
Foundation, sold 22 February 1982 for $1.5
million to; [Galerie Beyeler, Basel]; Beyeler
Foundation, Riehen, Switzerland.

Cat. 1166

Francisco de Goya y Lucientes
(Spanish, 1746–1828)
La Tauromaquia, 1st edition, 1816
Etching, aquatint, and drypoint, 33 plates
(Sale, London, Christie's, 2 July 1975 for
$48,128 to); Norton Simon Art Foundation,
sold 24 July 1978 as credit toward purchase
of Rembrandt van Rijn, *Landscape with
Trees, Farm Buildings and a Tower* and
*A Woman at the Bath with a Hat beside
Her* (cat. 1536A–B) to; [Greater India Co.
(Robert M. Light), Boston].

Cat. 1167

India, Uttar Pradesh, Mathura
Column from a Buddhist Stupa, 1st century
Sandstone, 91 x 8 ⅝ x 8 ¾ in.
(231.1 x 21.9 x 22.2 cm)
[Doris Wiener, New York, sold 2 July
1975 for $100,000 to]; The Norton Simon
Foundation (F.1975.7).

Cat. 1168

Jean-Louis Forain (French, 1852–1931)
Hidden Truth, c. 1900–1905
Oil on canvas, 19 ¹¹/₁₆ x 24 in. (50 x 61 cm)
[Galerie Barbizon, Paris, sold 3 July 1975 for
$3,682 to]; Norton Simon, gift 31 December
1979 to; Norton Simon Art Foundation
(M.1979.48).

Cat. 1169

Francisco de Goya y Lucientes
(Spanish, 1746–1828)
The Disasters of War (*Los Desastres de la
Guerra*), 1st edition, 1814–1820, printed 1863
Etching, aquatint, and drypoint, 80 plates
(Sale, London, Sotheby & Co., 3 July
1975 for $19,624 to); Norton Simon (sale,
London, Sotheby Parke Bernet & Co.,
16 May 1980, lot 223, for $25,300).

Cat. 1170

Henri Matisse (French, 1869–1954)
Jazz, 1947
Color stencil after collage and cut paper,
129/270, twenty plates, each 16 ½ x 12 ¾ in.
(41.9 x 32.4 cm)
[Zucker, New York, sold 8 July 1975 for
$22,500 to]; Norton Simon, by inheritance
2 June 1993 to; Jennifer Jones Simon Art
Trust, Los Angeles (N.1975.9.1–20).

Cat. 1171

India, Tamil Nadu
Shiva as the Supreme Teacher, c. 1250–1300
Granite, 36 x 20 in. (91.4 x 50.8 cm)
[Richard M. Heller, New York, sold 15 July
1975 for $15,000 to]; Norton Simon, by
inheritance 2 June 1993 to; Jennifer Jones
Simon Art Trust, Los Angeles (N.1975.10.2).

Cat. 1172

India, Tamil Nadu
Vishnu, mid-13th century
Granite, 47 ½ x 22 ½ in. (120.7 x 57.2 cm)
[Richard M. Heller, New York, sold 15 July
1975 for $6,000 to]; Norton Simon, by

inheritance 2 June 1993 to; Jennifer Jones
Simon Art Trust, Los Angeles (N.1975.10.1).

Cat. 1173

Claude Monet (French, 1840–1926)
The Artist's Garden at Vétheuil, 1881
Oil on canvas, 39 ½ x 32 in. (100.3 x 81.2 cm)
[Wildenstein & Co., New York, sold 25 July
1975 for $400,000 to]; The Norton Simon
Foundation (F.1975.9).

Cat. 1174

India, Rajasthan or Gujarat
Jina Neminatha with Ambika and Gomedha,
11th century
Marble, 14 ¾ x 9 ¾ in. (37.5 x 24.8 cm)
[Doris Wiener, New York, sold 28 July
1975 for $6,000 to]; Norton Simon, gift
28 December 1978 to; The Norton Simon
Foundation (F.1978.28).

Cat. 1175

Cambodia, Angkor Period
Lingam, 9th–12th century
Sandstone, 19 in. (48.3 cm)
[Yvonne Moreau-Gobard, Paris, sold
30 July 1975 for $1,840 to]; Norton Simon,
gift 18 October 1983 to; The Norton Simon
Foundation (F.1983.22).

Cat. 1176

Southeast Asia
Drum, 19th century or earlier
Bronze, 7 ½ x 10 ⅛ in. (19.1 x 25.7 cm)
[Yvonne Moreau-Gobard, Paris, sold 30
July 1975 for $460 to]; Norton Simon, by
inheritance 2 June 1993 to; Jennifer Jones
Simon Art Trust, Los Angeles (N.1975.14.2).

Cat. 1177

Thailand
Drum, 18th century
Bronze, 67.5 cm
[Yvonne Moreau-Gobard, Paris, sold
30 July 1975 for $1,151 to]; Norton Simon,
gift 27 March 1979 to; private collection,
Los Angeles.

1168

1173

1170

1174

1171

1175

1172

1176

1178

1183

1179

1184

1185

1180

1181

1186

1182

1187

Cat. 1178
Cambodia, Angkor Period
Head of Buddha, 13th century
Sandstone, 10 ½ in. (26.7 cm)
[Antiques and Coins of Siam, Bangkok, sold
5 August 1975 for $8,000 to]; The Norton
Simon Foundation (F.1975.10).

Cat. 1179
Cambodia, Angkor Period
Guardian Lion, 12th century
Sandstone, 42 x 21 ½ x 28 in.
(106.7 x 54.6 x 71.1 cm)
[Douglas Latchford, Bangkok, sold 5 August
1975 for $9,000 to]; Norton Simon, by
inheritance 2 June 1993 to; Jennifer Jones
Simon Art Trust, Los Angeles (N.1975.15).

Cat. 1180
Cambodia, Angkor Period
Pilaster with Figures, Animals, and Foliage,
c. 1100
Sandstone, 38 ½ x 10 ⅞ in. (97.8 x 27.6 cm)
[C. T. Loo, Paris, sold 6 August 1975 for
$9,616 to]; The Norton Simon Foundation
(F.1975.11.5).

Cat. 1181
India, Orissa, Ratnagiri
Head of Bodhisattva Avalokiteshvara,
9th century
Gneiss, 13 ½ x 7 in. (34.3 x 17.8 cm)
[C. T. Loo, Paris, sold 6 August 1975 for
$6,225 to]; The Norton Simon Foundation
(F.1975.11.2).

Cat. 1182
India, Rajasthan or Madhya Pradesh
Celestials and Lion Subduing an Elephant,
c. 900
Sandstone, 31 x 7 in. (78.7 x 17.8 cm)
[C. T. Loo, Paris, sold 6 August 1975 for
$7,147 to]; The Norton Simon Foundation
(F.1975.11.3).

Cat. 1183
India, Uttar Pradesh, Mathura
Male Head, 1st century
Sandstone, 9 x 6 ½ in. (22.9 x 16.5 cm)
[C. T. Loo, Paris, sold 6 August 1975 for
$2,997 to]; The Norton Simon Foundation
(F.1975.11.4).

Cat. 1184
Pakistan, Ancient Gandhara
Bath of the Newborn Siddhartha,
3rd–4th century
Schist, 5 x 7 ⅛ in. (12.7 x 18.1 cm)
[C. T. Loo, Paris, sold 6 August 1975 for
$692 to]; The Norton Simon Foundation
(F.1975.11.6).

Cat. 1185
South-Central Tibet
Chest, 18th–19th century
Gilt-copper repoussé inlaid with turquoise,
9 x 18 ⅞ x 11 ¼ in. (22.9 x 47.9 x 28.6 cm)
[C. T. Loo, Paris, sold 6 August 1975 for
$3,689 to]; The Norton Simon Foundation
(F.1975.11.1).

Cat. 1186
India, Madhya Pradesh
Vishnu with Personified Attributes,
c. 9th century or earlier
Sandstone, 66 x 27 in. (167.6 x 68.6 cm)
[Oriental Antiquities, London, sold 22
August 1975 for $60,000 to]; The Norton
Simon Foundation (F.1975.15.5).

Cat. 1187
India, Uttar Pradesh, Mathura
Balarama, 150–200
Sandstone, 63 x 29 in. (160 x 73.7 cm)
[Oriental Antiquities, London, sold
22 August 1975 for $45,000 to]; The Norton
Simon Foundation (F.1975.15.1).

Cat. 1188
India, Uttar Pradesh, Mathura, Gupta Period
Base of a Buddha Image with Adorants,
c. 500
Sandstone, 24 x 29 in. (61x 73.7 cm)
[Oriental Antiquities, London, sold 22
August 1975 for $5,000 to]; The Norton
Simon Foundation (F.1975.15.2).

Cat. 1189
India, Uttar Pradesh, Mathura, Gupta
Period
Shivalingam, 350–400
Sandstone, 21 in. (53.3 cm)
[Oriental Antiquities, London, sold 22
August 1975 for $15,000 to]; The Norton
Simon Foundation (F.1975.15.4).

Cat. 1190
India, Rajasthan
Durga with Attendants, 8th century
Schist, 56 ½ x 23 ½ in. (143.5 x 59.7 cm)
[Oriental Antiquities, London, sold
22 August 1975 for $35,000 to]; The Norton
Simon Foundation (F.1975.15.3).

Cat. 1191
India, Rajasthan
Table, 19th century
Wood decorated with incised copper plates,
8 x 47 in. (20.3 x 119.4 cm)
[C. T. Loo, Paris, sold 25 August 1975 for
$1,741 to]; Norton Simon, gift 28 December
1978 to; The Norton Simon Foundation
(F.1978.31).

Cat. 1192
China, Tang Dynasty
Meditating Buddha, 7th–8th century
Marble, 10 ⅜ in. (26.4 cm)
[Eskenazi, London, sold 3 September
1975 for $8,458 to]; Norton Simon, by
inheritance 2 June 1993 to; Jennifer Jones
Simon Art Trust, Los Angeles (N.1975.17).

Cat. 1193
Cambodia, Angkor Period
Head of a Temple Guardian, 11th century
Sandstone, 19 ½ in. (49.5 cm)
[William Wolff, New York, sold 9 September
1975 for $10,417 to]; The Norton Simon
Foundation (F.1975.13.3).

Cat. 1194
Cambodia, Angkor Period
Stele with Five Planetary Deities,
10th century
Sandstone, 17 ½ x 49 x 11 in.
(44.5 x 124.5 x 27.9 cm)
[William Wolff, New York, sold 9 September
1975 for $17,361 to]; The Norton Simon
Foundation (F.1975.13.2).

Cat. 1195
India, Bihar
Shivalingam with One Face, c. 750–800
Chlorite,
19 x 14 x 15 in. (48.3 x 35.6 x 38.1 cm)
[William Wolff, New York, sold 9 September
1975 for $17,361 to]; The Norton Simon
Foundation (F.1975.13.6).

Cat. 1196
India, Uttar Pradesh, Mathura
Frieze with Worshipers, c. 150
Sandstone, 11 ½ x 48 x 2 ½ in.
(29.2 x 121.9 x 6.4 cm)
[William Wolff, New York, sold 9 September
1975 for $17,361 to]; The Norton Simon
Foundation (F.1975.13.1).

Cat. 1197
India, Rajasthan
Archway of a Shaiva Shrine, 11th century
Sandstone, 14 ½ x 28 in. (36.8 x 71.1 cm)
[William Wolff, New York, sold 9 September
1975 for $3,333 to]; The Norton Simon
Foundation (F.1975.13.5).

1188

1193

1189

1194

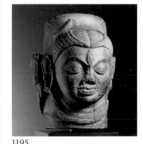
1195

1190

1196

1191

1197

1192

1198

1203

1199

1204

1200A   1200B

1201A   1201B

1202   1205

1207A   1207B   1206

Cat. 1198

Vietnam, Ancient Champa Kingdom
Shiva with Uma and Bull, 10th–11th century
Sandstone, 24 ¼ x 18 x 7 in.
(61.6 x 45.7 x 17.8 cm)
[William Wolff, New York, sold 9 September 1975 for $4,167 to]; The Norton Simon Foundation (F.1975.13.4).

Cat. 1199

Cambodia, Angkor Period
Palanquin Hooks and Rings, 12th century
Bronze: hooks, 7 in. (17.8 cm);
rings, 6 ½ in. (16.5 cm)
[Spink & Son, London, sold 18 September 1975 for $6,564 to]; The Norton Simon Foundation (F.1975.14.3.1–2).

Cat. 1200A-B

India, Andhra Pradesh, Amaravati
Relief Fragments with Flying Celestials,
c. 200
Limestone, 17 ½ in. (44.5 cm) and
14 ⅛ in. (35.9 cm)
[Spink & Son, London, sold 18 September 1975 for $8,865 to]; The Norton Simon Foundation (F.1975.14.1–2).

Cat. 1201A-B

India, Uttar Pradesh or Madhya Pradesh
Shiva and *Celestial Female*, 10th century
Sandstone, 33 ½ in. (85.1 cm) and 32 in.
(81.3 cm)
[Spink & Son, London, sold 18 September 1975 for $30,000 to]; The Norton Simon Foundation (F.1975.14.7–8).

Cat. 1202

Pakistan or Afghanistan
Woman Holding a Baby Elephant,
4th–5th century
Stucco, 9 ½ x 4 ½ in. (24.1 x 11.4 cm)
[Spink & Son, London, sold 18 September 1975 for $1,406 to]; The Norton Simon Foundation (F.1975.14.4).

Cat. 1203

Pakistan, Ancient Gandhara
Buddha Approaching the Bodhi Tree,
2nd–3rd century
Schist, 16 ½ x 18 ½ in. (41.9 x 44 cm)
[Spink & Son, London, sold 18 September 1975 for $2,625 to]; The Norton Simon Foundation (F.1975.14.5).

Cat. 1204

Pakistan, Ancient Gandhara
Buddha Subdues the Serpent and Converts Uruvilva Kasyapa, 2nd–3rd century
Schist, 8 ½ x 29 ¾ x 2 ½ in.
(21.6 x 75.6 x 6.4 cm)
[Spink & Son, London, sold 18 September 1975 for $2,625 to]; The Norton Simon Foundation (F.1975.14.6).

Cat. 1205

Burma
Eight Miraculous Events of the Buddha's Life,
13th century
Wood with pigment and gilding,
10 ½ x 6 in. (26.7 x 15.2 cm)
[Oriental Antiquities, London, sold 18 September 1975 for $500 to]; The Norton Simon Foundation (F.1975.16.16).

Cat. 1206

India, Bihar, Shahabad District
Durga with Kumara, 9th century
Schist, 35 ¼ in. (89.5 cm)
[Oriental Antiquities, London, sold 18 September 1975 for $40,000 to]; The Norton Simon Foundation (F.1975.16.10).

Cat. 1207A-B

India, Kerala
Hindu Goddesses, late 16th century
Bronze, 16 in. (40.6 cm) and 14 ½ in.
(36.8 cm)
[Oriental Antiquities, London, sold 18 September 1975 for $3,000 to];
The Norton Simon Foundation
(F.1975.16.18.1–2).

Cat. 1208
India, Madhya Pradesh
Ganesha with Siddhi and Buddhi, 1164
Sandstone, 47 x 26 in. (119.4 x 66 cm)
[Oriental Antiquities, London, sold
18 September 1975 for $45,000 to]; The
Norton Simon Foundation (F.1975.16.7).

Cat. 1209
India, Madhya Pradesh
Kubera, late 10th century
Sandstone, 34 ½ x 20 in. (87.6 x 50.8 cm)
[Oriental Antiquities, London, sold
18 September 1975 for $40,000 to]; The
Norton Simon Foundation (F.1975.16.3).

Cat. 1210
India, Madhya Pradesh
Vishnu, c. 1000
Sandstone, 42 x 17 in. (106.7 x 43.2 cm)
[Oriental Antiquities, London, sold
18 September 1975 for $35,000 to]; The
Norton Simon Foundation (F.1975.16.2).

Cat. 1211
India, Orissa
Vishnu, 15th century
Brass inlaid with silver, 12 ½ in. (31.8 cm)
[Oriental Antiquities, London, sold
18 September 1975 for $500 to]; The Norton
Simon Foundation (F.1975.16.19).

Cat. 1212
India, Rajasthan(?)
Ganesha with the Hindu Triad, 10th century
Limestone, 34 x 24 ½ in. (86.4 x 62.2 cm)
[Oriental Antiquities, London, sold
18 September 1975 for $10,000 to]; The
Norton Simon Foundation (F.1975.16.8).

Cat. 1213
India, Tamil Nadu
Shiva, 18th century
Bronze, 13 in. (33 cm)
[Oriental Antiquities, London, sold

18 September 1975 for $1,000 to]; The
Norton Simon Foundation (F.1975.16.17).

Cat. 1214
India, Tamil Nadu
Surya, 800–850
Granite, 58 ½ x 22 x 10 in.
(148.6 x 55.9 x 25.4 cm)
[Oriental Antiquities, London, sold
18 September 1975 for $15,000 to]; The
Norton Simon Foundation (F.1975.16.5).

Cat. 1215
India, Tamil Nadu
Vishnu, c. 1200
Granite, 46 x 25 x 18 in.
(116.8 x 63.5 x 45.7 cm)
[Oriental Antiquities, London, sold 18
September 1975 for $20,000 to]; The Norton
Simon Foundation (F.1975.16.4).

Cat. 1216
India, Uttar Pradesh or Haryana
Head and Torso of Buddha Shakyamuni,
3rd century
Sandstone, 12 x 9 in. (30.5 x 22.9 cm)
[Oriental Antiquities, London, sold
18 September 1975 for $2,000 to]; The
Norton Simon Foundation (F.1975.16.14).

Cat. 1217
India, Uttar Pradesh or Haryana
Vishnu as Vaikuntha, 10th century
Schist, 28 ⅜ x 16 ½ in. (72.1 x 41.9 cm)
[Oriental Antiquities, London, sold
18 September 1975 for $15,000 to]; The
Norton Simon Foundation (F.1975.16.9).

Cat. 1218
India, Uttar Pradesh, Mathura
Head of Buddha Shakyamuni, c. 200
Sandstone, 10 ½ x 6 ½ in. (26.7 x 16.5 cm)
[Oriental Antiquities, London, sold
18 September 1975 for $2,000 to]; The
Norton Simon Foundation (F.1975.16.13).

1208

1214

1209

1215

1210

1211

1216

1212

1217

1218

1213

1219

1225

1220

1226

1221

1222

1223

1227   1228

1229

1224

Cat. 1219

India, Uttar Pradesh, Mathura
Nimbus Fragment with Celestials and Bodhi Tree, c. 100
Sandstone, 21 ¾ x 39 in. (55.2 x 99.1 cm)
[Oriental Antiquities, London, sold 18 September 1975 for $10,000 to]; The Norton Simon Foundation (F.1975.16.1).

Cat. 1220

India, Uttar Pradesh, Mathura
Pillar Fragment with Lovers,
2nd–1st century B.C.
Sandstone, 9 ½ x 4 ¼ in. (24.1 x 10.8 cm)
[Oriental Antiquities, London, sold 18 September 1975 for $500 to]; The Norton Simon Foundation (F.1975.16.15).

Cat. 1221

India, Uttar Pradesh, Mathura
Vishnu as the Boar Avatar, 3rd century
Sandstone, 35 ½ x 16 in. (90.2 x 40.6 cm)
[Oriental Antiquities, London, sold 18 September 1975 for $110,000 to]; The Norton Simon Foundation (F.1975.16.6).

Cat. 1222

South-Central Tibet
Primordial Buddha Vajradhara, 15th century
Bronze, 15 ¼ x 9 in. (38.7 x 22.9 cm)
[Oriental Antiquities, London, sold 18 September 1975 for $500 to]; The Norton Simon Foundation (F.1975.16.20).

Cat. 1223

India, Bihar
Dancing Ganesha, 10th century
Schist, 16 ¾ x 10 in. (42.5 x 25.4 cm)
[Spink & Son, Zurich, sold 20 September 1975 for $1,250 to]; The Norton Simon Foundation (F.1975.17.16).

Cat. 1224

India, Bihar
Man-Lion Avatar of Vishnu, c. 1000
Chlorite, 46 ¾ x 23 in. (118.7 x 58.4 cm)

[Spink & Son, Zurich, sold 20 September 1975 for $80,000 to]; The Norton Simon Foundation (F.1975.17.47).

Cat. 1225

India, Gujarat
Attributed to the sculptor Govinda
(Indian, active c. 980–1110)
Jain Triad with Neminatha and Retinue,
c. 1000
Bronze, 11 ½ in. (29.2 cm)
[Spink & Son, Zurich, sold 20 September 1975 for $500 to]; The Norton Simon Foundation (F.1975.17.23).

Cat. 1226

India, Himachal Pradesh
Durga Killing the Buffalo Titan, 14th century
Bronze with orange pigment, 10 ⅜ in.
(26.4 cm)
[Spink & Son, Zurich, sold 20 September 1975 for $250 to]; The Norton Simon Foundation (F.1975.17.25).

Cat. 1227

India, Himachal Pradesh
Mohra with Shiva, 12th century
Bronze, 12 ¾ x 8 in. (32.4 x 20.3 cm)
[Spink & Son, Zurich, sold 20 September 1975 for $500 to]; The Norton Simon Foundation (F.1975.17.42).

Cat. 1228

India, Karnataka
Altarpiece with Anantanatha and Thirteen Jinas, 15th century
Bronze, 12 ⅝ in. (32.1 cm)
[Spink & Son, Zurich, sold 20 September 1975 for $400 to]; The Norton Simon Foundation (F.1975.17.45).

Cat. 1229

India, Karnataka
Digambara Jina, c. 1200
Bronze, 16 ½ in. (41.9 cm)
[Spink & Son, Zurich, sold 20 September

1975 for $1,000 to]; The Norton Simon
Foundation (F.1975.17.21).

Cat. 1230A-B
India, Karnataka
Digambara Yaksha Sarvahna and *Digambara
Yakshi Kushmandini*, c. 900
Schist, each 27 ½ in. (69.9 cm)
[Spink & Son, Zurich, sold 20 September
1975 for $40,000 to]; The Norton Simon
Foundation (F.1975.17.7–8).

Cat. 1231
India, Karnataka
Jina Suparsvanatha, c. 900
Schist, 32 ¼ x 14 in. (81.9 x 35.6 cm)
[Spink & Son, Zurich, sold 20 September
1975 for $25,000 to]; The Norton Simon
Foundation (F.1975.17.6).

Cat. 1232
India, Karnataka
Meditating Vishnu and Ten Avatars,
1100–1150
Schist, 49 ¼ x 27 ¼ in. (125.1 x 69.2 cm)
[Spink & Son, Zurich, sold 20 September
1975 for $10,000 to]; The Norton Simon
Foundation (F.1975.17.1).

Cat. 1233
India, Karnataka
Stele with Twenty-four Jinas,
late 13th century
Schist, 34 x 16 in. (86.4 x 40.6 cm)
[Spink & Son, Zurich, sold 20 September
1975 for $4,500 to]; The Norton Simon
Foundation (F.1975.17.12).

Cat. 1234
India, Kashmir or Ladakh, or western Tibet
Buddha with Two Bodhisattvas, 12th century
Bronze, 12 ¼ in. (31.1 cm)
[Spink & Son, Zurich, sold 20 September
1975 for $500 to]; The Norton Simon
Foundation (F.1975.17.24).

Cat. 1235
India, Madhya Pradesh
Celestial Musician, late 11th century
Sandstone, 19 ½ x 8 ½ x 5 in.
(49.5 x 21.6 x 12.7 cm)
[Spink & Son, Zurich, sold 20 September
1975 for $750 to]; The Norton Simon
Foundation (F.1975.17.15).

Cat. 1236
India, Madhya Pradesh
Woman with Bowl, 11th century
Sandstone, 20 ½ x 5 x 6 in.
(52.1 x 12.7 x 15.2 cm)
[Spink & Son, Zurich, sold 20 September
1975 for $500 to]; The Norton Simon
Foundation (F.1975.17.9).

Cat. 1237
India, Orissa
Celestial Female with Mangoes, 13th century
Gneiss, 48 ½ x 15 ¼ in. (123.2 x 38.7 cm)
[Spink & Son, Zurich, sold 20 September
1975 for $30,000 to]; The Norton Simon
Foundation (F.1975.17.2).

Cat. 1238A-B
India, Orissa
Jina Rishabhanatha with Attendants,
10th century
Bronze, 9 ⅝ in. (24.4 cm) and 9 ¼ in.
(23.5 cm)
[Spink & Son, Zurich, sold 20 September
1975 for $1,000 to]; The Norton Simon
Foundation (F.1975.17.19–20).

Cat. 1239
India, Orissa
Shiva as Lord of Dance and Music,
11th century
Sandstone, 45 x 17 in. (114.3 x 43.2 cm)
[Spink & Son, Zurich, sold 20 September
1975 for $10,000 to]; The Norton Simon
Foundation (F.1975.17.49).

1230A

1235

1236

1230B

1237

1231

1238A   1238B

1232

1239

1233   1234

1240

1246

1247

1241

1242

1248

1243

1249

1244   1245   1250

Cat. 1240
India, Rajasthan
Bracket with Celestial Dancer, 15th century
Schist, 29 x 12 in. (73.7 x 30.5 cm)
[Spink & Son, Zurich, sold 20 September 1975 for $500 to]; The Norton Simon Foundation (F.1975.17.13).

Cat. 1241
India, Rajasthan
Shivalingam with Faces and Figures, 15th century or earlier
Schist, 12 ¾ x 6 in. (32.4 x 15.2 cm)
[Spink & Son, Zurich, sold 20 September 1975 for $1,250 to]; The Norton Simon Foundation (F.1975.17.14).

Cat. 1242
India, Rajasthan or Gujarat
Altarpiece with Multiple Jinas, c. 1500
Bronze, 30 ¾ in. (78.1 cm)
[Spink & Son, Zurich, sold 20 September 1975 for $8,500 to]; The Norton Simon Foundation (F.1975.17.22).

Cat. 1243
India, Tamil Nadu
Buddha Shakyamuni, c. 1100
Granite, 50 x 37 in. (127 x 94 cm)
[Spink & Son, Zurich, sold 20 September 1975 for $25,000 to]; The Norton Simon Foundation (F.1975.17.3).

Cat. 1244
India, Tamil Nadu
Ganesha, late 16th century
Bronze, 14 in. (35.6 cm)
[Spink & Son, Zurich, sold 20 September 1975 for $6,500 to]; The Norton Simon Foundation (F.1975.17.37).

Cat. 1245
India, Tamil Nadu
Ganesha, 14th century
Bronze, 14 ½ in. (36.8 cm)

[Spink & Son, Zurich, sold 20 September 1975 for $50,000 to]; The Norton Simon Foundation (F.1975.17.51).

Cat. 1246
India, Tamil Nadu
Kali, 17th century
Bronze, 14 ¾ in. (37.5 cm)
[Spink & Son, Zurich, sold 20 September 1975 for $4,250 to]; The Norton Simon Foundation (F.1975.17.28).

Cat. 1247
India, Tamil Nadu
Krishna Dancing, 11th century
Bronze, 20 ¾ in. (52.7 cm)
[Spink & Son, Zurich, sold 20 September 1975 for $3,500 to]; The Norton Simon Foundation (F.1975.17.46).

Cat. 1248
India, Tamil Nadu
Parvati, 1050–1100
Bronze, 26 in. (66 cm)
[Spink & Son, Zurich, sold 20 September 1975 for $10,500 to]; The Norton Simon Foundation (F.1975.17.35).

Cat. 1249
India, Tamil Nadu(?)
Procession with Horse and Riders, 18th century
Bronze, 10 ¼ x 5 x 8 ½ in. (26 x 12.7 x 21.6 cm)
[Spink & Son, Zurich, sold 20 September 1975 for $250 to]; The Norton Simon Foundation (F.1975.17.34).

Cat. 1250
India, Tamil Nadu
Rama or Lakshmana, 11th century
Bronze, 30 ½ in. (77.5 cm)
[Spink & Son, Zurich, sold 20 September 1975 for $20,000 to]; The Norton Simon Foundation (F.1975.17.5).

Cat. 1251
India, Tamil Nadu
Shiva, 13th century
Bronze, 16 x 10 ¾ x 8 ¾ in.
(40.6 x 27.3 x 22.2 cm)
[Spink & Son, Zurich, sold 20 September
1975 for $1,450 to]; The Norton Simon
Foundation (F.1975.17.41).

Cat. 1252
India, Tamil Nadu
Shiva as King of Dance, c. 1200
Bronze, 29 ¼ x 23 ½ in. (74.3 x 59.7 cm)
[Spink & Son, Zurich, sold 20 September
1975 for $260,000 to]; The Norton Simon
Foundation (F.1975.17.52).

Cat. 1253
India, Tamil Nadu
Shiva with Uma and Skanda, c. 1500
Bronze, 23 ¾ in. (60.3 cm)
[Spink & Son, Zurich, sold 20 September
1975 for $140,000 to]; The Norton Simon
Foundation (F.1975.17.50).

Cat. 1254
India, Tamil Nadu
Sita(?), c. 1100–1150
Granite, 71 x 22 in. (180.3 x 55.9 cm)
[Spink & Son, Zurich, sold 20 September
1975 for $15,000 to]; The Norton Simon
Foundation (F.1975.17.4).

Cat. 1255
India, Tamil Nadu
Skanda, 12th century
Bronze, 8 in. (20.3 cm)
[Spink & Son, Zurich, sold 20 September
1975 for $750 to]; The Norton Simon
Foundation (F.1975.17.38).

Cat. 1256
India, Tamil Nadu
Sridevi, 14th century

Bronze, 23 in. (58.4 cm)
[Spink & Son, Zurich, sold 20 September
1975 for $2,100 to]; The Norton Simon
Foundation (F.1975.17.39).

Cat. 1257
India, Tamil Nadu
Sridevi, 12th century
Bronze, 15 ⅜ in. (39.1 cm)
[Spink & Son, Zurich, sold 20 September
1975 for $2,100 to]; The Norton Simon
Foundation (F.1975.17.40).

Cat. 1258
India, Tamil Nadu
Terrifying Form of Shiva, 15th century
Bronze, 22 in. (55.9 cm)
[Spink & Son, Zurich, sold 20 September
1975 for $4,500 to]; The Norton Simon
Foundation (F.1975.17.27).

Cat. 1259
India, Tamil Nadu
Uma, 13th century
Bronze, 12 ½ in. (31.8 cm)
[Spink & Son, Zurich, sold 20 September
1975 for $3,000 to]; The Norton Simon
Foundation (F.1975.17.32).

Cat. 1260
India, Tamil Nadu
Vishnu, c. 1200
Bronze, 20 ½ in. (52.1 cm)
[Spink & Son, Zurich, sold 20 September
1975 for $2,250 to]; The Norton Simon
Foundation (F.1975.17.36).

Cat. 1261
India, Tamil Nadu, Pudukottai Region
Horse and Rider, 15th–18th century
Bronze, 9 ⅜ in. (23.8 cm)
[Spink & Son, Zurich, sold 20 September
1975 for $250 to]; The Norton Simon
Foundation (F.1975.17.33).

1251

1257

1252

1258

1253

1259

1254

1260

1255

1256

1261

1262

1263

1264

1265

1266

1267

1268

1269

1270

1271

1272

Cat. 1262

India, Uttar Pradesh or Madhya Pradesh
Female Head, c. 1000
Sandstone, 5 ¼ x 3 ⅜ in. (13.3 x 8.6 cm)
[Spink & Son, Zurich, sold 20 September
1975 for $150 to]; The Norton Simon
Foundation (F.1975.17.44).

Cat. 1263

India, Uttar Pradesh
Lion Head, 6th century
Terracotta, 6 ¼ x 5 in. (15.9 cm)
[Spink & Son, Zurich, sold 20 September
1975 for $150 to]; The Norton Simon
Foundation (F.1975.17.43).

Cat. 1264

India, Uttar Pradesh
Vishnu with Personified Attributes, 750–800
Sandstone, 45 ¼ x 19 ½ in. (114.9 x 49.5 cm)
[Spink & Son, Zurich, sold 20 September
1975 for $70,000 to]; The Norton Simon
Foundation (F.1975.17.48).

Cat. 1265

India, West Bengal or Orissa
Krishna's Circular Dance, 19th century
Schist, 8 ⅛ x 8 ⅜ in. (20.6 x 21.3 cm)
[Spink & Son, Zurich, sold 20 September
1975 for $250 to]; The Norton Simon
Foundation (F.1975.17.10).

Cat. 1266

Pakistan, Ancient Gandhara
Bodhisattva Maitreya, 3rd century
Schist, 29 ½ x 13 in. (74.9 x 33cm)
[Spink & Son, Zurich, sold 20 September
1975 for $3,000 to]; The Norton Simon
Foundation (F.1975.17.11).

Cat. 1267

Pakistan, Ancient Gandhara
Siddhartha Meditating below the Jambu Tree,
3rd century
Schist, 23 x 17 in. (58.4 x 43.2 cm)

[Spink & Son, Zurich, sold 20 September
1975 for $2,750 to]; The Norton Simon
Foundation (F.1975.17.29).

Cat. 1268

Pakistan, Ancient Gandhara
Winged Figure, 3rd century
Schist, 15 ¾ x 14 x 7 in. (40 x 35.6 x 17.8 cm)
[Spink & Son, Zurich, sold 20 September
1975 for $1,500 to]; The Norton Simon
Foundation (F.1975.17.17).

Cat. 1269

Thailand, Buriram Province,
Prakhon Chai(?)
Bodhisattva, 8th century
Bronze, 8 ⅝ in. (21.9 cm)
[Spink & Son, Zurich, sold 20 September
1975 for $750 to]; The Norton Simon
Foundation (F.1975.17.30).

Cat. 1270

Thailand, Mon-Dvaravati Period
Buddha Shakyamuni, 8th century
Bronze, 8 ¼ in. (21 cm)
[Spink & Son, Zurich, sold 20 September
1975 for $750 to]; The Norton Simon
Foundation (F.1975.17.31).

Cat. 1271

Thailand, Sukothai Region
Buddha Shakyamuni, 15th century
Bronze, 21 in. (53.3 cm)
[Spink & Son, Zurich, sold 20 September
1975 for $750 to]; The Norton Simon
Foundation (F.1975.17.18).

Cat. 1272

Tibet
Buddha Shakyamuni or Akshobhya, c. 1200
Brass with traces of pigment, 10 ⅜ in.
(26.4 cm)
[Spink & Son, Zurich, sold 20 September
1975 for $750 to]; The Norton Simon
Foundation (F.1975.17.26).

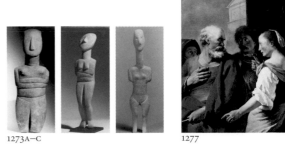
1273A–C

1277

1274

Cat. 1273A-C

Cycladic

Female Idols with Folded Arms

Marble, three figures: 15 ¾ in. (40 cm);
8 ⅝ in. (21.9 cm); and 7 in. (17.8 cm)
[Simone Monbrison, Paris, sold
22 September 1975 for $47,693 to]; Norton
Simon, by inheritance 2 June 1993 to;
Jennifer Jones Simon Art Trust, Los Angeles
(N.1975.18.1–3).

Cat. 1274

Cambodia, Angkor Period

Lintel with Reclining Vishnu and Retinue,
11th century

Sandstone, 18 x 57 x 8 ½ in.
(45.7 x 144.8 x 21.6 cm)
[Douglas Latchford, Bangkok, sold
6 October 1975 for $4,000 to]; Norton
Simon Art Foundation (M.1975.15.2).

Cat. 1275

Cambodia or Thailand, Angkor Period

Celestial Nymph, c. 1100

Sandstone, 37 x 21 in. (94 x 53.3 cm)
[Douglas Latchford, Bangkok, sold
6 October 1975 for $6,000 to]; Norton
Simon Art Foundation (M.1975.15.3).

Cat. 1276A-D

Thailand, Si Thep(?),
Mon-Dvaravati Period

Plaque with a Buddhist Triad and Symbols,
7th century

Gold repoussé, 2 ¼ x 3 ⅝ in. (5.7 x 9.2 cm)

Plaque with Bodhisattva, 7th–8th century

Gold repoussé, 4 ¾ x 2 ¾ in. (12.1 x 7cm)

Plaque with Lunar Deity, 7th century

Gold repoussé, 3 ¾ x 1 ⅞ in. (9.5 x 4.8 cm)

Plaque with Bodhisattva, 7th–8th century

Gold repoussé, 4 ¼ x 2 ⅞ in. (10.8 x 7.3 cm)
[Douglas Latchford, Bangkok, sold
6 October 1975 for $10,000 to]; Norton
Simon Art Foundation (M.1975.15.1.1–4).

Cat. 1277

Karel Du Jardin (Dutch, 1622–1678)

The Denial of Peter, c. 1663

Oil on canvas, 47 ⅛ x 41 ¼ in. (119.7 x 104.8 cm)
[G. Cramer, The Hague, sold 7 October
1975 for $31,820 to]; Norton Simon Art
Foundation (M.1975.16).

Cat. 1278

Thailand, Northeast Khorat Plateau: Ban
Chiang Cultural Tradition

Pedestaled Vessel, 1100–200 B.C.

Painted ceramic, 9 x 7 ½ in. (22.9 x 19.1 cm)
[Spink and Son, Zurich, sold 14 October
1975 for $3,045 to]; Norton Simon, by
inheritance 2 June 1993 to; Jennifer Jones
Simon Art Trust, Los Angeles (N.1975.19).

Cat. 1279A-B

India, Tamil Nadu

Bhudevi and *Sridevi,* c. 1025

Bronze, 26 ½ in. (67.3 cm) and 26 ¾ in.
(67.9 cm)
[William Wolff, New York, sold 12
November 1975 for $110,000 to]; Norton
Simon Art Foundation (M.1975.17.1–2).

Cat. 1280

Nepal

Dipankara Buddha with Two Monks,
dated 1801

Gilt bronze, 9 ¼ in. (23.5 cm)
[William Wolff, New York, sold
12 November 1975 for $4,200 to]; Norton
Simon, gift 28 December 1978 to; The
Norton Simon Foundation (F.1978.36).

Cat. 1281

Cambodia, Angkor Period

Head of Vishnu(?), 11th century

Sandstone, 21 in. (53.3 cm)
[Yvonne Moreau-Gobard, Paris, sold
3 December 1975 for $16,750 to]; Norton
Simon Art Foundation (M.1975.18.1).

1278

1275

1279A   1279B

1276A–D   1280

1281

1282

1287

1283

1288

1284

1289

1285

1290

1286

1291

Cat. 1282
Cambodia, Angkor Period
Palanquin Hook, 12th century
Gilt bronze, 7 ½ in. (19.1 cm)
[Yvonne Moreau-Gobard, Paris, sold
3 December 1975 for $8,118 to]; Norton
Simon Art Foundation (M.1975.18.4).

Cat. 1283
Cambodia, Pre-Angkor Period
Shiva's Bull, c. 800
Sandstone, 20 x 22 x 12 ½ in.
(50.8 x 55.9 x 31.8 cm)
[Yvonne Moreau-Gobard, Paris, sold
3 December 1975 for $9,244 to]; Norton
Simon Art Foundation (M.1975.18.5).

Cat. 1284
India, Uttar Pradesh
Head of Hanuman, 11th century
Sandstone, 15 ½ x 12 ½ x 9 in.
(39.4 x 31.8 x 22.9 cm)
[Yvonne Moreau-Gobard, Paris, sold
3 December 1975 for $11,120 to]; Norton
Simon Art Foundation (M.1975.18.2).

Cat. 1285
India, Uttar Pradesh, Mathura
Shiva's Bull, 7th–8th century
Sandstone, 6 ½ x 9 x 3 in. (16.5 x 22.9 x 7.6 cm)
[Yvonne Moreau-Gobard, Paris, sold
3 December 1975 for $1,362 to]; Norton
Simon Art Foundation (M.1975.18.3).

Cat. 1286
Rosa Bonheur (French, 1822–1899)
Sheep by the Sea, 1869
Oil on panel, 12 ½ x 18 in. (31.5 x 46 cm)
(Sale, New York, Sotheby Parke Bernet,
5 December 1975 for $3,250 to); Norton
Simon Art Foundation (sale, New York,
Sotheby Parke Bernet, 29 May 1980, lot
50, for $7,000). Wallace and Wilhelmina
Holladay, Washington, D.C., gift 1986 to;
National Museum of Women in the Arts,
Washington, D.C.

Cat. 1287
India, Rajasthan or Madhya Pradesh
Jina Parsvanatha with Attendants,
11th century
Sandstone, 36 ½ x 16 in. (92.7 x 40.6 cm)
(Sale, London, Sotheby & Co., 9 December
1975 for $2,018 to); Norton Simon, gift
31 December 1979 to; Norton Simon Art
Foundation (M.1979.86).

Cat. 1288
India, Uttar Pradesh, Gupta Period
Rama and Lakshmana, 6th century
Terracotta, 18 x 19 ¼ in. (45.7 x 48.9 cm)
(Sale, London, Sotheby & Co., 9 December
1975 for $1,681 to); Norton Simon, by
inheritance 2 June 1993 to; Jennifer Jones
Simon Art Trust, Los Angeles (N.1976.1.4).

Cat. 1289
India, West Bengal or Bangladesh
Vishnu with Retinue, 12th century
Chlorite, 29 ¼ x 14 ½ in. (74.3 x 36.8 cm)
(Sale, London, Sotheby & Co., 9 December
1975 for $1,121 to); Norton Simon, by
inheritance 2 June 1993 to; Jennifer Jones
Simon Art Trust, Los Angeles (N.1976.1.2).

Cat. 1290
Mainland Southeast Asia
Drum, 19th century
Bronze, 21 x 27 in. (53.3 x 68.6 cm)
(Sale, London, Sotheby & Co., 9 December
1975 for $986 to); Norton Simon, by
inheritance 2 June 1993 to; Jennifer Jones
Simon Art Trust, Los Angeles (N.1976.1.1).

Cat. 1291
Pakistan, Ancient Gandhara
Bodhisattva Maitreya, 3rd–4th century
Schist, 22 ¼ x 12 ½ in. (56.5 x 31.8 cm)
(Sale, London, Sotheby & Co., 9 December
1975 for $4,484 to); Norton Simon, by
inheritance 2 June 1993 to; Jennifer Jones
Simon Art Trust, Los Angeles (N.1976.1.5).

Cat. 1292

Antonio Joli (Italian, 1700–1777)

View of Paestum, 1759

Oil on canvas, 30 ¼ x 47 ½ in. (76.5 x 121 cm)

(Sale, London, Sotheby & Co., 10 December 1975 for $22,349 to); Norton Simon, gift 31 December 1979 to; Norton Simon Art Foundation (M.1979.52).

Cat. 1293

Master of Saint Cecilia

(Italian, active c. 1280–1330)

Madonna and Child Enthroned with Saint Francis, c. 1315

Tempera and gold leaf on panel, with pointed top, 49 ¾ x 27 ⅛ in. (126.4 x 68.9 cm)

(Sale, London, Sotheby & Co., 10 December 1975 for $86,625 to); Norton Simon, by inheritance 2 June 1993 to; Jennifer Jones Simon Art Trust, Los Angeles, gift 18 November 1994 to; Norton Simon Art Foundation (M.1994.2).

Cat. 1294

Corrado Giaquinto (Italian, 1703–c. 1766)

Marriage of the Virgin, 1764–1765

Oil on canvas, 112 x 70 in. (284.5 x 177.8 cm)

[P. & D. Colnaghi, London, sold 30 December 1975 for $67,865 to]; Norton Simon Art Foundation (M.1975.27).

1976

Cat. 1295

Claude Gellée, called Claude Lorrain

(French, 1600–1682)

Landscape with Jacob and Laban and His Daughters, 1659

Oil on copper, 10 ½ x 13 ⅞ in.

(26.7 x 35.2 cm)

[Edward Speelman, London, sold 29 January 1976 for $230,000 to]; Norton Simon Art Foundation (M.1976.1).

Cat. 1296

Attributed to Claude Gellée, called

Claude Lorrain (French, 1600–1682)

Classical Landscape

Oil on panel, 10 ¾ x 20 ¼ in. (27.3 x 51.4 cm)

(Sale, London, Sotheby & Co., 30 January 1976 for $3,800 to); Norton Simon, by inheritance 2 June 1993 to; Jennifer Jones Simon Art Trust, Los Angeles (N.1976.2.1).

Cat. 1297

Thomas-Germain-Joseph Duvivier

(French, 1735–1814)

An Architect's Table, 1772

Oil on canvas, 40 ⅜ x 31 in.

(102.6 x 78.7 cm)

[Richard Feigen, New York, sold 10 February 1976 for $14,500 to]; Norton Simon Art Foundation (M.1976.2).

Cat. 1298

Henry Moore (English, 1898–1986)

King and Queen, 1952–1953

Bronze, 64 ½ x 56 x 35 in.

(163.8 x 142.2 x 88.9 cm)

[Thomas Gibson, London, sold 15 February 1976 for $495,000 to]; Norton Simon Art Foundation (M.1976.3).

Cat. 1299

Émile Bernard (French, 1868–1941)

Leaving the Church at Medreac (formerly *Breton Women*), 1887

Oil on canvas, 28 x 36 in. (71.1 x 91.4 cm)

[Hirschl & Adler Galleries, New York, sold 23 February 1976 for $40,000 to]; Norton Simon (sale, New York, Christie's, 19 May 1981, lot 325, unsold), sold 16 June 1981 for $90,000 to; [Hirschl & Adler Galleries, New York, sold 10 September 1984 to]; Mrs. Charles Le Paul, Washington, D.C. [Charles Guy Le Paul, Pont-Aven]; [Didier Imbert Fine Art, Paris, 1985].

1292

1296

1293

1297

1294

1298

1295

1299

1300

1305

1301

1306

1302

1307

1303

1308

1304

Cat. 1300

Émile Bernard (French, 1868–1941)
Still Life with Flowers, 1887
Oil on canvas, 19 ¾ x 24 in. (50.2 x 61 cm)
[Hirschl & Adler Galleries, New York, sold 23 February 1976 for $25,000 to]; Norton Simon, by inheritance 2 June 1993 to; Jennifer Jones Simon Art Trust, Los Angeles, gift 12 August 1997 to; Norton Simon Art Foundation (M.1997.1.2).

Cat. 1301

Indonesia, Central Java
Torso of a Divinity, 9th century
Gneiss or volcanic stone,
21 ½ x 19 ½ in. (54.6 x 49.5 cm)
[Spink & Son, London, sold 25 February 1976 for $16,000 to]; Norton Simon, by inheritance, 2 June 1993 to; Jennifer Jones Simon Art Trust (N.1976.4).

Cat. 1302

Achille-Jacques-Jean-Marie Devéria
(French, 1800–1857)
Young Woman with a Rose, 1850
Oil on canvas, 33 ¾ x 27 ¼ in. (85.7 x 69.2 cm)
(Sale, Paris, Hôtel Drouot, 10 March 1976 for $4,045 to); Norton Simon, gift 18 October 1983 to; The Norton Simon Foundation (F.1983.8).

Cat. 1303

Salomon De Bray (Dutch, 1597–1664)
The Expulsion of Hagar and Ishmael, 1662
Oil on panel, 21 ⅜ x 18 ⅝ in. (54.3 x 47.3 cm)
(Sale, London, Christie's, 12 March 1976 for $8,489 to); Norton Simon, gift 31 December 1979 to; Norton Simon Art Foundation (M.1979.45).

Cat. 1304

China, Northern Qi Dynasty (550–577)
Torso of the Buddha, c. 577
Marble, 35 ½ x 13 ¾ in. (90.2 x 34.9 cm)
[Eskenazi, London, sold 12 March 1976 for

$19,398 to]; Norton Simon, gift 18 October 1983 to; The Norton Simon Foundation (F.1983.35).

Cat. 1305

Charles Natoire (French, 1700–1777)
Entry of Mark Antony into Ephesus, 1772
Oil on canvas, 42 x 76 ½ in. (106.7 x 194.3 cm)
[Galerie René Drouet, Paris, sold 16 March 1976 for $11,253 to]; Norton Simon, gift 31 December 1979 to; Norton Simon Art Foundation (M.1979.55).

Cat. 1306

Pablo Picasso (Spanish, 1881–1973)
Dora Maar, 1941
Oil on canvas, 31 ⅞ x 25 ⅝ in. (81 x 65 cm)
[Paul Kantor, Beverly Hills, Calif., sold 16 March 1976 for $150,000 to]; Norton Simon, sold 8 March 1978 for $172,000 to; [Paul Kantor, Beverly Hills, Calif.]. [Berggruen, Paris]. private collection. [Galerie Daniel Malingue, Paris, sold 1981 to]; private collection.

Cat. 1307

India, Andhra Pradesh
Bidri Bowl and Cover, 17th century
Zinc inlaid with silver,
5 ¾ x 4 ½ in. (14.6 x 11.4 cm)
(Sale, London, Sotheby & Co., 17 March 1976 for $322 to); Norton Simon, by inheritance 2 June 1993 to; Jennifer Jones Simon Art Trust, Los Angeles (N.1976.7).

Cat. 1308

Jacopo Palma il Vecchio (Italian, 1480–1528)
Venus and Cupid in a Landscape, c. 1515
Oil on canvas, 35 x 65 ¾ in. (88.9 x 167 cm)
(Sale, Goteborgs Auktionsverk, Gothenburg, Sweden, 23 March 1976 for $19,563 to); Norton Simon, by inheritance 2 June 1993 to; Jennifer Jones Simon Art Trust, Los Angeles, gift 9 May 1996 to; Norton Simon Art Foundation (M.1996.1).

Cat. 1309
Etruscan
Relief, c. 525–500 B.C.
Terracotta, 8 ¼ x 7 ¾ x 1 ⅜ in.
(21 x 19.7 x 3.5 cm)
[Simone de Monbrison, Paris, sold 25
March 1976 for $1,800 to]; Norton Simon,
by inheritance 2 June 1993 to; Jennifer Jones
Simon Art Trust, Los Angeles (N.1976.9.2).

Cat. 1310
Francisco de Goya y Lucientes
(Spanish, 1746–1828)
La Tauromaquia, 1st edition, 1816
Etching, aquatint, and drypoint, 33 plates
(plate 2 working proof)
(Sale, London, Sotheby & Co., 25 March
1976 for $73,561 to); The Norton Simon
Foundation (F.1976.3.1–33).

Cat. 1311
Greece
Antefix Head, late 6th century B.C.
Terracotta, 7 ⅛ x 5 ¼ in. (18.1 x 13.3 cm)
[Simone de Monbrison, Paris, sold 25 March
1976 for $5,400 to]; Norton Simon, by
inheritance 2 June 1993 to; Jennifer Jones
Simon Art Trust, Los Angeles (N.1976.9.3).

Cat. 1312A-C
Greece and Armenia
*Bracelet, Bracelet with Animal Head
Terminals, and Ring*, 3rd century B.C.
Gold, three pieces
[Christian Boursaud, Switzerland, sold
26 March 1976 for $10,300 to]; Norton
Simon, gift 18 October 1983 to; The Norton
Simon Foundation (F.1983.40–42).

Cat. 1313
Rome
Head of Cybele, 1st century
Marble, 11 x 7 x 9 in. (27.9 x 17.8 x 22.9 cm)
[Simone de Monbrison, Paris, sold

25 March 1976 for $5,400 to]; Norton
Simon, by inheritance 2 June 1993 to;
Jennifer Jones Simon Art Trust, Los Angeles
(N.1976.9.1).

Cat. 1314
Gerard Hoet (Dutch, 1648–1733)
Paris Presenting Helen at the Court of Priam
Oil on copper, 22 ³/₁₆ x 26 ¾ in.
(56.4 x 67.9 cm)
[Marianne Feilchenfeldt, Zurich, sold.
31 March 1976 for $9,500 to]; Norton Simon
Art Foundation (M.1976.4).

Cat. 1315
William-Adolphe Bouguereau (French,
1825–1905) or Elizabeth Gardner
Bouguereau (American, 1837–1922)
Allegory of the Arts, c. 1890–1895
Black and white chalk on buff paper, mounted
to linen, 20 x 52 ⅝ in. (50.8 x 133.7 cm)
(Sale, New York, Sotheby Parke Bernet, 2
April 1976 for $2,000 to); Norton Simon,
gift 31 December 1979 to; Norton Simon Art
Foundation (M.1979.62).

Cat. 1316
Jacob Jordaens (Flemish, 1593–1678) and Jan
Wildens (Flemish, 1585/1586–1653)
Mercury and Argus, early 1640s
Oil on canvas, 47 ¾ x 72 ¾ in.
(121.3 x 184.8 cm)
(Sale, London, Christie's, 2 April 1976 for
$36,650 to); The Norton Simon Foundation
(F.1976.1).

Cat. 1317
Francesco Solimena (Italian, 1657–1747)
The Personification of Faith
Oil on canvas, 19 ½ x 30 in. (49.5 x 76.2 cm)
(Sale, London, Christie's, 2 April 1976 for
$7,161 to); Norton Simon, gift 31 December
1979 to; Norton Simon Art Foundation
(M.1979.57).

1309

1311

1314

1315

1316

1312A

1312B

1312C

1317

1313

1318

1319

1320

1321

1322

1323

1324

1325

1326

Cat. 1318

Louis Tocqué (French, 1696–1772)
*Claude René Cordier de Launay de Montreuil,
President of the Parliament of Paris*
Oil on canvas, 32 ⅛ x 25 ¼ in. (81.6 x 64.1 cm)
(Sale, London, Christie's, 2 April 1976 for
$7,161 to); Norton Simon, gift 31 December
1979 to; Norton Simon Art Foundation
(M.1979.59).

Cat. 1319

Georges Braque (French, 1882–1963)
Artist and Model, 1939
Oil and sand on canvas, 51 ⅛ x 70 ⅞ in.
(129.9 x 180 cm)
[M. Knoedler & Co., New York, sold 6 April
1976 for $900,000 to]; Norton Simon Art
Foundation (M.1976.5).

Cat. 1320

Jean-Baptiste Camille Corot
(French, 1796–1875)
*Farm Building at Bois-Guillaume, near
Rouen*, c. 1823–1824
Oil and pencil on paper, laid down on
canvas, 10 x 13 in. (25.3 x 33 cm)
(Sale, London, Christie's, 6 April 1976 for
$24,232 to); Norton Simon, by inheritance
2 June 1993 to; Jennifer Jones Simon Art
Trust, Los Angeles (N.1976.18).

Cat. 1321

François-Hubert Drouais
(French, 1727–1775)
Young Girl Holding a Basket of Fruit
Oil on canvas, 28 ¾ x 23 ¼ in. (73 x 59.1 cm)
(Sale, Paris, Palais Galliera, 6 April 1976 for
$7,548 to); Norton Simon, gift 31 December
1979 to; Norton Simon Art Foundation
(M.1979.46).

Cat. 1322

Paul Liegeois (French, 17th century)
Still Life
Oil on canvas, 29 x 38 ⅜ in. (73.7 x 97.5 cm)

(Sale, Paris, Palais Galliera, 6 April 1976 for
$6,806 to); Norton Simon, gift 31 December
1979 to; Norton Simon Art Foundation
(M.1979.49).

Cat. 1323

Aert van der Neer (Dutch, 1603–1677)
*Soldiers and Villagers Leaving a Burning
Village*, 1637
Oil on panel, 14 ⁵/₁₆ x 20 ⁵/₁₆ in. (36.4 x 51.6 cm)
(Sale, Paris, Palais Galliéra, 6 April 1976 for
$24,863 to); Norton Simon, by inheritance
2 June 1993 to; Jennifer Jones Simon Art
Trust, Los Angeles (N.1976.17.3).

Cat. 1324

Gioacchino Assereto (Italian, 1600–1649)
David with the Head of Goliath
Oil on canvas, 31 ½ x 22 in. (80 x 55.9 cm)
(Sale, Paris, Laurin-Guilloux-Buffetaud,
7 April 1976 for $2,443 to); Norton Simon,
gift 31 December 1979 to; Norton Simon
Museum (P.1979.10).

Cat. 1325

Marie-Geneviève Bouliar
(French, 1772–1819)
Self-Portrait
Oil on canvas, 21 ⅞ x 18 ⅛ in. (55.6 x 46 cm)
(Sale, Paris, Palais Galliera, 7 April 1976 for
$5,075 to); Norton Simon, gift 31 December
1979 to; Norton Simon Art Foundation
(M.1979.43).

Cat. 1326

Niccolo di Pietro Gerini
(Italian, active 1368–1415)
Saints Anthony and Peter
Tempera on panel,
46 ¾ x 30 in. (118.7 x 76.2 cm)
(Sale, Paris, Palais Galliera, 7 April 1976
for $17,442 to); Norton Simon, gift
31 December 1979 to; Norton Simon Art
Foundation (M.1979.50).

Cat. 1327
Attributed to Louise Moillon
(French, 1610–1696)
Still Life with Peaches
Oil on canvas, 25 x 30 in. (63.5 x 76.2 cm)
(Sale, Paris, Palais Galliéra, 7 April 1976 for
$5,569 to); Norton Simon, gift 31 December
1979 to; Norton Simon Art Foundation
(M.1979.54).

Cat. 1328
Antoine Vestier (French, 1740–1824)
Portrait Presumed to Be Mlle de Lastelle
Oil on canvas, oval,
38 x 29 ¾ in. (96.5 x 75.5 cm)
(Sale, Paris, Laurin-Guilloux-Buffetaud,
7 April 1976 for $5,075 to); Norton Simon,
gift 18 October 1983 to; The Norton Simon
Foundation (F.1983.16).

Cat. 1329
Maurice Denis (French, 1870–1943)
Religious Pilgrimage, Brittany, 1939
Oil on canvas,
18 ¾ x 25 ¾ in. (47.6 x 65.4 cm)
(Sale, London, Sotheby & Co., 8 April
1976 for $17,164 to); Norton Simon, by
inheritance 2 June 1993 to; Jennifer Jones
Simon Art Trust, Los Angeles (N.1976.20.1).

Cat. 1330
Paul Sérusier (French, 1864–1927)
Synchromy in Yellow, 1900–1913 or 1915
Oil on canvas, 32 x 21 ½ in. (81.3 x 54.6 cm)
(Sale, London, Sothcby & Co., 8 April
1976 for $14,539 to); Norton Simon, by
inheritance 2 June 1993 to; Jennifer Jones
Simon Art Trust, Los Angeles, gift 11 April
2008 to; Norton Simon Art Foundation
(M.2008.1.2).

Cat. 1331
Émile Bernard (French, 1868–1941)
Court of Love, 1894

Oil on canvas, 35 x 46 ⅞ in. (89 x 119 cm)
(Sale, London, Christie's, 9 April 1976 for
$1,212 to); Norton Simon, sold 15 January
1977 for $1,212 to; Alvin E. Toffel, Los
Angeles, by descent to; private collection,
Los Angeles.

Cat. 1332
Claude Monet (French, 1840–1926)
Water Lilies, c. 1920
Oil on canvas, 51 x 59 ¾ in.
(129.5 x 151.8 cm)
[Arthur Tooth & Sons, London, sold
13 April 1976 (through David Geffen, Los
Angeles) for $350,000 to]; The Norton
Simon Foundation, used in trade 27
December 1978 with a value of $350,000
plus $310,000 as payment for repurchasing
Edgar Degas, *Woman Drying Herself after
the Bath* (cat. 172) to; [Wildenstein & Co.,
New York]. (sale, New York, Sotheby Parke
Bernet, 18 May 1983, lot 39, for $2,640,000).
private collection, Buenos Aires, c. 1996.
private collection, PA, 2008.

Cat. 1333
Constant Troyon (French, 1810–1865)
Thatched Cottage by the Sea, c. 1855–1860
Oil on panel, 10 ½ x 13 ¾ in.
(26.7 x 34.9 cm)
[Galerie Barbizon, Paris, sold 19 April
1976 for $2,574 to]; Norton Simon, by
inheritance 2 June 1993 to; Jennifer Jones
Simon Art Trust, Los Angeles (N.1976.15).

Cat. 1334
India, Orissa
Amorous Couple, 13th century
Gneiss, 69 x 28 in. (175.3 x 71.1 cm)
[Beurdeley, Paris, sold 28 April 1976 for
$77,297 to]; The Norton Simon Foundation
(F.1976.4).

1327

1332

1333

1328

1329

1334

1330

1331

1335

1337

1336

1338

1339

1345

1340

1341

1342   1343

1344

Cat. 1335
India, Himachal Pradesh
Buddha Shakyamuni, 11th–12th century
Bronze, 12 in. (30.5 cm)
[Ben Heller, New York, sold 29 April
1976 for $25,000 to]; The Norton Simon
Foundation (F.1976.5.12).

Cat. 1336
India, Uttar Pradesh, Gupta Period
Ganesha, late 6th century
Sandstone, 32 x 19 ½ in. (81.3 x 49.5 cm)
[Ben Heller, New York, sold 29 April
1976 for $25,000 to]; The Norton Simon
Foundation (F.1976.5.8).

Cat. 1337
India, Tamil Nadu
Ganesha, 12th century
Bronze, 13 in. (33 cm)
[Ben Heller, New York, sold 29 April
1976 for $30,000 to]; The Norton Simon
Foundation (F.1976.5.9).

Cat. 1338
India, Tamil Nadu
Uma, c. 1200
Granite, 51 ½ x 24 in. (130.8 x 61 cm)
[Ben Heller, New York, sold 29 April
1976 for $30,000 to];The Norton Simon
Foundation (F.1976.5.3).

Cat. 1339
India, Tamil Nadu
Vishnu, c. 850
Granite, 89 ½ x 31 x 14 ¼ in.
(227.3 x 78.7 x 36.2 cm)
[Ben Heller, New York, sold 29 April 1976
for $120,000 to]; The Norton Simon
Foundation (F.1976.5.4).

Cat. 1340
India, Uttar Pradesh, Mathura
Torso of a Male Divinity, c. 150–200
Sandstone, 22 ⅛ in. (56.2 cm)

[Ben Heller, New York, sold 29 April
1976 for $20,000 to]; The Norton Simon
Foundation (F.1976.5.13).

Cat. 1341
Nepal
Bodhisattva Avalokiteshvara, 14th century
Bronze with semiprecious stones,
17 ¾ in. (45.1 cm)
[Ben Heller, New York, sold 29 April
1976 for $50,000 to]; The Norton Simon
Foundation (F.1976.5.2).

Cat. 1342
Nepal or Tibet
Bodhisattva Avalokiteshvara, 14th century
Gilt copper, 24 in. (61 cm)
[Ben Heller, New York, sold 29 April
1976 for $30,000 to]; The Norton Simon
Foundation (F.1976.5.7).

Cat. 1343
Nepal
Buddha, 20th century
Gilt bronze, 12 ⅜ in. (31.4 cm)
[Ben Heller, New York, sold 29 April
1976 for $125,000 to]; The Norton Simon
Foundation (F.1976.5.6).

Cat. 1344
Nepal or Tibet
Buddha Akshobhya, 11th century
Gilt bronze with pigment, 7 ¼ in. (18.4 cm)
[Ben Heller, New York, sold 29 April 1976
for $100,000 to]; The Norton Simon
Foundation (F.1976.5.5).

Cat. 1345
Nepal or Tibet
Tara, c. 1300
Gilt bronze with semiprecious stones and
pigment, 34 ¾ in. (88.3 cm)
[Ben Heller, New York, sold 29 April 1976
for $200,000 to]; The Norton Simon
Foundation (F.1976.5.1).

Cat. 1346
Pakistan, Ancient Gandhara
Bust of a Male Figure, 4th–5th century
Stucco, 10 ¼ in. (26 cm)
[Ben Heller, New York, sold 29 April
1976 for $2,500 to]; The Norton Simon
Foundation (F.1976.5.11).

Cat. 1347
Pakistan or Afghanistan, Ancient Gandhara
Head of a Bodhisattva or Deity,
4th–5th century
Polychromed stucco, 6 ¼ in. (15.9 cm)
[Ben Heller, New York, sold 29 April
1976 for $2,500 to]; The Norton Simon
Foundation (F.1976.5.10).

Cat. 1348
Thailand, Mon-Dvaravati Period
Buddha Shakyamuni, 9th century
Bronze, 10 ⅛ in. (25.7 cm)
[Ben Heller, New York, sold 29 April
1976 for $10,000 to]; The Norton Simon
Foundation (F.1976.5.15).

Cat. 1349
Western Tibet
Bodhisattva Avalokiteshvara, 12th century
Brass inlaid with gold, silver, turquoise,
and pigment, 15 ¾ in. (40 cm)
[Ben Heller, New York, sold 29 April
1976 for $30,000 to]; The Norton Simon
Foundation (F.1976.5.14).

Cat. 1350A–C
Francisco de Goya y Lucientes
(Spanish, 1746–1828)
*The Moors Make a Different Play in the Ring
Calling the Bull with Their Bournous*; *Origin
of the Harpoons or Banderillas*; *Manly
Courage of the Celebrated Pajuelers in the
Ring at Saragosa*, plates 6, 7, and 22 from
La Tauromaquia, 1st edition, 1816
Etching, aquatint, and drypoint
(Sale, New York, Sotheby Parke Bernet,

5 May 1976 for $3,100 to); The Norton
Simon Foundation, gift 9 February 1983 to;
Norton Simon Museum in order to be sold
in the Museum store.

Cat. 1351
Francisco de Goya y Lucientes
(Spanish, 1746–1828)
Caritas, c. 1780
Etching and drypoint, 5 ⅛ x 3 ¾ in.
(13 x 9.5 cm)
(Sale, New York, Sotheby Parke Bernet,
5 May 1976 for $2,000 to); The Norton
Simon Foundation (F.1976.8.1).

Cat. 1352
Greece
Torso of Aphrodite
Marble, 8 ¼ in. (20.9 cm)
(Sale, New York, Sotheby Parke Bernet,
8 May 1976 for $6,300 to); Norton Simon,
by inheritance 2 June 1993 to; Jennifer Jones
Simon Art Trust, Los Angeles (N.1976.26).

Cat. 1353
Thailand, Ayutthaya Period
Buddha Shakyamuni, 16th century
Bronze, 15 ¾ in. (40 cm)
[Daibutsu Chinese and Japanese Arts,
San Francisco, sold 13 May 1976 for $629 to];
Norton Simon, gift 31 December 1979 to;
Norton Simon Art Foundation (M.1979.93).

Cat. 1354
Cambodia or Thailand, Angkor Period
Mythical Beast, c. 1200
Bronze, 16 ¾ x 6 ½ x 15 in.
(42.5 x 16.5 x 38.1 cm)
[Wheelock Marden (Douglas Latchford),
Thailand, sold 14 May 1976 for $65,000 to];
The Norton Simon Foundation, transferred
28 November 1980 to; Norton Simon Art
Foundation (M.1980.18).

1346

1351

1347

1352

1348

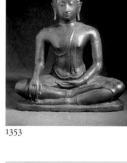
1353

1349

1354

1355

1359

1362

1356

1357

1363

1358

Cat. 1355
Henri Hayden (Polish, 1883–1970)
Still Life with Newspaper, 1918
Oil on canvas, 31 ½ x 23 ¼ in. (80 x 59.1 cm)
[Waddington Galleries, London, sold
14 May 1976 for $16,362 to]; Norton Simon
(sale, New York, Sotheby Parke Bernet, 1
November 1978, lot 45a, for $21,000 to);
[Galerie Daniel Malingue, Paris].

Cat. 1356
Rome
Pair of Earrings with Lions' Heads,
c. 3rd century
Gold, each 2 ½ x 1 ½ in. (6.4 x 3.8 cm)
[Simone de Monbrison, Paris, sold 14 May
1976 for $2,554 to]; Norton Simon, gift
18 October 1983 to; The Norton Simon
Foundation (F.1983.39).

Cat. 1357
Ceylon
*Mask of Grotesque Form with Cobra
Headdress*
Polychrome painted wood, 8 ¼ in. (21 cm)
(Sale, London, Sotheby & Co., 17 May
1976 for $117 to); Norton Simon, gift 28
December 1978 to; The Norton Simon
Foundation (F.1978.5).

Cat. 1358
Mainland Southeast Asia
Drum, 19th century or earlier
Bronze, 7 ½ x 10 ⅛ in. (19.1 x 25.7 cm)
(Sale, London, Sotheby & Co., 17 May 1976
for $254 to); Norton Simon, by inheritance
2 June 1993 to; Jennifer Jones Simon Art
Trust, Los Angeles (N.1976.30.2).

Cat. 1359
Francisco de Goya y Lucientes
(Spanish, 1746–1828)
Felipe IV, after Velázquez, 1st edition,
1778–1779
Etching, 14 ⁹/₁₆ x 12 ³/₁₆ in. (37 x 31 cm)

(Sale, London, Sotheby & Co., 20 May
1976 for $489 to); Norton Simon, gift 31
December 1979 to; Norton Simon Art
Foundation, sold 23 April 1981 for $3,500 to;
[William Schab, New York].

Cat. 1360
Francisco de Goya y Lucientes
(Spanish, 1746–1828)
Gaspar de Guzman, after Velázquez, 1st
edition, 1778–1779
Etching, plate, 14 ¹¹/₁₆ x 12 ⅜ in. (37.3 x 31.4
cm); sheet, 23 ⅝ x 16 ½ in. (60 x 41.9 cm)
(Sale, London, Sotheby & Co., 20 May 1976
for $489 to); Norton Simon, gift
31 December 1979 to; Norton Simon Art
Foundation (M.1979.66).

Cat. 1361
Francisco de Goya y Lucientes
(Spanish, 1746–1828)
La Tauromaquia, 1st edition, 1816
Etching, aquatint, and drypoint, 33 plates
(Sale, London, Sotheby & Co., 20 May
1976 for $64,393 to); The Norton Simon
Foundation (F.1976.9.1–33).

Cat. 1362
School of Fontainebleau
(French, 16th century)
Danae Sleeping
Oil on canvas, 34 ⅜ x 48 ½ in. (87.3 x 123.2 cm)
(Sale, Versailles, Palais des Congrès, 23 May
1976 for $3,031 to); Norton Simon, gift
31 December 1979 to; Norton Simon Art
Foundation (M.1979.47).

Cat. 1363
Claude-Joseph Vernet (French, 1714–1789)
The Embarkation of a Young Greek Woman
Oil on canvas, 22 ¾ x 24 in. (57.8 x 61 cm)
(Sale, Paris, Palais Galliéra, 25 May 1976 for
$9,159 to); Norton Simon, gift 31 December
1979 to; Norton Simon Art Foundation
(M.1979.61).

Cat. 1364

Louis Anquetin (French, 1861–1932)

Portrait of a Woman (Marguerite Dufay), 1891

Pastel, 24 ¾ x 20 in. (63 x 51 cm)

[La Cave–Galerie de Tableaux, Paris, sold 24 June 1976 for $5,281 to]; Norton Simon, gift 31 December 1979 to; Norton Simon Art Foundation (M.1979.42).

Cat. 1365

Maurice Denis (French, 1870–1943)

The Communicants, 1892

Pastel, 24 x 18 ½ in. (61 x 47 cm)

[La Cave–Galerie de Tableaux, Paris, sold 24 June 1976 for $5,280 to]; Norton Simon, sold 14 September 1976 for $5,280 to; David Mahoney, New York.

Cat. 1366

Maurice Denis (French, 1870–1943)

Hyacinths, 1900

Oil on canvas, 51 ¼ x 38 ½ in. (130.2 x 97.8 cm)

[La Cave–Galerie de Tableaux, Paris, sold 24 June 1976 for $12,673 to]; Norton Simon, sold 14 September 1976 for $12,673 to; David Mahoney, New York.

Cat. 1367

Maurice Denis (French, 1870–1943)

Procession, 1892

Oil on canvas, 18 x 14 ½ in. (45.7 x 36.8 cm)

[La Cave–Galerie de Tableaux, Paris, sold 24 June 1976 for $5,280 to]; Norton Simon, sold 14 September 1976 for $5,280 to; David Mahoney, New York.

Cat. 1368

Paul Sérusier (French, 1864–1927)

The Sea at Pouldu

Oil on canvas, 28 ¾ x 21 ¼ in. (73 x 54 cm)

[La Cave–Galerie de Tableaux, sold 24 June 1976 for $12,673 to]; Norton Simon, sold 14 September 1976 for $12,673 to; David Mahoney, New York.

Cat. 1369

Greece, Magna Graecia

Pair of Earrings with Lions' Heads, 4th century B.C.

Gold, each 1 ⅜ x 1 ⅛ in. (3.5 x 2.9 cm)

[Robin Symes, London, sold 6 July 1976 for $6,316 to]; The Norton Simon Foundation (F.1976.10a–b).

Cat. 1370

Luca Giordano (Italian, 1632–1705)

A Battle Scene

Oil on canvas, 79 x 127 ¾ in. (200.7 x 324.5 cm)

(Private sale, London, Sotheby & Co., 1 September 1976 for $18,830 to); The Norton Simon Foundation (F.1976.12).

Cat. 1371

Vincent van Gogh (Dutch, 1853–1890)

Dr. Gachet, 1890

Etching, 7 ³/₁₆ x 6 in. (18.3 x 15.2 cm)

[Private sale, Sotheby Parke-Bernet, New York, 8 July 1976 for $10,000 to]; The Norton Simon Foundation (F.1976.11).

Cat. 1372A-F

India, Himachal Pradesh

Six Mohras with Shivas and Goddesses

Brass, various sizes

(Sale, London, Sotheby & Co., 26 July 1976 for $360 to); Norton Simon, gift 31 December 1979 to; Norton Simon Art Foundation (M.1979.78, 79, 80. 1–3, 81).

Cat. 1373

Cambodia, Angkor Period

Lingam, 9th–12th century

Sandstone, 38 x 11 ¾ in. (96.5 x 29.8 cm)

[William Wolff, New York, sold 13 September 1976 for $5,000 to]; Norton Simon, by inheritance 2 June 1993 to; Jennifer Jones Simon Art Trust, Los Angeles (N.1976.33).

1364

1369

1370

1372A

1371

1372B

1373

1374

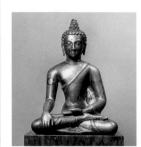

1379

1375

1380

1376

1381

1377A

1377B   1382

1378

1383

400

Cat. 1374

Cambodia, Koh Ker(?), Angkor Period
Temple Guardian, c. 925–950
Sandstone, 61 ¾ in. (156.8 cm)
[William Wolff, New York, sold
13 September 1976 for $175,000 to]; The
Norton Simon Foundation, transferred
28 November 1980 to; Norton Simon Art
Foundation (M.1980.15).

Cat. 1375

Roman Period
Venus
Marble, 44 in. (111.7 cm)
[Robin Symes, London, sold 13 September
1976 for $150,000 to]; Norton Simon, by
inheritance 2 June 1993 to; Jennifer Jones
Simon Art Trust, Los Angeles (N.1976.32).

Cat. 1376

Théodore Rousseau (French, 1812–1867)
The Fisherman, Early Morning, c. 1865
Oil on canvas, 39 ¼ x 53 in. (99.6 x 134.6 cm)
[Wildenstein & Co., New York, sold
13 September 1976 for $75,000 to]; The
Norton Simon Foundation (F.1976.14).

Cat. 1377A-B

Cambodia, Pre-Angkor Period
Lingams, 9th–12th century
Sandstone, each 18 x 5 ½ in. (45.7 x 14 cm)
[Beurdeley, Paris, sold 28 September 1976
for $2,042 to]; Norton Simon,
by inheritance 2 June 1993 to; Jennifer
Jones Simon Art Trust, Los Angeles
(N.1976.34.1–2).

Cat. 1378

Marino Marini (Italian, 1901–1980)
Dancer, 1954
Bronze, edition of 3, cast no. 3, 58 ¼ in.
(148 cm)
[Jeffrey H. Loria & Co., New York, sold
29 September 1976 for $43,000 to]; The
Norton Simon Foundation (sale, New York,

Sotheby Parke Bernet, 14 May 1980, lot 273,
for $48,000 to); [Galerie Ferrero, Nice].

Cat. 1379

Nepal
Seated Buddha, 9th–10th century
Gilt copper, 7 in. (17.8 cm)
[William Wolff, New York, sold 3 November
1976 for $6,000 to]; The Norton Simon
Foundation, returned 18 May 1979 for
full purchase price to; [William Wolff,
New York].

Cat. 1380

India, West Bengal or Bangladesh
Vishnu with Retinue, 12th century
Schist, 31 x 14 ½ in. (78.7 x 36.8 cm)
(Sale, London, Christie's, 10 November 1976
for $1,913 to); Norton Simon, gift
28 December 1978 to; The Norton Simon
Foundation (F.1978.33).

Cat. 1381

Pakistan, Ancient Gandhara
Head of Buddha, 2nd–3rd century
Schist, 7 ½ in. (19.1 cm)
(Sale, London, Christie's, 10 November
1976 for $1,000 to); Norton Simon, gift
31 December 1979 to; Norton Simon Art
Foundation (M.1979.76).

Cat. 1382

India, Rajasthan
Pediment with Adoring Celestials, c. 1000
Marble,
25 x 38 ½ x 10 in. (63.5 x 97.8 x 25.4 cm)
(Sale, London, Christie's, 10 November
1976 for $1,640 to); Norton Simon, by
inheritance 2 June 1993 to; Jennifer Jones
Simon Art Trust, Los Angeles (N.1976.35.1).

Cat. 1383

Francesco Guardi (Italian, 1712–1793)
*Godfrey of Boulogne Summons His Chiefs to
Council*, c. 1755
Oil on canvas, 98 ½ x 43 ¼ in.

(250.2 x 109.9 cm)
[Schaeffer Galleries, New York, sold 11
November 1976 for $57,500 to]; The Norton
Simon Foundation (F.1976.17).

Cat. 1384
Juan Rexach (Spanish, active 1443–1484)
*The Crucifixion and Madonna and Child
Enthroned with Angels*, c. 1465–1470
Tempera and gold leaf on panel,
68 ½ x 38 ½ in. (174 x 97.8 cm)
[Thomas Agnew & Sons, London, sold 21
November 1976 for $60,000 to]; The Norton
Simon Foundation (F.1976.18).

1384

Cat. 1385
India, Orissa
Head of Bhairava(?), 13th century
Gneiss, 15 ¾ x 13 in. (40 x 33 cm)
(Sale, New York, Sotheby Parke Bernet,
1 December 1976 for $2,900 to); The Norton
Simon Foundation (F.1976.19).

Cat. 1386
Indonesia, East Java
Zodiac Beaker, 1332
Bronze, 4 ½ x 5 ⅝ in. (11.4 x 14.3 cm)
(Sale, New York, Sotheby Parke Bernet,
1 December 1976 for $450 to); Norton Simon,
by inheritance 2 June 1993 to; Jennifer Jones
Simon Art Trust, Los Angeles (N.1976.36).

Cat. 1387
Raymond Bayless (American, 1920–2004)
Twenty-Dollar Bill, 1954
Gouache on board,
7 x 9 ½ in. (17.8 x 24.1 cm)
Date of purchase, price, and source
unknown (by 10 December 1976 with);
Norton Simon, gift 17 May 1977 to; Norton
Simon Museum (P.1977.4).

Cat. 1388
Francisco de Goya y Lucientes
(Spanish, 1746–1828)
La Tauromaquia, 1st edition, 1816

Etching, aquatint, and drypoint, incomplete
set of 31 plates
(Sale, London, Sotheby & Co., 16 December
1976 for $25,736 to); Norton Simon,
by inheritance 2 June 1993 to; Jennifer
Jones Simon Art Trust, Los Angeles
(N.1977.3.1–31).

Cat. 1389
Greece
Figure of a Goddess
Marble, 12 ¾ in. (32.4 cm)
(Sale, New York, Sotheby Parke Bernet,
23 December 1976 for $2,100 to); Norton
Simon, by inheritance 2 June 1993 to;
Jennifer Jones Simon Art Trust, Los Angeles
(N.1976.38).

Cat. 1390
India, Tamil Nadu
Shiva as King of Dance, 17th century
Bronze, 11 ¾ in. (29.8 cm)
Darryl Isley, Los Angeles, gift 25 December
1976 to; Norton Simon, by inheritance
2 June 1993 to; Jennifer Jones Simon Art
Trust, Los Angeles (N.1976.25).

Cat. 1391
Syria
Balustrade
Marble, 50 ½ x 25 ½ in. (128.3 x 64.8 cm)
[Simone de Monbrison, Paris, sold
31 December 1976 for $3,500 to]; Norton
Simon, by inheritance 2 June 1993 to;
Jennifer Jones Simon Art Trust, Los Angeles
(N.1976.39).

1977

Cat. 1392
Greece
Nereid, 2nd–3rd century B.C.
Marble, 52 x 19 ½ in. (132.1 x 49.5 cm)
[Robin Symes, London, sold 3 January
1977 for $200,000 to]; Norton Simon, by
inheritance 2 June 1993 to; Jennifer Jones
Simon Art Trust, Los Angeles (N.1977.2).

1389

1390

1385

1391

1386

1388

1392

1393A–C

1394

1395

1396

1397

1398

1399

1400

1401

1402

Cat. 1393A–C
India, Himachal Pradesh
Shiva with Parvati and Bull, c. 1960s
Brass with silver inlay, 37 in. (94 cm);
31 ½ in. (80 cm); and 17 in. (43.2 cm)
[J. J. Klejman, New York, sold 3 January
1977 for $25,000 to]; Norton Simon,
by inheritance 2 June 1993 to; Jennifer
Jones Simon Art Trust, Los Angeles
(N.1977.1.2.1–3).

Cat. 1394
Syria
Tetrarch, 3rd century A.D.
Limestone, 76 x 24 in. (193 x 61 cm)
[J. J. Klejman, New York, sold 3 January
1977 for $6,500 to]; Norton Simon, by
inheritance 2 June 1993 to; Jennifer Jones
Simon Art Trust, Los Angeles (N.1977.1.1).

Cat. 1395
Édouard Vuillard (French, 1868–1940)
Lucie Hessel, c. 1905
Oil on cardboard,
16 x 18 in. (40.6 x 45.7 cm)
[Alex Reid & Lefevre, London, 6 January
1977 for $30,000 to]; Norton Simon Art
Foundation (M.1977.1).

Cat. 1396
China, Tang Dynasty (618–907)
Bodhisattva, 7th–8th century
Marble, 12 in. (30.5 cm)
[C. T. Loo, Paris, sold 14 January 1977 for
$36,144 to]; Norton Simon, by inheritance
2 June 1993 to; Jennifer Jones Simon Art
Trust, Los Angeles (N.1977.4).

Cat. 1397
Edgar Degas (French, 1834–1917)
The modèle bronzes
Bronze, seventy in various sizes
and subjects
[Alex Reid & Lefevre, London, sold

4 January 1977 for $1.8 million to]; Norton
Simon Art Foundation (M.1977.2.1–70).

Cat. 1398
Louis Anquetin (French, 1861–1932)
Portrait of a Man, 1889
Pastel, 24 ½ x 20 in. (62.2 x 50.8 cm)
[La Cave–Galerie de Tableaux, Paris, sold
15 February 1977 for $6,443 to]; Norton
Simon Art Foundation (M.1977.3.1).

Cat. 1399
Cycladic
Collared Jar with Foot (Kandila),
c. 2400 B.C.
Marble, 4 ¾ in. (12.1 cm)
[Robin Symes, London, sold 15 February
1977 for $1,168 to]; Norton Simon, by
inheritance 2 June 1993 to; Jennifer Jones
Simon Art Trust, Los Angeles (N.1977.5.4).

Cat. 1400
Maurice Denis (French, 1870–1943)
The Entombment, 1893
Tempera on paper, mounted on canvas,
43 ½ x 52 in. (110.5 x 132.1 cm)
[La Cave–Galerie de Tableaux, Paris, sold
15 February 1977 for $16,510 to]; Norton
Simon Art Foundation (M.1977.3.3).

Cat. 1401
Egypt, Fayum
Portrait of a Man, 2nd century
Encaustic on wood, 12 ⅛ x 6 ⅝ in. (30.8 x
16.8 cm)
[Robin Symes, London, sold 15 February
1977 for $11,692 to]; Norton Simon, gift
28 December 1978 to; The Norton Simon
Foundation (F.1978.19).

Cat. 1402
Greece, Attic
Lekythos, late 4th century B.C.
Marble, 38 ¼ x 10 ½ in. (97.2 x 26.7 cm)
[Robin Symes, London, sold 15 February

1977 for $29,229 to]; Norton Simon, by inheritance 2 June 1993 to; Jennifer Jones Simon Art Trust, Los Angeles (N.1977.5.2).

Cat. 1403
Greece, Attic
Relief Head of a Woman, c. 320 B.C.
Marble, 8 x 6 in. (20.3 x 15.2 cm)
[Robin Symes, London, sold 15 February 1977 for $35,910 to]; Norton Simon, gift 18 October 1983 to; The Norton Simon Foundation (F.1983.38).

Cat. 1404
Ker-Xavier Roussel (French, 1867–1944)
Meeting of Women, c. 1893
Oil on canvas, 17 ⅞ x 29 ½ in. (45.4 x 75 cm)
[La Cave–Galerie de Tableaux, Paris, sold 15 February 1977 for $11,275 to]; Norton Simon Art Foundation (M.1977.3.2).

Cat. 1405
Paul Conrad (American, b. 1924)
Summit Meeting, 1971
Ink, 11 ½ x 9 ½ in. (29.2 x 24.1 cm)
Date of purchase, price, and source unknown (by 15 February 1977 with); Norton Simon, gift 17 May 1977 to; Norton Simon Museum (P.1977.6).

Cat. 1406
A. Velasco
Three Women Washing and Hanging Clothes
Oil on canvas, 28 ⅜ x 25 in. (72.1 x 63.5 cm)
Date of purchase, price, and source unknown (by 15 February 1977 with); Norton Simon, gift 17 May 1977 to; Norton Simon Museum (P.1977.7).

Cat. 1407
Edgar Degas (French, 1834–1917)
Arabesque over the right leg, left arm in line
Bronze, cast no. 3/HER.D, 11 ¼ in. (28.6 cm)
[Jeffrey H. Loria & Co., New York, sold 17 February 1977 for $25,000 to]; Norton

Simon Art Foundation (sale, New York, Sotheby Parke Bernet, 14 May 1980, lot 202, for $45,000). (sale, London, Christie's, 23 June 1997). private collection (sale, New York, Christie's, 7 November 2001, unsold; sale, New York, Christie's, 8 May 2002, lot 209, for $394,500).

Cat. 1408
Edgar Degas (French, 1834–1917)
Dancer (Battement in Second Position), 1874
Charcoal heightened with white and pale yellow pastel on gray-brown laid paper, 17 ¾ x 11 ⅞ in. (45.1 x 30.2 cm)
[Robert Schmit, Paris, sold 23 February 1977 for $48,100 to]; Norton Simon Art Foundation (M.1977.5).

Cat. 1409
Edgar Degas (French, 1834–1917)
Dancers in the Wings, c. 1876–1878
Pastel, gouache, distemper, and *essence* on paper, mounted on board, 27 ¼ x 19 ¾ in. (69.2 x 50.2 cm)
[Wildenstein & Co., New York, sold 19 March 1977 for $750,000 to]; Norton Simon Art Foundation (M.1977.6).

Cat. 1410
Aristide Maillol (French, 1861–1944)
Elisa, c. 1895
Oil on canvas, 23 ½ x 19 in. (59.7 x 48.3 cm)
(Sale, London, Sotheby & Co., 30 March 1977 for $17,226 to); Norton Simon Art Foundation (sale, New York, Sotheby Parke Bernet, 14 May 1980, lot 224, for $40,000 to); private collection.

Cat. 1411
Francisco de Goya y Lucientes (Spanish, 1746–1828)
La Tauromaquia, 1st edition, 1816
Etching, aquatint, and drypoint, 33 plates (Sale, London, Sotheby & Co., 27 April 1977 for $64,318 to); Norton Simon Art Foundation (M.1977.8.1.1–33).

1403

1408

1404

1409

1405

1410

1407

1411

1417

1413

1414

1418

1415

1419

1416A–C

1420

Cat. 1412
Francisco de Goya y Lucientes
(Spanish, 1746–1828)
They Plan Another with the Cape in an Enclosure, plate 4 from *La Tauromaquia*, 1st edition, 1816
Etching, aquatint, and drypoint
(Sale, London, Sotheby & Co., 27 April 1977 for $1,135 to); Norton Simon Art Foundation, gift 9 February 1983 to; Norton Simon Museum in order to be sold in the Museum store.

Cat. 1413
Pablo Picasso (Spanish, 1881–1973)
The Bull
Lithographs, eleven plates
(Sale, London, Sotheby & Co., 27 April 1977 for $160,795 to); Norton Simon Art Foundation (M.1977.8.3.1–11).

Cat. 1414
Pablo Picasso (Spanish, 1881–1973)
The Dove, January 9, 1949
Lithograph, 21 ½ x 27 ½ in. (54.6 x 69.9 cm)
(Sale, London, Sotheby & Co., 27 April 1977 for $7,945 to); Norton Simon Art Foundation (M.1977.8.4).

Cat. 1415
Pablo Picasso (Spanish, 1881–1973)
Youth, June 9, 1950
Lithograph, 2nd state, 19 ¾ x 25 ½ in. (50.2 x 64.8 cm)
(Sale, London, Sotheby & Co., 27 April 1977 for $5,297 to); Norton Simon Art Foundation (M.1977.8.5).

Cat. 1416A–C
South-Central Tibet
Milarepa or a Mystic with Two Royal Attendants, 15th century
Gilt bronze with semiprecious stones and pigment: 7 ½ in. (19 cm); 5 ½ in. (14 cm); 5 ½ in. (14 cm)
(Sale, London, Sotheby & Co., 9 May

1977 for $2,650 to); Norton Simon, by inheritance 2 June 1993 to; Jennifer Jones Simon Art Trust, Los Angeles (N.1977.6.4.1–3).

Cat. 1417
Nepal
Manjusri, c. 800
Gilt bronze, 5 in. (12.7 cm)
(Sale, London, Sotheby & Co., 9 May 1977 for $1,515 to); Norton Simon, by inheritance 2 June 1993 to; Jennifer Jones Simon Art Trust, Los Angeles (N.1977.6.3).

Cat. 1418
China, Qing Dynasty (1644–1911)
Shadakshari Lokeshvara, c. 1700
Lacquered wood with traces of gilding, 10 ¼ in. (26 cm)
(Sale, London, Sotheby & Co., 9 May 1977 for $1,609 to); Norton Simon, gift 31 December 1979 to; Norton Simon Art Foundation (M.1979.94).

Cat. 1419
Eastern Tibet(?)
Bodhisattva Shadakshari Lokeshvara, 17th century
Bronze with traces of pigment, 6 ½ in. (16.5 cm)
(Sale, London, Sotheby & Co., 9 May 1977 for $568 to); Norton Simon, by inheritance 2 June 1993 to; Jennifer Jones Simon Art Trust, Los Angeles (N.1977.6.1).

Cat. 1420
Edgar Degas (French, 1834–1917)
Horse trotting, the feet not touching the ground
Bronze, cast no. 49/HER, 8 ⅝ in. (22 cm)
(Sale, New York, Sotheby Parke Bernet, 11 May 1977 for $27,500 to); Norton Simon Art Foundation (sale, New York, Sotheby Parke Bernet, 7 November 1979, lot 534, for $32,500). [Robert Schmit, Paris]. private collection, Switzerland (sale, New York, Sotheby's, 9 November 1995).

Cat. 1421
Francisco de Goya y Lucientes
(Spanish, 1746–1828)
*The Rabble Hamstring the Bull with Lances,
Banderillas, and Other Arms*, plate 12 of
La Tauromaquia, 1st edition, 1816
Etching with aquatint
(Sale, New York, Sotheby Parke Bernet, 18
May 1977 for $1,400 to); Norton Simon Art
Foundation, gift 9 February 1983 to; Norton
Simon Museum in order to be sold in the
Museum store.

Cat. 1422
Giuseppe Bernardino Bison
(Italian, 1762–1844)
Parnassus
Oil on copper, 20 ½ x 19 in. (52.1 x 48.3 cm)
(Sale, New York, Sotheby Parke Bernet, 16
June 1977 for $4,750 to); Norton Simon,
gift 18 October 1983 to; The Norton Simon
Foundation (F.1983.4).

Cat. 1423
After Nicolaes Berchem (Dutch, 1620–1683)
*Evening Landscape with Tower and Figures,
and a Distant View of Mount Soratte, Rome*
Oil on canvas, 80 x 94 ½ in. (203.2 x 240 cm)
[Thomas Agnew & Sons, London, sold
24 June 1977 for $34,414 to]; Norton Simon
Art Foundation (M.1977.11).

Cat. 1424
Francisco de Goya y Lucientes
(Spanish, 1746–1828)
Landscape with Waterfall, before 1810,
trial proof, printed c. 1920
Etching and burnished aquatint (two plates
on one sheet): plate, 6 ½ x 5 ⅛ in. (16.5 x 13
cm); sheet, 12 ½ x 17 ¾ in. (31.8 x 45.1 cm)
[Reiss-Cohen, New York, sold 28 June 1977
for $2,000 to]; Norton Simon, sold 23 April
1981 for $10,000 to; [William Schab, New
York].

Cat. 1425
Pablo Picasso (Spanish, 1881–1973)
Long-haired Young Girl, November 1945
Lithographs, 2nd, 5th, and 6th states,
15 x 12 ½ in. (38.1 x 21.8 cm)
[E. V. Thaw & Co., New York, sold 28 June
1977 for $4,500 to]; Norton Simon, gift
17 January 1982, 20 December 1983, and
21 January 1984 to; private collection,
South America.

Cat. 1426A–E
Pablo Picasso (Spanish, 1881–1973)
Head of a Young Girl, 7 November 1945
Lithograph, 1st state, 12 ¾ x 10 ¼ in.
(32.4 x 26 cm)
Head of a Young Girl, 9 November 1945
Lithograph, 2nd state, 17 ¼ x 12 ⅝ in.
(43.8 x 32.1 cm)
Head of a Young Girl, 17 January 1946
Lithograph, 8th state, 17 ¼ x 12 ½ in.
(43.8 x 31.8 cm)
Head of a Young Girl, 6 February 1946
Lithograph, 9th state, 17 ¼ x 12 ½ in.
(43.8 x 31.8 cm)
Head of a Young Girl, 19 February 1946
Lithograph, 10th state, 17 ¼ x 12 ⅝ in.
(43.8 x 32.1 cm)
[E. V. Thaw & Co., New York, sold 28 June
1977 for $7,500 to]; Norton Simon, by
inheritance 2 June 1993 to; Jennifer Jones
Simon Art Trust, gift 18 May 2001 to; Norton
Simon Art Foundation (M.2001.1.1.1–5).

Cat. 1427
Georges Braque (French, 1882–1963)
Pitcher, Score, Fruits, and Napkin, 1926
Oil and sand on canvas, 14 ½ x 47 ¼ in.
(36.8 x 120 cm)
(Sale, London, Christie's, 28 June 1977,
through [Somerville & Simpson], for
$145,812 to]; Norton Simon Art Foundation
(M.1977.15.1).

1422

1423

1426A

1426C

1426B

1426D

1427

1428A

1428B

1429

1430B

1431

1432

1433

1434

1435

Cat. 1428A-B

Mainland Southeast Asia
Drums, 6th–10th century or later
Bronze, 14 ¼ x 20 ½ in. (36.2 x 52.1 cm) and
14 ¼ x 19 ¼ in. (36.2 x 48.7 cm)
[Beurdeley, Paris, sold 29 June 1977 for
$5,404 to]; Norton Simon, by inheritance
2 June 1993 to; Jennifer Jones Simon Art
Trust, Los Angeles (N.1977.10.1–2).

Cat. 1429

Pablo Picasso (Spanish, 1881–1973)
Bullfight under a Black Sun, 7 January 1946
Lithograph transfer, *bon à tirer* proof,
12 ⅛ x 16 ⅜ in. (30.8 x 41.6 cm)
(Sale, London, Christie's, 30 June 1977,
through [Somerville & Simpson], for
$2,620 to); Norton Simon Art Foundation
(M.1977.15.2.4).

Cat. 1430A-C

Pablo Picasso (Spanish, 1881–1973)
Composition with Glass and Apple
Three color lithographs, 1st state, 13 January
1946, 1/18: image, 9 ½ x 12 ½ in. (24.1 x 31.8
cm); sheet, 12 ¾ x 17 ½ in. (32.4 x 44.5 cm);
2nd state, 7 February 1946, 1/18: image, 9 ½
x 12 ½ in. (24.1 x 31.8 cm); sheet, 12 ¾ x 17 ½
in. (32.4 x 44.5 cm); 3rd state, 18 February
1946, 1/18: image, 11 x 13 ¾ in. (27.9 x 34.9
cm); sheet, 12 ¾ x 17 ½ in. (32.4 x 44.5 cm)
(Sale, London, Christie's, 30 June 1977,
through [Somerville & Simpson], for
$2,053 to); Norton Simon Art Foundation
(M.1977.15.2.6–8).

Cat. 1431

Pablo Picasso (Spanish, 1881–1973)
Head of a Man with a Pipe, 1911–1912
Etching, proof, 5 ⅛ x 4 ⅜ in. (13 x 11.1 cm)
(Sale, London, Christie's, 30 June 1977,
through [Somerville & Simpson], for
$5,459 to); Norton Simon Art Foundation
(M.1977.15.2.1).

Cat. 1432

Pablo Picasso (Spanish, 1881–1973)
Side View of Bull, 25 December 1945
Lithograph, crayon drawing transferred to
stone, 1/18: 12 ⅞ x 17 ½ in. (32.7 x 44.5 cm)
(Sale, London, Christie's, 30 June 1977,
through [Somerville & Simpson], for
$2,430 to); Norton Simon Art Foundation
(M.1977.15.2.5).

Cat. 1433

Pablo Picasso (Spanish, 1881–1973)
Still Life with Glass under the Lamp, 1962
Linocut, 15/50: image, 21 x 25 ¼ in.
(53.3 x 64.1 cm); sheet, 24 ½ x 29 ½ in.
(62.2 x 74.9 cm)
(Sale, London, Christie's, 30 June 1977,
through [Somerville & Simpson], for
$26,653 to); Norton Simon Art Foundation
(M.1977.15.2.9).

Cat. 1434

Pablo Picasso (Spanish, 1881–1973)
Still Life with Vase of Flowers,
14 December 1945
Lithograph, unique impression
(4 compositions on verso), 13 x 17 ⅝ in.
(33 x 44.8 cm)
(Sale, London, Christie's, 30 June 1977,
through [Somerville & Simpson], for
$2,809 to); Norton Simon Art Foundation
(M.1977.15.2.3).

Cat. 1435

Pablo Picasso (Spanish, 1881–1973)
Two Nude Women, 1945–1946
Lithograph, 14th state, trial proof:
image, 10 ⅜ x 14 ¼ in. (26.4 x 36.2 cm);
sheet, 13 1/16 x 17 7/16 in. (33.2 x 46.1 cm)
(Sale, London, Christie's, 30 June 1977,
through [Somerville & Simpson], for $2,649
to); Norton Simon Art Foundation, gift
7 February 1983 to; Norton Simon Museum
(P.1983.3.7).

Cat. 1436
Pablo Picasso (Spanish, 1881–1973)
Head of Woman, No. 3 (Dora Maar),
January–June 1939
Aquatint and scraper: plate, 11 ¾ x 9 ⅜ in.
(29.8 x 23.8 cm); sheet, 12 ⅞ x 9 ¾ in.
(32.7 x 24.8 cm)
[David Tunick, New York, sold 6 July
1977 for $23,845 to]; Norton Simon Art
Foundation (M.1977.12).

Cat. 1437
William-Adolphe Bouguereau
(French, 1825–1905)
Monsieur M., 1850
Oil on canvas, 34 ¼ x 27 ¾ in. (87 x 70.5 cm)
[Heim, London, sold 8 July 1977 for
$11,200 to]; Norton Simon Art Foundation
(M.1977.13.1).

Cat. 1438
Claude-Marie Dubufe (French, 1790–1864)
Portrait of a Young Woman, c. 1843
Oil on canvas, 51 ⅛ x 38 ⅜ in. (129.8 x 97.3
cm)
[Heim, London, sold 8 July 1977 for
$8,800 to]; Norton Simon Art Foundation
(M.1977.13.2).

Cat. 1439
China, Northern Wei Dynasty (368–534)
*Stele with Buddhas, Bodhisattvas, and
Donors*, dated 478
Limestone, 11 ¾ x 9 ¼ in. (29.9 x 23.5 cm)
(Sale, London, Christie's, 11 July 1977 for
$3,834 to); Norton Simon, by inheritance
2 June 1993 to; Jennifer Jones Simon Art
Trust, Los Angeles (N.1977.15.2).

Cat. 1440
India, Karnataka
Vishnu with Sridevi and Bhudevi,
late 12th century
Schist, 39 in. (99.1 cm)

(Sale, London, Sotheby & Co., 11 July
1977 for $3,832 to); Norton Simon, gift
31 December 1979 to; Norton Simon Art
Foundation (M.1979.75).

Cat. 1441
India, West Bengal or Bangladesh
Vishnu with Spouses and Other Deities,
late 11th century
Chlorite, 32 ¼ x 18 in. (81.9 x 45.7 cm)
(Sale, London, Sotheby & Co., 11 July
1977 for $5,000 to); Norton Simon, by
inheritance 2 June 1993 to; Jennifer Jones
Simon Art Trust, Los Angeles (N.1977.13.3).

Cat. 1442
Mainland Southeast Asia
Drum, 14th–17th century
Bronze, 13 x 22 ½ in. (33 x 57.2 cm)
(Sale, London, Christie's, 11 July 1977 for
$3,067 to); Norton Simon, by inheritance
2 June 1993 to; Jennifer Jones Simon Art
Trust, Los Angeles (N.1977.15.1).

Cat. 1443
Nepal
Lotus Mandala with Eight Mothers,
18th century
Bronze, 7 ¼ x 8 in. (18.4 x 20.3 cm)
(Sale, London, Sotheby & Co., 11 July 1977
for $863 to); Norton Simon, by inheritance
2 June 1993 to; Jennifer Jones Simon Art
Trust, Los Angeles (N.1977.14).

Cat. 1444
Tibet
Book Cover with Three Bodhisattvas,
11th century
Painted wood, 8 ½ x 27 in. (21.6 x 68.6 cm)
(Sale, London, Sotheby & Co., 11 July
1977 for $2,204 to); Norton Simon, by
inheritance 2 June 1993 to; Jennifer Jones
Simon Art Trust, Los Angeles (N.1977.13.1).

1436

1437

1438

1439

1441

1442

1443

1444

1440

1445

1446

1447

1448A

1448B

1449

1449

1451

1452

1453

Cat. 1445
Tibet
Buddha Bhaishajyaguru, 16th century
Gilt copper, 13 x 9 ½ x 8 ½ in.
(33 x 24.1 x 21.6 cm)
(Sale, London, Sotheby & Co., 11 July
1977 for $5,369 to); Norton Simon Art
Foundation (M.1977.22.2).

Cat. 1446
Tibet
Vajrapani with Consort, 16th century
Bronze with pigment, 7 in. (17.8 cm)
(Sale, London, Sotheby & Co.,
11 July 1977 for $5,177 to); Norton Simon
Art Foundation (M.1977.22.1).

Cat. 1447
Jérôme-Martin Langlois (French, 1779–1838)
Self-Portrait, c. 1830
Oil on canvas, 25 ⅜ x 21 ½ in. (64.5 x 54.6 cm)
[Heim, London, sold 13 July 1977 for
$34,000 to]; Norton Simon Art Foundation
(M.1977.14).

Cat. 1448A-B
Jean-Baptiste Deshays de Colleville
(French, 1729–1765)
Rest of the Shepherds and *Washerwoman*
Oil on canvas, oval, each 19 ½ x 16 ⅜ in.
(49.5 x 41.6 cm)
[Jean Cailleux, Paris, sold 18 July 1977 for
$20,700 to]; Norton Simon, gift 18 October
1983 to; The Norton Simon Foundation
(F.1983.7.1–2).

Cat. 1449
Pablo Picasso (Spanish, 1881–1973)
The Mourlot Lithographs
228 images of various states, including the
bon à tirer prints and the etching *Still Life
with Bottle of Marc*, 1911
[Berggruen, Paris, sold 19 July 1977 for
$450,000 to]; Norton Simon, gift of 69
prints, 18 October 1983 to; The Norton
Simon Foundation (F.1983.20.1–69),
remainder by inheritance 2 June 1993 to;

Jennifer Jones Simon Art Trust, Los Angeles,
gift of 44 prints, 18 May 2001 to; Norton
Simon Art Foundation (M.2001.1.6–44), gift
of 16 prints, 24 February 2006 to; Norton
Simon Art Foundation (M.2006.2.1–16), gift
of 58 prints, 28 February 2007 to; Norton
Simon Art Foundation (M.2007.1.1–58); gift
of 3 prints, 21 December 2007 to; Norton
Simon Art Foundation (M.2007.4.2–4).

Cat. 1450
Pablo Picasso (Spanish, 1881–1973)
Head of a Young Girl, 1945
Lithograph, 1st state, proof, 11 ¾ x 8 ¾ in.
(30 x 22 cm)
[David Tunick, New York, sold 21 July
1977 for $1,798 to]; Norton Simon Art
Foundation (sale, New York, Sotheby Parke
Bernet, 19 February 1981, lot 590, for $5,250).

Cat. 1451
Pablo Picasso (Spanish, 1881–1973)
Illustrations for Max Jacob's "Saint Matorel,"
1910
Etchings, group of 4, 2nd state, 7 ⅞ x 5 ⅝ in.
(20 x 14.3 cm)
[Margo P. Schab, New York, sold 29 July
1977 for $13,000 to]; Norton Simon Art
Foundation (M.1977.17.1–4).

Cat. 1452
Rembrandt van Rijn (Dutch, 1606–1669)
Etchings, group of 118
[Robert M. Light, Boston, sold 2 August
1977 for $1,770,510 to]; Norton Simon Art
Foundation (M.1977.32.1–118).

Cat. 1453
Francisco de Goya y Lucientes
(Spanish, 1746–1828)
The Disasters of War (*Los Desastres de la
Guerra*), working proofs, 1814–1820
Etching, aquatint, and drypoint, 82 prints
[P. & D. Colnaghi, London, sold 4 August
1977 for $130,260 to]; Norton Simon Art
Foundation (M.1977.18.1–82).

Cat. 1454A-B
Pablo Picasso (Spanish, 1881–1973)
Still Life with Fruit Stand, 6 November 1945
Lithograph, 1st state, trial proof: plate,
9 ¾ x 13 ¾ in. (24.8 x 34.9 cm)
Long-Haired Young Girl, 6 November 1945
Lithograph, first state, trial proof: image, 15
x 12 ¾ in. (38.1 x 32.4 cm); sheet, 16 ¼ x 14
in. (41.3 x 35.6 cm)
[P. & D. Colnaghi, London, sold 4 August
1977 for $24,740 to]; Norton Simon Art
Foundation (M.1977.18.2–3).

Cat. 1455
Pablo Picasso (Spanish, 1881–1973)
Paloma and Her Doll on Black Background,
14 December 1952
Lithograph, 36/50: image, 27 ½ x 21 ¾ in.
(69.9 x 55.2 cm); sheet, 29 ⅞ x 22 ⅜ in.
(75.9 x 56.8 cm)
[Reiss Cohen, New York, sold 5 August
1977 for $12,500 to]; Norton Simon Art
Foundation (M.1977.19).

Cat. 1456A-B
Vietnam, Ancient Champa Kingdom
Architectural Piece with Makara and
Celestial Female, c. 1100
Sandstone, 35 ½ x 41 ⅜ in. (90.2 x 105.1 cm)
and 28 x 13 ¼ x 9 in. (71.1 x 33.7 x 22.9 cm)
[Beurdeley, Paris, sold 8 August 1977 for
$24,558 to]; Norton Simon Art Foundation
(M.1977.20.1–2).

Cat. 1457
Pablo Picasso (Spanish, 1881–1973)
Italian Woman, 1953
Lithograph: image, 17 ½ x 13 ¾ in.
(44.5 x 34.9 cm); sheet, 25 ¼ x 19 ¼ in.
(64.1 x 48.9 cm)
[Blue Moon Gallery, New York, sold
22 August 1977 for $10,250 to]; Norton
Simon Art Foundation (M.1977.21).

Cat. 1458
Pablo Picasso (Spanish, 1881–1973)
Bust of a Woman with Hat, 1962

Color linocut, 25/50: image, 25 ¼ x 21 in.
(64.1 x 53.3 cm); sheet, 29 ⅝ x 24 ⅜ in.
(75.2 x 61.9 cm)
[Wallace Reiss, Old Greenwich, Conn., sold
13 September 1977 for $14,000 to]; Norton
Simon Art Foundation (M.1977.23).

Cat. 1459
Pablo Picasso (Spanish, 1881–1973)
*Illustrations for "Histoire Naturelle" by
Georges Louis Leclerc de Buffon*, 1936
Lift-ground aquatint etchings on vellum,
group of 31: plates various; sheets,
each 14 ⅜ x 11 in. (36.5 x 27.9 cm)
[Lucien Goldschmidt, New York, sold
24 October 1977 for $7,700 to]; Norton
Simon Art Foundation (M.1977.24.1–31).

Cat. 1460
Matthias Stom (Dutch, c. 1600–after 1651)
The Mocking of Christ, c. 1632–1635
Oil on canvas, 43 ½ x 63 ¼ in.
(110.5 x 160.7 cm)
[Richard Feigen, New York, sold 25 October
1977 for $42,500 to]; Norton Simon Art
Foundation (M.1977.25).

Cat. 1461
Antoine Favray (French, 1706–1791)
*The Submission of the Antipope Victor IV to
Pope Innocent II*, 1743
Oil on canvas, 63 ⅜ x 46 ¼ in.
(161 x 117.5 cm)
[Heim, London, sold 9 November 1977 for
$34,800 to]; Norton Simon Art Foundation
(M.1977.26.1).

Cat. 1462
Louis-Jean-François Lagrenée (French,
1725–1805)
Alcibiades on His Knees before His Mistress
Oil on panel, 20 ¾ x 25 ½ in.
(52.7 x 64.8 cm)
[Heim, London, sold 9 November 1977 for
$20,800 to]; Norton Simon Art Foundation
(M.1977.26.2).

1454A

1454B

1455

1458

1459

1460

1456A–B

1461

1462

1457

1463

1465A

1465B

1469

1466

1470

1467

1468

1471

1472

1473

Cat. 1463

Horace Vernet (French, 1789–1863)

A Soldier on the Field of Battle, 1818

Oil on canvas, 18 ¹/₁₆ x 21 ⅝ in. (46 x 55 cm)

[Heim, London, sold 9 November 1977 for $17,400 to]; Norton Simon Art Foundation (M.1977.26.3).

Cat. 1464

Edgar Degas (French, 1834–1917)

Grande arabesque, first time

Bronze, cast no. 18/M, 19 in. (48.2 cm)

[Stephen Hahn Gallery, New York, even trade with dealer 16 November 1977 for Edgar Degas, *Grande arabesque, first time*, cast no. 18/HER (cat. 416) to]; Norton Simon Art Foundation (sale, New York, Christie's, 19 May 1982, lot 11, unsold; sold privately for $45,000 to); Lorraine Pritzker (estate sale, London, Sotheby's, 26 June 2001). [Browse & Darby, London, May 2002; June 2004].

Cat. 1465A-B

Afghanistan, Ancient Gandhara, probably Hadda

Two Heads of Buddha, 4th century

Stucco, 6 ¾ in. (17.1 cm) and 6 in. (15.2 cm)

(Sale, London, Christie's, 16 November 1977 for $1,881 to); Norton Simon Art Foundation (M.1977.30.8–9).

Cat. 1466

India, West Bengal or Bangladesh

Surya with Dandi and Pingala, 8th century

Bronze, 7 ½ in. (19.1 cm)

(Sale, London, Christie's, 16 November 1977 for $3,343 to); Norton Simon Art Foundation (M.1977.30.13).

Cat. 1467

India, Karnataka

Jina Suparsvanatha, c. 900

Bronze, 6 in. (15.2 cm)

(Sale, London, Christie's, 16 November 1977 for $1,003 to); Norton Simon Art Foundation (M.1977.30.12).

Cat. 1468

India, Kashmir

Buddha Shakyamuni, 10th century

Bronze with silver inlay, 7 in. (17.8 cm)

(Sale, London, Christie's, 16 November 1977 for $2,298 to); Norton Simon Art Foundation (M.1977.30.18).

Cat. 1469

India, Kashmir

Buddha Vairochana, 11th century

Bronze, 7 in. (17.8 cm)

(Sale, London, Christie's, 16 November 1977 for $1,567 to); Norton Simon Art Foundation (M.1977.30.16).

Cat. 1470

India, Kashmir

Vishnu with Companions, 10th century

Brass, 8 ¼ in. (21 cm)

(Sale, London, Christie's, 16 November 1977 for $1,776 to); Norton Simon Art Foundation (M.1977.30.17).

Cat. 1471

India, Tamil Nadu

Krishna as a Crawling Infant, 16th century

Bronze, 3 ½ in. (8.9 cm)

(Sale, London, Christie's, 16 November 1977 for $209 to); Norton Simon Art Foundation (M.1977.30.10).

Cat. 1472

India, Uttar Pradesh, Mathura

Fragment from a "Birth of the Buddha" Stele, 2nd century

Sandstone, 8 ¾ in. (22.2 cm)

(Sale, London, Christie's, 16 November 1977 for $1,358 to); Norton Simon Art Foundation (M.1977.30.7).

Cat. 1473

India, Uttar Pradesh, Mathura

Head of Buddha Shakyamuni, c. 150

Sandstone, 8 ¾ in. (22.2 cm)

(Sale, London, Christie's, 16 November 1977 for $585 to); Norton Simon Art Foundation (M.1977.30.6).

Cat. 1474
India, Uttar Pradesh, Mathura
Head of a Jina, 3rd century
Sandstone, 8 ¼ in. (21cm)
(Sale, London, Christie's, 16 November
1977 for $2,925 to); Norton Simon Art
Foundation (M.1977.30.22).

Cat. 1475
Indonesia: Central Java
Buddha Shakyamuni, late 9th century
Bronze, 4 ½ in. (11.4 cm)
(Sale, London, Christie's, 16 November
1977 for $1,358 to); Norton Simon Art
Foundation (M.1977.30.11).

Cat. 1476
Nepal
Bodhisattva Manjusri Embracing His Spouse,
c. 1600
Gilt bronze, 2 ½ in. (6.4 cm)
(Sale, London, Christie's, 16 November
1977 for $1,086 to); Norton Simon Art
Foundation (M.1977.30.19).

Cat. 1477
Nepal
Buddha Shakyamuni, c. 600–800
Bronze, 3 in. (7.6 cm)
(Sale, London, Christie's, 16 November 1977
for $836 to); Norton Simon Art Foundation
(M.1977.30.5).

Cat. 1478
Pakistan, Ancient Gandhara
Fragment from a Narrative Relief,
2nd–3rd century
Schist, 8 ¾ in. (22.2 cm)
(Sale, London, Christie's, 16 November 1977
for $794 to); Norton Simon Art Foundation
(M.1977.30.21).

Cat. 1479
Thailand or Cambodia
Buddha Shakyamuni, c. 1200
Bronze, 11 ½ in. (29.2 cm)

(Sale, London, Christie's, 16 November
1977 for $2,298 to); Norton Simon Art
Foundation (M.1977.30.15).

Cat. 1480
Thailand or Cambodia
Ritual Conch with Buddhist Deity Hevajra,
12th century
Bronze, 10 in. (25.4 cm)
(Sale, London, Christie's, 16 November
1977 for $1,358 to); Norton Simon Art
Foundation (M.1977.30.14).

Cat. 1481
Tibet
Buddha Shakyamuni, 17th century
Gilt bronze with pigment, 7 in. (17.8 cm)
(Sale, London, Christie's, 16 November 1977
for $836 to); Norton Simon Art Foundation
(M.1977.30.2).

Cat. 1482
Tibet
Jambhala, late 15th century
Bronze inlaid with copper and semiprecious
stones, 4 ¼ in. (10.8 cm)
(Sale, London, Christie's, 16 November 1977
for $794 to); Norton Simon Art Foundation
(M.1977.30.4).

Cat. 1483
Tibet
Lama, 16th century
Bronze inlaid with copper and silver, 7 ¼ in.
(18.4 cm)
(Sale, London, Christie's, 16 November 1977
for $877 to); Norton Simon Art Foundation
(M.1977.30.3).

Cat. 1484
Tibet
Lama Jamyang Gonpo(?), c. 1500
Bronze, 4 ½ in. (11.4 cm)
(Sale, London, Christie's, 16 November 1977
for $731 to); Norton Simon Art Foundation
(M.1977.30.20).

1474 1479 1480

1475 1481

1476 1482

1477 1483

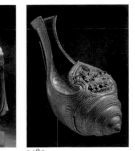
1478 1484

1485

1489

1486A

1486B

1486C

1487

1490

1491

1492

Cat. 1485
Tibet or Nepal
Ritual Dagger, 17th century
Painted wood, 13 in. (33 cm)
(Sale, London, Christie's, 16 November
1977 for $1,000 to); Norton Simon Art
Foundation (M.1977.30.1).

Cat. 1486A-C
Rembrandt van Rijn (Dutch, 1606–1669)
Bathers, 1651
Etching, only state: plate, 4 ⅜ x 5 ⁷/₁₆ in. (11.1
x 13.8 cm); sheet, 4 ½ x 5 ½ in. (11.4 x 14 cm)
Abraham Entertaining the Angels, 1656
Etching, drypoint, only state: plate, 6 ¼ x
5 ³/₁₆ in. (15.9 x 13.2 cm); sheet, 7 x 5 ⁹/₁₆ in.
(17.8 x 14.1 cm)
*Lieven Willemsz. van Coppenol,
Writing-Master*, 1658
Etching, drypoint, burin, 3rd state: plate,
13 ⅛ x 11 ⅛ in. (33.3 x 28.3 cm); sheet,
13 ⅛ x 11 ⅛ in. (33.3 x 28.3 cm)
(Sale, London, Sotheby & Co., 17 November
1977 for $27,368 to); Norton Simon Art
Foundation (M.1977.29.1–3).

Cat. 1487
Quiringh Gerritsz. van Brekelenkam
(Dutch, 1620–1668)
The Shoemaker's Shop, c. 1660
Oil on panel, 23 ⅜ x 32 ½ in. (59.4 x 82.6 cm)
[Essoldo Fine Arts, London, sold
16 December 1977 for $43,500 to]; Norton
Simon Art Foundation (M.1977.28).

Cat. 1488
Francisco de Goya y Lucientes
(Spanish, 1746–1828)
Los Caprichos, 1st edition, c. 1797–1799
Etching, aquatint, and drypoint with hand
coloring, 80 plates
[Baskett & Day, London, sold 16 December
1977 for $45,132 to]; Norton Simon Art
Foundation, sold 19 March 1980 for
$120,000 to; [Norman Leitman, London].

Cat. 1489
Rembrandt van Rijn (Dutch, 1606–1669)
*Portrait of a Bearded Man in a
Wide-Brimmed Hat*, 1633
Oil on oval panel, 27 ½ x 21 ½ in.
(69.9 x 54.6 cm)
[E. V. Thaw & Co., New York, sold
30 December 1977 for $1,150,000 ($430,000
cash and four works valued at $720,000:
Francesco Pesellino, *Virgin and Child* (cat.
D149); Jean-Antoine Watteau, *Head of
a Man, Two Studies of Hands* (cat. 549);
Rembrandt van Rijn, *Dido Divides the
Ox Hide* (cat. 596); Philips Koninck, *An
Extensive River Landscape* (cat. 970) to];
Norton Simon Art Foundation (M.1977.31).

1978

Cat. 1490
Francisco de Goya y Lucientes
(Spanish, 1746–1828)
Los Caprichos, 1st edition, c. 1797–1799
Etching, aquatint, and drypoint, 80 plates
[P. & D. Colnaghi, London, sold 3 January
1978 for $51,000 to]; Norton Simon Art
Foundation (M.1978.2.1.1–80).

Cat. 1491
Francisco de Goya y Lucientes
(Spanish, 1746–1828)
The Disasters of War (*Los Desastres de la
Guerra*), 1st edition, 1814–1820, printed 1863
Etching, aquatint, and drypoint, 80 plates;
8 in original yellow wrappers
[P. & D. Colnaghi, London, sold 3 January
1978 for $18,700 to]; Norton Simon Art
Foundation (M.1978.2.2.1–80).

Cat. 1492
Francisco de Goya y Lucientes
(Spanish, 1746–1828)
Little Bulls' Folly, additional plate from
Los Proverbios, trial proof, 1819–1820,
printed before 1877

Etching, aquatint, and drypoint: plate,
8 ¼ x 12 ½ in. (21 x 31.8 cm); sheet,
9 ⁹/₁₆ x 13 ¾ in. (24.3 x 34.9 cm)
[P. & D. Colnaghi, London, sold 3 January
1978 for $1,997 to]; Norton Simon Art
Foundation (M.1978.4.2).

Cat. 1493
Francisco de Goya y Lucientes
(Spanish, 1746–1828)
La Tauromaquia, 1st edition, 1816
Etching, aquatint, and drypoint, 33 plates
[P. & D. Colnaghi, London, sold 3 January
1978 for $55,250 to]; Norton Simon Art
Foundation, sold 30 November 1982 for
$108,880 to; [Artemis Fine Art, London].

Cat. 1494A-H
Pablo Picasso (Spanish, 1881–1973)
Etchings and lithographs: *Interior Scene*,
The Three Friends, *Dreams and Lies of
Franco* (2), *Head of a Young Boy*, *Heads of
Rams*, and *Shells and Birds* (2)
[P. & D. Colnaghi, London, sold 3 January
1978 for $8,936 to]; Norton Simon Art
Foundation (M.1978.3.1–6.2).

Cat. 1495
Rembrandt van Rijn (Dutch, 1606–1669)
The Angel Appearing to the Shepherds, 1634
Etching, 3rd state: plate, 10 ¼ x 8 ⅝ in.
(26x 21.9 cm); sheet, 10 ¼ x 8 ⅝ in.
(26 x 21.9 cm)
[P. & D. Colnaghi, London, sold 3 January
1978 for $2,733 to]; Norton Simon Art
Foundation (M.1978.4.1).

Cat. 1496
Rembrandt van Rijn (Dutch, 1606–1669)
Clement de Jonghe, Printseller, 1651
Etching, drypoint, burin, 3rd state:
plate, 8 ³/₁₆ x 6 ⅜ in. (20.8 x 16.2 cm);
sheet, 8 ¼ x 6 ⅜ in. (21x 16.2 cm)
[P. & D. Colnaghi, London, sold 3 January

1978 for $29,750 to]; Norton Simon Art
Foundation (M.1978.2.5).

Cat. 1497
Rembrandt van Rijn (Dutch, 1606–1669)
Self-Portrait Leaning on a Stone Sill, 1639
Etching and drypoint, 1st state:
plate, 8 ³/₁₆ x 6 ⅜ in. (20.8 x 16.2 cm);
sheet, 8 ³/₁₆ x 6 ⅜ in. (20.8 x 16.2 cm)
[P. & D. Colnaghi, London, sold 3 January
1978 for $25,500 to]; Norton Simon Art
Foundation (M.1978.2.4).

Cat. 1498
Pablo Picasso (Spanish, 1881–1973)
Salome, 1905
Drypoint, proof, before the steel facing of
the plate, on Arches paper:
plate, 15 ¾ x 13 ¾ in. (40 x 34.9 cm);
sheet, 24 x 17 ¼ in. (61 x 43.8 cm)
[Lumley Cazalet, London, sold 3 January
1978 for $40,000 to]; Norton Simon Art
Foundation (M.1978.5).

Cat. 1499
Pablo Picasso (Spanish, 1881–1973)
Woman Bullfighter, Last Kiss? 1934
Etching on vellum, 19 ⅝ x 27 ¼ in.
(49.8 x 69.2 cm)
[Jane Wade, New York, sold 3 January
1978 for $17,000 to]; Norton Simon Art
Foundation (M.1978.1).

Cat. 1500A-B
Pierre Bernard (French, 1704–1777)
Archduchess Elisabeth of Austria and
Archduchess Marie Anne of Austria, 1763
Pastel and gouache on vellum, oval, each
27 ¼ x 22 ¼ in. (69.2 x 56.5 cm)
(Sale, New York, Christie's, 12 January
1978 for $14,300 to); Norton Simon, gift
18 October 1983 to; The Norton Simon
Foundation (F.1983.17.1–2).

1494B

1497

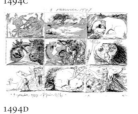
1494C

1498

1494D

1499

1495

1500A

1496

1500B

1501

1506

1503

1504

1505

1507A

1508

1507B    1507C

Cat. 1501

Jan Lievens (Dutch, 1607–1674)
Young Man with Red Beret, c. 1629–1630
Oil on panel, 27 ½ x 21 in. (69.9 x 53.3 cm)
(Sale, New York, Christie's, 12 January
1978 for $48,400 to); Norton Simon, by
inheritance 2 June 1993 to; Jennifer Jones
Simon Art Trust, Los Angeles, gift 12 August
1997 to; Norton Simon Art Foundation
(M.1997.1.1).

Cat. 1502A-B

Rome
Tabletop and Pedestal
Marble, two pieces: tabletop, 26 ⅜ in.
square (67 cm); pedestal, 22 ½ x 17 in.
(57.2 x 43.2 cm)
Capital
Stone, 9 ¾ x 13 ¾ x 14 ¾ in.
(24.8 x 34.9 x 37.5 cm)
[Simone de Monbrison, Paris, sold
8 February 1978 for $6,000 to); Norton
Simon, by inheritance 2 June 1993 to;
Jennifer Jones Simon Art Trust, Los Angeles
(N.1978.1.1a–b, 2).

Cat. 1503

Rembrandt van Rijn (Dutch, 1606–1669)
Christ Disputing with the Doctors: A Sketch,
1652
Etching and drypoint, 1st state:
plate, 5 x 8 ⁷/₁₆ in. (12.7 x 21.4 cm);
sheet, 5 ½ x 9 in. (14 x 22.9 cm)
[C. G. Boerner, Düsseldorf, sold
28 February 1978 for $47,043 to]; Norton
Simon Art Foundation (M.1978.6.2).

Cat. 1504

Rembrandt van Rijn (Dutch, 1606–1669)
The Entombment, c. 1654
Etching, drypoint and burin on China
paper, 1st state, 8 ¼ x 6 in. (21 x 15.2 cm)
[C. G. Boerner, Düsseldorf, sold
28 February 1978 for $54,357 to]; Norton
Simon Art Foundation (M.1978.6.1).

Cat. 1505

Vasily Kandinsky (Russian, 1866–1944)
Small Worlds I, 1922
Color lithograph on Japanese wove paper:
image, 9 ¾ x 8 ⅝ in. (24.8 x 21.9 cm);
sheet, 13 ⅝ x 11 ⅛ in. (34.6 x 28.3 cm)
[Alice Adams, Chicago, sold 1 March
1978 for $3,500 to]; Norton Simon Art
Foundation (M.1978.7).

Cat. 1506

Rembrandt van Rijn (Dutch, 1606–1669)
*Rembrandt with Plumed Cap and Lowered
Saber: Three-Quarter Length*, 1634
Etching, 3rd state: plate, 5 ⅛ x 4 ¼ in.
(13 x 10.8 cm); sheet, 5 ⁷/₁₆ x 4 ⁹/₁₆ in.
(13.8 x 11.6 cm)
[Craddock & Barnard, London, sold
8 March 1978 for $6,900 to]; Norton Simon
Art Foundation (M.1978.8).

Cat. 1507A-C

Rembrandt van Rijn (Dutch, 1606–1669)
Self-Portrait in a Heavy Fur Cap: Bust, 1631
Etching, only state: plate, 2 ½ x 2 ¼ in. (6.4
x 5.7 cm); sheet, 2 ⅝ x 2 ⁵/₁₆ in. (6.7 x 5.9 cm)
*A Peasant Calling Out: "Tis Vinnich Kout"
(It's Very Cold)*, 1634
Etching, only state: plate, 4 ½ x 1 ¹¹/₁₆ in. (11.4
x 4.3 cm); sheet, 4 ⅝ x 1 ⅞ in. (11.7 x 4.8 cm)
*A Peasant Replying: "Das Niet" (That's
Nothing)*, 1634
Etching, only state: plate, 4 ⁷/₁₆ x 1 ½ in. (11.3
x 3.8 cm); sheet, 4 ½ x 1 ⅝ in. (11.4 x 4.1 cm)
[R. E. Lewis, Larkspur, Calif., sold 14 March
1978 for $11,160 to]; Norton Simon Art
Foundation (M.1978.9.1–2.2).

Cat. 1508

Francisco de Goya y Lucientes
(Spanish, 1746–1828)
Old-Style Duel, c. 1819
Lithograph, proof, touched with brush and
black wash: image, 5 ⅜ x 6 ¾ in. (13.7 x 17.1
cm); mount: 8 x 9 ½ in. (20.3 x 24.1 cm)

[P. & D. Colnaghi, London, sold 28 March 1978 for $34,000 to]; Norton Simon Art Foundation (M.1978.10.2).

Cat. 1509
Francisco de Goya y Lucientes
(Spanish, 1746–1828)
Los Proverbios, trial proofs, 1819–1820, printed c. 1848
Etching, aquatint, and drypoint, 18 plates
[P. & D. Colnaghi, London, sold 28 March 1978 for $76,500 to]; Norton Simon Art Foundation (M.1978.10.1.1–18).

Cat. 1510
Rembrandt van Rijn (Dutch, 1606–1669)
Abraham's Sacrifice, 1655
Etching and drypoint, only state:
plate, 6 ⅛ x 5 ¼ in. (15.6 x 13.3 cm);
sheet, 6 ⁹/₁₆ x 6 ⅝ in. (16.7 x 16.8 cm)
[P. & D. Colnaghi, London, sold 28 March 1978 for $21,250 to]; Norton Simon Art Foundation (M.1978.10.3).

Cat. 1511
Pablo Picasso (Spanish, 1881–1973)
Head of Woman, No. 3 (Dora Maar), 1939
Aquatint, 12 ⅛ x 9 ¼ in. (30.8 x 23.5 cm)
(Sale, London, Sotheby Parke Bernet & Co., 26 April 1978, lot 347, for $5,513 to); Norton Simon Museum (Museum Purchase, Fellows Acquisition Fund) (P.1978.3).

Cat. 1512
Rembrandt van Rijn (Dutch, 1606–1669)
Landscape with a Road beside a Canal, c. 1652
Drypoint, only state, 3 ⅛ x 8 ⅜ in. (7.9 x 21.3 cm)
[Robert M. Light, Boston, sold 27 April 1978 for $55,000 to]; Norton Simon Art Foundation (M.1978.11.2).

Cat. 1513
Émile Bernard (French, 1868–1941)
Cupboard, 1891–1893

Carved and painted wood, 95 x 59 x 20 in. (241.3 x 149.9 x 50.8 cm)
[Sylvia Blatas, Paris, sold 28 April 1978 for $50,000 to]; Norton Simon, by inheritance 2 June 1993 to; Jennifer Jones Simon Art Trust, Los Angeles (N.1978.4).

Cat. 1514
Rembrandt van Rijn (Dutch, 1606–1669)
The Shell (Conus Marmoreus), 1650
Etching, drypoint and burin, 2nd state:
plate, 3 ¹³/₁₆ x 5 ³/₁₆ in. (9.7 x 13.2 cm); sheet, 3 ⅞ x 5 ³/₁₆ in. (9.8 x 13.2 cm)
[Robert M. Light, Boston, sold 28 April 1978 for $30,000 to]; Norton Simon Art Foundation (M.1978.11.1).

Cat. 1515
Rembrandt van Rijn (Dutch, 1606–1669)
The Presentation in the Temple: Oblong Print, c. 1639
Etching and drypoint, 2nd state:
plate, 8 ⅜ x 11 ⁷/₁₆ in. (21.3 x 29.1 cm); sheet, 8 ⅞ x 11 ⁷/₁₆ in. (22.5 x 29.1 cm)
(Sale, New York, Sotheby Parke Bernet, 3 May 1978 for $750 to); Norton Simon Art Foundation (M.1978.17).

Cat. 1516A-C
Pablo Picasso (Spanish, 1881–1973)
Still Life with Fruit Stand, 1945
Lithograph, 3rd state: image, 10 x 14 ⅛ in. (25.4 x 35.9 cm); sheet, 12 ¾ x 17 ⅜ in. (32.4 x 44.1 cm)
Head of Young Boy, 1945
Lithograph, image, 12 ⅛ x 9 in. (30.8 x 22.9 cm); sheet, 12 ¾ x 10 in. (32.4 x 25.4 cm)
Still Life with Three Apples, 1945
Lithograph: 1 of 2 impressions of black stone: image, 7 ½ x 12 in. (19.5 x 30.5 cm); sheet, 11 ¼ x 18 ¼ in. (28.6 x 46.4 cm)
(Sale, New York, Sotheby Parke Bernet, 4 May 1978 for $6,600 to); Norton Simon Art Foundation (M.1978.15.1–3).

1509

1514

1515

1510

1511

1516B

1512

1513

1517

1521

1518B

1518C

1522

1519

1523

1520

1524

1525

Cat. 1517

Pablo Picasso (Spanish, 1881–1973)
Two Nude Women, 1945–1946
Lithographs, group of six
(Sale, New York, Sotheby Parke Bernet,
4 May 1978 for $60,000 to); Norton Simon
Art Foundation, gift 7 February 1983 to;
Norton Simon Museum (P.1983.3.2–6, 8).

Cat. 1518A-C

Byzantium
Altarpiece, 6th century`
Marble, 4 ¾ x 42 ⅛ x 28 in.
(12.1 x 107 x 71.1 cm)
Rome
Capital (Corinthian Style), 2nd century
Stone, 15 ¾ x 17 ½ x 18 in. (40 x 44.5 x 45.7 cm)
Syria
Mortar, 2000–1000 B.C.
Stone, 7 ⅞ x 21 ¾ in. (20 x 55.2 cm)
[Simone de Monbrison, Paris, sold 9 May
1978 for $6,000 to]; Norton Simon, by
inheritance 2 June 1993 to; Jennifer Jones
Simon Art Trust, Los Angeles (N.1978.5.1–3).

Cat. 1519

Rembrandt van Rijn (Dutch, 1606–1669)
The Ship of Fortune, 1633
Etching, 2nd state: 4 ½ x 6 ⅝ in.
(11.4 x 16.8 cm)
[Paul Prouté, Paris, sold 12 May 1978 for
$3,450 to]; Norton Simon Art Foundation
(M.1978.12).

Cat. 1520

Edgar Degas (French, 1834–1917)
*The Rape of the Sabines (after Nicolas
Poussin)*, c. 1861–1862
Oil on canvas, 59 ⅛ x 81 ½ in. (150 x 207 cm)
[E. V. Thaw & Co., New York, sold 13 May
1978 for $48,000 to]; Norton Simon, gift
18 October 1983 to; The Norton Simon
Foundation (F.1983.6).

Cat. 1521

Rembrandt van Rijn (Dutch, 1606–1669)
The Phoenix or the Statue Overthrown, 1658
Etching and drypoint, only state:
plate, 7 ⅛ x 7 ³/₁₆ in. (18.1 x 18.3 cm);
sheet, 7 ¼ x 7 ⅜ in. (18.4 x 18.7 cm)
[P. & D. Colnaghi, London, sold 31 May
1978 for $108,000 to]; Norton Simon Art
Foundation (M.1978.14).

Cat. 1522

Pierre-Auguste Renoir (French, 1841–1919)
At Renoir's Home, rue St.-Georges (formerly
The Artist's Studio, rue St.-Georges), 1876
Oil on canvas, 18 ⅛ x 15 in. (46 x 38.1 cm)
[P. & D. Colnaghi, Zurich, sold 31 May
1978 for $266,000 to]; Norton Simon Art
Foundation (M.1978.13.1).

Cat. 1523

Henri de Toulouse-Lautrec
(French, 1864–1901)
*At the Cirque Fernando, Rider on a White
Horse*, 1887–1888
Pastel and drained oil paint on paperboard,
23 ⅝ x 31 ¼ in. (60 x 79.4 cm)
[P. & D. Colnaghi, London, sold 31 May
1978 for $352,800 to]; The Norton Simon
Foundation (M.1978.13.2).

Cat. 1524

Jan van Bijlert (Dutch, 1597/98–1671)
*Mars Vigilant (Man in Armor Holding
a Pike)*, c. 1630–1635
Oil on canvas, 33 x 26 ⅝ in. (83.8 x 67.6 cm)
[Robert Noortman, London, sold 6 June
1978 for $59,810 to]; Norton Simon Art
Foundation (M.1978.18).

Cat. 1525

Marcantonio Bassetti (Italian, 1588–1630)
Portrait of a Cleric
Oil on canvas, 31 ½ x 26 in. (80.1 x 66.4 cm)
(Sale, New York, Sotheby Parke Bernet,
7 June 1978 for $12,025 to); Norton Simon,

by inheritance 2 June 1993 to; Jennifer Jones Simon Art Trust, Los Angeles (N.1978.9.4).

Cat. 1526
Circle of François Desportes (French, 1661–1743)
Still Life with Game
Oil on panel, 16 ½ x 13 ½ in. (41.9 x 34.3 cm)
(Sale, New York, Sotheby Parke Bernet, 7 June 1978 for $1,325 to); Norton Simon, by inheritance 2 June 1993 to; Jennifer Jones Simon Art Trust, Los Angeles (N.1978.9.3).

Cat. 1527
Alonzo Sánchez Coello (Spanish, c. 1531–1588)
Portrait of a Young Noblewoman, 1593
Oil on canvas, 48 ¾ x 39 ¾ in. (123.8 x 101 cm)
(Sale, New York, Sotheby Parke Bernet, 7 June 1978 for $9,525 to); Norton Simon, by inheritance 2 June 1993 to; Jennifer Jones Simon Art Trust, Los Angeles (N.1978.9.1).

Cat. 1528
Venetian School
Saint Francis in Ecstasy, early 18th century
Oil on canvas, 22 x 14 ⅜ in. (53.4 x 34 cm)
(Sale, New York, Sotheby Parke Bernet, 7 June 1978 for $2,775 to); Norton Simon, gift 18 October 1983 to; The Norton Simon Foundation (F.1983.15).

Cat. 1529A-B
Claude-Marie Dubufe (French, 1790–1864)
Memories and *Regrets*, 1826–1827
Oil on canvas, oval, each 36 ¼ x 47 in. (92.1 x 119.3 cm)
(Sale, Paris, Palais d'Orsay, 13 June 1978 for $15,621 to); Norton Simon, by inheritance 2 June 1993 to; Jennifer Jones Simon Art Trust, Los Angeles (N.1978.7.1.1–2).

Cat. 1530
School of Fontainebleau
(French, 16th century)

Diane de Poitiers, c. 1550
Oil on panel, 16 ⅜ x 12 ⅞ in. (41.6 x 32.7 cm)
(Sale, Paris, Palais d'Orsay, 13 June 1978 for $17,620 to); Norton Simon, by inheritance 2 June 1993 to; Jennifer Jones Simon Art Trust, Los Angeles (N.1978.7.2).

Cat. 1531
Giovanni di Paolo (Italian, 1403–1482)
Branchini Madonna, 1427
Tempera and gold leaf on panel, 72 x 39 in. (182.9 x 99.1 cm)
(Sale, London, Sotheby Parke Bernet & Co., 21 June 1978 for $1,098,707 to); The Norton Simon Foundation (F.1978.1).

Cat. 1532A-D
Francisco de Goya y Lucientes (Spanish, 1746–1828)
Landscape with Buildings and Trees, trial proof, c. 1920 (plate executed before 1810)
Etching and burnished aquatint (two plates on one sheet): plate, 6 ½ x 5 ½ in. (16.5 x 14 cm); sheet, 10 ¼ x 13 ⅞ in. (26 x 35.2 cm)
Landscape with Waterfall, before 1810, trial proof, c. 1920
Etching and burnished aquatint (two plates on one sheet): plate, 6 ½ x 5 ⅛ in. (16.5 x 13 cm); sheet, 10 x 13 ¾ in. (25.4 x 34.9 cm)
Franco. Goya y Lucientes, Pintor, plate 1 from *Los Caprichos*, intermediate impression between 1st and 2nd editions, c. 1820
Etching, aquatint, and drypoint: plate, 8 ½ x 6 in. (21.6 x 15.2 cm); sheet, 12 ¾ x 9 in. (32.4 x 22.9 cm)
What a Golden Beak!, plate 53 from *Los Caprichos*, intermediate impression between 1st and 2nd editions, c. 1820
Etching, burnished aquatint and burin: plate, 8 ½ x 6 in. (21.6 x 15.2 cm); sheet, 12 ¾ x 9 in. (32.4 x 22.9 cm)
[P. & D. Colnaghi, London, sold 27 June 1978 for $10,700 to]; Norton Simon Art Foundation (M.1978.19.1–4).

1526

1528

1530

1531

1532A

1532B

1527

1529A

1529B

1533

1538

1534

1535

1539

1536A

1540

1536B

1541A

1537

1541B

1541C

Cat. 1533

Rembrandt Bugatti (Italian, 1885–1916)
Duck, c. 1910
Bronze, modèle cast, 5 ⅞ x 5 ½ x 2 ½ in.
(14.9 x 14 x 6.4 cm)
(Sale, London, Sotheby Parke Bernet & Co.,
29 June 1978 for $2,400 to); Norton Simon
Art Foundation (M.1978.24).

Cat. 1534

Jacob Isaac Meyer de Haan
(Dutch, 1852–1895)
Still Life with Ham, c. 1889
Oil on canvas, 13 x 18 ¼ in. (33 x 46 cm)
[La Cave–Galerie de Tableaux, Paris, sold
13 July 1978 for $13,500 to]; Norton Simon,
gift 18 October 1983 to; The Norton Simon
Foundation (F.1983.12).

Cat. 1535

Louis Roy (French, 1862–1907)
Figure in the Moonlight, 1887
Gouache, 9 ¼ x 11 ½ in. (23.5 x 29.2 cm)
[La Cave–Galerie de Tableaux, Paris, sold
13 July 1978 for $4,050 to]; Norton Simon,
by inheritance 2 June 1993 to; Jennifer Jones
Simon Art Trust, Los Angeles (N.1978.8.2).

Cat. 1536A-B

Rembrandt van Rijn (Dutch, 1606–1669)
*Landscape with Trees, Farm Buildings,
and a Tower*, c. 1651
Etching and drypoint, 3rd state: plate, 4 ⅞
x 12 ⅝ in. (20 x 32.1 cm); sheet, 5 ⅛ x 13 in.
(13 x 33 cm)
A Woman at the Bath with a Hat beside Her,
1658
Etching, drypoint, 2nd state:
plate, 6 ⅛ x 5 ⅛ in. (15.6 x 13 cm);
sheet, 6 ¼ x 5 ⅛ in. (15.9 x 13 cm)
[Robert M. Light, Boston, sold 24 July
1978 for $150,000 to]; Norton Simon Art
Foundation (M.1978.20.1–2).

Cat. 1537

Cycladic
Collared Jar with Foot (Kandila),

3200–2800 B.C.
Marble, 12 x 10 ¼ in. (30.5 x 26 cm)
[Simone de Monbrison, Paris, sold 25 July
1978 for $11,011 to]; Norton Simon, by
inheritance 2 June 1993 to; Jennifer Jones
Simon Art Trust, Los Angeles (N.1978.10.1).

Cat. 1538

Edgar Degas (French, 1834–1917)
Café-Concert Singer, c. 1877
Pastel on laid paper, 6 ⅜ x 4 ¾ in.
(16.2 x 12 cm)
[Wildenstein & Co., New York, sold 25 July
1978 for $85,000 to]; Norton Simon Art
Foundation (M.1978.21).

Cat. 1539

Pedro Fernández (Spanish, active first
quarter 16th century)
Saint John the Baptist, c. 1509–1510
Oil on panel: painted surface, 62 ¼ x 21 in.
(158.1 x 53.3 cm); panel, 62 ¼ x 26 ¾ in.
(189.2 x 87.6 x 8.3 cm)
[P. & D. Colnaghi, London, sold 25 July
1978 for $23,375 to]; The Norton Simon
Foundation (F.1978.2).

Cat. 1540

Greece
Headless Draped Woman, 3rd century B.C.
Marble, 12 ¾ in. (32.4 cm)
[Simone de Monbrison, Paris, sold 25 July
1978 for $12,012 to]; Norton Simon, by
inheritance 2 June 1993 to; Jennifer Jones
Simon Art Trust, Los Angeles (N.1978.10.2).

Cat. 1541A-C

Byzantium: Antioch
Tabletop, 6th century
Marble (U-shaped), 42 x 43 ½ in.
(106.7 x 110.5 cm)
Rome
Capital (Composite Style), late 2nd century
Marble, 22 ½ in. (57.2 cm)
Italy
Tabletop, 16th–17th century
Agate, 67 in. (170.2 cm)

[Robin Symes, London, sold 11 August 1978 for $28,784 to]; Norton Simon, by inheritance 2 June 1993 to; Jennifer Jones Simon Art Trust, Los Angeles (N.1978.11.1–3).

Cat. 1542

Edgar Degas (French, 1834–1917)
Seated Dancer Rubbing Her Leg, c. 1878
Charcoal with white and dark brown pastel on gray-brown laid paper, irreg.,
17 ⅝ x 12 ¼ in. (44.8 x 31.1 cm)
[E. V. Thaw & Co., New York, sold 22 August 1978 for $135,000 to]; Norton Simon Art Foundation (M.1978.23).

Cat. 1543

Nepal, Kathmandu Valley
Narrative Scroll Extolling Manavinayaka, c. 1575
Opaque watercolor on cotton, 14 x 72 ½ in. (35.6 x 184.2 cm)
Stephen Eckerd, W.Va., sold 26 October 1978 for $7,600 to; Norton Simon, gift 18 October 1983 to; The Norton Simon Foundation (F.1983.27).

Cat. 1544

Francisco de Goya y Lucientes (Spanish, 1746–1828)
May God Repay You, before 1804
Etching, aquatint, and drypoint: plate, 7 x 8 ½ in. (17.8 x 21.6 cm); sheet, 8 x 11 ⅜ in. (20.3 x 28.9 cm)
[Craddock & Barnard, London, sold 31 October 1978 for $196 to]; Norton Simon, by inheritance 2 June 1993 to; Jennifer Jones Simon Art Trust, Los Angeles (N.1978.13).

Cat. 1545

Aimé-Jules Dalou (French, 1838–1902)
Bacchus Consoling Ariadne
Bronze, 9 ½ in. (24.1 cm)
[Shepherd Gallery, New York, sold 1 November 1978 for $3,500 to]; Norton Simon Art Foundation (M.1978.22).

Cat. 1546A-C

Rembrandt van Rijn (Dutch, 1606–1669)
Diana at the Bath, c. 1631
Etching, only state: plate, 6 ¹⁵/₁₆ x 6 ⁵/₁₆ in. (17.6 x 16 cm); sheet, 7 x 6 ⁵/₁₆ in. (17.8 x 16 cm)
Bust of an Old Bearded Man, Looking Down, Three-Quarters Right, 1631
Etching, 2nd state, 4 ³/₁₆ x 4 ³/₁₆ in. (10.6 x 10.6 cm)
Polander Standing with Arms Folded, c. 1635
Etching, only state, 2 ¹/₁₆ x 1 ⁷/₁₆ in. (5.2 x 3.7 cm)
(Sale, London, Sotheby Parke Bernet & Co., 1 November 1978 for $7,593 to); Norton Simon Art Foundation (M.1978.29.1–3).

Cat. 1547

Rembrandt van Rijn and Others
A collection of etchings, published by J. Kay, London, 1826
Etchings, group of 199, various sizes
(Sale, London, Sotheby Parke Bernet & Co., 2 November 1978 for $1,317 to); Norton Simon Art Foundation (M.1978.29.4.1–199).

Cat. 1548

Edgar Degas (French, 1834–1917)
Woman Getting out of Her Bath, c. 1876–1877
Pastel over monotype on laid paper,
6 ¹¹/₁₆ x 8 ¹¹/₁₆ in. (17 x 22 cm)
[Walter Feilchenfeldt, Zurich, sold 3 November 1978 for $120,000 to]; Norton Simon Art Foundation (M.1978.26).

Cat. 1549

Edgar Degas (French, 1834–1917)
The Laundresses, c. 1879
Etching and aquatint on wove paper, 4th (final) state: plate, 4 ⅝ x 6 ¼ in. (11.7 x 15.7 cm); sheet, 8 x 9 ⁵/₁₆ in. (20.3 x 23.8 cm)
(Sale, New York, Sotheby Parke Bernet, 9 November 1978 for $12,000 to); Norton Simon Art Foundation (M.1979.1).

1546A

1542

1546B

1544

1546C

1543

1548

1545

1549

1555A   1555B

1550

1551A

1556

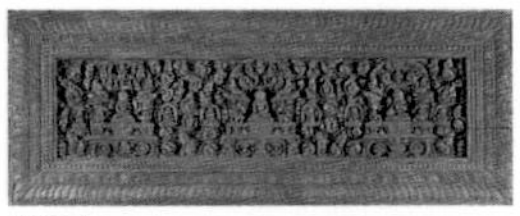

1551B

1557

1552A

1552B

Cat. 1550
Edgar Degas (French, 1834–1917)
Fan: Dancers on the Stage, 1879
Pastel with ink and wash, fan drawing:
image, 13 ⅞ x 24 ¼ in. (35.3 x 61.5 cm);
support, 15 ⅞ x 25 ¼ in. (40.3 x 64.1 cm)
[Galerie Beyeler, Basel, sold 13 November
1978 for $73,000 to]; Norton Simon Art
Foundation (M.1978.27).

Cat. 1551A-B
Tibet
Book Cover with Buddha and Deities,
15th century
Painted and gilded wood, 11 ⅜ x 29 in.
(28.9 x 73.7 cm)
Cover of a Prajnaparamita Manuscript,
16th century
Painted and gilded wood, 9 ½ x 25 ½ in.
(24.1 x 64.8 cm)
[Jane Werner, New York, sold 13 November
1978 for $7,400 to]; Norton Simon,
by inheritance 2 June 1993 to; Jennifer
Jones Simon Art Trust, Los Angeles
(N.1978.14.1–2).

Cat. 1552A-B
Claude-Marie Dubufe (French, 1790–1864)
Memories and Regrets
Engravings, each: image, 13 ½ x 18 ⅜ in.
(34.3 x 46.7 cm); sheet, 16 ¾ x 23 in.
(42.5 x 58.4 cm)
[Jean Cailleux, Paris, gift 27 November 1978
to]; Norton Simon, by inheritance 2 June
1993 to; Jennifer Jones Simon Art Trust, Los
Angeles (N.1978.7.1.3–4).

Cat. 1553
Rembrandt van Rijn (Dutch, 1606–1669)
Etchings, group of 13
(Sale, Munich, Karl & Faber, 23 November
1978 for $5,253 to); Norton Simon (sales,
New York, Sotheby Parke Bernet,
15 February 1980, six lots for $12,800; 16
May 1980, two lots for $1,370; 26 June 1980,
five lots for $5,700).

Cat. 1554
Francisco de Goya y Lucientes
(Spanish, 1746–1828)
The Disasters of War (*Los Desastres de la
Guerra*), 7th edition, printed 1937
Etching, aquatint, and drypoint,
53/150, 80 plates
(Sale, London, Christie's, 6 December
1978 for $3,520 to); Norton Simon Art
Foundation (M.1979.6.1–80).

Cat. 1555A-B
Francisco de Goya y Lucientes
(Spanish, 1746–1828)
A Dwarf (Sebastian de Morra), after
Velázquez, working proof, 1778
Etching, 8 ⅛ x 6 in. (20.6 x 15.2 cm)
Barbarroxa (Pernia), after Velázquez,
1st edition, 1778–1779
Etching and aquatint: plate, 11 ³/₁₆ x 6 ⅝ in.
(28.4 x 16.8 cm); sheet, 16 ⅜ x 12 ⅝ in.
(41.6 x 32.1 cm)
[P. & D. Colnaghi, London, sold 14
December 1978 for $12,788 to]; Norton
Simon Art Foundation (M.1978.28.1–2).

Cat. 1556
Rembrandt van Rijn (Dutch, 1606–1669)
*Illustrations to a Spanish Book: David and
Goliath*, 1655
Etching, burin, drypoint: 2nd state: plate,
4 ⅜ x 3 in. (11.1 x 7.6 cm); sheet, 4 ⅜ x 3 in.
(11.1 x 7.6 cm)
[P. & D. Colnaghi, London, sold 14
December 1978 for $7,834 to]; Norton
Simon Art Foundation (M.1978.28.3).

Cat. 1557
Edgar Degas (French, 1834–1917)
*Mary Cassatt at the Louvre: The Etruscan
Gallery*, 1879–1880
Softground etching, drypoint, aquatint,
and etching on Japan paper, 9th (final)
state, edition of 100: plate, 10 ½ x 9 ¼ in.
(26.7 x 23.5 cm); sheet, 14 x 10 ⅝ in.
(35.5 x 27 cm)

(Sale, London, Sotheby Parke Bernet &
Co., 14 December 1978, lot 127, for $9,286
to); Norton Simon Art Foundation
(M.1979.9.2).

Cat. 1558
Pakistan, Ancient Gandhara
Panel with Figure below a Tree,
3rd–4th century
Schist, 6 ⅞ x 3 x 1 ⅝ in. (17.5 x 7.6 x 4.1 cm)
(Sale, London, Sotheby Parke Bernet &
Co., 18 December 1978 for $451 to); Norton
Simon Art Foundation (M.1979.14.1).

Cat. 1559
Mainland Southeast Asia
Drum, 19th century or earlier
Bronze, 7 ¼ x 10 ⅛ in. (18.4 x 25.7 cm)
(Sale, London, Sotheby Parke Bernet &
Co., 18 December 1978 for $451 to); Norton
Simon Art Foundation (M.1979.14.2).

Cat. 1560
Henri Fantin-Latour (French, 1836–1904)
Andromeda
Oil on canvas, 20 ½ x 17 ½ in. (52 x 44.5 cm)
(Sale, Paris, Ader-Picard-Tajan,
21 December 1978 for $10,408 to); Norton
Simon Art Foundation (sale, London,
Sotheby Parke Bernet & Co., 18 June 1980,
lot 83a, for $15,155).

Cat. 1561
Léopold Survage
(French, b. Finland, 1879–1968)
Streets, 1913
Oil on board, 25 ½ x 21 ¼ in. (64.8 x 54 cm)
(Sale, Paris, Ader-Picard-Tajan,
21 December 1978 for $11,209 to); Norton
Simon Art Foundation (sale, Los Angeles,
Sotheby Parke Bernet, 23 June 1980, lot 212c,
for $12,000).

Cat. 1562
Thailand
Drum, c. 13th century

Bronze, 13 ¾ in. (34.9 cm)
[Beurdeley, Paris, sold 21 December 1978 for
$3,450 to]; Norton Simon, gift 25 December
1982 to; private collection, South America.

Cat. 1563
Francisco de Goya y Lucientes
(Spanish, 1746–1828)
Martin Miguel de Goicoechea, 1805–1806
Oil on copper, roundel, 3 ⅛ in. diameter
(8 cm)
[Sylvia Blatas, Paris, sold 26 December
1978 for $41,500 to]; The Norton Simon
Foundation (F.1978.3).

Cat. 1564
India, Kerala
Fluting Krishna with Retinue, 17th century
Bronze, 5 ¾ x 5 ½ in. (14.6 x 14 cm)
Anonymous gift 31 December 1978 to;
Norton Simon, by inheritance 2 June 1993
to; Jennifer Jones Simon Art Trust,
Los Angeles (N.1978.17).

1979

Cat. 1565
François Boucher (French, 1703–1770)
The Beautiful Country Woman, c. 1732
Oil on canvas, 16 ⅛ x 12 in. (41 x 30.5 cm)
[Wildenstein & Co., New York, sold 5
January 1979 for $50,000 to]; Norton
Simon, by inheritance 2 June 1993 to;
Jennifer Jones Simon Art Trust, Los Angeles,
gift 22 October 1999 to; Norton Simon Art
Foundation (M.1999.1).

Cat. 1566
Paul-Camille Guigou (French, 1834–1871)
Landscape in Southern France, 1870
Oil on panel, 7 ⅛ x 17 ⅞ in. (18.1 x 45.4 cm)
[Wildenstein & Co., New York, sold
5 January 1979 for $3,500 to]; Norton
Simon, by inheritance 2 June 1993 to;
Jennifer Jones Simon Art Trust, Los Angeles
(N.1979.1.2).

1558

1563

1560

1564

1565

1561

1566

1562

1567A   1567B

1568

1569A

1572

1573

1570

1574

1571

Cat. 1567A-B
Joseph Werner (Swiss, 1637–1710)
Louis XIV and *Mlle de la Valliere in Costume*, c. 1663
Gouache on parchment,
each 14 ⅜ x 10 ⅞ in. (36.5 x 27.6 cm)
[Wildenstein & Co., New York, sold
5 January 1979 for $30,000 to]; Norton
Simon, by inheritance 2 June 1993 to;
Jennifer Jones Simon Art Trust, Los Angeles
(N.1979.1.3–4).

Cat. 1568
Aimé-Jules Dalou (French, 1838–1902)
Woman with Arm Lifted
Bronze, edition size unknown, cast no. 1,
10 ½ in. (26.7 cm)
[Michel Kellermann, Paris, sold 5 January
1979 for $6,426 to]; Norton Simon Art
Foundation (M.1979.2).

Cat. 1569A-B
Circle of François Drouais
(French, 1727–1775)
Lady with Sprig of Blossom and
Lady with Pink Choker
Pastel on paper mounted to panel, oval,
each 21 x 17 in. (53.3 x 43.2 cm)
(Sale, New York, Christie's, 11 January
1979 for $2,090 to); Norton Simon,
by inheritance 2 June 1993 to; Jennifer
Jones Simon Art Trust, Los Angeles
(N.1979.6.1–2).

Cat. 1570
Rembrandt van Rijn (Dutch, 1606–1669)
Clement de Jonghe, Printseller, 1651
Etching, drypoint, burin, 1st state:
plate, 8 ³/₁₆ x 6 ⅜ in. (20.8 x 16.2 cm);
sheet, 8 ⁵/₁₆ x 6 ½ in. (21.1 x 16.5 cm)
[Robert M. Light, Boston, sold 12 January
1979 for $50,000 to]; Norton Simon Art
Foundation (M.1979.3.1).

Cat. 1571
Rembrandt van Rijn (Dutch, 1606–1669)
The Presentation in the Temple: In the Dark Manner, c. 1654
Etching and drypoint, only state:
plate, 8 ¼ x 6 ⅜ in. (21 x 16.2 cm);
sheet, 8 ⁵/₁₆ x 6 ⅜ in. (21.1 x 16.2 cm)
[Robert M. Light, Boston, sold 12 January
1979 for $110,000 to]; Norton Simon Art
Foundation (M.1979.3.2).

Cat. 1572
Odilon Redon (French, 1840–1916)
Peony, Geranium, and Lilacs
(formerly *Flowers in a Brown Vase*)
Oil on canvas, 21 ½ x 18 in. (54 x 45 cm)
[Paul Rosenberg & Co., New York, sold
17 January 1979 for $210,000 to]; Norton
Simon Art Foundation (sale, New York,
Sotheby Parke Bernet, 7 November 1979, lot
545, for $270,000). (sale, London, Sotheby's,
25 June 1985, lot 17, unsold) (sale, New York,
Christie's, 19 November 1986, lot 20, for
$495,000).

Cat. 1573
Edgar Degas (French, 1834–1917)
The Laundress, c. 1873
Oil on canvas, 9 ¹³/₁₆ x 7 ⁹/₁₆ in.
(24.8 x 19.2 cm)
[William Beadleston, New York, sold
24 January 1979 for $140,000 to]; Norton
Simon Art Foundation (M.1979.5).

Cat. 1574
Antonio Carnicero (Spanish, 1748–1814)
Collection of the Most Important Phases of a Bullfight
Etchings, group of 15: 13 color,
each 10 ½ x 15 ¼ in. (26.7 x 38.7 cm); 1 color,
18 ⅞ x 25 in. (47.9 x 63.5 cm); 1 black and
white, 14 ¾ x 9 ⅝ in. (37.5 x 24.4 cm)
[Fernando Berckemeyer, San Francisco,
sold 2 February 1979 for $1,000 to]; Norton
Simon, by inheritance 2 June 1993 to;
Jennifer Jones Simon Art Trust, Los Angeles
(N.1979.2.1–15).

Cat. 1575
Jean Perroneau (French, 1715–1783)
Portrait of a Man of the Journu Family, 1757
Pastel on paper, mounted on canvas,
23 x 18 ⅝ in.
[E. V. Thaw & Co., New York, sold
5 February 1979 for $160,000 to]; Norton
Simon, returned 16 November 1979 to;
[E. V. Thaw & Co., New York, sold to];
[Artemis and David Carritt Ltd., London].

Cat. 1576
Pablo Picasso (Spanish, 1881–1973)
The Hen, 1952
Scraped aquatint and drypoint, final state,
bon à tirer: plate, 20 ¼ x 26 in. (51.4 x 66
cm); sheet, 22 ⅛ x 30 in. (56.2 x 76.2 cm)
[P. & D. Colnaghi, London, sold 12 February
1979 for $4,643 to]; Norton Simon Art
Foundation (M.1979.9.1).

Cat. 1577
Pablo Picasso (Spanish, 1881–1973)
The Song of the Dead, 1945
Lithograph: cover, 19 ½ x 12 ⅞ in.
(49.5 x 32.7 cm); sheet, 16 ½ x 12 ⅝ in.
(41.9 x 32.1 cm)
[P. & D. Colnaghi, London, sold 12 February
1979 for $348 to]; Norton Simon Art
Foundation (M.1979.9.3).

Cat. 1578
Rembrandt van Rijn (Dutch, 1606–1669)
*Saint Jerome Kneeling in Prayer, Looking
Down*, 1635
Etching, only state: plate, 4 ⅝ x 3 ³/₁₆ in.
(11.7 x 8.1 cm); sheet, 4 ⅞ x 3 ⁷/₁₆ in.
(12.4 x 8.7 cm)
[C. G. Boerner, Düsseldorf, sold 12 February
1979 for $3,517 to]; Norton Simon Art
Foundation (M.1979.7).

Cat. 1579
Rembrandt van Rijn (Dutch, 1606–1669)
The Stoning of Saint Stephen, 1635
Etching, 1st state: plate, 3 ⅞ x 3 ⁷/₁₆ in.

(9.8 x 8.7 cm)
[Craddock & Barnard, London, sold
12 February 1979 for $3,548 to]; Norton
Simon Art Foundation (M.1979.8).

Cat. 1580
Pablo Picasso (Spanish, 1881–1973)
Nude with Crown of Flowers, 1929
Etching, *bon à tirer*: plate, 11 x 7 ⅝ in.
(27.9 x 19.4 cm); sheet, 17 ½ x 13 ¼ in.
(44.5 x 33.7 cm)
(Sale, New York, Sotheby Parke Bernet,
16 February 1979 for $5,170 to); Norton
Simon Art Foundation (M.1979.16.1).

Cat. 1581
Pablo Picasso (Spanish, 1881–1973)
*Standing Nude, Flutist and Young Girl
Kneeling*, 1938
Drypoint, *bon à tirer*: plate, 9 ¾ x 13 ⅝ in.
(24.8 x 34.6 cm); sheet, 13 ½ x 17 ⅝ in.
(34.3 x 44.8 cm)
(Sale, New York, Sotheby Parke Bernet,
16 February 1979 for $5,500 to); Norton
Simon Art Foundation (M.1979.16.2).

Cat. 1582
Pablo Picasso (Spanish, 1881–1973)
Two Line Figures, 1939
Engraving, *bon à tirer*: plate, 9 ¾ x 5 ⅛ in.
(24.8 x 13 cm); sheet, 17 ⅜ x 13 ¼ in.
(44.1 x 33.7 cm)
(Sale, New York, Sotheby Parke Bernet,
16 February 1979 for $2,860 to); Norton
Simon Art Foundation (M.1979.16.3).

Cat. 1583
Jacques Linard (French, 1600–1645)
Still Life: The Five Senses with Flowers, 1639
Oil on canvas, 21 ½ x 26 ¾ in.
(54.6 x 68 cm)
[E. V. Thaw & Co., New York, sold
21 February 1979 for $55,000 to]; Norton
Simon, by inheritance 2 June 1993 to;
Jennifer Jones Simon Art Trust, Los Angeles
(N.1979.4.1).

1575

1576

1580

1581

1582

1583

1577

1578

1579

1584

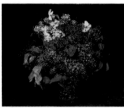

1585

1586

1587

1588

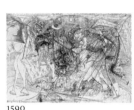

1589

1590

1591

1592

Cat. 1584

Pierre-Auguste Renoir (French, 1841–1919)
Bouquet of Lilacs, 1875–1880
Oil on canvas, 21 ¼ x 25 ¾ in. (54 x 65.5 cm)
[E. V. Thaw & Co., New York, sold
21 February 1979 for $110,000 to]; Norton
Simon, by inheritance 2 June 1993 to;
Jennifer Jones Simon Art Trust, Los Angeles
(N.1979.1.2).

Cat. 1585

Paul-Désiré Trouillebert
(French, 1829–1900)
Still Life with Plums, 1865–1880
Oil on panel, 6 ⅜ x 14 ¼ in. (16.2 x 36.2 cm)
[Abels Gemaelde Galerie, Cologne, sold
23 February 1979 for $7,700 to]; Norton
Simon Art Foundation (M.1979.11).

Cat. 1586

Edgar Degas (French, 1834–1917)
Singer at a Café Concert, c. 1876–1877
Lithograph, 1st state of 2: image, 10 ¹/₁₆ x 7 ⅝
in. (25.5 x 19.3 cm), sheet, 13 ¹³/₁₆ x 10 ¹³/₁₆ in.
(35.1 x 27.5 cm)
[Paul Prouté, Paris, sold 26 February
1979 for $15,896 to]; Norton Simon Art
Foundation (M.1979.12).

Cat. 1587A-F

Francisco de Goya y Lucientes
(Spanish, 1746–1828)
Six Plates from Los Caprichos, 1st edition,
c. 1797–1799
Etching, aquatint, and drypoint, plates 26,
50, 54, 76, 77, 78
[Paul Prouté, Paris, sold 26 February
1979 for $3,021 to]; Norton Simon Art
Foundation (M.1979.13.1–6).

Cat. 1588

Joan Miró (Spanish, 1893–1983)
Black and Red Series, 1938

Drypoint etching in red and black, *bon à
tirer*: plate, 6 ¾ x 10 ⅛ in. (17.1 x 25.7 cm);
sheet, 12 ¾ x 17 ½ in. (32.4 x 44.5 cm)
[Reiss-Cohen, New York, sold 26 March
1979 for $11,000 to]; Norton Simon Art
Foundation (M.1979.15.1).

Cat. 1589

Pablo Picasso (Spanish, 1881–1973)
Femme Torero I, 1934
Etching, late edition impression:
plate, 19 ⅛ x 27 in. (48.6 x 68.6 cm);
sheet, 22 ¼ x 30 ½ in. (56.5 x 77.5 cm)
[Reiss-Cohen, New York, sold 26 March
1979 for $4,375 to]; Norton Simon Art
Foundation (M.1979.15.2).

Cat. 1590

Pablo Picasso (Spanish, 1881–1973)
The Great Bullfight, with Woman Bullfighter,
1934
Etching: plate, 19 ⅛ x 27 in. (48.6 x 68.6 cm);
sheet, 22 ¼ x 30 ½ in. (56.5 x 77.5 cm)
[Reiss-Cohen, New York, sold 26 March
1979 for $4,375 to]; Norton Simon Art
Foundation (M.1979.15.3).

Cat. 1591

Pietro Antonio Rotari (Italian, 1707–1762)
Young Girl Writing a Love Letter, c. 1755
Oil on canvas, 33 ⅜ x 27 in. (84.8 x 68.6 cm)
[Paul Rosenberg & Co., New York, sold
2 April 1979 for $100,000 to]; Norton Simon
Art Foundation (M.1979.18).

Cat. 1592

Edgar Degas (French, 1834–1917)
Schoolgirl (Woman walking in the street)
Bronze, edition of 300, cast no. 37, 10 ⅝ in.
(27 cm)
[The Nelson Rockefeller Collection, New
York, sold 12 April 1979 for $800 to]; Norton
Simon Art Foundation (M.1979.38).

Cat. 1593
Francisco de Goya y Lucientes
(Spanish, 1746–1828)
This Is the Truth, plate 82 from *The Disasters of War* (*Los Desastres de la Guerra*),
1814–1820, trial proof, printed 1870
Etching, aquatint, and drypoint:
plate, 6 ⅞ x 8 ½ in. (17.5 x 21.6 cm);
sheet, 12 ¾ x 19 ¾ in. (32.4 x 50.2 cm)
[Paul Prouté, Paris, sold 26 April 1979 for
$2,102 to]; Norton Simon Art Foundation
(M.1979.30).

Cat. 1594
Antoine Etex (French, 1808–1888)
Bust of Alexandre Dumas the Elder, 1854
Bronze, 26 ¾ in. (68 cm)
[Heim, London, sold 1 May 1979 for
$16,500 to]; Norton Simon Art Foundation
(M.1979.19.1).

Cat. 1595
Alexandre Abel de Pujol (French, 1785–1861)
Portrait of a Magistrate, c. 1820
Oil on canvas, 39 ½ x 31 ⅞ in.
(100.3 x 81 cm)
[Heim, London, sold 1 May 1979 for
$23,500 to]; Norton Simon Art Foundation
(M.1979.19.2).

Cat. 1596
Michel Bouquet (French, 1807–1890)
Woodland Scene with Hunters, c. 1865
Oil on canvas, 16 ¼ x 22 ½ in.
(41.2 x 57.2 cm)
(Sale, New York, Sotheby Parke Bernet,
3 May 1979 for $5,775 to); Norton Simon,
gift 18 October 1983 to; The Norton Simon
Foundation (F.1983.5).

Cat. 1597
Émile-Gustave Couder (French, c.
1847–1903)
Floral Still Life with a Cat, 1872–1873

Oil on canvas, 46 x 58 in. (116.9 x 147.3 cm)
(Sale, New York, Sotheby Parke Bernet,
3 May 1979 for $2,200 to); Norton Simon,
by inheritance 2 June 1993 to; Jennifer
Jones Simon Art Trust, Los Angeles, gift
21 December 2007 to; Norton Simon Art
Foundation (M.2007.4.1).

Cat. 1598
Thomas Couture (French, 1815–1879)
Reverie, 1840–1841
Oil on canvas, 21 ⅝ x 20 ½ in. (54.9 x 52.1 cm)
(Sale, New York, Sotheby Parke Bernet, 3
May 1979 for $14,850 to); Norton Simon, by
inheritance 2 June 1993 to; Jennifer Jones
Simon Art Trust, Los Angeles (N.1979.11.5).

Cat. 1599
Narcisse-Virgile Diaz de la Peña
(French, 1807–1876)
The Approaching Storm, 1870
Oil on canvas, 33 ¼ x 41 ⅝ in. (84.4 x 105.6 cm)
(Sale, New York, Sotheby Parke Bernet,
3 May 1979 for $23,000 to); Norton Simon,
gift 18 October 1983 to; The Norton Simon
Foundation (F.1983.9).

Cat. 1600
Jules Dupré (French, 1811–1889)
Large Trees at Water's Edge, c. 1865
Oil on canvas, 38 x 30 in. (96.5 x 76.2 cm)
(Sale, New York, Sotheby Parke Bernet,
3 May 1979 for $19,800 to); Norton Simon,
gift 18 October 1983 to; The Norton Simon
Foundation (F.1983.11).

Cat. 1601
Charles-Émile Jacque (French, 1813–1894)
Return to the Fold, c. 1878–1880
Oil on canvas, 32 ¼ x 26 ¼ in. (81.8 x 66.6 cm)
(Sale, New York, Sotheby Parke Bernet,
3 May 1979 for $20,900 to); Norton Simon,
by inheritance 2 June 1993 to; Jennifer Jones
Simon Art Trust, Los Angeles (N.1979.11.3).

1593

1598

1594

1599

1595

1600

1596

1601

1597

1602

1607

1603

1608

1609

1604

1610

1605

1611

1606

Cat. 1602
Gaston Casimir Saint-Pierre
(French, 1833–1916)
Odalisque
Oil on canvas, 43 x 60 ½ in. (109.2 x 153.7 cm)
(Sale, New York, Sotheby Parke Bernet,
3 May 1979 for $18,150 to); Norton Simon,
sold 5 November 1979 at cost to; private
collection, Los Angeles.

Cat. 1603
Pierre Antoine Patel II (French, 1648–1707)
*A Capriccio Landscape with Ruins and
an Angler*
Oil on panel, 9 ¾ x 12 ¾ in. (24.8 x 32.4 cm)
(Sale, London, Christie's, 4 May 1979 for
$9,976 to); Norton Simon Art Foundation
(M.1979.40).

Cat. 1604
India, Rajasthan(?)
Bull with Shivalingam and Other Images,
16th century(?)
Schist, 20 ¼ x 28 x 9 in. (51.4 x 22.9 x 71.1 cm)
(Sale, New York, Sotheby Parke Bernet,
23 May 1979 for $5,940 to); Norton Simon
Art Foundation (M.1979.25).

Cat. 1605
Justus Sustermans (Flemish, 1597–1681)
Portrait of a Woman, c. 1650
Oil on canvas, 21 x 17 ¼ in. (53.3 x 43.8 cm)
(Sale, New York, Sotheby Parke Bernet,
30 May 1979 for S9,625 to); Norton Simon,
by inheritance 2 June 1993 to; Jennifer Jones
Simon Art Trust, Los Angeles (N.1979.12).

Cat. 1606
Louis Ducis (French, 1775–1847)
*Sappho Recalled to Life by the Charm of
Music,* c. 1811
Oil on canvas, 45 ⅜ x 57 ⅝ in.
(115.2 x 146.3 cm)
[Heim Gallery, London, sold 1 June 1979 for
$32,500 to]; Norton Simon, gift 18 October
1983 to; The Norton Simon Foundation
(F.1983.10).

Cat. 1607
Jean-Louis Forain (French, 1852–1931)
*At the Evening Party: Woman in White with
a Fan,* 1883–1884
Pastel, 21 ¾ x 18 in. (55.2 x 45.7 cm)
[Jean Cailleux, Paris, sold 11 June 1979 for
$32,761 to]; Norton Simon, by inheritance
2 June 1993 to; Jennifer Jones Simon Art
Trust, Los Angeles (N.1979.8).

Cat. 1608
Rembrandt van Rijn (Dutch, 1606–1669)
Cottage with a White Paling, 1648
Etching, drypoint; 3rd state, 5 ⅛ x 6 ¼ in.
(13 x 15.9 cm)
[Paul Prouté, Paris, sold 12 June 1979 for
$7,035 to]; Norton Simon Art Foundation
(M.1979.20).

Cat. 1609
Tibet
*Book Cover with Five Transcendental
Buddhas,* 15th century
Painted and gilded wood, 11 ¾ x 30 in.
(29.8 x 76.2 cm)
(Sale, London, Christie's, 13 June 1979 for
$2,606 to); Norton Simon, by inheritance
2 June 1993 to; Jennifer Jones Simon Art
Trust, Los Angeles (N.1979.13).

Cat. 1610
Berthe Morisot (French, 1841–1895)
Daydreaming, 1877
Pastel, mounted on canvas, 19 ¾ x 24 in.
(50.1 x 60.9 cm)
[E. V. Thaw & Co., New York, sold 18 June
1979 for $100,000 to]; Norton Simon,
returned 16 November 1979 to; [E. V. Thaw
& Co., New York, sold 1979 to]; The Nelson-
Atkins Museum of Art, Kansas City, Mo.

Cat. 1611
Berthe Morisot (French, 1841–1895)
In a Villa at the Seaside, 1874
Oil on canvas, 19 ¾ x 24 in. (50.2 x 61 cm)
[Hirschl & Adler Galleries, New York,

sold 22 June 1979 for $210,000 to]; Norton Simon Art Foundation (M.1979.21).

Cat. 1612
Roderic O'Conor (Irish, 1860–1940)
Landscape with Cows, 1890–1895
Oil on canvas, 25 ¾ x 32 in. (65.3 x 81.2 cm)
[La Cave–Galerie de Tableaux, Paris, sold 22 June 1979 for $12,608 to]; Norton Simon, by inheritance 2 June 1993 to; Jennifer Jones Simon Art Trust, Los Angeles (N.1979.10)

Cat. 1613
Edgar Degas (French, 1834–1917)
Schoolgirl (Woman walking in the street)
Bronze, edition of 20, cast no. 14, 10 ⅝ in. (27 cm)
[William Beadleston, New York, sold 27 June 1979 for $18,000 to]; Norton Simon Art Foundation (M.1979.22).

Cat. 1614
Guillaume Voiriot (French, 1713–1799)
Portrait of a Man, 1753
Pastel, 23 ¼ x 19 ⅛ in. (60 x 49.5 cm)
(Sale, London, Sotheby Parke Bernet & Co., 28 June 1979 for $7,945 to); Norton Simon, gift 18 October 1983 to; The Norton Simon Foundation (F.1983.19).

Cat. 1615
Pablo Picasso (Spanish, 1881–1973)
The Painter and His Model, 1926
Pen and ink, 11 ½ x 15 in. (29.2 x 39.1 cm)
(Sale, London, Sotheby Parke Bernet & Co., 3 July 1979 for $29,326 to); Norton Simon Art Foundation (sale, New York, Christie's, 20 May 1982, lot 143, for $35,000).

Cat. 1616
Pablo Picasso (Spanish, 1881–1973)
Table in Front of Shuttered Window, 1920
Oil on canvas, 8 ¾ x 5 in. (22.2 x 12.7 cm)
(Sale, London, Sotheby Parke Bernet & Co.,

3 July 1979 for $92,867 to); Norton Simon Art Foundation (sale, New York, Christie's, 19 May 1982, lot 40, for $120,000 to); private collection, Los Angeles, by inheritance to; private collection, Los Angeles.

Cat. 1617
Georges Lacombe (French, 1868–1916)
Autumn: The Chestnut Gatherers, 1894
Oil on canvas, 60 ⅛ x 93 ⅛ in. (152.7 x 236.3 cm)
(Sale, London, Sotheby Parke Bernet & Co., 4 July 1979 for $90,433 to); Norton Simon Art Foundation (M.1979.35).

Cat. 1618
Gustave Courbet (French, 1819–1877)
Vase of Lilacs, Roses, and Tulips, 1863
Oil on canvas, 25 ⅝ x 21 ⅜ in. (65 x 54.3 cm)
[Paul Rosenberg & Co., New York, sold 6 July 1979 for $300,000 to]; Norton Simon Art Foundation (M.1979.24).

Cat. 1619
Rembrandt van Rijn (Dutch, 1606–1669)
Christ Crucified between the Two Thieves: Long Oblong Plate (the "Three Crosses"), 1653
Drypoint and burin, 3rd state:
image, 13 ⅛ x 17 ¼ in. (33.3 x 43.8 cm);
sheet, 13 ⅛ x 17 ¼ in. (33.3 x 43.8 cm)
[David Tunick, New York, sold 19 July 1979 for $55,000 to]; Norton Simon Art Foundation (M.1979.26).

Cat. 1620
Rembrandt van Rijn (Dutch, 1606–1669)
The Rest on the Flight: Lightly Etched, 1645
Etching and drypoint, only state:
plate, 5 ⅛ x 4 ⁹/₁₆ in. (13 x 11.6 cm);
sheet, 5 ¾ x 5 ⅛ in. (14.6 x 13 cm)
[C. G. Boerner, Düsseldorf, sold 27 July 1979 for $25,809 to]; Norton Simon Art Foundation (M.1979.23).

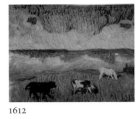
1612

1617

1613

1618

1614

1619

1615

1620

1616

1622

1623

1624

1625

1626

1627

1628

Cat. 1621A-D

Rembrandt van Rijn (Dutch, 1606–1669)
David in Prayer, 1652
Etching, late impression:
plate, 5 ⅝ x 3 ⅝ in. (14.3 x 9.2 cm);
sheet, 17 x 12 ¼ in. (43.2 x 31.1 cm)
The Flight into Egypt: A Night Piece, 1651
Etching, late impression: plate, 5 x 4 ⅜ in.
(12.7 x 11.1 cm); sheet, 17 x 12 ¼ in. (43.2 x
31.1 cm)
The Goldsmith, 1655
Etching, late impression:
plate, 3 x 2 ³/₁₆ in. (7.6 x 5.6 cm);
sheet, 17 x 12 ¼ in. (43.2 x 31.1 cm)
Jan Asselyn, Painter, c. 1647
Etching, late impression:
plate, 8 ⅝ x 6 ⅝ in. (21.9 x 16.8 cm);
sheet, 17 x 12 ¼ in. (43.2 x 31.1 cm)
[Frederick Mulder, London, sold 30 July
1979 for $805 to]; Norton Simon Art
Foundation (M.1979.27.1–4).

Cat. 1622

Cambodia, Pre-Angkor Period
Shivalingam with One Face, c. 700
Sandstone, 14 ¼ x 4 ⅜ x 4 ⅜ in.
(36.2 x 11.1 x 11.1 cm)
[L'Inde et la Chine, Paris, sold 1 August
1979 for $5,700 to]; Norton Simon, by
inheritance 2 June 1993 to; Jennifer Jones
Simon Art Trust, Los Angeles (N.1979.14).

Cat. 1623

Raoul Dufy (French, 1877–1953)
The Orchestra, Havre Theater, 1902
Oil on canvas, 44 ½ x 57 ½ in. (113 x 146 cm)
[Lee Ault, New York, sold 7 August 1979 for
$70,000 to]; Norton Simon, sold 1 April 1981
for $175,000 to; Ivan F. Boesky, New York,
by descent to; private collection, New York.

Cat. 1624

Rembrandt van Rijn (Dutch, 1606–1669)
*Christ Presented to the People: Large Oblong
Plate*, 1655

Drypoint, 4th state: plate, 14 x 17 ¹⁵/₁₆ in.
(35.6 x 45.6 cm); sheet, 14 ⅛ x 18 in.
(35.9 x 45.7 cm)
[Richard Day, London, sold 7 August
1979 for $58,050 to]; Norton Simon Art
Foundation (M.1979.28).

Cat. 1625

Rembrandt van Rijn (Dutch, 1606–1669)
*Illustrations to a Spanish Book:
The Image Seen by Nebuchadnezzar*, 1655
Etching, burin, drypoint, on Japan paper,
2nd state: plate, 3 ⅞ x 2 ¾ in. (9.8 x 7 cm);
sheet, 4 ⅛ x 2 ¾ in. (10.5 x 7 cm)
[Robert M. Light, Santa Barbara, Calif.,
sold 14 August 1979 for $6,500 to]; Norton
Simon Art Foundation (M.1979.29).

Cat. 1626

André Derain (French, 1880–1954)
Head of a Woman, c. 1935
Oil on canvas, 13 ¼ x 11 ¼ in. (33.7 x 28.6 cm)
[Michel Kellermann, Paris, sold
25 September 1979 for $8,302 to]; Norton
Simon Art Foundation (M.1979.36).

Cat. 1627

Edgar Degas (French, 1834–1917)
*Horse trotting, the feet not touching the
ground*
Bronze, cast no. 49/modèle, 9 x 10 x 2 ⁷/₁₆ in.
(22.9 x 25.3 x 6 cm); base, 10 ¹¹/₁₆ x 4 ¹⁵/₁₆ in.
(27.2 x 12.6 cm)
[Michel Kellermann, Paris, sold 3 October
1979 for $43,704 to]; Norton Simon Art
Foundation (M.1979.31).

Cat. 1628

Pablo Picasso (Spanish, 1881–1973)
Head of a Woman, 1971
Pastel on gray board, 11 ⅝ x 8 ¼ in.
(29.5 x 21 cm)
[Berggruen, Paris, sold 5 October 1979 for
$21,000 to]; Norton Simon Art Foundation
(M.1979.32).

Cat. 1629

Pablo Picasso (Spanish, 1881–1973)
The Moulin Rouge, 1901
China ink, 12 ¾ x 19 ½ in. (32.4 x 49.5 cm)
[Galerie Daniel Malingue, Paris, sold
11 October 1979 for $42,000 to]; Norton
Simon Art Foundation (M.1979.34).

Cat. 1630

Honoré Daumier (French, 1808–1879)
Le Charivari
Color lithographs, group of 20 on
newsprint, 1st state, sheet, 9 x 8 ½ in.
(22.9 x 21.6 cm)
[Paul Prouté, Paris, sold 5 November 1979
for $404 to]; Norton Simon, by inheritance
2 June 1993 to; Jennifer Jones Simon Art
Trust, Los Angeles (N.1979.18.1–20).

Cat. 1631

Rembrandt van Rijn (Dutch, 1606–1669)
Etchings, group of 27, Basan impressions
Various sizes
(Sale, New York, Sotheby Parke Bernet,
private sale 5 November 1979 for $13,200
to); Norton Simon Art Foundation (sales,
New York, Sotheby Parke Bernet,
14 November 1979, 11 lots for $10,800;
London, Sotheby Parke Bernet & Co.,
16 November 1980, 2 lots for $1,795, and
New York, Sotheby Parke Bernet, 25 June
1980, 3 lots for $2,750).

Cat. 1632

School of Nicolas de Largillière (French,
1656–1746)
Portrait of a Gentleman
Oil on canvas, 51 ¼ x 40 in. (130.2 x 101.6 cm)
(Sale, New York, Sotheby Parke Bernet,
16 November 1979 for $1,980 to); Norton
Simon Art Foundation (M.1980.4).

Cat. 1633

India, West Bengal or Bangladesh
Stele with Twelve Solar Deities, c. 1100
Chlorite, 28 ½ x 13 in. (72.4 x 33 cm)

(Sale, New York, Sotheby Parke Bernet,
19 November 1979 for $2,750 to); Norton
Simon Art Foundation (M.1980.1.2).

Cat. 1634

Pakistan, Ancient Gandhara
Worshipers Venerate the Buddha,
2nd–4th century
Schist, 9 ¼ x 22 ⅛ in. (23.5 x 56.2 cm)
(Sale, New York, Sotheby Parke Bernet,
19 November 1979 for $1,540 to); Norton
Simon Art Foundation (M.1980.1.1).

Cat. 1635

Thailand, Khorat Plateau(?)
Antefix with Five-headed Serpent, c. 1100
Sandstone, 42 ½ in. (108 cm)
(Sale, New York, Sotheby Parke Bernet,
19 November 1979 for $4,125 to); Norton
Simon, gift 18 October 1983 to; The Norton
Simon Foundation (F.1983.23).

Cat. 1636

Isaak Soreau (German, 1604–after 1638)
Still Life with Fruits and Flowers, c. 1638
Oil on panel, 28 ⅝ x 40 ¼ in. (72.7 x 102.2 cm)
[Paul Rosenberg & Co., New York, sold
29 November 1979 for $150,000 to]; Norton
Simon Art Foundation (M.1979.39).

Cat. 1637

Jean-Louis Forain (French, 1852–1931)
The Widow and the Orphans, c. 1910
Oil on canvas, 41 ⅛ x 32 ⅞ in. (104.5 x 83.5 cm)
[La Cave–Galerie de Tableaux, Paris, sold
4 December 1979 for $19,752 to]; Norton
Simon Art Foundation (M.1979.41).

Cat. 1638

Édouard Vuillard (French, 1868–1940)
Dressmakers under the Lamp, c. 1891–1892
Oil on cardboard, 9 ⅝ x 10 ½ in.
(24.5 x 26.7 cm)
[La Cave–Galerie de Tableaux, Paris, sold
4 December 1979 for $49,380 to]; Norton
Simon Art Foundation (M.1979.41.2).

1634

1629

1632

1635

1636

1633   1637

1638

1639

1644

1640

1645A

1645B

1641

1646

1642

Cat. 1639
Alexander Roslin (Swedish, 1718–1793)
Nikita Demidov, 1772
Oil on canvas, 29 x 23 ⅛ in. (73.7 x 58.7 cm)
(Sale, London, Sotheby Parke Bernet & Co.,
12 December 1979 for $16,713 to); Norton
Simon, by inheritance 2 June 1993 to;
Jennifer Jones Simon Art Trust, Los Angeles
(N.1980.2).

Cat. 1640
Francisco de Goya y Lucientes
(Spanish, 1746–1828)
She Fleeces Him, plate 35 from
Los Caprichos, 1st edition, c. 1798
Etching and burnished aquatint:
plate, 8 ½ x 6 in. (21.6 x 15.2 cm);
sheet, 12 ⅝ x 8 ½ in. (32.1 x 21.6 cm)
[P. & D. Colnaghi, London, sold
26 December 1979 for $1,530 to]; Norton
Simon Museum (Museum Purchase,
Fellows Acquisition Fund) (P.1979.8).

Cat. 1641
Pakistan or Afghanistan, Ancient Gandhara
Buddha Shakyamuni, 5th–6th century
Brass, 15 ⅝ in. (39.7 cm)
Date of purchase, price, and source
unknown (by 31 December 1979 with);
Norton Simon, by inheritance 2 June 1993
to; Jennifer Jones Simon Art Trust, Los
Angeles (N.1979.22).

1980

Cat. 1642
Claude-Émile Schuffenecker
(French, 1851–1934)
Fernand Quignon, c. 1885–1890
Oil on canvas, 31 ⅞ x 25 ⅝ in. (81 x 65 cm)
[Barbara Mathes, New York, sold 17 January
1980 for $36,000 to]; Norton Simon Art
Foundation (M.1980.2).

Cat. 1643
Albrecht Dürer (German, 1471–1528)
The Three Books, 1511, *Christ among the
Doctors*, c. 1503, and *Flagellation*, c. 1497
Woodcuts, group of 50, various sizes
[Paul Prouté, Paris, sold 29 January
1980 for $108,750 to]; Norton Simon Art
Foundation, used in trade 11 February 1980
as partial payment for Vincent van Gogh,
*Back Garden of Sien's Mother's House,
The Hague* (cat. 1644) to; [Robert M. Light,
Santa Barbara, Calif.].

Cat. 1644
Vincent van Gogh (Dutch, 1853–1890)
*Back Garden of Sien's Mother's House,
The Hague*, 1882
Sepia ink, gouache, and graphite on paper,
laid on Bristol board, 18 ¼ x 23 ⅞ in.
(46.3 x 60.7 cm)
[Robert M. Light, Santa Barbara, Calif., sold
11 February 1980 for $150,000 to]; Norton
Simon Art Foundation (M.1980.5).

Cat. 1645A-B
Giovanni Battista Tiepolo
(Italian, 1696–1770)
Female Satyr with House, Child, and a Putto
and *Female Satyr with Tambourine, Child,
and a Putto*, c. 1740–1742
Oil on canvas, oval, each 23 ⅝ x 37 ¾ in.
(60 x 95.9 cm)
[Jean Cailleux, Paris, sold 26 February
1980 for $305,366 to]; Norton Simon Art
Foundation (M.1980.6.1–2).

Cat. 1646
Dieric Bouts (Flemish, c. 1410–1475)
Resurrection, c. 1455
Distemper on linen, 35 ⅜ x 29 ¼ in.
(89.9 x 74.3 cm)
(Sale, London, Sotheby Parke Bernet & Co.,
16 April 1980 for $4,214,000 to); The Norton
Simon Foundation (F.1980.1).

Cat. 1647
Adolphe-Joseph-Thomas Monticelli
(French, 1824–1886)
Midsummer, 1860–1870
Oil on panel, 15 ⅝ x 23 ½ in. (39.7 x 59.7 cm)
[Paul Rosenberg & Co., New York, sold
23 April 1980 for $11,000 to]; Norton Simon,
gift 18 October 1983 to; The Norton Simon
Foundation (F.1983.13).

Cat. 1648
Francisco de Goya y Lucientes
(Spanish, 1746–1828)
Los Caprichos, 3rd or 4th edition,
printed 1881–1886
Etching, aquatint and drypoint, 80 plates
(Sale, New York, Christie's, 2 May 1980 for
$8,800 to); Norton Simon Art Foundation
(M.1980.10.1–80).

Cat. 1649
Aristide Maillol (French, 1861–1944)
The Three Nymphs, 1930–1937
Bronze, artist's proof, 62 x 56 ⅞ x 31 in.
(157.5 x 144.5 x 78.7 cm)
[Dina Vierny, Paris, sold 15 May 1980 for
$364,720 to]; Norton Simon Art Foundation
(M.1980.7).

Cat. 1650
Rembrandt van Rijn (Dutch, 1606–1669)
*Pierre-François Basan: Recueil de Quatre-
vingt-cinq Estampes Originaux*
Etchings, Basan impressions (82 by
Rembrandt, 5 by others), various sizes
(Sale, London, Sotheby Parke Bernet & Co.,
16 May 1980 for $114,675 to); Norton Simon
Art Foundation (M.1980.11.1–87).

Cat. 1651A-F
Pietro Antonio Rotari (Italian, 1707–1762)
Six Bust Portraits of Women
Oil on canvas, each 17 ¾ x 13 ¾ in.
(45.1 x 34.9 cm)

[P. & D. Colnaghi, London, sold 29 May
1980 for $50,000 to]; Norton Simon Art
Foundation (M.1980.8.1–6).

Cat. 1652
Pablo Picasso (Spanish, 1881–1973)
Two Nude Women, 1945
Lithograph, intermediate proof between
states 7 and 8, sheet, 13 x 18 in. (33 x 45.7 cm)
(Sale, New York, Sotheby Parke Bernet,
25 June 1980 for $3,740 to); Norton Simon
Art Foundation, gift 7 February 1983 to;
Norton Simon Museum (P.1983.3.1).

Cat. 1653
Adolphe-Joseph-Thomas Monticelli
(French, 1824–1886)
The Olive Oil Seller, c. 1880
Oil on panel, 20 x 15 ¾ in. (50.8 x 40 cm)
[E. V. Thaw & Co., New York, sold 8 July
1980 for $10,000 to]; Norton Simon Art
Foundation (M.1980.9).

Cat. 1654
Giovanni Francesco Barbieri, called
Il Guercino (Italian, 1591–1666)
Aldrovandi Dog, c. 1625
Oil on canvas, 44 x 68 ¼ in. (111.8 x 173.4
cm)
[Galerie Nathan, Zurich, sold 17 November
1980 for $1,153,600 to]; Norton Simon Art
Foundation, returned 22 March 1982 to;
[Galerie Nathan, Zurich]; [David Koetser,
Zurich (in partnership with Nathan), sold
20 June 1984 for $600,000 to]; The Norton
Simon Foundation (F.1984.2).

Cat. 1655
India, Himachal Pradesh(?)
Vishnu and Lakshmi, 14th–15th century
Bronze, 3 ¼ in. (8.3 cm)
(Sale, London, Sotheby Parke Bernet &
Co., 25 November 1980 for $179 to); Norton
Simon Art Foundation (M.1981.2.3).

1647

1653

1649

1654

1652

1655

1651A

1651D

1651B
1651E

1651C
1651F

1656

1657

1658

1659

1660

1664

1665

1666

Cat. 1656
Nepal or Tibet
Male Acolyte or Donor, 16th century
Bronze, 2 ⅛ x 1 ¾ in. (5.4 x 4.4 cm)
(Sale, London, Sotheby Parke Bernet & Co.,
25 November 1980 for $409 to); Norton
Simon Art Foundation (M.1981.2.1).

Cat. 1657
Nepal
Indra and Sachi, 18th century
Wood, 8 ¾ x 5 ½ in. (22.2 x 14 cm)
(Sale, London, Sotheby Parke Bernet & Co.,
25 November 1980 for $768 to); Norton
Simon Art Foundation (M.1981.2.2).

Cat. 1658
Tibet
Book Cover with Buddhist Deities,
15th–16th century
Wood, 8 ⅛ x 17 ¾ in. (20.6 x 45.1 cm)
(Sale, London, Sotheby Parke Bernet &
Co., 25 November 1980 for $921 to); Norton
Simon, by inheritance 2 June 1993 to;
Jennifer Jones Simon Art Trust, Los Angeles
(N.1981.2.1).

Cat. 1659
Tibet
Book Cover with Buddhist Deities,
15th century
Painted and gilded wood, 10 ⅝ x 27 ⅞ in.
(27 x 70.8 cm)
(Sale, London, Sotheby Parke Bernet & Co.,
25 November 1980 for $2,175 to); Norton
Simon, by inheritance 2 June 1993 to;
Jennifer Jones Simon Art Trust, Los Angeles
(N.1981.2.2).

Cat. 1660
Tibet or Nepal
Bovine, 18th–19th century(?)
Gilt bronze, 1 ¾ x 3 ¼ in. (4.4 x 8.3 cm)
(Sale, London, Sotheby Parke Bernet & Co.,
25 November 1980 for $2,647 to); Norton
Simon Art Foundation (M.1981.4).

Cat. 1661
Jean-Baptiste Audebert (French, 1759–1800)
Histoire naturelle des singes et des makis,
1798
Book, first edition, 62 hand-colored plates
(Sale, London, Christie's, 26 November
1980 for $3,136 to); Norton Simon Art
Foundation (sale, London, Christie's, 24
March 1982, lot 140, for $1,798).

Cat. 1662
James Bateman (English, 1811–1897)
The Orchidaceae of Mexico and Guatemala,
1837–1843
Book with 40 hand-colored plates
(Sale, London, Christie's, 26 November
1980 for $13,589 to); Norton Simon Art
Foundation (sale, London, Christie's, 24
March 1982, lot 141, for $10,785).

Cat. 1663
Cornelius Nozeman (Dutch, 1712–1786)
Nederlandische Vogelen
Book in three volumes with 147
hand-colored plates
(Sale, London, Christie's, 26 November
1980 for $13,067 to); Norton Simon Art
Foundation (sale, London, Christie's,
24 March 1982, lot 193, for $10,785).

Cat. 1664
Tristram Hillier (English, 1905–1983)
Blackmoor Vale from Pennard, 1980
Oil on board, 10 x 14 in. (25.4 x 35.6 cm)
[Alex Reid & Lefevre, London, sold
16 December 1980 for $4,192 to]; Norton
Simon Museum (P.1980.4.3).

Cat. 1665
Tristram Hillier (English, 1905–1983)
Palomas, 1976
Oil on board, 24 x 32 in. (61 x 81.3 cm)
[Alex Reid & Lefevre, London, sold
16 December 1980 for $8,384 to]; Norton
Simon Museum (P.1980.4.1).

Cat. 1666

Tristram Hillier (English, 1905–1983)
Still Life in the Studio, 1980
Oil on board, 16 x 20 in. (40.6 x 50.8 cm)
[Alex Reid & Lefevre, London, sold
16 December 1980 for $6,812 to]; Norton
Simon Museum (P.1980.4.2).

1981

Cat. 1667

Willem Reuter (Flemish, 1642–1681)
An Italian Market, 1669
Oil on canvas, 47 ⅝ x 77 in. (121 x 195.6 cm)
(Sale, New York, Sotheby Parke Bernet,
8 January 1981 for $63,250 to); Norton Simon,
by inheritance 2 June 1993 to; Jennifer Jones
Simon Art Trust, Los Angeles (N.1981.1).

Cat. 1668

Jan Baptist Huysmans (Flemish, 1654–1716)
A Wooded Italianate Landscape, 1690
Oil on canvas, 67 ⅝ x 95 ¾ in. (171.8 x 243.2 cm)
(Sale, New York, Christie's, 9 January 1981
for $31,900 to); Norton Simon National
Institute, sold 30 December 1982 for
$31,900 to; Norton Simon Art Foundation
(M.1982.7.2).

Cat. 1669

Attributed to Justus Juncker
(German, 1703–1767)
Sportsmen in a Tavern, c. 1735
Oil on canvas, 9 x 14 ½ in. (22.9 x 36.8 cm)
(Sale, New York, Christie's, 9 January 1981
for $8,250 to); Norton Simon National
Institute, sold 30 December 1982 for
$8,250 to; Norton Simon Art Foundation
(M.1982.7.1).

Cat. 1670A-B

Pablo Picasso (Spanish, 1881–1973)
Two Nude Women, 30 September 1930
Etching, *bon à tirer*: plate, 12 ⁷/₁₆ x 8 ⅞ in.
(31.6 x 22.5 cm); sheet, 22 ¾ x 18 in.
(57.8 x 45.7 cm)

The Diver (Marie-Thérèse), December 1932
Etching printed over collage of colored
papers, 5 ½ x 4 ⅜ in. (14 x 11.1 cm)
(Sale, New York, Christie's, 15 January 1981,
lot 201, for $13,200 to); Norton Simon
Museum (P.1981.1.1–2).

Cat. 1671

Nicolas Poussin (French, 1594–1665)
*The Holy Family with the Infant Saint John
the Baptist and Saint Elizabeth*
Oil on canvas, 39 ⅝ x 52 ⅛ in.
(100.6 x 132.4 cm)
(Sale, London, Christie's, 10 April 1981,
through [Wildenstein & Co., New York]
for $3,433,894 [$1,716,947 each] to); Norton
Simon Art Foundation (M.1981.6) and
The J. Paul Getty Museum, Los Angeles.

Cat. 1672

Edgar Degas (French, 1834–1917)
Jockey on a Horse, c. 1882–1888
Charcoal and pastel on tracing paper,
mounted on board, 7 ½ x 8 ¼ in. (19 x 21 cm)
[La Cave–Galerie de Tableaux, Paris, sold
13 April 1981 for $11,762 to]; The Norton
Simon Foundation (F.1981.1).

Cat. 1673

Vietnam
Drum, 3rd century B.C.–1st century A.D.
Bronze, 20 x 26 in. (50.8 x 66 cm)
[Beurdeley, Paris, sold 1 May 1981 for
$21,054 to]; Norton Simon, by inheritance
2 June 1993 to; Jennifer Jones Simon Art
Trust, Los Angeles (N.1981.4).

Cat. 1674

Pablo Picasso (Spanish, 1881–1973)
Nu debout (Standing Nude), c. 1935
Aquatint, *bon à tirer*: image, 9 ¼ x 4 ¾ in.
(23.5 x 12.1 cm); sheet, 17 ⅝ x 13 ½ in.
(44.8 x 34.3 cm)
(Sale, New York, Sotheby Parke Bernet,
5 May 1981, lot 416, for $5,500 to); Norton
Simon Museum (P.1981.2).

1667

1668

1669

1671

1673

1672

1676

1676

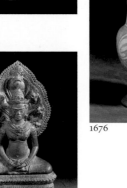

1678

1679

1683

Cat. 1675
Circle of Giovanni Francesco Romanelli
(Italian, 1610–1662)
Saint Catherine of Alexandria
Oil on canvas, 35 ½ x 29 in. (90.2 x 73.7 cm)
(Sale, New York, Sotheby Parke Bernet,
16 July 1981 for $1,870 to); Norton Simon
Art Foundation (sale, London, Sotheby
Parke Bernet & Co., 7 July 1982, lot 306,
for $1,219).

Cat. 1676
Thailand, Ban Chiang Culture
Six Pots, 1st century or earlier
Ceramic, various sizes
Francine Rothdach, Ventura, Calif., sold
30 July 1981 for $6,250 to; Norton Simon,
gifts of two, 25 December 1982 to; private
collection, Los Angeles, gifts of four
18 October 1983 to; The Norton Simon
Foundation (F.1983.30.1–4).

Cat. 1677
India and Thailand
Village Gods from Tamil Nadu and *Pots*
from the Ban Chiang region
30 bronzes and ceramics
[William Wolff, New York, sold
22 September 1981 for $9,200 to]; Norton
Simon, gifts of seven 18 October 1983
to; The Norton Simon Foundation
(F.1983.31.1–7); remainder by inheritance
2 June 1993 to; Jennifer Jones Simon Art
Trust (N.1981.6.1–20, 28–30).

Cat. 1678
Cambodia, Angkor Period
Buddha Sheltered by the Serpent, c. 1200
Bronze, 9 ¾ in. (24.8 cm)
[William Wolff, New York, sold
22 September 1981 for $16,250 to]; Norton
Simon Art Foundation (M.1981.5.1).

Cat. 1679
Indonesia, Central Java
Chunda, 9th–10th century

Bronze, 5 ⅛ in. (13 cm)
[William Wolff, New York, sold
22 September 1981 for $4,000 to]; Norton
Simon Art Foundation (M.1981.5.2).

Cat. 1680
Pablo Picasso (Spanish, 1881–1973)
Head of a Young Girl, 15 November 1945
Lithograph, 4th state, *bon à tirer*,
17 ½ x 12 ⅞ in. (44.5 x 32.7 cm)
(Sale, Los Angeles, Sotheby Parke Bernet,
22 September 1981, lot 375, for $3,025 to);
Norton Simon Museum (P.1981.3).

Cat. 1681
Pablo Picasso (Spanish, 1881–1973)
Woman in an Armchair, No. 4, 10 December
1948–3 January 1949
Lithograph, 5th state, 38/ 50,
30 ⅛ x 22 ¼ in. (76.5 x 56.5 cm)
(Sale, Los Angeles, Sotheby Parke Bernet,
22 September 1981, lot 379, for $9,500 to);
Norton Simon Museum (P.1982.1).

Cat. 1682
Hubert Robert (French, 1733–1808)
The Cloister of the Augustinian Nuns
Oil on canvas, 51 ¼ x 41 ⅜ in. (130.2 x 105.1 cm)
[E. V. Thaw & Co., New York, sold
5 November 1981 for $185,000 to]; The
Norton Simon Foundation (F.1981.2).

Cat. 1683
Francisco de Goya y Lucientes
(Spanish, 1746–1828)
Another Madness of His in the Same Ring,
plate 19 from *La Tauromaquia*, 1st edition,
1816
Etching, aquatint, and drypoint:
plate, 9 ⅞ x 13 ⅞ in. (25.1 x 35.2 cm);
sheet, 10 ⅞ x 14 ⅞ in. (27.6 x 37.8 cm)
(Sale, New York, Sotheby Parke Bernet,
14 November 1981 for $2,200 to); Norton
Simon, by inheritance 2 June 1993 to;
Jennifer Jones Simon Art Trust, Los Angeles
(N.1981.7).

Cat. 1684
Francisco de Goya y Lucientes
(Spanish, 1746–1828)
Dona Francisca Vicenta Chollet y Caballero,
1806
Oil on canvas, 40 ½ x 31 ⅞ in. (102.9 x 80.9 cm)
[Thomas Agnew & Sons, London, sold
31 December 1981 for $2,018,750 to]; Norton
Simon Art Foundation (M.1981.7).

Cat. 1685
India, Tamil Nadu
Kali, 11th century
Bronze, 26 ⅛ in. (66.4 cm)
Date of purchase, price, and source
unknown (by 31 December 1981) to; Norton
Simon, by inheritance 2 June 1993 to;
Jennifer Jones Simon Art Trust, Los Angeles
(N.1981.8).

Cat. 1686
Tibet
Cover of a Prajnaparamita Manuscript, 12th
century
Painted and gilded wood, 10 ⅝ x 28 ⅛ in.
(27 x 71.4 cm)
Date of purchase, price, and source
unknown (by 31 December 1981) to; Norton
Simon, by inheritance 2 June 1993 to;
Jennifer Jones Simon Art Trust, Los Angeles
(N.1981.9).

1982

Cat. 1687
Francesco Guardi (Italian, 1712–1793)
Venetian Capriccio, 1760–1765
Oil on canvas, 20 ⅝ x 15 ⅛ in. (52.4 x 38.4 cm)
[E. V. Thaw & Co., New York, sold
21 January 1982 for $200,000 to]; Norton
Simon Art Foundation (M.1982.1.1).

Cat. 1688
Jan van der Heyden (Dutch, 1637–1712)
Townscape with Gothic Church, c. 1670
Oil on panel, 13 ⅜ x 15 ¾ in. (34 x 40 cm)
[E. V. Thaw & Co., New York, sold
21 January 1982 for $250,000 to]; Norton
Simon Art Foundation (M.1982.1.2).

Cat. 1689A–G
Pablo Picasso (Spanish, 1881–1973)
The Diver, 29 November 1932
Etching over collage of sand and papers:
plate, 5 ½ x 4 ⁷/₁₆ in. (14 x 11.3 cm); sheet,
12 ⅞ x 9 ¾ in. (32.7 x 9.5 cm)
Heads of Rams, 7 December 1945
Lithograph, proof impression:
image, 9 ½ x 13 ¾ in. (24.1 x 34.9 cm);
sheet, 11 ¼ x 17 ⅝ in. (28.6 x 44.8 cm)
Still Life with Three Apples, 17 December 1945
Lithograph in five colors:
image, 9 ⅛ x 13 ⅝ in. (23.2 x 34.6 cm);
sheet, 12 ¾ x 20 in. (32.4 x 50.8 cm)
Still Life with Three Apples, 17 December 1945
Lithograph in black: image, 8 ¾ x 12 in.
(22.2 x 30.5 cm); sheet, 11 x 18 ¼ in.
(27.9 x 46.4 cm)
Composition with Glass and Apple,
13 January 1946
Lithograph, 1st state: image, 9 ½ x 12 ½ in.
(24.1 x 31.8 cm); sheet, 12 ¾ x 17 ½ in.
(32.4 x 44.5 cm)
Composition with Glass and Apple,
7 February 1946
Lithograph, 2nd state: image, 10 ½ x 13 ½ in.
(26.7 x 34.3 cm); sheet, 12 ¾ x 17 ½ in.
(32.4 x 44.5 cm)
Composition with Glass and Apple,
18 February 1946
Lithograph, 3rd state: image, 10 ⅞ x 13 ¾ in.
(27.6 x 34.9 cm); sheet, 12 ¾ x 17 ½ in.
(32.4 x 44.5 cm)
(Sale, New York, Sotheby Parke Bernet,
17 February 1982, lots 327, 339, 341–342,
for $6,985 to); Norton Simon Museum
(P.1982.2.1–7).

1684

1685

1686

1687

1689A

1688

1690

1694

1691

1695

1692

1696

1693

1697

Cat. 1690

Georges-Pierre Seurat (French, 1859–1891)
Angelica at the Rock (after Ingres), 1878
Oil on canvas, 32 ⅝ x 26 ⅛ in. (83 x 66.2 cm)
[Wildenstein & Co., New York, sold 16 April
1982 for $64,000 to]; Norton Simon, by
inheritance 2 June 1993 to; Jennifer Jones
Simon Art Trust, Los Angeles, gift 12 August
1997 to; Norton Simon Art Foundation
(M.1997.1.4).

Cat. 1691A-F

Pablo Picasso (Spanish, 1881–1973)
The Pipers, August–September 1946
Six etchings, states 1–6, 1st state, 1/2: plate,
10 ⅝ x 14 in. (27 x 35.6 cm); sheet, 12 ⅞ x 19 ¾
in. (32.7 x 50.2 cm); 2nd state, 1/2: plate, 10
¾ x 13 ⅞ in. (27.3 x 35.2 cm); sheet, 14 ¾ x
22 in. (37.5 x 55.9 cm); 3rd state, edition of 1:
plate, 10 ¾ x 13 ⅞ in. (27.3 x 35.2 cm), sheet,
14 ⅞ x 22 in. (37.8 x 55.9 cm); 4th state, 1/2:
plate, 10 ¾ x 13 ⅞ in. (27.3 x 35.2 cm), sheet,
14 ¾ x 20 ¼ in. (37.5 x 51.4 cm); 5th state,
edition of 1: plate, 10 ¾ x 14 in. (27.3 x 35.6
cm); sheet, 13 x 19 in. (33 x 48.3 cm); 6th
state, 2/2: plate, 10 ¾ x 13 ⅞ in. (27.3 x 35.2
cm); sheet, 18 ⅜ x 20 ½ in. (46.7 x 52.1 cm)
[Wolfgang Wittrock, Düsseldorf, sold
10 June 1982 for $57,000 to]; Norton Simon
Museum (P.1982.3.1–6).

Cat. 1692

Pablo Picasso (Spanish, 1881–1973)
Françoise on a Gray Background,
5 November 1950
Lithograph on zinc, 1st state, *bon à tirer*:
image, 25 ⅝ x 19 ½ in. (65.1 x 49.5 cm);
sheet, 30 x 22 ¼ in. (76.2 x 57.2 cm)
(Sale, New York, Sotheby Parke Bernet,
17 November 1982, lot 43, for $11,000 to);
Norton Simon Museum (P.1983.1.1).

Cat. 1693

Pablo Picasso (Spanish, 1881–1973)
The Italian Woman, 21 January 1953
Lithograph, 2nd state, proof: image,

17 ½ x 14 ⅞ in. (44.5 x 37.8 cm); sheet,
25 ¾ x 19 ¾ in. (65.4 x 50.2 cm)
(Sale, New York, Sotheby Parke Bernet,
17 November 1982, lot 49, for $6,600 to);
Norton Simon Museum (P.1983.1.2).

Cat. 1694

Francisco de Goya y Lucientes
(Spanish, 1746–1828)
*The Forceful Rendon Stabs a Bull with the
Pique…*, plate 28 from *La Tauromaquia*,
1st edition, 1816
Etching, aquatint, and drypoint:
plate, 9 ⅞ x 13 ⅞ in. (25.1 x 35.2 cm);
sheet, 10 ⅞ x 14 ⅞ in. (27.6 x 37.8 cm)
(Sale, New York, Sotheby Parke Bernet,
19 November 1982 for $1,100 to); Norton
Simon, by inheritance 2 June 1993 to;
Jennifer Jones Simon Art Trust, Los Angeles
(N.1982.2).

Cat. 1695

Guido Cagnacci (Italian, 1601–1663)
Martha Rebuking Mary for Her Vanity,
after 1660
Oil on canvas, 90 ¼ x 104 ¾ in.
(229.2 x 266.1 cm)
[P. & D. Colnaghi, London, sold
22 November 1982 for $524,000 to]; Norton
Simon Art Foundation (M.1982.5).

Cat. 1696

Nicolas de Largillière (French, 1656–1746)
Portrait of Lambert de Vermont, c. 1697
Oil on canvas, 57 ½ x 44 ¾ in. (146.1 x 113.7 cm)
[P. & D. Colnaghi, London, sold
23 November 1982 for $121,688 to]; Norton
Simon Art Foundation (M.1982.6.1).

Cat. 1697

Louis Tocqué (French, 1696–1772)
Presumed Portrait of Alexis Piron, c. 1737
Oil on canvas, 50 ½ x 38 in. (128.3 x 96.5 cm)
[P. & D. Colnaghi, London, sold
23 November 1982 for $56, 788 to]; Norton
Simon Art Foundation (M.1982.6.2).

Cat. 1698

India, Kashmir or Panjab

Table, late 19th century

Wood, 40 x 54 ¼ x 24 ¾ in. (101.6 x 137.8 x 62.9 cm)

(Sale, London, Sotheby Parke Bernet & Co., 29 November 1982 for $5,040 to); Norton Simon, by inheritance 2 June 1993 to; Jennifer Jones Simon Art Trust, Los Angeles (N.1983.1.2).

Cat. 1699

Southern Tibet

Segment of a Throne or Aureole, 16th century

Gilt-copper repoussé, 16 ½ x 13 ½ in. (41.9 x 34.3 cm)

(Sale, London, Sotheby Parke Bernet & Co., 29 November 1982 for $3,528 to); Norton Simon, by inheritance 2 June 1993 to; Jennifer Jones Simon Art Trust, Los Angeles (N.1983.1.1).

Cat. 1700

Pablo Picasso (Spanish, 1881–1973)

Two Nude Women, 5 January 1946

Lithograph, 8th state, unique impression: image, 10 x 13 in. (25.4 x 33 cm); sheet, 13 x 18 in. (33 x 45.7 cm)

[Wolfgang Wittrock, Düsseldorf, sold 15 December 1982 for $10,245 to]; Norton Simon Museum (P.1982.4).

Cat. 1701

Pablo Picasso (Spanish, 1881–1973)

Head on a Black Background, 9 May 1953

Etching: image, 27 ¼ x 21 ½ in. (69.2 x 54.6 cm); sheet, 29 ⅞ x 22 ¼ in. (75.9 x 56.5 cm); Lithograph, proof: image, 27 ¼ x 21 ½ in. (69.2 x 54.6 cm); sheet, 29 ⅞ x 22 ¼ in. (75.9 x 56.5 cm)

[Wolfgang Wittrock, Düsseldorf, sold 21 December 1982 for $23,237 to]; Norton Simon Museum (P.1982.5.1–2).

1983

Cat. 1702

Édouard Vuillard (French, 1868–1940)

The Pitch Pine Room (formerly *Denise Natanson and Marcelle Aron in the Summerhouse at Villerville, Normandy*), summer 1910

Oil on canvas, 18 ¼ x 25 ⅜ in. (46.4 x 64.4 cm)

(Sale, New York, Christie's, 17 May 1983 for $104,500 to); The Norton Simon Foundation (F.1983.1).

Cat. 1703

Edgar Degas (French, 1834–1917)

Olive Trees against a Mountainous Background, c. 1890–1892

Pastel over monotype: image, 10 x 13 ⅝ in. (25.4 x 34.6 cm); sheet, 10 ⅝ x 14 ⅛ in. (27 x 35.9 cm)

(Sale, New York, Sotheby Parke Bernet, 18 May 1983 for $71,500 to); The Norton Simon Foundation (F.1983.2.1).

Cat. 1704

Edgar Degas (French, 1834–1917)

Waiting, c. 1879–1882

Pastel, 19 x 24 in. (48.2 x 61 cm)

(Sale, New York, Sotheby Parke Bernet, 18 May 1983 for $3,740,000 [$1,870,000 each]to); Norton Simon Art Foundation (M.1983.1) and The J. Paul Getty Museum, Los Angeles.

Cat. 1705

Edgar Degas (French, 1834–1917)

Wheat Field and Green Hill, c. 1890–1892

Pastel over monotype in oil colors: image, 10 x 13 ⅝ in. (25.4 x 34.6 cm); sheet, 10 ⅝ x 14 ⅛ in. (27 x 35.9 cm)

(Sale, New York, Sotheby Parke Bernet, 18 May 1983 for $132,000 to); The Norton Simon Foundation (F.1983.2.2).

1698

1702

1699

1703

1700

1704

1705

1710

1706

1707

1711

1708

1712

1709

1713

1714

Cat. 1706

Jean-Auguste-Dominique Ingres
(French, 1780–1867)
Baron Joseph-Pierre Vialètes de Mortarieu,
1805–1806
Oil on canvas, 24 ⅛ x 19 ¾ in.
(61.2 x 50.2 cm)
[Sarec, S.A., Geneva, 21 July 1983 for $1.1
million to]; The Norton Simon Foundation
(F.1983.3).

Cat. 1707

India, Gujarat
Altarpiece with Vishnu and Other Deities,
10th century
Bronze, 12 x 6 ⅞ x 3 ⅝ in.
(30.5 x 17.5 x 9.2 cm)
Date of purchase, price, and source
unknown (by 31 December 1983) to; Norton
Simon, by inheritance 2 June 1993 to;
Jennifer Jones Simon Art Trust, Los Angeles
(N.1983.2).

1984

Cat. 1708

Pablo Picasso (Spanish, 1881–1973)
The Bull, 24 December 1945
Lithograph, 5th state, 1/18: 12 ⅞ x 17 ½ in.
(32.7 x 44.5 cm)
(Sotheby's, New York, sold privately
4 January 1984 for $15,000 to); Norton
Simon Art Foundation (M.1984.1).

Cat. 1709

Auguste Rodin (French, 1840–1917)
Jean de Fiennes, Dressed, 1884–1895
Bronze, edition of 4, cast no. I,
81 ⅞ x 31 x 47 in. (208 x 78.7 x 119.4 cm)
Musée Rodin, Paris, sold 4 June 1984 for
$83,216 to; The Norton Simon Foundation
(F.1984.1.3).

Cat. 1710

Auguste Rodin (French, 1840–1917)
Pierre de Wissant, Dressed, 1884–1895
Bronze, edition of 4, cast no. I,
84 ¼ x 39 ½ x 47 ¾ in. (214 x 100.3 x 121.3 cm)
Musée Rodin, Paris, sold 4 June 1984 for
$83,216 to; The Norton Simon Foundation
(F.1984.1.1).

Cat. 1711

Auguste Rodin (French, 1840–1917)
Pierre de Wissant, Nude, 1884–1895
Bronze, edition of 4, cast no. II,
77 ¾ x 38 ½ x 44 ¾ in. (197.5 x 97.8 x 113.7 cm)
Musée Rodin, Paris, sold 4 June 1984 for
$77,339 to; The Norton Simon Foundation
(F.1984.1.2).

Cat. 1712

Pablo Picasso (Spanish, 1881–1973)
Woman with Mandolin, 1925
Oil on canvas, 51 ⅜ x 38 ½ in. (130.5 x 97.8 cm)
(Sale, New York, Christie's, 13 November
1984, lot 143, for $1,925,000 to); Norton
Simon Museum (P.1984.2).

Cat. 1713

Vincent van Gogh (Dutch, 1853–1890)
*Head of a Peasant Woman in a White
Bonnet,* 1885
Oil on canvas, 18 ½ x 13 ¾ in. (47 x 35 cm)
(Sale, New York, Sotheby Parke Bernet,
14 November 1984 for $220,000 to); The
Norton Simon Foundation (F.1985.1).

Cat. 1714

Gustave Caillebotte (French, 1848–1894)
Canoe on the Yerres River, 1878
Oil on canvas, 25 ⅞ x 31 ⅞ in. (65.7 x 81 cm)
(Sale, New York, Sotheby Parke Bernet,
16 November 1984 for $220,000 to); Norton
Simon, by inheritance 2 June 1993 to;
Jennifer Jones Simon Art Trust, Los Angeles
(N.1984.1.1).

Cat. 1715
Gustave Caillebotte (French, 1848–1894)
The Yellow Boat, 1891
Oil on canvas, 28 ¾ x 36 ⅜ in. (73 x 92.5 cm)
(Sale, New York, Sotheby Parke Bernet,
16 November 1984 for $77,000 to); The
Norton Simon Foundation (F.1985.2.1).

Cat. 1716
Albert Marquet (French, 1875–1947)
Algiers, the Balcony, 1944
Oil on panel, 13 x 9 ¼ in. (33 x 23.5 cm)
(Sale, New York, Sotheby Parke Bernet,
16 November 1984 for $22,000 to); Norton
Simon, by inheritance 2 June 1993 to;
Jennifer Jones Simon Art Trust, Los Angeles
(N.1984.1.3).

Cat. 1717
Albert Marquet (French, 1875–1947)
Poissy, the White Fence, 1929
Oil on canvas, 25 ⅝ x 32 in. (65.1 x 81.3 cm)
(Sale, New York, Sotheby Parke Bernet,
16 November 1984 for $104,500 to); The
Norton Simon Foundation (F.1985.2.2).

Cat. 1718
Albert Marquet (French, 1875–1947)
Saint Jean de Luz, the Fisherman, 1927
Oil on canvasboard, 12 ¾ x 16 in.
(32.4 x 40.6 cm)
(Sale, New York, Sotheby Parke Bernet,
16 November 1984 for $46,750 to); Norton
Simon, by inheritance 2 June 1993 to;
Jennifer Jones Simon Art Trust, Los Angeles
(N.1984.1.2).

Cat. 1719
Albert Marquet (French, 1875–1947)
Saint Raphael, the Terrace, 1932
Oil on canvas, 24 x 19 ¾ in. (61 x 50.2 cm)
(Sale, New York, Sotheby Parke Bernet,
16 November 1984 for $71,500 to); The
Norton Simon Foundation (F.1985.2.3).

Cat. 1720A-B
Attributed to Ferdinand van Kessel
(Flemish, 1648–after 1696)
Still Life with Fruits and a Vase of Flowers
and *Still Life with Fruit and a Bird*
Oil on copper, each 6 ⅝ x 8 ⅝ in.
(16.8 x 21.9 cm)
[Galerie Sanct Lucas, Vienna, sold 20
December 1984 for $67,000 to]; Norton
Simon Art Foundation (M.1984.3.1–2).

1985
Cat. 1721
Jean-Baptiste Pater (French, 1695–1736)
Fête Champêtre, c. 1730
Oil on canvas, 22 ⅛ x 26 in. (56.2 x 66 cm)
[Paul Rosenberg & Co., New York, sold
25 January 1985 for $190,000 to]; The
Norton Simon Foundation (F.1985.3).

Cat. 1722
Pierre-Paul Prud'hon (French, 1758–1823)
*The Abduction of Psyche by Zephyrus
to the Palace of Eros*, after 1808, probably
before 1820
Oil on canvas, 39 ¾ x 32 ½ (101 x 82.5 cm)
[Paul Rosenberg & Co., New York, sold
25 January 1985 for $110,000 to]; Norton
Simon Art Foundation (M.1985.1).

1986

Cat. 1723
Paul Paulin (French, c. 1850–c. 1932)
Bust of Degas, 1907
Bronze, 18 ¼ x 16 ¼ x 12 ¼ in.
(46.4 x 41.3 x 31.1 cm)
[Marianne Feilchenfeldt, Zurich, sold
28 April 1986 for $10,000 to]; Norton Simon
Art Foundation (M.1986.1).

1715

1720A

1720B

1716

1721

1717

1722

1718

1723

1719

1724

1729

1725

1726

1731

1727

1728

1730B

1732

1987

Cat. 1724
Naum Lvovich Aronson
(Russian, 1872–1943)
Count Leo Tolstoy
Pencil and brown chalk, 12 ¾ x 9 ½ in.
(32.4 x 24.1 cm)
(Sale, London, Sotheby's, 1 May 1987 for
$1,278 to); Norton Simon Art Foundation
(M.1987.1.1).

Cat. 1725
Mstislav Valerianovich Dobujinsky
(Russian, 1875–1957)
A Courtyard in Novgorod, 1904
Watercolor and pencil, 9 ½ x 12 in.
(24.1 x 30.5 cm)
(Sale, London, Sotheby's, 1 May 1987 for
$1,825 to); Norton Simon Art Foundation
(M.1987.1.2).

Cat. 1726
Boris Dmitrievich Grigoriev
(Russian, 1886–1930)
Portrait of a Seated Woman
Oil on panel, 35 ⅜ x 39 in. (89.9 x 99.1 cm)
(Sale, London, Sotheby's, 1 May 1987 for
$8,214 to); Norton Simon Art Foundation
(M.1987.1.3).

Cat. 1727
Alexander Alexandrovich Kiselev
(Russian, 1838–1911)
The Mill, 1890
Oil on canvas, 29 ½ x 49 ⅛ in. (75 x 125 cm)
(Sale, London, Sotheby's, 1 May 1987 for
$25,554 to); Norton Simon Art Foundation
(M.1987.1.4).

Cat. 1728
Boris Mikhailovich Kustodiev
(Russian, 1878–1927)
Two Young Women Seated on a Balustrade,
1914

Gouache over pencil: image, 8 ¹/₁₆ x 10 ⁹/₁₆ in.
(20.5 x 26.8 cm); mount, 8 ⅛ x 10 ⅞ in.
(20.6 x 27.6 cm)
(Sale, London, Sotheby's, 1 May 1987 for
$5,111 to); Norton Simon Art Foundation
(M.1987.1.5).

Cat. 1729
Philippe Andreevich Maliavin
(Russian, 1869–1940)
A Peasant Woman
Oil on canvas, 41 ½ x 27 ¾ in. (105.4 x 70.5 cm)
(Sale, London, Sotheby's, 1 May 1987 for
$31,029 to); Norton Simon Art Foundation
(M.1987.1.6).

1988

Cat. 1730A-E
Cornelis van Kittensteyn
(Dutch, c. 1600–1663)
The Five Senses, after Dirk Hals
Engravings, group of 5
(Sale, London, Sotheby's, 1 December
1988 for $2,372 to); Norton Simon, by
inheritance 2 June 1993 to; Jennifer Jones
Simon Art Trust, Los Angeles (N.1989.1.1–5).

1989

Cat. 1731
Various artists
Artists' Letters, group of 42
[William Schab, New York, sold 13 February
1989 for $90,000 to]; Norton Simon Art
Foundation (M.1989.1.1–42).

Cat. 1732
Gustave Courbet (French, 1819–1877)
Peasant Girl with a Scarf, c. 1849
Oil on canvas, 23 ⅝ x 28 ¾ in. (60 x 73 cm)
[Acquavella Galleries, New York, sold
22 December 1989 for $900,000 to]; Norton
Simon Art Foundation (M.1989.2).

The Duveen Inventory

ARTWORKS IN THE
SIMON COLLECTIONS

Duveen Brothers stock numbers are in brackets. Unless stated otherwise, the works are in the collection of The Norton Simon Foundation; the foundation's accession number appears in parentheses.

PAINTINGS

Cat. D1
Workshop of Fra Angelico (Italian, 1387–1455)
Madonna and Child
Tempera and gold leaf on panel,
18 ⅛ x 15 in. (46 x 38.1 cm)
[29831] (F.1965.1.1)

Cat. D2
Fra Antonio da Monza (Italian, active 1480–1505)
The Flagellation of Christ
Tempera on vellum,
17 ½ x 13 ½ in. (44.5 x 34.3 cm)
[30434] (F.1965.1.101)

Cat. D3
Follower of Bartolomeo Veneto
(Italian, active 1502–1531)
Portrait of a Man
Oil on panel, 20 ⅝ x 15 ⅝ in. (52.4 x 39.7 cm)
[29350] (F.1965.1.69)

Cat. D4
Circle of Jacopo Bassano (Jacopo da Ponte)
(Italian, 1510–1592)
Portrait of a Lady, after 1570
Oil on canvas, 30 x 25 ¾ in. (76.2 x 65.4 cm)
[29351] (F.1965.1.2)

Cat. D5
Follower of Giovanni Bellini
(Italian, c. 1430–1516)
Virgin and Child
Oil on panel, 33 ¾ x 26 ¾ in. (85.7 x 67.9 cm)
[28717] (F.1965.1.3)

Cat. D6
Follower of Giovanni Bellini
(Italian, c. 1430–1516)
Virgin and Child in a Landscape
Oil on panel, 26 ⅞ x 18 ¾ in. (68.3 x 47.6 cm)
[29444] (F.1965.1.4)

Cat. D7
Francesco Bissolo (Italian, 1470/72–1554)
The Annunciation, c. 1500
Oil on panel, transferred to canvas,
43 ¾ x 39 ½ in. (111.1 x 100.3 cm)
[29838] transferred 19 November 2004 to; Norton
Simon Art Foundation (M.2004.2)

Cat. D8
Sandro Botticelli (Italian, c. 1444–1510)
Madonna and Child with Adoring Angel, c. 1468
Tempera on panel, 35 x 26 ¾ in. (88.9 x 68 cm)
[29467] transferred 27 November 1987 to; Norton
Simon Art Foundation (M.1987.2)

Cat. D9
Francesco Botticini (Italian, 1446–1497)
Virgin and Child with Four Angels and Two Cherubim, c. 1470–1475
Tempera on panel,
25 ¾ x 19 ½ in. (65.4 x 49.5 cm)
[29351] (F.1965.1.9)

Cat. D10
Attributed to Vittore Carpaccio
(Italian, 1455–1526)
Portrait of a Venetian Nobleman, c. 1510
Oil on panel, 14 x 10 ¾ in. (35.6 x 27.3 cm)
[30101] (F.1965.1.12)

D1

D6

D2

D7

D3

D8

D4

D9

D5

D10

D11

D12

D13

D14

D15

D16

D17

D18A   D18B

D19

D20

D21

D22

Cat. D11

Attributed to Vincenzo Catena
(Italian, c. 1470–1531)
Madonna and Child with Saint Peter and Saint Catherine of Alexandria, early 16th century
Oil on panel, transferred to canvas,
32 ½ x 42 in. (82.6 x 106.7 cm)
[28204] (F.1965.1.14)

Cat. D12

Vincenzo Catena (Italian, c. 1470–1531)
(formerly attributed to Giovanni Bellini)
The Rest on the Flight into Egypt,
early 16th century
Oil on panel, 32 x 43 in. (81.3 x 109.2 cm)
[29531] transferred 24 November 2008 to; Norton
Simon Art Foundation (M.2008.2)

Cat. D13

Gerard David (Netherlandish, c. 1460–1523)
The Coronation of the Virgin, c. 1520
Oil on panel, 27 ⅞ x 21 ¼ in. (70.8 x 54 cm)
[30108] (F.1965.1.17)

Cat. D14

Circle of Eugène Delacroix, possibly Richard
Parkes Bonington (English, 1801–1828)
The Crucifixion, c. 1825
Oil on canvas, 19 ¾ x 25 ¾ in. (50.2 x 65.4 cm)
[30351] (F.1965.1.6)

Cat. D15

School of Fontainebleau (French, 16th century)
The Birth of Adonis
Oil on panel, 38 x 30 ⅜ in. (96.5 x 77.2 cm)
[30143] (F.1965.1.26)

Cat. D16

Attributed to Girolamo Forabosco
(Italian, 1604/5–1679)
The Lace Maker
Oil on canvas, 32 ½ x 26 in. (82.6 x 66 cm)
[29351] (F.1965.1.148)

Cat. D17

Jean-Honoré Fragonard (French, 1732–1806)
Happy Lovers, c. 1760–1765
Oil on canvas, 35 ½ x 47 ¾ in. (90.2 x 121.3 cm)
[29712] (F.1965.1.21)

Cat. D18A-B

Francesco d'Antonio (Italian, 1394–c. 1433)
The Archangel Gabriel and *The Virgin Annunciate*,
c. 1420–1430
Tempera and gold leaf on panel, a pair,
each 13 x 10 ¼ in. (33 x 26 cm)
[29826] (F.1965.1.41.1–2)

Cat. D19

Francesco di Giorgio Martini (Italian, 1439–1501/2)
Fidelity, c. 1485
Fresco transferred to canvas, mounted on wood
panel, 49 ½ x 29 ¾ in. (125.7 x 75.6 cm)
[30093] (F.1965.1.22)

Cat. D20

Francesco Francia (Italian, c. 1450–after 1526)
*Madonna and Child with Saints Jerome and
Francis*, c. 1500
Oil on panel, transferred to canvas, retransferred
to panel, 24 ¾ x 18 ⅝ in. (62.9 x 47.3 cm)
[28203] (F.1965.1.23)

Cat. D21

French School, 18th century
Portrait of a Lady
Pastel on paper, 22 ½ x 18 in. (57.2 x 45.7 cm)
[29933] (F.1965.1.73)

Cat. D22

French School, c. 14th century
Saint Anthony
Fresco transferred to panel,
39 ¼ x 33 ½ in. (99.7 x 85.1 cm)
[29946] (F.1965.1.25)

Cat. D23
After French School, 15th century
(19th-century copy)
Royal Banquet Scene
Tempera on vellum, 13 ¼ x 8 ¼ in. (33.7 x 21 cm)
[30436] (F.1965.1.103)

Cat. D24
After French School, 15th century
(19th-century copy)
A Tournament Scene
Tempera on vellum, 13 ¼ x 8 ¼ in. (33.7 x 21 cm)
[30435] (F.1965.1.102)

Cat. D25
Possibly John De Critz (English, 1551/1552–1642)
(formerly attributed to Marcus Gheeraerts the
Younger (Flemish, 1561–1635)
Portrait of a Woman, c. 1605–1610
Oil on canvas, 71 x 39 in. (180.3 x 99.1 cm)
[29986] (F.1965.1.27)

Cat. D26
Attributed to Giorgione (Italian, 1477/1478–1510)
Bust Portrait of a Courtesan, c. 1509
Oil on panel, transferred to canvas,
12 ½ x 9 ⅜ in. (31.8 x 23.8 cm)
[29643] (F.1965.1.28, see also cat. 152)

Cat. D27
After Hans Holbein the Younger
(German, 1497–1543)
Sir Brian Tuke, 17th century copy
Oil on panel, 19 ½ x 15 ¼ in. (49.5 x 38.7 cm)
[30330] (F.1965.1.30)   .

Cat. D28A–B
Nathaniel Hone (English, 1718–1784)
William Henry and *Charlotte Augusta Matilda*,
1776
Oil on canvas, a pair, 30 x 25 in. (76.2 x 63.5 cm)
and 30 ¼ x 24 ¼ in. (76.8 x 61.6 cm)
[30139] (F.1965.1.31.1–2)

Cat. D29A–G
Circle of Jacques de Lajoue (French, 1687–1761)
Fête Champêtre
Suite of seven panels, oil on canvas: *Music*, 75 x
100 ½ in. (190.5 x 255.3 cm); *The Picnic*, 75 x 98
in. (190.5 x 248.9 cm); *Bird Nesting*, 75 ¼ x 47 in.
(191.1 x 119.4 cm); *The Musician*, 75 x 24 in. (190.5
x 61 cm); *The Pet Goat*, 33 ¾ x 38 ¾ in. (85.7 x
98.4 cm); *The Luncheon*, 28 x 44 ¼ in. (71.1 x 112.4
cm); *Picking Flowers*, 28 x 44 ¼ in. (71.1 x 112.4 cm)
[30089] (F.1965.1.033.1–7)

Cat. D30
Nicolas de Largillière (French, 1687–1761)
The Marquis d'Havrincourt, c. 1713
Oil on canvas, 32 x 25 ½ in. (81.3 x 64.8 cm)
[30141] (F.1965.1.34)

Cat. D31
Nicolas de Largillière (French, 1687–1761)
The Sculptor Pierre Lepautre, 1689
Oil on canvas, 64 ¼ x 50 ¾ in. (163.2 x 128.9 cm)
[30352] (F.1965.1.35)

Cat. D32 A–B
Bernardino Luini (Italian, c. 1481/82–1532)
Saint Alexander and *Saint Catherine of
Alexandria*, 1525
Oil on panel, a pair,
each 24 ⅝ x 13 ½ in. (62.5 x 34.3 cm)
[30014] (F.1965.1.39.1–2)

Cat. D33A–E
Bernardino Luini (Italian, c. 1481/82–1532)
The Story of the Val di Non, 1525
Suite of five, oil on panel: *The Vow of the Three
Friends*, 12 ⅝ x 18 ½ in. (32.1 x 47 cm); *The
Ordination*, 12 ⅝ x 11 in. (32.1 x 27.9 cm); *The
Altar of Saturn*, 12 ¾ x 16 ½ in. (32.4 x 42 cm);
The Martyrdom of Martyrius and Alexander, 12
½ x 11 ¼ in. (31.8 x 28.6 cm); *The Martyrdom of
Sisinnius*, 12 ½ x 18 ¼ in. (31.8 x 46.4 cm)
[29351] transferred 19 November 2004 to; Norton
Simon Art Foundation (M.2004.3.1–5)

D29A

D23

D24

D29B

D30

D31

D25

D26

D27

D32A

D32B

D33A

D28A

D28B

D33B

D34   D40   D35   D41   D42   D36   D43   D37   D44   D38   D45   D39   D46

Cat. D34
Bernardino Luini (Italian, c. 1481/82–1532)
Virgin and Child with Saint Catherine, 1525
Oil on canvas, mounted to panel,
48 x 35 in. (121.9 x 88.9 cm)
[29108] (F.1965.1.37)

Cat. D35
After Sebastiano Mainardi (Italian, c. 1460–1513)
Portrait of a Lady, late 15th century
Oil on canvas, transferred to panel,
23 ¼ x 12 ¾ in. (59.1 x 32.4 cm)
[29775] (F.1965.1.40)

Cat. D36
South German Master (formerly Follower of the
Master of Karlsruhe Passion)
(German, 2nd half of the 15th century)
Christ Bearing the Cross, c. 1490
Oil on panel, 20 x 14 ¾ in. (50.8 x 37.5 cm)
[30275] (F.1965.1.36)

Cat. D37
In the Style of Daniel Mijtens the Elder
(Dutch, 1590–1642)
Portrait of a Young Noblewoman, c. 1620
Oil on canvas, 77 ⅛ x 48 ½ in. (195.9 x 123.2 cm)
[29987] (F.1965.1.42)

Cat. D38
Neroccio de' Landi (Italian, 1447–1500)
Madonna and Child
Tempera and gold leaf on panel,
18 1/8 x 12 in. (46 x 30.5 cm)
[29970] (F.1965.1.45)

Cat. D39
Neroccio de' Landi (Italian, 1447–1500)
*Madonna and Child with Saints John the Baptist
and Catherine of Alexandria*, c. 1480–1485
Tempera and gold leaf on panel,
29 ½ x 24 ⅜ in. (74.9 x 61.9 cm)
[29490] (F.1965.1.44)

Cat. D40
Jean-Baptiste Oudry (French, 1686–1755)
Duchess of Choiseul as Diana, c. 1704
Oil on canvas, 54 ½ x 42 ¼ in. (138.4 x 107.3 cm)
[30185] (F.1965.1.47)

Cat. D41
Juan Pantoja de la Cruz (Spanish, 1554–1608)
*Don Diego Gomez de Sandoval y Rojas, Count of
Saldana*, c. 1598
Oil on canvas, 73 x 41 ⅛ in. (185.4 x 104.5 cm)
[30031] (F.1965.1.48)

Cat. D42
Giovanni Ambrogio da Predis (Italian, 1455–1522)
Profile of a Lady, late 15th–early 16th century
Tempera on sheepskin on panel,
23 3/16 x 12 ⅝ in. (58.9 x 32.1 cm)
[30107] (F.1965.1.51)

Cat. D43
Puccio di Simone (Italian, active c. 1343–c. 1362)
Madonna and Child with Angels
Tempera on panel, 38 x 22 ½ in. (96.5 x 57.2 cm)
[30126] (F.1965.1.46)

Cat. D44
Jusepe de Ribera (Spanish, 1591–1652)
The Sense of Touch, c. 1615–1616
Oil on canvas, 45 ⅝ x 34 ¾ in. (115.9 x 88.3 cm)
[30164] (F.1965.1.52)

Cat. D45
Hyacinthe Rigaud (French, 1659–1743)
Antoine Paris, Conseiller d'État, 1724
Oil on canvas, 58 ½ x 45 in. (148.6 x 114.3 cm)
[30140] (F.1965.1.54)

Cat. D46
After Hubert Robert (French, 1733–1808)
The Fountain, c. 1775
Oil on canvas, 26 x 20 in. (66 x 50.8 cm)
[30393] (F.1965.1.55)

Cat. D47
Antoniazzo Romano (Italian, active 1461–1508)
Madonna and Child with Infant Saint John the Baptist, c. 1480
Oil and gold leaf on panel,
18 ¾ x 13 ⅛ in. (47.6 x 33.3 cm)
[29997] (F.1965.1.057)

Cat. D48
Antoniazzo Romano (Italian, active 1461–1508)
Madonna and Child with Two Cherubim,
c. 1475–1480
Tempera on panel, 21 x 16 ½ in. (53.3 x 41.9 cm)
[29743] (F.1965.1.56)

Cat. D49
George Romney (English, 1734–1802)
Lady Hamilton as "Medea," c. 1786
Oil on canvas, 29 ¼ x 25 ¼ in. (74.3 x 64.1 cm)
[28636] (F.1965.1.58)

Cat. D50A–B
Peter Paul Rubens (Flemish, 1577–1640) and Workshop
Louis XIII and Anne of Austria, King and Queen of France, c. 1622
Oil on canvas, a pair, 46 ½ x 38 in. (118.1 x 96.5 cm) and 47 ¼ x 38 ⅛ in. (120 x 96.8 cm)
[29280 and 29761] (F.1965.1.059–60)

Cat. D51
Spinello Aretino (Italian, c. 1346–1410)
Saint Christopher with the Christ Child and Saints Anthony, Catherine, and Lucy
Tempera and gold leaf on panel,
8 x 13 ¼ in. (20.3 x 33.7 cm)
[30373] (F.1965.1.62)

Cat. D52
Follower of Jacopo Robusti, called Tintoretto (Italian, 1518–1594)
Portrait of a Venetian Nobleman
Oil on canvas, 51 x 36 ½ in. (129.5 x 92.7 cm)
[27935] (F.1965.1.63)

Cat. D53
Follower of Tiziano Vecellio, called Titian
(Italian, c. 1485–1576)
Portrait of a Man
Oil on canvas, 38 x 32 in. (96.5 x 81.3 cm)
[29351] (F.1965.1.64)

Cat. D54
Follower of Tiziano Vecellio, called Titian
(Italian, c. 1485–1576)
Portrait of a Venetian Nobleman
Oil on canvas, 42 ½ x 36 in. (108 x 91.4 cm)
[29396] (F.1965.1.65)

Cat. D55
Follower of Tiziano Vecellio, called Titian
(Italian, c. 1485–1576)
Salome with the Head of John the Baptist
Oil on canvas, 34 x 29 in. (86.4 x 73.3 cm)
[30053] (F.1965.1.066)

Cat. D56
Follower of Tiziano Vecellio, called Titian
(Italian, c. 1485–1576)
Virgin and Child with Saint John the Baptist
Oil on canvas, 38 ¼ x 32 ¼ in. (97.2 x 81.9 cm)
[29521] (F.1965.1.67)

Cat. D57
Venetian School (Italian, 14th century)
Scenes in the Life of Christ with Patron Saints,
c. 1300
Tempera and gold leaf on panel,
16 ⅜ x 26 ⅜ in. (41.6 x 67 cm)
[27262] (F.1965.1.20)

Cat. D58
Claude-Joseph Vernet (French, 1714–1789)
Bay of Naples, 1762
Oil on canvas, 28 ½ x 38 in. (72.4 x 96.5 cm)
[30444] (F.1965.1.70)

D47

D53

D48

D54

D49

D55

D50A

D50B

D56

D51

D57

D52

D58

D59

D60

D64

D65

D66

D67

D61

D68

D62

D69

Cat. D59

Follower of Antoine Vestier (French, 1740–1824)
The Countess d'Estrades
Oil on canvas, 39 x 29 ¼ in. (99.1 x 74.3 cm)
[30146] (F.1965.1.71)

Cat. D60

Adriaen Ysenbrandt (Flemish, c. 1480–1551)
Young Man with a Rosary, c. 1550
Oil on canvas, transferred to panel,
16 ¾ x 12 ½ in. (42.5 x 31.8 cm)
[30020] (F.1965.1.32)

DRAWINGS AND PRINTS

Cat. D61

Circle of Edmé Bouchardon (French, 1698–1762)
Three Girls by a Fountain
Watercolor and black chalk,
14 ½ x 6 ¾ in. (36.8 x 17.2 cm)
[30389] (F.1965.1.74)

Cat. D62

Follower of Annibale Carracci
(Italian, 1560–1609)
Three Peasants
Pen and brown ink, 10 x 7 ⅜ in. (25.4 x 18.7 cm)
[30451] (F.1965.1.76)

Cat. D63

Joshua Reynolds (English, 1723–1792)
The Earl of Erroll
Engraving, 23 ½ x 14 ¾ in. (59.7 x 37.5 cm)
(F.1965.1.143)

SCULPTURE

Cat. D64

Attributed to Agostino di Giovanni
(Italian, 1310–1347)
The Virgin Annunciate, 2nd quarter of the
14th century
Marble, 37 in. (94 cm)
[29974] (F.1965.1.104)

Cat. D65

China, 19th century
Standing Figure of a Court Lady
Porcelain, 37 in. (94 cm)
[28947] (F.1965.1.134)

Cat. D66

China, 19th century
God of Rank
Porcelain, 16 ¼ in. (41.3 cm)
[28808] (F.1965.1.135)

Cat. D67

China, 19th century
Statuette of a Priest
Porcelain, 18 ⅛ in. (46 cm)
[28812] (F.1965.1.136)

Cat. D68

Claude Michel, called Clodion
(French, 1738–1814)
Bacchante Supported by Bacchus and a Faun, 1795
Terracotta, 20 in. (50.8 cm)
[30287] (F.1965.1.105)

Cat. D69

Attributed to Desiderio da Settignano
(Italian, 1428–1464)
Beauregard Madonna, c. 1455
White Carrara marble, 20 in. (50.8 cm)
[30135] (F.1965.1.108)

Cat. D70

Martin Desjardins (French, c. 1640–1694)
Bust Portrait of Pierre Mignard
Marble, 31 in. (78.7 cm)
[29990] (F.1965.1.109)

Cat. D71

After Donatello (Italian, c. 1386–1466)
Madonna and Child
Terracotta, 27 in. (68.6 cm)
[29947] (F.1965.1.119)

Cat. D72

Flanders, 16th century
Venus with a Dolphin, c. 1560–1600
Bronze, 25 ¼ in. (64.1 cm)
[29764] (F.1965.1.121)

Cat. D73A–B

France, 16th century
A Pair of Andirons Depicting a Male and a Female
Bronze, 35 ¾ in. (90.8 cm) and 36 in. (91.4 cm)
[30258] (F.1965.1.128.1–2)

Cat. D74

Giambologna (Flemish, 1529–1608)
Rape of Proserpina (or Rape of the Sabine Woman), c. 1579
Bronze, 38 ½ in. (97.8 cm)
[28799] (F.1965.1.127)

Cat. D75

François Girardon (French, 1628–1715)
The Grand Dauphin
Marble, 38 in. (96.5 cm)
[30006] (F.1965.1.111)

Cat. D76A–B

Italy, early 17th century
War and Peace (andirons)
Bronze, a pair, 21 ¼ in. (54 cm) and
21 ½ in. (54.6 cm)
[24039] (F.1965.1.116.1–2)

Cat. D77

Jean-Louis Lemoyne (French, 1665–1755)
The Fear of Cupid's Arrows
Terracotta, 70 ½ in. (179.1 cm)
[27776] (F.1965.1.112)

Cat. D78

Leone Leoni (Italian, 1509–1590)
Bust of Giovanni Francesco Martignone
Bronze, 19 in. (48.3 cm)
[25876] (F.1965.1.123)

Cat. D79

In the Style of Mino da Fiesole (Italian, 1431–1484)
The Madonna Adoring the Child, 19th century
Marble, 23 ¼ in. (59.1 cm)
[29969] (F.1965.1.120)

Cat. D80

Northern Europe, 17th century
Flying Mercury
Bronze, 27 in. (68.6 cm)
[27970] (F.1965.1.110)

Cat. D81

Northern Italy, late 14th–early 15th century
The Virgin Annunciate
Marble, 19 ½ in. (49.5 cm)
[29530] (F.1965.1.118)

Cat. D82

Pierino da Vinci (Italian, 1530–1553)
Nilus, God of the River Nile, 16th century
Bronze, 5 ½ x 12 ½ in. (14 x 31.8 cm)
[27960] (F.1965.1.122)

Cat. D83A–C

Pisan School (Italian, 14th century)
Angel Playing Timbrels, marble, 19 ¾ in. (50.2 cm)
Angel Playing Bagpipe, marble, 20 in. (50.8 cm)
Angel Playing Zither, marble, 20 in. (50.8 cm)
[30013, 30016] (F.1965.1.113–116)

D70

D77

D78

D79

D71

D72

D73A–B

D74 D75 D80 D81

D82

D83A–C

D76A–B

D84

D85

D86

D87A–B

D88

D89

D90

D91

D92

D93

D94

D95

Cat. D84

Reims School

(French, late 13th–early 14th century)

*Saint Michael and the Dragon as
Virtue Overcoming Vice*

Polychromed wood, 36 ½ in. (92.7 cm)

[29984] (F.1965.1.126)

Cat. D85

Attributed to Luca della Robbia (Italian,
1400–1482)

Madonna and Child

Polychromed stucco bas-relief,

26 x 18 ¼ in. (66 x 46.4 cm)

[30130] (F.1965.1.107)

Cat. D86

Cast from a model by Luca della Robbia
(Italian, 1400–1482)

Virgin and Child with Six Angels

Glazed terracotta roundel, diameter 15 ¾ in. (40
cm)

[30007] (F.1965.1.106)

Cat. D87A–B

Nicolò Roccatagliata (Italian, active 1593–1636)

Mars and Minerva (andirons)

Bronze, a pair, 38 ½ in. (82.6 cm) and 37 ¾ in.
(95.9 cm)

[28051] (F.1965.1.117.1–2)

Cat. D88

In the Style of Alessandro Rondoni
(Italian, c. 1562–1634)

Don Juan of Austria

Marble, 34 in. (86.4 cm)

[25264] (F.1965.1.125)

Cat. D89

Circle of Antonio Rossellino (Italian, 1427–1478)

Tabernacle, 2nd half of the 15th century

Marble and porphyry with gilt bronze,

26 ¾ in. (67.9 cm)

[29530] (F.1965.1.124)

TAPESTRIES

Cat. D90

Flanders, Brussels

Holy Family with Music-Making Angels, c. 1520

Wool tapestry with silk and gold threads,

102 x 116 in. (259.1 x 294.6 cm)

[29628] (F.1965.1.130)

Cat. D91

Flanders, Brussels

Justice of the Emperor Trajan, c. 1510

Wool and silk tapestry with gilt silver threads,

129 x 145 in. (327.7 x 368.3 cm)

[27567] (F.1965.1.132)

Cat. D92

Flanders, Tournai

*The Arrival of Paris and Helen at the Court of
Priam, King of Troy*, c. 1500

Wool and silk tapestry,

152 x 164 in. (386.1 x 416.6 cm)

[27433] (F.1965.1.129.1)

Cat. D93

Flanders, Tournai

*Embassy of Ulysses and Diomedes from the Greeks
to the Trojans*, c. 1500

Wool and silk tapestry, 158 x 145 in. (401.3 x 368.3
cm)

[27433] (F.1965.1.129.3)

Cat. D94

Flanders, Tournai

Esther and Ahasuerus, c. 1500

Wool and silk tapestry,

134 x 120 in. (340.4 x 304.8 cm)

[27433] (F.1965.1.129.4)

Cat. D95

Flanders, Tournai

The Marriage of Paris and Helen, c. 1500

Wool and silk tapestry,

134 x 133 in. (340.4 x 337.8 cm)

[27433] (F.1965.1.129.2)

D96

Cat. D96

Flanders, Tournai
Surrender of Rome to Brennus, British King of Gaul, c. 1480
Wool tapestry with gold threads, 100 x 167 in. (254 x 424.2 cm)
[28074] (F.1965.1.131)

DECORATIVE ARTS

Cat. D97

France, 18th century
Garden Vases with Garlands and Rams' Heads
Marble, pair, each 66 in. (167.6 cm)
[27737] (F.1965.1.139.1–2)

Cat. D98

Italy
Vase and Pedestal
Marble, 17 in. (43.2 cm)
[28050] (F.1965.1.138)

Cat. D99

Spain, 18th century
Embroidered Cape with Girdle
Blue silk and silver threads,
58 x 152 in. (147.3 x 386.1 cm)
[28084] (F.1965.1.149)

DUVEEN ARTWORKS DEACCESSIONED 1965–1985

Catalogue information and correspondence on the following objects can be found in the Norton Simon Museum curatorial archives. However, for many of those works deaccessioned between 1965 and 1969, material is sparse or nonexistent. When available, the sales information is given and, whenever possible, their later history and present locations. Auction sales appear in parentheses. Dealers and Duveen stock numbers are enclosed in brackets.

PAINTINGS

Cat. D100
Anglo-Flemish School, 17th century
Lieutenant-Colonel Sir John Burlacy, c. 1620
Oil on canvas, 84 x 45 in. (213.4 x 114.3 cm)
[30002] (sale, London, Sotheby & Co.,
27 June 1973, lot 1, for $4,410)

Cat. D101
Anglo-Flemish School, 17th century
Captain Sir Edward Harwood, c. 1620
Oil on canvas, 84 x 43 ¼ in. (213.4 x 109.9 cm)
[30000] (sale, London, Sotheby & Co.,
27 June 1973, lot 2, for $1,960)

Cat. D102
Anglo-Flemish School, 16th century
Portrait of a Noblewoman, c. 1570
Oil on panel, 16 ½ x 13 in. (41.9 x 33 cm)
[30407] Sold February 1970 to; private collection,
California.

Cat. D103
Jean-Baptiste Belin the Elder (French, 1653–1715)
A Still Life of Flowers
Oil on canvas, 50 x 39 ⅜ in. (127 x 100 cm)
[30395] (sale, New York, Parke-Bernet Galleries,
8 May 1971, lot 214, for $2,000)

D99

D101

D100

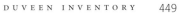
D103

D104

D110

D105

D111

D106

D112

D107

D113A

D108

D113B

D109

D114

Cat. D104
Alexis Simon Belle (French, c. 1674–1734)
Duc de Chartres
Oil on canvas, 32 ½ x 26 in. (82.6 x 66 cm)
[30328] Sold December 1966 for $600 to;
[David Colombo, Milan].

Cat. D105
Attributed to Giovanni Bellini
(Italian, c. 1430–1516)
Virgin and Child
Oil on panel, 30 ⅜ x 21 ¼ in. (77.2 x 54 cm)
[28208] Sold 2 May 1967 for $22,500 to;
[David Colombo, Milan].

Cat. D106
Biagio d'Antonio (Italian, 1446–1516)
Virgin and Child with Saint John
Oil on panel, 22 ¾ x 15 ¾ in. (57.8 x 40 cm)
[29512] (sale, London, Sotheby Parke Bernet
& Co., 16 July 1980, lot 77, for $38,000)

Cat. D107
Jan Frans van Bloemen (Flemish, 1662–1740)
A Landscape
Oil on canvas, 19 ⅞ x 26 ¼ in. (50.5 x 66.7 cm)
[30447] Sold March 1966 for $800 to; [De Castro,
London].

Cat. D108
Jan Baptist Bosschaert (Flemish, 1667–c. 1746)
A Still Life of Flowers
Oil on canvas, 46 x 39 in. (116.8 x 99.1 cm)
[28287] (sale, New York, Parke-Bernet Galleries,
8 May 1971, lot 213, for $2,600). (sale, Munich,
Hampel Kunstauktionen, 4 July 2008, lot 231, for
$27,700).

Cat. D109
Sandro Botticelli (Italian, c. 1444–1510)
(previously attributed to Piero di Cosimo)
*The Adoration with the Arrival of the Shepherds
and the Flight into Egypt*, c. 1500
Oil on panel, diameter 47 ½ in. (120.7 cm)
[29962] Sold 27 December 1974 for $177,500 to;
[Spencer Samuels, New York, for] the Sarah
Campbell Blaffer Foundation, Houston.

Cat. D110
Attributed to Sandro Botticelli
(Italian, c. 1444–1510)
Man in a Red Coat
Oil on panel, 18 x 13 ½ in. (45.7 x 34.3 cm)
[28211] Sold 9 September 1969 for $20,000 to;
[David Colombo, Milan].

Cat. D111
Attributed to Sandro Botticelli
(Italian, c. 1444–1510)
Virgin and Child
Tempera on panel, 14 ¾ x 11 ¼ in. (37.5 x 28.6 cm)
[29537] Sold 14 June 1977 for $50,000 to; [Spencer
Samuels, New York]. (sale, New York, Christie's,
11 January 1991, lot 4, for $231,000).

Cat. D112
Attributed to Sandro Botticelli
(Italian, c. 1444–1510)
Virgin and Child with Saint John
Oil on panel, diameter 33 ½ in. (85.1 cm)
[29532] Sold June 1970 for $27,500 to; [David
Colombo, Milan].

Cat. D113A–C
François Boucher (French, 1703–1770)
*Flora (The Floral Crown), Helen (The Love Letter),
Pomona (The Basket of Fruit)*, c. 1745
Oil on canvas, three panels: 46 x 38 in.
(116.8 x 96.5 cm); 45 ¾ x 58 ¼ in. (116.2 x 148 cm);
45 x 36 in. (114.3 x 91.4 cm)
[30112] Sold 11 April 1966 for $150,000 to;
[Wildenstein, New York]; private collection,
New York.

Cat. D114
Attributed to François Boucher
(French, 1703–1770)
The Old Mill
Oil on canvas, 23 ¾ x 25 in. (60.3 x 63.5 cm)
[30160] (sale, London, Sotheby Parke Bernet
& Co., 16 April 1980, lot 46, for $6,663)

Cat. D115
Attributed to Domenico Campagnola
(Italian, c. 1500–1564)
A Woody Landscape with Saint Jerome
Oil on canvas, 28 x 38 ¾ in. (71.1 x 98.4 cm)
[30063] (sale, London, Sotheby Parke Bernet
& Co., 16 July 1980, lot 17, for $3,332)

Cat. D116
Conrad von Soest (German, c. 1360–1422)
Saint Peter the Apostle
Oil on panel, 23 x 14 in. (58.4 x 35.6 cm)
[30263] (sale, London, Sotheby Parke Bernet
& Co., 16 April 1980, lot 33, for $6,663)

Cat. D117
Richard Cosway (English, 1742–1821)
Portrait of a Lady
Oil on canvas, 30 x 25 in. (76.2 x 63.5 cm)
[30248] (sale, London, Sotheby & Co.,
27 June 1973, lot 22, for $2,450)

Cat. D118
Attributed to Lucas Cranach the Younger
(German, 1515–1586)
The Conversion of Saint Paul
Oil on panel, 37 x 32 ⅝ in. (94 x 82.9 cm)
[30153] (Sale, London, Sotheby Parke Bernet
& Co., 9 December 1981, lot 45, for $61,380 to);
anonymous foundation (sale, London, Sotheby's,
9 July 2008, lot 63, unsold).

Cat. D119
Carlo Crivelli (Italian, c. 1435–c. 1495)
Madonna and Child
Tempera on panel,
17 ½ x 15 ⅛ in. (44.5 x 38.4 cm)
[29973] Sold 9 September 1969 for $10,000 to;
[David Colombo, Milan].

Cat. D120
Bernardo Daddi (Italian, c. 1280–1348)
Virgin and Child
Tempera on panel, 35 ½ x 20 in. (90.2 x 50.8 cm)
[28186] Sold 29 December 1978 for $80,000 to;
[Spencer Samuels, New York, for] the Sarah
Campbell Blaffer Foundation, Houston.

Cat. D121
Nathaniel Dance-Holland (English, 1735– 1811)
(formerly attributed to Thomas Gainsborough)
*John Russell, Fourth Duke of Bedford, and His
Grandson*
Oil on canvas, 91 ½ x 58 ¼ in. (232.4 x 148 cm)
[28582] (sale, London, Sotheby & Co.,
27 June 1973, lot 18, for $17,150)

Cat. D122
Attributed to Domenico di Michelino
(Italian, 1417–1491)
Madonna and Child with Four Saints
Tempera and gold leaf on panel,
37 x 22 ½ in. (94 x 57.2 cm)
[29996] Sold September 1969 for $17,500 to;
[David Colombo, Milan].

Cat. D123
Dosso Dossi (Italian, c. 1490–1542)
Man with a Large Hat
Oil on canvas, 28 ¾ x 23 ¼ in. (73 x 59.1 cm)
[30358] Sold 21 February 1975 for $45,000 to;
[Dino Fabbri, New York].

Cat. D124
Attributed to Circle of Duccio di Buoninsegna
(Italian, c. 1260–c. 1318)
Madonna and Child
Oil on panel with gold leaf,
37 x 24 ½ in. (94 x 62.2 cm)
[30276] (sale, London, Sotheby's, 3 July 1985, lot 4,
sold after the sale for $7,663)

D115

D120

D116

D121

D117

D122

D123

D118

D124

D119

D125

D126

D127

D128

D129

D130

D131

D132

D133

D134

D135

D136

Cat. D125
Anthony van Dyck (Flemish, 1599–1641)
Amalia, Princess of Orange
Oil on canvas, 45 x 38 in. (114.3 x 96.5 cm)
[29611] (sale, London, Sotheby & Co.,
12 December 1973, lot 42, for $42,500). (sale,
London, Sotheby's, 1 November 1978, lot 66,
unsold). [Brain Trust, Inc., Tokyo, sold 1 December
1990 to]; the Tokyo Fuji Art Museum.

Cat. D126
Anthony van Dyck (Flemish, 1599–1641)
Ann Carr, Countess of Bedford
Oil on canvas, 41 ½ x 32 in. (105.4 x 81.3 cm)
[29695] (sale, London, Sotheby & Co.,
27 June 1973, lot 3, for $83,300). [Mai Trading
Company, sold 30 November 1989 to]; the Tokyo
Fuji Art Museum.

Cat. D127
Anthony van Dyck (Flemish, 1599–1641)
George Hay, Second Earl of Kinnoul
Oil on canvas, 86 x 52 in. (218.4 x 132.1 cm)
[28505] (sale, London, Sotheby & Co.,
27 June 1973, lot 4, for $9,800)

Cat. D128
Francesco Francia (Italian, c. 1450–after 1526)
Virgin and Child with Saint Catherine
Oil on panel, 25 ½ x 20 ¾ in. (64.8 x 52.7 cm)
[29476] (sale, London, Sotheby Parke Bernet
& Co., 16 July 1980, lot 125, for $19,005)

Cat. D129
Thomas Gainsborough (English, 1727–1788)
Sir Francis Bassett, Baron de Dunstanville
Oil on canvas, 30 x 25 in. (76.2 x 63.5 cm)
[29607] (sale, London, Sotheby & Co.,
27 June 1973, lot 7, for $2,695)

Cat. D130
Thomas Gainsborough (English, 1727–1788)
The Cruttenden Sisters, Elizabeth and Sarah
Oil on canvas, 44 ¼ x 58 ¾ in. (112.4 x 149.2 cm)
[29400] (sale, London, Sotheby & Co.,
27 June 1973, lot 5, for $269,500)

Cat. D131
Thomas Gainsborough (English, 1727–1788)
Theodosia Magill, Countess Clanwilliam, 1765
Oil on canvas, 50 x 40 in. (127 x 101.6 cm)
[29756] (sale, London, Sotheby & Co.,
27 June 1973, lot 6, for $58,800 to); [Roy Miles
Fine Paintings, London, sold to]; [the trade,
London, sold to]; private collection.

Cat. D132
Thomas Gainsborough (English, 1727–1788)
The Watering Place, c. 1773
Oil on canvas, 40 x 50 in. (101.6 x 127 cm)
[30326] (sale, London, Sotheby & Co.,
28 November 1973, lot 87, for $1,880)

Cat. D133
Attributed to Thomas Gainsborough
(English, 1727–1788)
A Gentleman in Outdoor Costume
Oil on canvas, 50 ¾ x 40 in. (128.9 x 101.6 cm)
[30149] (sale, New York, Parke-Bernet Galleries,
23 February 1968, lot 92, for $832)

Cat. D134
Attributed to Thomas Gainsborough
(English, 1727–1788)
A View of Suffolk with Cattle and Figures
Oil on canvas, 47 ½ x 58 ½ in. (120.7 x 148.6 cm)
[30005] (sale, London, Sotheby & Co., 28
November 1973, lot 74, for $700)

Cat. D135
Attributed to Giorgione (Italian, 1477/1478–1510)
Portrait of a Man
Oil on canvas, 26 ½ x 20 ½ in. (67.3 x 52.1 cm)
[28611] Sold June 1970 for $30,000 to; [David
Colombo, Milan].

Cat. D136
Francesco Granacci (Italian, 1477–1543)
(previously attributed to Mariotto Albertinelli)
Virgin and Child Enthroned
Tempera on panel, 64 x 34 ¼ in. (162.6 x 87 cm)
[27736] Traded 4 March 1974, in partial payment
for Jan Lievens, *Panoramic Landscape* (cat. 1007),
to; [Newhouse Galleries, New York].

Cat. D137
John Hoppner (English, 1758–1810)
Elizabeth, Countess of Mexborough
Oil on canvas, 40 x 30 in. (101.6 x 76.2 cm)
[29370]] (sale, London, Sotheby & Co.,
27 June 1973, lot 8, for $17,150)

Cat. D138
John Hoppner (English, 1758–1810)
Harriet Serle as Bo-Peep
Oil on canvas, 50 x 40 in. (127 x 101.6 cm)
[28004] (sale, London, Sotheby & Co.,
27 June 1973, lot 9 for $14,700). (sale, London,
Sotheby's, 27 November 2003, lot 167, unsold).
(sale, Edinburgh, Lyon & Turnbull, 7 May 2008,
lot 271, unsold).

Cat. D139A–I
Italy, 15th-century style
Illuminated Initials from an Antiphonary
2 items [30428–29], gifts 1965 to; Elmer Belt
Library of Vinciana, University of California,
Los Angeles; 7 items [30413–14, 30416, 30419,
30424–25, 30431] (sale, London, Sotheby & Co.,
8 July 1974, lots 18–24, for $6,700)

Cat. D140
Johannes Janson (Dutch, 1729–1784)
The Swanenburg House
Oil on panel, 13 ⅞ x 17 ¼ in. (35.2 x 43.8 cm)
[30083] Sold February 1970 to; private collection,
California.

Cat. D141
Thomas Jones (Welsh, 1742–1803)
Lake Avernus in Campania
Oil on canvas, 37 x 47 ¼ in. (94 x 120 cm)
[30158] (sale, London, Sotheby & Co., 28
November 1973, lot 81, for $1,057)

Cat. D142A–B
Nicolas Lancret (French, 1690–1743)
The Love Song and *Lovers in a Landscape
with a Dog*
Oil on canvas, a pair, each 24 x 28 ¾ in.
(61 x 73 cm)
[30345] Sold June 1966 for $10,000 to; The Union
Bank of Switzerland.

Cat. D143
Jean-Baptiste Le Prince (French, 1734–1781)
A Seascape Caprice
Oil on canvas, 21 ¾ x 16 ¼ in. (55.3 x 41.3 cm)
[30408] Sold 1 March 1966 for $2,800 to;
[De Castro, London].

Cat. D144
Attributed to Jean-Michel Liotard
(Swiss, 1702–1796)
Innocence
Oil on canvas, 17 ½ x 22 ½ in. (44.5 x 57.2 cm)
[30442] Sold February 1970 to; private collection,
California.

Cat. D145
Attributed to Gabriel Metsu (Dutch, 1629–1667)
A Sportsman Presenting Game to a Lady
Oil on canvas, 22 x 16 ¾ in. (55.9 x 42.6 cm)
[30347] Sold February 1970 to; private collection,
Los Angeles. (sale, Saint-Dié, France, Morel A &
G, 17 June 2007, lot 276, for $2,000).

Cat. D146A–B
George Morland (English, 1763–1804)
The Peddler and *The Woodcutter*, c. 1792
Oil on canvas, 34 x 46 ¾ in
(86.4 x 118.8 cm) and 23 x 27 in. (58.4 x 68.6 cm)
[30318; 30150] (sale, London, Sotheby & Co., 27
June 1973, lot 26, for $6,125 and lot 27 for $2,450)

Cat. D147
Jean-Marc Nattier (French, 1685–1766)
Countess de Brac as Aurora
Oil on canvas, 51 ½ x 38 ½ in. (130.8 x 97.8 cm)
[27274] (sale, London, Sotheby Parke Bernet,
& Co., 16 July 1980, lot 75, for $8,330)

Cat. D148
Thomas Patch (English, 1725–1782)
A Panoramic View of Florence
Oil on canvas, 37 ¼ x 62 ½ in. (94.6 x 158.8 cm)
[30449] (sale, London, Sotheby & Co.,
27 June 1973, lot 25, for $22,050)

D137

D143

D138

D144

D139C

D146B

D141

D147

D142A

D148

D142B

D149

D150

D151

D152

D153

D154

D155

D156

D157

D158

D159

Cat. D149
Francesco Pesellino (Italian, 1422–1457)
Virgin and Child
Tempera on panel, 9 ⅛ x 6 ¾ in. (23.2 x 17.2 cm)
[29530] Used in trade 30 December 1977 with
a value of $85,000 as partial payment for
Rembrandt, *Portrait of a Bearded Man in a
Wide-Brimmed Hat* (cat. 1489) to;
[E. V. Thaw & Co., New York, sold, 1983 to];
private collection, U.S.A. (sale, New York,
Sotheby's, 24 January 2002, lot 143, unsold), (sale,
London, Sotheby's, 10 July 2002, lot 55, unsold).

Cat. D150
Matthew William Peters (English, 1741–1814)
Marie Antoinette Herry
Oil on canvas, 52 ½ x 41 ½ in. (133.4 x 105.4 cm)
[27301] (sale, London, Sotheby & Co.,
27 June 1973, lot 19, for $6,321)

Cat. D151
Henry Raeburn (Scottish, 1756–1823)
Mrs. John Hutchinson Ferguson
Oil on canvas, 35 x 27 in. (88.9 x 68.6 cm)
[28654] (sale, London, Sotheby & Co.,
27 June 1973, lot 20, for $7,350 to); McLaren. (sale,
London, 27 November 1974, lot 75 to: [Old Hall
Gallery, London, to]; private collection, U.K.
(sale, London, Sotheby's, 29 April 2009, lot 1, for
$24,845).

Cat. D152
Henry Raeburn (Scottish, 1756–1823)
James Harrower with His Wife and Son
Oil on canvas, 51 ½ x 41 ¾ in. (130.8 x 106.1 cm)
[28073] (sale, London, Sotheby & Co.,
27 June 1973, lot 21, for $2,450)

Cat. D153
Attributed to Joshua Reynolds (English,
1723–1792)
James, 15th Earl of Erroll
Oil on canvas, 93 ¾ x 58 in. (238.1 x 147.3 cm)
[29529] (sale, London, Sotheby & Co.,
27 June 1973, lot 23, for $4,900 to); private
collection, U.K. (sale, London, Christie's, 20 April
1990, lot 29 for £150,000 to); private collection,

U.K. (sale, London, Christie's, 7 December 2007,
lot 228, for $121,644).

Cat. D154
Attributed to Joshua Reynolds (English,
1723–1792)
Miss Frances Shepherd
Oil on canvas, 30 ½ x 25 in. (77.5 x 63.5 cm)
[29638] (sale, London, Sotheby's, 17 July 1985, lot
549, for $1,055)

Cat. D155
Johan Richter (Swedish, 1665–1745)
Church of San Giorgio Maggiore
Oil on canvas, 23 x 38 in. (58.4 x 96.5 cm)
[30445] (sale, London, Sotheby Parke Bernet
& Co., 16 April 1980, lot 40, for $16,657)

Cat. D156
George Romney (English, 1734–1802)
Miss Kitty Calcraft, c. 1787
Oil on canvas, 49 x 39 in. (124.5 x 99.1 cm)
[28390] (sale, London, Sotheby & Co.,
27 June 1973, lot 10, for $24,500 to); [Sotheby
Parke Bernet & Co., London (sale, New York,
Sotheby Parke Bernet, 6 March 1975, lot 24, for
$8,000 to)]; Mr. and Mrs. Arch Madsen, Salt
Lake City, gift, 1975 to; Brigham Young University
Museum of Art, Provo, Utah.

Cat. D157
George Romney (English, 1734–1802)
Barbara, Marchioness Donegal, c. 1792
Oil on canvas, 94 ¾ x 58 ½ in. (240.7 x 148.6 cm)
[28376] (sale, London, Sotheby & Co.,
27 June 1973, lot 15, for $2,450 to); J. G. Hood
(sale, London, Christie's, 19 November 1976,
lot 82, unsold). private collection, U.S.A. (sale,
New York, Sotheby's, 24 January 2008, lot 67, for
$577,000).

Cat. D158
George Romney (English, 1734–1802)
Madame de Genlis
Oil on canvas, 23 ½ x 20 in. (59.7 x 50.8 cm)
[29792] (sale, London, Sotheby & Co.,
27 June 1973, lot 14, for $17,150)

Cat. D159
George Romney (English, 1734–1802)
Lady Hamilton as a Bacchante
Oil on canvas, 30 x 25 in. (76.2 x 63.5 cm)
[29192] (sale, London, Sotheby & Co.,
28 November 1973, lot 77, for $700)

Cat. D160
George Romney (English, 1734–1802)
Lady Hamilton as a Bacchante
Oil on canvas, 50 x 40 in. (127 x 101.6 cm)
[29115] (sale, London, Sotheby & Co.,
27 June 1973, lot 12, for $4,410)

Cat. D161
George Romney (English, 1734–1802)
Lady Hamilton as Mirth
Oil on canvas, 56 ¼ x 45 ¼ in. (142.9 x 114.9 cm)
[29757] (sale, London, Sotheby & Co.,
27 June 1973, lot 16, for $4,900)

Cat. D162
George Romney (English, 1734–1802)
The Milner Sisters
Oil on canvas, 68 x 52 in. (172.7 x 132.1 cm)
[27769] (sale, London, Sotheby & Co.,
27 June 1973, lot 11, for $2,450)

Cat. D163
George Romney (English, 1734–1802)
Georgiana Anne, Marchioness Townshend
Oil on canvas, 50 x 40 in. (127 x 101.6 cm)
[29366] Sold 5 July 1973 for $32,000 to;
Earl Townshend.

Cat. D164
George Romney (English, 1734–1802)
Georgiana Anne, Marchioness Townshend
Oil on canvas, 29 x 24 in. (73.7 x 61 cm)
[28513] (sale, London, Sotheby & Co.,
27 June 1973, lot 17, for $2,450)

Cat. D165
Peter Paul Rubens (Flemish, 1577–1640)
*Triumph of the Sacrament over Ignorance
and Blindness*
Oil on canvas, transferred from panel,
21 ½ x 35 ⅞ in. (54.6 x 91.1 cm)

[30152] Traded 3 March 1970 for $37,000 in
partial payment for Francisco de Goya, *Saint
Jerome in Penitence* (cat. 728) to; [Spencer
Samuels, New York].

Cat. D166
Jean-Frédéric Schall (French, 1752–1825)
The Dancer (Mlle Colombe)
Oil on canvas, 12 ¼ x 9 ½ in. (31.1 x 24.1 cm)
[29863] (sale, New York, Parke-Bernet Galleries,
8 May 1971, lot 215, for $8,000)

Cat. D167
Attributed to Joseph Mallord William Turner
(English, 1775–1851)
A Visionary Scene of Carthage, c. 1835–1840
Oil on canvas, 40 ½ x 50 in. (102.9 x 127 cm)
[30288] (sale, London, Sotheby & Co.,
28 November 1973, lot 84, for $1,645)

Cat. D168
Alfred Vickers (English, 1786–1868)
A Pastoral Landscape
Oil on panel, 11 ½ x 16 ½ in. (29.2 x 41.9 cm)
[30353] Sold February 1970 to; private collection,
California.

Cat. D169
Attributed to Jan de Vos (Flemish, 1460–1533)
Mystic Marriage of Saint Catherine
Oil on panel, 27 ¾ x 22 in. (70.5 x 55.9 cm)
[30237] (sale, London, Sotheby Parke Bernet
& Co., 16 April 1980, lot 27, for $84,398)

Cat. D170
Thomas Wijck (Dutch, 1616–1677)
A Country Inn
Oil on panel, 22 x 26 ⅜ in. (55.9 x 67 cm)
[30446] Sold February 1970 to; private collection,
California.

Cat. D171
Attributed to Richard Wilson (English, 1714–1782)
Stratford-on-Avon
Oil on canvas, 21 x 30 ¼ in. (53.3 x 76.8 cm)
[28056] Sold February 1970 to; private collection,
California.

D160

D161

D166

D162

D163

D167

D164

D169

D171

D165

D172

D173

D174B

D174C

D174D

D175

D177

D179A

D179B

D180A

D181A

D181B

DRAWINGS AND WATERCOLORS

Cat. D172
Agostino Carracci (Italian, 1557–1602)
Jesus and Magdalene
Brown ink, heightened with white,
3 ¾ x 3 ⅛ in. (9.5 x 7.9 cm)
[30392] (sale, London, Christie's,
11 December 1980, lot 49, for $78)

Cat. D173
John Sell Cotman (English, 1782–1842)
Shimmering Water
Watercolor, 10 ¾ x 18 ¼ in. (27.3 x 46.4 cm)
[30452] (sale, London, Christie's,
16 December 1980, lot 30, for $79)

Cat. D174A–F
David Cox (English, 1783–1859)
Blarney Castle and *Woodland Scene*
Watercolor, two, each 4 x 6 ¼ in. (10.2 x 15.9 cm)
Coast, River, Castles, Castles
Watercolor, four, each 3 x 4 ½ in. (7.6 x 11.4 cm)
[30453; 30454] (sale, London, Christie's,
16 December 1980, lot 18, for $129)

Cat. D175
Antoine Coypel (French, 1661–1722)
Two Female Figures
Red chalk, 6 ⅛ x 3 ½ in. (15.6 x 8.9 cm)
[30391] (sale, London, Christie's,
11 December 1980, lot 49, for $100)

Cat. D176A–B
Copley Fielding (English, 1787–1855)
Near Glengyle
Watercolor, two, each 9 x 13 ¼ in. (22.9 x 33.7 cm)
[30456] (sale, London, Christie's,
16 December 1980, lot 6, for $159)

Cat. D177
John Gendall (English, 1790–1865)
Exmouth, Devon
Watercolor, 4 ¾ x 7 ¼ in. (12.1 x 18.4 cm)
[30455] (sale, London, Christie's,
16 December 1980, lot 30, for $100)

Cat. D178
Attributed to Giacomo Guardi
(Italian, 1764–1835)
Arch with Figures
Drawing, dimensions unknown
[30388] (sale, London, Christie's,
11 December 1980, lot 49, for $100)

Cat. D179A–B
Jean-Baptiste Mallet (French, 1759–1835)
Artist Painting (The Little Donatrix) and *Musicale*
Gouache, 12 x 15 in. (30.5 x 38.1 cm) and 12 x 17 in.
(30.5 x 43.2 cm)
[29789] (sale, London, Sotheby & Co.,
27 June 1974, lots 44 and 45, for $10,965)

Cat. D180A–B
Jean-Baptiste Pillement (French, 1728–1808)
River Scenes
Colored chalk, two, each 13 ¼ x 17 in.
(33.7 x 43.2 cm)
[30397] (sale, London, Sotheby & Co.,
27 June 1974, lots 50 and 51, for $8,343)

Cat. D181A–E
François Quesnel (French, c. 1543–1619)
Five Portraits
Pencil and colored crayon on paper, 12 x 8 ½ in.
(30.5 x 21.6 cm); 10 ¾ x 8 ¼ in. (27.3 x 21 cm);
11 ½ x 8 ¼ in. (29.2 x 21 cm); 12 x 8 ½ in.
(30.5 x 21.6 cm); 9 ½ x 7 ½ in. (24.1 x 19.1 cm)
(sale, London, Sotheby & Co., 27 June 1974,
Christine of Lorraine [24952], lot 8, for $6,198;
Nobleman [30174], lot 9, for $6,674; *Diane
d'Estrées* [26315], lot 10, for $700; *Henrietta
de Balzac* [26315], lot 11, for $763; *Françoise de
Montmorency* [26315], lot 12, for $1,907)

Cat. D182
Salvatore Rosa (Italian, 1615–1673)
Scene from Ancient History
Brown ink, 7 ⅛ x 7 ¾ in. (18.1 x 19.7 cm)
[30387] (sale, London, Christie's,
11 December 1980, lot 50, for $219)

Cat. D183
Louis Rolland Trinquesse (French, 1746–1800)
Family Scene
Brown ink, 9 ¼ x 7 in. (23.5 x 17.8 cm)
[30396] (sale, London, Christie's,
11 December 1980, lot 83, for $596)

SCULPTURE

Cat. D184
After Benedetto da Maiano (Italian, 1442–1497)
Relief of the Madonna and Child
Stucco, diameter 23 in. (58.4 cm)
[30183] (sale, New York, Parke-Bernet Galleries,
7 May 1971, lot 113a, for $700)

Cat. D185
After Jean-Jacques Caffieri (French, 1725–1792)
Bust of the Prince de Condé
Terracotta, 30 ½ in. (77.5 cm)
[29980] (sale, New York, Parke-Bernet Galleries,
7 May 1971, lot 130, for $4,500)

Cat. D186
Attributed to Giovanni da Campione
Madonna and Child
Marble, 13 ½ in. (34.3 cm)
[30038] (sale, New York, Parke-Bernet Galleries,
7 May 1971, lot 107, for $2,200)

Cat. D187
Attributed to Étienne-Maurice Falconet
(French, 1716–1791)
Figure of a Bather
Marble, 41 ½ in. (105.4 cm)
[25895] (sale, New York, Parke-Bernet Galleries,
7 May 1971, lot 127, for $4,600)

Cat. D188
Attributed to Étienne-Maurice Falconet
(French, 1716–1791)
The Toilet of Venus
Polychromed wax, 17 in. (43.2 cm)
[29249] (sale, New York, Parke-Bernet Galleries,
7 May 1971, lot 128a, for $1,800)

Cat. D189
Florence, late 15th century style (formerly
attributed to Andrea del Verrocchio [Italian,
1435–1488])
Bust of a Lady
Terracotta, 23 ½ in. (59.7 cm)
[30111] (sale, New York, Parke-Bernet Galleries,
7 May 1971, lot 111, for $1,200)

Cat. D190A–B
France, 16th century style
Saint Claude and *Saint Sylvester*
Limestone, 31 in. (78.7 cm) and 37 in. (94 cm)
[30125] (sale, New York, Parke-Bernet Galleries,
7 May 1971, lot 117, for $850)

Cat. D191
France, 16th century style
Saint Adrian and the Lion, 19th century
Limestone, 34 in. (86.4 cm)
[29999] (sale, New York, Parke-Bernet Galleries,
7 May 1971, lot 118, for $300)

Cat. D192A–B
France, Gothic style
Two Figures of the Madonna and Child
Limestone, 69 in. (175.3 cm) and 70 in. (177.8 cm)
[29196, 29344] (sale, New York, Parke-Bernet
Galleries, 7 May 1971, lot 109, for $400, and lot
110, for $700)

Cat. D193
France, Gothic style
Head of a King
Marble, 13 ½ in. (34.3 cm)
[29527] (sale, New York, Parke-Bernet Galleries,
7 May 1971, lot 106, for $400)

D182

D183

D184

D188

D189

D185

D190A–B

D186

D191

D192B

D187

D193

D194

D200

D195

D197

D198A-B

D201A-B

D202

D199

D203A-B

D205

Cat. D194
After Giambologna (Flemish, 1529–1608)
Mercury
Bronze, 28 ½ in. (72.4 cm)
[30386] (sale, New York, Parke-Bernet Galleries,
7 May 1971, lot 120, for $1,200)

Cat. D195
Jean-Antoine Houdon (French, 1741–1828)
Voltaire, c. 1778
Marble, 18 ¾ in. (47.6 cm)
[29518] (sale, New York, Parke-Bernet Galleries,
7 May 1971, lot 133, for $9,000)

Cat. D196
Italy, 17th century
Bust of a Roman Emperor
Bronze and marble, 31 ½ in. (80 cm)
[27957] (sale, New York, Parke-Bernet Galleries,
7 May 1971, lot 124, for $12,000)

Cat. D197
Attributed to Pierre Julien (French, 1731–1804)
A Young Girl Holding Two Doves
Terracotta, 67 ½ in. (171.5 cm)
[29517] (sale, New York, Parke-Bernet Galleries,
7 May 1971, lot 129, for $2,200)

Cat. D198A–B
After Pierre Legros (French, 1666 1719)
Earth and *Water*, late 17th century
Bronze, a pair, each 7 ¼ in. (18.4 cm)
[25622] (sale, New York, Parke-Bernet Galleries,
7 May 1971, lot 126, for $1,300)

Cat. D199
Jean-Baptiste Lemoyne (French, 1704–1778)
Bust of Jean-Florent de Vallières, c. 1753
Terracotta, 28 in. (71.1 cm)
[30033] (sale, New York, Parke-Bernet Galleries,
7 May 1971, lot 131, for $1,900)

Cat. D200
Jean-Baptiste Lemoyne (French, 1704–1778)
Bust of Madame Victoire, c. 1775
Marble, 27 in. (68.6 cm)
[30015] (sale, New York, Parke-Bernet Galleries,
7 May 1971, lot 132, for $4,000)

Cat. D201A–B
After Joseph Charles Marin (French, 1759–1834)
Busts of Bacchantes, 19th century
Bronze, a pair, each 19 in. (48.3 cm)
[30035] (sale, New York, Parke-Bernet Galleries,
7 May 1971, lot 128, for $950)

Cat. D202
Northern Italy, 16th century style
Relief of a Young Man, 19th century
Marble, 13 in. (33 cm)
[29530] (sale, New York, Parke-Bernet Galleries,
7 May 1971, lot 112, for $1,000)

Cat. D203A–B
Lower Rhine, early 16th century
The Virgin and *Saint John*
Wood, a pair, each 53 ½ in. (135.9 cm)
[30163] (sale, New York, Parke-Bernet Galleries,
7 May 1971, lot 115, for $1,400)

Cat. D204A–B
Upper Rhine, 15th century
Unidentified Saint and *Saint Florian*
Wood, a pair, each 46 in. (116.8 cm)
[29377] (sale, New York, Parke-Bernet Galleries,
7 May 1971, lot 114, for $5,600)

Cat. D205
School of Nicolò Roccatagliata
(Italian, active 1593–1636)
Group of a Warrior and a Demon
Bronze, 30 in. (76.2 cm)
[25877] (sale, New York, Parke-Bernet Galleries,
7 May 1971, lot 121, for $4,200)

TAPESTRIES

Cat. D206
Flanders, Brussels
The Justice of Trajan, early 16th century
Wool and silk tapestry,
140 x 162 in. (355.6 x 411.5 cm)
[28284] (sale, New York, Parke-Bernet Galleries,
8 May 1971, lot 225, for $16,000)

Cat. D207
Flanders, Brussels
The Prodigal Son, early 16th century
Wool and silk tapestry,
130 x 158 in. (330.2 x 401.3 cm)
[28570] (sale, New York, Parke-Bernet Galleries,
8 May 1971, lot 226, for $18,000)

Cat. D208
Flanders, Brussels
The Return of the Prodigal Son (The Fountain),
early 16th century
Wool and silk tapestry,
156 x 123 in. (396.2 x 312.4 cm)
[28504] (sale, New York, Parke-Bernet Galleries, 8
May 1971, lot 227, for $18,000)

Cat. D209
Flanders, Brussels
King Solomon and the Queen of Sheba, early 16th
century
Wool and silk tapestry,
136 x 188 in. (345.4 x 477.5 cm)
[28569] (sale, New York, Parke-Bernet Galleries, 8
May 1971, lot 228, for $20,000)

Cat. D210
Flanders, Tournai
The Lord of the Manor (Return from the Hunt),
late 15th century
Wool and silk tapestry,
136 x 156 in. (345.4 x 396.2 cm)
[28503] (sale, New York, Parke-Bernet Galleries, 8
May 1971, lot 224, for $45,000)

Cat. D211A–D
France, 16th century
*The Story of King David: David and Bathsheba
Reproached by Nathan, Bathsheba at the Bath;
Uriah Killed in Battle*, 156 x 192 in. (396.2 x 487.7
cm); *David Hears of the Death of Saul*, 136 x 186
in. (345.4 x 472.4 cm); *The Death of Absalom;
David Instructs Joab, Abishai, and Ittai*, 140 x 124
in. (355.6 x 315 cm); *David and the Gideonites;
David Returns to Jerusalem*, 133 x 128 in.
(337.8 x 325.1 cm)
Wool and silk tapestry, 4 panels
[29718] Sold 3 November 1967 with a Persian rose
ground carpet [27544] for $30,000 to; [Sarkis
Yakoubian, New York].

Cat. D212A–B
France, Aubusson, after cartoons by François
Boucher (French, 1703–1770) and floral borders
by Jean-Baptiste Huet (French, 1745–1811)
Swing and *Maypole*, c. 1780
Wool and silk tapestry, 2 panels, 86 x 70 in.
(218.4 x 177.8 cm) and 86 x 92 in.
(218.4 x 233.7 cm)
[28581] (sale, London, Christie's, 13 December
1973, lot 153, for $2,315)

Cat. D213
France, Beauvais
The Basket of Fruit (after François Boucher),
mid-18th century
Wool and silk tapestry,
130 x 95 in. (330.3 x 241.3 cm)
[27566] (sale, New York, Parke-Bernet Galleries,
8 May 1971, lot 231, for $10,000)

Cat. D214A–D
France, Beauvais
Set of four tapestries, late 18th century
The Cherry Pickers, 97 x 71 in. (246.4 x 180.3 cm);
The Swing, 98 x 99 in. (248.9 x 251.5 cm);
The Bird Nesters, 98 x 88 in. (248.9 x 223.5 cm);
The Maypole, 98 x 100 in. (248.9 x 254 cm)
[27770] (sale, New York, Parke-Bernet Galleries,
8 May 1971, lot 231a, for $17,000)

D206

D212A

D207

D213

D208

D209

D214A

D210

D218

D215B

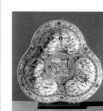

D219

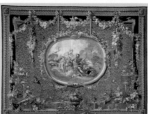

D216B

D219

D217

D220

Cat. D215A–B
France, Gobelins
January and *May*, early 18th century
Wool and silk tapestries, 143 x 130 in. (363.2 x 330.3 cm) and 143 x 142 in. (363.2 x 360.7 cm)
[27771] (sale, New York, Parke-Bernet Galleries, 8 May 1971, lots 229 and 330, for $32,000)

Cat. D216A–D
France, Gobelins
Set of four tapestries, after cartoons by François Boucher (French, 1703–1770), 1775–1778
Venus Emerging on the Waters, 150 x 127 in. (381 x 322.6 cm); *Venus at the Forge of Vulcan*, 150 x 195 in. (381 x 495.3 cm); *Aurora and Cephalus*, 151 x 125 in. (383.5 x 317.5 cm); *Jupiter Disguised as Diana* and *Vertumnus and Pomona*, each 151 x 246 in. (383.5 x 624.8 cm)
[29618] (sale, New York, Parke-Bernet Galleries, 8 May 1971, lot 233, for $190,000 to); The J. Paul Getty Museum, Los Angeles.

Cat. D217
France, probably Touraine
The Annunciation, late 15th century
Wool and silk tapestry,
43 x 85 ½ in. (109.2 x 217.2 cm)
[28168] Sold, March 1971 to; The Metropolitan Museum of Art, New York.

FURNITURE AND DECORATIVE ARTS
[Duveen stock numbers available in the Norton Simon Museum archives]

Cat. D218
China, miscellaneous porcelain (111 items)
14 items, sold October 1966–December 1967 to unknown buyers; one item (sale, Los Angeles, Sotheby Parke Bernet, 1 July 1974, lot 30, for $1,650); 97 items (sale, New York, Parke-Bernet Galleries, 7 May 1971, lots 1–78, for $119,570; photographs and descriptions appear in the sales catalogue)

Cat. D219
Italy, miscellaneous majolica, 18 items (sale, New York, Parke-Bernet Galleries, 7 May 1971, lots 79–93a, for $42,250; photographs and descriptions appear in the sales catalogue)

Cat. D220
Europe, miscellaneous pottery and porcelain (29 items)
10 items sold 1 December 1967 to unknown buyers;
17 items (sale, New York, Parke-Bernet Galleries, 7 May 1971, lots 94–105, for $5,130); one item (sale, New York, Sotheby Parke Bernet, 2 March 1974, lot 52, for $1,800); one item (sale, New York, Sotheby Parke Bernet 18 April 1975, lot 18, for $1,800) Photographs and descriptions appear in the sales catalogues.

Cat. D221
Europe: miscellaneous works of art, stained glass, carpets, and rugs (103 items)
63 items sold October 1965–December 1967 to unknown buyers; 44 items (sale, New York, Parke-Bernet Galleries, 7 May 1971, lots 116, 119, 122–123, 125, for $23,850; 8 May 1971, lots 135–153, 217–223, for $90,145); one item (sale, Los Angeles, Sotheby Parke-Bernet, 18 February 1974, lot 243, for $3,500) Photographs and descriptions appear in the sales catalogues.

D221

D221

D221

Cat. D222
Miscellaneous textiles (31 items)
(sale, New York, Parke-Bernet 84,
22 September 1971)

Cat. D223
Italy and France, miscellaneous furniture,
15th–16th century (8 items)
Six chairs; cassone; carved table
Gift 1965 to; Elmer Belt Library of Vinciana,
University of California, Los Angeles.

Cat. D224
Italy and France, miscellaneous furniture,
16th–17th century (23 items)
Table; 14 chairs; chair bench; two cabinets;
chimneypiece and mantel; 4 swords
Sold October and December 1966 for $2,600 to;
[David Colombo, Milan].

Cat. D225
Italy, 17th century
Savonarola Chair
Gift 1967 to; [French & Co., New York].

Cat. D226
Europe, miscellaneous furniture and decorative
objects, (18 items)
Sold October 1965–September 1968 to unknown
buyers.

Cat. D227
France, 16th–19th century; England, 18th century;
Italy, 16th century
Furniture (73 items) (sale, New York, Parke-
Bernet Galleries, 8 May 1971, lots 154–197 and
232, for $165,480; photographs and descriptions
appear in the sales catalogue). *Right:* lot 193,
Burgundian cabinet, to; The J. Paul Getty
Museum, Los Angeles.

Cat. D228
Oak and pine paneled rooms (3 items)
Sold September 1968 to unknown buyers.

Cat. D229
Miscellaneous wall lights and chandeliers (8
items)
Sold 4 November 1965 and 1 December 1966 to
unknown buyers.

D223

D223

D228

D224

D226

D229

D227

Appendix

ACQUISITION EXPEDITURES BY YEAR

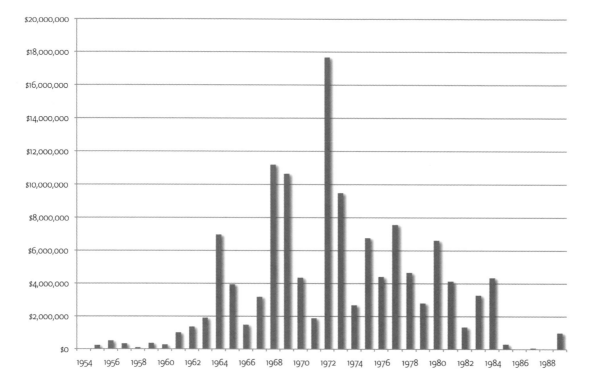

NUMBER OF ACQUISITIONS BY YEAR

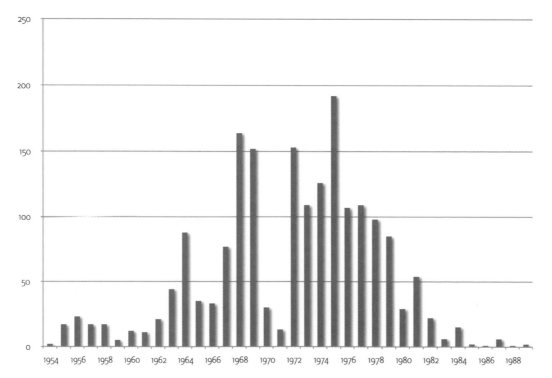

References

Anderson, 1996
Anderson, Jaynie, *Giorgione: Peintre de la "Brièvete Poétique,"* Paris, 1996.

Ashton, 1972
Ashton, Dore, *Picasso on Art: A Selection of Views,* New York, 1972.

Baldass, 1929
Baldass, Ludwig, "Ein unbekanntes Hauptwerk des Cariani," *Jahrbuch der Kunsthistorischen Sammlungen in Wein,* vol. 3, 1929.

Barnett, 2002
Barnett, Vivian Endicott, *The Blue Four Collection at the Norton Simon Museum,* New Haven, 2002.

Barrett, 1965
Barrett, Douglas, *Early Cola Bronzes,* Bombay, 1965.

Berenson, 1957
Berenson, Bernard, *Italian Pictures of the Renaissance: Venetian School,* vol. 1, 1957.

Berges, 1965
Berges, Marshall, "The Corporate Cézanne," *Time* 85, no. 23 (4 June 1965), cover and pp. 74–80.

Berges, 1974
Berges, Marshall, "Home Q and A: Jennifer Jones and Norton Simon," *Los Angeles Times Home Magazine,* 15 December 1974, pp. 58–63.

Berges, 1975
Berges, Marshall, unpublished interviews with Norton Simon, 5 January, 2 February, 23 February 1975.

Boggs et al., 1958
Boggs, Jean Sutherland, et al., *Edgar Hilaire Germain Degas* [Exh. cat. County Museum, Los Angeles.] Los Angeles, 1958.

Braham, 1981
Braham, Helen, *The Princes Gate Collection,* London, 1981.

Bredius, 1936
Bredius, Abraham, *The Paintings of Rembrandt,* Vienna, 1936.

Bredius and Gerson, 1969
Bredius, Abraham, and Horst Gerson, *Rembrandt: The Complete Edition of the Paintings,* London, 1969.

Brettell and Eisenman, 2006
Brettell, Richard R., and Stephen F. Eisenman, *Nineteenth-Century Art in the Norton Simon Museum, Vol. 1,* New Haven, 2006.

Bruyn et al., 1989
Bruyn, Josua, Bob Haak, S. H. Levie, P. J. J. van Thiel, and Ernst van de Wetering, *A Corpus of Rembrandt Paintings,* vol. 3, *1635–1642,* The Hague, 1989.

Campbell, 1976
Campbell, Sara, ed., *The Blue Four Galka Scheyer Collection,* Pasadena, 1976.

Campbell, 1995
Campbell, Sara, "A Catalogue of Degas' Bronzes," *Apollo* 142, no. 402 (August 1995).

Campbell, 1996
Campbell, Sara, "Norton Simon's Enquiring Eye: The Evolution of a Collection," *Orientations* 27, no. 7 (July–August 1996), pp. 30–34.

Campbell et al., 1989
Campbell, Sara, et al., *Masterpieces from the Norton Simon Museum,* Pasadena, 1989.

Campbell et al., 2009
Campbell, Sara, Richard Kendall, Daphne Barbour, and Shelley Sturman, *Degas in the Norton Simon Museum: Nineteenth-Century Art, Vol. 2,* New Haven, 2009.

Collins, 1948
Collins, James H., "From Shoestrings to Millions: The Strategy behind Hunt Foods," *Sales Management,* 15 December 1948, pp. 52–60.

Connoisseur, 1976
"The Norton Simon Museum of Art at Pasadena,"
Connoisseur 193, no. 777 (November 1976), pp. 161–240.

Conrad, 1968
Conrad, Barnaby, MS draft for an unpublished *New York Times* article on Norton Simon, c. October–November 1968.

Coplans, 1975
Coplans, John, "Diary of a Disaster," *Artforum* 13, no. 6 (February 1975), pp. 28–45.

Daily Telegraph, 1959
"Degas Sold for £100,000 in California," *Daily Telegraph*, 1 June 1959, p. 1.

Davis, 2007
Davis, Margaret Leslie, *The Culture Broker: Franklin D. Murphy and the Transformation of Los Angeles*, Berkeley, 2007.

Dortu, 1971
Dortu, M. G., *Toulouse-Lautrec et son oeuvre*, New York, 1971.

Esterow, 1964
Esterow, Milton, "Norton Simon Foundation to Buy Mansion and $15 Million Art Collection of Duveen Gallery," *New York Times*, 21 April 1964.

Esterow, 1965
Esterow, Milton, "Available, Say Many," *New York Times*, 24 November 1965.

Friedländer, 1967–1976
Friedländer, Max, *Early Netherlandish Painting*, 14 vols., New York, 1967–1976.

Glueck, 1968
Glueck, Grace, "$1.5 Million for Renoir Sets World Mark," *New York Herald Tribune*, 11 October 1968.

Gordon, 2003
Gordon, Dillian, *National Gallery Catalogues*, vol. 1, *The Fifteenth Century Italian Paintings*, London 2003.

Graham et al., 1973, 1974
Graham, Lanier, et al., *Three Centuries of French Art: Selections from The Norton Simon, Inc. Museum of Art and The Norton Simon Foundation*. [Exh. cat. California Palace of the Legion of Honor, San Francisco.] San Francisco, vol. 1, 1973; vol. 2, 1974.

Harvey, 1970
Harvey, Mary, ". . . And a Quixotic Bid by Simon the Silent," *Los Angeles* 15, no. 5 (May 1970), pp. 36–37, 88.

Hofstede de Groot, 1916
Hofstede de Groot, Cornelis, *A Catalogue Raisonné of the Most Eminent Dutch Painters of the 17th Century*, 8 vols., London, 1916.

Hoving, 2008
Hoving, Thomas, "LACMA's Loss That Isn't," *Los Angeles Times*, 14 January 2008.

Isenberg, 1971
Isenberg, Barbara, "Pasadena Museum: Ambition vs. Endowment," *Wall Street Journal*, 30 August 1971.

Isenberg, 1978
Isenberg, Barbara, "Simon Museum Board Holdovers to Quit," *Los Angeles Times*, 12 June 1978.

Jaworska, 1972
Jaworska, Wladyslawa, *Gauguin and the Pont-Aven School*, New York, 1972.

Joannides, 2001
Joannides, Paul, *Titian to 1518*, New Haven, 2001.

Joyant, 1926
Joyant, Maurice, *Henri de Toulouse-Lautrec, 1864–1901*, Paris, 1926.

Kamm, 1965
Kamm, Henry, "$6 Million Refused for Leonardo," *New York Times*, 24 November 1965.

Kuh, 1965
Kuh, Katharine, "Los Angeles: Salute to a New Museum," *Saturday Review*, 3 April 1965, pp. 29–30, 35.

Lee, 1969
Lee, Sherman E., *Ancient Cambodian Sculpture*, New York, 1969.

Lefevre Gallery, 1946
Lefevre Gallery, *Delacroix to Dufy: French Paintings of the 19th and 20th Centuries, in Aid of the Contemporary Art Society*. [Exh. cat. Lefevre Gallery, London.] London, 1946.

Lemoisne, 1946–1949
Lemoisne, Paul-André, *Degas et son oeuvre*, 4 vols., Paris, 1946–1949.

Lincoln, 1953
Lincoln, Freeman, "Norton Simon—Like Him or Not," *Fortune*, December 1953, pp. 142–180.

Los Angeles Times, 1965
"Land Acquired for Art Museum," *Los Angeles Times*, 26 January 1965.

Los Angeles Times, 1971
"Norton Simon and Jennifer Jones on Secret Honeymoon," *Los Angeles Times*, 1 June 1971.

Los Angeles Times, 1974a
"Drawings, Watercolors to Be Sold," *Los Angeles Times*, 3 March 1974.

Los Angeles Times, 1974b
"Statue Dispute Cancels Simon Show at Met," *Los Angeles Times*, 3 June 1974.

Lucco, 1995
Lucco, Mauro, *Giorgione*, Milan, 1995.

Luthi, 1974
Luthi, Jean-Jacques, *Émile Bernard, l'initiateur*, Paris, 1974.

Mariacher, 1968
Mariacher, Giovanni, *Palma il Vecchio*, Milan, 1968.

McGuinness, 1969
McGuinness, Liz, "County Cities Still Hope to Get Valuable Art Collection," *Los Angeles Times*, 11 August 1969.

Morassi, 1942
Morassi, Antonio, *Giorgione*, Milan, 1942.

Moreau-Nélaton, 1926
Moreau-Nélaton, Étienne, *Manet raconté par lui-même*, 2 vols., Paris, 1926.

Mourlot, 1970
Mourlot, Fernand, *Picasso Lithographs*, 4 vols., Boston, 1970.

Muchnic, 1990
Muchnic, Suzanne, "Simon Finally Breaks the Silence," *Los Angeles Times*, 24 June 1990.

Muchnic, 1993
Muchnic, Suzanne, "Industrialist, Art Collector Norton Simon Dies at 86," *Los Angeles Times*, 4 June 1993.

Muchnic, 1998
Muchnic, Suzanne, *Odd Man In: Norton Simon and the Pursuit of Culture*, Berkeley, 1998.

Newsweek, 1964
"Exit Lord Pengo," *Newsweek*, 4 May 1964, p. 61

Newsweek, 1965
"Colossus in L.A.," *Newsweek*, 5 April 1965, pp. 84, 86.

New York Times, 1965
"Simon's Painting Gets Exit Permit," *New York Times*, 13 May 1965.

Nicolson, 1963
Nicolson, Benedict, "Venetian Art in Stockholm," *Burlington* 105, no. 718 (January 1963).

Pace, 1993
Pace, Eric, "Norton Simon, Businessman and Collector, Dies at 86," *New York Times*, 4 June 1993.

Pal, 2003a
Pal, Pratapaditya, *Asian Art at the Norton Simon Museum*, Vol. 1, *Art from the Indian Subcontinent*, New Haven, 2003.

Pal, 2003b
Pal, Pratapaditya, *Asian Art at the Norton Simon Museum*, Vol. 2, *Art from the Himalayas and China*, New Haven, 2003.

Pal, 2004
Pal, Pratapaditya, *Asian Art at the Norton Simon Museum*, Vol. 3, *Art from Sri Lanka and Southeast Asia*, New Haven, 2004.

Pardo, 1974
Pardo, Ed, "Outgoing Chief Cites Woes of Pasadena Art Museum," *Pasadena Star-News*, 13 February 1974.

Pignatti, 1955
Pignatti, Terisio, *Giorgione*, Milan, 1955.

Rewald, 1996
Rewald, John, *The Paintings of Paul Cézanne*, New York, 1996.

Richter, 1937
Richter, George M., *Giorgio da Castelfranco, called Giorgione*, New York, 1937.

Roberts, 1970
Roberts, Steven V., "Why a 63-Year-Old Tycoon Worth $100 Million Wants to Run for the Senate," *New York Times Magazine*, 31 May 1970, pp. 10–12, 26–28.

Rosenberg, 1948
Rosenberg, Jakob, *Rembrandt*, 2 vols., Cambridge, Mass., 1948.

Rouart and Wildenstein, 1975
Rouart, Denis, and Daniel Wildenstein, *Édouard Manet: Catalogue raisonné*, 2 vols., Lausanne and Paris, 1975.

Rylands, 1989
Rylands, Philip, *Palma il Vecchio: L'opera completa*, Milan, 1989.

Sander et al., 2006
Sander, Gloria Williams, et al., *The Collectible Moment: Catalogue of Photographs in the Norton Simon Museum*, New Haven, 2006.

San Francisco Examiner, 1941
"Hunt Bros. Packing Co. Stock Block Bought," *San Francisco Examiner*, 22 November 1941, p. 20.

Seidenbaum, 1965
Seidenbaum, Art, "A Man to Move a Museum," *Los Angeles Times Magazine*, 28 March 1965, pp. 28–29, 64–65.

Seilern, 1959
Seilern, Antoine, *Italian Paintings and Drawings at 56 Princes Gate London SW7*, London, 1959.

Seldis, 1965a
Seldis, Henry J., "An Achievement 50 Years in the Making," *Los Angeles Times Magazine*, 28 March 1965, pp. 25, 38.

Seldis, 1965b
Seldis, Henry J., "Titus' Display in Capital Reflects L.A.'s Problems," *Los Angeles Times*, 6 June 1965, pp. 2, 33.

Seldis, 1965c
Seldis, Henry J., "Simon Offer for Work by Da Vinci Reported," *Los Angeles Times*, 25 November 1965.

Seldis, 1967a
Seldis, Henry J., "Norton Simon and the World of Art," *Los Angeles Times*, 23 July 1967, *West* magazine, pp. 10–19.

Seldis, 1967b
Seldis, Henry J., "Famed Museum Builder Selected as Hunt Art Director," *Los Angeles Times*, 18 November 1967.

Seldis, 1968
Seldis, Henry J., "Simon's Loans Challenge to Art Museum Future," *Los Angeles Times*, 18 August 1968.

Seldis, 1969
Seldis, Henry J., "After Four Years, Goals Undefined," *Los Angeles Times*, 5 March 1969.

Seldis, 1972a
Seldis, Henry J., "County Museum to Exhibit Simon Art Treasures," *Los Angeles Times*, 11 June 1972.

Seldis, 1972b
Seldis, Henry J., "Simon Says: 'Under One Roof, We'd Rank among the Top Museums in the Country,'" *Art News* 71, no. 8 (December 1972), pp. 24–28.

Seldis, 1973
Seldis, Henry J., "Simon Denies He Admitted Buying Smuggled Statue," *Los Angeles Times*, 13 May 1973.

Seldis, 1974
Seldis, Henry J., "Pasadena Museum Turns down an Invitation to Disaster," *Los Angeles Times*, 24 March 1974.

Seldis, 1977
Seldis, Henry J., "Lithographs by Picasso: Less Becomes More," *Los Angeles Times*, 4 December 1977.

Shirey, 1973
Shirey, David, "Norton Simon Bought Smuggled Idol," *New York Times*, 12 May 1973.

Simon, 1974
Simon, Norton, "Musings of an Art Collector," MS of an article written for the *New York Times*, c. March–April 1974.

Southwest Art Gallery Magazine, 1972
"Houston Museum of Fine Arts Hosts Norton Simon Collection," *Southwest Art Gallery Magazine*, October 1972.

Steadman et al., 1972
Steadman, David W. et al., *Selections from the Norton Simon, Inc. Museum of Art*. [Exh. cat. Princeton University Art Museum, Princeton, N.J.] Princeton, 1972.

Suida, 1933
Suida, Wilhelm, *Tizian*, Rome, 1933.

Time, 1945
"Tin Can King," *Time* 46, no. 15 (8 October 1945), pp. 86–88.

Time, 1955
"The Raiders: Challenge to Management," *Time* 66, no. 4 (25 July 1955), pp. 80–81.

Time, 1963
"The Tomato Philosopher," *Time* 82, no. 8 (23 August 1963), pp. 64–65.

Time, 1964
"The Abstract Businessman," *Time* 83, no. 23 (5 June 1964), pp. 90–95.

Troche, 1932
Troche, Gunter, "Giovanni Cariani als Bildnismaler," *Pantheon*, vol. 9 (January 1932).

Valcanover, 1960
Valcanover, Francesco, *All the Paintings of Titian*, New York, 1960.

Valentiner, 1931
Valentiner, Wilhelm R., *Paintings in the Collection of Joseph Widener at Lynnewood Hall*, Elkins Park, Pa., 1931.

Venturi, 1936
Venturi, Lionello, *Cézanne: son art—son oeuvre*, 2 vols., Paris, 1936.

Vollard, 1924
Vollard, Ambroise, *Degas*, Paris, 1924.

Wall Street Journal, 1969
"Simon Resigns from Norton Simon Inc., May Consolidate Art Collection in a Museum," *Wall Street Journal*, 2 December 1969.

Walsh, forthcoming
Walsh, Amy, *Northern European Paintings in the Norton Simon Museum*, New Haven, forthcoming.

Wernick, 1966
Wernick, Robert, "Wars of the Instant Medicis," *Life*, 28 October 1966, pp. 102–112.

Whalen, 1965
Whalen, Richard J., "Norton Simon Says Thumbs Down," *Fortune*, June 1965, pp. 146–159, 224–243.

Whitman, 1979
Whitman, Alden, "The Collector," *New West* 4, no. 10 (7 May 1979), pp. SC-30–35.

Wildenstein, 1933
Wildenstein, Georges, *Chardin*, Paris, 1933.

Wilson, 1981
Wilson, William, "Museums Pool Resources to Buy Poussin Painting," *Los Angeles Times*, 29 April 1981.

Exhibitions Devoted to the Norton Simon Collections

Detroit, 1974
The Detroit Institute of Arts, *Italian Art from the Norton Simon Collections*, August 1974–October 1975.

Houston, 1972
The Museum of Fine Arts, Houston, *Masterpieces of Five Centuries: Paintings and Sculpture from The Norton Simon Foundation and Norton Simon, Inc. Museum of Art*, 4 October 1972–November 1973.

Irvine, 1967
Irvine, University of California, *A Selection of Nineteenth and Twentieth Century Works from The Hunt Foods and Industries Museum of Art Collection*, 7–22 March 1967 (traveled to Davis, University of California, 3–28 April 1967, Riverside, University of California, 10–30 May 1967, and San Diego, Fine Arts Gallery, 7 July–1 October 1967).

Los Angeles, 1965
Los Angeles, County Museum of Art, *A Selection from the Mr. and Mrs. Norton Simon Collection Honoring the College Art Association*, 18 January–7 March 1965.

Los Angeles, 1968
Los Angeles, County Museum of Art, *Sculpture from the Collections of Norton Simon Inc. and the Hunt Industries Museum of Art*, opened 20 August 1968.

Los Angeles, 1972
Los Angeles, County Museum of Art, *Selections from the Norton Simon Foundation and the Norton Simon, Inc. Museum*, 16 June 1972–June 1974.

Los Angeles, 1988a
Los Angeles, County Museum of Art, *American Art of the 1950s and 1960s from the Collection of the Norton Simon Museum*, 11 August 1988–3 April 1994.

Los Angeles, 1988b
Los Angeles, Museum of Contemporary Art, *American Art of the 1960s from the Norton Simon Museum*, 4 October 1988–13 June 1990.

New Orleans, 1973
New Orleans Museum of Art, *Henry Moore: Fifteen Bronzes from the Collections of The Norton Simon Foundation and the Norton Simon, Inc. Museum of Art*, 3 December 1973–23 October 1974.

Pasadena, 1972
Pasadena Art Museum, *Modern Sculpture from the Norton Simon, Inc. Museum of Art and The Norton Simon Foundation*, 1 August 1972–16 September 1973.

Philadelphia, 1969
Philadelphia, Museum of Art, *Recent Acquisitions by the Norton Simon, Inc. Museum of Art*, 24 January–23 June 1969.

Portland, 1968
Portland, Oregon, Portland Art Museum, *Recent Acquisitions by the Norton Simon, Inc. Museum of Art*, 12 November 1968–20 April 1969.

Princeton, 1972
Princeton, University Art Museum, *Selections from the Norton Simon, Inc. Museum of Art*, 3 December 1972–17 July 1974.

Richmond, 1970
Richmond, Virginia Museum of Fine Arts, *Recent Acquisitions of the Norton Simon, Inc. Museum*, 27 May 1970–10 July 1972.

San Francisco, 1970
San Francisco, The California Palace of the Legion of Honor, *The Claude Lorrain Album in the Norton Simon, Inc. Museum of Art*, 2 May–5 July 1970 (traveled to Zurich, Kunsthaus, 30 October–28 November 1971; Los Angeles County Museum of Art, 16 June–October 1972; Princeton University Art Museum, 27 April–3 July 1973; Cambridge, Mass., Fogg Art Museum, Harvard University, 21 September–21 October 1973; Northampton, Mass., Smith College Museum of Art, 1 November–20 December 1973; Chapel Hill, Ackland Memorial Art Center, University of North Carolina,

6–27 January 1974; Oberlin, Ohio, Allen Memorial Art Museum, Oberlin College, 16 February–31 March 1974; Wellesley, Mass., Wellesley College Museum, 8 April–8 June 1974; Berkeley, University Art Museum, University of California at Berkeley, February–March 1975).

San Francisco, 1973
San Francisco, California Palace of the Legion of Honor, *Three Centuries of French Art: Selections from The Norton Simon, Inc. Museum of Art and The Norton Simon Foundation*, 3 May 1973–15 June 1976.

San Francisco, 1974
San Francisco, California Palace of the Legion of Honor, *Three Centuries of French Art: Selections from The Norton Simon, Inc. Museum of Art and The Norton Simon Foundation*, 19 October 1974–15 June 1976.

PHOTOGRAPHY ACKNOWLEDGMENTS

Unless otherwise noted, all figure illustrations are courtesy of the Norton Simon Art Foundation, Pasadena. All images of artworks in the Norton Simon Art Foundation, The Norton Simon Foundation, the Norton Simon Museum, and the Jennifer Jones Simon Art Trust are copyrighted to their respective owning entity. A good faith effort has been made to secure permission from copyrights holders. In instances where no copyright holder has been located, any information is appreciated and will be included in future editions.

All works by Josef Albers: © 2010 The Josef and Anni Albers Foundation/ Artists Rights Society (ARS), New York; Jean Arp, Lyonel Feininger, Georg Kolbe, Käthe Kollwitz, Fritz Winter: © 2010 Artists Rights Society (ARS), New York/ VG Bild-Kunst, Bonn; Emile Bernard, Pierre Bonnard, Constantin Brancusi, Georges Braque, Nicolas de Staël, Maurice Denis, André Derain, Jean Dubuffet, Raoul Dufy, Marcel Gromaire, Henri Hayden, Vasily Kandinsky, Henri Laurens, Fernand Léger, Aristide Maillol, Marc Chagall, Albert Marquet, Jean Metzinger, Georges Rouault, Ker-Xavier Roussel, André Dunoyer de Segonzac, Chaim Soutine, Léopold Survage, Maurice Utrillo, Kees Van Dongen, Jacques Villon, Maurice de Vlaminck, Edouard Vuillard: © 2010 Artists Rights Society (ARS), New York/ ADAGP, Paris; Alexander Calder: © 2010 Calder Foundation, New York/Artists Rights Society (ARS), New York; Paul Conrad: © Paul Conrad; Ronald Davis: © Ron Davis; Willem de Kooning: © 2010 The Willem de Kooning Foundation/ Artists Rights Society (ARS), New York; Leonard Edmondson: © Estate of Leonard Edmondson, courtesy Tobey C. Moss Gallery; Nese Erdok: © Nese Erdok; Helen Frankenthaler: © 2010 Helen Frankenthaler/Artists Rights Society (ARS), New York; Alberto Giacometti: © 2010 Artists Rights Society (ARS), New York/ADAGP/FAAG, Paris; Arshile Gorky, Erich Heckel: © 2010 Artists Rights Society (ARS), New York; Barbara Hepworth: © Bowness, Hepworth Estate; Tristram Hillier: Courtesy of the artist's estate/Bridgeman Art Library; Hans Hofmann: © 2010 Renate, Hans & Maria Hofmann Trust/ Artists Rights Society (ARS), New York; Oskar Kokoschka: © 2010 Fondation Oskar Kokoschka/Artists Rights Society (ARS), New York/ProLitteris, Zürich; Jacques Lipchitz: © Estate of Jacques Lipchitz /Marlborough Gallery, NY; Giacomo Manzu, Marino Marini: © 2010 Artists Rights Society (ARS), New York/SIAE, Rome; Henri Matisse: © 2010 Succession H. Matisse/Artists Rights Society (ARS), New York; Joan Miro: © 2010 Successió Miró/Artists Rights Society (ARS), New York/ ADAGP, Paris; Henry Moore: Reproduced by permission of the Henry Moore Foundation, www.henry-moore-fdn.co.uk; Edvard Munch: © 2010 The Munch Museum/The Munch-Ellingsen Group/Artists Rights Society (ARS), New York; Ben Nicholson, Walter Richard Sickert: © 2010 Artists Rights Society (ARS), New York/DACS, London; Emil Nolde: Stiftung Seebüll Ada und Emil Nolde; Pablo Picasso: © 2010 Estate of Pablo Picasso/Artists Rights Society (ARS), New York; Jackson Pollock: © 2010 The Pollock-Krasner Foundation/Artists Rights Society (ARS), New York; David Smith: © Estate of David Smith/Licensed by VAGA, NY

© Bettmann/CORBIS: p.106
Boston, Museum of Fine Arts, Bequest of William A. Coolidge, 1993.40, photo © 2010 Museum of Fine Arts: p. 58 fig.9
Cambridge, photo © Fitzwilliam Museum: cat. 536
Canberra, National Gallery of Australia, Purchased 1973: p. 148, cat. 118
© Christie's Images/Bridgeman Art Library: Cat. 173
Claremont, CA, Pomona College Museum of Art: cat. 59
Düsseldorf, Kunstsammlung Nordrhein-Westfalen, photo © Erich Lessing/Art Resource, NY: cat. 583
Fort Worth, Kimbell Art Museum, photo © Kimbell Art Museum, Fort Worth, Texas/Art Resource, NY: p. 199 fig. 8, cat. 558
Fort Worth, Kimbell Art Museum, photo Bob Wharton: p. 20
Fort Worth, The Burnett Foundation, photo the Kimbell Art Museum, Fort Worth: p. 86, cat. 328A-D
Houston, TX, The Museum of Fine Arts, Gift of Mrs. Harry C. Hanszen: cat. 81
Kansas City, MO, The Nelson-Atkins Museum of Art, Acquired through the generosity of an anonymous donor, F79-47, photo by Mel McLean: cat. 1610
Kansas City, MO, Nelson-Atkins Museum of Art, Purchase: the Kenneth A. and Helen F. Spencer Foundation Acquisition Fund, F73-30, photo E. G. Schempf: p. 77 fig. 10, cat. 271
London, National Gallery, photo © National Gallery, London/ Art Resource, NY: p. 37 fig. 3
London, National Portrait Gallery: p. 43 fig. 11
London, Private collection: p. 172 fig. 12
London, Sotheby's Picture Library: p. 220 fig. 1
London, Thomas Agnew & Sons: p. 43 fig. 10
Los Angeles County Museum of Art, Gift of Lucille Ellis Simon and family in honor of the museum's twenty-fifth anniversary, photo © 2010 Museum Associates/LACMA: p. 19 fig. 3, cat. 7
Los Angeles, David Abdo: p. 220 fig. 2; p. 223 fig. 4; p. 224 fig. 5; p. 462
Los Angeles Times, Tony Barnard: p. 193, fig. 2
Los Angeles, photo courtesy Evelyn Prell: p. 12
Los Angeles, The Armand Hammer Collection. Gift of the Armand Hammer Foundation. Hammer Museum: pp. 40 fig. 6, 109 fig. 6; cats. 63, 99, 212, 421
Los Angeles, The Eli and Edythe L. Broad Collection, photo Douglas M. Parker Studio, Los Angeles: p. 90 fig. 10, cat. 515
Los Angeles, The J. Paul Getty Museum: pp. 21, 87 fig. 7, 110, 171 fig. 9, cats. 29, 348, 1005, D216B
Madrid, Thyssen-Bornemisza Collection, photo © Museo Thyssen-Bornemisza: pp. 27, 45, cats. 31, 140
New York, Barbara Goldenberg: p. 221
New York, Alexander Hammid: p. 163 fig. 1
New York, Elaine Rosenberg: p. 37 fig. 1
New York, Eugene V. Thaw: p. 136 fig. 3
New York, Private collection, photo © Erich Lessing/Art Resource, NY: p. 61 fig. 13, cat. 258
New York, The Metropolitan Museum of Art, Gift of Janice H. Levin, 1991. Image © The Metropolitan Museum of Art/Art Resource, NY: p. 109 fig. 5, cat. 123

New York, The Metropolitan Museum of Art, Lucille Ellis Simon. Walter H. and Leonore Annenberg, 1993. Image © The Metropolitan Museum of Art/Art Resource, NY: cat. 406
New York, The Metropolitan Museum of Art, Purchase, special contributions and funds given or bequeathed by friends of the Museum, 1961. Image © The Metropolitan Museum of Art/Art Resource, NY: p. 39
New York, The Metropolitan Museum of Art, Purchase, special contributions and funds given or bequeathed by friends of the Museum, 1967. Image © The Metropolitan Museum of Art/Art Resource, NY: p. 91 fig. 12
New York, The Metropolitan Museum of Art, The Walter H. and Leonore Annenberg Collection, Gift of Walter H. and Leonore Annenberg, 1993, Bequest of Walter H. Annenberg, 2002. Image © The Metropolitan Museum of Art/Art Resource, NY: p. 175 fig. 16, cat. 406
New York, The Metropolitan Museum of Art, The Walter H. and Leonore Annenberg Collection, Gift of Walter H. and Leonore Annenberg, 2001, Bequest of Walter H. Annenberg, 2002. Image © The Metropolitan Museum of Art/Art Resource, NY: cat. 725
New York, Wildenstein and Co: p. 18
Ottowa, National Gallery of Canada, Purchased 1975: cat. 160
Paris, Musee d'Orsay, photo © Erich Lessing/Art Resource, NY: p. 31 fig. 14
Parkland, Florida, Dorothy Rabin: p. 239 fig. 5
Pasadena, George Abdo: pp. 11 fig. 1, 166 figs. 3-4
Pasadena, Sara Campbell: pp. 220 fig. 2, 223, 224
Pasadena, Norton Simon Art Foundation, photos by Darryl Isley: pp. 83-84 figs. 1-3
Provo, UT, Brigham Young University Museum of Art. All rights reserved: p. 55 fig. 6, cat. D156
Raleigh, North Carolina Museum of Art, Purchased with funds from the State of North Carolina: cat. 108
Riehen, Switzerland, Fondation Beyeler: p. 199 fig. 7, cat. 1165
Santa Barbara, Robert M. Light: p. 184 fig. 7
Sharon, CT, Ben Heller: p. 126 fig. 10
Stanford, CA, Iris & B. Gerald Cantor Center for Visual Arts at Stanford University, Mortimer C. Levintritt Fund and Committee for Art Acquisitions Fund, 1973.23: cat. 519
The Art Institute of Chicago, Searle Family Trust, 1986.137: cat. 226
Time & Life Pictures/Getty Images, Ralph Crane: p. 63 fig. 16
Time & Life Pictures/Getty Images, Terrence Spencer: p. 72
Washington, D.C., The National Gallery of Art, Ailsa Mellon Bruce Fund. Image courtesy of the Board of Trustees, National Gallery of Art: p. 78
Washington, D.C., National Gallery of Art, The Armand Hammer Collection: cats. 137, 198, 199
Washington, D.C., National Gallery of Art, The Stephen Hahn Family Collection (Partial and Promised Gift), 1995.29.21. Image courtesy of the Board of Trustees, National Gallery of Art: cat. 39

Index

Note: Catalogue numbers in **bold** denote artworks still in the collections; those that are illustrated in the text are denoted with page numbers in ***bold italics.*** Other illustrations are denoted with page numbers in *italics.* Page ranges in the Catalogue section (pp. 244 *ff*) indicate isolated references on each page, not a continuous discussion. Where, traditionally (as, particularly, in Asian art), the makers of works of art are unnamed, the works are indexed by their place of origin. To distinguish them from works of art, texts are annotated with the date of publication.

A

Abdo, George, 177 n. 18

Abels Gemaelde Galerie, Cologne, 424

Acosta, Edgardo, Gallery, Beverly Hills, Calif., 259

Acquavella, William (dealer), New York, 63 n. 8, 87, 205, 262

Acquavella Galleries, New York, 87, 88, 246, 257, 277, 293, 313, 317, 326, 332, 343, 378, 440

acquisitions, annual, 1954–1988 (graph), *462*

Adams, Alice (dealer), Chicago, 414

Ader-Picard-Tajan (auction house), Paris, 363, 421

Adler, Rachel, Fine Art, New York, 325

advertising, NS as innovator in, 13–14, *14*, 15 n. 15, 20

Afghanistan, ancient Gandhara

    Two Heads of Buddha (**cat. 1465A–B**), 410, *410*

    see also Pakistan or Afghanistan

Africa

    Benin, *Melon-shaped Cover* (**cat. 902**), 350, *350*

    Nigeria, *Seated Queen* (**cat. 760**), 336, *336*

Agee, William, 164

Agnew, Geoffrey (dealer), London, 28–29, 43, *43*, 45, 70–71, 92, 193, 220

Agnew, Julian (dealer), London, 197, 223

Agnew, Thomas, & Sons, London, 27, 28, 70–71, 220, 309, 311

    acquisitions through, 29, 44, 51, 141, 197–98, 252–54, 260, 264, 276, 323, 327, 348, 357–59, 401, 405, 435

    sales to, 116, 333

Agostino di Giovanni, attrib., *The Virgin Annunciate* (**cat. D64**), 446, *446*

Ahmanson, Howard, 30

Albers, Josef, 229

    Set of Four Centennial Prints (**cat. 744 A–D**), 310, 334, *334*

Albertinelli, Mariotto, attrib. (formerly). *See* Granacci, Francesco

Altman, Ralph C. (dealer), Los Angeles, 268

Ambassador Hotel, Los Angeles, 17, 33 n. 2

American Association of Museum Directors, 159

American Association of Museums, 207 n. 31

Ammann, Thomas, Fine Art, Zurich, 280, 320

Angelico, Fra, *Madonna and Child* (**cat. D1**), 63 nn. 3, 5, 441, *441*

Anglo-Flemish school

    Captain Sir Edward Harwood (**cat. D101**), 449, *449*

    Lieutenant-Colonel Sir John Burlacy (**cat. D100**), 449, *449*

    Portrait of a Noblewoman (**cat. D102**), 449

Angulo Íñiguez, Diego, 112, 113, 119 n. 50

Annenberg, Walter H. and Leonore, 294, 332

anonymous Dutch artist, *The Great Tulip Book* (**cat. 1060**), 168, 169, 367, *367*

    Admirael Der Admiraels de Gouda, **168**

Anquetin, Louis

    Portrait of a Man (**cat. 1398**), 402, *402*

    Portrait of a Woman (Marguerite Dufay) (**cat. 1364**), 399, *399*

Antiques and Coins of Siam (dealer), Bangkok, 380

Antonio da Monza, Fra, *The Flagellation of Christ* (**cat. D2**), 441, *441*

Apollo magazine, 95, 101 n. 61

Armand Hammer Museum of Art and Culture Center, Los Angeles, 108, 118 n. 35, 252, 256, 271, 296, 298

Armenia. *See* Greece and

Aronson, Naum Lvovich, *Count Leo Tolstoy* (**cat. 1724**), 205, 440, *440*

Arp, Jean, 229

    Classical Sculpture (**cat. 546**), 310–11, *310*

Ars Antiqua (auction house), Lucerne, 254

Artemis Fine Art, London, 357, 413

    and David Carritt Ltd., London, 423

Art Institute of Chicago, 18, 26, 100 n. 28, 137, 149 n. 25, 156, 189 n. 18, 273, 281

artists, representation of in the collections (table), 224

artists' letters, group of 42 (**cat. 1731**), 440

    Honoré Daumier, *440*

Art News (periodical), 155

Art Salon Takahata, Osaka, 277

Arts Anciens et Modernes, Galerie des, Schaan, Liechtenstein, 261, 262, 263, 284, 285, 296, 301, 318, 332, 333

    see also Marlborough Gallery, New York

Asian art, 25, 121–33, 167, 170, 171, 177 n. 34, 179, 188, 220, 228

    catalogues of the NS collection, 133 n. 7

    galleries, *176*, 215, 228

    loan exhibitions of, 158–59, 165, 175

    see also under countries of origin

Assereto, Gioacchino, *David with the Head of Goliath* (**cat. 1324**), 394, *394*

Ast, Balthasar van der, *Still Life with Fruits and Flowers* (**cat. 858**), 141, 345, *345*

Audebert, Jean-Baptiste, *Histoire naturelle des singes et des makis* (cat. 1661), 432

Ault, Lee (dealer), New York, 428

Averkamp, Barent, *Family Group* (cat. 366), 289, *289*

Avery, Stanton, 211

Azcárraga, Emilio, 299, 352

B

Baciccio. *See* Gaulli, Giovanni Battista

Bader, Alfred and Isabel, 247

Bader, Franz (dealer), New York, 321

Baer, Martha, 101 n. 35

Balen, Hendrick van, the Elder, *Mythological Scene* (cat. 205), 270, *270*

Bandinelli, Baccio, *Hercules* (cat. 206), 65 n. 18, 270, *270*

Bangladesh. *See* India, West Bengal or

Bar, Jules (dealer), Zurich, 265

Barbieri, Giovanni Francesco. *See* Guercino

Barbizon, Galerie, Paris, 379, 395

Barlach, Ernst

    The Avenger (**cat. 251**), 276, *276*

    Der Tote Tag (cat. 292), 281

    Reading Monks III (cat. 259), 277, *277*

    Singing Man (cat. 167), 265, *265*

Barr, Daniel, 250

Bartolomeo Veneto, follower of, *Portrait of a Man* (**cat. D3**), 441, *441*

Baskett & Day, London, 268, 412

Bassano, Jacopo (Jacopo da Ponte called)

    The Flight into Egypt (**cat. 702**), 95–96, *95*, 101 nn. 62, 64, 140, 329, 329

    —circle of, *Portrait of a Lady* (**cat. D4**), 441, *441*

Bassetti, Marcantonio, *Portrait of a Cleric* (**cat. 1525**), 416–17, *416*

Bateman, James, *The Orchidaceae of Mexico and Guatemala* (cat. 1662), 432

Battson, Leigh, 107

Bauhaus, the, 163

Bayless, Raymond, *Twenty-Dollar Bill* (**cat. 1387**), 401

Bazille, Jean-Frédéric, *Woman in a Moorish Costume* (**cat. 709**), 96, 330, *330*

Beadleston, William (dealer), New York, 87, 293, 422, 427

Beale, Arthur, 189 n. 9

Beatty, Sir Alfred Chester, 31–32, 38, 41–42

Beatty, Edith Dunn, n.

Beckmann, Max, *Jahrmarkt (The Fair)* (cat. 580), 314–15

Behram, Boman, 130

Beit, Sir Alfred, 60

Belin, Jean-Baptist, the Elder, *A Still Life of Flowers* (cat. D103), 449, *449*

Bellange, Jacques, *The Annunciation* (cat. 939), 354, *354*

Belle, Alexis Simon, *Duc de Chartres* (cat. D104), 450, *450*

Bellini, Giovanni

    Joerg Fugger (**cat. 584**), 93, ***93***, 315, *315*

    —attrib., *Virgin and Child* (cat. D105), 450, *450*

    —follower of

        Virgin and Child (**cat. D5**), 441, *441*

        Virgin and Child in a Landscape (**cat. D6**), 441, *441*

Bellini, Galleria Luigi, Florence, 349

Bellotto, Bernardo, 57

    A Capriccio of Padua (cat. 255), 276, *276*

Benedetto da Maiano, after, *Relief of the Madonna and Child* (cat. D184), 457, *457*

Bensinger, Mr. and Mrs. B. Edward, 281

COLLECTOR WITHOUT WALLS:
NORTON SIMON AND HIS HUNT FOR THE BEST

was edited by Fronia Simpson and
designed and managed by Lilli Colton.
Type was set in Minion and Formata Light.
The index is by Frances Bowles.
The book was printed and bound in China
by Artron through Overseas Printing.

For more information about the
Norton Simon collections, please visit
www.nortonsimonmuseum.org